1932

Also by David Pietrusza

1948:
Harry Truman's Improbable Victory and the Year That
Transformed America

1960: LBJ vs. JFK vs. Nixon:
The Epic Campaign That Forged Three Presidencies

1920:
The Year of the Six Presidents

Rothstein:
The Life, Times, and Murder of the Criminal Genius Who
Fixed the 1919 World Series

Judge and Jury:
The Life and Times of Judge Kenesaw Mountain Landis

Silent Cal's Almanack:
The Homespun Wit and Wisdom of Vermont's Calvin Coolidge

Calvin Coolidge:
A Documentary Biography

Calvin Coolidge on The Founders:
Reflections on the American Revolution & the Founding Fathers

1932
The Rise of Hitler and FDR—
Two Tales of Politics, Betrayal, and Unlikely Destiny

DAVID PIETRUSZA

Guilford, Connecticut

An imprint of Rowman & Littlefield

Distributed by NATIONAL BOOK NETWORK

Copyright © 2016 by David Pietrusza

British Library Cataloguing in Publication Information Available

Library of Congress Cataloging-in-Publication Data
Pietrusza, David, 1949-
  1932 : the rise of Hitler and FDR ; two tales of politics, betrayal, and unlikely destiny / David Pietrusza.
    pages cm
  Includes bibliographical references and index.
  ISBN 978-0-7627-9302-0 (hardcover : alk. paper) — ISBN 978-1-4930-0944-2 (pbk. : alk. paper) — ISBN 978-1-4930-1805-5 (electronic)
  1. Roosevelt, Franklin D. (Franklin Delano), 1882-1945. 2. United States—Politics and government—1933-1945. 3. United States—Foreign relations—1933-1945. 4. New Deal, 1933-1939. 5. Hitler, Adolf, 1889-1945. 6. Germany—Politics and government—1933-1945. 7. Germany—Foreign relations—1933-1945. 8. National socialism. I. Title. II. Title: Nineteen thirty-two.
  E806.P54 2015
  973.917—dc23
                                                    2015016456

∞™ The paper used in this publication meets the minimum requirements of American National Standard for Information Sciences—Permanence of Paper for Printed Library Materials, ANSI/NISO Z39.48-1992.

CONTENTS

CAST OF CHARACTERS

Newton Diehl Baker Jr. (1871–1937): Woodrow Wilson's secretary of the army. Dark-horse, unannounced, and largely unwilling possibility for 1932's Democratic nomination. Acceptable to most party factions. Long beset by heart problems. "Our salvation lies largely in [Roosevelt's] nomination," calculates Herbert Hoover. "I am afraid of Baker."

Bernard Mannes "The Lone Eagle" Baruch (1870–1965): Legendary lonewolf Wall Street financier. Like Joe Kennedy, one of the very fortunate few to sell—and profit—before the Crash. Winston Churchill's friend and patron. Favoring Newton Baker in 1932, the elegantly aloof South Carolinian derides FDR as "wishy-washy" and "the Boy Scout Governor."

Eva Anna Paula Braun (1912–1945): Assistant to Heinrich Hoffmann, Adolf Hitler's official photographer. She has her sights on Hitler. In 1932, despairing of his indifference, she attempts suicide. "The girl did it for love of me. . . . ," Hitler confesses to Hoffmann. "Obviously I must now look after the girl."

Wilhelm Brückner (1884–1954): Hitler's hulking adjutant. Former Munich SA leader. Survivor of the 1923 Beer Hall Putsch.

Heinrich Brüning (1885–1970): Depression-wracked Weimar Germany's "Hunger Chancellor." Centre Party (*Zentrum*) member. His rule by presidential emergency decree unwittingly presages Hitler's dictatorship. "The best chancellor since Bismarck," says *Reichspräsident* Hindenburg—before firing him.

Anton Joseph "Ten Percent Tony" Cermak (1873–1933): Czech-born, Protestant, Democratic mayor—and corrupt boss—of Chicago. "The wettest man in Chicago." He packs the hall for fellow "wet" Al Smith at 1932's Democratic Convention.

Winston Spencer Churchill (1874–1965): Hero of the Boer War. Architect of Allied disaster at Gallipoli. Eyewitness to Wall Street's Black Thursday. Visiting Munich in the summer of 1932, the ardent anti-Bolshevik ("it is not a creed; it is a pestilence"), Churchill is invited to meet Hitler. Snaps

Churchill: "Tell your boss from me that anti-Semitism may be a good starter, but it is a bad sticker."

John Calvin "Silent Cal" Coolidge (1872–1933): Hoover's conservative Yankee predecessor. Reluctantly backing Hoover in 1932. "I no longer fit with these times," he concludes at year's end. "Great changes can come about in four years. These socialistic notions of government are not of my day."

Father Charles Edward Coughlin (1891–1979): Spellbinding Canadian-born, Detroit-area radio priest. Anti-Prohibition and anti-Hoover. Pro-silver and very pro-FDR. "I am with you to the end," Coughlin wires the newly nominated Roosevelt. "Say the word and I will follow."

Father James Renshaw Cox (1886–1951): Stocky, bespectacled pastor of Pittsburgh's Old St. Patrick's parish. In January, Cox leads twenty thousand jobless in a protest to Washington. Founder of the "Blue Shirts" movement. Presidential nominee of the short-lived "Jobless Party." Running on a platform of federal control of banks and an end to usury.

James Michael "The Mayor of the Poor" Curley (1874–1958): Boston's ex-convict, pro–public works, pro-FDR mayor. Defeated by Smith's forces in April's Commonwealth of Massachusetts presidential primary, he mysteriously appears at June's Democratic National Convention as delegate "Alcade [Mayor] Jaime Miguel Curleo"—representing the Commonwealth of Puerto Rico.

Charles "Indian" Curtis (1860–1936): Hoover's aged and part-Kaw vice president. Former Senate majority leader. An ardent "dry." The model for *Of Thee I Sing*'s ineffectual Vice President Alexander Throttlebottom. Hoover wants Curtis off the 1932 ticket. Reputed poker cheat. "Well," as Alice Roosevelt Longworth observes, "we just don't come in when Charlie deals. . . ."

Theodor Duesterberg (1875–1950): A leader of Germany's right-wing Stahlhelm veterans' group. Allied with Hitler and the DNVP's Alfred Hugenberg in 1931's short-lived Harzburg Front. His slim chances fizzle in March 1932's presidential election when gleeful Nazis reveal his secret: a Jewish great-grandfather.

Lt. Col. Dwight David Eisenhower (1890–1969): Aide to Army Chief of Staff Douglas MacArthur ("I studied dramatics under MacArthur for seven years"). Participant in clearing 1932's Bonus March. "Best clerk I ever had," says MacArthur of Ike. "I've been called 'Dictator Ike,'" Ike says as 1932 mercifully concludes, "because I believe that virtual dictatorship must be exercised by our President."

James Aloysius "Big Jim" Farley (1888–1976): Charming and highly effective chairman of New York State's Democratic Party. FDR's 1928, 1930—and 1932—campaign manager. "His lameness," Farley explains regarding Roosevelt's paralysis, "which is steadily getting better, has no more effect on his general condition than if he had a glass eye or was prematurely bald."

Edward Joseph "Boss" Flynn (1891–1953): Chairman of the Bronx Democratic Committee. New York State secretary of state. A key—but extremely low-key—member of the Roosevelt team. Publicly, Flynn defers to the more personable Jim Farley. "I realized my own limitations," says Flynn, "I . . . found it quite difficult to move about with facility among strange people."

Henry Ford (1863–1947): Creator of the Model "A," the Model "T," and the five-dollar work day. Pre–World War I peace activist. Prominent postwar anti-Semite. "Every year sees [the Jews] emerging as rulers of the work-force of [an American] population of 120 million people," Hitler had observed. "A single great man, Ford, stands there today independent, much to their anger." In March 1932, a Communist-led "Hunger March" to Ford's River Rouge Complex leads to tear gas, shooting, and four deaths. He campaigns with Hoover.

William Zebulon Foster (1881–1961): Stalinist general secretary of the Communist Party USA. Leader of 1932's "Ford Hunger March." The CPUSA's 1932 presidential candidate. His running mate: the black James William Ford. "George Bernard Shaw is right," proclaims Foster, "the time will surely come when the victorious toilers will build a monument to Lenin in New York."

Dr. Joseph Irwin France (1873–1939): Former US senator. Challenging Hoover's "administrative dictatorship," the obscure "wet" France bests Hoover in six of seven head-to-head primaries—but loses his home state of Maryland. Forcibly ejected from the GOP convention when he attempts to nominate ex-President Coolidge. "This is a colossal piece of political racketeering," charges France. ". . . The nomination of this man Hoover is invalid."

André François-Poncet (1887–1978): France's elegant envoy to Germany; called by William L. Shirer, "the best informed ambassador in Berlin."

Dr. Wilhelm Frick (1877–1946): Jailed for his role in the 1923 Beer Hall Putsch. A rare colorless figure in the bizarre Nazi pantheon. Supports

Gregor Strasser's December 1932 abortive plot to join Kurt von Schleicher's government.

John Nance "Cactus Jack" Garner IV (1868–1967): Democratic Speaker of the House of Representatives. A reluctant presidential aspirant. The bushy-browed Garner, says historian Arthur Schlesinger Jr., "presented at once an appearance of an infinitely experienced sage and of a new-born baby." A backroom convention deal transforms him into Roosevelt's running mate.

Dr. Paul Joseph Goebbels (1897–1945): Nazi *gauleiter* of Berlin. Editor of *Der Angriff*. A leader of the radical socialistic wing of Hitler's NSDAP. "A clubfoot," says Goebbels's hated rival Gregor Strasser. "This is Satan in human form."

Hermann Wilhelm Göring (1893–1946): World War I flying ace. Morphine addict. As *Reichstag Präsident* he illegally blocks Chancellor von Papen's move to dissolve parliament. "Half executioner, half clown," judges one disgusted foreign observer.

Gen. Wilhelm Gröner (1867–1939): Former chief of the defeated Imperial General Staff. Heinrich Brüning's minister of defense. Kurt von Schleicher's patron. Forced from power by Göring's taunts—and his unfaithful protégé Schleicher's intrigues. "Scorn and rage boil within me," Gröner writes to Schleicher, "because I have been deceived in you, my old friend, disciple, adopted son."

Ernst Franz Sedgwick "Putzi" Hanfstaengl (1887–1975): Der Führer's clownish American-descended intimate ("Hitler's Piano Player"). FDR's old friend from New York City's posh Harvard Club. "Roosevelt made himself by conquering an infirmity of the body," says Hanfstaengl, "Hitler by conquering the infirmity of the German people."

William Randolph Hearst (1863–1951): Controversial American press baron. His own presidential ambitions long frustrated, Hearst still covets the king-maker position. Hating Al Smith and Newton Baker ("there are in the United States . . . approximately 125,000,000 persons and among the least desirable of these as a candidate for President is Newton D. Baker"), Hearst booms John Nance Garner—and, later—after Joe Kennedy's prodding—FDR.

Edmund Heines (1897–1934): Deputy *Sturmabteilung* ("storm battalion" or "storm troopers") leader under Ernst Röhm. Reichstag deputy. Convicted murderer. Notorious homosexual.

Lorena Alice Hickok (1893–1968): Associated Press reporter covering the Roosevelt family. Eleanor's beefy (5'8", 200 pounds), cigar-smoking, tough-talking, hard-drinking lesbian lover. "I trust you," Eleanor tells her.

Heinrich Luitpold Himmler (1900–1945): Reichsführer of Hitler's elite *Schutzstaffel* (the "Protection Squad" or "SS"). Bookish, occult-oriented, rabid anti-Semite. Tenacious rival of Oberster SA-Führer Ernst Röhm. "I have never been served so much political nonsense in such a concentrated form," recalls one gauleiter on meeting Himmler.

Major Oskar von Beneckendorff und von Hindenburg (1883–1960): Son of *Reichspräsident* Paul von Hindenburg. His father's influential aide-de-camp. A protégé of Kurt von Schleicher. Crucial in eventually arguing for Hitler as chancellor. Have the Nazis blackmailed him?

Paul Ludwig Hans Anton von Beneckendorff und von Hindenburg (1847–1934): German *Reichspräsident*. Victor at August 1914's key battle of Tannenberg. An increasingly infirm national hero. Running for re-election in 1932 only to checkmate Hitler. "You demand power," the aged Hindenburg informs him. "I can only offer you the Post Office."

Adolf Hitler (1889–1945): Austrian-born Führer of Germany's National Socialist German Workers Party—the Nazis. Failed artist. Austrian draft dodger. Temporarily blinded German army veteran. Charismatic orator. Rabid militarist and anti-Semite. Nazi presidential candidate. "Before 1932," Hitler will recall, "our domestic foes never saw where we were going or that our oath of legalism was just a trick. . . . They could have suppressed us. They could have arrested a couple of us in 1925 and that would have been that, the end. No, they let us through the danger zone."

Herbert Clark Hoover (1874–1964): Embattled American president. Iowa-born orphan. Wealthy international mining engineer. Savior of starving millions throughout Europe, Russia, and the Middle East. Harding and Coolidge's energetic and innovative commerce secretary. A success at everything—except in combatting America's Great Depression. Seeking re-election in 1932, Hoover is "a solemn and sad, an unhappy man, a man without hope. Instead of radiating confidence and good cheer in the presence of the economic crisis, his portraits made one want to sell short, get the money in gold, and bury it."

Lou Henry Hoover (1874–1944): Wife of Herbert Hoover. A survivor of the Boxer Rebellion, she and her husband often converse in Chinese to foil

White House eavesdroppers. "Her only departures from sweet urbanity," her husband recalls, "were in outrage at some unfairness in our opponents—and that in private. . . ."

Louis McHenry Howe (1871–1936): FDR's disheveled, chain-smoking, adoring campaign manager. "[A]lmost at that very first meeting," said the 5'4" Howe of his idol, "I made up my mind that he was Presidential timber and that nothing but an accident could keep him from becoming President of the United States."

Alfred Ernst Christian Alexander Hugenberg (1865–1951): German press and film baron. Former Krupp Steel executive. Stuffy, block-headed leader of the ultra-nationalist, anti-Semitic German National People's Party (DNVP). Opposed to Brüning's chancellorship. Briefly allied with the Nazis in 1931's Harzburg Front, he backs Theodor Duesterberg against Hitler and Hindenburg in March 1932. Hugenberg's DNVP siphons votes from the faltering Nazis in November 1932's crucial Reichstag election.

Sen. Cordell Hull (1871–1955): "Dry," anti-tariff freshman Tennessee Democrat. Former chairman of the Democratic National Committee. Log cabin–born. Tall (6'0") and lean, shy and lisping—and angling to be secretary of state under FDR.

Harold LeClair "The Old Curmudgeon" Ickes (1874–1952): Acerbic Chicago progressive "Republican." Ickes reluctantly organizes Gifford Pinchot's stillborn challenge to Herbert Hoover. "I can see no reason why the Republican Party should deliberately run into a smashing defeat to satisfy one man's ambition," says the pudgy Ickes of the paunchy Hoover.

Theodore Goldsmith "Ted" Joslin (1890–1944): Herbert Hoover's press secretary. Former *Boston Transcript* Washington correspondent. Joslin's March 1931 appointment, notes one clearly unimpressed reporter, was the "first known instance of a rat joining a sinking ship."

Joseph Patrick Kennedy (1888–1969): Boston-based investor and film magnate. Son-in-law of former Boston mayor John "Honey Fitz" Fitzgerald. He helps deliver the Democratic nod to FDR, but when Joe tries to impress Gloria Swanson, his former mistress, with his connections to the newly minted nominee ("I want you to say hello to him"), she hangs up on both of them.

Count Harry Clément Ulrich Kessler (1868–1937): Reputed son of his godfather, Germany's Kaiser Wilhelm I. Renowned patron of the arts. Acerbic observer of Weimar's fall and Hitler's rise.

Hubert Renfro "Red" Knickerbocker (1898–1949): Angular, red-headed, Texas-born *New York Post* and the *Philadelphia Public Ledger* Berlin correspondent.

Fiorello Henry "The Little Flower" La Guardia (1882–1947): East Harlem–based progressive Republican congressman. Defeated for mayor in a landslide in 1929. Co-author of 1932's pro-labor Norris-La Guardia Act. "I never could pronounce his first name," recalls "Cactus Jack" Garner, "so I just called him 'Frijole'—he liked that."

Marguerite Alice "Missy" LeHand (1898–1944): FDR's statuesque, blue-eyed, and intensely devoted private secretary. "There was no attempt to conceal their relationship . . . ," admits Franklin's son Elliott.

Walter Lippmann (1889–1974): Olympian *New York Herald-Tribune*–based syndicated columnist—"a Manhattan Zeus." An old Wilsonian, unimpressed with—if not depressed by—his fellow Harvard-alum Franklin Roosevelt ("a pleasant man without any important qualifications for the office").

Huey Pierce "The Kingfish" Long Jr. (1893–1935): Brash US senator. Former Louisiana governor. Dictatorial boss of his state. For FDR—but his anti–two-thirds rule convention antics threaten FDR's substantial southern support. An unexcelled—if unorthodox—demagogue. "A mob is coming here in six months to hang the other ninety-five of you damned scoundrels," Long informs the Senate, "and I'm undecided whether to stick here with you or go out and lead them."

Alice Roosevelt "Princess Alice" Longworth (1884–1980): TR's intractable daughter. Widow of House Speaker Nicholas Longworth. Veteran of a well-publicized protocol war with Vice President Curtis's sister "Dolly" Gann—and hell-bent on replacing Curtis on the ticket (and thus creating a Hoover-Roosevelt slate) with her younger half-brother Teddy Jr.

Louis Ferdinand, Prince of Prussia (1907–1994): The Kaiser's doctorate-holding grandson. Ford Motor Company employee. FDR, he recalls, was "like a father to me . . . a true aristocrat. . . ."

Kurt Lüdecke (1890–1960): Hitler's early financial supporter. Reputed "con man" and homosexual blackmailer. Hitler's early 1930s representative in America.

General Douglas MacArthur (1880–1964): Vain but brilliant US Army chief of staff. Commander of July 1932's controversial eviction of "Bonus

Army" marchers from their Anacostia Flats shanties. Huey Long, says FDR, is one of the two most dangerous men in the country: "The other is Douglas MacArthur."

William Gibbs McAdoo (1863–1941): Woodrow Wilson's son-in-law— and also his highly capable secretary of the treasury. Failed in 1920 and 1924 presidential bids. A "dry." Running for the Senate from California in 1932. A key to Garner's stunning upset of FDR in that state's primary. "California came here to nominate a President of the United States," McAdoo proclaims as he delivers the nomination to FDR. "She did not come here to deadlock this convention or to engage in another disastrous contest like that of 1924."

Rep. Louis Thomas McFadden (1876–1936): Pennsylvania Republican congressman. Former chair of the House Banking Committee. Anti-Semitic foe of international bankers, a reparations moratorium, the Federal Reserve— and Herbert Hoover. "I am," he alleges, "being watched in every move I make. . . ."

Otto Meissner (1880–1953): Hindenburg's scheming secretary of state—"a ruddy, flushed, well-set up, chubby person always too tightly encased in his clothes, his glance lurking behind goggles, at home with all regimes. . . ."

Henry Louis "The Sage of Baltimore" Mencken (1880–1956): Iconoclastic *Baltimore Sun* columnist and *American Mercury* editor. "Mr. Hoover is almost as sure of re-election next year," the rarely prescient Mencken writes in July 1931, "as he was in 1928."

Sgt. Earl R. Miller (1897–1973): Eleanor Roosevelt's New York State Police bodyguard. "Mrs. R," Miller reveals decades later, "was going to stick with [the] Governor until he was elected and then she and the Sergeant were going to get married."

Raymond Charles Moley (1886–1975): Columbia University law professor. Charter member of FDR's famed "Brains Trust." "I came to know one of the loveliest facets of Roosevelt's character: he stood by his people when they got into a jam—," Moley will recall, "sometimes even when they got him into a jam."

William Henry Davis "Alfalfa Bill" Murray (1869–1956): Toadsuck, Texas– born, irascible, rumpled, populist, racist Oklahoma governor. Actively seeking 1932's Democratic nomination. His slogan: "Bread, Butter, Bacon, and Beans."

John T. Pace (1899–1972): Detroit-based leader of the Bonus March's Communist faction. "I was told," reveals Pace, "to use every trick to bring about bloodshed. . . ."

Franz Joseph Hermann Michael Maria von Papen (zu Köningen) (1879–1969): German spymaster in the United States during the World War. Heinrich Brüning's replacement as chancellor in June 1932. His appointment "met with incredulity," noted French ambassador André François-Poncet. "No one smiled or tittered or laughed because Papen enjoyed the peculiarity of being taken seriously by neither his friends or his enemies. . . ."

John William Wright Patman (1893–1976): Populist East Texas congressman. He fights to deliver a World War veterans bonus.

Maj. George Smith Patton Jr. (1885–1945): Former aide-de-camp to General "Black Jack" Pershing. In 1932, a valued member of Douglas MacArthur's general staff. Hit by a brick as he leads six tanks ("a distasteful form of service") to smash the "Bonus Marchers."

Konrad Pietrzuch (1897–1932): Ethnically Polish Communist worker beaten to death at his Silesian home—in full view of his own mother. "My comrades!" Hitler exhorts his storm trooper murderers, "I am bound to you in unlimited loyalty in the face of this most hideous blood sentence. You have my picture hanging in your cells. How could I forsake you?"

Gifford Pinchot (1865–1946): Progressive Republican Pennsylvania governor. Former TR ally. Prohibitionist. Angling to replace Hoover in 1932. "No man in American politics," it is observed, "has had so many good issues and handled them so ineptly."

John Jakob Raskob (1879–1950): Democratic national chairman. DuPont and General Motors executive; developer of the new Empire State Building. Ardently "wet" and just as ardently Catholic (the father of twelve). For Al Smith. "I am firm in my belief," he announces in August 1929, "that anyone not only can be rich, but ought to be rich."

Angela Maria "Geli" Raubal (1908–1931): Adolf Hitler's half-niece. A resident in his plush Munich apartment. She was, said Hitler's friend and official photographer Heinrich Hoffmann, "an enchantress. . . . each and every one of us was devoted to her—especially her uncle. . . ."

Samuel Taliaferro "Sam" Rayburn (1882–1961): East Texas congressman. Shepherding the absent John Nance Garner's Democratic Convention forces.

"We have come to Chicago to nominate . . . Garner for the Presidency if we can. . . . ," Rayburn gingerly informs "Big Jim" Farley, "but we don't intend to make it another Madison Square Garden."

Helene Bertha Amalie "Leni" Riefenstahl (1902–2003): Captivating star of director G. W. Pabst's mountaineering film *Das Blaue Licht* (*The Blue Light*). "I had an almost apocalyptic vision that I was never able to forget," she recalls of first hearing Hitler speak. "It seemed as if the Earth's surface were spreading out in front of me, like a hemisphere that suddenly splits apart in the middle, spewing out an enormous jet of water, so powerful that it touched the sky and shook the earth."

Albert Cabell Ritchie (1876–1936): Democratic Maryland governor. A conservative, states-rights "wet" favorite son dark horse. Handsome ("It is no reflection to suggest that there would be fewer headlines were he less handsome")—but divorced. "In vagueness lies his one hope of victory," notes one observer of Ritchie, "and he is victoriously vague."

Joseph Taylor Robinson (1872–1937): US Senate minority leader. Al Smith's 1928 running mate. An Arkansas "dry" ("You cannot write on the banner of the Democratic party . . . the skull and crossbones emblematic of an outlawed trade"). "More than any other individual, perhaps," notes one observer, "he is responsible for the belief that there is no difference between the two major parties."

William Penn Adair "Will" Rogers (1879–1935): Oklahoma-born cowboy, vaudeville, Broadway, and motion picture star. America's favorite homespun philosopher and wise-cracker. Drawls Rogers: "I am not a member of an organized political party. I am a Democrat." Proving the point, Rogers secures twenty-two votes on the Democratic Convention's second ballot.

Ernst Julius Günther Röhm (1887–1934): Radical leader of Hitler's Sturmabteilung. Returned to Germany—and the NSDAP—after a self-imposed Bolivian exile. His flagrant homosexuality roils many. "All revolutions," Röhm presciently notes, "devour their own children."

Anna Eleanor Roosevelt Roosevelt (1884–1962): Theodore Roosevelt's niece. Still married to Franklin despite his wartime infidelities with her former social secretary. On the eve of his presidential nomination, she despairs for her future and threatens to flee Franklin and the White House to commence a new life with her State Police bodyguard Sgt. Earl Miller. "Now I will have no identity," Eleanor mourns even on election night.

Franklin Delano Roosevelt (1882–1945): Democratic governor of New York. Woodrow Wilson's assistant secretary of the navy. TR's fifth cousin. Undeterred by polio. A straddling "moist" on Prohibition. How will the cannily elusive FDR govern if elected president? "Philosophy?" he says. "I am a Christian and a Democrat—that's all."

Sara Delano Roosevelt (1854–1941): Franklin's doting, aristocratic mother. "Once I said to him: 'My son, don't give the orders all of the time. Let the other boys give them sometimes,'" she recalled. "'Mummie,' he said . . . 'if I didn't give the orders nothing would happen.'"

Theodore Roosevelt Jr. (1887–1944): TR's son, Alice Longworth's younger half-brother, Al Smith's 1924 gubernatorial opponent, and Herbert Hoover's governor-general of Puerto Rico and the Philippines.

Samuel Irving "Sammy the Rose" Rosenman (1896–1973): Texas-born former New York State assemblyman. Now FDR's gifted speechwriter. "Where shall we turn for advice?" FDR asks Rosenman. "Why not go to the universities of the country?" Rosenman answers. The result: the "Brains Trust."

Frederic Moseley Sackett Jr. (1868–1941): Former Republican US senator from Kentucky. US ambassador to Berlin. After secretly meeting Hitler, he dismisses him as "certainly not the type from which statesmen evolve."

Hjalmar Horace Greeley Schacht (1877–1970): Former *Reichsbank* president. Despite his parents' longtime residency in the United States, he vehemently opposes the American-created Young Plan for German reparations. An influential Hitler ally. "I [soon] learned what all of us experienced later," Schacht recalled, "that in a discussion with Hitler, his associates contributed only 5 per cent; Hitler himself supplied the remaining 95 per cent. . . ."

Gen. Kurt Friedrich Hermann Ferdinand von Schleicher (1882–1934): Master intriguer (incredibly, his surname literally means "schemer") of the unraveling Weimar Republic. His power stems largely from his friendship with his protégé Oskar von Hindenburg. Manipulates the rise and fall of both the Brüning and Papen Cabinets. Appointed chancellor himself in December 1932. "If there were no Nazis," he cynically decides, "it would be necessary to invent them."

Judge Samuel Seabury (1873–1958): Patrician investigator ("The Seabury Commission") of Mayor Jimmy Walker's corrupt Tammany regime. For Newton D. Baker. "This fellow Seabury," FDR privately complains to

Col. Edward House, "is merely trying to perpetrate another political play to embarrass me."

Franz Seldte (1882–1947): The one-armed founder and president of the German nationalist veterans' organization, the anti-republican ("We hate the present form of the German state with all our hearts . . .") *Stahlhelm*. Ally of the DNVP's Alfred Hugenberg. Seldte's deputy, Theodor Duesterberg, judges Berlin journalist Bella Fromm, "has background, vitality, and courage—all of which Franz Seldte . . . seems to lack."

Alfred Emanuel "The Happy Warrior" Smith (1873–1944): Picturesque Lower East Side–born former New York governor. Landslide loser to Hoover in 1928. Catholic, "wringing wet" ("To the millions who ask food he would give a drink"), and Tammany. Running again in 1932. "I will take off my coat and vest and fight to the end against any candidate," he now says of his erstwhile ally Franklin Roosevelt, "who persists in any demagogic appeal to the masses . . . to destroy themselves by setting class against class and rich against poor."

Luise Solmitz (1889–1973): Hanover schoolteacher. A budding Hitlerite—married to a Jew. "I decided to vote for the . . . Nazis," she writes in 1930, "it is a dangerous experiment. . . ."

Gregor Strasser (1892–1934): Left-wing former NSDAP leader of propaganda, now its powerful political director. Frustrated by 1932's continuing electoral deadlock and fearful of a Nazi collapse, he plots to join Kurt von Schleicher's shaky new government—enraging Hitler. "I am," bemoans Strasser, "a man marked by death."

Otto Johann Maximilian Strasser (1897–1974): Gregor Strasser's younger brother. Expelled from the NSDAP in July 1930, he forms the left-wing (but still anti-Semitic) anti-Hitler "Black Front."

Ernst Thälmann (1886–1944): Stalin-installed leader of the German Communist Party (KPD). His 1925 presidential campaign helps bestow the presidency on the doddering, reactionary Hindenburg. In 1932, Thälmann runs again and plays an even more dangerous game, deriding the Socialist SPD as "Social Fascists." The KPD's inflexible slogan: "A vote for Hindenburg is a vote for Hitler; a vote for Hitler is a vote for war."

Norman Mattoon Thomas (1884–1968): Presbyterian minister. Anti-Tammany crusader. As the Socialist Party's 1932 presidential candidate, Thomas garners 884,000 votes, but others on the left demand a more radical vision. Voting Socialist, says hard-line leftist John Dos Passos, is as satisfying "as drinking a bottle of near beer."

Dorothy Thompson (1893–1961): American journalist. Wife of Nobel Prize winner Sinclair Lewis. "It took [less than fifteen seconds] to measure the startling insignificance of this man . . . ," she writes of meeting Hitler. "Oh, Adolf! Adolf! You will be out of luck!"

Rexford Guy Tugwell (1891–1979): Columbia University agricultural expert. Among the more radical "Brains Trusters," advocating "collectivized progressivism." "Hoover's failures," noted Tugwell, "were more of an asset than Roosevelt's promises."

James John "Gentleman Jimmy" Walker (1881–1946): Captivating, but lazy and simply crooked, Tammany mayor of Jazz Age New York. Investigated for widespread corruption by Judge Seabury and FDR. "Beau James" hopes to charm his way free. His old friend Al Smith bluntly warns him: "Jim, you're through. You must resign for the good of the party."

Walter W. "Hot" Waters (1898–1959): The Portland, Oregon–based former Army sergeant commanding 1932's "Bonus Expeditionary Force" march on Washington. "My chief problem with the Communists," says Waters, "was to prevent the men of the B.E.F., literally, from almost killing any Communist they found among them."

James Eli "Sunny Jim" Watson (1864–1948): Old guard, backslapping, formerly Klan-backed Republican US Senate majority leader. When Democrats achieve gains (but not a majority) in 1930's elections, the artless Hoover shocks the GOP by suggesting Watson turn over the Senate to them. Hoover, grouses Watson, "knows less than a child about politics."

Bernhard "Isidor" Weiss (1880–1951): Berlin's SPD police commissioner. Mercilessly pilloried by Goebbels. "We felt," Weiss fatalistically sighs, "that what must be, must be."

Wilhelm II (Friedrich Wilhelm Viktor Albrecht von Preussen; Frederick William Victor Albert of Prussia) (1859–1941): Germany's exiled last Kaiser. Still hoping for a restoration, but soon to abandon hope in Hitler.

Owen D. Young (1874–1962): Self-made chairman of General Electric. Founder of RCA. Creator of the controversial "Young Plan" for German wartime reparations. *Time's* 1929 "Man of the Year." A 1932 Democratic dark horse.

Giuseppe Zangara (1900–1933): Down-on-his-luck Italian immigrant. In February 1933, the unstable 5'1" bricklayer ("I hate all presidents") comes closer than anyone to derailing the New Deal. But he will miss.

Major German Political Parties

National Socialist German Workers Party (*Nationalsozialistische Deutsche Arbeiterpartei*—NSDAP): the "Nazis."

Social Democratic Party of Germany (*Sozialdemokratische Partei Deutschlands*—SPD): the "Social Democrats" or "Socialists."

Communist Party of Germany (*Kommunistische Partei Deutschlands*—KPD): the Communists.

Centre Party (*Deutsche Zentrumspartei*—**Zentrum**): the major Catholic party.

German National People's Party (*Deutschnationale Volkspartei*—DNVP): the "Nationalists."

Bavarian People's Party (*Bayerische Volkspartei*—BVP): the Bavarian and more conservative branch of the Zentrum.

German People's Party (*Deutsche Volkspartei*—DVP): a right-wing liberal party.

German State Party (DStP) (until 1930 the **German Democratic Party** [*Deutsche Staatspartei*]-DDP): a more left-wing liberal party.

Christian Social People's Service (*Christlich-Sozialer Volksdienst*—CSVD): a conservative Protestant Party.

Reich Party of the German Middle Class (*Reichspartei des deutschen Mittelstandes*—WP) (until 1925 the **Economic Party of the German Middle Classes** [*Wirtschaftspartei des Deutschen Mittelstandes*]—WP): the "Economic Party," a conservative party.

Conservative People's Party (*Konservative Volkspartei*—KVP): an ill-fated, more moderate offshoot of the DNVP.

CHAPTER ONE

"A gentleman cast himself down fifteen stories"

HE WAS NOT THEN AT ALL A MAN OF DESTINY.

Or, if he was, it may have all been past tense.

Plump, ruddy, and balding, he currently counted only among history's more spectacular walking disasters, vaingloriously presiding over a heady mix of bloody military and domestic debacles and ultimately ruinous monetary policies. Reduced now to politics' mere outskirts, he stared glumly into their guarded precincts through a triad of foggy prisms: scotch, cigar smoke, and his current career—journalism.

Meet the Rt. Hon. Winston Spencer Churchill, mastermind of London's bloody Siege of Sidney Street and of far-gorier Gallipoli, architect of his nation's badly executed return to the gold standard,[1] and presently persona non grata in Britain's Conservative Party.

. . . and tourist to America.

He arrived in September 1929, and though his political wardrobe might be in tatters, he still sported the mantle—and enjoyed the prerogatives—of simply being Winston Churchill. He delivered speeches and secured a fabulous £40,000 worth of writing contracts. His friend, the Wall Street speculator Bernard Baruch, provided him with a private train car and accommodations.[2] In California, he chatted with the great Chaplin as The Little Tramp ("bolshy in politics but delightful in conversation"[3]) shot *City Lights.*[4] At Santa Barbara, he stayed with former Treasury Secretary William Gibbs McAdoo.[5] At San Simeon, he met with publishing mogul William Randolph Hearst ("A grave simple child"[6]) and Hearst mistress Marion Davies and swam in their heated marble pool.[7] Returning to Manhattan, he accepted *Mrs.* Hearst's hospitality at her Riverside Drive quintuplex penthouse, serenaded all the while by Rudy Vallee's orchestra.[8] At publisher Condé Nast's glass-enclosed

Park Avenue rooftop he rubbed elbows with such luminaries as Cole Porter, George Jean Nathan, Gloria Swanson, Walter Lippmann, and Jascha Heifetz.[9] There, Winston's traveling companion, his younger brother, Major John "Jack" Churchill, chanced upon a marvelous dancing companion. "I can only dance well with a good partner," recalled Jack, "and that night I danced superbly. My partner was Adele Astaire. She attracted me so much that next morning I followed up our meeting with a visit to her home."[10]

Winston also desired to meet with New York's newly elected governor, a chap named Franklin Roosevelt, but Roosevelt, being in office, while Churchill was not, was just too busy—too busy even to respond personally, palming off the task to the mere chairman of the New York State Agricultural Advisory Committee, his Hudson Valley chum, Henry Morgenthau Jr.[11] FDR instead attended to a Democrat banquet in nearby Springfield, Massachusetts.

That, however, was not too great a disappointment. Winston's Democrat of choice was not Franklin at all, but his gubernatorial predecessor, "The Happy Warrior," Alfred E. Smith, and Smith had proved more obliging than FDR, even allowing Churchill—and Baruch—to escort him onstage at Manhattan's Tammany Hall, where he rousingly excoriated longshot mayoral challengers Republican Fiorello La Guardia and Socialist Norman Thomas ("Do they take the citizens of this city for mental defectives?"[12]) for their attacks on his flamboyant ally Mayor James J. "Gentleman Jimmy" Walker.[13]

In Washington, the far less flamboyant President Herbert Hoover also took a meeting with Churchill.[14] Their conversation, while hardly edifying, was, at least, polite—quite the achievement considering that during the Great War Churchill had attempted having "The Great Humanitarian" Hoover arrested for shipping foodstuffs beyond enemy German lines.[15] Time heals some wounds.

Things were stirring when Churchill returned to Manhattan in late October—stirring and shaking and crashing.

Following an early lunch, he found himself strolling about lower Manhattan. "I happened to be walking down Wall Street at the worst moment of the panic, and a perfect stranger who recognized me invited me to enter the gallery of the Stock Exchange," Churchill would recall. It was packed—with a record 722 visitors—as the once-booming stock market collapsed before their very eyes. Minutes later, nervous authorities shuttered gallery doors, and Winston Spencer Churchill, as so often his practice, now possessed a position at history's ringside.

"I expected to see pandemonium," he soon wrote, "but the spectacle that met my eyes was one of surprising calm and orderliness. There are only 1,200 members of the New York Stock Exchange, each of whom has paid over £100,000 for his ticket. These gentlemen are precluded by the strongest rules from running or raising their voices unduly. So there they were, walking to and fro like a slow motion picture of a disturbed ant heap, offering each other enormous blocks of securities at one-third of the old prices and half their present value, and for many minutes together finding no one strong enough to pick up the sure fortunes they were compelled to offer."[16]

On Fifth Avenue, that morose evening, Churchill dined with Bernard Baruch and with forty of Baruch's associates, among them the most influential and wealthiest of New York bankers and investors. This October 24, 1929—"Black Thursday"—the stock market plunged 11 percent before steadying itself to close at a relatively less disastrous loss of 6.38 percent. Baruch, either on to something or not, jokingly addressed his guests as "Friends and *former* millionaires."[17]

In Springfield, on Monday, October 28, Franklin Roosevelt wasted no time in converting the Crash into political capital. "If such a market debacle ever took place in a Democratic administration," he maintained, "it would immediately be hailed as the result of business bungling by the party in power." As if on cue, a telegram ("Will they blame the Stock Market on the Democrats?—Al"[18]) arrived. Most present assumed it from Al Smith. It was a hoax.[19]

Democrats in Springfield might chuckle. So might Bernard Baruch. He, after all, had already fled the market.[20] Others with far fewer resources behind them found it more difficult to laugh, among these being a fellow guest at Churchill's own Savoy Plaza hostelry. "Under my very window," Churchill recalled, "a gentleman cast himself down fifteen stories and was dashed to pieces, causing a wild commotion and the arrival of the fire brigade."[21]

Churchill lingered in New York. Wall Street had sustained a roundhouse punch that Thursday. It wobbled but remained on its feet. On Black Tuesday, October 29, 1929, it crumpled down for the count.

The great boom was over. So was Churchill's American expedition. The next morning, at Manhattan's West 14th Street pier, he and Major Jack boarded the Cunard steamship *Berengaria*, bound for Southampton and home. Winston maintained a strange silence, refusing all farewell interviews. Jack curtly informed the press that his brother was asleep and had been interviewed "forty-two times already," but, perhaps there was more to it than that.[22] Prohibition was the rule, if not the practice, for America. It was neither for Winston Churchill.

Scant weeks previously, Winston debarked in America in bright and rich and gay 1929. He set sail now for a world headed straight for . . . 1932.

CHAPTER TWO

"I won't be ready until 1932"

FRANKLIN DELANO ROOSEVELT WAS, INDEED, A VERY BUSY MAN IN 1929—and had been for a very long time.

Busy with politics, busy with government—but, above all, busy with ambition.

Like Winston Churchill, he seemed born to rule, born into an aristocratic Hudson Valley family in January 1882. It was his father James's second marriage, his bride being the much-younger (by a good twenty-six years), but, at least, equally aristocratic, Sara Ann Delano. They were sixth cousins,[1] but that was of no concern, for, after all, James's first bride had been his first cousin once removed.[2]

Though Franklin possessed a half-brother, James Roosevelt "Rosey" Roosevelt, "Rosey" was nearly twenty-eight years older than he. Pampered young Franklin was essentially an only child to his parents, and, more important, literally an only child to his doting mother.

It remains difficult to identify a future president—or anyone, for that matter—bred under more pleasant circumstances than Franklin Roosevelt. There was, of course, the family's significant wealth, their pleasant river estate and great house at Hyde Park, rafts of servants, a twenty-eight-foot ice yacht, a thirty-four-room "cottage" at Campobello on Canada's Bay of Fundy,[3] their annual excursions to the continent. But there was something much more to it than that. Franklin Roosevelt was loved and cherished. Very late in his life he wrote, "In thinking back to my earliest days I am impressed by the peacefulness and regularity of things. . . ."[4]

There was, however, a rather significant blot on the family escutcheon. James Roosevelt, for all his virtues, was a Democrat.[5] This circumstance, however, not only earned half-brother "Rosey" a consular appointment[6] from President Grover Cleveland, but also facilitated five-year-old Franklin's 1887 visit to the White House. "My little man," said Cleveland, "I am making a strange wish for you. It is that you may never be President of the United States."[7]

There seemed little chance of that, or, even of Franklin replicating his father's election as Democratic supervisor of Hyde Park.[8] Privately educated, Franklin had little contact with children his own age. His first true "classroom" experiences occurred not at Hyde Park or New York City, but rather, abroad, at summer *Stadtschule* sessions[9] at Germany's Bad Nauheim, where his sixty-ish father, in deteriorating health, took the spa's waters.[10]

It was then that Franklin's placid cocoon turned inside-out. In the fall of 1896, he exited the world of private tutors to enter Groton, a premier Episcopalian boarding school.[11] He did not fit in easily. Worse, hot springs do only so much for ailing hearts. James Roosevelt died in December 1900.

Franklin entered Harvard (his father had graduated from Harvard Law[12]) in September 1900, only to repeat his Groton experience. Drawing a "gentlemanly C" average,[13] he failed to gain membership to the exclusive Porcellian Club ("the greatest disappointment he ever had"[14]). To ease her son's existence (or, perhaps just to oversee it), young widow Sara took up residency at Cambridge. It was a pattern to be repeated. Yet, Franklin had his triumphs. He emerged as editor-in-chief of the *Harvard Crimson*.[15] His fifth cousin, Theodore Roosevelt (who *had* made Porcellian), had become vice president, and, in September 1901, upon William McKinley's assassination, president himself. Even cousin Ted's mere vice-presidency had so thrilled Franklin that he momentarily abandoned the Democratic Party, to, in 1900, join Harvard's Republican Club, so as in some small way to boost Rough Rider TR's chances.[16]

Most significant, the century's first decade witnessed his courtship. On March 17, 1905, in the family tradition he married his own sixth cousin: the gangly Anna Eleanor Roosevelt. The date had nothing to do with St. Patrick's Day, but once more on family. Giving away the orphaned twenty-year-old bride was her late father's brother—President "Uncle Ted" Roosevelt, and the date had to be reset again and again for his convenience.[17] He, not they, was the star of this—and *every*—show. "After the ceremony," FDR recalled to his eldest son, James, "when TR moved into the library for a sip of punch, the crowd followed him as if he were the Pied Piper, leaving your mother and me standing all alone and forlorn."[18]

But cousin-bride or not, the marriage upset FDR's protective mother. To Sara, her only child wrote reassuringly: "Dear Mummy, you know that nothing can ever change what we have been and always will be to each other."[19]

FDR attended, but did not graduate from, Columbia School of Law. Nonetheless, he passed the bar, entering into practice with the small but prestigious firm of Carter, Ledyard & Milburn. His personally drafted business card proclaimed:

> Franklin D. Roosevelt
> Counselor at Law
> 54 Wall Street
> New York
>
> *I beg to call your attention to my own excellent facilities for carrying on every description of legal business. Unpaid bills a specialty. Briefs on the liquor question furnished free to ladies. Race suicides cheerfully prosecuted. Small dogs chloroformed without charge. Babies raised under advice of expert grandmother etc., etc.[20]*

He was, shall we say, not in love with the law—nor in any sense, particularly familiar with it. "I went to a big law office in New York," he recalled, "And somebody the day after I got there said, 'Go up and answer the calendar call in the supreme court tomorrow morning. We have such and such a case on.'

"Then the next day somebody gave me a deed of transfer of some land. He said, 'Take it up to the county clerk's office.' I had never been to the county clerk's office. And there I was, theoretically a full-fledged lawyer."[21]

The great tidal waves of history may often raise up the most obscure pebbles. So it was in 1910 when "Uncle Ted" broke with his White House successor William Howard Taft, sundered the Republican Party wide-open, and ultimately elected not merely Woodrow Wilson but a host of otherwise unelectable Democrats to public office.

Among these was a young Wall Street lawyer who might otherwise have found his practice restricted to chloroforming small dogs.[22]

Dutchess County Democrats nominated Franklin to an invariably suicidal run for the state senate.[23] He surprised everyone, most likely even himself, by winning, thus emulating TR's own experience in the New York legislature. Arriving in Albany, his great good fortune only continued. Their 1910 landslide gave Democrats rare control of the legislature, and, thus, the ability to name the state's next US senator. Tammany Hall offered its machine hack choice, a Buffalo assemblyman turned Wall Street lawyer named "Blue-Eyed Billy" Sheehan. A small coterie of reform (and largely upstate) Democrats demurred—and held the balance of power. Deadlocking the process, they defeated Sheehan, and, though, Tammany still managed to designate Blue Eyed Billy's replacement,[24] the tussle earned freshman senator FDR a place in the headlines, thanks, in part, to adulatory coverage from *New York Herald* reporter Louis McHenry Howe.

Few then found young Senator Roosevelt particularly compelling. Even the gnome-like (just 5'4"[25]), often unsanitary Howe thought him to be a "spoiled silk-pants kind of guy."[26] New York Consumers League reformer Frances Perkins noted a disturbing "streak of vanity and insincerity,"[27] but Howe uncannily looked beyond that. "[A]lmost at that very first meeting," said Howe, "I made up my mind that he was Presidential timber and that nothing but an accident could keep him from becoming President of the United States."[28]

FDR supported TR in 1904.[29] He might have supported him yet again in 1912. Other Democrats, such as Louisiana's John M. Parker, had. But Franklin threw in his lot not with "Uncle Ted." Perhaps he found himself—despite his battles with Tammany—comfortable as an elected Democrat in Albany. Perhaps he merely settled back into a permanent relationship with the party of his own branch of the Roosevelts. Or perhaps Franklin had concluded that one might only rise so far as the next Roosevelt in the Republican or Progressive parties. The field was too crowded, his credentials decidedly tenuous. One would have to crawl over too many direct descendants of the Rough Rider. In the Democratic Party, one had the Roosevelt field to oneself.

Franklin Roosevelt cast his still small lot with Woodrow Wilson.

Politics has its rewards. Unsure of how long he might maintain his senate seat in Dutchess County's rock-ribbed GOP environs, upon Wilson's election, he fairly jumped at the chance to again emulate TR and assume the post of assistant secretary of the navy.

When war came in April 1917, FDR played his part in victory, but, personally, he remained less adroit. He schemed, and not always well, against his superiors and, still at odds with Tammany, badly lost a 1914 primary for the US Senate.[30] Worse still, he became far too social with Eleanor's social secretary, the comely and charming Lucy Mercer. Upon his return from a European inspection trip in the fall of 1918, he took sick. It was then that Eleanor discovered and inspected a cache of love letters from Lucy to her husband.[31] Divorce would have ruined Franklin politically (Secretary of the Navy Josephus Daniels would have fired him) and financially (Sara would have cut him off; maternal love then had its limits). Eleanor and Franklin remained together, but only in a most awkward, and, if not loveless—sexless—alliance.

Such peccadillos proved no barrier to a vice-presidential nomination in 1920. The Democratic Party possessed little chance of victory, and so second billing on a hopelessly second-place ticket was not worth much. Besides, Tammany Hall wanted him shunted away from state politics, and this was as good a way as any to do it. More positively, FDR brought not only the Roosevelt name to the slate, his nomination also tossed a tangible bone to the battered Wilson wing of the party. On the campaign trail, he, nonetheless, made his mistakes. Boasting often outpaced veracity, particularly in regard to his official actions regarding Latin America ("You know I have had a little something to do with the running of a couple of little republics. The facts are that I wrote Haiti's Constitution myself, and if I do say it, I think it a pretty good constitution."[32]). Mendacity ("I was wholly erroneously reported"[33]) often followed boasting. But, with Sara helping to finance his campaign tour, he proved remarkably energetic and enthusiastic. Still, FDR and his running mate, Ohio governor James Middleton Cox, lost in a spectacular debacle, the greatest Democratic defeat since 1860, in fact, up to that point its greatest ever.

The *Baltimore Sun's* dyspeptic H. L. Mencken dismissed him as "a pale and somewhat pathetic caricature of his late relative, Theodore . . . resembling the Rough Rider much as a wart resembles the Matterhorn,"[34] but, all in all, Franklin had not performed too badly. He had seen the country. It had seen him—conceivably, not the last of him—and, perhaps sufficiently chastened by events, he finally seemed to be learning patience. The story goes that in 1922 FDR predicted to Wilson's highly capable former solicitor general John W. Davis that Davis might emerge as 1924's nominee.

"You might get it yourself," Davis remarked, perhaps more from politeness than sound political calculation.

"No," Roosevelt countered, "I won't be ready until 1932."[35]

He, in fact, wouldn't—because *it* happened.

Polio. Contracted, most likely in late July 1921 while visiting a Boy Scout encampment at Palisades Park, New Jersey, its symptoms struck FDR two weeks later at Campobello, following his swim in the Bay of Fundy's freezing waters. A 102-degree fever raged. He lost control of first his left and then his right leg. His once-smiling face suffered partial paralysis.[36] Death beckoned. But he survived, with permanently withered, largely useless, legs, relying upon heavy metal braces to even stand, dependent on others for virtually any mobility. He might have easily given up and been hidden away at Hyde Park, collecting stamps and prints of War of 1812 naval vessels. Sara counseled that. Eleanor and Louis Howe, to their credit, did not.[37]

The experience took away half of the man, though many said it made him whole.

"There are times," thought Howe, "when I think that Franklin might never have been President if he had not been stricken. You see, he had a thousand interests. You couldn't pin him down. He rode, he swam, he played golf, tennis, he sailed, he collected stamps, he politicked, he did everything under the sun a man could think of doing. Then, suddenly, there he was, flat on his back with nothing to do but think. He began to read, he talked, he gathered people around him—his thoughts expanded. He began to see the other fellow's point of view. He thought of others who were ill and afflicted and in want. He dwelt on many things that had not bothered him much before. Lying there, he grew bigger, day by day."[38]

There was, it went without saying, much more to polio than presidential ambitions or an ability to suddenly focus upon public policy. There was the terrible human toll, both upon Franklin and upon those who knew him, most especially on his family. Son James would not see his now-crippled father until returning home from Groton for Christmas 1921. James, fearful of what to expect, stood frozen at the door of his father's bedroom, his legs as paralyzed as his father's, his lip quavering in both fear and immeasurable sorrow.

FDR would have none of that.

"'Come here, old man!" Franklin bellowed. "I rushed over and received his embrace," James recalled, "and I learned right then and there that whatever had happened to his legs had not affected the power in his arms. Then, even though I was a Roosevelt and a Grotonian, I cried a bit, but, with Pa squeezing me and slapping me on the back and carrying on enthusiastically about how 'grand' I looked, I soon was chattering along with him."[39]

Such a man could not easily be beaten.

"There had been a plowing up of his nature," Frances Perkins now observed. "The man emerged completely warm-hearted, with new humility of spirit and a firmer understanding of philosophical concepts."[40]

Yet, it was an odd sort of humility. Said Brains Truster Rexford Tugwell, "humiliation had not made him a humble man,"[41] and by that, presumably, he meant that FDR's faith in himself had not diminished, it had only grown perhaps exponentially. "He was never a man of little faith;" Tugwell also later explained, "after his sickness he was a man of unassailable confidence. If so terrible a disease had not stopped his progress, if he had been allowed to go on, surely nothing could stop him . . . He had no doubts, no qualms about asking for power and then more power."[42]

All things considered, he waited remarkably little for his chance of a comeback. In 1924, New York's Democratic governor, Alfred E. Smith, sought the presidency and needed a stentorian voice to place his name in nomination. His first choice, the eloquent Tammany congressman Bourke Cockran (it was said Churchill modeled himself in part upon Cockran) had inconveniently died before he might perform the honors.[43] It was only then that Franklin delivered his memorable peroration of Smith as "the Happy Warrior of the political battlefield," though the words were not his, and he, in fact, hated such "poetry."[44] But it was not poetry that won him the day. It was sheer grit, the sight of him painfully yet triumphantly making his way down the aisle to the podium on his son James's arm, "gripping . . . so hard it hurt."[45]

"Here on the stage," the rising young author Will Durant wrote glowingly, "was Franklin Roosevelt—beyond question the finest man that has appeared at either convention. Beside him the master minds who held the platform . . . were crude bourgeois, porters suddenly made rich.

"A figure tall and proud, even in suffering, pale with years of struggle against paralysis, a frame nervous and yet self-controlled with that tense, taut unity of spirit which lifts the complex soul above those whose calmness is mere stolidity; most obviously a gentleman and a scholar, a man softened and cleansed and illumined with pain.

"This is a civilized man; he could look Balfour and Poincaré in the face. For the moment we are lifted up."[46]

Roosevelt, himself, however, could only lift up so much. The convention itself was a great squabbling train wreck, rambling on for 104 ballots, rent by controversies over Prohibition and the Klan (though Roosevelt dodged both). It ultimately denied the Catholic and "wet" Smith the nomination—delivering it to, of all people, the obscure sacrificial lamb John W. Davis. FDR bided his time, for, after all, not only was he crippled, so was the Democratic Party, buried under a dozen years of GOP ascendancy. FDR maintained his contacts within the party but sidestepped a chance to run in 1926 for the US Senate.[47]

Returning to Wall Street, to the Fidelity & Deposit Company of Maryland, he utilized his formidable political skills to peddle surety bonds.[48] He invested in strange sorts of things, like newfangled (but still unprofitable) vending machines[49] and placing cameras in rail stations and stores.[50] He lost twenty-five thousand dollars in a lobster-freezing scheme[51] and hoped to profit personally from the hyper-inflation then wracking Germany.[52] It was not lobsters or worthless deutschmarks, however, that brought him financial stability. It was his seventy-three-year-old half-brother Rosey's death in May 1927[53] and the $100,000 in securities left to him.[54]

There was the oddest of moments when FDR might have tossed politics away. In April 1923, consistent with his love for the sea, he dashed off a screenplay on the life of John Paul Jones and, like any other first-time author, packed it off for acceptance. He was, of course, not like any other writer. He was even then Franklin Roosevelt, and when Paramount's Adolf Zukor received his query Zukor instructed his staff "to let him down easy." Studio functionary Jane West visited FDR's townhouse to string him along, and the charade proceeded for three full months. Finally, the letdown had to come.

Years later, he met West once more and confided, "I think, at the time, I wanted to sell my story . . . and become a professional writer more than anything else in my life. My darkest moment was when you told me Paramount had rejected it."[55]

It was, of course, perhaps not, what he wanted most.

He wanted most to walk.

In October 1924, FDR, Eleanor, and his twenty-six-year-old secretary, Miss Marguerite "Missy" LeHand, first visited a ramshackle resort at rustic Warm Springs, Georgia.[56] It might have been the tales told him by the locals of the curative powers of such warm, bubbling waters—or recollections of his father's days at Bad Nauheim. But, for whatever reason, Franklin (using the bulk of his inheritance from half-brother Rosey) grew convinced that if anything might heal him, it would be these waters, this place. Wrote FDR to Sara: "I feel that a great 'cure' for infantile paralysis and kindred diseases could well be established here."[57]

He would often so expound, to his family, to the outside world, and most of all, to his fellow invalids. It was, as he knew, always best to hold out the hand of hope to the desperate and the frightened. False hope is better than real despair.

One day, a nurse at Warm Springs asked him about his own goal.

His face, invariably so beaming, hardened. "I'll walk into a room without scaring everybody half to death," he vowed. "I'll stand easily enough in front of people that they'll forget I'm a cripple!"[58]

Decades later, the historians Peter Collier and David Horowitz perceptively observed: "Warm Springs became [FDR's] equivalent of TR's Badlands experience—a place where he found that he had something in common with common men and women and where he toughened his soul as well as his body. No one would again charge him with being effeminate after his days at the resort. The 'streak of vanity and insincerity' that Frances Perkins saw as his chief quality was still there, but it had been subordinated and controlled. He learned lessons of sensibility as well as survival as a result of his involvement with others."[59]

In 1928, Al Smith summoned him again and not merely for a nominating speech. "The Happy Warrior" had finally received his presidential nomination (at a dull convention termed "the longest wake any Irishman ever attended"[60]) and now begged Roosevelt to run to succeed him as governor. FDR demurred. He was not yet ready, he felt, physically. Nor did the political times seem propitious. Whether Smith—or his Republican opponent Herbert Hoover—was elected, Roosevelt calculated they would serve two terms. His time for the governorship would come, not in 1928, but rather four years hence—in 1932. There was, Franklin calculated, no need to rush.

He ducked Smith's calls. He wired him: "My physicians are very definite in stating that the continued improvement in my walking is dependent on my avoiding the cold climate of winter and taking the exercises here in the winter months. It probably means getting rid of my leg braces within the next two years and that would be impossible at Albany."[61] He might have even believed that.

Finally, connected only through Eleanor's intervention,[62] Roosevelt, grudgingly agreed to accept the nomination if state Democrats tendered it to him. He prayed they wouldn't. "Well," FDR finally informed his family, "if I've got to run for Governor there's no use in all of us getting sick about it!"[63]

Missy LeHand[64] ("Don't you dare! Don't you dare!"[65]) and Louis Howe[66] ("MESS IS NO NAME FOR IT"[67]) were yet to be convinced, but Sara Roosevelt now needed no prodding. "Now what follows is *really private*," she wrote her son on the day of his nomination. "In case of your election, I know your salary is smaller than the one you get now. I am prepared to make the difference up to you."[68]

Al Smith ("a governor doesn't have to be an acrobat"[69]) advised Franklin that if elected he might still sojourn as long as he wished at Warm Springs. Lieutenant governor running mate Herbert Lehman could ably handle matters in his absence. It was no great vote of confidence in either Franklin's physical—or mental—powers. FDR was, in fact, being cast in the now-familiar role of patrician front-man. Largely Catholic Tammany had tapped Protestants Robert Anderson Van Wyck, George B. McClellan Jr., and William Jay Gaynor as its front-men for mayor at the turn of the century. Boston Irish Democrats had backed wealthy WASPs such as Andrew J. Peters for mayor, Joseph B. Ely for governor, and Marcus A. Coolidge for US senator. New Jersey machine Democrats captured the governorship via an icy Presbyterian college president—Thomas Woodrow Wilson.[70] FDR merely followed in this handy tradition: one, it must be confessed, practiced not only by Democrats. Republicans like New York's Tom "The Easy Boss" Platt and Ohio's Marcus Alonzo Hanna also resorted to it—with another Roosevelt: Theodore. As the Wilson and TR cases demonstrated, even if the stratagem proves successful (perhaps especially if it is successful), it involves substantial dangers.

Thus, was Alfred Emmanuel Smith cursed. Once committed to a new campaign, FDR's old war horse galloped again. By election's end, Roosevelt was mocking his opponents for their "concern" regarding his health. In town after town, he addressed huge crowds. "And then, for good measure," he famously crowed, "we just dropped into Schenectady and spoke there earlier in the evening, and now here we are in Troy. Too bad about this unfortunate sick man, isn't it?"[71]

Election Night, November 6, 1928, found Al Smith as hopelessly vanquished as James M. Cox or John W. Davis. Four times elected governor, the very Catholic Smith forfeited even his own state to Herbert Hoover. That FDR might triumph as Smith stumbled seemed implausible at best. But when the final votes had been counted Roosevelt miraculously squeaked through to a narrow victory—by just 25,608 votes out of more than four million cast.[72]

A star pointing at the White House still shone over Albany's Executive Mansion.

But no longer over Al Smith.

CHAPTER THREE

"Everything should be blown up"

A MUCH OLDER, PREVIOUSLY MARRIED HUSBAND.

A far younger wife, this, her first marriage.

A doting mother. A much-loved son. A, shall we say, messy genealogy.

Such are the similarities in the beginnings of our tales. Many, many are the differences.

— ◦ ~ —

Adolf Hitler. How might we understand this man? Others have come from similar spaces and times. They reached neither his heights nor his depths. He is simply beyond our grasp. For, after all, who can understand *anyone*, even the most ordinary of us? In most instances, we cannot even comprehend our very selves—our motives, our accomplishments, our failings. Compared to Hitler, understanding an FDR or a Churchill is 2 + 2 = 4.

No, let us not even pretend to fathom or explain him.

Let us merely narrate what we can—and hope for the best.

— ◦ ~ —

Our story begins on a river—one not so nearly as broad as Franklin Roosevelt's Rhine-like Hudson, but similarly bound by magnificent mountainscapes. At Braunau-am-Inn, on Holy Saturday, April 20, 1889, twenty-eight-year-old Klara Pölzl Hitler ("a beautiful woman to the day of her death"[1]), wife of a fifty-one-year-old Austrian customs official named Alois Hitler, gave birth. In the New World, the van Rosenvelts had quickly become the Roosevelts. In hardscrabble, rural Austria, Alois Hitler's family surname followed a more tortured—and far less grand—evolution. Alois, himself born illegitimate to the forty-two-year-old servant Maria Anna Schicklgruber, had until age thirty-nine been "Alois Schicklgruber." At that age, he adopted the surname "Hitler," a variant of his itinerant and impecunious stepfather's, the miller,

Johann Georg Hiedler. Johann Georg Hiedler *might* have been Alois's actual father. Or not. That "honor" may, by right, have belonged to Johann Georg's younger brother, Johann Nepomuk, who actually raised young Alois.

Alois entered government service early—at age eighteen. He married late—at thirty-six. We know little about that marriage, though its basic facts are strange enough. His bride Anna Glasl-Hörer, the adopted daughter of a high customs official, was fifty. Soon, she became an invalid, and, perhaps even sooner, Alois took up with his kitchen maid Franziska "Fanni" Matzelsberger. In January 1882, Fanni gave birth to their illegitimate son, Alois Jr.[2] First wife Anna died that April, leaving Alois free to marry second wife Fanni thirteen months later. A daughter, Angela, soon followed, as did Fanni's own death in August 1884. By now, Alois was involved with yet another young servant girl (and third wife), the aforementioned Klara Pölzl. She was five months pregnant—by Alois, but not with Adolf. He would not arrive until April 1889. By then she had delivered three other children—Gustav, Ida, and Otto. All died very young.[3]

If Alois Hitler's background was not enough a version of a backwater Austrian soap-opera, his consanguinity with Klara Pölzl was more than enough. Klara's mother, Johanna Hiedler, was Johann Nepomuk Hiedler's daughter. If Johann Georg Hiedler (Alois's official father) was his actual progenitor, Klara was Alois's first cousin once removed. Bad enough. But if, as many believed, Johann Nepomuk Hiedler was indeed, Alois's actual father, Klara was actually Alois's niece.[4] Throughout their marriage she continued to address her husband as "uncle."[5]

The Hitler/Hiedler/Schicklgruber family certainly contained not only a too ample share of inbreeding but also the mental illness and disabilities that often accompanies it.[6] A mentally ill second cousin, Aloisia Veit, even found herself euthanized in 1940 in a Nazi gas chamber.[7] In part for such reasons—illegitimacy, infidelity, and incest—Adolf Hitler never appreciated attempts to pry into his background. "People must not know who I am," he exploded to half-brother Alois's son Patrick in 1930, "They must not know where I come from and who my family is. . . ."[8]

"I'll kill myself," he sobbed as he sprang from the room, "I'll put a gun to my head."[9]

But was Adolf merely inbred—or also half-bred? Not fully German at all? A strain of Czech blood in this muddled border region was hardly out of the question.[10] Worse, some said his grandfather was not a Hiedler at all, but a Jew named Frankenberger or Frankenreiter.[11] Few now credit that latter possibility, but the theory's significance may not lay in its actual truth, but whether Hitler believed it true.[12] As his biographer, R. G. Waite, theorized,

Hitler conceived "Jewishness to be an evil within himself, a poison to be purged, a demon to be exorcised."[13]

The ray of light in all this darkness was, as is often the case, the love between mother and son. As Franklin Roosevelt enjoyed an unusually close relationship with his mother, Adolf Hitler's was, conceivably, closer still. "My stepmother always took his part," his half-brother Alois recalled. "He would get the craziest ideas and get away with it. . . . He had no friends, took to no one and could be very heartless. He could fly into a rage over any triviality."[14] The family doctor, the Jewish Dr. Eduard Bloch, contended that he had "never witnessed a closer attachment"[15] between mother and son.

While Franklin's relationship with his much-older father was, indeed, truly loving, the relationship between the demanding father Alois Sr. and rebellious son Adolf proved tension-filled and often violent. Adolf, recalled his younger sister Paula, "challenged my father to extreme harshness and . . . got his sound thrashing every day. He was a scrubby little rogue, and all attempts of his father to thrash him for his rudeness and to cause him to love the profession of an official of the state were in vain."[16]

Yes, the artistically inclined Adolf rebelled against his father's demands to follow him into the civil service, but it was not the case that the son rebelled against all the father stood for. While Klara was devoutly Catholic, Alois was not.[17] And, though the very young Hitler served in both the parish choir and at the altar, what little religiosity he possessed soon passed. "At thirteen, fourteen, fifteen, I no longer believed in anything, certainly none of my friends still believed in the so-called communion, only a few totally stupid honor students! Except, at the time, I thought everything should be blown up."[18] His early biographer Konrad Heiden reports a "legend" that, at age fourteen, Hitler spat out the consecrated Host as a deliberate sacrilege.[19]

He read voraciously and went to the opera—to Wagner,[20] of course, entranced by the music and the drama of the old Norse myths and heroes. Though Austrian, his sympathies lay not at all with that tottering empire. He found it to be a mongrelized aberration. His loyalties lay across the border, to the freshly consolidated German *Reich* and to a triumphant pan-Germanism that might finally unite all his people.[21]

But would he play any great part—or any part at all—in realizing that dream? His personal vision involved not politics but art. His schoolwork deteriorated, and he dropped out of school. A teacher recalled him as "Distinctly talented, though rather one-sided, lacking self-discipline and being regarded, at least, as intransigent, obstinate, high-handed, and hot-tempered."[22] He applied twice for Vienna's Academy of Fine Arts. Twice it rejected him, judging his talents for painting deficient ("Few heads. Test drawing unsatisfactory"[23]). Its officials thought he might have possibilities as an architect,[24] but having dropped out of school, that too was a dead end. He loafed incessantly. "Your father cannot rest in his grave," the widowed Klara chided him, "because you do absolutely nothing that he wanted for you. Obedience is what distinguishes a good son, but you do not know the meaning of the word. That's why you did so badly at school and why you're not getting anywhere now."[25] He who would demand the unquestioning obedience of tens of millions could not himself obey the most natural of authorities.

He shuffled off for Vienna in 1905, living off his orphan's pension.[26] His mother's death from breast cancer in December 1907 left him heartbroken. "In all my forty years of practice," recalled Dr. Bloch, "I had never seen a young man broken by grief and bowed down by suffering as young Adolf Hitler was that day."[27]

His Vienna days remain a profound mystery, the facts of his anonymity hidden not only by his very obscurity—as well as by his own later deviousness. The details of where he lived (sometimes in flophouses) and how he survived remain fuzzy and often shrouded in controversy. In *Mein Kampf*, he claimed to have worked as a common laborer,[28] though, that seems problematical at best. He continued to paint, and his income, though never large, grew to a sufficient amount to keep the wolf from his door. How his political ideas formed is the still greater rub. His solitary boyhood friend, the slightly older August "Gustl" Kubizek, claimed that Adolf had already become a convinced anti-Semite while living at Linz.[29] Others believe that that virus bit him only in Vienna ("Wherever I went, I began to see Jews . . ."[30]), a hotbed of such ideas. As an artist, he rebelled against bourgeois convention (particularly the conventions that kept him out of art school), but as the son of a middle-class government official, he possessed little sympathy for the growing working class–based socialist movement ("a pestilential whore"[31]). And though, he could not help but admire the socialists' talent for propaganda and their success in wooing the masses ("the endless columns of mass demonstrations"[32]), he could also not fail to notice something else: "I gradually became aware that the Social Democratic press was directed predominantly by Jews; . . . From the publisher on down, they were all Jews. . . . The names of the Austerlitzes, Davids, Adlers, Ellenbogens, etc., will remain forever graven in my memory."[33]

He remained the loner and voracious reader he had been in boyhood (and would remain forever) but read only to re-enforce existing ideas and prejudices. Hitler, noted Kubizek, "absorbed with great fervor everything he could lay his hands on, but he took great care to keep at a safe distance anything that might put him to the test. . . . He was not interested in 'another opinion,' not in any discussion of the book. . . . He was a seeker, certainly, but even in his books he found only what suited him."[34]

Yet, though the printed page so attracted him, he instinctively grasped its limitations, conceding its necessity for reaching intellectuals but reckoning that converting the unwashed, unlettered masses required a more visceral approach: the spoken word, wielded by an orator, ideally shouted by a master demagogue raised up from the depths of the people themselves, sharing not merely their hopes but their hatreds. In *Mein Kampf*, he would contend:

> *For let it be said to all our present-day fops and knights of the pen: the greatest revolutions in this world have never yet been directed by a goose-quill!*
>
> *No, to the pen it has always been reserved to provide their theoretical foundations.*
>
> *But the power which has always set the greatest religious and political avalanches in history rolling has from time immemorial been the magic power of the spoken word, and that alone.*
>
> *Particularly the broad masses of the people can be moved only by the power of speech. And all great movements are popular movements, volcanic eruptions of human passions and emotional sentiments, stirred either by the cruel Goddess of Distress or by the firebrand of the word hurled among the masses; they are not the lemonade-like outpourings of literary aesthetes and drawing-room heroes.*
>
> *Only a storm of hot passion can turn the destinies of peoples, and he alone can arouse passion who bears it within himself.*
>
> *It alone gives its chosen one the words which like hammer blows can open the gates to the heart of a people.*
>
> *But the man whom passion fails and whose lips are sealed—he has not been chosen by Heaven to proclaim its will.*[35]

Whether he fancied himself at those flophouse and men's hostel-lodging moments as the man who might wield that hammer one can only surmise.

Other influences entered his psyche, more ideas shaped his basic ideology. He visited Austria's parliament (*Reichsrat*), perched in its ornate visitors' gallery, witnessing the endless wranglings of "a majority of ignoramuses and incompetents."[36] The spectacle—and particularly the fractious Czech delegates—disgusted him.[37] He concluded that a parliament's diffusion of responsibility only guaranteed its failure. Individual judgment was the key, and that judgment could only be implemented through the concentration of power within a single individual.[38]

No operas, after all, were ever composed about a committee.

Thus, was born the *Führer* Principle—the dictum driving his rise to power. "Sooner," he would eventually write, "will a camel pass through a needle's eye than a great man be 'discovered' by an election."[39]

Yet, elections were realities, and Hitler learned from a profound realist in that endeavor, Vienna's Christian Social Party mayor, Dr. Karl Lueger. While Hitler may have recoiled from Lueger's fervent Catholicism, two of Lueger's attributes mightily attracted him: his anti-Semitism and his appeal to Vienna's broad masses,[40] though eventually "Handsome Karl" tempered his anti-Semitism into what Hitler considered a "sham."[41] Earlier, Hitler had found himself attracted to Georg Ritter von Schönerer's Pan-German Party, but its middle-class and openly anti-Catholic ("away from Rome") biases precluded it from any genuine mass appeal.[42] Eventually, polyglot, cosmopolitan Vienna, chock full of Jews and Czechs ("Did you hear, Gustl? Czech!"[43]), Poles and Italians ("incest incarnate"[44] he termed it), proved too much for young Hitler.

Such was the world of young Hitler's mind, a hodgepodge of (mostly) not-so-grand theories, delusions, and hatreds. He had, at some point, mysteriously disappeared from his friend Kubizek, vanishing into the depths of Meidlingen Strasse's "Home for Men." "Only loafers, drunkards, and the like stay for a long time in such a home,"[45] noted one contemporary observer, and true enough Hitler did not remain there very long at all, descending yet again, now to the deeper, sadder recesses of sheer homelessness, of nights spent outdoors, of begging upon city streets. From the nuns at Landstrasse-Hauptstrasse he received meat patties, some soup, or perhaps even a stray coin or two. The Merciful Brothers (*Barmherzige Bruder*) provided him with medical care.[46]

That was his very bottom.

His recovery (what there was then of it) commenced at Meidlingen Strasse in late 1909 when he made the acquaintance of fellow tramp Reinhold Hanisch. "On the very first day," recalled the Sudetenland-born Hanisch, "there sat next to the bed . . . allotted to me a man who had nothing on except an old torn pair of trousers—Hitler. His clothes were being cleaned of lice, since for days he had been wandering about without a roof and in a terribly neglected condition."[47]

Hitler confided to Hanisch that he was no mere hobo but an accomplished painter (and lied about attending the Art Academy). Hanisch conceived a partnership: Hitler to paint and Hanisch to peddle. Once Hitler acquired the necessary funds for artistic supplies (probably from his hunchbacked[48] maternal aunt, Joanna Pölzl, his "Haniaunt"[49]), that is exactly what they did. Hanisch busily sold every humble little work Hitler produced, hectoring him ("It was impossible to make Hitler work"[50]) to produce more. By February 1910 Hitler enjoyed quarters in far more tolerable accommodations, the six-story men's hostel at 27 Meldemannstrasse. Keeping Hitler from his easel were two avocations: devouring the daily newspapers ("in the morning he wouldn't begin work until he'd read several newspapers, and if anyone should come in with another newspaper he'd read that too"[51]) and political debates ("When he got excited Hitler couldn't restrain himself. He screamed, and fidgeted with his hands"[52]).

"I believe," Hitler admitted in *Mein Kampf*, "that those who knew me in those days took me for an eccentric."[53]

He still dealt with individual Jews, indeed, often having to. He enjoyed quite good relations with a locksmith at 27 Meldemannstrasse, Simon Robinsohn (borrowing money from him),[54] and with the art dealers Jakob Altenberg[55] and Josef Neumann, accepting a used coat from the latter and even briefly living with him.[56] To Hanisch, he explained "it was only with the Jews that one could do business, because they were willing to take chances."[57]

He soon quarreled with Hanisch, sued him, and even had him jailed (with the help of a Moravian Jewish acquaintance Siegfried Löffner[58]). But other opportunities arose.[59] Through a sign-painter named Josef Greiner (an associate of the Jew Josef Neumann), he produced a number of advertising illustrations: a bed-feathers shop, for shoe polish and hair tonic and ladies' corsets, and even one for "Teddy" antiperspirant:

Ten thousand steps day in day out,
Is an enormous pain!
Ten thousand steps, dear brother,
Is a joy with Teddy powder![60]

Yet, he could not entirely hide his raging prejudices. Meldemannstrasse resident Karl Honisch recalled his rages against the Jesuits and the "Reds."[61] He held that Jews were "a different race" possessing "a different smell."[62] In his modest Meldemannstrasse lodgings he carefully hung two framed mottoes:

Without Jews, without Rome
We build Germany's Cathedral. Heil!

and:

We gaze freely and openly, we gaze unflinchingly
We gaze happily over there into the German fatherland. Heil![63]

Toward his supposed comrades of the working classes he felt no better. In 1930, he snorted, "The whole mass of workers wants nothing else but bread and games; they have no ideals."[64]

He enjoyed cheap rent at the Meldemannstrasse. He neither smoked nor drank. His only luxuries were the opera and as many pastries as he might stuff into his mouth. Kubizek and Hanisch and Greiner all vanished, but in February 1913 a nineteen-year-old pharmacist's apprentice, Rudolf Häusler, entered the now twenty-three-year-old Adolf's life. Both young men's fathers had been customs officials. Both Hitler and Häusler had played their cards wrong enough to end up at 27 Meldemannstrasse. Like Kubizek, Häusler acted the docile disciple to the domineering Hitler. Hitler, Häusler recalled decades later, "enlightened me politically, and thus laid the foundation for my political and general education."[65]

They might have stayed at the Meldemannstrasse forever, but The Fatherland beckoned. Hitler's antipathy to the racially mixed Hapsburg Empire had finally reached the breaking point, and fueled by pan-German propaganda, Hitler determined to relocate to Munich. "He was," noted one report, "full of praise for that city and never forgot to mention its great galleries, beer parlors, radishes, etc."[66] Munich indeed boasted fine radishes. It also boasted something quite different: the absence of the Austrian draft—and military service with the Hapsburg monarchy's too generous quotients of Slavs and Jews.[67] On his twenty-fourth birthday, April 20, 1913,[68] Hitler finally cleared his paternal inheritance, and with eighty kronen in his pocket[69] emigrated to Bavaria. Munich—"Athens on the Isar"—was German but still boasted its share of Jews—and more than its share of anti-Semitism.[70]

Häusler accompanied him, and though their circumstances remained straightened,[71] at least, they no longer resided in men's shelters, sharing instead a twenty-mark-per-month[72] room rented from local master tailor Josef Popp[73] in the city's Bohemian Schwabing district. Difficulty still dogged Hitler, even in Germanic Munich. Austrian authorities tracked him down for draft dodging. He pled ignorance and ill health and barely escaped deportation home.[74] Häusler tired of his roommate's odd hours and odder (and sloppy) political harangues. "Come on Adi, stop spitting!" Häusler complained, "Otherwise I'll get an umbrella!"[75] But Häusler didn't get an umbrella; he simply left.

And then came war.

Austria declared war on Serbia, Russia on Austria, and Germany on Russia, and the world was ablaze. Hitler stood in the massive crowd at Munich's Odeonsplatz to hear the news, as thrilled and excited as any native German.[76] "To me," he would write, "those hours seemed like a release from the painful feelings of my youth. Even today I am not ashamed to say that, overpowered by stormy enthusiasm, I fell down on my knees and thanked Heaven from my overflowing heart for granting me the good fortune of being permitted to live at this time."[77]

He would not fight directly for Austria but wasted no time in volunteering to fight for Germany, which fought for Austria. No one bothered to check if he was a citizen, and he was assigned to the 1st Company of the 16th Bavarian Reserve Regiment—the List Regiment—[78] as a *meldeganger* or dispatch runner.[79] It was dangerous work. He saw thirty-six major battles,[80] was both wounded and gassed, and received the Iron Cross First Class, a rare honor for an enlisted man.[81] The official recommendation for that decoration read:

> *As a runner his coolness and dash in both trench and open warfare have been exemplary, and invariably he has shown himself ready to volunteer for tasks in the most difficult situations and at great danger to himself. Whenever communications have been totally disrupted at a critical moment in a battle, it has been thanks to Hitler's unflagging and devoted efforts that important messages continued to get through despite every difficulty. Hitler received the Iron Cross 2nd Class for gallant conduct during the fighting at Wytschaete on 1 Dec. 1914. I consider that he fully deserves the Iron Cross 1st class.*[82]

He had found himself. His previous existence had been aimless, hand-to-mouth. Now, he was engaged, albeit as a very small part, in a very grand endeavor. "For Pfc. Hitler," a superior recalled, "the List Regiment was his homeland."[83] Yet, he was changed without being changed at all. He still played the dreamy, bookish,[84] far-too-serious loner (his closest companion may have been his small, white terrier *Fuchsl* ["Foxl"], a deserter from British ranks[85]). He still painted.[86] On his single wartime furlough he visited not brothels[87] ("We always called him the 'woman-hater'"[88]) but museums (no opera, though; Wagner was not on the bill).[89] No promotion beyond the rank of lance corporal came his way, no great or even the most minute hint of leadership manifested itself.[90]

Some have intimated that he did not desire any promotion, not from any humility or lack of ambition but from courser motives: assuming officer or even NCO status meant abandoning his role as a courier. One former comrade, Josef Stettner, contended:

> *Some worshippers of Hitler have pointed out now that the job of a dispatch runner was more dangerous than that of a soldier in the trenches.*

While the troops in the first line could calmly lie under cover, it is said in Hitler's defence, the dispatch runners would have been much more exposed to enemy fire while on duty. However, I can accept that only for dispatch runners of companies or maybe also of battalions. In the worst-case scenario, the regimental dispatch runner had to go to the dugout of a battalion which still lay far behind the first line. And even in those cases, it was for the most part the dispatch runners of the battalion themselves who had to pick up the messages at the regimental headquarters, particularly when things were getting dangerous. All the duties of a regimental dispatch runner lay outside the dangerous zone of machine-gun fire.[91]

Stettner continued in some detail in this vein:

Hitler had worked out for himself how to get out of the line of fire on time. He had already managed to get a small post as regimental dispatch runner behind the front at the end of 1914. At first he lay with the regimental staff in the underground vaults and basements of Fromelles [in northern France]. For months, the infantry companies that lay in reserve behind the front and pioneers that had specially been deployed for this task had to make the shelters of the regimental staff bomb-proof. While we had to lie in the wet trenches at the front line for seven to ten days without a break or while we stood up to our stomachs in the mud, Hitler lay on a warm, lice-free stretcher and had several metres of protective stone above his hero's body.

But it did not take very long before the entire regimental staff set itself up even more comfortably in Foumes, approximately 10 kilometres behind the first line. There for more than a year the dispatch runners had a room of their own in a former Estaminet (small pub or cafe). Every one of us in the trench would have given his eye teeth to swap with the hero Hitler even just for eight days.

. . . The front experience of Private Hitler consisted more in the consumption of artificial honey and tea than of the participation in any combat. He was separated from the actual combat zone by a zone some 10 kilometres deep. Thousands of family fathers would have filled Hitler's little post behind the front just as well as him: however, at the time Hitler did not display any sign that he felt driven towards military front-line action, as he is trying to tell the blinded German youth today. He did, as we front-line soldiers used to say at the time, "keep his position."[92]

To his comrades Meldeganger Hitler soft-pedaled his anti-Semitism.[93] He had his reasons: His direct superior—and the officer recommending him for

Iron Cross First Class—was the Nürnberg Jew, Lt. Hugo Gutmann.[94] In February 1915, however, in the one surviving document revealing his wartime political vision (a letter to a Munich judge who had sent him two food packages) Hitler wrote:

> *I think of Munich so often, and each of us has only one wish, that it should soon come to a final reckoning with this gang, to get at them no matter what the cost, and that those of us who are lucky enough to see their homeland again will find it a purer place, less riddled with foreign influences, so that the daily sacrifices and sufferings of hundreds of thousands of us and the torrent of blood that keeps flowing here day after day against an international world of enemies, will not only help to smash Germany's foes outside but that our inner internationalism, too, will collapse. This would be worth much more than any territorial gains.[95]*

It takes only the smallest leap of hindsight to envision that "foreign influences" and "inner internationalism" translated into Germany's Jews.

And, yet, some extremely significant changes did occur within him. War now captivated and entranced him. "We learn casually from Kubizek that in his Vienna days, Hitler was a pacifist;" observes the noted historian Hugh Trevor-Roper, "and certainly the ruthlessness of his later worship of war becomes more comprehensible when he realize that it was the religion of a convert."[96] He ruminated at length on the value of propaganda—both the effectiveness of the Allied efforts and on Berlin's failures.[97] He still maintained a strange aloofness from those surrounding him. But when the spirit moved him, "Comrade Laced Shoe"[98] might abandon his normal silence to unleash veritable lectures. "There is almost no subject about which he did not talk," recalled Cpl. Ignaz Westenkirchner. "He mastered each theme and spoke fluently. We simple fellows were very much impressed, and we liked it. His favorite subject was art. . . ."[99] Some said he had already harbored ambitions to become a political orator.[100]

He acquired a sense of purpose—that he, so wretched and discarded for so long, was meant for something greater, perhaps even for greatness itself. "I was eating my dinner in a trench with several comrades," Hitler later recalled of an incident of September 1915. "Suddenly a voice seemed to be saying to me: 'Get up and go over there' I rose at once to my feet and walked 20 metres along the trench. . . Hardly had I done so when a flash and deafening sound came from the part of the trench I had just left. A stray shell had burst over the group in which I had been sitting, and every member of it was killed."[101]

That Christmas he confided to List Regiment dispatch rider Hans "Ghost Rider" Mend of his burgeoning destiny. "[H]e said that we would hear much about him," recollected Mend. "We should just wait until his time had arrived."[102]

The war ended badly for Hitler—and for his adopted Fatherland. South of Ypres in mid-October 1918, a British chlorine gas attack enveloped his unit. By morning his "eyes had turned into glowing coals."[103] Totally blind and with hope of only a partial recovery, he was shipped off to Pasewalk military hospital, northeast of Berlin.

There exists some very great issue regarding his blindness. Was it physical? Or psychological and psychosomatic? Historian Thomas Weber, the premier student of Hitler's war record, argues for the latter verdict ("war hysteria"), pointing out that Hitler was treated at Pasewalk's psychiatric ward—not its ophthalmology ward.[104] "Hitler was diagnosed as a psychopath with symptoms of hysteria," contends Weber.[105] Hysteria was certainly in the air at Pasewalk. So was revolution. The Kaiser had abdicated, and Social Democrats in Berlin had fumblingly proclaimed a republic. A pastor visited Pasewalk to convey the news. "I could stand it no longer—," Hitler recalled. "It became impossible for me to sit still one minute more. Again everything went black before my eyes; I tottered and groped my way back to the dormitory, threw myself on my bunk, and dug my burning head into my blanket and pillow. Since the day when I had stood at my mother's grave, I had not wept."[106]

Almost miraculously, his vision returned. His hatred never departed. The Kaiser, he concluded had been a fool to have dealt with Social Democrats and, worse, with Jews ("the Jews organized the revolution and smashed Prussia and Bavaria at once"[107]). Such errors must never be repeated. "There is no making pacts with the Jews," he concluded, "there can only be the hard either–or. I, for my part, decided to go into politics."[108]

CHAPTER FOUR

"Miracle Man, Washington, D.C."

FRANKLIN ROOSEVELT AND ADOLF HITLER DREAMT OF COMMANDING A nation.

Herbert Hoover's nightmare was to already command one.

And, until he entered command's gilded confines, his life had been neither a puzzlement nor a tragedy. It inspired tens of millions.

Born to Quaker parents, a blacksmith father and a schoolteacher mother, in a tiny white, wooden cottage in equally tiny West Branch, Iowa, at six "Bertie" Hoover saw his father die. His mother (to whom he bore a great resemblance)[1] followed three years later. Eventually he was packed off to a maternal uncle in Newberg, Oregon, with a dime sewed into his clothing and carrying with him "an enormous supply of fried chicken, ham, bread, and meat pies."[2] Apprenticed to his uncle's real estate office, he never attended high school,[3] perhaps explaining why, save for mathematics, he initially failed his college entrance exams.[4] Nonetheless, he eventually gained admittance to newly formed Stanford University's initial class, where, ever practical, he majored in geology. Finding, however, no "white collar" positions in his field upon graduation, he drifted over to the Nevada gold mines, taking two-dollar-per-day work pushing a heavy underground mining cart.[5]

But even that dried up ("I learned what the bottom levels of real human despair are paved with"[6]). He finally obtained an engineering post in the Colorado and New Mexico mines, before securing a six-hundred-dollar-a-month position with the British firm of Bewick, Moreing and Company in western Australia's far-off gold fields.[7]

Here he found fortune—and himself. By 1899, he oversaw mines in China (stopping off in California to pick up—and marry—fellow Stanford geology major Miss Lou Henry[8]). Chinese mines were lucrative—but dangerous. At least, the Boxer Rebellion was, and, at Tientsin, the Hoovers found themselves smack in the middle of its fighting, besieged for a solid month by twenty-five thousand Boxers (firing sixty thousand shells)—until relieved by a combined force of fifteen hundred American Marines and Welsh Fusiliers.[9] Hoover designed the surrounded western enclave's battlements. His wife toted a .38-caliber Mauser pistol.[10]

By 1901 he had assumed a junior partnership at Bewick, Moreing. Just twenty-seven, he had already been "The Chief" to his men since his Australian days—at a mere twenty-three.[11] Now, he acquired a new sobriquet—"The Great Engineer,"[12] globetrotting for Bewick, Moreing to India and Russia, Egypt and France, to Hawaii and to Ceylon. He was soon rich—his fortune an estimated $30 million.[13] Within a decade he boasted a firm of his own.

And, suddenly, everything changed.

For the entire world, and, yes, for Herbert Hoover.

When war erupted in August 1914, it trapped thousands of Americans overseas. Hoover organized their return, within two months, hustling-up $400,000 for that purpose.[14] But fund-raising proved decidedly simple compared to the task awaiting him: feeding a million starving Belgians trapped behind invading German lines. America's ambassador to the Court of St. James, Walter Hines Page, tapped Hoover for the task. He raised a million more dollars per week. Again, that was the easy part of the job.

Hoover's "Commission for Relief in Belgium" controlled railways, ships, and factories—and alienated statesmen and generals and politicians—primarily British—on both sides of the trenches. He was not pleasant, but he got the job done. His inspiring success transformed a dour "Great Engineer" into (a still dour) "Great Humanitarian."

"He told us of his big work in Belgium," recalled Navy secretary Josephus Daniels, "as coldly as if he were giving statistics of production. From his words and his manner he seemed to regard human beings as so many numbers."[15]

Others cared less about Hoover's personality—at least, not so long as he delivered results. "He's a simple, modest, energetic little man," Ambassador Page informed Woodrow Wilson in January 1915, "who began his career in California and will end it in Heaven; and he doesn't want anybody's thanks."[16] Wilson himself gushed to his future wife in November 1915 regarding Hoover: "He is a real man . . . Such men stir me deeply and make me in love with duty!"[17]

America joined the fight in April 1917, and Hoover returned home to oversee an unprecedented food rationing campaign. "Food will win the war,"[18] he exhorted, and his stateside efforts elevated his reputation ever more. He might have easily been blamed for shortages. He was not. In fact, to "Hooverize"—to economize—emerged as a catchphrase of great praise. Read one wartime Valentine's Day poem:

I can Hooverize on dinner,
And on lights and fuel too,
But I'll never learn to Hooverize,
When it comes to loving you.[19]

Such tribute turns the heads of even "simple, modest" men. And soon, Republicans and Democrats alike were booming "The Great Humanitarian" for the White House. Hoover had been raised a Republican (though bolting the party for TR in 1912[20])—and, as far as anyone knew, might still be one. Yet, now proudly serving the Democratic Woodrow Wilson, he publicly supported Wilson's ultimately disastrous partisan appeal to elect a Democratic Congress in 1918. Numbered among Hoover's friends within that administration was Navy Under Secretary Franklin Roosevelt. In January 1920, Franklin privately wrote that there would be "none better" than the "wonder" Hoover for president. Shortly thereafter FDR endorsed a scheme to field a Hoover-FDR Democratic ticket. Hoover, however, not the total political naïf, recognized that 1920 spelled disaster for Democrats and wanted no part of the idea. He cast his lot with his ancestral party.[21]

He went nowhere that year for the presidency (though winning the New Hampshire and Michigan *Democratic* primaries). But along the way he impressed ("The smartest gink I know"[22]) incoming President Warren Harding enough to earn appointment as secretary of commerce. It was not much of a department, but the energetic Hoover made it one and for good measure earned a not-always-complimentary reputation as "secretary of commerce and under-secretary of all other departments."[23] In 1922, he penned a volume, *American Individualism*, outlining his hybrid philosophy of private property and collective "associated activities." Franklin Roosevelt congratulated his old friend: "I have taken great pleasure in reading it."[24]

Hoover's frenetic energies may have charmed Franklin Roosevelt, college undergraduates, and the headline writers—but not Harding's successor, Calvin Coolidge. The normally circumspect "Silent Cal" retained Hoover, but privately derided him as "Wonder Boy" and "that superman," confiding to associates, "That man has offered me unsolicited advice every day for six years, all of it bad."[25]

Most Republican leaders joined in Coolidge's assessment, recalling Hoover's support of Wilson and his League of Nations, his progressivism, and his lack of real political experience. On convention eve in 1928, Senate Majority Leader Charles Curtis pronounced, "The Republican Party cannot afford to nominate Herbert Hoover. It would be apologizing for him from the moment of nomination until the polls close in November."[26] Intellectuals shared H. L. Mencken's dismissal of "Lord Hoover" as "a pious old woman, a fat Coolidge."[27]

A quartet of old guard US senators challenged Hoover for the nomination: the aforementioned Charles Curtis, Indiana's amiable James E. Watson, Ohio's Frank B. Willis, and West Virginia's former senator Guy Goff. "In such an array," conceded a highly critical early biographer, "Hoover's worst enemy granting an elemental sense of patriotism could hardly wish him anything but success."[28] Willis, the strongest of the bunch, literally dropped dead while delivering his campaign's opening address. The 1928 nomination virtually fell into Hoover's lap—and so, unfortunately, did Charles Curtis as his running mate.

It was, nonetheless, a heady time to be Herbert Clark Hoover. His election, in a time of Republican prosperity and facing the largely un-electable Al Smith, seemed fore-ordained. And so, on August 11, 1928, in his formal acceptance speech at Palo Alto, he declared: "We in America today are nearer to the final triumph over poverty than ever before in the history of any land. The poorhouse is vanishing from among us."[29]

So it seemed. Hoover's reputation soared yet again. An envelope reached him, simply bearing the mere inscription: "Miracle Man, Washington, D. C."[30] In July 1929, the Associated Press reported that explorer Nicholas Roerich had in his expedition to remote Tibet discovered that Hoover "is regarded as a kind of god by Tibetan tribes. . . . President Hoover's work seems to have penetrated by word of mouth into Tibet, where he is looked upon as a supernatural and beneficent being, Mr. Roerich added. He said that the name 'Hoover' had been distorted by Tibetans into 'Koovera' which is their name for the god of happiness. He found an old picture of Mr. Hoover, taken many years ago, enshrined in a Tibetan home."[31]

And, then came . . . the Crash.

At first, the Crash seemed more like a Thud. Yes, events were bad, but not necessarily catastrophic—and Mr. Hoover had been very lucky to have them transpire so very early in his tenure. Normally, the economy should have recovered by November 1932—and with it Hoover's chances for re-election. In May 1930, Democrat Bernard Baruch groused that Hoover would be "fortunate enough, before the next election, to have a rising tide and then he will be pictured as the great master mind who led the country out of its economic misery."[32]

By June 1930, unemployment, steadily declining from a disturbing 9 percent in December 1929, improved to a more manageable 6.3 percent.[33]

Such data inspired Hoover to utter a series of optimistic statements ("we have passed the worst and with continued effort we shall rapidly recover"[34]) that by 1932 marked him as either callous, clueless, or both.

And so, compared to his frenetic activities of 1931-32 when he instituted the Reconstruction Finance Corporation (RFC), the Home Loan Bank, signed the Glass-Steagall and Norris-La Guardia acts, and expended hundreds of millions on public works, in 1930 Hoover did comparatively little (save for banning immigration by executive fiat[35]) regarding the limping economy. He did not even call the Congress into special session.

He was, nonetheless, busy—with other things. Of course, Herbert Hoover was *always* busy. But 1930 found him preoccupied with two great disasters he himself had instigated even before the Crash. Whatever his failings, Herbert Hoover did *not* trigger said Crash. He did, however, set in motion the Smoot-Hawley Tariff and the Wickersham Commission.

Agriculture, suffering from wartime overplanting and overinvestment, had lagged behind the '20s general prosperity. Throughout the decade, farm states' legislators lobbied for federal relief—most prominently proposing the controversial McNary-Haugen Act. Twice, Calvin Coolidge vetoed the measure, vigorously scoring its largely unworkable features.[36] Hoover, supported in 1928 by such farm block senators as Idaho's William Borah, determined, nonetheless, to provide some assistance to hard-put American agriculture. Eschewing newfangled McNary-Haugen style methods, he now applied a more traditional Republican economic tool—the tariff—to a segment of the economy traditionally opposed to protectionism—agriculture. Hoover initially proposed merely raising tariffs on agricultural imports. But by the time Congress had passed Hoover's bill (now termed Smoot-Hawley), it had added to the mix increased rates on all manner of manufactured imports. More than a thousand economists petitioned Hoover to veto this concoction,[37] and it was not merely academics in opposition. "I almost went down on my knees to beg Herbert Hoover to veto the asinine Hawley-Smoot tariff,"[38] recalled J. P. Morgan's head Thomas W. Lamont. "NOT ONLY A DISGRACE TO THE PARTY IN POWER BUT A BRAKE UPON THE WHEELS OF RETURNING PROSPERITY,"[39] headlined William Randolph Hearst (who *thought* in capital letters).

Hoover, however, having created the monster, refused to slay it. Flourishing six gold pens, he signed Smoot-Hawley into law on June 17, 1930[40]— *June 1930*, when joblessness bottomed out at 6.3 percent. By December it had exploded to 14.4 percent.[41]

Hoover had authorized the Wickersham Commission (officially the "National Commission on Law Observance and Enforcement"; less officially the "Liquorsham Commission"[42]) to ameliorate the continuing controversy regarding Prohibition. Calvin Coolidge and Warren Harding had addressed this politically dangerous issue with asbestos gloves, wisely saying (and doing) as little as possible about it. Hoover, lacking political experience, also lacked political sense. In his acceptance speech, he employed one of his more (of many) deleterious phrases, terming the Eighteenth Amendment "an experiment noble in purpose." Both sides detested his characterization. "Dry" forces resented the word "experiment." To them there was nothing "experimental" about Prohibition at all. The issue was settled. Period. To "wets," favoring repeal, there was nothing "noble" about the amendment. It was wrongheaded, bigoted, and destructive of manners and morals. Having stumbled in word, Hoover then proceeded to stumble in deed. Creation of the Wickersham Commission triggered a raging dispute about a dangerous but hitherto largely manageable issue—a debate that would begin the process of sundering the staunchly GOP (but highly "wet") Northeast from its ancestral Republican roots.

And that was the mere beginning of Hoover's political ineptitude.

The man was incredibly sensitive to criticism. Coolidge had noticed it.[43] So had Wilson.[44] Even before Wall Street's bottomless bottom dropped out from under him, Hoover termed holding public office a "hair shirt."[45]

He displayed the arrogance of the self-made man who peered down upon his creation and scorned others not made so well. "On the day after his nomination," wrote one observer, "he expressed a low opinion of the financiers and politicians who had opposed him."[46]

"I owe nothing to them," he boasted upon his triumph, "and they know it."[47]

And he would not admit anything. "No President," he cautioned an old friend, must ever admit he has been wrong."[48]

Insecurity, self-pity, and arrogance are a dangerous combination.

If Al Smith was "The Happy Warrior," Herbert Hoover seemed always unhappily at war with himself. Chief White House usher Irwin "Ike" Hoover's (no relation) recollection was by no means fond:

> He would go about, never speaking to any of the help. Never a Merry Christmas or a Happy New Year. All days were alike to him. Sunday was no exception . . . There was always a frown on his face and a look of worry. Of all the administrations, the hardest to work for was that of . . . Hoover . . . the Hoovers were dictatorial, attempted to do more than any

of the rest . . . All of the employees at the White House were glad when
they were gone; . . . He reminded one of a fellow who was always afraid
of losing his job and must hang around in an effort to hold on.[49]

More missteps accompanied Smoot-Hawley and the Wickersham Commission. In November 1929, Hoover petulantly excluded the prickly isolationist progressive, California's Hiram Johnson, from a White House dinner for Senate Foreign Relations Committee members.[50] To fill a Supreme Court vacancy, he designated North Carolina judge John H. Parker. It was a disastrous continuation of Hoover's short-sighted 1928 "southern strategy." Hoover, first requiring southern rotten-borough convention delegates, and then coveting superfluous southern electoral votes to pad his massive landslide over the unfortunate Al Smith, decided to woo southern votes. Short-term, both strategies worked. But they contained the seeds of ultimate disaster. Refusing to effectively decry the anti-Catholic sentiment opposing Smith, he alienated previously Republican Catholic northeastern voters. In 1928, such tactics cost him normally Republican (but substantially Catholic) Massachusetts and Rhode Island. In the South he transmitted a not-very-subtle message to white Democratic supporters ("Hoovercrats") that he would shift federal patronage away from black Republicans,[51] assisting him in carrying Virginia, North Carolina, Texas, Florida, Kentucky, and Tennessee. Blacks still voted for him in 1928, but with considerably less enthusiasm—and trust—than tendered to previous Republicans.

Judge Parker enjoyed a reputation as both anti-union and anti-black.[52] Senate Majority Leader Watson, Attorney General William D. Mitchell, and even Parker himself, advised Hoover to withdraw his embattled nomination. Hoover refused.[53] In May 1930, the Senate rejected Parker 41–39.[54] Compounding his disaster, Hoover fumed the "rejection is an outrage. I don't know what the country is coming to if things are to be run by demagogues and Negro politicians."[55]

Such was Hoover. Said Treasury Secretary Andrew W. Mellon to Majority Leader Watson: "Hoover is an engineer; he wants to run a straight line, just one line, and then say to everyone, 'This is the only line there is, and you must come up to it, or else keep out.'"[56]

The savvy Watson agreed. Never impressed by Hoover, and badly burned in one egregious legislative incident ("How in hell can a man stand behind this President, unless he has St. Vitus Dance!"[57]), he angrily concluded that Hoover "knows less than a child about politics."[58]

His boorishness manifested itself in ways great—the Great Depression—and small. Touring the Virgin Islands on a 1932 good-will tour, he

departed by insulting its inhabitants by complaining about the US possession's purchase from Denmark. The United States had, he sneered, bought "an
effective poorhouse" in acquiring the militarily strategic archipelago.[59]

Pressured on all sides (including Democratic ones) to cut federal spending, Hoover responded with a brace of measures implying criticism of his
predecessor, the still-respected Coolidge: scrapping the *Mayflower*, the presidential yacht much favored by the frugal Vermonter, and packing off the
horses from the White House stables to Fort Myer, Virginia.[60] "How much
less hay will the horses eat at Fort Myer?" Coolidge retorted.[61]

There was, unfortunately, more. In the spring of 1930, the hyper-sensitive
Hoover received a report contending that the Democrats (not exactly shy
about sullying his name) had obtained documents so destructive of his reputation that they would also damage the national government. Thus, was set in
motion a pre-Watergate plot to break into Democratic National Committee
offices and retrieve said documents—a cabal ultimately involving Hoover;
his chief of staff, Larry Richey (a former Secret Service agent and TR's own
bodyguard); New York banker (and former Hoover private secretary) Lewis
L. Strauss; and various Office of Naval Intelligence personnel.

"Strauss told me that the President is anxious to know what the contents
of the mysterious documents are," ONI District Intelligence Officer Glenn
Howell recorded in his diary, "and Strauss is authorized by the President to
utilize the services of any one of our various government secret services."

By the time ONI actually burgled, however, Democrats had vacated the
office in question. A frustrated Howell and his civilian assistant Robert J.
Peterkin, a former police inspector, tracked down the premises' former ten-
ant, the muckraking Democratic publicist (and former police officer) James J.
O'Brien. "We shadowed him for a bit and then came to the conclusion that
no President of the United States need be afraid of a ham-and-egger like this
O'Brien," Howell noted, "All these beliefs I conveyed to Lewis Strauss who
transmitted them to Larry Richey . . . who informed the President [who]
told Larry to tell Lewis to tell me to call off my watch and consider the case
closed."[62]

But that was not the end of the Hoover team's skullduggery. In January 1931, the rapidly rising radio firebrand, Royal Oak, Michigan's populist
Roman Catholic priest, Fr. Charles E. Coughlin, busied himself drafting
a CBS network address on the allegedly sinister forces behind the treaty
ending the world war, the Treaty of Versailles—and more so how Versailles
had triggered the worldwide Depression. A Coughlin aide phoned Pennsylvania Republican congressman Louis T. McFadden, an equally volatile
Hoover critic, to confirm his data. The White House intercepted their

call (McFadden would later say: "I am being watched in every move I make and even my friends are being watched and analyzed. I even have to be careful in what I say over the telephone, because undoubtedly some one is listening"[63]). McFadden may indeed have been paranoid, but even paranoid people have enemies. Soon CBS somehow knew the contents of Coughlin's address, and, alleging complaints from two affiliate stations, a CBS vice president placed a mysterious late-night call to Coughlin advising him to "temper and restrain" any "controversial" content. Coughlin had his quick revenge, acceding to CBS's request—and then publicly lacerating their censorship over their own airwaves. A week later he gave it anyway.[64] By February 1932, Coughlin was publicly excoriating Hoover as "the banker's friend, the Holy Ghost of the rich, the protective angel of Wall Street."[65]

Such contretemps failed to daunt Hoover's camp, as his underlings continued toiling furiously to right his capsizing presidency. Postmaster General Walter F. Brown publicly banned any patronage for Rep. McFadden.[66] Larry Richey maintained a "black list" of the President's enemies, even keeping Hoover's Medal of Honor–winning former speech writer (and former Coolidge assistant attorney general) William J. "Wild Bill" Donovan under surveillance.[67] A Hoover assistant postmaster general informed Missouri postmasters:

> *Get out on the firing line in support of President Hoover. I'll be back in Washington Monday and I'll be glad at that time to take the resignation of any of you postmasters who don't want to do it.*
>
> *You are a part of this Administration. When you hear anybody assailing that man Hoover, remember what I said [in Springfield, Missouri] or go read a book and answer them. As long as you do that you are filling the job of postmaster.*
>
> *To make the world safe again for democracy, you must stand behind that man of peerless leadership—of brains, ability and steadfastness. I ask your faith in God, that our country shall not fail.*[68]

In January 1931, Republican National Committee executive director Robert H. Lucas (an architect of the "Hoovercrat" strategy—and the former commissioner of Internal Revenue) wrote to his former Internal Revenue Bureau field agents soliciting any political information they might possess.[69] Fumed New Mexico's progressive Republican senator Bronson Cutting: "These men check the income tax returns of all taxpayers . . . Does that not confirm the view I took some years ago that the Commissioner of Internal Revenue can control the politics of the country?"[70]

Hoover's "trouble," Senator James Watson concluded, "was that he thought he was just as strong all the way through his administration as he had been in 1928 when practically the whole country was for him. He did not think that party organization was necessary because he confidently believed that the name Hoover would be sufficient to take all hurdles and overcome all obstacles. I very plainly told him that if he were elected . . . in 1932, it would be as 'the Republican candidate for president' and not as Herbert Hoover, and he didn't like that suggestion at all."[71]

It was not bad advice. No longer did anyone speak admiringly of "Hooverizing." Through clenched teeth, they spoke of "Hoovercarts" (gasless autos drawn of necessity by mules or horses), "Hoovervilles" (homeless shanty towns), "Hoover blankets" (newspapers for those sleeping on park benches), "Hoover leather" (the cardboard lining an old shoe), "Hoover Pullmans" (freight cars for transporting vagrants), and "Hooverflags" (empty pants pockets drawn inside-out).[72] The man's name was a curse: his pasty, pudgy face simultaneously a cruel and clueless specter of heartless ineptitude.

By January 1931, the *Rockford Register-Republican*, published by Ruth Hanna McCormick[73] (daughter of Republican kingmaker Marc Hanna and a member by marriage of the prominent McCormick family), openly advocated dumping him. So did the aggrieved Hiram Johnson.[74] Progressives like Idaho's William Borah (alienated by administration farm policy) and Pennsylvania's Governor Gifford Pinchot (himself a former Hoover aide[75]) similarly excoriated Hoover. "We in Pennsylvania," said Pinchot in January 1932, "are doing more than one half of what Mr. Hoover is doing nationally in this respect. I cannot believe that a national government will stand by while its citizens freeze and starve, without lifting a hand to help."[76] The Great Humanitarian, concluded Pinchot, was simply "vicious."[77] That April, J. P. Morgan's Thomas W. Lamont joined with fellow financier Otto Kahn and former Republican national chairman Charles D. Hilles in a secret, but still-born, draft-Coolidge movement. The previous September Hilles had even floated the fanciful idea of a Hoover-Coolidge ticket, hoping against hope that the convention might ultimately then stampede and re-nominate the still-popular former president.[78]

By June 1931 yet another 1928 Hoover booster,[79] the mercurial press baron William Randolph Hearst, had also turned upon his former candidate's "reactionary" and "do-nothing administration."[80] Hearst, an erstwhile radical Democrat, also tried and failed to entice "Silent Cal" ("Back Coolidge and Americanism, Coolidge and Patriotism, Coolidge and Confidence"[81]) back on the ticket.[82] Hearst not only accelerated his anti-Hoover offensive ("Only a strange mind, with artificial water-tight compartments, can be closed to the acute suffering of his own people, while asking generous gestures to those overseas"[83]), he kept looking for a replacement. If that meant returning to the Democratic Party ("It has no leaders and apparently no principles"[84]), so be it.

"Not one Republican in ten wants President Hoover re-nominated and hardly anyone believes he can be re-elected," noted the prickly Chicago progressive Harold Ickes, hoping not for a Coolidge restoration but for a Pinchot boomlet. "I can see no reason why the Republican Party should deliberately run into a smashing defeat to satisfy one man's ambition."[85]

It was not that Hoover did not try to repair the economy. He did. And many of his initiatives presaged those of his ultimate successor. He spent on public works and he spent on corporations and banks. He lent money to states. But, faithful to his notion of "rugged individualism," he resisted virtually all efforts to spend on direct relief. "I once made a list of New Deal ventures began during Hoover's years as secretary of commerce and then as president," wrote FDR Brains Truster Rexford Guy Tugwell. "I had to conclude that his policies were correct."[86] Correct, perhaps by later liberal economic orthodoxy but not in preventing the horrible downward spiral that haunted the nation and Hoover himself. It was an odd form of correct.

Republicans fared badly in 1930's midterm elections, pinning false hopes on the Prohibition issue, and narrowly losing the House. They retained a slim Senate majority, though thanks to the long-standing progressive dissension within their ranks, effectively forfeited de facto control. Hoover advised Jim Watson to surrender his majority leader's post to Arkansas Democrat Joseph T. Robinson to saddle Democrats with full responsibility for events. Watson, aghast, refused.[87] Hoover, comprehending nothing of the legislative process, later sniped that Senate Republicans merely wanted to retain "the nicer offices in the Capitol."[88]

Despair piled upon misery upon despondency. In November 1930, Hoover's patrician secretary of state Henry L. Stimson confided to his diary regarding "the ever present feeling of gloom that pervades everything connected with the administration":

I really never knew such unenlivened occasions as our Cabinet meetings. When I sat down today and tried to think it over, I don't remember that there has ever been a joke cracked in a single meeting of the last year and a half, nothing but steady, serious grind, in a group of men sitting around the table who apparently had no humanity for anything but business. . . .

How I wish I could cheer up the poor old President and make him feel the importance of a little brightness and recreation in his own work.[89]

Or, as Mount Rushmore sculptor Gutzon Borglum tartly observed, "If you put a rose in Hoover's hand it would wilt."[90]

The Depression sunk from one level of quicksand to another. Anti-Hoover gossip kept pace with the deathly length of the breadlines and the sickening brutality of foreclosures. Among the tamer, yet really harsher, apocryphal tales was this one. Hoover, momentarily short of cash, needed a nickel to treat a friend to a soda and turned to the fabulously wealthy Andrew Mellon to borrow one.

"Here's a dime—," Mellon is said to have responded, *"treat 'em all."*[91]

CHAPTER FIVE

"They will remain hanging until they stink"

ADOLF HITLER HAD NO FRIENDS AT ALL, HARDLY TEN PFENNIGS TO HIS name, barely his eyesight—and, in November 1918, no longer much of a country, nor even much left of a continent. "Russia," Winston Churchill, then minister of munitions, orated, "is being rapidly reduced by the Bolsheviks to an animal form of Barbarism. . . . Civilization is being completely extinguished over gigantic areas, while Bolsheviks hop and caper like troops of ferocious baboons amid the ruins of their cities and the corpses of their victims."[1]

Further west, the glittering but fragile Hapsburg mosaic had fallen to the ground and shattered into a half-dozen jagged pieces. In Budapest, Bolsheviks imposed a Hungarian Soviet Republic—and a consequent deadly "Red Terror"—under the charismatic thirty-three-year-old half-Jewish Transylvanian Béla Kun.[2] In January 1919, Rosa Luxemburg and Karl Liebknecht mounted a Spartacist (Communist) coup against Weimar Germany's Social Democratic regime, which pled for rightist *Freikorps* troops to save their infant government. Luxemburg and Liebknecht ended up with bullets to their brains.[3] Weimar's Communists and Socialists ended up hating each other with a hate beyond reason. That same month, Moscow radio issued a call for an international revolutionary congress, the "Comintern." Delegates dedicated to a Marxist world uprising attended from virtually all European nations.[4]

In the meantime, Hitler's superiors shipped him back to Munich,[5] which even by the standards of the times was an outright mess. Independent Social Democrat Kurt Eisner had proclaimed his own Bavarian republic. In February 1919, the reactionary (but half-Jewish[6]) Count Anton von Arco-Valley shot the bearded, fully Jewish Eisner dead.[7] An hour later a Communist butcher's apprentice named Alois Lindner entered the Bavarian *Landtag* (parliament), calmly drew his pistol, steadied himself against a railing and shot (but failed to kill) a Social Democrat delegate, the Eisner rival Erhard Auer. An army officer tried halting Lindner's exit. Lindner shot him dead—and strolled out of the chamber just as calmly as he had entered.[8] In April, a largely insane group of artists, communists, and anarchists (led by the Jewish playwright Ernst Toller) seized power, proclaimed a "Bavarian Soviet Republic," declared war on Switzerland, mandated a knowledge of Walt Whitman "by heart," and complained to Comrade Lenin that the previous regime had departed with the washroom key.[9] A handful of days later, less-fanciful Communists led by Eugen Leviné seized power, raided the offices of the right-wing, racialist, neo-pagan Thule Society, and shot eight hostages including Prince Gustav of Thurn und Taxis and Countess Hella von Westarp.[10] Rightist military forces poured into Munich. Massacres reigned left and right. In this fashion, "order" was finally restored.

Munich's armed command, realizing that it required the loyalty of its enlisted men, embarked upon properly indoctrinating them, placing the anti-Semitic Capt. Karl Mayr in charge of its "Education and Propaganda Department." Among Mayr's recruits was the still-only twenty-nine-year-old Corp. Adolf Hitler.[11] Hitler later contended that he had intensely opposed Munich's revolutionary crazy-quilt (and others verified that[12]), but Mayr, nonetheless, found him to be "totally unconcerned about the German people and their destinies."[13]

"When I first met him he was like a tired stray dog looking for a master . . . ," Mayr recalled of Hitler "ready to throw in his lot with anyone who would show him kindness. . . ."

Whatever Corporal Hitler's true sympathies, he quickly emerged as Mayr's star pupil, capable and trustworthy enough to be dispatched to spy upon the welter of political parties now forming. Thus, on Friday evening, September 12, 1919, at Munich's former Sterneckerbräu beer hall's "Leiber Room," Adolf Hitler surveilled his first meeting of the German Workers Party (the *Deutsche Arbeiterpartei*—the "DAP").[14] Barely twenty persons attended,[15] and though Hitler found the group largely sympathetic to his own ideas, he also judged it profoundly unimpressive, "neither good nor bad."[16]

"The founder for the most part," he concluded, "had no idea what it means to make a party—let alone a movement—out of a club."[17]

He might have silently departed without making any impression at all, but in the evening's "free discussion period," a Professor Baumann proposed an independent Bavarian-Austrian union, free of the greater Reich. Hitler detested such ideas and unleashed a tirade against him.[18] A week later he received notice of being "accepted" into the DAP. The missive "astonished" him. He had "no intention of joining a ready-made party but wanted to found one of my own."[19]

He joined anyway (or, at least, eventually[20]), and on October 16, 1919 at Munich's Hofbräuhauskeller, delivered his first speech for his new party. A mere 111 persons attended,[21] but Hitler held them in the palm of his hand. "I could speak!" he marveled in *Mein Kampf*. "After 30 minutes the people in the small room were electrified and the enthusiasm was first expressed by the fact that my appeal to the self-sacrifice of those present led to the donation of three hundred marks."[22] That fistful of marks, in fact, turned out to be of lasting importance, for it was the gate receipts from Hitler's histrionic performances that would help carry the party forward on its often halting, stumbling road to power. Adolf Hitler—the one-time, longtime, sullen, ignored loner—was to become the rock star of German political orators.

Soon he was more than a guest speaker, more than the party's top box office draw. He seized this hitherto wretched "party" and made it into his plaything, his army of evil toy soldiers marching ever forward. In February 1920, he arranged the movement's truly first mass meeting in Munich, moving from the Hofbräuhaus basement ("keller") to its two-thousand-seat main venue. To highlight his triumph, he (along with party co-founder, the Munich railway locksmith Anton Drexler and its early economic guru, the self-taught anti-interest crank Gottfried Feder) cobbled together a party program, a nationalist-racist-populist-socialist mish-mosh of twenty-five points, that Hitler would soon ignore—yet still proclaim to be "unalterable":[23]

1. Union of all Germans in a Greater Germany on the basis of the right of self-determination.

2. Equality of rights for the German people in its dealings with other nations, and the revocation of the peace treaties of Versailles and St. Germain.

3. Land and territory (colonies) to feed our people and to settle our surplus population.

4. Only people of German blood may be citizens of the State . . . accordingly, no Jew may be a member of the nation.

5. Those who are not citizens must live in Germany as foreigners and must be subject to the law of aliens.

6. The right to choose the government and determine the laws of the State shall belong only to citizens. We therefore demand that no public office, of whatever nature, whether in the central government, the province, or the municipality, shall be held by anyone who is not a citizen.

We wage war against the corrupt parliamentary administration whereby men are appointed to posts by favor of the party without regard to character and fitness.

7. Foreign nationals (non-citizens) must be deported from the Reich.

8. All non-German immigration must be prevented.

9. All citizens shall have equal rights and duties.

10. It must be the first duty of every citizen to perform physical or mental work.

11. Abolition of incomes unearned by work and the breaking of the interest slavery (Zinsknechtschaff).

12. Personal enrichment from war must be regarded as a crime against the nation . . . ruthless confiscation of all war profits.

13. Nationalization of all businesses which have been formed into corporations (trusts).

14. Profits from the wholesale trade be shared.

15. The extensive development of provision for old age.

16. Creation and maintenance of a healthy middle class, the immediate communalizing of big department stores.

17. Land reform suitable to our national requirements . . . expropriation of land for communal purposes without compensation, abolition of ground rent, and prohibition of all speculation in land.

18. Common criminals, usurers, profiteers, etc., must be punished with death, whatever their creed or race.

19. That Roman Law, which serves a materialistic world order, be replaced by a German common law.

20. The State must consider a thorough reconstruction of our national system of education (with the aim of opening up to every able and hard-working German the possibility of higher education and of thus obtaining advancement). The curricula of all educational establishments must be brought into line with the requirements of practical life. The aim of the school must be to give the pupil, beginning with the first sign of intelligence, a grasp of the nation of the State (through the study of civic affairs). We demand the education of gifted children of poor parents, whatever their class or occupation, at the expense of the State.

21. The nation's health standards must be raised by protecting mothers and infants, by prohibiting child labour, by promoting physical strength . . . through compulsory gymnastics and sports.

22. Abolition of mercenary troops and formation of a people's army.[24]

23. Legal warfare against conscious political lying and its dissemination in the press. . . .

24. Liberty for all religious denominations in the state, so long as they are not a danger to it and do not militate against the moral feelings of the German race.

The party, as such, stands for positive Christianity . . . It combats the Jewish-materialist spirit within us . . .

25. That all the foregoing may be realized we demand the creation of a strong central power of the state. . . .[25]

It was clap-trap, but it foretold a future of dictatorship, censorship, foreign aggression, and, most of all, anti-Semitism. It also foretold the present, for on that very day, Hitler also unveiled his own "people's army, the *Ordnerdienst*[26]—soon known to history as the Nazi brown-shirted, strong-arm squad, the *Sturmabteilung* or "storm troopers." Within a week the party formally became the "National Socialist German Workers Party"—the *Nationalsozialistische Deutsche Arbeiterpartei* or NSDAP—and adopted its new symbol, the swastika.[27]

Yet, Hitler's "movement" remained just a localized cog in a great, noisy, dangerous, disunited mob of nationalists and/or racists. In March 1920, other armed rightists marched on Berlin. Captain Mayr ordered Hitler (still in the army) and the journalist and DAP founder Dietrich Eckart (a morphine-addicted Thule Society member[28]) to fly north to join this so-called "Kapp Putsch." On arrival, the putsch's official spokesman, Ignaz Trebitsch-Lincoln—a Hungarian Jew—greeted them. "Come on Adolf," the paunchy Eckart groused, "We have no further business here."[29]

It had been a trip from hell. Hitler became airsick.[30] Forced to land at Jüterbog, the duo was surrounded by hostile Communists, produced false papers, and barely escaped alive.[31] The Communists indeed played rough.

They had flopped abysmally in January 1919's Spartacist Revolt, but a year later they struck again, this time in Prussia's Saxony region, posting these placards in whatever towns they occupied:

> *DICTATORSHIP OF THE PROLETARIAT!*
> *We have occupied the area with our Red troops and hereby*
> *proclaim proletarian martial law, to the effect that*
> *EVERY INHABITANT WILL BE SHOT*
> *who does not comply with the ordinances of the Military*
> *Command. The moment reports reach us that the Security*
> *Police or the army are approaching, we will at once*
> *SET FIRE TO THE ENTIRE CITY AND SLAUGHTER THE*
> *BOURGEOISIE*
> *without distinction as to sex or age.*[32]

That proved to be the last bloody gasp of armed Communist insurrection within Germany. But Hitler was only getting started, now addressing crowds of sixty-five hundred at Munich's Circus Krone[33] ("Entry one mark. War invalids free"[34]). His skyrocketing popularity enabled him to issue an ultimatum to his fellow party leaders: either he would rule the NSDAP as its dictator—or leave.[35] In July 1921, the party supinely conveyed this cringing message to the one-time tramp: "In recognition of your vast knowledge, of your rare gift of oratory and of the services you have rendered with rare self-sacrifice in an honorary capacity for the advancement of the movement, this committee hereby accords you dictatorial powers."[36] The vote was 554–0 for dictatorship.[37] A month later, Dietrich Eckart would hail Hitler as "the Leader" (*Der Führer*)[38] in the NSDAP's recently acquired official newspaper, the *Völkischer Beobachter*.[39]

How had Adolf Hitler achieved such untrammeled power? And so easily?

To those who knew him and followed him he was something beyond the mere demonic shouter and hater we recall from newsreels, something very different. The devil, after all, does not corrupt souls by being repulsive but rather through charm and by being oh-so-very reasonable. Portions of the Hitler persona seemed charming, even diffident. He came from nothing. That only accentuated his greatness. His grievances were *your* grievances. He cared—about you and, above all, about wounded, betrayed Germany.

"Here [in Germany]," the youthful American journalist William Chapman White observed in April 1932, "are many other groups from all classes who blame their personal misfortunes and the misfortunes of the Fatherland on the Jews, on France, on Christianity, on machinery, on the unwillingness of municipalities to issue their own currency, on the failure of the German people to recognize the virtues of vegetarianism and to eat sausage made from beets—and all would like to see something done about it."[40]

How Adolf Hitler might accomplish said diverse program remained quite another story. Neither he—nor his mesmerized disciples—agonized over such bothersome details. "His critics charge him with having no concrete programme," White further explained. "That criticism is unimportant. Moses never offered his followers a detailed relief map of the Promised Land. It was enough to assure them that there was such a land. 'And Hitler has no economic programme,' the critics say. That, for his followers, also means little. No one who believes in heaven worries whether heaven maintains the gold standard or not."[41]

And, yet, as satisfying as his vague oratory might be, there was something distinctly *off* about this rising messiah. "A strange man this Adolf Hitler," noted an early biographer. "He is infinitely polite and courteous in his interviews pausing perceptibly after every statement in case there is something his questioner wishes to add. He is punctilious to the point of quixotism in acknowledging the salute of his men and then himself saluting the standards. . . . [H]e never seems at ease in formal gatherings or when being spoken to. He seems a hunted being and is always ready to find refuge in making a miniature speech, even when one asks him a question that could be answered by a single word. In making a speech he is at least on firm ground. There he does not have to think, there he can let himself go for he has said it all thousands of times and will keep on saying it until he dies."[42]

He was, if not at all educated, nonetheless, quite knowledgeable—at least, on those subjects and what facts he deemed worthwhile. As FDR knew his ships and the name of every Democrat ward healer from coast to coast (or, at least, he could heartily pretend he knew each name), Hitler knew his architecture and his Wagner and his guns and armaments and regimental formations. And he only discussed what he thought he knew. He had read voraciously as a youth, though what he read and how he read was quite another matter. "His was the attitude of total prejudice," noted his biographer Joachim Fest, "which only 'reads' what it already knows better, only absorbs what endorses its views and resists any questioning of knowledge it has already absorbed."[43]

He was also mysterious, not merely regarding his shadowy past, but regarding his current appearance, at first strangely refusing to allow any photographs of himself and having supporters smash the cameras of any photographer who dared breach his privacy.[44]

His inner circle would contain a varied bunch: rabid haters (ideo-logues Alfred Rosenberg and Julius Streicher), hopeless hero-worshippers (Rudolf Hess and Joseph and Magda Goebbels), upper-class deal-makers (Dr. Hjalmar Schacht and Franz von Papen), drunks (Dietrich Eckart,[45] offi-cial photographer Heinrich Hoffmann—the *Reichstrunkenbold* or "National Drunkard in Chief,"[46] the roly-poly economist Walther Funk,[47] Reich Minis-ter of Science, Education, and Culture Bernhard Rust,[48] and German Labor Front [*Deutsche Arbeitsfront*] leader Robert Ley[49]), craven opportunists (the future diplomat Joachim von Ribbentrop), bureaucrats gone mad (SS leader Heinrich Himmler and Hitler's own private secretary Martin Bormann), and outright brigands (the SA's Ernst Röhm ["I am an immature and wicked man"[50]], party co-founder Hermann Esser [Hitler: "I know Esser is a scoun-drel"[51]], and, of course, Hermann Göring). There was, for good measure, even the occasional convicted accomplice to murder (Bormann[52]) and an actual murderer (the SA's Edmund Heines). Göring, brilliant in his own way and shameless in his evil, provided the best, frankest, and most frightening, expla-nation (and to an interrogator at Nürnberg, no less) of what brought the lot of them together:

> *If you really want to do something new, the good won't help you with it. They are self-satisfied, lazy, they have their God and their own pig-headedness—you can't do it with them. "Let me have men about me that are fat." An anointed king can say that but not a leader who has made himself. Let me have men about me that are errant knaves. The wicked who have something on their conscience are obliging, quick to hear threats because they know how it's done, and for booty you can offer them things because they will take them. Because they have no hesitations. You can hang them if they get out of step. Let me have men about me that are utter villains—provided that I have the power of absolute power over life and death. The sole and single leader, whom no one can interfere with. What do you know of the possibilities and evil! Why do you write books and make philosophy when you only know about virtue and how to acquire it, whereas the world is fundamentally moved by something quite different?[53]*

They *were* evil. They were also young. Hitler's movement was a youth move-ment: a young top leadership, a young Führer, a young party filled with young veterans and younger students. Its youth gave it energy—as well as impetuosity, impatience ("Make room, you old ones!"[54]), and intolerance. "National Socialism," boasted the party's official slogan, "is the organized will of youth."[55]

In this, the movement mimicked the man, for in Hitler it was not so much the child that was father to the man but rather the adolescent who fathered the man—his adolescent ideas and attitudes, his obsessions and hatreds of that crucial timeframe fixed forever within him. As developmental psychologist Erik Erikson noted:

> *Psychologists overdo the father attributes in Hitler's historical image; Hitler, the adolescent who refused to become a father by any connotation, or, for that matter, a kaiser or a president. He did not repeat Napoleon's error. He was the Führer: a glorified older brother, who took over prerogatives of the fathers without over-identifying with them . . . he reserved for himself the new position of the one who remains young in possession of supreme power. He was the unbroken adolescent who had chosen a career apart from civilian happiness, mercantile tranquility, and spiritual peace: a gang leader who kept the boys together by demanding their admiration, by creating terror, and by shrewdly involving them in crimes from which there was no way back. And he was a ruthless exploiter of parental failures.*[56]

But even youth and adolescence require a ritual—and Hitler provided his followers with a dazzling array of ceremonies and trappings drawn in some not inconsequential way from his own beginnings.

Unable to posit any value to his ancestral Church's actual teachings—sprung, after all, originally from the Jews and permeated with what he dismissed as intolerable "weakness"—he attributed its power and its resilience to mere structure—to vestments and hymns and architecture and, above all, to hierarchical organization. "The Nazi Party was to be built upon the model of the Catholic Church," former Hamburg *gauleiter* (regional leader) Albert Krebs recalled Hitler lecturing Krebs's fellow gauleiters in late June 1930. "Upon a broad pediment of preachers and 'political pastors' living and working among the people, the structure should ascend the leadership pyramid of the party from the county leaders over the Gauleiters to the senators and ultimately to the Führer-Pope. Hitler did not shrink from a comparison between Gauleiter and Bishop, future senators and cardinals, no more than he was concerned about shifting the concept of authority, obedience, and faith out of the realm of the spiritual into the temporal without even indicating how those concepts changed in the process."[57]

Thus, Adolf Hitler fashioned a movement based on hatred, youth, trappings, and ritual—and, yes, outright violence. As early as January 1921, he proclaimed, "The National Socialist Movement in Munich will in future ruthlessly prevent—if necessary by force—all meetings or lectures that are likely to distract the minds of our former countrymen."[58] He soon backed up his threats with an actual Löwenbräukeller assault upon the Bavarian separatist Otto Ballerstedt, serving a month in Stadelheim Prison for his efforts.[59] Bavaria's conservative interior minister Franz Schweyer mulled his deportation to Austria,[60] but Nazi violence only grew, with Hitler's storm troopers overly eager to flex their muscles, for not only in 1920s America did gangland violence run wild. It ran wilder in Germany, its most vicious gang being Hitler's. In *Mein Kampf,* he described the SA's first great battle (or rather brawl)—in November 1921, at Munich's Hofbräuhaus:

> *I made it clear to the lads that today probably for the first time they would have to show themselves loyal to the movement through thick and thin, and that not a man of us must leave the hall unless we were carried out dead . . . if I should see anyone playing the coward, I myself would personally tear off his armband and take away his insignia . . . In front of me, especially to the left of me, only enemies were sitting and standing. They were all robust men and young fellows, in large part from the Maffei [railway] factory, from Kustermann's [iron and steel works], from Isaria Meter Works . . . In a few seconds the whole hall was filled with a roaring, screaming crowd, over which, like howitzer shells, flew innumerable beer mugs . . . It was an idiotic spectacle . . . I should have liked to see a bourgeois meeting under such circumstances . . . For twenty minutes the hellish tumult lasted, but then our enemies, who must have numbered seven or eight hundred men, had for the most part been beaten out of the hall and chased down the stairs by my men, numbering not even fifty . . . Then suddenly two shots were fired from the hall entrance towards the platform, and wild shooting started. Your heart almost rejoiced at such a revival of old war experience.*[61]

Violence proved intoxicating. It fed upon itself. The nationalist right might have learned from 1920's disastrous Kapp Putsch. It did not—and neither did political neophyte Hitler. In September 1922, Munich rightists, commanded by Regensburg public health inspector Dr. Otto Pittinger, the head of the paramilitary *Bund Bayern und Reich,* prepared yet another putsch. Hitler, still simply one among many rabble rousers, showed up, prepared for action. Virtually no one else bothered. The fiasco taught him yet another lesson. Coalitions were out. "I was ready—my men were ready!" Hitler explained to his wealthy (but truly shady) early patron Kurt Lüdecke. "From now on I go my way alone. No more Pittingers, no more Fatherland societies! One party. One single party. These gentlemen, these counts and generals—they won't do anything. I shall. I alone."[62] He would now lead not just the NSDAP but *everything.*

And lead them against the Jews.

The chaos of 1918–1920 only emboldened his existing antipathies to the "Jewish menace"—the Marxes, Trotskys, Luxemburgs, Eisners, Kuns, Tollers, Levinés et al. His early talks had been liberally peppered not merely against the "November Criminals," who had plotted German wartime defeat and the founding of the hated Weimar Republic, but with anti-Semitic screeds and fantasies. "Once I really am in power, my first and foremost task will be the annihilation of the Jews," he confided in 1922 to journalist Josef Hell, a former major. "As soon as I have the power to do so, I will have gallows built in rows—at the Marienplatz in Munich, for example—as many as traffic allows. Then the Jews will be hanged indiscriminately, and they will remain hanging until they stink; they will hang there as long as the principles of hygiene permit. As soon as they have been untied, the next batch will be strung up, and so on down the line, until the last Jew in Munich has been exterminated. Other cities will follow suit, precisely in this fashion, until all Germany has been completely cleansed of Jews."[63]

A year later, the American journalist (and former paid German propagandist) George Sylvester Viereck interviewed him. Viereck found his subject "more like a poet than a politician," but when Viereck dared to defend Germany's Jews, Hitler retorted, "The fact that a man is decent is no reason why we should not eliminate him."[64]

As November 1923 approached, Hitler plotted his own coup. By now he had recruited such men as Hermann Göring (a world war ace) Rudolf Hess (a List Regiment officer[65]), Ernst Röhm (a former superior during his indoctrination class period[66]), and, most interesting, two other notables designed to broaden his appeal to more elevated circles. The first was Ernst Franz Sedgwick "Putzi" Hanfstaengl, son of a Munich art publisher and an American mother. The 6'5" Hanfstaengl had graduated Harvard ('09) with columnist Walter Lippmann[67] and palled about New York's Harvard Club with both Franklin Roosevelt[68] and TR Jr.,[69] even visiting TR himself at Washington and at Oyster Bay.[70] His Madison Avenue art shop numbered the avid collector William Randolph Hearst among its clientele.[71] In July 1921, he returned home and soon fell under Hitler's widening spell, ironically tipped off to Hitler's potential by America's attaché in Berlin, the Yale man Capt. Truman Smith.[72] "His technique," Hanfstaengl marveled of Hitler, "resembled the thrusts and parries of a fencer or the perfect balance of a tightrope walker. Sometimes he reminded me of a skilled violinist, who never coming to the end of his bow, always left just the faint anticipation of a tone—a thought spared the indelicacy of utterance."[73] He amused Hitler (as he had FDR) with his piano stylings, introduced the still gangsterly attired Führer to high society, and provided a badly needed thousand-dollar interest-free loan for purchasing the fledging Nazi newspaper, *Völkischer Beobachter*.[74] Last, and certainly not least, he adopted the Harvard fight song into a raucous "Sieg Heil" chant.[75] Hanfstaengl possessed his charms, but as American journalist Quentin Reynolds observed, "You had to know Putzi to really dislike him."[76] Reynolds's fellow journalist, Dorothy Thompson, found Hanfstaengl to be "an immense, high-strung, incoherent clown."[77]

Clown or not, Putzi provided cash and respectability. Gen. Erich Friedrich Wilhelm Ludendorff provided *ancien régime* star power.

Ludendorff had teamed with Field Marshal Paul von Hindenburg to command German armed forces in the war, eventually emerging as the nation's de facto dictator. He was, however, a crackpot, not just in the sense of his rabid militarism, but in his opposition to Catholics, Jesuits, Masons, and to Christianity in general and to his belief in esoteric theories such as that Mozart and Schiller had been assassinated by "the Cheka of the supranatural secret society." War—and Wotan—were his gods.[78] Nonetheless, he was still a very big herring in the still middling pond of a former lance corporal.

Germany was astir, ablaze. Organization Consul, a secret ultra-nationalist group, conducted a wave of high-profile assassinations, commencing with the August 1921 murder of the Catholic Centre (the *Deutsche Zentrumspartei* or "*Zentrum*") Party's Matthias Erzberger, a signer of the hated Armistice.[79] In April 1922, nationalist plotters fatally machine-gunned Foreign Minister Walther Rathenau ("Kill off Walther Rathenau, The goddamned Jewish sow"[80]), a signatory to the Treaty of Rapallo, formally ceding territory lost in the war.[81] That June, two Organization Consul thugs flung prussic acid into the face of former chancellor (*Reichskanzler*) Philipp Scheidemann.[82]

At that unruly November 1921 Hofbräuhaus rally, Hitler himself had nearly missed death. Pro- and anti-Hitler partisans had descended to hurling beer steins and then chairs at each other. Storm troopers evicted opponents from the hall. Two shots were fired at Hitler. Someone (perhaps even the invariably pistol-packing Führer) fired back. Unharmed and unrattled, Hitler orated for another twenty minutes at full throttle.[83]

Unemployment reached 23 percent.[84] Hyper-inflation raged, wreaking havoc—particularly on the middle class (*Mittelstand*). An American dollar bought 4.2 marks in 1914; on November 19, 1923, 4.2 billion.[85] That September, a young student named Albert Speer wrote home from the Black Forest, "Very cheap here! Lodgings 400,000 marks and supper 1,800,000 marks. Milk 250,000 marks a pint."[86] Soon a restaurant dinner cost Speer ten to twenty billion marks—even in the student cafeteria, more than a billion. A theater ticket fetched between three and four hundred million marks.

"I had a monthly salary of 200 billion marks," mused a character in novelist Erich Maria Remarque's *Drei Kameraden*, "we were paid twice a day, and then everybody had a half hour's leave so that he could rush to the stores and buy something before the next quotation on the dollar came out, at which time the money would lose half its value."[87]

A vengeful France occupied Germany's industrial Ruhr region in January 1923, uniting a humiliated nation in patriotic rage.[88] Fueling German anger was France's deployment of black colonial troops in the job.[89] Berlin declared a state of emergency. Bavarian authorities refused to abide by it—and proclaimed their own.[90] Later that month, "Black *Reichswehr*" troops under Maj. Bruno Buchrucker (a future Nazi) seized three forts east of Berlin.[91] Communists gained entrance to governments in Saxony and Thuringia[92] and rioted in Hamburg and Muelheim.[93] Hitler believed the time had finally come for his own coup. In the fashion of Italy's former Socialist journalist Benito Mussolini, he would march on his own nation's capital and install a fascist regime.

But not alone. He required the backing of Bavarian's rightist government. But as much as Munich's leaders opposed Berlin's often socialist-dominated regimes, they were hardly prepared to forcibly supplant them—or to tolerate Hitler in such a mad effort. They had their reasons. At a March 1922 meeting with Ludendorff, Otto Pittinger, local Reichswehr commander Gen. Otto von Lossow, and Gustav Ritter von Kahr, Bavaria's monarchist (though Protestant[94]) minister president, Hitler had advocated a most un-rightist position, a strategic alliance with the Communists "for the purpose of delivering them from the hands of the Jews and of making use of them later to get the power into our own hands." Hitler's prospective allies rejected the idea. "You will live to regret the treachery which you are committing against the German race today," he stormed. "You will recognize too late what power I have behind me."[95]

They may not have perceived his power. He had none, save for the power of his lungs. But many discerned his menace. The alarmed General Lossow extracted a pledge from Hitler "on his word of honor . . . [to] never make a putsch."[96] Such vows, as the world soon learned, remained operative only at his convenience. Hitler's Baltic German advisers, the pompous Alfred Rosenberg and the prissy Max von Scheubner-Richter[97] accordingly developed a crack-brained scheme to kidnap Lossow, Kahr, and Bavarian State Police chief Col. Hans Ritter von Seisser and compel them to join a Nazi-led march on Berlin.

On Friday evening, November 9, 1923, Hitler struck, invading Munich's vast Bürgerbräukeller, where Kahr (with Lossow and Seisser alongside) addressed a capacity (but drowsy) audience of three thousand. Six hundred storm troopers surrounded the hall. The cutaway-clad Hitler ("a cross between Charlie Chaplin and a headwaiter"[98]) mounted a chair. Firing his Browning pistol into the air, he placed Bavaria's ruling triumvirate under arrest before entreating them—and all present—to enlist in his grand crusade. "The National Revolution has begun! . . . ," he shouted. "I have a machine gun posted in the gallery. The barracks of the Reichswehr and police are occupied. The Army and the Police are marching on the city under the swastika banner."[99] His audience reacted with fright, puzzlement, and, then, with sheer annoyance. Sensing their hostility, Hermann Göring tramped to the platform to calm them, "There is nothing to fear. We have the friendliest intentions. For that matter, you've no cause to grumble, you've got your beer!"[100]

The National Revolution had already descended to the level of a bad joke.

Yes, a joke. Neither the army nor the police had joined Hitler's adventure. Kahr, Lossow, and Seisser all assured Hitler and Ludendorff of their support, and thanks to Ludendorff's naïveté speedily exited. Once free, they organized armed resistance against their former captors. Immeasurably aiding them was Bavarian vice premier Franz Matt, the highest ranking Bavarian not trapped inside the Bürgerbräukeller. That night Matt (simply unwilling to suffer any more of Kahr's speeches) dined with Munich's Cardinal Michael von Faulhaber—as well as with Papal Nuncio Eugenio Pacelli (later Pius XII).[101] In their earliest days, the Nazis had placed considerable emphasis on wooing Bavarian Catholics to their cause. Assisted by a number of anti-Semitic clergy, they attained some measure of success. But their burgeoning alliance with Ludendorff and north German quasi-pagan *völkisch* ("racial tribalist") elements soon alienated Bavaria's devout population.[102] Just five days preceding Hitler's putsch, Faulhaber (no liberal at all[103]) had even publicly expressed sympathies with "our fellow Israelite citizens."[104]

By mid-morning November 10, the die had been cast. Kahr, Matt, and their allies had rallied their forces. This coup was going nowhere. An idea seized Ludendorff. National Socialist forces (now numbering three thousand) would march upon the Bavarian Defense Ministry. But as they warily crossed the Odeonsplatz, a hundred of Colonel Seisser's "Green Police" blocked their way. Shots rang out. Bullets ricocheted wildly off the plaza's granite paving. Sixteen Nazis and three soldiers died. A shot through the lungs instantly killed Max von Scheubner-Richter, marching arm-in-arm with Hitler. His falling lifeless body jerked Der Führer to the ground, dislocating his shoulder. Hitler's bodyguard Ulrich Graf fell upon his chief to shield him from further police fire. Eleven bullets riddled Graf's chest, arms, stomach, and thighs. He survived.[105] Flying granite splinters lacerated Göring's groin and thigh. A Jewish furniture dealer's wife, Frau Ilse Ballin (and her sister; both trained war nurses), treated his wounds.[106] Only Ludendorff and his adjutant maintained their dignity, marching forward, stiffly and alone into captivity.[107] His fellow putschists ingloriously fled. Hitler ("the first to get up and turn back"[108]) scrambled into a waiting yellow Fiat[109] to speed him into hiding thirty miles away at Putzi Hanfstaengl's chalet at Uffing. "This is the end!" he screamed to Putzi's American-born wife Helene, as police surrounded the house, "I will never let those swine take me! I will shoot myself first!"[110] Helene knocked the pistol from his hand—sending it flying into a barrel of flour—as he prepared to make good the threat, saving his life. He trudged downstairs to a police car, wearing only a pair of oversized white pajamas and a blue terrycloth robe belonging to his hostess's 6'4" husband[111]—with his Iron Cross incongruously pinned to it.[112]

The putsch had unmade Hitler's dreams, unmasking him as a hopeless dreamer, a bungler, and (despite his war record) a coward. The trial that followed redeemed him. Authorities placed him, Ludendorff, Captain Röhm, Wilhelm Frick, Munich SA leader Wilhelm Brückner, and four others on the dock for treason. The *Chicago Daily News*'s Edgar Ansel Mowrer recalled: "It was before the Munich judges that I first saw [Hitler]—and marveled. Was this provincial dandy, with his slick dark hair, his cutaway coat, his awkward tongue, the terrible rebel? He seemed for all the world like a traveling salesman for a clothing firm."[113]

Somewhere between Hitler's capture and his trial at Landsberg am Lech, he recovered his nerve. The Weimar Republic, and not he, would face history's judgment. Seizing full advantage of a sympathetic court, he exculpated his actions ("I am not a traitor but a German"[114]) and damned not only the Republic but also Kahr ("I trusted him like a brother"[115]), Lossow, and Seisser. Assuming his own defense, "at the top of his lungs,"[116] he concluded:

> *The army we have formed is growing from day to day, from hour to hour, and faster. Especially in these days I nourish the proud hope that one day the hour will come when those rough companies will grow to battalions, the battalions to regiments, the regiments to divisions, and the old cockade will be taken out of the filth, and the old flag will wave again, and there will be a reconciliation at the Last Judgment, which we are prepared to face. Then will the voice of the real Court of Justice speak from our bones and our graves. For it is not you, gentlemen, who pronounce judgment upon us. Instead, the judgment of the eternal court*

of history will pronounce against this prosecution which has been raised against us. As for your verdict—I know it already. The eternal court will not ask us: "Did you commit high treason, or not?" That court will judge us, the Quartermaster-General of the old Army [Ludendorff], his officers and soldiers, as Germans who wanted the good of their own people and Fatherland, who wanted to fight and die. You may judge us guilty a thousand times over, but the Goddess of Eternal Justice will smile and tear to tatters the brief of the state's attorney and the verdict of this court. For she acquits us![117]

Those who crushed Hitler's revolt might have killed him on the spot. That fate, after all, befell Luxemburg and Liebknecht. They didn't. The judges who tried Hitler might very well have hung—or, at least, deported—him. His own party platform, after all demanded that, "Foreign nationals (non-citizens) must be deported from the Reich." But they neither shot nor deported him. Instead, they gave him five years in Landsberg prison. Brückner received a year-and-a-half sentence; Ernst Röhm, a year of parole; Frick, a suspended sentence. Ludendorff (who in actuality had not known in advance of Hitler's plans[118]) went free.[119] In his cozy prison lodgings, Hitler dictated his memoirs to the dimwitted though faithful Rudolf Hess. He wanted to title his work *Four and a Half Years (of Struggle) Against Lies, Stupidity and Cowardice.* His publisher, the former List Regiment staff sergeant (*feldwebel*), Max Amann, judiciously shortened that mouthful to *My Struggle* (*Mein Kampf*). Out of prison by December 1924,[120] he was free—but damaged goods. The United Press's Berlin correspondent had already pronounced "the end of the hip-hip-hooray methods" of this "spectacular former sign painter."[121] Who might logically have argued with that hypothesis?

His party had skidded downward with him. In May 1924's *Reichstag* contests, the NSDAP, temporarily renamed the National Socialist Freedom Movement (*Nationalsozialistische Freiheitsbewegung* or "NSFB"), received 1,918,329 votes (6.55 percent), winning thirty-two seats, including those captured by Ludendorff and Röhm.[122] That December's Reichstag balloting saw the movement plummet to a puny 907,242 votes (3 percent) and fourteen seats.[123]

The following February, the pudgy, ex-saddlemaker Reich president (*Reichspräsident*) Friedrich Ebert died. Ludendorff, running to succeed him, garnered just 285,793 votes, an infinitesimal 1.1 percent.[124]

The nation was pulling out of its funk. Inflation ceased. Industrial production skyrocketed. The League of Nations admitted Germany to membership. The NSDAP's malaise accelerated. Ludendorff broke with Hitler.

Ernst Röhm abruptly withdrew from public life.[125] Hermann Göring, beset by morphine addiction, found himself confined to the Langbro lunatic asylum.[126] In local elections the Nazi vote proved almost nonexistent—1.6 percent in Saxony,[127] 1.5 percent in Hamburg,[128] and 3.7 percent in Braunschweig (Brunswick).[129]

Unemployment dropped from 18.1 percent in 1926 to 8.8 percent in 1927 and then again to 8.4 percent.[130] In May 1928's Reichstag vote, the Hitlerite vote sunk yet again, to 810,000 votes (2.6 percent), entitling the party to just twelve deputies.[131] In Berlin, it drew a measly 16,478 votes—1.4 percent.[132] The left, meanwhile, only increased its strength. The Socialists (*Sozialdemokratische Partei Deutschlands*, the "SPD") were stronger than ever. Communists (*Kommunistische Partei Deutschlands*, the "KPD") gained a half million votes.[133]

And, yet . . .

Below the surface of Reichstag and Landtag votes, something sinister gnawed within the German heart. The Nazi Party was not dying at all. It was not stagnant. It grew steadily all the while, thriving despite failed putsches and speaking bans and disappointing showings at the ballot box. Consider its membership rolls throughout the decade[134]:

1920	3,000
1925	27,000
1926	49,000
1927	72,000
1928	108,000
1929	178,000

And *then* came *Der Krasch*.

The Depression hit Germany as hard as anywhere, still harder, with the nation shouldering the burden of wartime reparations. Even before October 1929, German rightists had temporarily united in a "Reich Committee" to oppose the new Young Plan to restructure such payments. Press baron Alfred Hugenberg of the intransigently nationalist German National People's Party (*Deutschnationale Volkspartei* or "DNVP"), Franz Seldte of the major rightist veterans group, the *Stahlhelm*, and Pan-German League (*Alldeutscher Verband*) president Heinrich Class were the movement's more natural leaders, but the group sensed it required street muscle to succeed. Enter Adolf Hitler.[135] The Reich Committee's plebiscite fizzled, attracting only 13.8 percent of voters,[136] but, in the process, Hitler's more prosperous and respectable rightist allies had pumped new funds and publicity into his supposedly stagnating movement.

It was a time for ruffians. Unemployment reached two million[137] as early as January 1930; three million by late summer.[138] By 1931, the unemployment rate had jumped to 33.7 percent—and 43.7 by 1932.[139] Communists rioted in the cities.[140] SPD-controlled Prussia banned outdoor meetings and demonstrations.[141] The Prussian Ministry of the Interior decreed NSDAP or KPD membership to be incompatible with holding public or civil service positions.[142]

Chaos reigned within the NSDAP as well. Ideological divisions had long sundered Nazi ranks. Some took the "Socialist" portion of "National Socialist" far more seriously than Hitler, now eager to court such moneybag allies as Hugenberg or Seldte. Events climaxed in July 1930 as Hitler expelled Otto Strasser (younger brother of party propaganda leader Gregor Strasser) and his leftist followers "ruthlessly and without exception. . . ."[143] Meanwhile, the movement's purely street-tough wing, the SA, roiled with discontent over insufficient pay and the party leadership's perceived lack of fighting spirit. That August, its Berlin SA leader Walther Stennes (a cadet classmate of Hermann Göring) occupied and trashed the NSDAP's Berlin headquarters.[144] Hitler reacted by reaching into the party's past, appointing Ernst Röhm (soldiering in Bolivia since 1928) as *Oberster SA Führer*.[145]

Chancellor Hermann Heinrich Müller, a colorless, sickly Social Democratic,[146] headed a "Grand Coalition" in weaker health composed of SPD, Zentrum, German Democratic Party (DDP), and German People's Party (DVP) members. In March 1930, Müller resigned over the issue of funding of unemployment benefits.[147] Reichspräsident Paul von Hindenburg (no friend of the SPD) replaced him with the Zentrum's conservative Heinrich Brüning. When Brüning attempted to raise taxes to deal with the Depression, the Reichstag defeated his measure 256–204.[148] Hindenburg called for new elections.

Hitler's putsch had taught him two hard lessons: Putsches rarely succeed, and the most pleasant of prisons were still unpleasant places to be avoided. From 1923 forward, he preached a sneering willingness to work within the established system—to destroy it. Though his subsequent lack of success at the polls hardly validated that strategy, he stuck with it, thus, aggravating the intra-party frictions leading to the Stennes and Otto Strasser ousters. With new Reichstag elections approaching in 1930, he held fast to that strategy.

He would need to. And he would need to increase his base from its motley collection of rabid racists, neo-pagans, and crackpot socialists. He would need to steal votes from the nationalist right, from the old monarchists, from more sensible anti-Communists. "Will Nationalist Socialist ideas cleanse?" a Hamburg schoolteacher named Luise Solmitz pondered in her diary. Solmitz was not merely a middle-class Protestant conservative wary of Brüning (a "petty Jesuit"[149]), and an admirer of the Hugenberg/Hindenburg stripe of politics. She had married a Jew (albeit a convert to her faith) and mothered a *mischling* daughter, Gisella. Yet, even she felt the appeal of this strangely energetic new movement. "Will salvation come from the unity of the people [*Volksgemeinshaft*] in harmony with the *Bürgertum* [middle class]? Will we today place fatherland above private interests? One thing is for sure, the strong attraction of National Socialism."

Frau Solmitz joined Hitler's camp that September. "I decided to vote for the two Nazis," she wrote, "it is a dangerous experiment. . . ."[150]

Nazi party membership doubled in 1930—from 178,000 to 389,000.[151] Millions more now voted National Socialist. In a campaign marred by street fighting between Hitlerite storm troopers and the KPD's Alliance of Red Front Fighters (*Roter Frontkämpfer-Bund* or "RFB"), September 1930's polling saw both Müller's SPD and Hugenberg's DNVP forfeit seats. The more centrist German People's (DVP) and German State (DStP) parties crumbled. The Communist KPD gained twenty-three delegates. Now with seventy-seven seats, it emerged as Weimar's fourth largest party, sliding past the Zentrum. The great, the earth-shaking, change came from the Nazis. Their popularity simply exploded. Party vote totals skyrocketed from 810,127 to 6,379,672, moving them from ninth place to second, trailing only the wounded SPD. From 2.6 percent they surged to 18.25 percent, their Reichstag representation ascending from a mere twelve delegates to a fearsome 107.[152] Hitler no longer merely lurked as the leader of a vague, unlikely tomorrow. He stood loudly knocking at the gates of power today.

But how might he employ that power?

For all his force and bluster, his white-hot heat of hatreds, he was disturbingly vague about what he stood for—and, most pressing, how he might sever the Gordian Knot of his Fatherland's economic morass. "Our solution depends upon confidence," Braunschweig's Nazi minister of interior and education Dietrich Klagges alibied to the *New York Post*'s Berlin correspondent H. R. "Red" Knickerbocker, "the solution will be more effective the less is known about it in advance."[153]

"If we give away our method of getting out of the economic crisis," contended another party leader, "our enemies will take it up and use it and take the credit for it."[154]

It was all very Alice-in-Wonderland—a party claiming the ability to solve everything—but strangely lacking the ability to even hint at how they might do it; a leader coveting votes but hating voting.

"We know that no election can finally decide the fate of nations—," Hitler lectured his party leadership in July 1930, "they can destroy nations. But we know that in these elections democracy must be destroyed with weapons of democracy."[155]

He would now wield a cynical sledgehammer of destruction upon a system he so despised.

CHAPTER SIX

"He has never consulted me
about a damn thing"

Electoral triumphs filled the air.

In 1928 Hitler's Nazis had flopped at the ballot box. September 1930 witnessed him vault nearly to the top of the Reichstag pack.

In November 1928 Franklin Roosevelt won—but by the skin of his teeth and running behind Herbert Lehman and the entire statewide Democratic slate.[1] It was a different story in 1930. Barely six weeks following Hitler's 1930 triumph, Franklin won re-election by a purely stupendous margin, well exceeding anything recorded by the popular Al Smith.[2] "I do not see," crowed one FDR aide, "how Mr. Roosevelt can escape being the next presidential nominee of his party, even if no one should raise a finger to bring it about."[3]

Or as Will Rogers put it: "The Democrats nominated their President yesterday, Franklin D. Roosevelt."[4]

Yes, FDR surely wanted the presidency, but a gleaming smile ("his Christian Science smile"[5] as H. L. Mencken for some reason put it) and a famous surname might only carry one so far. Roosevelt needed an organization—an organization bigger than Louis Howe, Eleanor, and his normal coterie of hangers-on. Remarkably, he soon enjoyed one—certainly, not particularly large by later standards but big enough and certainly larger and far more effective than any competitor possessed.

In fact, it was actually very good.

Three key additions came early: Samuel ("Sammy the Rose" in FDR parlance) Rosenman, a former Al Smith aide, who proved both remarkably adept at research and speechwriting—and, of course, at switching loyalties; Edward Flynn, the Democratic boss of the Bronx, an invaluable counterweight to corrupt and unreliable Manhattan-based Tammany Hall; and, most essential of all, James A. Farley.

Farley, another Smith administration veteran, was no city slicker, hailing from New York's rural Rockland County. Where Ed Flynn was introverted and Howe too irascible to peddle FDR to the rest of the nation, the 6'2"[6] "Big Jim" Farley, a man of immense good will and political skills, was just what the doctor ordered. Serendipitously, the intensely jealous[7] Howe (who truly hated Rosenman[8]—and nearly everyone else) proved strangely tolerant of this affable Irishman.

It was, however, the despised Rosenman, who sparked one of FDR's more famous innovations, a team of academic policy advisers soon known to history as the "Brains Trust."

"Where shall we go for advice?" FDR, wary of relying too heavily on the usual coterie of politicians or businessmen for policy guidance, had asked. "Why not," answered Rosenman, "go to the universities of the country?"[9]

Roosevelt did, first tapping Columbia University's Raymond Moley, an expert on criminal justice, and, perhaps more significantly a veteran of midwestern progressive politics. The pipe-puffing Moley in turn recruited two other Columbia faculty: agricultural specialist Rexford Guy Tugwell and Adolf A. Berle, a precocious thirty-something authority on corporate governance. Berle, who entered Harvard at age fourteen, was that university's youngest graduate. The startlingly handsome and dapper Tugwell, Moley recalled, possessed an "original and speculative turn of mind [which] made him an enormously exhilarating companion. Rex was like a cocktail. His conversation picked you up and made your brain race along."[10] In his youth, he had written with all the pompous hubris of youth:

I have gathered my tools and my charts;
My plans are fashioned and practical;
I shall roll up my sleeves—make America over![11]

In the intervening years he had rolled down his sleeves—but not his dreams.

The less impassioned Moley had actually been with Roosevelt since 1928.[12] Rosenman found him "devious" and "morose"; he found Rosenman "smug" and "obsequious."[13] But more important, Moley, in 1932, judged FDR to be "patient, amenable to advice, moderate and smilingly indifferent to criticism."[14] Further, Franklin's indomitable will ("he is hard, stubborn, resourceful, relentless") and energy impressed the hell out of him. "The stories about his illness and its effect upon him are the bunk," Moley wrote to his sister in April 1932. "Nobody in public life since T. R. has been so robust, so buoyantly and blatantly healthy as this fellow. He is full of animal spirits and keeps himself and the people around him in a rare good humor. . . ."[15]

That was Moley. Tugwell and Berle, however, took their time in warming to their new candidate. Berle alibied to Moley that he actually supported another candidate (Tugwell surmised that to be former Wilson secretary of war Newton D. Baker[16]). For his part, Tugwell assessed Franklin as "not a handsome fellow," despite "overdeveloped muscles that rippled under his well-coat cut." A receding hairline marred his features, Tugwell observed, "as did a discoloration under his eyes," "irregular" teeth, and a discernible paunch. FDR, he thought, "despite his exercises, showed more deterioration than normal for his age."[17]

Still, FDR, confidently booming away from behind any podium, looked better, healthier, and stronger than the hopelessly bedraggled Herbert Hoover. From behind a radio microphone he outshone *all* comers. "He wasn't . . . a good extemporaneous speaker," Jim Farley later recalled, "but he read beautifully, and the intonation of his voice and everything else went over. Made him, I think, one of the outstanding campaigners of all time. He wasn't an orator in the way [Adlai] Stevenson was, and he didn't have the type of oratory that Smith had or any of the other men of his time, but he read a speech well and got it over, and he did it with a great deal of sincerity, and it got across."[18]

But *was* he sincere? Even Farley, who claimed FDR "never lied to me except about the third term," had to admit that "a lot of people accuse him of lying or being careless with the truth"[19]—Rexford Tugwell being among them ("He had learned what I did not yet know, that the record is seldom cited and claiming to be right is a political habit").[20] Veracity aside, much of FDR's personality profoundly disquieted Tugwell, including his tendency to treat people as disposable ("Roosevelt would organize endeavors only if he could close them out simply by not mentioning them again. His custom of consulting many and diverse people was already known to us"[21]) and his general ingratitude ("He seldom said anything that showed the least appreciation. . . ."[22]).

And what, in fact, did Franklin actually know about anything? What lay beyond his dazzling smile, the well-formed words, the often-forced banter? Fiorello La Guardia praised Roosevelt as "aldermanic" in remembering political details,[23] and Tugwell conceded that he possessed "amazingly detailed"[24] knowledge of utility valuations. But that was about it. "One of the characteristics most puzzling to those who met him first as late as 1932," Tugwell would later confess, "was the completeness of his assurance, especially since it seemed to proceed from a less than sufficient competence. There were many matters about which his lack of knowledge was total. There were issues about which the groundwork had not been laid. Even his general attitude of liberal progressivism, sufficient until now for expedients, was suddenly irrelevant and obsolete."[25]

Reservations aside, Tugwell—and Berle—stayed on.

For not only at day's end, but at its dawn, Franklin Roosevelt remained simply the party's best, most electable candidate. Other Democrats *wanted* the nomination and *might want it* if a deadlocked convention dropped it into their lap. But FDR not only wanted it, he *worked* for it. And so did his team, primarily Howe and Farley, but all of them, really. And that made a difference.

For more than a decade, FDR, through Howe, had maintained a tidal wave of correspondence with rank-and-file Democrats nationwide. A goodly numbers of such letters, FDR never saw (and certainly never signed; forgery was a highly cultivated art form in Howe's efficient operation), but they worked to remarkably good effect. In June 1931, however, Jim Farley's personal glad-handing approach went into high gear to augment Howe's correspondence-driven approach. Touring the country, ostensibly in his capacity as an active national officer of the Benevolent and Protective Order of Elks, in nineteen days, Farley met eleven hundred Elk.[26] In reality, he rode the rails not for Elk but for bigger game: delegates. The enthusiastic response he received only further convinced him that his boss was unstoppable.

But then again, who would stop him? Who dispatched their own version of "Big Jim" Farley to lasso support? What caliber of Democrat waited in the wings to snatch the nomination from FDR and vanquish the now-pathetic Hoover in November 1932? As one Iowa delegate explained that June, "Well, Jim Farley came out and asked us and nobody else did."[27]

FDR's opposition featured a ragbag of longshots, dark horses, and outright fantasies. The aforementioned Newton D. Baker was a darling of the party's eastern elite. Maryland governor Albert C. Ritchie was a true Jeffersonian, to the right of Hoover—perhaps of Coolidge. On Prohibition, he may have been "wetter" than Smith.[28] Oklahoma governor "Alfalfa Bill" Murray, a cigar-chomping, mustachioed Wild West populist (just back from Bolivia[29]—like Ernst Röhm), had declared martial law in his state[30] and nearly went to war with Texas. Behind this unlikely trio were the even longer longshots: Illinois's US senator J. Hamilton "Pink Whiskers" Lewis, famous (or perhaps merely infamous) for his pink whiskers (obviously), his spats, and his rather too detectable toupee; the acerbic former Missouri senator James A. Reed, a bitter opponent of the late Woodrow Wilson, a dripping "wet"[31]— and Henry Ford's attorney against charges of anti-Semitic libel[32]; Arkansas senator Joseph T. Robinson, Smith's 1928 running mate and the current Senate minority leader; General Electric chairman Owen D. Young, author of the Young Plan for German reparations ("a most likely dark horse,"[33] thought Farley), and a smattering of even less distinguished favorite sons.

Not yet running was John Nance "Cactus Jack" Garner, newly minted Speaker of the US House of Representatives and an acknowledged leader in the fine art of pork-barrel legislation ("Every time one of those Yankees get a ham, I am going to do my best to get a hog"[34]). The bushy-browed South Texan found himself in contention not from any desire or action on his own, but rather from a very big push provided by the very big William Randolph Hearst, the controversial press baron who commanded not only magazines (including *Good Housekeeping, Harper's Bazaar,* and *Cosmopolitan*), the Hearst-Metrotone News newsreels, the International News Service, a film studio (Cosmopolitan Productions), and twelve radio stations,[35] but, most significant, twenty-five daily papers in eighteen major cities controlling 13.9 percent of America's total daily circulation—and 22.5 percent of Sunday circulation.[36] Broadcasting nationwide from Los Angeles's KFI on January 2, 1932, "W. R." unleashed a truly Hearstian blast on just about anyone who might dare seek the presidency: Roosevelt, Baker, Young, and Hoover ("a Wilsonite . . . he has led the Republican Party to join the Democratic wreckage at the end of Mr. Wilson's political blind alley"[37]), as well as three previous Democratic nominees: Al Smith, John W. Davis, and the aforementioned very dead Woodrow Wilson. He praised but one individual: Garner, whom he termed "a loyal American citizen, a plain man of the plain people, a sound and sincere Democrat; in fact, another Champ Clark."[38]

Roosevelt and Ritchie might look presidential; the taciturn, rumpled "Cactus Jack" seemed quite the rube—at best. The historian Arthur Schlesinger Jr. thought he "presented at once an appearance of an infinitely experienced sage and of a new-born baby."[39] Party liberals and progressives regarded him with profound suspicion. Rex Tugwell saw him as "a confused Texan who, as the most prominent congressional Democrat, had had the responsibility for shaping alternatives to Hoover policies. He was, however, so conservative and so lacking in imagination that nothing occurred to him that Hoover had not thought of first."[40]

But Garner was no mere sagebrush cipher or relic of the Democrats' long minority status within the House. His potential had been grasped years earlier—and by none other than the hyper-intellectual Woodrow Wilson. Wilson despised the House's Democratic majority leader North Carolina's Claude Kitchin. But, of all the Democrats Wilson might have chosen as his unofficial pipeline to that legislative body, he selected Garner, conferring twice weekly with him, their sessions often stretching into several hours.[41]

Boosted now so loudly by Hearst, the hitherto uninterested Garner now exhibited moderate interest, and *voila!* a presidential candidacy (of sorts) was born.

Also poised to enter the fray was Al Smith. Tensions between him and Roosevelt had smoldered since Franklin's first gubernatorial victory and Al's concurrent presidential debacle. Smith had calculated that he might remain as the power behind Roosevelt's throne/wheelchair. He had even engaged a suite at the city's DeWitt Clinton Hotel to make himself instantly available when the call came from the Capitol or the Executive Mansion.[42]

It never came.

Smith thought Roosevelt would rely on him for advice. He didn't. He thought FDR would retain two of his closest aides, his secretary (chief of staff) Belle Moskowitz and his brilliant secretary of state Robert Moses. FDR wasn't interested in keeping either—particularly Moses, with whom he had previously tussled regarding the state's Taconic Parkway Commission.[43] Worse, Moses had refused FDR's request to provide Howe with a $5,000 state sinecure, so Louis might continue promoting his master's political work on the public dime.[44] When Smith personally begged FDR to retain the ultra-capable Moskowitz, Roosevelt countered that he was tapping upstate assemblyman Guernsey Cross for the job. "You know I need a great, big, strong man as secretary," said Roosevelt. "I need someone whom I can lean on physically, if necessary, and I think it will be better, Al."[45]

It was not so much that Franklin desired a big, strong man, as much as he did not desire a big, strong woman—particularly one so devoted to "The Happy Warrior." And—despite all her once-blazing affection for Smith—neither did Eleanor. "By all signs I think Belle and Bob Moses mean to cling to you," she wrote her husband, "and you will wake up to find R. M. Secretary of state and B. M. running Democratic publicity at the old stand unless you take a firm stand."[46] A week later, Eleanor wrote regarding Moses and Moskowitz, "Gosh, the race has nerves of iron and tentacles of steel."[47]

Ill-will simmered between Smith and his one-time protégé, never quite bursting into open warfare, but bubbling, nonetheless, upon the very surface of their relationship, visible to whomever chose to even casually glance in its direction. In December 1931, Smith conferred at his Empire State Building offices with *Atlanta Constitution* publisher Clark Howell, "Do you know, by God," Smith seethed, "that he [FDR] has never consulted me about a damn thing since he has been governor? He has taken bad advice and from sources not friendly to me. He has ignored me."[48]

Other Democrats possessed other gripes. They dismissed FDR as a lightweight. Bernard Baruch derided him as "wishy-washy"[49] and "the Boy

Scout Governor."[50] They derided him as a waffler. They distrusted his intentions (if they could discern them at all) regarding Prohibition (particularly vexing to such ardent wets as Smith), the League of Nations (he withdrew his longtime support instantly and ingloriously after a very public blast from the isolationist Hearst[51]), or regarding the burgeoning scandals enveloping Mayor "Gentleman Jimmy" Walker's New York City administration.

"[T]he banquet to which he bids us is merely a meal of parsnips and fine words," scoffed *New York World-Telegram* columnist Heywood Broun, a passionate liberal, a recent Socialist Party Silk Stocking District congressional candidate,[52] and, generally, a great fan of Smith.[53] "To be sure," Broun continued, "there is a little chestnut stuffing. Though it is true that fine words do not butter parsnips, they may contrive to make them seem more succulent. That is, until one gets his teeth into the roots. . . . I would much prefer to entrust the task of [the nation's] revision to somebody who does not approach the job on his hands and knees."[54]

A particularly significant blast emerged in January 1932 when *New York Herald Tribune* columnist Walter Lippmann unleashed this long-recalled salvo: "Franklin D. Roosevelt is no crusader. He is no tribune of the people. He is no enemy of entrenched privilege. He is a pleasant man without any important qualifications for the office, who would like very much to be President. . . . The notion which seems to prevail in the west and south, that Wall Street fears him is preposterous. Wall Street thinks he is too dry, not that he is too radical."[55] The *New Republic* similarly found him to be "not a man of great intellectual force or supreme moral stamina."[56]

In retrospect was FDR merely a master trimmer? Or a practical master strategist? Biding his time so he might do what he wished when he wished? Or as historian Elliot Rosen concluded, "Roosevelt . . . had no penchant for lost causes. The Hyde Park squire knew when to equivocate, lacking the intellectual's gift for consistency and political suicide."[57]

High-toned criticism emanated from the intellectuals. The bare-knuckled kind emerged from the back rooms and the gutters. In October 1930, delegates to 1928's Democratic convention received anonymous letters contending that FDR suffered not from polio—but from syphilis.[58] Yet, FDR continued to collect delegates. His star maintained its ascent, while Smith's troubles only multiplied. Never a rich man, "The Happy Warrior" had accepted a position managing the new Empire State Building—just before the Depression collapsed the Manhattan real estate market. Further, he had been struck by the November 1929 suicide of his friend and supporter James J. Riordan, president of Manhattan's failing County Trust Company. Compounding Smith's grief was the fact that in 1928, vaingloriously anticipating a Smith victory, Riordan had foolishly advanced a million dollar loan to the Democratic National Committee—leaving many of Smith's other friends on the hook for its repayment.[59]

Such financial entanglements should have kept Smith out of the race in 1932. That, at least, is what he confided to such visitors—and erstwhile supporters—as Ed Flynn and Lt. Gov. Herbert Lehman.[60] And because he had lost so horrendously in 1928, he was perhaps the least likely candidate to either defeat Hoover for re-election or to derail an FDR candidacy. True, Democrats had thrice nominated William Jennings Bryan, but that was so long ago, and the party, smelling blood in 1932, had since accumulated greater practicality. It had also discerned that hopelessly deadlocked conventions, such as the one that had derailed both Smith and William Gibbs McAdoo in 1924, only guaranteed defeat, even in the best of circumstances.

But bitterness now outweighed Smith's caution. Inflaming his already very real wounds was a report emanating from June 1931's National Governors' Conference. "Smith was a rotten Governor," Franklin had supposedly informed his colleagues. "I didn't know that until I got into the governorship myself."[61] FDR vehemently denied any such utterance. But Smith did not believe him. Al set to work—in tandem with party chairman John Jakob Raskob to again secure the nomination, not so much in revenge against Hoover, but rather to finally repeal the Eighteenth Amendment—and, more so, to avenge himself against the fiendishly grinning, ungrateful upstart residing in Hyde Park and in Albany.

The shy, mumbling Raskob, Smith's fellow Catholic, had his uses—and his money, having made a ton of it with the DuPonts and with General Motors. "I am firm in my belief," he had famously announced to the *Ladies Home Journal* in August 1929, "that anyone not only can be rich, but ought to be rich."[62]

Riches were not necessarily a bad thing. After all, Franklin Roosevelt was rich, though not so rich that he hadn't needed a $100,000 gift from Raskob to fund his Warm Springs Foundation.[63] But many thought that consorting with the Croesus-like Raskob (a 1924 Coolidge supporter[64] and until 1928 a Republican[65]) had transformed the 1932 version of Smith into something far removed from his salt-of-the-earth Lower East Side and Fulton Fish Market roots. "His heart still beats for the common people," assessed syndicated columnist Frank R. Kent, a conservative Democrat, of Smith in March 1932, "but he talks the big-business language."[66]

Raskob was wealthy. But more than gold blinded him. His softness on the tariff alienated traditional Democrat free-traders like Tennessee's freshman senator Cordell Hull.[67] But, above all, his obsession with repealing

Prohibition rendered him oblivious to virtually all other issues. The nation might have sunk into economic collapse. Bread lines and hunger marches might fill the streets. But to Raskob, classically still "fighting the last war," liquor remained the great issue of the times. Yes, the nation was clearly galloping toward repeal (a May 1930 *Literary Digest* poll showed a growing majority in its favor[68]), but Democratic National Convention rules still required a two-thirds vote to nominate. Delegate-rich swatches of the West and South, as well as many prominent Democratic office-holders (including senators Hull, Joe Robinson, Thomas Walsh of Montana, Claude Swanson and Carter Glass of Virginia, and Alben Barkley of Kentucky) remained steadfastly "dry." Glass and FDR's old boss Josephus Daniels, another ardent "dry," had even plotted to draft FDR in 1928 to block Smith.[69] An unabashed push for a "wet" 1932 platform plank might only propel such men and women away from Smith and Raskob—and into the evasive, but waiting, arms of Franklin Delano Roosevelt.

And that is just what happened.

In February 1931 Raskob summoned an unprecedented meeting of the Democratic National Committee.[70] Traditionally, the committee had been quite moribund between presidential elections. The year previously, however, Raskob—to his credit—had shattered such inertia by hiring former *New York World* Washington correspondent Charles Michelson as DNC publicity director. Michelson (salary: $25,000) generated an unending stream of criticism (and vitriol) toward Herbert Hoover, making the job of any upcoming Democratic nominee all the easier.[71] But what Raskob now desired was to craft a "wet" plank for the 1932 platform. The party's remaining "dry" elements—led by Senators Robinson ("You cannot inscribe on the banner of the Democratic party the skull and crossbones of an outlawed trade"[72]), Hull, Swanson, and Virginia's Governor Harry Flood Byrd—revolted.[73]

Raskob didn't get his plank. He was, as Frank Kent noted, "just a naive amateur with an inaccurate idea of the importance his money mortgage on the party gives him and an amazing awkwardness at the political game. He is a party liability, not an asset. Incidentally, he seems in a fair way to get most of his money back, which, even in this time of unemployment, is a good thing. Immediately after the convention, regardless of who the nominee may be, the obscurity from which he sprang in 1928 will completely envelop him again."[74]

Roosevelt, however, remained woefully weak in the populous Northeast (even in his own state), paying the price in the nation's "least dry" region for being his party's "least wet" serious contender. He suffered as well from questions regarding his progressive principles. But temporizing had its advantages. Delegate after delegate trooped into his camp, as he quietly assembled a powerful western- and southern-based alliance of delegates, some conservative, some populist, some "wet," some "dry"—but all craving one thing: to back a winner in 1932.

In April 1931, Jesse I. Straus, co-owner of Macy's department store and a key Roosevelt ally,[75] polled his fellow New York businessmen concerning their presidential preferences. FDR trounced Owen D. Young 562 votes to 256, while Smith (115), Joe Robinson (95), Albert Ritchie (85), and Newton Baker (16) all trailed badly.[76] More significant, a month earlier, Straus had sampled 844 delegates from 1928's convention. They favored Roosevelt even more: 478 for FDR, followed by Smith (125), Young (73), Ritchie (39), Robinson (38); Baker (35), and James A. Reed (15).[77]

Whispers continued about FDR's health. "I'm not going to mention the word paralysis unless I have to," Louis Howe had informed Eleanor in 1921. "If it's printed, we're sunk. Franklin's career is *kaput*, finished."[78] The issue had remained strangely quiet in the 1920s. FDR would cheerfully inform newsreel cameramen, "No movies of me getting out of the machine [his car] boys!"[79]—and remarkably they deferentially averted their lenses. But tolerance had its limits, and, occasionally, mere murmurs erupted into shouts. Even as Jesse Straus unveiled his business poll, at a national "dry" Democratic women's conference, Maryland's Mrs. Jesse W. Nicholson contended that "while mentally qualified for the presidency, [Franklin Roosevelt] is utterly unfit physically." Her quote made *Time* magazine.[80] William Gibbs McAdoo bluntly informed the bespectacled pro-FDR Nebraska Democrat Arthur Mullen: "We don't want a dead man on the ticket."[81]

Roosevelt swung into action. Within days, a medical panel descended upon FDR's Manhattan townhouse to conduct a rigorous physical examination.[82] That July, *Liberty* magazine published a glowing report on his health.[83] "I had noted the alertness of his movements, the sparkle of his eyes, the vigor of his gestures," reporter Earle Looker noted. "I had seen his strength under the strain of long working periods. In so far as I had observed him, I had come to the conclusion that he seemed able to take more punishment than many men ten years younger. Merely his legs were not much good to him."[84]

Looker, though touted as a Republican, was, in fact, no dispassionate observer, being Roosevelt's ghostwriter for an entire series of *Liberty* articles—and a year later the actual author of an official Roosevelt campaign tome.[85] But in July 1931, Looker's words helped to silence FDR's less-decorous critics and to reassure those already on board—or about to board—the Roosevelt express. Louis Howe mailed fifty thousand copies of Looker's prose to potential supporters.[86]

And there were already many of them. "Roosevelt's supporters were a remarkably varied lot—," observed historian James MacGregor Burns, "a strange assortment of old Harvard friends, city bosses, millionaires, Western radicals, Southern Bourbons, opportunistic Midwesterners who knew how to jump on the right bandwagon, Ku Kluxers, old Wilsonites, old Bryanites, professors, high tariff men, low tariff men."[87]

For the longest time Franklin played his game with exasperating coyness ("I have seen so much of the White House ever since 1892 that I have no hankering, secret or otherwise, to be a candidate."[88]). Finally, in January 1932, he declared his unsurprising candidacy.[89] Soon, a seething Smith proclaimed his own "availability."[90]

Their battle—Smith versus Roosevelt—was on.

CHAPTER SEVEN

"Are you frightened of me?"

ADOLF HITLER NOW HELD SOME VERY GOOD CARDS, BUT NOT ALL OF them.

Reichskanzler Heinrich Brüning held just one card—a very large one—the support of Reichspräsident Paul von Hindenburg.

Like Hitler, Brüning remained a bachelor. Raised Catholic, despite a fragile constitution he had enlisted in the Great War. Twice wounded, he earned both the Iron Cross first and second class.

There, the similarities ended. The ascetic Brüning (as reichskanzler he still lived in two rooms at a Berlin Catholic retreat[1]) had remained fervently monarchist, devoutly Catholic, and now headed the Catholic Centre (Zentrum) Party. He was a man of substance, of little show, of no shouting whatsoever—and he meant to combat Germany's woes not by street fighting or rabid nationalism, but by balanced budgets and fiscal belt-tightening, by slashing public sector wages and salaries by between 25 and 30 percent.[2] Such moves only cemented a man's unpopularity. Nazis and Communists naturally withheld their support. So did Alfred Hugenberg's obstinate (and quite often anti-Catholic) Nationalists, as well as the Zentrum's longtime allies, the SPD. "Hunger Chancellor"[3] Brüning enjoyed neither public support for his policies—nor for remaining in office. But who would replace him? Certainly not Hitler or the KPD's Stalinist stooge Ernst Thälmann.[4] Hugenberg, clueless and intransigent ("A block [i.e., party], not a jelly"[5]), remained out of the question. The SPD might conceivably return to power but only if it somehow regained a working Reichstag majority. Hindenburg would certainly not assist their cause. He'd won election against the Social Democrats in 1925 and still despised them—as he personally despised most Catholics, Hugenberg,[6] and the upstart "Bohemian Corporal"[7] Hitler. Brüning remained one of the few national politicians (or Catholics) The Old Gentleman could tolerate. In fact, he more than tolerated Brüning, deeming him "the best chancellor since

Bismarck."[8] But even if Brüning remained more "Hunger Chancellor" than "Iron Chancellor," he would have to do—and do it without a parliamentary majority or anything approaching one.

Saving Herr Brüning's Cabinet was the Weimar constitution, often praised as the "most democratic in the world," but like all enterprises crafted by the hand of man, it contained a fatal flaw, in its case a combination of two provisions investing Germany's president with powers more reminiscent of Hohenzollern Kaisers than American-style chief executives. Article 48 bestowed upon the nation's Reichspräsident (and his chancellor) the authority to issue emergency decrees. Such power had been used scores of times prior to Brüning, but said chancellors had enjoyed parliamentary majorities and utilized their Article 48 authority more sparingly. Still, the Reichstag could override such decrees—and might well have save for Article 25 of Weimar's constitution, which empowered the Reichspräsident to dissolve parliament at will. Article 48, combined with Article 25, enabled Hindenburg and Brüning to defy the laws of majoritarian gravity.[9]

Weimar authorities assured American officials that 1930's Reichstag elections would barely amount to a ripple in the republic's storm-tossed history. Recently appointed Ambassador Frederic M. Sackett, yet another Hoover wartime associate, thus felt no compunction about returning to his Kentucky home as Germans voted. When they had, neither Sackett nor his embassy *chargé d'affaires* George Anderson Gordon could easily explain the ominous result. Career diplomat Gordon wired the State Department:

> *Any constructive element in [the Nazis'] so-called program is difficult to discern . . . [W]hen seeking to win votes from the Communists the National Socialist orators declared that, as their social theories were similar, they appealed to them to vote for a Communist form of government directed by Germans rather than . . . Moscow; when invading Nationalist territory, [they] emphasized their adherence to the principle of private ownership of property. Throughout the land their program consisted of asseverations that all the country's evils flowed from Semitism, international banks, the Young Plan, the Treaty of Versailles and all other international treaties . . . , the remedy being repudiation pure and simple of any written obligations, and a march on Berlin, for the purpose of establishing a reactionary dictatorship with, however, not even a suggestion as to the alternative measures contemplated for remedying the conditions complained of.[10]*

Most foreign observers found Hitler as unimpressive as he was incomprehensible. In December 1931, the influential American journalist Dorothy

Thompson interviewed him for William Randolph Hearst's *Cosmopolitan*. "When finally I walked into Adolf Hitler's [Kaiserhof Hotel] salon . . . I was convinced that I was meeting the future dictator of Germany," she wrote. "In something less than fifty seconds I was quite sure I was not. It took just about that time to measure the startling insignificance of this man who has set the world agog. He is formless, almost faceless, a man whose countenance is a caricature, a man whose framework seems cartilaginous, without bones. He is inconsequent and voluble, ill-poised, insecure. He is the very prototype of the Little Man. . . ."[11]

But, then again, Dorothy Thompson may have been drunk.[12]

Hitler's deputies wasted no time in using their newfound Reichstag strength to turn that body upside-down. Even in 1928, Hermann Göring had brazenly trumpeted the Nazis' attitude toward parliamentarianism. "We become Reichstag deputies in order to paralyze the Weimar democracy with its own assistance," he blared. "If democracy is stupid enough to give us free travel privileges and per diem allowances for this service, that is its affair. . . .We come as enemies! Like the wolf tearing into a flock of sheep, that is how we come. Now you are no longer among yourselves."[13]

Wolves indeed.

Heinrich Himmler, *Reichsführer* of Hitler's newly formed elite bodyguard, the *Schutzstaffel* (SS), was among them. The sallow-chested, chinless Himmler seemed an odd choice for anyone's bodyguard, more in need of protection than capable of providing it. Still, this former Gregor Strasser protégé offered Hitler unwavering loyalty, and that counted for something in the messy world of internal Nazi politics. His unprepossessing physique, however, was not his only shortcoming. In the spring of 1929, former Hamburg Gauleiter Albert Krebs "traumatically" shared a six-hour train ride from Eberfeld to Hamburg with Himmler ("ostentatiously crude and lower class [marked by] social insecurity"). Krebs was, to say the least, not impressed:

> . . . *What made [Himmler] practically unbearable company on that trip was the stupid and fundamentally empty claptrap to which he ceaselessly subjected me.*
>
> *Even today I think I may say without exaggeration that I have never been served so much political nonsense in such a concentrated form, and that from a man with a university education and a professional involvement with politics. Himmler's exegesis was a remarkable mixture*

of martial bombastics, petty-bourgeois barber-shop prattle, and the zeal-
ous prophecy of a revivalist preacher.[14]

South Hanover-Braunschweig Gauleiter Dr. Bernhard Rust, unlike Himmler still a Strasserite, also won a seat. Earlier that very year, he had been
dismissed from his teaching position after being charged with indecently
assaulting a female student. Rust—examined by Dr. Edmund Forster, the
same neuropathologist who had treated both Hitler at Pasewalk and Göring
for morphine addiction—pled temporary insanity from a wartime head
wound.[15]

In February 1932, Reichstag State Party deputy August Weber rose to
denounce yet another disreputable Nazi delegate:

> *In 1920 a poor farm worker, falsely suspected of intending to inform the*
> *Prussian police of local illegal traffic in arms, was murdered; the murderer*
> *pressed a pistol to the man's face and discharged the weapon twice. At a*
> *trial in Stettin in May 1928, the murderer was sentenced to five year's*
> *imprisonment. After the Stettin decision, the National Socialist Party . . .*
> *expelled the murderer from its ranks. Today, however, the murderer is*
> *once more a member of the . . . Party—and a member of its Reichstag*
> *delegation.[16]*

Meet SA man Edmund Heines.

In the streets and boulevards outside, it was hardly much better. Wrote
one observer:

> *The whole afternoon and evening great Nazi masses who demonstrated*
> *and, during the afternoon in the Leipzigerstrasse, smashed the windows*
> *of the department stores of Wertheim, Grünfeld, etc. In the evening, in*
> *the Potsdamer Platz, crowds . . . shouted "Deutchland erwache!", "Juda*
> *verrecke!" "Heil! Heil!" And were continually dispersed by the Schupo*
> *[Schutzpolizei or "state police"], patrolling in vans and on horses. . . . The*
> *scene in the streets reminded me of the days shortly before the revolu-*
> *tion, the same crowds, the same Catilanarian types lounging about and*
> *demonstrating.[17]*

American *chargé d'affaires* George Anderson Gordon watched the formal
Nazi entrance, exit, and ominous re-entrance into the Reichstag in October
1930. All filed into the chamber in proper civilian garb. All (save Goebbels, then no great lover of uniforms, at least, not for himself) then trooped
out, before quickly returning, in defiance of Reichstag rules, in full storm
trooper garb.[18] Their sartorial indiscretions affronted Gordon as much as any

ideological inconsistencies, and he informed Washington of their "astounding lack of dignity. The Hitlerites in their so-called uniforms of no coats, brown shirts with a swastika armlet and—in the majority of cases—with a single shoulder strap worn in the guise of a suspender, and a simulacrum of golf trousers as a crowning touch, presented the appearance of an overgrown troop of boy scouts."

Gordon, however, also thought he detected "a certain amount of shame-faced embarrassment" in their buffoonish attire and boorish behavior.[19] In that, of course, he was quite wrong. Outside, Nazi ruffians smashed Jewish shop windows.[20] Not long afterward, Universal Studios' *All Quiet on the Western Front* (*Im Westen nichts Neus*), based upon Erich Maria Remarque's anti-war novel, premiered in Germany, its pacifist message (a "Jewish provocation"[21]) outraging National Socialists (self-proclaimed "bearers of state morality"[22]). Berlin Gauleiter Joseph Goebbels commanded 150 storm troopers to harass patrons outside Nollendorfplatz's Mozartsaal theater.[23] Inside, Hitlerites released snakes, stink bombs, and hundreds of white mice.[24] Six days later, the government banned not the Nazis but the film.[25]

⌇

By February 1931, Hermann Göring marched his 107 delegates out of the Reichstag. Nationalist and Communist deputies followed.[26] The KPD proved a particular thorn in the Republic's side. Ostensibly the party most opposed to Hitler's Nazis, the KPD was, in fact, its closest kin. Both parties featured top-down, authoritarian leadership. KPD hatred for—nay, its obsession with—the Social Democrats rivaled and perhaps exceeded the loathing festering within Hitler since his Vienna days. The KPD's uniformed street thugs, often intimately connected to underworld gangs,[27] seized effective control of large urban neighborhoods ("red districts"[28]), battled Nazis, and provided a facile excuse for those frightened by this Bolshevik horde to seek safe harbor under Hitler's swastika banner.

Fueling the street violence was, of course, unemployment. By 1932, well over a third of the work force was unemployed.[29] A full 6,127,000 persons officially suffered joblessness.[30] The real total may have reached 7.6 million—perhaps more.[31] By 1932, only 15 percent of KPD members had a job.[32] In Hamburg's grim working-class suburb of Altona, it was less than 10 percent.[33] The unemployment rate in some Berlin SA units reached 67 percent.[34] Desperate men and women did desperate acts. The nation's suicide rate reached 260 per million in 1932—twice America's.[35] Tens of thousands of desperate men streamed into the uniformed paramilitary armies of the nation's radical parties.

Germany perched uneasily upon a huge, sputtering powder keg. Forty percent of its democratically elected Reichstag deputies—Nazis, Communists, and Nationalists—fully despised democracy. They just couldn't agree on what to replace it with—a Führer, a commissar, or a Hohenzollern. "Every conversation I had in Germany with anyone under the age of thirty," recalled Dorothy Thompson, "ended with this phrase: '*Es kann nicht weiter. Es muss etwas geschehen.*' 'It can't go on. Something must happen.'"[36]

In March 1931, Brüning utilized Article 48 powers to ban the wearing of military-style uniforms and to require permission for all outdoor political meetings.[37] Hitler continued his charade of legality, publicly threatening to expel any SA member not obeying the ban.[38] "I understand your distress and your rage," he exhorted his brownshirts, even before Brüning's action, "but you must not bear arms."[39] His words meant little. Violence only accelerated on the Reich's streets.

Meanwhile, Brüning struggled on the international front. His stillborn plans for a customs union with Austria[40] ultimately crashed Vienna's Kreditanstalt.[41] Tensions increased with Warsaw. In March 1931, Ernst Röhm promised Reichswehr leadership that should Poland invade (or domestic Reds rebel) Nazi storm troopers would fight alongside them.[42] In late May 1931, 150,000 paramilitary Stahlhelm members provocatively paraded at Breslau, just thirty-five miles from the Polish frontier.[43] Germany threatened to default on reparations. That June, Hindenburg personally begged Hoover to intervene.[44] "The need of the German people . . . compels me to adopt the unusual step of addressing you personally. . . . ," he wrote. "All possibilities of improving the situation by domestic measures without relief from abroad are exhausted."[45] Hoover responded with a one-year debt moratorium.

A year earlier, panic-stricken Düsseldorf industrialists had urged Brüning to assume a formal dictatorship.[46] Such magnates were now also ripe for Hitler's blandishments. True, he had never abandoned (and never would reject) his contempt for bourgeois society and its economic systems. But he now needed such support (or, at least, neutrality) to carry him across the last finish line. As he despised Reichstag democracy but exhibited no compunction in exploiting it, he now pandered to the Reich's capitalists. Turning on his considerable charms, toning down his rhetoric, he masked the harsh voice of destruction with reassuring tones of mutual interest.

To court such establishment leaders—as well as the great, broad mass of the German upper and middle classes—Hitler trimmed his economic sails. In October 1930, Nazi Reichstag deputies Gregor Strasser, Gottfried Feder, and Wilhelm Frick introduced a measure calling for a 4 percent cap on interest rates, as well as for the seizure of the property of "Eastern Jews." However, their measure also demanded nationalization of the nation's banks. The latter move horrified not merely the nation's upper crust but also Hitler, who ordered the resolution withdrawn. Communist deputies, sensing an opportunity to embarrass their Brown rivals, re-introduced the measure—without alteration. Hitler ordered NSDAP deputies to vote against it. They did,[47] and, by December, Feder was publicly disavowing the party's socialist tendencies.[48]

Firing Gregor Strasser's radical brother Otto was a key step in Hitler's often confusing march to the middle. Connecting with the brilliant economist Dr. Hjalmar Horace Greeley Schacht (his parents had lived in America; two of his brothers were born there[49]) was another. Schacht, formerly a member of the center-left German Democratic Party (and excoriated by the Nazi press as being in reality "Hajum Schachtl," a Budapest Jew[50]—"the father of the greatest fraud on the public of all time"[51]), had resigned as president of the *Reichsbank* to protest the Young Plan.[52] Schacht first met Hitler at Hermann Göring's flat for dinner. Steel magnate Fritz Thyssen, a long-standing Hitler admirer, accompanied Schacht.[53] The diminutive Berlin Gauleiter Joseph Goebbels escorted Hitler, and along with Göring maintained what Schacht considered to be an odd silence.[54] "At this first meeting," Schacht recalled, "I learned what all of us experienced later, that in a discussion with Hitler, his associates contributed only 5 per cent; Hitler himself supplied the remaining 95 per cent of the conversation. His skill in exposition was most striking. Everything he said he demonstrated as incontrovertible truth; nevertheless his ideas were not unreasonable and were entirely free from any propagandist pathos. He spoke with moderation and was obviously anxious to avoid anything that might shock us in our capacity as representatives of a more traditional society . . . Even [then] it was obvious to me that Hitler's power of propaganda would have a tremendous pull with the German population if we did not succeed in overcoming the economic crisis and weaning the masses from radicalism. Hitler was obsessed by his own words, a thorough fanatic with the most powerful effect on his audience; a born agitator in spite of a hoarse, sometimes broken and not infrequently croaking voice."[55] Schacht soon lobbied Brüning to include this croaking Führer in his creaking Cabinet.[56]

Such sessions complimented Hitler's breakthrough to hitherto standoffish elements of the ultra-nationalist Right: Hugenberg's DNVP, the one-armed Franz Seldte's Stahlhelm, the Junker-dominated *Reichslandbund* ("National Rural League"), and Heinrich Class's old-line, but still anti-Semitic and anti-Polish, "Pan-German League." In October 1931 they combined with Hitler in the so-called Harzburg Front. Their alliance soon crumbled, but Hitler's appearance alongside not only Hugenberg, Seldte,

Class, Schacht, and Thyssen, but also former Reichswehr chief of staff Gen. Hans von Seeckt and two of the exiled Kaiser Wilhelm's half-dozen sons, the stocky wounded war veteran Eitel Friedrich ("Fritz") and the homosexual August Wilhelm (Wilhelm II disgustingly thought there "very little manliness in his entire manner"[57]) enabled the *déclasse* bohemian Hitler to slither up yet another rung upon the ladder of respectability.[58]

Yet, one should not overemphasize such maneuverings. True, by the summer of 1931, Hitler "suddenly decided to concentrate systematically on cultivating the influential economic magnates."[59] But the Harzburg Front immediately collapsed. High society remained high society. Hitler's men remained street thugs. Much of big business still shunned him. Industrialists like Thyssen and the bearded and aged Ruhr coal baron Emil Kirdorf[60] provided support, but, on the whole, their compatriots retained a proper wariness. Hitler's National Socialists might be nationalists, they reasoned, but they were also socialists. They had indeed introduced that dreaded bank nationalization measure. They supported striking Berlin metalworkers as well as other strikes.[61] They harbored a serious left-wing component—not merely the Strasser brothers and Walther Stennes's brownshirts but also such rising members of the hierarchy as Berlin Gauleiter Goebbels. Far more typical than Thyssen or Kirdorf were Hamburg America shipping line director-general Dr. Wilhelm Cuno (a former chancellor)[62] and steel magnate Gustav Krupp von Bohlen und Halbach.[63] Both remained unimpressed by Hitler.

So was the Catholic Church. Wary of the party's anti-Christian biases (flaunted most conspicuously by Alfred Rosenberg and his best-selling monstrosity, 1930's *The Myth of the Twentieth Century*[64]) the Church's hierarchy still vociferously resisted Hitler. In February 1931, German bishops, while gingerly avoiding a total membership ban, barred their priests from any participation in the movement.[65] The following month, the Reich's three cardinals—Bertram of Breslau, Faulhaber of Munich, and Schulte of Köln (Cologne)—each condemned Nazi ideology. As Cardinal Karl Schulte (ironically, Walther Stennes's uncle) declared his opposition, storm troopers savagely disrupted a Zentrum meeting within his archdiocese, severely beating two priests.[66] That September, Mainz's Bishop Ludwig Maria Hugo not only prohibited party membership, he vetoed even the laying of Nazi wreaths in Catholic cemeteries.[67]

Hitler himself maintained a cautious, calculating, strangely patient, attitude against any head-to-head confrontations against Germany's established churches. "[I]f you want to see my meaning illustrated," he lectured Kurt Lüdecke in the fall of 1932, "you need only go to the funeral of a fallen Nazi and watch the Storm-Troopers ranked about the grave. Watch their faces, blank while the priest is reading the service"—and here he stopped long enough to imitate a priest mumbling the litany, fingering an imaginary rosary and spreading hands in blessing (an excellent performance, as always)—and then see them light up when the Nazi leader lifts the flag and begins to speak words of flame over the dead.

"Yes, National Socialism is a form of conversion, a new faith, but we don't need to raise that issue—it will come of itself. Just as I insist on the mathematical certainty of our coming to power, because might always attracts might, and the traditional wings, whether they be Right or Left, constructive or destructive, will always attract all the activist elements, leaving only a juiceless pulp in the middle—just so do I insist on the certainty that sooner or later, once we hold the power, Christianity will be overcome and the *Deutsche Kirche* established. Yes, the German Church, without a Pope and without the Bible—and Luther, if he could be with us, would give us his blessing.

"Of course, I myself am a heathen to the core!"[68]

❦

Survival of Weimar democracy now rested on one very shaky—and old—pillar: Paul von Hindenburg. Elected with Nationalist backing to foil the Social Democrats in 1925, his term expired in March 1932. His world had since turned upside down. Nationalists, chagrined not only by his failure to fully overturn the hated republic but also from his reluctant acceptance of the hated Young Plan,[69] now detested him. "Field-Marshal von Hindenburg has forfeited the right to wear the field-grey uniform of the army and be buried in it," fulminated his long-erstwhile comrade Ludendorff. "Herr Paul von Hindenburg had destroyed the very thing he fought for as Field-Marshal."[70] The SPD, however, fearful of the growing National Socialist and KPD menace, suddenly gazed upon their old adversary with new favor.

Hindenburg, himself, was rapidly failing, not merely physically but also mentally. At one July 1930 meeting, he could not even recognize Brüning. Nearing eighty-four in September 1931, he suffered a ten-day mental breakdown. A month later, he failed to identify either Brüning or Brüning's trusted Conservative People's Party (KVP) minister without portfolio Gottfried Treviranus.[71] Yet, Hindenburg's nation still needed him, and an old soldier never abandons his post. He would consent to another term.

Brüning realized what all but Hindenburg realized: The Old Gentleman would never live out a second term. One might place a nation's fate in the trembling hands of an octogenarian—but not in the lifeless hands of a corpse. Brüning accordingly devised a scheme to restore the monarchy—ultimately placing one of the exiled Kaiser Wilhelm II's numerous male descendants on the throne. Hindenburg torpedoed the plan. "I am the trustee of the Emperor," he insisted, "and can never give my consent to anyone succeeding to the throne save the Emperor himself."[72]

❦

Germany tottered on the brink. Banks failed. Desperate men battled more desperate men in the streets and alleys. But Adolf Hitler grew more personally comfortable than ever. He received funding from such industrialists as Thyssen, gifts from such personal admirers as the Munich publisher Hugo Bruckmann and the piano manufacturer Edwin Bechstein and his Hitler-worshipping wife Helene,[73] increased royalties from *Mein Kampf*,[74] fees for articles commissioned by the Nazi[75] and foreign press ("Adolf Hitler's Own Story: He Tells What Is the Matter with Germany and How He Proposes to Remedy It"[76]),[77] interviews granted to foreign reporters (netting as much as two to three thousand dollars per sitting),[78] and later even from sales of Hitler phonograph records—as much as twenty thousand dollars from a single recording.[79] Even unemployed SA men had to fork over their unemployment benefits for the food and shelter provided them.[80] But, above all, Hitler and his growing party were funded by dues and from admission fees to mass rallies.[81] Hitler was the first "rock star" politician. His huge audiences yelled themselves hoarse. Young (and not so young) women swooned. The beat-beat-beat of drums and the pulsating beams of light shows sliced the air, taking audiences to heights (or depths) that no other politician might.

He was, of course, not physically attractive, certainly not in any conventional sense. Putzi Hanfstaengl thought the early Führer "looked like a suburban hairdresser on his day off or a waiter in a railway-station restaurant."[82] In uniform, and glowering more than any public personage ever should, he looked hardly better. One author described him as resembling a "boy scout leader with a grudge."[83]

He, nonetheless, excited crowds, whipping them to orgiastic frenzy. And he excited individuals. Elisabetta Cerruti, wife of Italy's ambassador, hardly cared for him. Yet even she recalled:

> *When dinner was announced he offered me his arm. As I touched his arm, curiously enough, I received a strong electric shock. I was so keyed up with excitement it unnerved me a little and even though I'm a skeptic and don't believe in the supernatural, I became convinced that he possessed some mystic, magnetic power that he could exercise at will. The shock was so strong I looked up in astonishment. He stood there as pale and calm as ever. Somewhat shaken, I walked in with him to the dining hall.*[84]

＿～＿

In Vienna, Hitler had dwelt in hostels and boarding houses. In the early 1920s, he still lived reasonably modestly—from May 1920 in a shabby furnished two-room apartment above the pharmacy at 41 Thierschstrasse.[85] But by the late 1920s, even before the Depression struck and his party's fortunes finally ascended, Herr Hitler was doing quite well, quite well, indeed. In 1925, he rented (for a hundred marks per month[86]) a modest mountain chalet (Haus Wachenfels) on the Obersalzberg, engaging his older half-sister Angela—improbably then serving as a cook at Vienna's Mensa Academica Judaica[87]—as its housekeeper.[88] By September 1929, he relocated from cold and dingy Thierschstrasse to spectacularly different lodgings, a nine-room second-floor flat at 16 Prinzregentenplatz, in Munich's highly fashionable Bogenhausen district.[89] He might have brought sister Angela there.

He did not.

To Prinzregentenplatz he brought her daughter—his half-niece—"Geli."

＿～＿

If Hitler's political ascent was a mystery, his sexual nature—then and now—remains the greater riddle. We do not know everything (nor should we) regarding Franklin Roosevelt's intimate moments. We do not even care about such things regarding Herbert Hoover. But Adolf Hitler's private moments remain an unsolvable puzzle. Was he heterosexual? Homosexual? Or bisexual? Normal or abnormal in his practices? Or even in his anatomy? The record provides tantalizing clues—that, in the end, fully resolve nothing.

His early life seems virtually bereft of even the most casual contact with the opposite sex. His friend August Kubizek narrates the tale of a thin, blonde girl in Linz, Stefanie Isak, who Hitler worshipped from afar—but never dared approach.[90] His wartime trenchmates found him to be a misogynist, with no use at all for the fairer sex—or less fair prostitutes. Yet, his political testament *Mein Kampf* obsesses incoherently for page after page on prostitution's dangers ("this Jewification of our spiritual life . . . the vices of the parents are revealed in the parents of the children"[91])—and, perhaps even more strangely, of the menace of syphilis[92] ("in the insane asylums, and . . . unfortunately, in our—children"[93]). Commencing a political career, he professed such a vocation to be incompatible with romantic entanglements. "My bride is Germany,"[94] he proclaimed, half in jest, more than half seriously. Nonetheless (or perhaps *because* of his reputed unattainability), female party members threw themselves at him. As early as 1921 a young Munich housewife, Suzi Liptauer, attempted to hang herself over Hitler.[95]

In the fall of 1926, he devoted significant attention to a blonde Berchtes-gaden sixteen-year-old tailor's daughter named Maria "Mimi" Reiter (his "woodland sprite"). The relationship may later have been consummated ("I let anything happen to me"). It may not have. She attempted suicide by hanging in 1927.[96]

Angela "Geli" Raubal was just seventeen when she accompanied her mother and younger sister Elfriede ("Friedl") to Germany in 1925 to oversee Haus Wachenfels. Geli remains as much a mystery as Hitler. On the one hand, history records her as a magical, entrancing figure. "She was a princess who forced people to turn round and look at her," recalled Hitler's chauffeur, Emil Maurice, "a thing that was not often done in Munich."[97]

In Vienna, she had generated the same effect. Decades later, a woman who had then been a child in her apartment building recalled, "I was walking down the street outside our apartment building, and I heard her singing. I saw her, and I just stopped dead. She was just so tall and beautiful that I was speechless. And she saw me standing frozen and said, "Are you frightened of me?"

"No," the child answered, "I was just admiring you."

"She was just so tall and beautiful; I had never seen anyone like that."[98]

Hitler's longtime adjutant Julius Schaub described Geli as "a brown-eyed brunette, 5 feet 6 tall, well-built with a blooming appearance, animal spirits and a pleasing voice . . . extraordinarily self-possessed."[99] She was, said Hitler's friend and official photographer Heinrich Hoffmann, "an enchantress. In her artless way and without the slightest suspicion of coquetry, she succeeded, by her mere presence, in putting everybody in the best of good spirits; each and every one of us was devoted to her—especially her uncle. . . ."[100]

He certainly was. "Only Geli can laugh like that with her eyes,"[101] Uncle Adolf marveled, clearly enchanted by her. "[F]or a while," thought Putzi Hanfstaengl, "Hitler behaved like a youngster in love."[102]

"If Geli wanted to go swimming . . . ," recollected Hoffmann's teenage daughter Henriette ("Henny"), "it was more important to Hitler than the most important conference. Picnic baskets were packed, and we drove to the lake."[103] He meekly followed her shopping, noted Hoffmann himself, "he always followed her like a faithful lamb."[104]

"He loved her," thought Emil Maurice, "but it was a strange affection that did not dare to show itself, for he was too proud to admit the weaknesses of an infatuation."[105]

And, yet, there may have been nothing quite extraordinary about the object of these avuncular affections at all. Henriette Hoffmann conceded that Geli was "irresistibly charming" but also "coarse, provocative and a little quarrelsome."[106] Hanfstaengl ultimately considered her "an empty-headed little slut."[107] And surviving photographs reveal nothing that would have compelled anyone, anywhere, "to turn round and look at her." No lithe, blonde Aryan goddess, she is dark-haired and pudgy-faced. In posed portraits her smile is merely forced and insipid. It is all very much like the Hitler phenomenon itself: one can only conclude that *one simply had to be there*. . . . "Geli's charm couldn't be photographed," conceded Henriette. "It wasn't present in any of the pictures that my father took of her."[108]

We know—or we think we know—Hitler's attitude toward Geli: worshipful, moonstruck at best; something much more diabolical at worst ("My uncle is a monster. You would never believe the things he makes me do"[109]). But what was her attitude toward him? She may have been honored and flattered by the attentions of such an important man. She may have merely seen him as a meal ticket, one treating her to dinners out, the opera, clothes, voice lessons (despite no appreciable talent), and a more than comfortable room in an opulent apartment in one of Munich's most fashionable neighborhoods. "After we became better friends," Frau Ada Dort, wife of Geli's voice instructor, recounted, "Geli told me about her uncle and how he gave her expensive gifts whenever she was 'nice' to him. When I learned that her uncle was Adolf Hitler, the radical politician, I warned her she was asking for trouble. Geli just laughed at me. She said she could wind him around her little finger when she was alone with him."[110] But such trinkets came with a cost, the proverbial flightless perch within the gilded cage. Hitler demanded that Geli be strictly chaperoned on leaving their apartment. Once, when she wanted to attend a Munich Shrovetide ball, he instructed Heinrich Hoffmann and his publisher Max Amann to not only accompany her—but to escort her home by eleven. Even Hoffmann rebelled. "Herr Hitler," Hoffmann dared inform his Führer, "the restraint under which Geli is living is not only a great strain on her, but it is also making her thoroughly unhappy. That much was quite obvious at the ball. Far from giving her any pleasure by permitting her to go to it, all you've done has been sharply to accentuate the intolerable restraint you impose on her."

"You know, Hoffmann," Hitler responded, "Geli's future is so dear to my heart, that I feel myself in duty bound to watch over her. Right! I love Geli, and I could marry her; but you know my views and you know that I am determined to remain a bachelor. Therefore I reserve to myself the right to watch over the circle of her male acquaintances until such a time as the right man comes along. What Geli now regards as restraint is in reality wise precaution. I am quite determined to see that she does not fall into the hands of some unworthy adventurer or swindler."[111]

Yes, young women have their inclinations: not merely dress balls but the young men who attend them, and Geli Raubal was no different in this regard than any other Jazz Age *mädchen*. Very soon after her arrival in Munich she took up with Hitler's muscular chauffeur, the strapping Emil Maurice. By Christmas Eve 1928, she wrote to Maurice, "Uncle Adolf is insisting that we should wait two years. Think of it, Emil, two whole years of being only to kiss each other now and then and always having Uncle Adolf in charge. I can only give you my love and be unconditionally faithful to you. I love you so infinitely much. Uncle Adolf insists that I should go on with my studies."[112]

They became engaged. When Maurice informed his boss, Maurice thought Hitler would shoot him then and there.[113] The engagement was off.

But if Maurice could not be on the scene, others might. "Many times when Hitler was away for several days at a political rally or tending to party matters in Berlin or elsewhere," his SA bodyguard Wilhelm Stocker recalled, "Geli would associate with other men. I liked the girl myself so I never told anyone what she did or where she went on these free nights. Hitler would have been furious if he had known that she was out with such men as a violin player from Augsburg or a ski instructor from Innsbruck . . . She was a girl who needed attention and needed it often. And she definitely wanted to remain Hitler's favourite girlfriend."[114] Or, as Otto Strasser observed, "I used to pay her attentions. She was no prude."[115]

So, both uncle and niece played at very dangerous games: Hitler, risking a grave scandal, which might capsize his career as he now stood perched upon the brink of power; Geli perhaps pursuing one even more perilous.

And what was really going on here? Was the relation merely a case of fixation and platonic infatuation on Hitler's part? Or was it something more sinister? And at what level did such darkness stop? At incest? Or at something worse? Putzi Hanfstaengl[116] and Otto Strasser[117] later painted pictures of outright, sordid, disgusting perversion. Bodyguard Wilhelm Stocker—in less detail—confirmed that.[118] Hanfstaengl and Otto Strasser, however, had by then irretrievably broken with Hitler, both hiding in exile and fearful for their lives. They had their reasons to not merely circulate tales—but to invent them. Beyond that, the greater question arises: *How might they really know such things?* And by whom might we confirm their allegations?

We do know this: Hanfstaengl related a story of certain pornographic drawings of Geli composed by her "Uncle Alf," retrieved by party treasurer Franz Xaver Schwarz with the connivance of a former Munich priest, Fr. Bernhard Stempfle, who had assisted Hitler in the hopeless task of editing *Mein Kampf*. Again, there remains no way to confirm the bitter Hanfstaengl's story, but this is certain: In 1934's bloody settling of Hitler's scores—"The

Night of the Long Knives"—Fr. Stempfle was among the victims, shot three times in the heart, his body dumped in the woods near Munich. Emil Maurice oversaw his murder.[119]

Whatever occurred at Prinzregentenplatz, whether mere suffocating possessiveness—or something worse—climaxed in mid-September 1931. Hitler, having just a few hours in Munich before departing to deliver speeches in north Germany, summoned Geli from Obersalzberg.[120] They argued. Some say she desired to travel to Vienna. A servant supposedly heard her declare "I can shoot myself."[121] Hitler responded, "For the last time, no!"[122]

Hitler motored off. As he did, he confided to Heinrich Hoffmann: "I don't know why but I have a most uneasy feeling."[123] On Prinzregentenplatz Geli angrily remarked to Hitler's housekeeper Frau Anni Winter, "Really, I have nothing at all in common with my uncle."[124] That evening she attended the Munich Playhouse. Her companion, Julius Schaub's wife, Wilma, found her sullen, distracted, on the edge of tears.[125]

The next day, as Hitler's black Mercedes sped north from Nürnberg's Deutscher Hof Hotel to Bayreuth, a taxi raced up behind him. A hotel pageboy carried urgent instructions for Hitler to return to the Deutscher Hof. Rudolf Hess had phoned with an urgent message.

Hitler dashed into a telephone booth, not even bothering to close its door. "Hitler here—has something happened?" he demanded, "Oh God! how awful!" His tone quickly shifted from desperation to despair. "Hess! answer me—yes or no—is she still alive?. . ." he screamed. "Hess! on your word of honour as an officer—tell me the truth—is she alive or dead? . . . Hess! . . . Hess!"[126]

He sped south to Munich. Geli was by now twenty hours dead. It all made so little sense. She was, as Hoffmann found her, "the reverse of the hysterical, suicidal type."[127] Following Hitler's departure she had chatted on the phone with a friend, Elfie Samthaber. The conversation concerned itself with trivialities—and not a hint of unpleasantness.[128]

Rumors filled the air. Some said that she was pregnant by a Jewish art teacher in Linz (or a half-Jewish music teacher in Vienna).[129] Or even by Hitler.[130] Some said Hitler himself had killed her[131]—though a speeding ticket he had earned at Ebenhausen while hurrying back to Munich put the lie to that account.[132] Still others contended that Heinrich Himmler, either upon the orders of nervous party leaders—or even on Hitler's behalf—had done the deed.[133] Theories of foul play made little sense. Murdering Hitler's niece in his own apartment with his own gun could hardly safeguard either party or Führer. In fact, even a mere suicide threatened to permanently derail Hitler's suddenly revivified career. It was, in the words of his biographer Ron Rosenbaum, "Adolf Hitler's Chappaquiddick."[134]

Munich police officers Sauer and Forster interrogated the grieving Führer, and they reported:

She [Geli] had previously belonged to a society that had séances where tables moved, and she had said to Hitler that she had learned that one day she would die an unnatural death. Hitler went on to add that she could have taken the pistol very easily because she knew where it was, where he kept his things. Her dying touches his emotions very deeply because she was the only one of his relatives who was close to him. And now this must happen to him.[135]

Certain details emerged but hardly clarified events. The day before her death, Geli's canary "Hansi" had died and she had forlornly carried it about the apartment in a small wooden box.[136] It also transpired that Geli had wrapped her gun—Hitler's Walther 6.35 pistol—in a damp towel to muffle the sound of the fatal shot.[137] Police found a letter that she had been writing. Barely begun, it was never finished, not even its last word: "When I come to Vienna—hopefully soon—we'll drive together to Semmering an. . . ."[138]

Perhaps Geli wrote to a young admirer. Perhaps not, perhaps merely to a friend or an old classmate. She might have wished to escape her uncle—or perhaps she feared not his clutches but his abandonment, the loss of his affections and the favors he might bestow. Bodyguard Wilhelm Stocker had already picked up on her apprehensions. "At the beginning of 1931," he would recall, "I think she was worried that there might be another woman in Hitler's life because she mentioned to me several times that her uncle didn't seem to be as interested in her as he once was."[139] And there was a letter, not by her but found by her within her uncle's coat pocket when she and Wilma Schaub returned from the playhouse.[140] It read:

Dear Mr. Hitler,

Thank you again for the wonderful invitation to the theater. It was a memorable evening. I am most grateful to you for your kindness. I am counting the hours until I may have the joy of another meeting.[141]

Geli, recounted Frau Schaub, turned chalk-white.

Wild reports filled the daily press. The *Münchener Neueste Nachrichten* reported:

Some say that Miss Raubal had met a singer in Vienna but that her uncle would not allow her to leave Munich. Others affirm that the poor girl killed herself because she was supposed to make her debut as a singer but did not believe herself capable of facing the public.[142]

The Social Democrat *Münchener Post* contended that, "The dead woman's nose was broken, and there were other serious injuries on the body. From a letter to a female friend living in Vienna, it is clear that Fraulein Geli had the firm intention of going to Vienna. The letter was never posted."[143] There had, of course, been a letter. Its contents were inconclusive. There were no broken bones or injuries. The official report had deflated that allegation, but none could dispel what another *Münchener Post* account contended: "What drove the student to kill herself is unknown. She was Angela Raubal, the daughter of Hitler's half-sister. On Friday 18 September there was once again a violent quarrel between Herr Hitler and his niece. What was the reason? The vivacious 23-year-old music student, Geli, wanted to go to Vienna, she wanted to become engaged. Hitler was strongly opposed to this. The two of them had recurrent disagreements about it. After a violent scene, Hitler left his flat on the second floor of 16 Prinzregentenplatz."[144]

The situation portended so great a danger for Hitler that he took a highly unusual step: formally responding to the allegations. The September 20 *Münchener Post* contained his heated denials:

> It is untrue that I had either "recurrent disagreements" or a "violent quarrel" with my niece Angela Raubal on Friday 18 September or previously.
>
> It is untrue that I was "strongly opposed" to my niece's travelling to Vienna.
>
> It is untrue that my niece wanted to become engaged in Vienna or that I had some objection to my niece's engagement.[145]

Hitler retained enough presence of mind for that—but for little else. His niece's death—whatever caused it—left him dumbstruck, burdened with a very real and immense grief. "Hitler was at his wits' end," recalled Anni Winter. "He really wanted to kill himself, to commit suicide. He locked himself in Haus Wachenfeld, in Geli's room, would not eat, wanted to kill himself: the loaded pistol was lying on the table."[146] For two days he thus cloistered himself. Finally, he summoned the strength to phone Hoffmann to entreat him to join him at an associate's home on the Tegernsee just south of Munich. They would be alone. Not even Hitler's look-alike chauffeur Julius Schreck, who had taken the precaution of hiding Hitler's pistol from him, accompanied them. Through the night Hitler paced the floor like a caged beast. All the while he would not eat. "Geli's death had shaken my friend to the depths of his soul," wrote Hoffmann, "Had he a feeling of guilt? Was he torturing himself with remorseful self-reproach? What would he do? All of these questions went hammering through my head, but to none of them could I find an answer."[147]

An outstanding Austrian arrest warrant kept him from her Requiem Mass at Vienna, though Himmler and Ernst Röhm had represented him at the ceremonies[148] and at her burial in Catholic ground (a very rare—and suspicious—occurrence for an official suicide),[149] and Hitler seemingly regained control of his emotions. Authorities, nonetheless, granted him twenty-four hours in his homeland to visit her grave. He reached Catholic Central Cemetery in the hours of early morning. Franz Xaver Schwarz and Julius Schaub awaited him. Some said he stood at her grave for a full half hour. Some said he remained for hours, unable to speak. Returning to his car, this unnatural muteness still possessed him, unnerving his aides.

Finally—finally—he spoke.[150]

"*So, now let the struggle begin—the struggle which must and shall be crowned with success.*"[151]

And with that Adolf Hitler returned to Germany.

CHAPTER EIGHT

"I will take off my coat and vest"

DEMOCRATIC NATIONAL CHAIRMAN JOHN JAKOB RASKOB BELIEVED that the great struggle confronting America remained Prohibition. So did his testy "dry" rival, the Methodist Episcopal bishop James Cannon Jr. The millions of unemployed, the underemployed, the foreclosed, the bankrupt, and the thoroughly frightened contended otherwise. They judged the day's great issue to be the Great Depression—and there New York's Franklin Roosevelt pledged to act. Exactly how, observers remained unsure. But FDR could point to at least one concrete measure in his gubernatorial résumé. In September 1931, he and New York's Republican-controlled legislature created a new Temporary Emergency Relief Administration. Headed by Franklin's political ally Jesse Straus, TERA distributed a mere $20 million in unemployment funds.[1] But in an era of halting relief efforts, the pioneering agency, nonetheless, burnished Roosevelt's reputation in the nation's flagging fight against want.

Yet, FDR might also play the conservative. On taking office, though never enamored of Calvin Coolidge's presidency, he proposed emulating it, advocating a 20 percent decrease in New York's income tax.[2] "I am opposed to any form of dole. I do not believe the state has any right to hand out money," he vowed in October 1928.[3] To Young Democrats in April 1932, he railed against an alleged "orgy of [government] spending" prevailing prior to 1929, vowing to slash state spending even further ("now we have to be penny foolish. We have been pound foolish in the past") than he already had—by a full 10 to 20 percent more if necessary.[4]

His first significant public reaction to the Crash—on November 24, 1929—was to wire Herbert Hoover from Warm Springs supporting The Great Engineer's call for increased public works spending. With his support, however, came a very significant—and fiscally conservative—caveat: Such Depression-fighting expenditures must be "limited only by estimated receipts from revenues without increasing taxation."[5]

Like Hoover, FDR initially failed to fully grasp what dislocation and suffering the Depression might eventually wreak. Barely a week later, he instructed Louis Howe to hike over to Park Avenue and to the Anderson Galleries' "final liquidation sale." "It is just possible," he chortled, "that *the recent little Flurry down town* [emphasis added] will make prices comparatively low. I have marked several items."[6]

So perhaps this was not the politician to radically—or even merely effectively—combat the Depression. Perhaps Lippmann, Broun, and Baruch were indeed right about him after all. "Alfalfa Bill" Murray derided him as "without courage."[7] Newcomer Huey Long dismissed him as the Democrat easiest for Hoover to beat.[8] The *New York World-Telegram*'s Ray Tucker pronounced: "Mr. Roosevelt, once a dry and a liberal and a reformer, has listed with every political wind that has blown within the last twenty years. He has stood in every camp; he has fought on every firing line. He is the soldier of fortune of American politics."[9]

Did such "soldiering" result from a lack of interest? From mere cowardice? Or, instead, from sheer calculation? The first duty of a patriot, an old maxim held, was to get elected. William Jennings Bryan had been forthright. So had TR in 1912, and The Happy Warrior in 1928. What good had it provided them? Or the country? Or anyone, for that matter?

Or did FDR have more up his sleeve than merely salving the wounds of the nation's millions of unemployed? He hinted as much at the National Democratic Club's April 1930 Jefferson Day Dinner. "If Thomas Jefferson were alive," he told the crowd of two thousand, excoriating the nation's bankers, "he would be the first to question this concentration of economic power."[10] Did Franklin envision more than stop-gap measures? Did he, in fact, aim to uproot an entire economic system, to transplant power from Wall Street to Pennsylvania Avenue—and never let it move back again?

Yet, as governor, FDR had done little to reform the banking or the financial system. The New York stock market, then as now, oversaw most national stock trading. No federal Securities and Exchange Commission existed to oversee it. Most observers still viewed stock regulation as a state responsibility, specifically New York's responsibility—Al Smith and Franklin Roosevelt's responsibility. FDR himself had worked on Wall Street, rubbing shoulders with traders and the big customers of the traders. He knew the system. Yet, how had he moved to regulate the market, either before or after the crash?

On Sunday evening, March 2, 1930, he took to the NBC Blue Network's airwaves to categorically condemn any notion of federal responsibility in such matters. "Wisely or unwisely, people know that under the Eighteenth Amendment Congress has been given the right to legislate on this particular subject," he contended, "but this is not the case in the matter of a great number of other vital problems of government, such as the conduct of public utilities, of banks, of insurance, of business, of agriculture, of education, of social welfare and of a dozen other important features. In these, Washington must not be encouraged to interfere."[11]

As economist John Kenneth Galbraith would later point out, "Roosevelt, too, was following a laissez-faire policy, at least, on the matter of the stock market."[12]

And as the stock market went in 1929, so did the banks a year later.

Even in the booming '20s seven thousand banks had failed. Most were rural and, save to those lives ruined by their collapse, largely insignificant institutions. Ninety percent boasted under a hundred thousand dollars in assets.[13] In 1929, 659 banks had collapsed. A year later, 1,352; by 1931, 2,294.[14] In January 1932 alone, 342 more folded.[15] Just 1.5 percent of the nation's businesses failed in the Depression's first three years. Banks (mostly state regulated) collapsed at near 25 percent.[16]

The Depression shifted banking insolvency to the cities. But trouble in New York City predated the Crash. On Friday, February 1, 1929, Francesco M. (Frank) Ferrari, the forty-four-year-old Naples-born founder and president of the City Trust Company,[17] one of the many financial institutions then serving specific ethnic communities, died. Nothing seemed amiss, but ten days later FDR's banking superintendent, the Smith holdover, Frank H. Warder, shuttered the bank.[18] Again, nothing appeared suspicious. Nor did it when Warder shortly resigned[19] or even when he headed for Europe. But, in fact, he had long been on the take from the deceased Signor Ferrari, and this would soon become known.[20]

When it did, FDR was on one of his extended vacations at Warm Springs. Just as Al Smith had envisioned, Lt. Gov. Herbert Lehman swung into action, ordering a Moreland Act investigation of the situation. That Lehman dared to appoint FDR's bête-noir, the unceremoniously cashiered Robert Moses, as commission chairman, was remarkable then and remarkable now.[21]

Lehman never consulted FDR on Moses's appointment. But, as Lehman could ignore Roosevelt, Roosevelt could ignore Moses and his findings. He appointed a *new* banking commission, which recommended oversight of private banks but little else.[22]

Among the appointments on FDR's new commission was Manhattan's former state senator Henry W. Pollock, a vice president of the state-chartered Bank of United States. Like the Italian-oriented City Trust Co., the "Bank of United States" was another of the many ethnic-based financial institutions dotting the city and, indeed, the country, the "Bank of United States" being Jewish. Thanks to a series of mergers in the late 1920s, it ranked as perhaps the largest of all ethnic banks. By 1929, it served 450,000 depositors,[23] boasted $200 million in deposits,[24] was the city's third-largest bank, and the twenty-eighth-largest nationwide. Not bad at all for a mere "pants pressers" bank.

In December 1930, it too spectacularly crashed, accelerating (if not triggering) a nationwide banking disaster. Its might not have crashed at all—had Franklin Roosevelt heeded Robert Moses's recommendations for reform. Moses had specifically highlighted this very bank's unsteadiness.[25] A July 1929 report by a full hundred State Banking Department and Federal Reserve auditors concurred.[26] Until it was far too late, FDR and his newly appointed banking superintendent Joseph A. Broderick did nothing.[27]

"Why had Governor Roosevelt ignored Robert Moses' emphatic warnings in the report on City Trust?" FDR's favorable biographer Frank Freidel would ask, "Why had he failed to fight through reform legislation which would have prevented the Bank of United States debacle? These are the sharp questions that critics of Roosevelt asked at the time and later."[28]

Or, as another sympathetic biographer, Conrad Black, concluded, "with a proper monitoring and regulatory system, the depositors, at least, of the Bank of the United States would have been rescued. This was the beginning of the rockslide of the banking system in New York, as the Chelsea Bank and the State Bank of Binghamton folded a few weeks later."[29]

Panic built upon panic. The city and then the state and then the national banking systems eventually split apart like rotted logs. A billion dollars poured out of banks, where they might have fueled a recovery, into inert hoards of cash secured under mattresses, buried in back yards, and locked into private safes across a panicked land.[30] Compounding the chaos was outright subversion, with Communist Party agitators taking to the streets to trigger further collapses.[31]

Adding very real insult to injury was this: the indictment of FDR's banking superintendent Joseph A. Broderick for neglect of duty and conspiracy in the matter of the Bank of United States.[32]

Yet, such embarrassments failed to halt (or even substantially slow) Roosevelt's presidential juggernaut.

Beyond TERA, a forty-hour, six-day week for women and children, a passion for public electric power, and a modest expansion in the state's workers' compensation program, FDR had few items on his reformist résumé. Even his adulatory earlier biographer James MacGregor Burns conceded that "the actual legislation passed was almost trifling compared with the enormity of the problem" facing the nation.[33] Perhaps that is why in May 1932, FDR along with TERA administrator Harry Hopkins announced a program of "subsistence farms" for the unemployed, the state to pay their rent, and furnish them with tools and seeds; 244 such farms were, said FDR, already in place. It was an odd, fanciful touch of utopianism, which even Rex Tugwell found economically impractical,[34] though not necessarily politically impractical—a scheme concocted to counteract not Herbert Hoover or such rising populists as "Alfalfa Bill" Murray or "The Kingfish" Huey Long—but rather Pennsylvania's mustached Gifford Pinchot.[35]

Both Pinchot and Roosevelt were aristocratic to their very core. They moved in the same rarified circles. Cornelia Pinchot and Eleanor Roosevelt had even attended dancing school together.[36] As a freshman state legislator in 1912, FDR had invited the then much more celebrated Pinchot to address the state senate Forest, Fish, and Game Committee.[37] In 1929 Pinchot requested Franklin to support his application to the New York Yacht Club.[38]

By 1932, it was Pinchot, the former conservationist ally of Uncle Ted, and not FDR, who boasted bragging rights as the Northeast's most progressive and activist governor. FDR had requested a measly $20 million for TERA. Pinchot (though he finally received only $10 million) requested $60 million from his legislature to care for his state's poor, following that up with a seven-month 1 percent tax on gross-income from sales to finance another $12 million in aid.[39] He put men to work building "Pinchot Roads." FDR provided conflicting messages regarding where to lead the nation. Pinchot left no doubts. To Illinois Republicans in February 1932, he exclaimed, "Today the United States is in the hands of big business and the great international bankers,"[40] claiming that Lincoln would not be nominated by the current GOP. "Where would he get with the controlling powers of the Republican Convention in Chicago?" challenged a discernibly bitter[41] Pinchot. "He wouldn't get to first base."[42] Headlined the *New York Times* in June 1931: "[George] Norris Hails Pinchot for '32; Prefers Him to Hoover 500 to 1."[43]

Gifford had the substance. Franklin had the breaks. Pinchot, at sixty-seven, seemed far too old for the White House. Franklin Roosevelt, at fifty, seemed just right. Herbert Hoover controlled the levers of power in Pinchot's Republican Party. Despite frantic pro-Smith maneuvering by John Jakob Raskob, the doors of the Democratic Party lay wide-open to FDR. Worst of all, Gifford Pinchot was as confirmed and genuine a "dry" as one might still find in 1932. Franklin was as "dry"—or as "wet"—as he had to be.

By early 1932, the time had finally arrived for FDR to speak out, to assure a skeptical world that he was more than a "Boy Scout" or an amiable, glad-handing "feather duster."

And that is why he had instituted his own noble experiment, the "Brains Trust"—not so much for brains but for words.

He set Moley, Tugwell, and Berle to work crafting a series of speeches designed to convince a wary electorate that he was, indeed, not balsa wood but sturdy presidential timber. On April 7, 1932, Raymond Moley[44] fashioned a ten-minute address for FDR to deliver during NBC's "Lucky Strike Hour."[45] It contained yet another dose of Rooseveltian conservatism, particularly as he skewered Herbert Hoover's unprecedented levels of public works spending. "It is the habit of the unthinking to turn in times like this to the illusions of economic magic," said FDR, "People suggest that a huge expenditure of public funds by the Federal Government and by State and local governments will completely solve the unemployment problem. But it is clear that even if we could raise many billions of dollars and find definitely useful public works to spend these billions on, even all that money would not give employment to the seven million or ten million people who are out of work. Let us admit frankly that it would be only a stopgap. A real economic cure must go to the killing of the bacteria in the system rather than to the treatment of external symptoms."

That is how he began. But he lurched leftward, for this was, in fact, FDR's famed "Forgotten Man" address. "These unhappy times," he orated, "call for the building of plans that rest upon the forgotten, the unorganized but the indispensable units of economic power, for plans like those of 1917 that build from the bottom up and not from the top down, that put their faith once more in the forgotten man at the bottom of the economic pyramid."[46]

The "forgotten man" was hardly a new concept. Laissez-faire economics advocate and Yale professor William Graham Sumner[47] had coined the phrase in the 1870s. In April 1932, FDR's use of it generated significant public interest, promising as he did to use wartime-style federal authority to assist the millions now trapped "at the bottom of the economic pyramid."

It also spawned a furious backlash from FDR's own "forgotten man," one Alfred Emanuel Smith.

To Smith, the phrase and the very speech betrayed Franklin's real agenda, a re-ordering of the economic system to be achieved by pitting the jealousies of the poor against the rich, the have-nots versus the remaining haves. Five days following Roosevelt's "Forgotten Man" talk, Smith highlighted an otherwise exceedingly dull Jefferson Day Dinner at Washington's Willard Hotel. "This is no time for demagogues," Smith ripped into FDR. "At a time like this, when millions of men, women and children are starving throughout the land, there is always a temptation to some men to stir up class prejudice, to stir up the bitterness of the rich against the poor, and the poor against the rich. Against that effort I set myself uncompromisingly.

"I have recently stated that, while I would accept the nomination for the presidency if it were tendered me by the Convention, that before the Convention assembled, I would not be for or against any candidate. I announce tonight an exception to that statement. I will take off my coat and vest and fight to the end against any candidate who persists in any demagogic appeal to the masses of the working people of this country, to destroy themselves by setting class against class and rich against poor."[48]

All present—Governor Ritchie, John Nance Garner, Sen. Joe Robinson, Newton Baker, John Jakob Raskob—all feigned bafflement, if not outright befuddlement, concerning to whom Smith's barbed comments might refer. Smith, himself, solemnly averred that his gibes were not aimed at anyone in particular.[49]

But they—and everyone else in the country, including Franklin Roosevelt—knew better.

CHAPTER NINE

"A poison-painted monkey on a stick"

GELI RAUBAL WAS GONE, BUT A NEW YEAR—1932—REMAINED UPON the horizon.

For Hitler's National Socialists, still aglow from the light of 1930's Reichstag results, the months ahead lay filled with hope and promise.

To his diary one Nazi leader confided:

> *The year has ended as it began, with work. Up to the last day worries and difficulties. Reading, writing, and endless conferences.*
>
> *At 12 p.m. motor out to Spandau . . . to visit the Storm Troopers. Great jubilations at midnight. I address them earnestly but full of hope and confidence. 1932 must be the decisive year.*
>
> *It will be a year of hard and inexorable struggle. Only a strong man who takes his stand on firm ground will get it through. Main thing: always to be amidst one's men. One must never fall out of touch with the people. The people are the beginning, middle and end of all our endeavours.*
>
> *The first day of the new year brings some respite. But it is merely the hush before the storm: We must toughen ourselves to weather crises ahead. The day after tomorrow work begins again.[1]*

The writer was Joseph Goebbels. His work: a new presidential election.

There might not be an election at all, at least, not one that featured millions of voters trooping to the polls. Observers widely agreed that Weimar was "the most democratic democracy in the world,"[2] yet the republic's constitution harbored not only articles 25 and 48, it contained yet another anti-democratic provision, short-circuiting any popular vote for presidential re-election if two-thirds of both the Reichstag and the nation's invariably forgotten upper legislative house, the Reichsrat, opted to extend any incumbent's tenure.[3] Such was the scenario the aged and autocratic Hindenburg preferred over facing another election's democratic indignities. Securing legislative approval fell, however, not to Hindenburg but to his chancellor, Heinrich Brüning. KPD support (their demands were mere anti-SPD propaganda[4]) was out of the question, but backing quickly emerged from the SPD itself.

In 1925, SPD-Zentrum coalition candidate Wilhelm Marx seemed poised to win the presidency over the leading rightist candidate, the German People's Party's Karl Jarres, mayor of Duisberg in the Ruhr. At the last moment Hindenburg supplanted the lackluster Jarres to snatch victory from Marx.[5] In 1932, however, both the SPD and the Zentrum desperately wanted to block the ascending NSDAP, essentially switching sides, shifting their still substantial support to their old enemy Hindenburg.[6] Such patronage should have cleared his path to an unopposed second term. It did not. His exceedingly grudging support for both the republic in general and the hated Young Plan specifically had alienated the nationalist Right—led now by the DNVP's intransigent, blundering Alfred Hugenberg. The National Socialists' 107 Reichstag delegates also remained in question, with Hitler still dancing nervously not only upon the tightrope of legality versus revolution, but also upon how forcefully he dared go in opposing the venerable Reichspräsident. Hitler might not enjoy the votes of Hindenburg's admirers today, but knew he would need them soon enough. Flinging mud upon the field marshal's field-gray uniform was no way to secure them.

In January 1932, Brüning commenced negotiating with Hugenberg and a gleeful Hitler ("Now I have them in my pocket"[7]) for Hindenburg's second term. Hugenberg quickly refused, arguing that to assent would signify support for Brüning's minority government and for Brüning's having "dragged [Hindenburg] into the party and parliamentary discussions which do not do justice to the constitutional position and high esteem which the Reichspräsident enjoys among his people."[8] Hitler, invariably the procrastinator, proceeded more cautiously. With unusual delicacy, he addressed his response not to Brüning but to Hindenburg, couching his objections solely on constitutional (and even democratic) grounds. Would he support Hindenburg in the election that now must ensue? He did not say yes. He did not say no.[9]

Such equanimity, however, could not last. Hugenberg had positioned himself to Hitler's right, and Hitler could not stand for that—not with his movement's more fiery elements pounding the war drums for action. Within days, he issued two statements, equal in invective ("I shall never believe that flabbiness constitutes a political asset . . . everything hinges on overthrowing the present regime . . ."[10]) to Hugenberg's.[11]

Hindenburg grew testier.[12] But, after much pleading, he reluctantly announced his candidacy:[13] "In full consciousness of my great responsibility I have resolved to offer myself for re-election, as the request that I should do so does not come from any party but from the broad masses of the nation, I feel it is my duty to do so. . . . If I am defeated, I shall at least not have incurred the reproach that of my own accord I deserted my post in an hour of crisis."[14]

Would either the Nazis or the Nationalists now support The Old Gentleman? Or offer their own candidates? Hugenberg's DNVP continued its electoral slippage. The NSDAP retained its momentum. Between 1930 and 1931 they had increased their vote in Bremen from 12 to 25.4 percent. In Mecklenburg, they jumped from 22 to 41 percent.[15] Solid gains occurred in Hamburg, Hesse, and Oldenburg.[16] In the state of Lippe's January 1932 balloting, Nazi representation surged from zero seats to nine.[17] "No other way offers but to appoint our own candidate," Goebbels recorded in his diary. "A difficult and disagreeable struggle, but one that has to be carried through."[18]

But by whom? In hindsight, the logical answer is, of course, Hitler. It was not then. Speculation centered on two of the party's less seedy luminaries, Gregor Strasser's colorless ally Wilhelm Frick and retired war hero and Freikorps veteran Gen. Franz Xaver Ritter von Epp.[19] After all, an immense roadblock still obstructed Hitler's destiny: He was not yet a German citizen. For all intents and purposes, he remained an undocumented Aryan.

Hitler dithered. He hobnobbed with actors,[20] attended the cinema (a Greta Garbo film[21] and the pioneering lesbian drama *Mädchen in Uniform*),[22] and live productions of *Die Fledermaus* and *The Merry Widow*,[23] even busied himself planning a new party headquarters as well as completely revitalizing Berlin.[24] Goebbels ("Everyone is nervous and strained . . . They fear that the Führer is waiting too long"[25]) went on the attack. From the Reichstag in mid-February, he issued a scathing, almost inconceivably reckless (yet, thoroughly premeditated) jeremiad against the Reichspräsident. "I protest against the charge [that] the National Socialist movement that it has abandoned Hindenburg," he began. "No, Hindenburg has abandoned the case of his one-time voters. We entrusted him with the highest office of the Republic in the belief that at least in basic questions he would adopt the policies which the national Germany considered vital. He has done the opposite. He has unequivocally sided with the middle, he has sided as openly with the Social Democrats.

"We National Socialists," he finally roared, "have a saying which has never failed to prove true: Tell me who praises you, and I will tell you who you are! Praised by the [Berlin] asphalt press, praised by the party of deserters—."[26] An uproar ("You bastard!" "Mongrel"[27]) interrupted his words. SPD delegate Kurt Schumacher (severely crippled in the war) sarcastically congratulated him for having succeeded for the first time in recorded history "in effecting the total mobilization of human stupidity."[28] Defense minister Gen. Wilhelm Gröner denounced Goebbels for having finally gone too far. Goebbels refused to withdraw his remarks. The body expelled him.[29]

By now Hitler had decided on a presidential run. So had the Nationalists. Initially, Hugenberg considered himself—and then two members of the Hohenzollern royal family, the dissolute Crown Prince (*Kronprinz*) Wilhelm and the Kaiser's fifth son, the wounded war veteran, Prince Oskar (eventually a Nazi Party member[30]). Their father vetoed their candidacy. So, when Hugenberg's Stahlhelm allies nominated their capable but colorless second-in-command, the bald-pated Prussian Theodor Duesterberg, Hugenberg meekly acceded in their selection.[31]

But what of Hitler's citizenship? Like everything in this unloved republic, there seemed a way around any inconvenience, any truth. In Hitler's case, he might achieve citizenship via an appointment to some minor provincial post. In 1930, Wilhelm Frick, now Thuringia's minister of interior and education, suggested appointing him as Hildburghausen town police chief.[32] That struck Hitler as beneath his dignity. On February 26, 1932, however, with the clock ticking on his candidacy, Braunschweig's Nazi minister of interior and education, the former *Realschule* teacher Dietrich Klagges, proposed to grant him citizenship through appointment as a professor of "Politics and Organic Sociology" (whatever that was—and no one really knew) at its local technical college. Again, Hitler refused.[33] Braunschweig finally did appoint him as a counselor (*Regierungsrat*), assigned as an attaché to its Berlin legation. An ex-Austrian became a German—and soon a candidate.[34]

Goebbels—fresh from blasting Hindenburg—had already announced his chief's candidacy.[35] "Four weeks ago," he informed a packed hall at Berlin's huge Sportpalast, "15,000 people spontaneously leapt to their feet and hailed the name of our Führer. I myself stood with them with palpitating heart and I dared not speak . . . Hitler will be our Reichspräsident."[36]

But it requires far more than words to win an election. It takes cash, and Nazi balance sheets ran far more red than black. "Money is wanting everywhere," Goebbels had already complained to his diary on January 5. "It is very difficult to obtain. Nobody will give us credit. Once you get the power you can get the cash galore, but then you need it no longer. Without the power you need the money, but then you can't get it!"[37]

Soon, Goebbels would have his money.

Either by design or by luck, Hitler's rhetoric now took a more measured tone. Sitting for an extended interview at Munich's Brown House with the American correspondent, H. R. Knickerbocker, he patiently explained why American investments would be not just safe, but safest—almost guaranteed—under his forthcoming regime. Hitler "looked like an actor or artist," thought the Texas-born Knickerbocker, "or he might have been a rising young district attorney in one of our Southern States, a man with his eye on the governorship." He played the "courteous host," pulling up his guest's chair, even smiling "engagingly."[38] But, all the while Putzi Hanfstaengl ("the best diplomat in Hitler's service"[39]) sat at his master's elbow to guard against misquotation. From the grander topics of debt and reparation, Knickerbocker eventually honed in on less macro-economic matters: the Nazis' long-standing antipathy to department stores—and not merely to those under Jewish ownership, but also to the American Woolworth dime-store chain that boasted a string of outlets throughout Germany. "We shall not let German-American relationships depend upon department stores," Hitler joked before quickly and firmly defending orthodox National Socialist doctrine. "But seriously the existence of such undertakings is an encouragement for Bolshevism. They represent a concentration of capital that Marx has taught us is the condition for the coming of Communism. They destroy many small existences. Therefore we shall not approve of them, and be assured that your undertakings of this character will be treated precisely as are similar German undertakings."[40]

That was in Munich. In Düsseldorf, the prestigious (though no longer so swank[41]) Industry Club had permitted the Jewish Social Democrat economist Max Cohen-Reuss to address it. Club member Fritz Thyssen—a recent Nazi party member[42] but a longtime sympathizer—countered this SPD incursion by proposing an invitation to a prominent National Socialist. He set his sights on Gregor Strasser, who despite his leftist sympathies, Thyssen still considered as educated, reasonable, and well respected. Soon afterward, however, Thyssen ran into Hitler in Berlin,[43] who convinced him that the opportunity might be better served if he rather than any underling attended.

The result was a Hitler tour-de-force. Outside, SPD and KPD demonstrators threatened to storm the venue.[44] Inside, Hitler delivered a measured performance, perfectly calculated to curry favor not only from the thousand club members before him, but from business and industrial leaders throughout the Reich.[45] He began, not ranting (he did not even mention the Jews[46]) but modestly. "People say to me so often," he informed his audience, "'You are only the drummer of national Germany.' And supposing that I were only the drummer? It would today be a far more statesmanlike achievement to drum once more into this German people a new faith than gradually to squander the only faith they have . . . The more you bring a people back into the sphere of faith, of ideals, the more will it cease to regard material distress as the one and only thing that counts."[47]

He painted himself as the nation's only effective counterweight—its last hope—against domestic and foreign Bolshevism. "Bolshevism will, if its advance is not halted," he warned, "expose the world to a transformation as complete as the one Christianity once effected. In 300 years people will no longer say: this is a new idea in production. In 300 years people might already know that it is almost a new religion, though based upon other principles! In 300 years, if this movement continues to develop, people will see in Lenin not only a revolutionary of the year 1917, but the founder of a new world doctrine, worshipped perhaps like Buddha."[48]

Coincidentally or not, within the fortnight, Goebbels chortled: "Money affairs improve daily. The financing of the electoral campaign is practically assured."[49]

Adolf Hitler could indeed be a *very* persuasive man.

—✦—

And so could Dr. Goebbels.

Hitler's disciples all boasted too-ample shares of hate and ambition and hero-worship. None quite fit that mold as much as Paul Joseph Goebbels.

His path to such a warped honor had been neither easy nor direct.

Herr Doktor Goebbels was Exhibit "A" in the case of Nazi leadership failing to meet ideal Aryan standards. Slight of build (just 5'5" at best), rat-faced, and club-footed, he was not even of pure German blood, his mother being of Dutch extraction (and perhaps even Javanese[50]). Kurt Lüdecke thought him "a poison-painted monkey on a stick."[51]

He had not always even been an anti-Semite, though eventually such sentiments accelerated within him, perhaps even eclipsing those of his master. One hesitates (to put the matter mildly) to ever quote Holocaust denier David Irving, but when Irving states: "There's no question that whatever tragedy befell the Jews in Germany during the Third Reich, Dr. Goebbels himself was the prime moving force behind it," Irving might be on to something.[52] Except, of course, that he was merely only the *second*-largest moving force.

And, yet, in his hometown Goebbels had long dated a half-Jewish[53] sports teacher named Else Janke ("She is good and without guile . . . . She is good to me and makes me happy"[54]). In February 1919, a letter from another early girlfriend, Anka Stalherm, contained a fairly mild anti-Semitic remark. He fired back this broadside: "As you know, I can't stand this exaggerated anti-Semitism. My view is you don't get rid of them by huffing and puffing, let alone by pogroms, and even if you could do so, that would be both highly ignoble and unworthy."[55]

By the mid-1920s, however, he had, nonetheless, become virulently anti-Semitic. Perhaps the feeling was genuine, or, quite possibly, it was to compensate for his decidedly getting off on the wrong club-foot with his Führer, for he had always been quite the extreme left-winger, part-and-parcel of Gregor Strasser's north German socialist faction. "National and socialist! What goes first, and what comes afterwards?" he argued, "With us . . . there can be no doubt. First socialist redemption, then comes national liberation like a whirlwind . . . Hitler stands between both opinions. . . ."[56]

He went so far as to describe himself as a "German Communist,"[57] opposed to "stock exchange capital,"[58] fuming at the sight of how Germany "gives in and sells out to the capitalist west. A horrible prospect: Germany's sons will bleed to death on the battlefields of Europe as the mercenaries of capitalism. Perhaps probably in a 'holy war against Moscow!'"[59]

"In the last analysis," he concludes, "better go down with Bolshevism than live in eternal capitalist servitude."[60]

Aligned with Gregor Strasser ("A splendid fellow. A massive Bavarian"[61]), Goebbels clashed violently with Hitler on economic issues ("I feel devastated. What sort of Hitler? A reactionary? Amazingly clumsy and uncertain. . . . Gruesome! . . . Not rattle the question of private property!"[62]). At a meeting in Hanover, the exasperated Goebbels finally dared to demand "that the petty bourgeois Adolf Hitler shall be expelled from the party."[63]

Feuding northern and southern Nazi cliques collided at a February 1926 party conference Hitler summoned to Bamberg. The Führer's grip on his party held firm—"hard as Krupp steel," as he might have put it. Strasser and Goebbels ("I want to cry . . . We are socialist"[64]) folded completely. Beaten, they might have deserted the movement, joined the Communists, or founded their own "national Bolshevik" party. They did none of these things. Retaining his NSDAP membership, Strasser, soft-soaped by Hitler ("Listen, Strasser, you really mustn't go on living like a wretched official. Sell your pharmacy, draw on Party funds and set yourself up properly as a man of your worth should"[65]), remained in an increasingly uneasy alliance with Hitler. But there was nothing uneasy or uncertain about the twenty-eight-year-old Goebbels's new attitude.

It was akin to love.

"I stand shaken before [Hitler]," he gushed to his diary. "That is how he is: like a child, dear, good, compassionate. Sly like a cat, clever and skillful, magnificently roaring like a gigantic lion. A fine fellow, a real man. . . . That's how he is! Yes, that's how he is!"[66]

Yes, love.

"How I love him!" he scribbled, "What a fellow! . . . How small I am! He gives me his photograph. . . . Heil Hitler! I want Hitler to be my friend. . . ."[67]

And, in Augsburg . . .

"Hitler and I smothered in flowers . . . Hitler gives me a bunch of flowers to take away with me: red, red roses. Farewell from him. My heart aches. . . ."[68]

Yes, Hitler ("those big blue eyes. Like stars"[69]) had successfully courted Goebbels. He had recognized the immense talent and energy—"A man who burns like a flame"[70]—residing in this young, misshapen man. He would put Goebbels to work.

In November 1926, he appointed Goebbels as gauleiter ("responsible to me alone"[71]—not, as would normally be the case, to Gregor Strasser[72]) of Berlin.[73] It was both an immense honor and a thankless task. Goebbels would lead the struggle in the nation's capital, the veritable "New York of Europe"[74]—in Goebbels's words "a self-important hydrocephalus, a repulsive accumulation of pirates, pederasts, gangsters and their like, a city which for the best must disappear from German soil."[75] And those were its *good* points. Berlin was rife with socialists and communists. The KPD boasted 250,000 members (in four thousand cells) and twenty-five newspapers.[76] It contained the Reich's largest component of Jews (4 percent of its population).[77] "The only fly in the ointment," noted British ambassador Sir Horace Rumbold upon his appointment, "is the number of Jews in the place."[78] Beyond that, the city was nearly bereft of Nazis—just two thousand of them in 1926.[79] Recall that in 1928's Reichstag elections, the party had drawn a measly 1.5 percent within city precincts.[80] "A Babylon of sins!" Goebbels groused, "And into this I shall throw myself."[81]

Throw himself, indeed. In July 1927, he established a weekly newspaper, *Der Angriff* (*"The Attack"*); its slogan: "Germany awake, Judaism be damned." In 1928, alongside Strasser, Göring, and Frick, Goebbels ("Do you really want to elect me?"[82] he dared voters) emerged as one of the party's meager quotient of Reichstag deputies.[83] By November 1930, he had transformed *Der Angriff* into a daily.[84]

In January 1929, Hitler designated Goebbels as *Reichspropagandaleiter*—party propaganda chief—replacing Gregor Strasser's assistant Heinrich Himmler.[85] The assignment only angered Strasser, now loathing Goebbels as "the scheming dwarf."[86]

Reichspropagandaleiter counted as no small sinecure. Propaganda's black arts had long obsessed Hitler. *Mein Kampf* expounded at length upon its subtleties—or more accurately the proper lack thereof (and collaterally revealed its author's immense, sneering contempt for those he eventually hoped to lead). "The receptivity of the great masses is very limited, their intelligence is small," Hitler wrote, "but their power of forgetting is enormous. In consequence of these facts, all effective propaganda must be limited to a very few points and must harp on these in slogans until the last member of the public understands what you want him to understand by your slogan. As soon as you sacrifice this slogan and try to be many-sided, the effect will piddle away, for the crowd can neither digest nor retain the material offered. In this way the result is weakened and entirely cancelled out."[87] Such slogans, Hitler added, need not always be true, here developing the theory and practice of the Big Lie: "something of the most insolent lie will always remain and stick—a fact which all the great lie-virtuosi and lying clubs in this world know only too well . . ."[88]

Goebbels proved himself more than capable of administering liberal doses of propaganda—and outright falsehoods—to German audiences. "ANTI-SEMITISM is UN-CHRISTIAN," he fulminated in 1930. "That means that he is a Christian who looks while the Jew sews straps around our necks. TO BE A CHRISTIAN MEANS: LOVE THY NEIGHBOR AS THYSELF! MY NEIGHBOR IS ONE WHO IS TIED TO ME BY BLOOD. IF I LOVE HIM I MUST HATE HIS ENEMIES. HE WHO THINKS GERMAN MUST DESPISE THE JEWS."[89]

All the while, he remained the hard-core revolutionary ("we still have too many philistines in the party. . . . I'll stick to the straight and narrow path . . ."[90]). In October 1930, he supported a massive Berlin metal-workers strike.[91] "The struggle is for daily bread versus the Dawes and Young policy. . . . ," he proclaimed (he was, after all, always *proclaiming*). "No wheel must turn and no hand must move a tool. Anyone working as a strike breaker will be expelled from the National Socialist Party. . . ."[92] *Der Angriff* echoed his leftist slant: "The stock-market hyenas are sitting in London and New York's Wall Street for whose benefit the German worker is expected to accept a cut in his already meager living standard."[93]

Goebbels had once admired the Communists ("we have far more in common with Eastern Bolshevism than with Western capitalism . . . Russia's freedom shall be our freedom . . ."[94]). Now, his back-alley thugs battled their back-alley thugs. Previously an ally of Gregor and Otto Strasser, he now reviled them. In June 1930, he convened a raucous Sportpalast session to attack the Strassers' "literary clique."[95] The movement's always fractious atmosphere turned even uglier. Goebbels's ally, the caricaturist Hans Schweitzer (soon *Der Angriff*'s star cartoonist), suggested Otto Strasser must "have Jewish blood in his veins," as witnessed by his "reddish, kinky hair, his hooked nose, his puffy, fleshy face."[96] Goebbels' SA hirelings roughed up Strasser's.[97]

He damned all his opponents, taking fiendish glee ("And he who had laughter on his side, was always right"[98]) in incessantly ridiculing Berlin's tiny, bespectacled—but exceedingly brave and honest—Jewish police commissioner, Dr. Bernhard Weiss, as "Isidor" Weiss.[99] Reichskanzler Hermann Müller he dismissed as "a traveler in water closets."[100] To Goebbels, Germany's brilliant foreign minister Philipp Scheidemann was a mere "salon simpleton."[101] Sometimes-ally Alfred Hugenberg emerged as *Hugenzswerg,* "Hugendwarf."[102] Occasionally, his propaganda machine turned its attentions to real grievances, to actual scandals. When it did, and when said scandals involved either political enemies—and/or Jews—so much the better. His most such spectacular opportunity involved Berlin's Sklarek brothers. Eastern Jewish (*Ostjuden*) clothing merchants Max, Leo, and Willy Sklarek enjoyed a virtual monopoly in supplying the city with uniforms, clothing, and hospital linen. They resorted to widespread bribery, mostly small-scale stuff, but with a cut-rate fur jacket thrown in for Lord Mayor Gustav Böss's wife—and a full coat for his actress mistress. Piquantly, His Honor was visiting New York's similarly corrupt Mayor Walker when the scandal exploded with the Sklareks September 1929 arrests. Two former mayors and two Communist city counselors went to jail.[103] "The rise of the Nazis," recalled SPD Berlin city councilor Dr. Käte Frankenthal, "began with these 'Sklarek elections.'"[104]

Yet, neither maestro Goebbels—nor the full Nazi propaganda orchestra—restricted their concertos to their keyboard's anti-Semitic notes. Nor did they always perform at full, eardrum-shattering volume. The movement had a bad product to sell, but even bad products—particularly bad products—still required selling. Effective marketing requires an ear for its customers' needs—or, at least, their wants. Thus, Hitler might jettison anti-Semitism in speaking to Düsseldorf's Industry Club. But to those already infected with the virus, Nazi Jew-hating remained high octane ("THE JEW IS OUR GREATEST MISFORTUNE"[105]). Xenophobia could even shift away from Jews to more hot-button targets—say Poles or even Danes—in specific localities.[106] As the general population was not yet ready to fully abandon traditional Christianity for a secular völkisch creed, no such demands would be made—at least, not consistently, at least, not yet.[107] When economic problems might be the bigger draw, they would be properly highlighted. When nationalism was in play, that was the Nazi missive. Though, even that message might be diluted or disguised, if necessary, often thus maddening their opponents. "Hitler," complained the KPD, "says payment of the Versailles tribute only to the extent that is possible. We say not one penny of tribute. Which position is the more consistent one?"[108]

Yes, skillful, successful propaganda required fine tuning its many aspects, and Goebbels (once a devout Catholic and perhaps even bound for the priesthood[109]) grasped the immense value of any cult of martyrology. References to fallen Nazis or nationalists had roused the greatest response to his earliest speeches. Twenty-eight-year-old saboteur Albert Leo Schlageter, shot by the French in the occupied Ruhr,[110] had inspired not merely Nazis but virtually all Germans—even the Communists.[111] The sixteen early fighters who fell at Munich's Feldherrnhalle became the party's "blood martyrs." Their bullet-riddled, blood-stained battle flag—the *Blutfahne*[112] ("blood flag") became its holiest relic. November 9 transformed itself into a "National Reich Day of Mourning"—with an accompanying Munich passion play.[113] For good measure, Nazis celebrated an additional martyrs and battlefield heroes day—complete with bonfire leaping and *Feuersprüche* ("fire speeches")—each summer solstice.[114]

As storm troopers continued to battle Communists, new martyrs—and new myths—arose. Certainly enough dead Nazis existed to choose from. Five died in 1928 street fighting. Seventeen the next year, forty-three the next, cresting to eighty-four in 1932.[115] Often, prospective myths foundered on facts. Not all "Party comrades" fell bravely before an enemy fusillade or the blows of their truncheons. Berlin SA-man Hans-Georg Kütemeyer, for one, embarrassingly turned out to be a mere suicide.[116] Another Berlin "martyr," Walther Fischer, was, in truth, merely an apostate Nazi caught in the path of a stray barroom bullet.[117]

Goebbels fared far, far better with the fifteen-year-old Hitler Youth member, Herbert Norkus, whose mother had gone insane following repeated KPD attacks on her milk shop. In January 1932, Communists in Berlin's left-wing Moabit neighborhood set upon him as he distributed Nazi pamphlets. Fleeing to a nearby home for safety, Norkus found the door slammed in his face. His pursuers stabbed him six times.[118] "The delicate head is trampled to a bloody pulp," the trenchcoat–clad[119] Goebbels orated at Norkus's massive funeral. "Long, deep wounds go into the slender body, and a mortal gash penetrates heart and lungs. . . . Wearily, black night descends. From two glassy eyes stares the emptiness of death."[120]

A best-selling novel (*Hitlerjunge Quex*) and later a popular film commemorated the boy's passing. But, as luck would have it, young Norkus would not emerge as First Martyr of the Reich, for that position was already occupied: by SA *Sturmführer* ("Storm Leader") Horst Wessel.

Wessel's passing was immeasurably more complicated—and messier—than Norkus's. He had been a friend, protégé, and special project of Gauleiter Goebbels ("A fine boy who speaks with incredible idealism"[121]), even contributing verse to *Der Angriff*. But Wessel was primarily a street fighter, and by the standards of such things a pretty good one. So much so that Communists issued a wanted poster for him: "Note the face!" it screamed, "Horst Wessel Storm leader—Murderer of Workers."[122]

Affairs of the heart too often prove more dangerous than those of politics. By 1929, Wessel, son of a Lutheran minister, had taken a live-in girl-friend, one Erna Jaenicke. Many eventually claimed that he was also her pimp, and though Fraulein Jaenicke had indeed previously toiled as one of Berlin's many, many prostitutes, this was not the case. What was true, was this: Their Grosse Frankfurter Strasse landlady, the twenty-nine-year-old widower Elisabeth Salm (herself a petty criminal), desired the couple evicted from their apartment. She had friends—Communists—more than willing to lend a hand since their arch-foe Wessel came with the assignment. At least eight Red Front Fighters trudged upstairs to the twenty-year-old Wessel's third-story flat. They knocked. A thirty-one-year-old, heavily tattooed petty criminal (and, as luck would have it, an actual pimp) Albrecht "Ali" Höhler exclaimed, "You know what this is for!"[123] At close range, he fired his Luger P08 repeatedly into Wessel's mouth.[124]

The KPD nervously attempted to downplay the incident's political aspects. "SA Leader Gunned Down Out of Jealousy,"[125] headlined its paper *Die Rote Fahne*. Goebbels conversely hastened to proclaim Wessel, "A new martyr for the Third Reich."[126]

Hideously wounded, Horst Wessel took a full five weeks to die. When he did, *Der Angriff* cynically and sacrilegiously eulogized:

> *He went forth as a preacher in the wilderness . . . harvesting hate rather than gratitude, and only persecution instead of recognition. . . . They laughed at him, mocked him, spat at him, wherever he came among them, and turned their backs on him with abhorrence. . . . In the end he was prepared . . . to forsake his mother and the parental home, going among those who mocked and spate at him. . . . Beyond, in a proletarian quarter, high above in a mansard room of a block of flats he created an austere young man's existence. A Christian socialist! One who through his deeds cries: 'Come to me. I will redeem you' . . . Five weeks long he lay in agony close to death. . . . He did not complain. . . . And in the end, tired and wracked with pain, he gave up the ghost. They bore him to the grave . . . those he sought to save threw stones at the dead. . . . He drank the pain-filled chalice down to the dregs. . . . The deceased who is with us, raises his weary hand and points into the dim distance: Advance over the graves! At the end lies Germany!*[127]

Joseph Goebbels was indeed creating a new religion, and, though, Horst Wessel might sound like he was the propagandist leader's Christ, he was merely another mass-produced Nazi John the Baptist. Goebbels's real gangland leader-god, Adolf Hitler, would not even bother attending Wessel's March 1930 funeral,[128] but he was running—running very hard—for Reichspräsident in 1932.

CHAPTER TEN

"The half-witted yokels of the cow and cotton States"

A<small>L</small> S<small>MITH</small> <small>WAS NOT ABOUT TO BE MOLLIFIED.</small>

And Franklin Roosevelt was not about to be silenced.

Following FDR's "Forgotten Man" speech and Smith's fiery "coat and vest" response, Roosevelt again took up his oratorical cudgels, this time at a Monday evening, April 18, 1932, Jefferson Day Dinner at St. Paul, in part designed to skewer Hoover's tariff policies. Raymond Moley, author of Roosevelt's "Forgotten Man" salvo, again performed the speechwriting honors.[1] Unlike FDR's former address, however, this effort generated little policy controversy.

It should have. FDR had prefaced his St. Paul thoughts by reassuring the party and the nation's more conservative elements, "I am not speaking of an economic life completely planned and regimented."[2] But, he soon flung such pious sentiments overboard by vowing, "I favor economic planning not for this period alone but for our needs for a long time to come."[3]

That should have triggered alarm bells. It did not in part thanks to a particularly odd piece of the Roosevelt luck.

The Brains Trust, it seemed, was invaluable but not infallible—and recruitment for it was not invariably "brainy."

Exhibit A: Thirty-five-year-old American Molasses Company[4] president Charles W. Taussig.

Taussig had accosted FDR on board the train from New York to Warm Springs, tendering to FDR his business card, and proceeded to fill Roosevelt's ears with his ideas regarding tariffs (Taussig was as low tariff as Tennessee's Cordell Hull) and the Caribbean. In the course of this accidental conversation, Taussig learned of the newly formed Brains Trust's existence and asked to sit in on it. Much to Ray Moley's chagrin, FDR readily agreed.[5]

Taussig was merely an annoyance. It was, Moley, however, who recruited the more dangerous Columbia University economics professor Lindsay Rogers. And it was Rogers who supplied Moley with these lines for FDR's St. Paul speech:

> *The consequences of the Hawley-Smoot bill have been tremendous, both directly and indirectly. Directly, American foreign trade has been steadily dwindling. Indirectly—the high schedules of the Hawley-Smoot bill caused European nations to raise their own tariff walls, and these walls were raised not only against us but against each other.*[6]

Anti-tariff men like Cordell Hull certainly admired those words. So did Alfred E. Smith. In fact, Smith, in his blistering April 13 response to Roosevelt's "Forgotten Man" address had employed virtually identical verbiage:

> *The consequences of the Hawley-Smoot bill have been tremendous, both directly and indirectly. Directly, American foreign trade has been steadily dwindling. Indirectly, the high schedules of the Hawley-Smoot bill caused European nations to raise their own tariff walls, not only against us but against each other.*[7]

It appeared that Professor Rogers, like Berle or Tugwell, was not, as yet, fully convinced of the inevitability or perhaps even the basic desirability, of a Roosevelt candidacy. Rogers, also in active communication with the Smith camp, had supplied the material to them for a March speech. When The Happy Warrior never used his words, Rogers peddled them to Moley. In the interim, however, Smith *had* employed them. He had, however, not utilized them in any mundane Tammany Hall assembly district banquet, but rather in the most famous public blast yet issued against Franklin Roosevelt. No one noticed in the Roosevelt camp. But the Republican *New York Post* did,[8] providing Smith with a field day of gibes ("I don't know where Roosevelt got it. This is mine"[9]) and proof to pundits like Messrs. Lippmann and Broun that FDR was indeed the unprincipled lightweight they supposed him to be. "Either Roosevelt does not read his opponent's speeches," concluded the *Post*, "or he doesn't read his own."[10]

The episode embarrassed Roosevelt but not enough to can Moley, who (even more embarrassed than FDR) conceded that his swift termination would have been profoundly justified. Roosevelt, however, merely indicated that it was simply time to move on—and forward. "So," recalled Moley, "I came to know one of the loveliest facets of Roosevelt's character: He stood by his people when they got into a jam—sometimes even when they got him into a jam."[11]

Rogers, however, quickly vanished into the mists of historical footnotes, the Pete Best of Brains Trusters.

⌐⌐

In late April, the Roosevelt-Hoover relationship took a new turn—for the worse. The nation's governors had assembled this year at Richmond, and then, FDR, Albert Ritchie, and Gifford Pinchot among them, convened again for dinner at the White House. Franklin and Eleanor, as was their habit, arrived early. Hoover uncharacteristically arrived twenty minutes late. The Roosevelts waited—with Franklin awkwardly, painfully, standing the whole time. Aides twice offered him a chair. But buckling and unbuckling his braces was embarrassing. Sweating profusely in unseasonable heat, he refused both offers.[12] Eleanor later fumed that she was "absolutely convinced" that Hoover made her husband stand simply and callously to demonstrate his physical unfitness for the presidency. Franklin shared her suspicions.[13]

This was nonsense (FDR biographer Frank Freidel, among many others, dismisses the supposition as "absolutely preposterous"). Hoover had simply misplaced a governor, Minnesota's Floyd Bjørnstjerne Olson, and was frantically trying to locate him. The left-wing Farmer-Labor Partyite Olson had wired on short notice that he would not be attending, a development somehow escaping the notice of the invariably efficient Hoover White House. Not until the hard-drinking Olson was located (and still refused his presidential invitation) did Hoover troop downstairs.[14]

But thoughts of his rival's infirmities did cross Hoover's mind. "Back in the office tonight," his press secretary Ted Joslin's diary recorded, "we discussed the [recent primary] elections . . . [FDR] shouldn't think of running. He wouldn't live a year in the White House."[15]

And, yet, Roosevelt, as so often the case, had the last laugh—a hearty one. The thin-skinned Hoover quickly reviewed newsreels of the dinner— and hit the roof. "They were horrible," he complained to Joslin. "My worst fears were realized. They make me look as though I was 82 years old. Worst of all, posed pictures of Roosevelt and Ritchie were woven into them. They looked young and vigorous. I was made to appear aged and decrepid [sic]. They were entirely misrepresented to you. This is the end of indoor Movie-tones. Mrs. Hoover was so disturbed that she broke down and cried."[16]

⌐⌐

It may have been the Lindsay Rogers plagiarism fiasco that caused the *New York Herald Tribune*'s Ernest K. Lindley to criticize FDR's speech-making efforts. The *Herald Tribune* was Republican. But Lindley, author of an early

FDR biography (1931's *Franklin D. Roosevelt: A Career in Progressive Democracy*), was hardly hostile to his candidacy. In fact, he was as ardently Rooseveltian as any Brains Truster. FDR dared Lindley to do better—if he could.[17] Lindley recruited the *New York Times*'s James M. Kieran to assist him, and the result was, what Rexford Tugwell believed was, "the sincerest, most unpolitical statement of [FDR's] real attitudes and convictions."[18]

Thus, while accepting an honorary Doctor of Laws degree at Atlanta's Oglethorpe University, on May 22, 1932, FDR signaled the approach that later critics would term "unfocused" and "opportunistic" but which admirers would term "flexible" and "pragmatic."

"The country needs," FDR declared, "and, unless I mistake its temper, the country demands bold, persistent experimentation. It is common sense to take a method and try it: If it fails, admit it frankly and try another. But above all, try something. The millions who are in want will not stand by silently forever while the things to satisfy their needs are within easy reach."[19]

Less noticed was his clarion call for a redistribution of wealth—"the reward of a day's work will have to be greater; and the reward to capital, especially capital which is speculative, will have to be less."[20] "[T]he Oglethorpe speech," calculated Tugwell, "represented the high tide of collectivism"[21] in the election. But, befitting FDR's zig-zagging approach to both governance—and political maneuvering—his Oglethorpe address, in fact, "presented the last of [collectivism] in the campaign."[22]

Herbert Hoover, meanwhile, was not standing still. That same day, responding to American Society of Civil Engineers president Richard S. Parker, he unveiled a twelve-point program for dealing with the Depression; an energetic program, nonetheless, limited by several powerful caveats. Hoover advocated loans, but not grants, to the individual states, standing against make-work programs and warning that "only self-liquidating programs can be justified."[23]

History recalls the Oglethorpe speech. It ignores Hoover's effort. At the time, however, that was hardly the case. "Mr. Hoover is precise, concrete, positive," noted the *New York Times*. "Governor Roosevelt is indefinite, abstract, irresolute. . . . As a matter of experience, the man most to be avoided in a time of crisis is one who goes about wringing his hands and demanding that something be done without explaining or knowing what can or ought to be done."[24]

Many Republicans, however, remained less impressed with Mr. Hoover. Gifford Pinchot (or rather his party) had decided against a challenge to The Great Engineer, but progressive dissatisfaction against him still festered. In 1928, conservatives—Watson, Mellon, et al.—had opposed his nomination.

Progressives seemed better disposed to him. True, two Progressive Republican senators, Wisconsin's John J. Blaine[25] and Nebraska's George W. Norris,[26] traversed the gossamer (if nonexistent) boundaries of their party loyalty to endorse Al Smith, but Idaho's William E. Borah, Oregon's Charles McNary, South Dakota's Peter Norbeck, and Iowa's Smith Wildman Brookhart stumped prodigiously for The Great Engineer.[27]

By 1932, they had all thoroughly sickened of the man, in part from his failure to carry through upon his promises to the farm block, in part from his greater failure to vanquish the Depression. In historical hindsight, Borah, the original "Lion of the Senate," was their logical standard bearer. But for all his white-maned bluster, Borah remained at heart a party man. Where a Hiram Johnson might bolt the party in 1916, a La Guardia[28] or a La Follette Sr. in 1924, or a Norris or a Blaine in 1928, Borah always faithfully remained aboard the Republican ship. With 1932 approaching, even with growing doubts about Hoover's loyalty to the "dry" cause festering in Borah's mind, he again refrained from either an outright bolt—or an outright challenge.

Pondering a challenge was, however, the blathering Father Charles Coughlin's ally, the veteran Canton, Pennsylvania, congressman Louis T. McFadden, until recently chairman of the House Banking Committee and, interestingly enough, survivor of 1928 and 1932 primary challenges from Gifford Pinchot's wife, Cornelia.[29] Hoover's December 1931 proposal to place German war debts on hold—his "moratorium"—finally pushed McFadden over the edge. Hoover, charged McFadden, had "sold out"[30] the country "and paid his debt to the German international bankers."[31]

Few Republicans dared to buck Hoover on the moratorium. Only four other GOP congressmen joined McFadden and ninety-five Democrats in opposition. Even such inveterate mavericks as East Harlem's Fiorello La Guardia supported Hoover. "If you don't grant this moratorium Hitler will be in power in Germany in two months," the partially Jewish "Little Flower" warned. "You don't want a Hohenzollern back in power there."[32]

Hoover's minions threatened retaliation versus McFadden. Postmaster General Walter F. Brown publicly cut off his patronage.[33] The "dry"[34] McFadden responded by entering the North Dakota primary.[35]

The volatile McFadden may have been principled—or, most likely, simply nuts—and rabidly anti-Semitic;[36] when he railed against "German international bankers," he really meant "Jewish international bankers." By mid-February, he had, however, mercifully dropped out of the presidential sweepstakes.[37] By this time, however, another progressive challenger had jumped in: former Maryland US senator Dr. Joseph I. France.

France, "wet,"[38] isolationist,[39] and wealthy,[40] was not crazy. He had never done anything particularly offensive as a member of the Senate, save, in 1922, to lose his seat after a single term. France, noted Frank R. Kent, "stands for every Progressive principle and policy [but] is entirely without Progressive support. They just do not seem to care for the good Doctor . . . And they are embarrassed and annoyed when his candidacy is mentioned."[41] Republican progressives may have been embarrassed not so much by him but by their own lack of courage and energy in opposing a one-time comrade who was now merely a huge millstone upon their principles, their party, and, not negligibly, their own chances for re-election.

The unknown France, bereft of meaningful backing, launched a series of primary challenges versus Hoover. He won North Dakota,[42] Nebraska,[43] West Virginia,[44] New Jersey,[45] and Oregon.[46] But his "victories" came with immense caveats. In North Dakota, he defeated not Hoover but the nearly seventy-eight-year-old Massillon, Ohio, mayor Jacob S. Coxey of 1894 "Coxey's Army" fame.[47] In West Virginia, he ran unopposed. In Oregon, Hoover was a mere write-in candidate. Beyond that France's triumphs yielded a mere four delegates,[48] being mere "beauty contests," that Hoover, controlling each state party convention, might easily avoid. Most embarrassing was France's solitary loss to Hoover: in Maryland, his home state.[49]

When not politicking, Hoover was governing—badly. Sick economies only sicken government balance sheets. Pressures rise for relief spending. Revenues vanish. Red ink is writ large. On May 31, 1932, Hoover uncharacteristically broke with tradition. Startling Senate members, he personally barged into their chamber to upbraid their lack of a budget and, in what the *New York Times*'s Arthur Krock termed "the monotone which is his oratorical vehicle,"[50] to demand that they forthwith slash expenditures and raise revenues.[51] His oration (if it might be called that) warned against the danger of hiking income tax rates to where they would yield "diminishing returns,"[52] but the resulting Revenue Act of 1932 skyrocketed the highest marginal rate from 25 to 55 percent and instituted new or increased excise taxes on just about everything—cars, gasoline, tobacco, long-distance telephone calls, telegrams (with newspapers exempt), radios, phonographs, jewelry, furs, refrigerators, cameras, sporting goods, candy, chewing gum, matches, soft drinks, firearms and ammunition, bank checks and safety-deposit boxes, stock transfers, wine-making and brewing materials (quite legal, though their products were often dubious), and movie and theater tickets. It raised first-class postage by 50 percent[53] and imposed a two-cent-per-gallon tax on mineral water.[54]

Supposedly free-trade House Democrats even tacked on entirely new tariffs on coal and oil.[55] About the only things missing from this bloated, destructive mess were a tax on gold dental work[56] and a national sales tax (supported for a while by Hoover; strenuously opposed by Fiorello La Guardia). America had not dodged either by much.[57] A fiscal replay of the train-wrecks Hoover had triggered with Hawley-Smoot and the Wickersham Commission, once again he accepted no personal blame. This jerry-built, log-rolling, counterproductive mess was, in his mind, Congress's pickle, not at all his. "He contented himself with saying that many of the taxes were not as he desired," wrote White House press secretary Ted Joslin of his boss, "and let it go at that." He let it go, and he signed it.

And the deficit only grew.

Joseph France won primaries. Hoover won delegates—and some reassuring news of public opinion. Unemployment breached the 20 percent mark[58] in February 1932, but the following month, *Pathfinder* magazine, a journal appealing largely to rural and small-town readers and which had successfully predicted 1928's results, released tallies from its current straw poll.

The results were, on their face, startling. Hoover led his nearest rival, Franklin Roosevelt, by a better than two-to-one margin. FDR carried no state outside the South but Arizona. Hoover took even New York two-to-one over the combined Roosevelt–Al Smith total.[59]

Die-hard Republicans took heart. *Pathfinder*, itself, pointed out that "If there is any faction popularly believed antagonistic to Hoover policies it is the agricultural element,"[60] thus auguring well for Hoover among the general populace. "One could take these figures and prove almost anything by them . . . . ," theorized upstate New York's *Amsterdam Recorder*, "but much will depend upon the progress of business in the next few months and on the outcome of the congressional action on taxation. Present behavior of the Democratic Insurgents in the capitol at Washington is helping the administration and materially boosting Mr. Hoover's stock. If this continues, the Republican candidate will have little difficulty next November."[61]

In actuality, in themselves, *Pathfinder*'s Hoover and Roosevelt numbers signified almost nothing. FDR had yet to win the hearts and minds of his party. But neither had anyone else. The darlings of the party's intellectual and financial smart sets—Baker, Young, Ritchie—attracted abysmally negligible support. Even FDR's most energetic rival, Al Smith, ran woefully behind FDR, behind the reluctant Texan John Nance Garner, and barely ahead of the Sooner State barbarian, "Alfalfa Bill" Murray.

And, speaking of runner-ups, the pitiful totals recorded for such supposedly strong Hoover challengers as Borah, Pinchot, Norris, La Follette Jr., former Vice President Dawes—even Calvin Coolidge—revealed their own fatal weakness.

But the most revealing number was this: add up *all* the numbers and Hoover wins not by a romp but by the slimmest of majorities. And what Roosevelt or Borah or Ritchie or Garner supporter was about to join the Hoover economic funeral cortege if his own candidate foundered?

None.

Factor in all the big city voters who had already in 1928 abandoned the GOP—and did not read *Pathfinder*—and factor in all those who could no longer afford a magazine subscription or a stamp to respond to a poll, and Herbert Hoover was in very deep trouble.

But sometimes majorities are not enough. Franklin Roosevelt required two-thirds of convention delegates to acquire nomination. If he failed to secure that number early enough, he might never secure it. Front-runners stumble, such as 1844's Lewis Cass; 1860's William H. Seward; 1876's James G. Blaine; 1916's Champ Clark; 1920's William Gibbs McAdoo, A. Mitchell Palmer, Gen. Leonard Wood, and Frank Lowden; or 1924's Smith and McAdoo. Dark horses emerge: not only hopeless losers like 1904's Alton B. Parker, 1920's James M. Cox, or 1924's John W. Davis, but future presidents like James Knox Polk, James A. Garfield, and Warren Harding. The same pattern might repeat in this year of crisis. Crises breed surprises.

Had Roosevelt enjoyed Smith's support, Frank Kent had noted that March, "he would be nominated by acclamation. Even with an inactive, neutral, uninterested Al, he probably would be named on an early ballot. But with an Al militantly determined that he shall not be named, actively asserting his power, leading the fight against him, why then he is sunk and a compromise candidate—Baker or Ritchie—will be inevitable."[62]

And Al Smith was just getting going.

❧

Organized to an extent that his opponents were not, FDR counted on Farley and Howe to round up enough delegates in state conventions to move him near the nomination in early ballots and to secure it soon enough thereafter. Primaries were also part-and-parcel of the Roosevelt strategy, not so much for the delegates they might deliver, but for the sense of momentum and inevitability they would create. Here, in the early going, Roosevelt had the field virtually to himself. Ritchie and Young and Baker were not about to compete, so "Alfalfa Bill" Murray materialized as FDR's competition—a marvelously welcome gift to the Roosevelt forces. FDR rolled over Murray in rural North Dakota[63] and Nebraska,[64] by a 9–1 margin in West Virginia,[65] by 3–1 in Oregon,[66] and 5–1 in Florida.[67] In Georgia, FDR crushed a Garner surrogate 8–1. He carried Warm Springs 218–1.[68] At Norfolk, Nebraska, "Alfalfa Bill" fulminated, "You Nebraska Democrats have a national committeeman named Arthur Mullen who brought $50,000 here from the east to buy convention delegations for Gov. Roosevelt. You can sell out if you want to, but you'll never elect him." But the charge was bunk. It wasn't easy money—but a chance for easy victory—that motivated delegates from New England to Oregon and back again to Nebraska.

Which was all well and good for FDR—save for Al Smith entering the race.

Smith, limitations notwithstanding, was the candidate best able to exploit Franklin Roosevelt's weaknesses in the Northeast and in urban areas. FDR might have his Farley and his Howe, but Smith retained strong ties with his former Tammany cohorts. They might have to walk a tricky balancing act between their old hero and a sitting governor, but they would not betray Smith. Quickly added to the Smith alliance were corrupt big city bosses Frank Hague of Jersey City (and of the entire New Jersey Democratic Party), Chicago mayor "Ten Percent Tony" Cermak, Albany's Edward J. O'Connell,[69] as well as powerful elements of the Catholic-dominated New England party. There, FDR drew first blood, easily besting Smith in March 6's snow-blanketed New Hampshire primary, taking 61.7 percent of the vote and capturing all eight delegates.[70]

The ease of their New Hampshire triumph, plus additional victories in Wisconsin[71] and Maine,[72] emboldened the FDR camp—emboldened them too much. Louis Howe privately derided the Smith campaign as "largely a fake movement."[73] Jim Farley dared predict a first-ballot victory.[74]

But first—or rather, next, was Massachusetts.

Massachusetts was Smith country, heavily Catholic, and dominated by his supporters. Jesse Straus's poll had revealed immense rank-and-file Smith support within the commonwealth.[75] The party's dominant wing, primarily Bay State governor Joseph B. Ely,[76] US senator David I. Walsh,[77] and former Boston mayor John F. "Honey Fitz" Fitzgerald,[78] all retained substantial, even fanatical, loyalty to The Happy Warrior.

The best FDR might toss into the Massachusetts fray was his son James,[79] now engaged at Boston in the insurance trade—and that city's mayor, one James Michael Curley.[80]

. . . and the slightly more distinguished Col. Edward M. House.

The Texas-born House had earned his fame as Woodrow Wilson's brilliant but shadowy *éminence grise*—and Franklin Roosevelt—and Roosevelt's family[81]—had been on his radar screen for a very long time. When Louis Wehle (Louis Brandeis's nephew) had first concocted the idea of a Hoover-FDR ticket, it was to Colonel House that Wehle first consulted. "It is a wonderful idea," exulted the diminutive House, "and the only chance the Democrats have in November."[82] As FDR's post-1920 march to the White House continued, he courted House, and the colonel courted him. FDR required House's blessings to validate his Wilson Administration credentials. House needed to hitch his eclipsed wagon to another perhaps greater, rising star.

And so House advised FDR and Howe[83] on campaign management, busied himself in subtly knifing potential FDR opponents, most egregiously in the case of that most favored ex-Wilsonite, Newton D. Baker,[84] and most directly by attempting to corral a most reluctant Massachusetts Democratic Party into the growing FDR fold. On June 4, House's Beverly, Massachusetts, summer estate "Magnolia" hosted a star-studded luncheon in Franklin's honor.

House's guests: Senators Walsh and Marcus Coolidge, *Boston Evening Transcript* publisher Robert M. Washburn, *Boston Post* political editor Robert L. Norton, *Atlantic Monthly* editor Ellery Sedgwick (Ernst Franz Sedgwick "Putzi" Hanfstaengl's Groton- and Harvard-educated maternal relation), railroad attorney William H. Coolidge, House's own son-in-law, Randolph Tucker, and FDR's own Hyde Park associate Henry Morgenthau Jr.[85]

The purpose: in House's words, "to discourage Smith and his followers and to show how hopeless it was to oppose our man."[86]

Missing was Governor Ely, speechifying across the state at Williamstown.[87] Added late to the list was Boston's Mayor Curley.[88] Smith was not yet in the race, and those present seemed, if not enthusiastic about, at least, resigned, to a Roosevelt candidacy.

The event went along as well as might be expected, save for the presence of Mayor Curley, the bitter and buffoonish adversary of Ely (Curley had vehemently opposed him in 1930[89]), Walsh, and "Honey Fitz" Fitzgerald (Curley had blackmailed him out of the 1914 mayor's race[90]).[91] Until recently Curley (like fellow mayors Hague, Walker, and Cermak[92]) had been plumping for Owen D. Young.[93] But though he was buffoonish—and an actual jailbird[94]—he was also savvy enough to discern that the Young ship might never sail and that the USS Roosevelt boasted sixteen-inch guns. It was time to enlist.

And so he did.

His Honor arrived with an entourage of his own, a squadron of local reporters, and even a Movietone newsreel crew. "We have been making history here today," the tall, handsome Curley piously intoned. "Franklin Delano Roosevelt is the hope of the nation. His splendid administration of the affairs of the Empire State makes him outstanding as the man to nominate for the Presidency."[95]

Franklin smiled broadly[96] at Curley's words—but then again, his reassuring grin often masked his real feelings. He was not so much a silent sphinx but a grinning sphinx.[97] In Beverly, however, Roosevelt might have better kept his smiles to himself. Curley was a self-propelled incendiary device, about to be hurled into the FDR campaign. If anything could stampede the bulk of the Massachusetts Democrat Party into Smith's camp, it was the grand entrance of James Michael Curley into FDR's.

All of which translated into the wisdom of a discreet FDR absence from Massachusetts's April 26 primary.

Friends warned him to stay out. His Harvard classmate H. LaRue Brown of the Jeffersonian Society had said so.[98] New Hampshire Democrat Robert H. Jackson, the architect of his narrowly won Maine convention triumph, similarly advised him.[99] A Massachusetts backer, Patricia Van Dorn, tersely warned: "We strongly advise against any entry in primary there. It would be political suicide to oppose Smith there. New Hampshire and Vermont will be carried by you and would minimize Massachusetts outcome, and furthermore escape bitter conflict and leave no scars. Curley could not carry Boston by a sufficient margin to offset [the] upstate vote."[100]

FDR digested her warning then merely scribbled, "Please prepare a soft answer for the lady."[101]

He would contest Smith in Massachusetts.

Unmitigated disaster followed. Not only could Curley not sway western Massachusetts voters, his apostasy in betraying Smith infuriated Boston Catholic voters. The Ancient Order of Hibernians passed a resolution condemning him.[102] On St. Patrick's Day, a barrage of snowballs—not cheers—greeted his and James Roosevelt's parade appearance.[103]

Smith defeated FDR 3–1 in the Bay State, capturing all thirty-six delegates, sweeping all thirty-nine of its cities, and every congressional district.[104]

The floodgates had opened. The unstoppable Mr. Roosevelt had been stopped, not just in Massachusetts, but suddenly, seemingly, everywhere. At May 2's Rhode Island state convention, Smith captured all ten delegates[105]—and, for good measure, an FDR-backed resolution flopped by a whopping 172–23 margin.[106] Connecticut FDR backers predicted that their candidate would win as many as twelve of the state's sixteen delegates. He secured none.[107]

But, all that was New England, and might be alibied as such. Worse news arrived from Pennsylvania, where the Smith effort was disorganized at best and where former national committeeman Joe Guffey forecast FDR snaring sixty-six of seventy-six delegates.[108] Instead, Smith, running well in "wet" urban areas, held FDR to a mere forty-four delegates.[109] "It was not, in fact" Rexford Tugwell ruefully admitted, "an impressive win."[110] At the White House, Hoover crowed to Ted Joslin that FDR's Massachusetts and Pennsylvania setbacks spelled his "elimination."[111]

But unimpressive wins were, nonetheless, preferable to any sort of loss, and FDR was not done with either. At Trenton, Frank Hague delivered New Jersey's thirty-six delegates to Smith.[112] At Houston on the same day, Texas Democrats boisterously instructed their forty-six delegates to vote for John Nance Garner "and none other" until "released by him."[113] Graver still, at Albany, a Tammany-dominated convention designated all ninety-four delegates as "uncommitted," pushed through a resolution demanding outright repeal of Prohibition—and designated Al Smith and John W. Davis (now privately convinced that "If that man [FDR] is elected he will ruin the United States"[114]) as delegates-at-large.[115]

"Everything is lovely," chirped FDR of events in Albany, "Everything is harmonious. The wet resolution is in complete accord with my views."[116] But then he said nothing further, for not all was right at all.

"Massachusetts and Pennsylvania show that [Roosevelt] still has a heavy fight on his hands," observed H. L. Mencken, "and we may have every confidence that fight will be carried on in berserker and suicidal fashion. No one, in fact, really likes Roosevelt, not even his own ostensible friends, and no one quite trusts him. He is a pleasant enough fellow, but he has no more visible conscience than his eminent kinsman, Theodore Dentatus. His chief strength at this moment does not lie among people of his own place and kind, but among the half-witted yokels of the cow and cotton States, and these hinds prefer him, not because they have any real confidence in him, but simply because they believe they can split New York, and so beat Al Smith and the Pope. That beating Al and the Pope will also, in all probability, involve losing New York altogether, and maybe most of the other essential Northern States with it—that fact since they are Democrats, does not concern them for an instant."[117]

Still, FDR continued to pick up delegates in uncontested venues. Such support, while crucial, nonetheless, failed to counteract the growing impression that if the wheels had not quite fallen off the Roosevelt victory train, they were, at the very least, dangerously wobbly.

. . . which made California's forty-four delegates even more significant.

Roosevelt's forces initially oozed optimism regarding their candidate's chances. "I am convinced we won't even have a contest," said the pro-FDR chairman of the state executive committee, San Franciscan Justus S. Wardell, "but if we do, the result will be so overwhelmingly in our favor it will indicate most impressively what the sentiment is among the Democrats of the state."[118]

Yet, trouble percolated on any number of fronts. William Randolph Hearst retained a huge amount of influence in his native state (he controlled five big city papers boasting 42.6 percent of the state's daily circulation and 56 percent of its Sunday circulation[119]) and was now about to employ it in favor of his newest pet project, John Nance Garner. Soon, William Gibbs McAdoo, now running for US Senate in the state, was also endorsing Garner, denouncing both Smith and FDR as "Tammany candidates from New York."[120] Completing the local Garner coalition was the hundred-thousand-member Texas State Society of California,[121] overwhelmingly for their bushy-browed compatriot.

And, here, FDR's longtime prevarication on the Prohibition issue finally caught up to him. A year before, it aided him immeasurably in shoring up "dry" southern support. But now, caught between the "dry" McAdoo-Garner forces and their "wet" Smith counterparts, FDR possessed precious little to offer. "If you are Wet, vote for Smith," jeered one Smith pamphlet, "If you are Dry, vote for Garner,—If you don't know what you are, Vote for Roosevelt."[122]

Most people knew where they stood.

Louis Howe first pooh-poohed FDR's Massachusetts fiasco;[123] now he characterized the situation in California as "chaotic"[124] and proposed divvying up Golden State delegates.[125] Again, however, the Roosevelt camp suffered from bad intelligence on the ground. Their Southern California chief, the state's national committeeman Isidore B. Dockweiler (a "wet" and a longtime McAdoo foe[126]), advised that the "Roosevelt delegation will win,"[127] and talk of compromise vanished.

Roosevelt carried thirty-five of the state's fifty-eight counties, but ran abysmally in the Hearst-dominated cities. Smith won San Francisco. Garner carried Los Angeles (headquarters of the Texas Society), nearly tripling FDR's vote. Garner sailed to victory with 41.3 percent of the vote to 32.5 percent for Roosevelt and 26.3 percent for Smith.[128]

The result, said McAdoo, had dealt a "perhaps irreparable blow"[129] to FDR.

It was not a good day at all for the Roosevelt forces.

CHAPTER ELEVEN

"Dear old man . . . you must step aside"

HERBERT HOOVER THOUGHT HINDENBURG WOULD BEAT HITLER.

At least, that is what he was told when he received the Kaiser's one-time foreign minister Dr. Richard von Kühlmann at the White House in February 1932. In their "pleasant chat," Kuhlmann informed The Great Engineer that the DNVP's Theodor Duesterberg and the KPD's Ernst Thälmann counted for little, the race was between the field marshal and the corporal. "It will be an exciting election," Kühlmann told the press afterward, "and may be very close."[1]

Hoover had already received word of an extraordinary secret American outreach to Hitler. On Saturday afternoon, December 5, 1931, Ambassador and Mrs. Frederic Sackett chatted at the home of *Deutsche Bank*'s pro-Nazi Emil Georg von Strauss. As if by coincidence, though that was hardly the case (Hjalmar Schacht had, in fact, arranged everything), four more visitors arrived—Putzi Hanfstaengl, Hermann Göring, Rudolf Hess, and an individual introducing himself as merely "Herr Wolff"—in reality, of course, Hitler himself, who, as was his habit, engaged more in endless harangue than polite hello. Sackett tendered "Herr Wolff" points for "intensity and forthrightness," but otherwise found him to be a "fanatical crusader . . . certainly not the type from which statesmen evolve." Should these National Socialists by some wild chance assume power, Sackett informed Secretary of State Stimson, Germany would find itself "on the rocks."[2]

Kühlmann and Sackett's calculations made great sense. The absurdity of a great nation turning to a former nobody from nowhere like Hitler aside, Hindenburg simply had the numbers on his side. His former opponents, the Zentrum and the SPD, backed him. And, despite what Hugenberg's DNVP and Franz Seldte's Stahlhelm might desire, many of their organization's members might logically still turn to the hero of Tannenberg.

Still, all the energy—all the momentum—lay on Hitler's side. Party membership rolls had continued their dizzying growth, skyrocketing from 293,000 in September 1930, to 398,000 at year's end to 862,000 in December 1931 and then again to 920,000 in just another month.[3] The rush of newcomers was so huge—and on one level so unwelcome—that Joseph Goebbels nastily derided them as "Septemberlings."[4] Hundreds of trained NSDAP speakers invaded city and countryside. Money—from wherever, whether newfound funds from craven industrialists or the party's normal income from dues and public events—seemed available for the fight, even while the Hindenburg-Brüning camp struggled for funding and even had to rely on one million marks drawn upon a secret Reichswehr account.[5] And though Hindenburg might possess Socialist and Catholic votes, he did not possess their hearts. Hitler *owned* the hearts of his supporters.

And, of course, it was an advantage to not be governing in 1932—nor to have ever comprised even the smallest portion of this forlorn and despised republic's star-crossed governing history. "National Socialism," Gregor Strasser would soon boast, "is the opposite of what there is today."[6] Today was not very good in Germany—or just about anywhere else—in 1932.

Less than a week after Goebbels had unofficially proclaimed his Führer's candidacy, Hitler formally jumped into the race.[7] Addressing twenty-five thousand rapturous Nazis, from that same Sportpalast podium, Hitler jeered at his opponents, "I know your slogan. You say, we will stay [in office] at any cost. And I tell you: We will overthrow you in any case!"[8] To Prussia's SPD interior minister Albert Grzesinski who had only recently vowed to drive him from the country with a dog whip,[9] he countered, "Go ahead and threaten me with the dog whip. We shall see whether at the end of the struggle the whip is still in your hands." And he challenged not merely Grzesinski but also Hindenburg: "Dear old man, . . . With our deep regret, therefore, you must step aside, for they want to fight us and we want to fight them."[10]

The crowd exploded at his challenge, and among those swept up in the frenzy was a thirty-one-year-old actress hearing Hitler speak for the first time: Leni Riefenstahl. Devouring *Mein Kampf* while working on her latest film, *Das Blaue Licht* (*The Blue Light*), she found it "made a tremendous impression on me. I became a confirmed National Socialist after reading the first page."[11]

Assistant cinematographer Heinz von Jaworsky recalled that she was "fascinated" by Hitler's masterwork and "tried to convince me that it was a beautiful book. I laughed and we got into an argument. Then she said, 'You'll see. They are right.'"[12] To *Das Blaue Licht*'s co-producer Harry Sokal— a Romanian-born Jew—she insisted, "Harry, you must read this book. This is the coming man."[13] To the dubious von Jaworsky, she vowed: "I'll work for them"[14]—the Nazis.

Yet, *Mein Kampf* could never prepare her for the Sportpalast—the crowds, the bands, the fluttering black-white-red sea of swastikas, and, yes, the man Hitler himself. "I had an almost apocalyptic vision that I was never able to forget," she confessed decades later. "It seemed as if the earth's surface were spreading out in front of me, like a hemisphere that suddenly splits apart in the middle, spewing out an enormous jet of water, so powerful that it touched the sky and shook the earth. I felt quite paralyzed."[15] She stayed paralyzed, dazed and confused, freezing to the bone on Potsdamer Strasse, unable even to unscramble her thoughts—and her emotions—enough to summon a cab to take her home.[16] "I was infected," she admitted, proudly then, not so proudly later, "no doubt about it."[17]

❧

Heinrich Brüning was not paralyzed. He would fight back. He had to because Hindenburg himself was neither able—nor willing—to take the fight to Hitler. The Old Gentleman could have been forty-eight rather than eighty-four, and it would have been the same. Political campaigning was simply beneath him. Hindenburg would consent to only two appearances even remotely capable of being judged campaign events. At Moabit, in early March, with sound newsreel cameras rolling, the ancient, 6'5" field marshal reviewed ten companies of the Reichswehr's Berlin Guard Regiment.[18] The *New York Times* found him to be "a veritable mountain of a man whose black and gold spiked helmet towered a full head above even the tall and slimmer figures of his grey-green clad staff, his keen old eyes losing no details."[19] Within the week, he broadcast over the radio from his study. "I cannot believe that Germany is to be plunged into domestic feuds and civil war," he informed voters. "I recall to you the spirit of 1914 and the frontline attitude which was concerned with the man and not with his social status or party. . . . I will not give up the hope that Germany will come together again in new unity."[20]

Brüning took up the slack, rushing about Germany—from Berlin to Breslau to Köln to Düsseldorf to Dortmund to Breslau to Weimar—in the latter city he spoke in a hall so freezing he orated in his overcoat.[21] Nazis attempted to disrupt his campaign appearances, even loosing white mice in the halls to frighten women voters.[22] Hindenburg campaign aircraft showered Berlin with anti-Hitler leaflets, at one point dropping them directly into a Nazi rally in the Lustgarten. "A vote for Hitler means voting for hatred, inexperience, nepotism and ruin for the German people," their message read. "Vote for Hindenburg and you vote for wisdom, tradition, impartiality, responsibility, union, right, freedom and preservation and a new rise of the Reich and the people."[23]

Yet, when the conservative *Münchener Illustrierte Presse* printed Hindenburg's portrait, readers denounced its editor for featuring the "vicious traitor Hindenburg."[24] Berlin's similarly conservative *Deutsche Zeitung* proclaimed, "The present issue is whether the international traitors and pacifist swine, with the help of Hindenburg, are to bring about the ruin of Germany."[25] Rumors flew that the Reichspräsident's son (and confidant) Major Oskar von Hindenburg, as well as his state secretary, Dr. Otto Meissner, had become Social Democrats.[26] Even wilder rumors accused Oskar of converting to Catholicism[27]—and still more improbably that The Old Gentleman's two middle-aged daughters had joined the Socialist Students League.[28] Worse, money ran dangerously low in the Hindenburg camp; his slapdash campaign even still owed printers five million marks from his 1925 effort.[29]

Hindenburg had always ostentatiously pledged his fealty to the Hohenzollerns. Now, even they turned upon him. "He betrayed my father," Kronprinz Wilhelm curtly complained to Brüning, "and he betrayed Ludendorff. When the time comes he will betray you too."[30] The presumptive heir to Germany's vacant throne supported Duesterberg, not Hindenburg.

Hitler opposed both—as well as two others who achieved the twenty-five thousand signature ballot threshold, the KPD's Ernst Thälmann (official occupation: "transport worker") and attorney Gustav Winter of the People's Revalorization League. Winter, an outright con man, campaigned even less than Hindenburg, inconveniently jailed as he was on fraud charges.[31] Thälmann, however, committed the greater fraud, professing there to be no difference whatsoever between Hitler and the SPD-backed Hindenburg. The SPD, of course, thought otherwise. "Every vote against Hindenburg is a vote for Hitler," warned the SPD Berlin newspaper *Vorwärts*. "Every vote snatched away from Thälmann . . . and given to Hindenburg is a blow against Hitler."[32]

Gustav Winter campaigned not at all. Hindenburg campaigned by proxy. Hitler campaigned like a demon—from Hamburg to Stettin to Breslau to Leipzig to Bad Blankenburg to Weimar and Frankfurt (on the same day) to Nürnberg to Stuttgart and on to Köln and Dortmund and Godesberg and Hanover.[33] His *Völkischer Beobachter* claimed he addressed a half million people in just eleven days.[34] The Nazi journalist Heinz Heinz would boast (and with only some inaccuracy):

> *Hitler's activities were such as political life in Germany or elsewhere has never before witnessed. To address three or four meetings a day was*

nothing to him. Most of these were held in the open air, when he might have an audience of anything from one hundred thousand to three hundred thousand men. Everything had to be arranged and brought off strictly to time if his terrific programme, daily, was to be carried out.[35]

Heinz might embellish the crowd numbers (Nazis almost always did) but he did not exaggerate the incredible power of Hitler's whirlwind campaign. Nazis staged three thousand meetings. They distributed eight million pamphlets.[36] Their Führer might keep them waiting for hours, but, still, vast crowds remained to hear him. He scored with references to unemployment ("Things have come to such a pass that two workingmen must feed one unemployed"[37]) and Germany's weakness, and, as always, touted his own rise from the depths ("a man who comes of the nameless mass of the people"[38]). His personal miracle resonated with desperate voters. "What has this man achieved from nothing . . .?" the Hamburg schoolteacher Luise Solmitz marveled in her diaries. "He is able to catch hold of the poorest and most miserable for the national ideal, who may have never followed this course—except in war. May Hitler's way be blessed. At least he brings us hope of a new dawn."[39]

The Hindenburg camp exhorted voters that their own candidate "hath kept faith with you; be ye faithful unto him."[40]

"Honor Hindenburg," NSDAP posters countered. "Vote for Hitler."[41]

More disturbing blows rained down upon Der Führer. In early March, fifteen thousand Duesterberg supporters (Crown Prince Wilhelm among them) rallied at the Sportpalast. The meeting's chairman, the former Freikorps leader Major Franz von Stephani, mocked Hitler as "foreign to Nordic Prussian feeling."

"Adolf Hitler's face is Roman," sneered the arch-Prussian Stephani, "and his dogma of infallibility is Roman. He is a weakling."[42]

The potshots were many. Germany had not yet been silenced. In late February, Hamburg's SPD paper, *Echo der Woche*, had impugned his war record. Hitler sued—and surprisingly won—though largely due to the paper's refusal to reveal its source.[43]

Summoned to another hearing at Weimar in mid-March, he and Wilhelm Frick defended his recent naturalization. Infuriated, trembling in anger, he stormed from the courtroom.[44] As he, Frick, and Goebbels sped back to Munich, a projectile shattered a window of one of their train's third-class coaches. It might have been a shot. It might have been a mere stone.[45] Goebbels, as usual, made the most of it. "On the way revolver shots are fired at the express," he boasted in his diary. "No harm ensues."[46]

He increasingly counted upon street violence from his SA goons. "Berlin was in a state of civil war," recorded the British-expatriate novelist Christopher Isherwood, then subsisting as a private tutor. "Hate exploded suddenly, without warning, out of nowhere; at street corners, in restaurants, cinemas, dance halls, swimming baths; at midnight, after breakfast, in the middle of the afternoon. Knives were whipped out, blows were dealt with spiked rings, beer mugs, chair legs or leaded clubs; bullets slashed the advertisements on the poster columns, rebounded from the iron roofs of latrines. In the middle of a crowded street a young man would be attacked, stripped, thrashed and left bleeding on the pavement; in fifteen seconds it was all over and the assailants had disappeared. . . . The newspapers were full of death-bed photographs of rival martyrs, Nazi, Reichsbanner and Communist. My pupils looked at them and shook their heads, apologizing to me for the state of Germany. 'Dear, dear!' they said, 'it's terrible. It can't go on.'"[47]

It did, growing worse each day. Suddenly, the press peered beyond the violence and into more personal aspects of the SA leadership. On March 7, the left-wing *Welt am Montag* published three incriminating letters that SA chief Ernst Röhm had addressed from Bolivia to former Freikorps member Dr. Karl-Günther Heimsoth in Berlin regarding his own "peculiarities"[48] and the dreadful loneliness to be endured in La Paz "where they know nothing of this sort of love."[49] The battle-scarred warrior Röhm was, in fact, far less manly than he first appeared, being since at least 1924[50] an active homosexual. Two days later, the *Münchener Post* reprinted his incriminating correspondence,[51] causing the KPD's *Die Rote Fahne* to chortle: "The Hitlerian party is a nest of informants and spies, of intrigues between the leaders and the most horrible corruption."[52] The furor sparked Walter Buch (head of the party's secret disciplinary "Investigation and Adjustment Committee"—as well as Martin Bormann's father-in-law) to issue stillborn orders to assassinate Röhm and his staff.[53]

All of which dropped the issue clearly into presidential candidate Adolf Hitler's uncomfortable lap. When his personal attorney, the young former Munich Freikorps member Hans Frank, brought the matter to his attention, he exclaimed, "Such a horrible mess! It's not human, it's bestial, worse, even animals would not do such a thing." He inquired if pedophilia was involved. Frank said no. "That would be utterly intolerable," Hitler responded, suddenly much calmer. "As long as it is between grown men—what Röhm does. Children are not his victims. . . . Well, then we can at least consider whether to keep him or not, but God help him if he abuses young boys! Then he must go."[54]

He did indeed engage in such abuse—even once admitting that his sexuality "often had to do with young boys in that direction."[55] Worse, he involved the party in it, engaging one of his lovers, the twentyish Peter Granninger, on the SA intelligence unit's payroll at two hundred marks per month to procure them—but not before he tested them out for himself before passing them on to Röhm. Eleven of their victims came from a single Munich school, the Gisela High School.[56] Yet, Hitler launched no move against Röhm, who, in fact, fit neatly into his SA, the organization's top leadership being riddled with homosexuality—including the aforementioned political murderer/Reichstag deputy Edmund Heines,[57] Berlin SA supreme leader Karl Ernst (a bisexual),[58] Count Wolf von Helldorf,[59] and the fair-haired, fast-rising young Breslau group leader Hans Walter Schmidt. Lust was hardly their only vice. "Fraulein Schmidt" once drunkenly shot a waiter in a restaurant and sneered, "You'd better put the waiter on the bill."[60]

Nor, should Hitler by *any* means have evinced such wide-eyed surprise concerning his old comrade. Röhm, after all, had been among his earliest mentors, their relationship stretching back even before Hitler even knew of the infant Nazis. Röhm retained an informality with Hitler that no other party member might still boast of—the ability to address him with the familiar "du."[61] Otto Wagener, Röhm's predecessor as SA commander, had, in fact, warned Hitler of Röhm's proclivities. Hitler reported back to Wagener with Röhm's assurances that such activity was a thing of the past.[62] In June 1931, anti-Röhm Berlin SA leader Paul Schulz (Gregor Strasser's closest ally[63]) wrote directly to Hitler warning of "the dangers . . . necessarily entailed . . . by the employment of morally objectionable persons in positions of authority. . . . Captain Röhm makes absolutely no secret of his disposition; on the contrary, he prides himself on his aversion to the female sex and proclaims it in public."[64] Yes, Hitler's outrage was all for show for Hans Frank. As Hitler's early benefactor the international adventurer (and blackmailer) Kurt Lüdecke would state point-blank: "Hitler had long known of the existence of [the Röhm-Heimsoth] correspondence."[65]

Beyond that, Hitler counted any number of suspected (and actual) homosexuals and bisexuals among his inner circles ("a lot of wavy-haired bugger-boys,"[66] thought Dorothy Thompson), including Kurt Lüdecke himself,[67] as well as Rudolf Hess (aka "Fraulein Anna")[68], Hitler Youth leader Baldur von Schirach (Heinrich Hoffmann's son-in-law),[69] the bespectacled pretty-boy NSDAP business manager Philipp Bouhler,[70] his adjutant Wilhelm Brückner[71] and his bodyguards Ulrich Graf and Christian Weber,[72] economist Walther Funk,[73] and, yes, even his attorney—Hans Frank.[74]

If Hitler's reaction was a mystery, more so were other questions concerning Röhm's embarrassing missives to Heimsoth. Heimsoth had departed the

Nazi Party in 1930 to join Otto Strasser's Black Front. They soon quarreled, and Otto gleefully tipped off Berlin prosecutors to the Röhm-Heimsoth relationship. In July 1931, authorities raided Heimsoth's home and seized the incriminating documents.[75] Their text, however, was not explicit enough to trigger convictions under Paragraph 175 of the German Criminal Code ("Unnatural fornication, whether between persons of the male sex or of humans with beasts, is to be punished by imprisonment; a sentence of loss of civil rights may also be passed"), but was sufficient to cause more than enough mischief. Prussian prime minister Otto Braun transmitted photostatic copies to Heinrich Brüning (who did nothing with them),[76] while the head of Prussia's political police Rudolf Diels passed the documents onto SPD journalist (and former Nazi) Helmuth Klotz. It required Diels's persistent hectoring to finally convince Klotz to indeed print them.

Here, we tread yet deeper into the bizarre world of National Socialist intra-party intrigue. Diels (possessor, in the words of one future lover, of the "the most sinister, scar-torn face I have ever seen"[77]) was even less what he seemed to be than our usual run of double-dealing characters. Though he claimed membership in the fast-expiring German State Party,[78] he was, in reality, a secret National Socialist and, for good measure, an SA man who would later boast of collecting dirt on Röhm upon Hitler's direct orders.[79]

Hitler possessed worries, not just about homosexual storm troopers or even about winning a presidential election. In early March, he breakfasted with Hamburg Gauleiter Albert Krebs and revealed that his recent conversion to a vegetarian diet had little to do with concern for animals, and everything to do with his recurrent stomach cramps and his fear of cancer—and an early death. "I have no time to wait!" he exclaimed. "If I had time, I would never have run for the presidency at all. The old man won't last much longer anyway. But I can't lose a single year more. I must come to power soon to be able to finish the gigantic tasks in the time left to me. I must! I must!"[80]

In the midst of all this hypochondria, street-fighting, mud-slinging, and ideological confusion, at one point, everything came to a quiet, dignified, unified—but highly fleeting—halt. The date was Sunday, March 6, and, on that day, the Reichstag paused . . . to honor George Washington.

It was, of course, the bicentennial of Washington's birth, though why the Reichstag tarried for nearly two full weeks following the actual anniversary of his nativity seriously belied any concept of German efficiency. Delegates festooned their packed chamber with evergreens and American flags, enthroned a bust of Washington where their presiding officer usually stood, and heard Reichskanzler Brüning and US Ambassador Sackett expound upon America's first chief executive's very real virtues. Few, however, escaped the suspicion that Brüning was in actuality alluding to Reichspräsident Hindenburg when he spoke "on what, for a nation in distress, is finally decisive, the greatness of its chief leader." National Socialists most likely harbored visions of another "chief leader." When Brüning concluded, in Berlin, in 1932, all stood—Nazi and Communist and Catholic and Social Democrat and Nationalist alike—to hear a band play "The Star-Spangled Banner."[81]

Hindenburg pledged to bring unity to the nation—though his own coalition may have been the most fractious and, indeed, incoherent in history. Hitler, of course, pledged a very different sort of cohesion, that of the jackboot and truncheon. This day in the Reichstag was, however, not only the campaign's most harmonious moment, as transitory and meaningless as that might be, it was very likely the most unified in Weimar's unhappy tenure.

Which meant that on Sunday, March 13, 1932, a very disjointed nation marched to the polls.[82] Its practice of strange politics and stranger bedfellows was still in force, with one unnamed Nazi leader revealing that, "Our tactics are to induce the workers to stay at home or to vote Communist, thus cutting down the Socialist vote [for Hindenburg]."[83]

National Socialists hoped for the best. Hitler himself apprised foreign journalists that he and Hindenburg would each gather roughly twelve million votes. Heinrich Himmler confidently issued orders limiting alcohol consumption at scheduled SS victory parties.[84] That February, Goebbels, ever the fanatic, assured the American diplomat John Wiley of Hitler's inevitable triumph. "He was obviously hypnotized by his own logic," Wiley wired Washington. "In the first of the forthcoming presidential elections he has estimated that the Nazi candidate will receive 13,500,000 votes. . . . Hindenburg would get 10,000,000; Thälmann, . . . 7,000,000; Hugenberg or the Nationalist candidate 2,500,000; and the Stahlhelm candidate, if any, 500,000 votes. In the second election the Nationalist Opposition together (this presupposes that Hugenberg and the Stahlhelm will bow before the inevitable and support unconditionally the Nazi candidate . . .) 18,000,000 votes; Hindenburg 10,000,000; Thälmann 6,000,000. I have frequently seen bright-eyed people figure out with pencil and paper that a certain horse must win. I have somewhat the same feeling with regard to Dr. Goebbels' estimated calculation. In other words, I am not yet ready to bet on Hitler or against Hindenburg!"[85]

In *Der Angriff*, as the election drew near Goebbels exhorted every National Socialist on to victory:

In the desperate misery of the postwar years a new political faith has come to life. It is founded on a glowing, dedicated idealism. . . . This is the work of Adolf Hitler! In him the masses see their last hope, and to millions his name has become the shining symbol of Germany's will to freedom. . . . Those who wish that everything remain as it is in Germany simply yield to despair. We can't blame them for giving their vote to the representative of the existing system. We, however, want to see everything changed in Germany. Those who do not want class struggle and fratricide, those who are looking for a way out of the errors and the confusion of our time cast their vote for Adolf Hitler. He embodies the awakening young German idealism, he is the spokesman of national activism, he is the exponent of a dawning social and economic revival. Therefore we call on you: Give power to Adolf Hitler so that the German people will once more secure the right to live. For freedom and bread![86]

"Tomorrow," Goebbels's paper headlined, "Hitler will be elected President of the Reich."[87]

The atmosphere proved tense—for Nazis and for the authorities. "Newspapers have been forbidden to post election returns in their windows . . . or to project them on [outdoor] lantern screens," noted the *New York Post*'s "Red" Knickerbocker. "Citizens have been urged to sit in the safety of their homes and listen to the election returns over the radio."[88]

But Nazi dreams were not to be. In his diary, Goebbels wrote:

Everyone confident of the victory. I remain skeptical. Large party in the evening at home. Everybody who has got any legs to come on, young and old, seems to have turned up.

We listen to the results of the election on the wireless. News comes slowly trickling through. Things look queer for us. At about ten o'clock the situation receives a general summing up. We are beaten; awful outlook for the future! We have not so much miscalculated our own votes as underrated those of our opponents. They only lack 100,000 votes to have secured an absolute majority. The Communists have failed completely. We have gained 86 per cent since September, 1930; but that is no consolation. . . .[89]

Goebbels, for once, spoke an unvarnished truth. National Socialists had badly underestimated Hindenburg's strength. The KPD had flopped horribly. The totals told the story[90]:

Candidate	Party	*Votes*	*Percent*
Paul von Hindenburg	Independent	18,651,497	49.6
Adolf Hitler	National Socialists	11,339,446	30.1
Ernst Thälmann	Communists	4,938,341	13.2
Theodor Duesterberg	Stahlhelm-DNVP	2,557,729	6.8
Gustav Winter	People's Revalorization League	116,304	0.3
Total		37,603,317	100
Registered voters / percentage of turnout		43,949,681	85.6

The Brown tide of 1930 and in the state elections that followed finally halted upon a rock called Hindenburg—and as long as he lived there seemed no way around him. The Old Gentleman had missed formal re-election but only by the merest eyelash. A second Hitler campaign risked absolute humiliation.

"The Party," Goebbels confessed, "is deeply depressed and discouraged."[91] As was Hitler. Putzi Hanfstaengl thought his leader "the image of a disappointed, discouraged gambler who had wagered beyond his means."[92] From the ranks of the opposition, Otto Strasser's Black Front chortled, "The Grand Army is annihilated. His Majesty the Emperor is in good health."[93]

"Only a bold stroke can retrieve matters," Goebbels posited, and Hitler soon provided it. He had never been short of recuperative—if often delusional—powers. Strike him blind—and his sight is restored. Imprison him for treason—and he fortifies his grasp on a movement he has led to disaster. In seemingly hopeless despair for his beloved dead niece, he lifts his head and vows, "Now let the struggle begin. . . ."[94]

The Great Procrastinator had in this crisis wavered not an instant. Delay and indecision might doom him, reinforcing the portrait of the immense defeat just endured. "Phone to the Leader late at night," noted Goebbels. "He is entirely composed and is not at all upset. I never expected anything else of him. We had set ourselves too difficult a task; nevertheless it was all to the good to have been through this experience."[95]

"We must resume attack immediately and most ruthlessly," Hitler announced to the party and to the nation, stunning both with his boldness. "The National Socialist, recognizing his foe, does not relent till his victory is complete. I command you to begin this instant the fight for the second election! I know that you, my comrades, have accomplished superhuman tasks during the past weeks. Only to-day, there can be no pause for reflection. Previous sacrifices only serve to prove further necessity for battle. The work shall and must be increased, if necessary redoubled. Already this evening, orders are being issued to our organizations for the continuation and rein-forcement of the struggle. The first election campaign is over, the second has begun to-day. I shall lead it!"[96]

CHAPTER TWELVE

"The nomination of this man Hoover is invalid"

PAUL VON HINDENBURG WAS A HAIR SHORT OF A BARE MAJORITY.

Franklin Roosevelt was stuck short of the necessary two-thirds majority. Republicans were stuck with Herbert Hoover.

"The Republican national convention," wrote sportswriter turned political columnist Westbrook Pegler, "called to re-nominate Mr. Hoover . . . seems to have much in common with a heavyweight championship wrestling match, which represents a maximum of bother and expense for a minimum of benefit. It never matters who wins the heavyweight wrestling championship . . . and there are those who hold the belief that nothing will matter any more, either, if Mr. Hoover should be reelected."[1]

Only two cities had even wanted the Republican Convention: the recently convicted Alphonse Capone's Chicago and Enoch Johnson's Atlantic City. The "Windy City" won and hoped that mid-June's GOP gathering—and the Democratic convention to follow on its down-turned heels—might bring a badly needed economic boost. "[I]n the days of five-cent beers and the bunny hug," reported the United Press, the convention's Coliseum area was "a wide-open, roaring square mile of saloons, vice resorts, ten-by-twelve dance halls, and bullet-pocked gambling houses [where] the girls wore their paint thick and their knives in their stockings.

"Several gaudy cabarets have opened up on the near North Side. Owners admit frankly that they are angling for convention trade. Prices are down, gin from $25 to $18 a case of twelve fifths, and alcohol can be bought for $4, $5, and $6 a gallon, depending on quality. Canadian Bourbon, costing bootleggers $65 a case, sells to the consumer for $5 a pint delivered. American Bourbon comes at $5.50 a pint. Canadian Scotch is priced at $7 a pint."[2]

Amid such a lively illicit trade, Hoover had pretty much lined up all his ducks—at least, regarding his own nomination. But too many other key elements remained chaotic. Regarding Prohibition, outright chaos reigned. And, if delegates possessed little enthusiasm for Hoover, they possessed less for his running mate, Vice President Charles Curtis.

Can one impress anyone as vice president? The three-eighths Indian[3] Curtis (one-eighth each of Kaw, Osage, and Pottawatomie blood) certainly did not, serving as the model for "Alexander Throttlebottom," the memorably forgettable veep in George Gershwin's 1932 musical-comedy *Of Thee I Sing*.[4] Curtis, nonetheless, found himself enmeshed in a classic inside-the-beltway tempest, swirling around the personages of two of Washington's grandest grande dames: Mrs. Permelia Theressa Curtis Gann and Mrs. Alice Lee Roosevelt Longworth.

Mrs. Gann was his younger half-sister, "Dolly." Alice Longworth was, in fact, none other than "Princess Alice," TR's rambunctious only daughter and the wife of the fast-living Republican Speaker of the House Nicholas Longworth ("He'd rather be tight than be President,"[5] sayeth Alice). The Longworths' marriage had not been sanguine. Each enjoyed their respective affairs, most amazingly, the one between Alice and Sen. William Borah, an assignation resulting in the Valentine's Day 1925 birth of their daughter at Chicago's Lying-in Hospital. Alice desired to name the child Deborah—a play on "de Borah." Mr. Longworth, his liberality finally exhausted, objected.[6] They named her instead Paulina.

Aside from widower Curtis's cheating at poker ("Well," recalled Alice, "we just don't come in when Charlie deals . . ."[7]), he tread considerably more demurely at Washington, residing modestly with Dolly and her husband, Edward Everett Gann. Upon Curtis's 1928 election, however, a crisis of protocol arose, as Curtis insisted on bestowing the honors normally accorded a "Second Lady" to "Second Sister" Dolly. Alice Roosevelt conversely thought she, as the House Speaker's wife, deserved pride of place. In April 1929, when financier Eugene Meyer hosted a dinner marking his retirement from the Federal Farm Loan Board, nobody knew who would sit where, causing both the Longworths and the Curtises to both remain sitting at their respective homes and detonating a very public feud among what passed for society along the Potomac.[8]

Nicholas Longworth's sudden April 1931 death should have rendered such a dispute moot. It did not. Hell hath no fury like Alice Roosevelt Longworth. Period. As 1932's Republican convention approached, Princess Alice pushed herself to the front ranks of the many (including even Hoover[9]) plotting Charles Curtis's forced retirement.

Her plan: to supplant Mrs. Gann's older half-brother with *her* younger half-brother, Teddy Jr.,[10] now residing at Manila as governor-general of the Philippines,[11] following his ill-considered and ill-executed 1924 gubernatorial run versus Al Smith.[12]

Alice's idea might also have crossed TR Jr.'s own mind as well, for he wrote to his wife, Eleanor (not, of course, to be confused with *the* Eleanor Roosevelt; Mrs. FDR was merely TR Jr.'s first cousin): "To nominate [Curtis] would be a crime. He is such an old man now that should Hoover die it might be a national calamity to have him as President. Furthermore, it seems to me that what the Republican ticket will need next autumn is not an old gentleman, dry from Kansas, but an active, younger man, preferably an ex-service man with wet leanings, possibly from the Northeast. . . ."[13]

TR Jr. added, of course, that he could *not* possibly be referring to himself.

Some even considered Alice herself as a proper substitute for the seventy-two-year-old Curtis. "She would," posited South Dakota's Rep. William Williamson, "add color and pep."[14]

Indeed, she would, but it was not to be.

Dolly Gann proved far more efficient in working a convention than the imperious (and inconveniently whooping cough–wracked[15]) Alice. Moreover, a movement arose to return Charles Curtis's jaunty predecessor, Charles Gates Dawes (severely hampered by questions of RFC loans to his Chicago bank) to the post. It finally required Dawes's pointed refusal,[16] pleading from Hoover (who, in the end, saw no utility in knifing Curtis if the process was too visibly bloody),[17] and pressure on seventy-five Pennsylvania delegates to switch their votes to shove the beleaguered Curtis over the top.[18]

Of even greater vexation, however, was the infernal, and, seemingly eternal, issue of Prohibition. Democrats—with their big-city base—leaned increasingly toward repeal, but so did many northeastern Republicans. Hoover did not, but it was difficult to understand exactly where he stood. First he praised Prohibition, then he instituted the Wickersham Commission, and, now, as much as anyone, he clearly witnessed the ever-burgeoning antipathy toward the "noble experiment." And yet he could not bring himself to act in any decisive or coherent manner. His strategy seemed to be, as the *New Republic* gibed, "Don't change barrels while going over Niagara."[19]

Now, with his re-nomination fast approaching, his party's Prohibition plank reflected their nominee's befuddlement:

> *We do not favor a submission limited to the issue of retention or repeal, for the American nation never in its history has gone backward, and in this*

case the progress which has been thus far made must be preserved, while the evils must be eliminated.

We therefore believe that the people should have an opportunity to pass upon a proposed amendment the provision of which, while retaining in the Federal Government power to preserve the gains already made in dealing with the evils inherent in the liquor traffic, shall allow the States to deal with the problem as their citizens may determine, but subject always to the power of the Federal Government to protect those States where prohibition may exist and safeguard our citizens everywhere from the return of the saloon and attendant abuses.[20]

Four years previously, such gobbledygook might have constituted some level of boldness. Now, it represented hardly anything. "The Hoover plank," noted H. L. Mencken, "at least has the great virtue of being quite unintelligible to simple folk."[21]

The wheels had indeed fallen off the "dry" Model T. Once, not that long ago, the "best" people supported national Prohibition, but as the activities of such folk as John Jakob Raskob (and the ultra-chic, ultra-wealthy Mrs. Pauline Joy Sabin, head of the Women's Organization for National Prohibition Reform[22]) demonstrated, "society" had discovered that it liked its cocktails better than dealing with bootleggers or peering nervously over its shoulders for the constabulary. Such hostility was hardly restricted to the Raskobs, Sabins, or DuPonts. Between 1927 and 1931, Women's Christian Temperance Union (WCTU) membership plummeted from a peak of 766,000[23] to just 372,355.[24]

The heaviest blow fell just as Republican delegates gathered. Bigger even than the DuPonts—bigger financially than anyone—were the Rockefellers, and like their fellow financial titans Henry Ford, Andrew Carnegie, dime-store pioneer S. S. Kresge, and Philadelphia department store magnate John Wanamaker,[25] the Rockefeller tribe had long sustained the "dry" cause. On Monday, June 6, 1932, John D. Rockefeller Jr. dispatched an open letter to the prominent Republican "wet," Columbia University president Nicholas Murray Butler. "My position may surprise you," Rockefeller began, "as it will many of my friends. I was born a teetotaler; all my life I have been a teetotaler on principle. Neither my father nor his father ever tasted a drop of intoxicating liquor, nor have I. . . . [F]rom the year 1900 up to and including the date of the passage of the eighteenth amendment, the contributions of my father and myself to all branches of the antisaloon league, federal and state,—the only contributions made by us in support of prohibition legislation—aggregated $350,000." That's how he began. He finished by announcing his abandonment of the prohibition cause.[26]

At the convention, Butler[27] and Connecticut's aristocratic, white-maned, and already officially censured[28] US senator Hiram Bingham ("We adopted the 18th Amendment in order to help win the war. We must repeal it in order to help win the depression"[29]) offered a substitute plank calling for outright repeal. Condemning the administration's majority version as "almost the worst proposal that has been made for dealing with this subject,"[30] Butler blasted it for not merely continuing but exacerbating the role of the federal government in the liquor question, "What the word 'slavery' was seventy years ago," he thundered, "what the word 'gold' was thirty-six years ago, the word 'repeal' is today."[31]

Nevada governor Fred B. Balzar stepped to the microphone, claiming to represent "the only free State left in the Union . . . where men are men and women are glad of it" and spoke for Butler's plank. "[W]e have in my State put the cards on the table," said Balzar, who had already legalized gaming in the state (as well as liberalized divorce). "We do not in my State pussyfoot."[32]

The heavily arm-twisted convention was, however, happy to pussyfoot, prevaricate, or pusillanimate—however, one wished to phrase it—voting down Butler, Bingham—and the very manly Balzar—690$\frac{19}{36}$–420$\frac{5}{6}$.[33] As they did, the *New York Times* reported, "men with half-glasses of beer paraded the aisles."[34] Butler, along with San Francisco banker William H. Crocker, had already bolted Chicago in disgust.[35]

Which left everyone else with the re-nomination of Herbert Clark Hoover.

Little drama or glory enveloped said event, only a residue of sullen weariness. Sen. Lester J. "Hell Raising Dick" Dickinson, an Iowa "dry," provided what passed for a keynote address. "Mr. Dickenson [sic]," observers Roy Peel and Thomas Donnelly noted equally drily, "gained for himself the distinction of being the first Republican keynoter in some time who has not dealt upon prosperity."[36] Hoover—ever the busybody—had edited Dickinson's talk.[37]

A huge portrait of Washington festooned the Chicago Coliseum, though none yet of Hoover himself.[38] A pair of "Press On with Hoover" banners, nonetheless, graced the hall. When convention factotums realized that adding a mere two vowels and a single consonant changed their message to "Depression with Hoover,"[39] down they went.

An English-born gentleman from Pasadena answering to the name of Joseph L. "Plain Joe" Scott[40] placed Hoover in nomination.[41] The bushy-browed Scott, the father of two priests,[42] promised to eschew any "hifalutin" oratory, instructing listeners "to think of [Hoover] as I think of him in the study of the White House, in the room where Lincoln signed the Emancipation Proclamation, working through ceaseless hours over the problems that

are your problems, seeking solutions that will aid mankind."[43] Scott meandered from Lincoln to "the Fathers of our Nation" to Edmund Burke, on
to the Gettysburg Address, the Declaration of Independence, the dough-
boys, Nero and the (original) Coliseum, *plus* the Sermon on the Mount. His
address, suffice it to say, was not long on current public policy. All in just two
thousand words.

Will Rogers thought "Plain Joe" "a triple-tongued elocution hound,"[44]
and, listening via radio at the White House, Hoover dispiritedly praised
Scott's effort as being "as good as could be expected in the circumstances."[45]
But as "Plain Joe" Scott rumbled ever onward, three Cabinet members
(Treasury's Ogden Mills, War's Patrick Hurley, and State's Henry Stimson)
gingerly exited the hall. Postmaster General Brown did not. He was asleep.
Will Rogers wanted to know why Secretary of the Interior Ray Lyman Wilbur hadn't left. "Oh, it's not so bad here," Wilbur cheerfully explained, "I
can't hear a word."[46] Rogers meandered over to California delegate Louis B.
Mayer, head of production at M-G-M Studios, a close Hoover ally,[47] and
his first overnight guest at the White House in 1929.[48] "I accused [Mayer],"
said Rogers, "of stealing [Scott's speech] out of Metro-Goldwyn-Mayer's
scenario department that had been sent in as a comedy. Louie said he didn't,
but that he would buy it and take it back."[49]

Mayer's Hollywood staff hadn't drafted Scott's encomium, but they fashioned a huge (but "ghostly") Hoover slide show[50] to follow his act. "The grand
climax [came] when His master's Voice poured out of the loudspeakers and a
moving picture of the rotund features of the Great Engineer flicked vaguely
on two huge screens, owing to bad lighting and stage management," wrote
the *New Republic's* John Dos Passos. "The Presence failed to materialize."[51]

So stultified, few among the crowd noticed when Portland, Oregon,
delegate Lawritz Bernard Sandblast rose to place Senator Joseph I. France
in nomination.[52] But from within ennui's drowsy mists, a specter of high
drama (or was it just low comedy?) materialized. France now bounded
toward the podium. His goal: to foreswear his own campaign, to nominate
former President Coolidge, and to stampede the convention away from
the hated Hoover. The convention chair, House Minority Leader Bertrand
Snell, contested France's credentials. France's microphone went dead. So
did the klieg lights illuminating him. The convention's normally ponderous
sergeant-at-arms Everett Sanders and one of his assistants muscled France
backward. "You will have to carry off a presidential candidate if you want
to stop me," France yowled. "I have a right to talk and intend nominating Coolidge."[53] Private security guards, augmented by two Chicago police,
swarmed him. A cop grabbed France's arm, yanking him down the rear

podium steps, and hustling him into the coliseum's small temporary police station.[54]

"The treatment was absolutely illegal and outrageous," France fumed, "[showing] how tyrannical men can be who have power. They were afraid to allow me to place Mr. Coolidge in nomination for fear he would win. There were over 500 votes favorable to him. I was treated illegally."[55]

"The nomination of this man Hoover is invalid,"[56] he raged to Hearst reporters, as he distributed copies[57] of the nominating speech he had failed to deliver. It was all to no avail. Joe France's fifteen minutes of obscurity were up.

Hoover's steamroller rumbled forward. Even then diversity ruled the day. Four women and a black (he spoke of standing at Lincoln's tomb and seemed to hear The Great Emancipator request, "Say to Hoover, if by chance you see him, that I once travelled the path now trod by him"[58]) assisted in seconding his nomination. Hoover's vote was nearly unanimous, 1126½ to 13 for Wisconsin progressive Sen. John J. Blaine, 4½ for the still un-nominated Coolidge, four for the un-seconded France, and one apiece for Charles Dawes and the "wet" ex–New York senator James W. Wadsworth.[59]

Herbert Hoover had vanquished Joe France. He had won his nomination. How much it was worth depended upon who the Democrats would soon nominate.

Herbert Clark Hoover hoped so very much that it would be Franklin Delano Roosevelt.[60]

CHAPTER THIRTEEN

"There was little opportunity for air-sickness"

HITLER AGAIN FACED PAUL VON HINDENBURG.

Their March 1932 skirmish had been the proverbial war without a victor.

The DNVP? Theodor Duesterberg's disastrous showing only distressed his Stahlhelm comrades and their Alfred Hugenberg–led Nationalist allies.

The KPD? Extrapolating from 1930's Reichstag totals, observers forecast that Ernst Thälmann would garner 6.2 million votes.[1] He received but 4.9 million. The Soviet press alibied that his disappointing total was "much more important than appears at first sight." But even Moscow had to concede that too many Germans remained "influenced by sentiments of bourgeois nationalism."[2]

Der Reichspräsident? Hindenburg hadn't performed badly at all. In a five-man race—and essentially without campaigning—he nearly achieved an outright majority. Yet, monarchist that he was, he hated elections—even those he won. Desiring coronation not election, enduring a second round of balloting only soured his Prussian tastes.

And, then there was Hitler. *Der Angriff* boldly predicted outright victory. Hitler, a bit more cautiously, forecast a tight race. Instead, he lost badly. Round two might prove no better. "In . . . the Government," Ambassador Sackett wired Washington, "a somewhat malicious joy . . . is evident that a supplementary ballot will be necessary to complete the election formalities. It implies for Hitler the chagrin of suffering the same defeat a second time. Moreover, the second ballot involves a further drain of Hitler's campaign resources, already . . . at a low ebb."[3] Nazi leadership tried its best to lie its way out of a discouraging defeat. "Yesterday," averred Goebbels's *Der Angriff*, "proved irrefutably that all national aims can be represented exclusively by the National Socialist party."[4]

"The fight goes on," Putzi Hanfstaengl bluffed to foreign reporters. "Hitler will yet be President. Of this there is no doubt. The Steel Helmet organization will merge with the Nazis on the next ballots. Besides, we shall win over enough von Hindenburg supporters to win the next ballot, when Hitler will have 16,300,000 votes. Von Hindenburg would have had at least 3,000,000 votes less than he obtained if the Communists had not passed out the word that the younger membership should work for him. We are quite satisfied with the results."[5]

Rank-and-file Hitlerites—intoxicated by recent triumphs and gulled by overzealous party propaganda—weren't satisfied at all. March's balloting threatened to permanently cripple party morale and shrink its electoral strength to lackluster pre-1930 levels. The club that grew into a cult that became a movement and nearly seized a government might now be lurching back down the same dizzying stairway.

Party leadership—even its vaunted propagandists—was even more dispirited than its rank-and-file. At a March 31 Berlin meeting of Hitler's press chiefs, defeatism and dissension ruled. "Never before had I heard so much oppositional spirit, so openly expressed," recalled former Hamburg Gauleiter Albert Krebs, now editor of the Nazi *Hamburger Tageblatt*, "—not even the Führer's person was immune."[6]

Then *he* spoke. Hitler's address (Krebs thought it "a real masterpiece"[7]) alternately flattered and excoriated his minions. He pointed to his campaign's many highlights. Then he lowered the boom. "The individual elements of the party . . . ," summarized Krebs, "the Gaue, the Local Groups, the NSBO [*Nationalsozialistische Betriebszellenorganisation*—National Socialist Factory Cell Organization; essentially the Nazi labor union], Women's groups, and so on, let him down to a shameful extent. Everything that they did was stupid, petty-bourgeois, uninspired, small time, clumsy, and therefore, of necessity, also useless. The party had left him, Hitler, in the lurch!"[8]

It requires more than harangues and blame-shifting to resuscitate a wounded party. Hitler needed to reinvigorate his lacerated movement. He needed votes. And he needed to gain them minus access to the national airwaves. Heinrich Brüning and even Paul von Hindenburg reached millions of listeners via radio addresses. So did Herbert Hoover or Franklin Roosevelt. But a government ukase banned Hitler—and his followers—from that medium.[9] In person, he might be the most mesmerizing speaker in all history. But how many persons could anyone so reach, no matter how large the venue? No matter how packed the hall? Beyond that, this latest presidential canvass was exceedingly short. Second-round voting occurred on Sunday, April 10, with all electioneering barred during the intervening Holy Week.

The campaign deciding Germany's fate—and Hitler's—found itself reduced to not even a single week.

Hitler, desperate for attention, would have to go over the head of such barriers—*literally* over German heads.

He would fly.

How his idea developed we do not know. Furiously nomadic, Hitler had long criss-crossed the *Vaterland* by both train and car. But even his boundless energy would fail this latest challenge. Flight was the only answer. And so, in late March, Lufthansa pilot Hans Baur (a National Socialist since 1926) reported to Hitler at party headquarters in Munich. His airsick jaunt to Berlin to join the ill-fated Kapp Putsch still rankled Hitler, but Baur reassured his potential passenger that aircraft had progressed mightily since 1920. "[I]n any case," thought Baur, "he didn't look to me like a type who would easily get airsick. As a matter of fact I have a very keen eye for that sort of thing; I have often astonished my crews by taking a quick look at our passengers and telling them just who was likely to be sick, and I was usually right. But, just in case, I suggested that Hitler should sit next to me in the mechanic's seat, because there was so much to be seen and so much to take the interest there, that there was little opportunity for air-sickness, which is largely psychological."[10]

But even with the experienced Baur at the controls, Hitler faced trouble. His usual marathon addresses were out of the question. He needed to jump from city to city to city in a single day, limiting himself to (for him) relatively brief harangues, speaking day and night—*flying* day and night. In *Mein Kampf,* he described the hidden magic of events held at night ("The same lecture, the same speaker, the same theme have an entirely different effect at ten o'clock in the morning, at three o'clock in the afternoon or at night"[11]). He could not now surrender the power of darkness even if it made each landing and take-off ever more perilous.

His flights (the "*Deutschlandflug*"[12]) commenced on Sunday, April 3, with favorable weather. At least, that is how Baur recalled it. Others found that first flight simply hair-raising. From Dresden's Reick Cycle Track on April 3, Hitler flew on to Leipzig's Exhibition Hall and to Chemnitz and Plauen. "At the end of the first day," Baur recalled, "Hitler picked out the biggest of all the numerous bunches of flowers with which he had been presented during the day and handed it to me with the words: 'Baur, you've done your job well. I'm enthusiastic about air travel from now on!'"[13] The next day saw him in Berlin moving feverishly about from the Lustgarten, to Potsdam and the Sportpalast and then to Berlin-Friedrichshain. Thus, one frantic day would follow another.

It's unsure who conceived the idea of this unprecedented "Hitler Over Germany" campaign. Perhaps it was Göring or perhaps Hess, both experienced pilots. Perhaps it was the (now unlike Hitler) airsick-prone Putzi Hanfstaengl.[14] Perhaps Hitler himself. We can surmise from the short shrift the braggart Joseph Goebbels's diary provides to his leader's innovation that it was not he.[15] But his Monday, April 4, entry does provide a snapshot of the campaign's whirlwind-like pace:

> *Berlin . . . is hardly recognizable. Our posters blaze forth on all advertising pillars. Everything is taking its course.*
>
> *The Leader speaks in Saxonia [Leipzig, Chemnitz, and Plauen], on Monday, to 20,000 people. He is very fit and ready.*
>
> *One hundred and fifty thousand march to the Lustgarten. I deliver the first address. Then the Leader appears. Undescribable [sic] enthusiasm prevails. He makes a wonderful speech. Motor to Potsdam at eighty miles an hour. There he speaks in the Stadium to 50,000. Potsdam is itself again. Late at night at the Sportpalast in Berlin. A crush of 18,000 people; they receive the Leader with frantic ovations.*
>
> *At midnight at Friedrichshain, the poorer quarter of the town. The people here are profoundly touched by the Leader's address.*[16]

After Friedrichshain Hitler moved east, to the Free City of Danzig (where he reviewed the police), and then further on, to Elbing and Königsberg in East Prussia. Politics—not weather—forced an emergency detour, back to Berlin. Local authorities had issued a crackdown upon the SA. Allegations regarding Ernst Röhm's sexual proclivities ("Röhmosexuality"[17]) reached a public boiling point. "For the moment," Goebbels laments, "our propaganda chiefly consists in contradicting lies. A disgusting task, but it has to be done."[18] Complicating matters, thought the *Daily Express*'s Sefton "Tom" Delmer, was the "strangely delicate . . . almost effeminate" nature of Hitler's Deutschlandflug bodyguards. "I began to wonder whether the *Stabschef* [Röhm] had a hand in their selection," Delmer mused, particularly when he observed them ostentatiously exhibiting wallet photos of their boyfriends ("Isn't he sweet!").[19]

The scar-faced Röhm wasn't particularly sweet, but he was useful, and Hitler strongly defended him: "For quite transparent reasons," he thundered, "the rumor has been circulating frequently during the campaign that I am planning to dismiss my Chief of Staff. In this respect I may explicitly state once and for all: Lieutenant Colonel Röhm is now and will remain my Chief of Staff after the elections. Not even the dirtiest and most disgusting smear campaign, which does not stop at misrepresentations, violations of the law or abuse of office and which will be lawfully atoned for, can change this fact."[20]

"Hitler Over Germany" accelerated, as Hitler chartered a second Lufthansa plane, a Junkers F.13, allowing his strong-arm, but oddly genial[21], chief bodyguard Josef "Sepp" Dietrich ("You couldn't get close to Hitler as far as private conversations are concerned. Nor even Göring"[22]), along with one or two journalists, to precede him.[23] The candidate spoke at Wurzburg's Frankenhalle, Nürnberg's Festhalle, and under a tent at Regensburg on April 6. The next day, he flew to Frankfurt, Darmstadt and Ludwigshafen, and on to Düsseldorf. He spoke at cycle tracks at Essen and Münster on the 8th.[24] Bad weather—snow and hail—caught up with him.

Scheduled for Düsseldorf, Hitler ordered Baur to press on. "It wasn't a flight," recalled press aide Otto Dietrich. "It was a whirl. First we passed over a squall, then we tore into the clouds, then an invisible whirlpool sucked us down, then we felt as if we were drawn steeply upward by some lofty crane. Snow and hail pattered upon the wings of our [triple-engined Junkers] D1720 and against the cabin windows. Sometimes we flew so low that our operator had to pull in the antenna to prevent it from catching in the treetops or in the telephone wires." Hitler, despite all his original misgivings about flight, remained calm throughout, ignoring everything, working on his next oration.[25]

"On Furth airfield we had to fasten our machine to the ground to prevent its being blown away," Baur recalled. "Hitler was worried about his speaking tour and wanted to fly, and I told him that it was possible but that it wouldn't be pleasant. I thought I could get over the Spessart [mountain range in Bavaria], but mountains were a real problem in such weather. Hitler . . . told me to carry on. I took off without difficulty, but over Neustadt we ran into the first hail showers. I flew fairly low, but even then we were flying practically blind as far as Wurzburg, where [it] improved. But as we came nearer the Spessart the hail grew worse. . . . Despite the rough passage Hitler was not air-sick. He told me that he had been deeply impressed by the sight of the Spessart below us, lashed by rain and hail against a dark background of threatening clouds. It had reminded him forcibly of the 'Walkure,' he said."[26]

All was not *sturm und drang*. Far from it. In late March, Hitler paused to witness the Munich wedding of Heinrich Hoffmann's now nineteen-year-old daughter Henriette to the sycophantic ("loyalty is everything and everything is the love of Adolf Hitler"[27]) twenty-four-year-old Hitler Youth leader Baldur von Schirach. Like Putzi Hanfstaengl and Hjalmar Schacht, the violently anti-Christian Schirach boasted distinctly American roots—a thoroughly American mother, a German national but American-born father, and descent from *two* signers of the Declaration of Independence. Less decorously, his anti-Semitism similarly featured American antecedents, springing, he said, from a reading of Henry Ford's *The International Jew.*[28]

Hitler hosted the newlyweds' reception at his Prinzregentenplatz apartment.[29] The vegetarianism he embraced following niece Geli's suicide loudly manifested itself, as he instructed the bride and her somewhat flabby groom regarding any future visits he might make to their abode: "I eat everything that Nature yields of her own accord: fruit, vegetables, vegetable oil. Please, spare me everything that animals give up against their will: meat, milk and cheese. From animals [I eat] only eggs."[30]

Diets change. Hairstyles change. The foreign press took increased notice of him, doing what the daily press does best: focusing on the non-essentials. "Vast implications for Germany's future have been detected in the change in Adolf Hitler's hair-cut," reported the Associated Press's Berlin Bureau on April 2. "On the eve of the presidential election the Fascist leader took to parting his hair on the left instead of the right, so that the mass of locks fell on the right side of his forehead. The implication is that Hitler will hereafter emphasize the rightist or nationalistic tenets of his National Socialist programme to the exclusion of the leftist or Socialist."[31]

A Hitlerite swing to the right hardly concerned the Communist KPD. Oblivious to any danger confronting the republic, the nation, and, indeed, themselves, the Reds continued their peculiar ideological games, fretting far more about their socialist SPD cousins than their radical cousins of the NSDAP. As Stalinist Dmitry Manuilsky proclaimed at Moscow's Comintern session: "In order to deceive the masses, the Social Democrats deliberately proclaim that the chief enemy of the working class is Fascism, it is not true that Fascism of the Hitler type represents the chief enemy. . . ."[32] *Pravda* similarly pretended that the "Social Fascists" (i.e, the SPD) supporting Hindenburg and the real fascists supporting Hitler were "in reality twins."[33]

No, the KPD would *never* cooperate with the forces of democracy, particularly socialist democracy, even to stop an Adolf Hitler. By January 1932, its attitude had advanced from mere intransigence to outright death-wish. Germany's democratic Left had finally founded a well-funded, broadly based anti-Hitler coalition—the "Iron Front" (*Eiserne Front*). KPD activist Richard Krebs (aka Jan Valtin) recalled that:

> *The daily Nazi average of two thousand mass meetings was to be countered by an equal number of "Stop Hitler" rallies. . . . Shock-brigades of trade unionists—Hammerschafren—[were] formed to protect the meetings and propaganda squads of the Iron Front against storm troop raids.*

No sooner had the Iron Front launched its counter-offensive than all the units of the Communist Party received instructions to sabotage [it] at every turn. This we did. Propaganda detachments of the Iron Front were forcibly relieved of their arms and of the leaflets and papers they had set out to distribute. Iron Front meetings were disrupted by packing the halls in advance with storm troopers and communists. Communists professing to be democrats entered the Iron Front organizations by the hundreds for the sole purpose of creating confusion. And accompanying these under-handed jabs was a tremendous campaign in the . . . communist press.

Communists played their games. The nationalist Right tumbled into mere dispirited confusion. Alfred Hugenberg's DNVP fielded no candidate in this second round of presidential balloting, instead allowing its members to support Hindenburg or Hitler, whomever they preferred.[34] Personal insult, however, had compounded Theodor Duesterberg's electoral injury. Not only had he fared poorly in March's balloting, but, in its course, gleeful Nazis had circulated an embarrassing (though true) accusation: His paternal great-grandfather had been a Jew. Duesterberg, less enamored of Hitler than ever, endorsed Hindenburg.

The Hohenzollerns meanwhile lurched in the opposite direction. Kronprinz Wilhelm had proudly attended Duesterberg's March 4 Sport-palast rally,[35] but Duesterberg's candidacy was now dead. Hitler's candidacy remained more than alive—it was airborne—yet, he may still have remained ambivalent regarding the best path to power. The details are murky, but in late March, the Kronprinz was approached regarding a possible Nazi-backed royal candidacy. Just as Hindenburg substituted for the DVP's Karl Jarres in 1925, the Kronprinz would now pinch-hit for Hitler (and, with luck, even force Hindenburg himself out). Whether this idea originated with Hitler, or, much more likely, was merely broached by extremely low-level Nazis with-out his knowledge, remains unclear. Whatever the case, Wilhelm, though cognizant that the Nazis only turned to him as an anti-Hindenburg ploy, nonetheless, thought the tactic possessed merit. Had not, after all, an elected presidency once paved the way for a Bonaparte restoration?

Future Reichspräsident or not, however, the Kronprinz still knew it essential to run the idea past his father. He did not call him, instead entrust-ing the matter to a courier, Eberhard von Selasinsky. The exiled Kaiser's sec-ond wife, the much younger Princess Hermine, barred Selasinsky's direct access to Wilhelm II and, though herself pro-Nazi (she had even attended Party Day in 1929[36]), convinced her husband to veto the Crown Prince's candidacy.[37] "Princess Hermine saw Germany's future in Hitler and trusted him completely," recalled Selasinsky. "She seemed fairly convinced that when he held the power of Germany in his hands it would be only . . . a short time until she would see her husband return to his hereditary place. In any event, . . . in the Princess I had the strongest opponent of the plan . . . in her I had a convinced disciple of National Socialism before me. . . ."[38]

Kronprinz Wilhelm folded. By April 2, he proclaimed: "Abstention at the second ballot . . . is incompatible with the concept of the Harzburg Front. Because I believe that it is absolutely essential that the national front stand united, I will vote for Adolf Hitler. . . ."[39] His younger brother, the effeminate storm trooper Prince August Wilhelm ("Auwi") headed the Nazi list for Prussia's upcoming Landtag elections.[40] "Adolf Hitler," August Wilhelm had proclaimed a year previously, "is God's gift to Germany."[41]

Nationalists on the Right. Communists on the Left. National Socialists where? The Right? The Left? The Middle? Nowhere at all? Or everywhere at once? "In our movement the two extremes come together," Hitler once expounded, "the Communists from the Left and the officers and the students from the Right. . . . it was the greatest crime that they used to oppose each other in street fights. The Communists were the idealists of socialism; through years of persecution they saw their mortal enemy in the officer; while the officers fought the Communists because they inevitably saw the mortal enemy of their fatherland in the proletarian led astray by the Jew. Our party has already succeeded in uniting these two utter extremes within the ranks of our storm troops. They . . . will stand together when the day comes to say: The nation arises, the storm is breaking!"[42]

It broke now in 1932 because of the Depression—and, not inconsequentially, because people were sick of the electioneering, sick of the politics, sick of the squabbling and the historic divisions that had torn their nation apart. "Germany has for years been divided sharply in two," Joseph Goebbels privately explained to the American embassy's John Cooper Wiley that February. "On one side of the dividing line were the bourgeois elements; on the other were the Marxists. . . . National-Socialism was created on the outside. It represented no caste or class or precise political or economic policy . . . a synthesis of all national elements. Its principal objective was to break down this line . . . [I]t had broken through into the bourgeois ranks as the point of least resistance. From within the bourgeois ranks it was encroaching on the Marxist ranks. To the same degree as the Communists were eating into the Social Democrats, the National-Socialists were nibbling away at the Communists."[43]

Germans voted. Morning "rainstorms and dismal weather"[44] kept many indoors. By noon only a quarter of those eligible had balloted—down from 40 to 50 percent a month earlier. Brüning, fresh from East Prussian campaigning, voted in Berlin by 9:00 a.m. Hindenburg, disdainful as ever of democracy, didn't bother. Hitler balloted, not in Munich, but in Stuttgart, where he had spoken the previous night. Both the Nazis and their "Iron Front" rivals desperately instituted a get-out-the-vote "drag service." Berlin Communists posted placards over existing street signs, confusing motorists by temporarily renaming thoroughfares with such names as "Thälmannstrasse" or "Leninstrasse." Polls closed everywhere at 6:00 p.m. In the voting's last hour, turnout surged.[45]

Hindenburg won.

And so did Hitler.

The results[46]:

Candidate	Party	Votes	*Percent*
Paul von Hindenburg	Independent	19,359,983	53.0
Adolf Hitler	National Socialist	13,418,547	36.8
Ernst Thälmann	Communist	3,706,759	10.2
Other candidates		5,472	0.0
Total		36,490,761	100.0
Registered voters / percentage of turnout		44,063,958	82.9

Hindenburg had indeed crossed the finish fine, but no one contested the fact that Hitler's tide had not abated at all. Its ominous ascent persisted—by a good 2.1 million votes. When—or if—it might recede no one now dared predict. Hindenburg's vote had, by comparison, barely budged, rising from 18,651,497 votes to 19,359,983. Ernst Thälmann's tanked, from 4.9 million to just 3.7 million. "Thälmann has failed miserably," Goebbels chortled. "His defeat is our greatest success. In Berlin alone our following has increased by 200,000 votes."[47] Hitler had stolen votes simultaneously and significantly from both the far right *and* the far left. This, indeed, was a candidate and a phenomenon to be reckoned with.

He "won" this round—and he knew it.

"National Socialists! Party Comrades!" he exclaimed. "You have fought a great and difficult battle. I knew that your loyalty is unshakeable. Still I must thank you for your tremendous faith, your willingness to make sacrifices, and your diligence!

"In spite of all the acts of suppression and persecution, our Movement has won a new victory through you which justifies it in regarding itself as a vanguard of national liberty and thus of the national future. Tomorrow the new struggle will begin. I know that you will continue to be the best guard of the German Volk in the future."[48]

He thundered that, "Tomorrow the new struggle will begin." He spoke not metaphorically, but literally. Another election campaign—in the German Lander or provinces now unfolded, with state elections scheduled in Prussia, Bavaria, Württemberg, and Anhalt for Sunday, April 24, plus municipal elections slated for Hamburg. As Otto Strasser mocked, "The game of dupers duped began once more."[49]

Catholics and Social Democrats still refused to be suckered by the Hitler game. So too did many key industrial magnates, refusing service in the Hitler juggernaut. On April 12, Hjalmar Schacht bluntly explained to Hitler why he had failed to get their support: They are unclear on your economic program."[50]

Nonetheless, the war began again. "Gramophone records are being prepared," noted Goebbels, "talking films made, posters and placards designed."[51] Hitler rode not only a Junkers D1720—he rode a tiger and could not get off. His second "Germany Flight" began at Augsburg on April 16. In the days and nights to come, he would deliver another twenty-five major speeches.[52]

At the Hamburg suburbs he addressed 120,000. Schoolteacher Luise Solmitz stood among them. To her diary she gushed:

> No one calls him Hitler only "the Leader." . . . The hours passed, the sun shone, the expectation mounted . . . It got to 3 o'clock. "The Führer's coming!" A thrill goes through the masses. Around the platform hands could be seen raised in the Hitler greeting . . . There stood Hitler in a simple black coat, looking expectantly over the crowd. A forest of swastika banners rustled upwards. The jubilation of the moment gave vent to a rousing cry of 'Heil.' Then Hitler spoke. Main idea: out of the parties a people (Volk) will emerge, the German people. He castigated the 'system' . . . For the rest, he refrained from personal attacks and also unspecific and specific promises. His voice was hoarse from speaking so much in previous days. When the speech was over, there were roars of jubilation and applause. Hitler was helped into his coat. Then he went. How many look to him in touching faith as the helper, the savior, the redeemer from overgreat distress. To him, who rescues the Prussian prince, the scholar, the clergyman, the peasant, the worker, the unemployed out of the party into the people.[53]

His were not political campaigns. They were something utterly new, absolutely different—frightening to some, the Fatherland's final hope to others. The American journalist Edgar Ansel Mowrer had observed of these gatherings' attendees, that Hitler was "asking them for their votes and support—but you would never know it. By making them pay to enter, by his stage craft and decorations and mass suggestion, . . . they who are appealing to him. So far as I know, aside from a few successful revivalists, no one else in the contemporary world can do this."[54]

Hitler's two presidential campaigns delivered moral victories. This third campaign produced tangible results. In Württemberg, the Nazi vote skyrocketed from a miniscule 1.8 percent in 1928 to 26.4 percent. Bavaria's soared to 32.5 percent, just a hair below the dominant Bavarian Peoples Party (BVP). In Anhalt, in north-central Germany, National Socialists drew 40.9 percent. Even in proletarian Hamburg Hitlerites garnered 31.2 percent.[55]

But it was in massive, staunchly SPD Prussia that the earth shook. Nazis won just 2.9 percent of the vote and six delegates in 1928. In 1932, they captured 162. The SPD stumbled from 137 to a relatively paltry ninety-three. The Zentrum ("Back to Brüning"[56]) won sixty-seven seats; the KPD, fifty-seven; the DNVP, thirty-one; German People's Party (DVP), seven; and the fast-fading centrist State Party (DstP) just two.[57] The Nazis owned a solid 36.6 percent[58] plurality in Prussia. They might not form a government—but neither could anyone else in what passed for Prussia's Weimar democracy.

"It's a fantastic victory that we've attained," crowed Goebbels before reflecting on not merely how far his party had traveled but how much further it need go. "Something must happen now. We *must* shortly come to power," he cautioned himself, "otherwise our victory will be a Pyrrhic one. . . . Now we must have our wits about us, and keep our heads screwed on particularly tight. This is the time to test what sort of stuff one is made of."[59]

CHAPTER FOURTEEN

"Dammit, Louis, I'm the nominee!"

AND WHAT MANNER OF STUFF COMPOSED FRANKLIN DELANO ROOSEVELT?

Disaster descended upon Franklin Roosevelt—in Massachusetts and Connecticut and Rhode Island and New Jersey and Indiana[1] and Texas, and, above all, in California. Primary and convention voters suddenly resisted his charms. So did both ward healers and progressive intellectuals. Preceding his Bay State humiliation, old-line Boston politico Martin Lomasney lambasted him as "an aristocrat, a demagogue, and a double-crosser who had capitalized his invalidism and was using it to excite sympathy."[2] Jersey City boss Frank Hague damned him as the party's feeblest hopeful. "[H]e (Roosevelt) cannot carry a single state east of the Mississippi, and very few in the Far West," charged Hague. "The Democratic Party has a golden opportunity . . . but . . . to select its weakest man . . . cannot bring the party success."[3] The left-leaning Scripps-Howard newspaper chain (for La Follette Sr. in 1924[4]), not only endorsed Smith, it blasted Franklin's "delay" and "inaction." "In Franklin Roosevelt," Roy Howard editorialized, "we have another Hoover."[5]

Progressives barely found Franklin more palatable. In January 1932, *The Nation* termed FDR "a charming person . . . who does not advance the cause of reform one bit."[6] In the June 1 *New Republic*, though editor Bruce Bliven credited FDR for being "notably progressive for one of his background," he counseled, "if you don't want four years of disappointment as the result of your vote, I suggest that you might well vote for the Socialist candidate, whatever individual (named Norman Thomas) he happens to be!"[7]

And literally as the Democrats' convention opened, columnist Heywood Broun blasted "Fearless Frank" as:

the corkscrew candidate of a convoluting convention.

To him the presidency is a prize somewhat after the nature of a brass ring which can only be captured by someone who approaches it whirling furiously in circles.

From the very beginning of his dervish drive . . . no consideration except expediency has governed any one of his decisions. And yet even this does not tell the whole story. He is not as good as that.

If Roosevelt has weighed the main chance upon every occasion and then ridden on ruthlessly toward his objective his conduct would be deplorable. And it would also arouse a sneaking admiration in the heart of every man.

But even expediency has not been sufficient to enable Roosevelt to cut a straight line. After throwing every scruple overboard he still bogged and tacked. In all too many instances he has been bewildered at the problem of deciding just what moral attitude and what fearless decision would be the best for Franklin Roosevelt.

The slightest hint of opposition has seemed to him sufficient to cancel every obligation. But that is not all. He has been mean to his adversaries but he has squared that up by betraying his friends.[8]

Yet, far greater calamities—polio, his 1914 and 1920 runs, a near divorce—had visited FDR before. They killed him not. Neither would these setbacks and brickbats. All the while he accumulated delegates at state conventions. In March, in Minnesota,[9] Maine, and Iowa.[10] In April, in Michigan and Kentucky.[11] In May, in Alabama,[12] Kansas,[13] Montana,[14] Vermont,[15] South Carolina,[16] Nevada,[17] Delaware,[18] Utah,[19] Tennessee,[20] Oregon,[21] and West Virginia.[22] In mid-June, North Carolina.[23] Such victories may not have generated the banner headlines that greeted his Massachusetts or California debacles, but the delegates they produced counted as much as any selected via primary. "Colonel House," noted one Roosevelt biographer, "was right when he said that Roosevelt was a student of American geography who profited by his knowledge of the existence of Nebraska, Minnesota, Iowa, the two Dakotas, and the other foster States of the Union."[24]

Among the last states fitting itself into FDR's now-vexing pre-convention puzzle was Louisiana, until very recently merely a bayou and bordello backwater, but with the ascent of Governor (and then Senator) Huey Pierce "The Kingfish" Long, among the more intriguing destinations on the American political landscape.

Louisiana's delegates came late and came expensive—their price necessarily including association with the brash upstart Long. Like a cyclone, The Kingfish had emerged from rural northern Louisiana to seize the governorship, dodge impeachment, forge an unprecedented (and many said dictatorial) political machine, and quickly promote himself to the US Senate—all such stops, of course, being in his nimble mind, mere way stations on his own frenetic path to the White House. Brazenly eschewing all Senate committee assignments,[25] he quickly and spectacularly lampooned not only Republicans but also fellow Democrats: "the two foghorns, Baruch on the one hand and [Eugene] Meyer on the other, [Joe] Robinson on the left and somebody else on the right."[26]

Long initially regarded Roosevelt as negligibly as he might any landed aristocrat or waffling rival politico. But pressure from FDR's first great Senate ally, Montana Democrat Burton K. Wheeler (Long: "I didn't like your sonofabitch but I'll be for him"[27]) and counsel from Nebraska Republican George W. Norris[28] ("Well, if Norris will tell me he's for him, I'll be for him"[29]) shoehorned the fractious Long aboard the Roosevelt train. His normal incivility, however, only presaged his bomb-throwing on arrival, with Long hijacking a late June conference of sixty-five prominent FDR supporters. His goal: to abolish the party's longstanding "two-thirds" rule,[30] a bylaw too often hopelessly deadlocking convention proceedings, as witnessed by 1924's infamous 103-ballot fiasco.

The rule, however, preserved Dixie's influence within the party. Predictably, his gambit outraged fellow southerners of all ideological stripes. "I wouldn't support any man who takes the short cut [to nomination] that way," threatened Virginia's aristocratic conservative Sen. Carter Glass. "If the Democrats want to recommend abolition of the rule at the next convention, that's different but to pull a snap play like this in the middle of the game is not playing the game. . . ."[31] The often-prickly[32] Glass damned any nomination so obtained as "damaged goods obtained by a gambler's trick."[33]

"Why, we'll destroy our party if we destroy the two thirds rule," warned "Alfalfa Bill" Murray. "If the Roosevelt people put it over, it will mean a third party."[34]

Freshman North Carolina senator Josiah Bailey assailed Long's proposal as "foolhardy and asinine."[35] Bailey "stormed into our headquarters," recalled Ed Flynn, "and told us that we would not only lose . . . North Carolina, but we would alienate every other southern state . . . Farley and I took a lesson in national politics then and there."[36]

FDR, however, had not learned the lesson quickly enough. He supported the reform. Then he retreated.[37] As Heywood Broun wrote:

> *the sensational announcement was made that Straight-From-the-Shoulder Frank demanded the abolition of the two-thirds rule. He was*

determined to throw down an ancient custom because he was a raring, tearing radical and the man with the most votes. Opposition developed and the great untrammeled Governor took one step to the left and two quick hops to the rear. He telegraphed his cohorts to quit the fight and seek a new rule which "will avoid the catastrophe of a deadlock and prolonged balloting."

The army which had marched so bravely up the hill under the banner of "Excelsior and Franklin D. Roosevelt" marched half way down again after changing the slogan to read "2.75 per cent excelsior and maybe Franklin D. Roosevelt."

After a bitter fight the devoted followers of Fearless Frank forced through by a vote of 30 to 20 the provision that after the sixth ballot the convention might abrogate the two-thirds rule. Came the dawn and a statement from the Governor that he had neither been consulted in the matter nor authorized the change.

Any man who proposes to fight shoulder to shoulder with Franklin Roosevelt must have the speed of [sprinter Charley] Paddock and the endurance of [Paddock's fellow sprinter, the Olympic gold medalist Paavo] Nurmi. I do not believe that even Houdini could have explained Governor Roosevelt's ability to disappear from the center of a controversy. Moreover, he can slip out of a promise with twice the speed of any handcuff king escaping fine steel bracelets.[38]

Other controversies exploded. On Tuesday, June 21, 1932, Wisconsin Democratic National Committeeman John M. Callahan, a Smith stalwart, released correspondence between FDR and two Georgia supporters F. B. Summers and C. W. Jones—both active Klansmen.[39] "[W]ith such damaging information in circulation," charged Callahan, "it will be impossible to win election in November unless another candidate is selected at the convention in Chicago."[40]

From Wisconsin came charges of Klan support. From the East came very few Roosevelt supporters. The New York Central's 20th Century Limited transported to Chicago a constellation of eastern Democratic luminaries—Bernard Baruch, Walter Lippmann, Frank Kent, former *New York World* editor Herbert Bayard Swope, journalist Clare Boothe Brokaw (not until 1935 Clare Boothe Luce, but already the quite-married Baruch's girlfriend[41]), and the widowed Mrs. Woodrow Wilson. None particularly cared for Roosevelt. Swope (favoring Owen D. Young), wrote to his younger brother General Electric president Gerard Swope: "Roosevelt has most of the delegates but no friends; the others have most of the friends but no delegates."[42] The divorced

Mrs. Brokaw toyed with forming a "New National Party," even serving as its executive director (young Dillon, Read executive James V. Forrestal served as treasurer[43]). It supported repeal (of both Prohibition *and* the tariff) and recognizing Red Russia. In its support *Vanity Fair* proclaimed: "WANTED, A DICTATOR!"[44] Arriving at Chicago, Lippmann called out to Clare, "If Roosevelt gets the nomination, you can put me down as a member. . . ."[45]

Critical to FDR—and to all Democrats—was the festering Prohibition issue. The party remained deeply divided on the controversy. FDR himself had vacillated on the matter with good political reason, delaying his ultimate call for repeal until that February 20.[46] On Wednesday, June 29, however, the party's Resolutions Committee adopted a thoroughly straightforward "wet" plank. It read:

> We advocate the repeal of the Eighteenth Amendment. To effect such repeal we demand that the Congress immediately propose a Constitutional Amendment to truly representative conventions in the states called to act solely on that proposal. We urge the enactment of such measures by the several states as will actually promote temperance, effectively prevent the return of the saloon and bring the liquor traffic into the open under complete supervision and control by the states.
>
> We demand that the Federal Government effectively exercise its power to enable the states to protect themselves against importation of intoxicating liquors in violation of their laws.
>
> Pending repeal, we favor immediate modification of the Volstead Act to legalize the manufacture and sale of beer and other beverages of such alcoholic content as is permissible under the Constitution and to provide therefrom a proper and needed revenue.[47]

That language passed 32–17. But among the committee's seventeen "nays" was a disturbingly wide array of party heavyweights: not only William Gibbs McAdoo, "Alfalfa Bill" Murray, and Carter Glass, but also a quartet of Roosevelt loyalists: former attorney general A. Mitchell Palmer (also a former FDR neighbor) and United States senators Cordell Hull (Tennessee), Clarence C. Dill (Washington State), and Joseph O'Mahoney (Wyoming).[48]

"Has the prohibition plank been finished?" Carter Glass bewailed. "Yes, it has been finished, and it may finish the Democratic party. They have adopted a barroom plank."[49]

The *New York Times* described Senator Hull as "disconsolate" and warning that the decision might wreck his party that November. "This," the log cabin–born Hull advised, "is the culmination of four years of use of the Democratic organization, with affiliated organizations, equipped with vast moneys to quietly hand-pick many delegations and pack the Democratic national convention with reference to the anti-prohibition movement."[50]

Others certainly disagreed. At the Gold Room of Chicago's Congress Hotel, Virgin Islands alternate delegate, Judge Lucius J. M. Malmin cornered "dry" leader Methodist bishop James Cannon Jr. "Bishop," grinned Malmin, as he bestowed a bottle of Virgin Islands rum upon him, "here's a present for you."

Photographers' shutters snapped furiously. "I'll smash that," the sixty-eight-year-old Cannon howled, jumping from his seat in alcophobic panic, "I'll smash that."[51]

Precious little hubbub surrounded the platform's lesser planks. Crafted by the physically ailing A. Mitchell Palmer, the document's brevity (a trim 1,489 words; the briefest of any major party ever[52]), if not the soul of wit, was at least the essence of discretion—and even of a pronounced fiscal conservatism:

> We advocate an immediate and drastic reduction of governmental expenditures by abolishing useless commissions and offices, consolidating departments and bureaus, and eliminating extravagance, to accomplish a saving of not less than twenty-five per cent in the cost of federal government, and we call upon the Democratic Party in the States to make a zealous effort to achieve a proportionate result.
>
> We favor maintenance of the national credit by a federal budget annually balanced on the basis of accurate executive estimates within revenues, raised by a system of taxation levied on the principle of ability to pay. . . .
>
> [We favor t]he removal of government from all fields of private enterprise except where necessary to develop public works and natural resources in the common interest.[53]

Such words spelt conservatism writ large. Yet, the Resolutions Committee also took testimony from radical Detroit radio priest Charles E. Coughlin (bounced from CBS in late 1931, now more popular than ever on his own ad hoc radio network, and enthusiastically supporting—"Roosevelt or Ruin"[54]—FDR) regarding the unemployment question.[55] The remainder of the platform boasted vague talk of tariff reform (Cordell Hull's influence[56]), opposition to cancelling foreign debts (a Hearst-McAdoo bugaboo[57]), aid to agriculture, regulation of the financial industry, control of interstate power rates, and, most significant, regarding Roosevelt's real future path: "unemployment and old age insurance."[58] But even these latter initiatives were not to emerge via any burgeoning federal leviathan, but rather, in proper

Jeffersonian manner, "under state laws."[59] FDR personally vetoed a federal guarantee of bank deposits. "These bankers here in New York think that I'm a Communist now," Roosevelt informed his floor manager, former Nebraska attorney general Arthur Mullen, "so let's leave that plank out of the platform. I'll take care of it later."[60]

The Roosevelt coalition superlatively demonstrated the ancient adage regarding politics and strange bedfellows, composed as it was of respectable old southern gentlemen (Hull), big city bosses (Ed Flynn and James Curley), western radical progressives (Burton J. Wheeler and Clarence Dill), merchant princes (Jesse Straus), and outright demagogues (Coughlin and Long). But two sides could play that game of odd alliances. On Sunday, June 26, 1932—the day before Democrats convened—Bernard Baruch toiled to broker a marriage of desperate convenience between the stop-Roosevelt movement's most disparate branches: Alfred Emanuel Smith and William Gibbs McAdoo.

They met warily over lunch at Chicago's Blackstone Hotel.

"Bernie," Smith confessed to Baruch, "I don't like him [McAdoo], I don't trust him, but in this fight I would sleep with a Chinaman to win and I'll come."

The feeling was mutual. As liberal syndicated columnist Rodney Dutcher reported: "Smith still disliked McAdoo at Chicago, but perhaps he didn't realize that McAdoo disliked Smith much more intensely."[61]

Lower East Side–born, Catholic, and "wet" Smith and Georgia-born, Klan-supported, and "dry" McAdoo had battled to bloody standstills at the 1920 and 1924 conventions. The tall, lanky, hawk-visaged McAdoo hadn't bothered running in 1928, but the embers of his always powerful ambitions still flickered in 1932. "I am foolish enough," McAdoo confided to publisher W. M. Kiplinger in June 1930, "[to consider myself able to] come nearer [to] winning a victory for the Democrats than any other man now in sight. I say this without egotism."[62]

McAdoo may have lacked egotism. He, nonetheless, possessed a passel of similar vices. Federal Reserve chairman Charles Sumner Hamlin considered him "the most selfish man I ever met."[63] Washington observers suspected that McAdoo had not only leaked information concerning his father-in-law's administration to the *Washington Post*—he by-lined it under a pseudonym.[64] Newton Baker found his former Cabinet colleague to possess "the greatest lust for power I ever saw."[65] Jim Farley deemed him "selfish" *and* "arrogant."[66] And, perhaps that is why McAdoo had already begun his scheming, meeting at New York's Waldorf-Astoria Hotel to backstab Hearst and Garner and— highly ironically—to back former Secretary Baker.[67]

And for good measure he truly detested Al Smith's New York: "the citadel of privilege . . . ," he termed it, "reactionary, sinister, unscrupulous, mercenary, and sordid."[68]

Such was the ally the ultimate New Yorker Al Smith now courted.

"How're you, how're you?" queried McAdoo as they settled in at the Blackstone.

"Out of sight, out of sight," came Smith's noncommittal reply.

"Well, what are you going to do out here?"

"I'm going to be on the level with you," Smith answered. "We're both against Roosevelt or you wouldn't be here. Is that right?" McAdoo assented, and Smith replied, "All right, if we work together we can beat this fellow."[69]

McAdoo demanded to know Smith's strategy. It was the obvious one: a stall followed by a deadlock followed by a compromise candidate. "If we go to the fifth ballot we've got him licked all right," strategized The Happy Warrior. "Then my candidacy is out the window. I can't be nominated, but we can sit down around a table and get together on a candidate."

McAdoo's ears pricked up. But he demanded assurances that he would be a player: "When you sit around the table will I be there?"

"If you're not there," Smith reassured his perennial adversary, "I won't be there either."[70]

All around them others scrambled just as feverishly for even the smallest advantage. Jim Farley knew damned well the truth of Smith's stall-to-a-deadlock strategy. He and Louis Howe (deathly ill from asthma virtually the whole time[71]) enticed delegates to their Congress Hotel headquarters for conference calls featuring their candidate, still in far-off Albany.[72] More significant, Farley and his operatives dangled the vice-presidential nod before anyone capable of pushing FDR over the top: primarily Ritchie[73] and Garner,[74] but even Virginia governor Harry Byrd.[75] None of these second-slot overtures bore fruit, but Garner floor manager Sam Rayburn offered a glimmer of hope. "We have come to Chicago to nominate Speaker Jack Garner for the Presidency if we can," Rayburn advised. "We are not against any other candidate and we are not for any other candidate. Governor Roosevelt is the leading candidate and naturally he must be headed off if we are to win. But we don't intend to make it another Madison Square Garden."[76] Rayburn hadn't said yes to Roosevelt, but he hadn't said no.

Garner stayed in. Illinois senator Hamilton "Pink Whiskers" Lewis dropped out. "This is the beginning of the end," Farley trumpeted. "Roosevelt will be nominated on the first ballot."[77] He was wrong. Chicago mayor Anton Cermak calmly substituted another stop-FDR front-man for Lewis: Windy City banker Melvin "Honest Mel . . . the new Abe Lincoln"[78] Traylor. Farley quickly offered Traylor secretary of the treasury.[79] As the convention opened, however, Traylor's First National Bank lurched toward insolvency, and an embattled "Honest Mel" rushed to his institution to literally mount a marble pillar to beg his panic-stricken depositors not to crash First National.[80]

Al Smith's political skills—or, at least, his temperament—had already crashed. A Chippewa chief tried to present the erstwhile Fulton Fish Market alumnus with a bass. Smith petulantly refused. "I've been posing nine hours. . . . ," he snarled. "Take one of the other pictures and paint a fish on it."[81] When reporters queried Al if he had spoken with FDR, he snapped, "No, I know [the Executive Mansion] number well. It didn't call me."[82] He phoned Sam Rayburn to see if the stop-FDR lines were holding. Rayburn said they weren't, and Smith slammed the receiver down on him.[83]

The convention finally opened on Monday, June 27. The Salvation Army's Evangeline Booth, a still ardent "dry,"[84] delivered the unabashedly Christian opening prayer, "In this tragic hour of world history," she begged her Redeemer, "we wonder if there is an interpretation of Thy will written upon the walls of the nations in letters of want and sorrow which we have not caught . . . give us the light that will show the way."[85] She was right to speak of "a tragic hour." In 1932, between twelve and thirteen million unemployed Americans walked the streets. Millions more suffered mere partial employment. Salaries had dropped 40 percent; wages, 60 percent. Business lost somewhere between five and six billion dollars. The Federal Reserve Board's Adjusted Index of Industrial Production had tumbled from 125 to fifty-eight. Business and industry badly required capital, but the amount of securities fueling such investment had plummeted by $23/24$. Gross agricultural income had declined from $12 to $5¼ billion. By year's end a million jobless, homeless persons were on the march across America. Marching to where or to what they knew not. An estimated two hundred thousand were children.[86] That spring, in Chicago itself, a horrified observer witnessed "a crowd of some fifty men fighting over a barrel of garbage which had been set outside the back door of a restaurant. American citizens fighting for scraps of food like animals."[87]

. . . and *each* national convention still focused on . . . Prohibition.

Hypocrisy accompanied attention. Perhaps it always had—on both sides, in both parties—but the phenomenon now notched new records as the ground shifted dangerously under formerly "dry" feet.

The Democratic keynote speaker, Kentucky senator Alben Barkley, had been quite the "dry."[88] In Chicago, however, he now jeered: "Two weeks ago in this place, the Republican party promulgated what it called a plank on the Eighteenth Amendment. It is not a plank. It is a promiscuous agglomeration of scrap-lumber. (APPLAUSE) Nicholas Murray Butler condemns it because it is dry, Senator Borah condemns it because it is wet, and the American people will condemn it because it is a fraud. . . . This convention should . . . recommend the passage by Congress of a resolution repealing the Eighteenth Amendment of the Constitution. . . ."[89]

A few "dry" die-hards remained. Cordell Hull proposed scaling back the party's now dripping "wet" plank. Delegates debated for four full hours, spent ten minutes cheering the mere entrance of ultra-"wet" Al Smith,[90] and then voted down Hull's motion 934¾–213¾.[91] Hull thought Smith's address on the subject was filled with "demagogy and discourtesy" against him—no doubt payback for four years of anti-Smith activities on Hull's part.[92]

In Albany, FDR listened on "a portable radio set"[93] as his supporter, the Catholic Montana senator Thomas J. Walsh, defeated Raskob, Smith, and John W. Davis's man, Democrat National Committee executive director Jouett Shouse, for the post of the permanent convention chairman,[94] but seventy-three-year-old Walsh's narrow 626–528 victory margin[95] only augured future difficulties. As did the 638¾–514¼ seating of white-suited Huey Long's pro-Roosevelt Louisiana delegation.[96] FDR clearly possessed a comfortable convention majority, but, even more clearly, he lacked the necessary two-thirds of delegates—770 votes—necessary for nomination.

His forces grew nervous. Their runner might yet stumble. In truth, they had recorded little progress since Jim Farley's confident forecasts that January. Still, some observers retained that belief. In Washington, on Tuesday, June 28, Herbert Hoover asked his press secretary, Ted Joslin, if Roosevelt would still be nominated. "Absolutely," Joslin replied, "he'll get it on the second or third ballot."

"I hope so," Hoover replied, "Our salvation lies largely in his nomination . . . .," before adding, "I am afraid of Baker."[97]

Newton D. Baker's specter simply would not vanish. Walter Lippmann boosted him as "the man of the hour" for president. "My impression," Lippmann argued, "is that he [Baker] is the real first choice of more responsible Democrats than any other man, and . . . an acceptable second choice to almost every one. Although there is not a single delegate instructed to vote for him, he is the man who, once preconvention pledges have been fulfilled, could most easily be nominated."[98] Columnist Mark Sullivan (a Hoover crony) concurred, confidently pronouncing Baker the "most probable nominee."[99]

Baker wasn't the only high-hat dark horse. Many, including the supposed Smith loyalist John J. Raskob, pinned their hopes on Owen D. Young.

Raskob, it transpired, was far more realistic than sentimental regarding Smith's chances. Just before the convention opened he wrote to an associate: "There is no better candidate and should we be able to nominate [Young] I am certain the country would concede his election and immediately start to pull itself out of the Depression."[100] Young, like Baker, however, desired the nomination served to him upon a silver platter, but such servings are rarely rendered without heaping and unappetizing side portions of sacrificial lamb. No lambs dwelt among the donkeys in 1932.

The convention's opening day's program boasted the inevitable Will Rogers, fast-talking sportscaster Ted Husing, the ostentatiously erudite former heavyweight champion Gene Tunney ("As a speaker, Gene is a good heavyweight boxer"[101]), the wiry, little former vaudevillian Massachusetts representative William P. Connery Jr., and famed Chicago defense attorney Clarence Darrow (champion of both evolution and its twin counterarguments Leopold and Loeb). Transforming the day, however, into easily the least politically correct in convention history (at least to twenty-first century eyes) were newly minted blackface radio stars Amos 'n Andy ("two boys who have given more clean, wholesome entertainment than anyone . . ."[102] to which Andy responded: "I'se regusted"[103]), and Fr. Charles Coughlin, who argued that "the Carpenter from Nazareth" should replace "an engineer from Palo Alto."[104]

The time finally arrived for nominations. Of the lesser candidates, "Alfalfa Bill" Murray's twenty-four-minute-long demonstration generated the most razzmatazz. Both Will Rogers (wearing a "Garner" hat secured from the Texas delegation) and Heywood Broun (also to enlist in the Smith demonstration and even here shouting "Smith, Smith, Smith!") enrolled in the "Alfalfa" brouhaha.[105]

Former New York State Supreme Court judge John E. Mack, Roosevelt's ally since nominating him for state senator in 1910, again performed his man's nominating honors. When not merely plodding, Mack recklessly risked overstatement. "Country-born and country-loving, this man's whole political life is an open book," Mack orated, ignoring, among other things, his candidate's near divorce. "His reputation is unsullied, his character spotless. . . . As a young man, as a student, as a lawyer, as a son, as a husband, as a father, as a legislator, and an executive, he has measured up to the traditions of true American manhood."[106]

Such twaddle, nonetheless, generated an often excruciating forty-three-minute demonstration,[107] hardly more fun than Mack's leaden oratory. Aggravating matters was nine-fingered stadium organist Al Melgard's funereal rendition of FDR's personal musical selection for the occasion, the nautical

"Anchors Aweigh." Finally, Louis Howe wheezed. "For God's sake tell 'em play something else!" Which left the question of what to play after tossing "Anchors Aweigh" overboard. Ed Flynn advanced a suggestion, and that is how "Happy Days Are Here Again" became the Roosevelt theme song.[108]

Not happy at all, however, was Massachusetts governor Joseph B. Ely. He had pledged not to seek re-election if his party nominated FDR.[109] Now, he outshone all in his passionate nomination of Al Smith. "After his defeat, who reorganized the party machinery?" Ely demanded. "Who carried on the battle? Who has set the course? Brains, force, leadership, human interest, organization, color, contrast, votes. Why pause? Why hesitate?

"Is there a ghost of other years hovering about this convention hall to dominate your mind, your heart, your conscience? Does the ghost of fear dominate you? . . .

"I speak for the Commonwealth of Massachusetts. . . . I believe that I voice the sentiments of the industrial East. The prejudices of our Protestant ancestors against entrusting government to those of a different religious faith have long since been wiped away by many a successful experience through which we have found that a man imbued with faith in God, whatever the creed, may be entrusted safely with the reins of government. . . .

". . . He who guides the destiny of nations looks upon both the home-lands of the South and the sidewalks of New York. I am the small voice of the inarticulate souls of the millions of Americans begging you to respond to their cry for the leadership of one of their own. I but voice his nomination, moved by deeper, more fundamental, more vital powers. As I stand here, I devoutly believe that a Divine Providence has given us this man and pre-served him so that you might make him the instrument for the preservation of popular government and democratic freedom.

"Let us end government by doubt, let us establish a government of deci-sion, of action, and of progress. For the Democratic party, for the United States of America, for the needs of humanity, I give to this convention the name of Alfred E. Smith."[110]

It was not so much what Ely said, but how he said it. The crowd sat enthralled at his performance—cheering for fifty-two minutes when he was done. Herbert Bayard Swope compared Ely's address to that of spellbinder Robert G. "The Great Agnostic" Ingersoll for James Abram Garfield in 1880. Others likened it to Bryan's famed "Cross of Gold" speech of 1896. Al Smith embraced Ely. Tears welled up in Al's eyes. Some said he kissed him.[111]

Delegates' hearts may (or may not) have been with Smith. Their heads were not; 1928 was a thousand years ago.

And while Joseph Ely drew tears and applause, other Bay Staters toiled less conspicuously and, perhaps more effectively, for their own candidate—Franklin Roosevelt.

Boston mayor James Michael Curley had sufficiently recovered his wits following his bruising primary defeat to travel to Chicago and even to obtain credentials "in conformity with an old Spanish custom"[112]—as an alternate delegate from Puerto Rico. Puckishly billing himself as "Alcalde [Mayor] Jaime Miguel Curleo,"[113] he busily hectored Farley and Howe (who disliked Curley perhaps more than he normally disliked anyone) with the idea that he should phone William Randolph Hearst out in California to switch Hearst's support to FDR. Farley and Howe remained unconvinced, but Curley called anyway, arguing that Garner was not so much a dark horse as a dead horse, that Hearst should swing to FDR, and that such a maneuver might easily win Garner the ticket's second slot. "You have the opportunity to name the next President and Vice-president of the United States," Curley hectored Hearst, but "W. R." remained unmoved. Curley called again and then again before morning broke. Coincidentally or not, that afternoon's *Chicago American* exhibited more tolerance for FDR than any Hearst paper had hitherto exhibited. Curley scooped up every available copy and scurried to distribute them around the hall.[114]

As Curley badgered Hearst, the seemingly endless parade of nominating and seconding speeches droned on. Their attendant floor demonstrations processed with ever less real enthusiasm but plodded forward, nevertheless. Desperate to speed the process, Jim Farley ordered those delivering FDR's seconding speeches to trim their orations. He had no luck. "I learned something on that occasion," he later recalled, "that perhaps we should have learned before: a thorough-going Democrat will give you his support, his loyalty, his vote, and his money—but never his radio time."[115] Not until 4:28 a.m.—to near abandoned galleries—did first ballot voting finally commence.[116] Two hours later the totals stood at 666¼ for Roosevelt, followed by Smith at 201½, Garner 90¼, Ohio favorite son Gov. George White 52, the embattled banker Melvin Traylor 42¼, Virginia's Harry Byrd 25, Missouri favorite son former senator James A. Reed 24, "Alfalfa Bill" Murray 23, Albert Ritchie 21, and—clearly not yet out of the starting gate—dark horse Newton D. Baker 8½.[117]

Before balloting began, however, an increasingly nervous Farley once more conferred with Garner floor manager Sam Rayburn. Farley again dangled the vice-presidency, proposing that Garner's votes switch to FDR following the first ballot. Rayburn responded that his 360 Texas delegates and alternates had traveled north to Chicago to vote for their man—and that is what they proposed to do. He was not exaggerating. "Garner for President" may have originally been the solitary and unrealistic brainchild of William Randolph Hearst, but once Texans savored the idea, they grasped it with Alamo-like devotion to their breasts. Shifting them into Roosevelt's column would be no easy task. Rayburn demanded to know how long FDR's forces could hold together. "Three ballots," Farley ruefully admitted, "four ballots, and maybe five"[118] before Franklin's candidacy slowly, but inevitably, collapsed.

"Well," drawled Rayburn, playing what cards he held very carefully, "we must let the convention go for a while, even if we are interested in the Vice-Presidency, and I'm not saying that we are."[119]

Farley's pessimism was indeed justified. FDR's 666¼ first-ballot vote total was weaker than it looked. Numerous state delegations featured bare Roosevelt majorities, but bound by the so-called "unit" rule, they voted unanimously for Roosevelt. A mere handful of delegates shifting within a given state (or more ominously a series of states) would trigger a dangerous reverse momentum for front-runner FDR, his situation particularly perilous in Alabama, Mississippi, Arizona, and Arkansas, each of which contained significant cores of Garner—and even Baker—sympathizers.[120] Mississippi was key. If it defected, Arkansas would soon follow.[121] Its newly elected governor Sennet Conner favored Baker, but Sen. Pat Harrison worked mightily to hold it for FDR. Sentiment for a bolt to Baker grew even stronger following John W. Davis and Al Smith's visit to its delegation. Charging to FDR's rescue was Huey Long, threatening to invade the state and defeat any politico who dared abandon Franklin.[122] At work more discreetly was FDR's 1914 senate primary opponent, James W. Gerard. Voting loyally for Smith as a New York delegate, his heart was, nonetheless, for fellow-patrician Roosevelt, and he ponied up eight hundred dollars to a western delegate to keep his wobbly pro-FDR delegation entertained (presumably drunk) and in line.[123]

Second ballot voting saw Roosevelt rise—just barely—to 677¾ votes. Smith declined to 194¼. Texas held steady for Garner. Not much happened elsewhere along the line, save that the comical "Alfalfa Bill" Murray's candidacy suddenly evaporated, with twenty-two of his twenty-three first ballot votes defecting to actual comic Will Rogers.[124] More significant, however, was what transpired as already-weary delegates voted. Others besides James Michael Curley had been dialing William Randolph Hearst's San Simeon mansion. Joseph P. Kennedy—united to "W. R." by mutual interests of immense wealth, alternating delusions and realities of political grandeur, film studio investments, and, yes, film industry mistresses—was also on the phone to Hearst.

Joe Kennedy had known Franklin Roosevelt since the Great War. "He was a tough guy in those days," Kennedy recalled. "He didn't let anything stand in the way of the output of warcraft and materials. . . ."[125] Roosevelt was the hardest trader I'd ever run up against. When I left his office, I was so disappointed and angry that I broke down and cried."[126]

Kennedy's tears, nonetheless, had sufficiently dried for him to count as an early enlistee in the Roosevelt cause. "Joe called me one day from California—" Greenwich, Connecticut, investment banker Jeremiah Milbank, a close friend of Herbert Hoover, recollected. "I think he was staying at Hearst's ranch—and in the course of our conversation he asked me if I had a notebook. I said yes, 'Well,' he said, 'jot down the name of the next president. You're not hearing much about him now, but you will in 1932. It's Franklin D. Roosevelt. And don't forget who told you.'"[127] A crucial $5,000 pre-convention contribution followed.[128] Wall Street wolf Joe Kennedy always bought low and sold high.

In mid-April 1932, Kennedy again visited San Simeon, peddling Roosevelt. He failed.[129] Now, he phoned "W. R.," not so much to tout the still unmarketable FDR, but to knock the alternatives. "Do you want that man Baker running our country, that great defender of the League of Nations, that ardent internationalist whose policies you despise?" Kennedy urged Hearst, "No, of course you don't. But that's just who you're going to get if you keep holding out your delegates from Roosevelt, for if the convention cracks open, it'll surely be Baker. And then where will you be?"[130]

Still powerfully wary of Roosevelt, Hearst countered, "Can't I get Ritchie?"[131]

Kennedy plotted; others fretted. Discouraged by Roosevelt's second ballot stall, his floor manager Arthur Mullen moved to adjourn, hoping to provide his forces with time to regroup, swing deals, and twist arms. Jersey City's Frank Hague and Tammany Hall's Dudley Field Malone (in his younger days quite the physical ringer for Winston Churchill and still bearing some resemblance) objected and forced a voice vote. Convention chairman Thomas Walsh ruled it inconclusive. Privately, however, he advised Mullen that the anti-Roosevelt "nays" really had triumphed and warned that a roll-call vote would only spark an embarrassing—and perhaps ultimately fatal—defeat for FDR. Mullen ingloriously withdrew his motion.[132]

Tallies hardly budged on the third ballot, save that Will Rogers's support vanished as quickly and as totally as it had appeared. Garner posted the biggest gain, from 90¼ to 101¼. FDR moved from 677¾ to the unlikely total of 682.79.[133]

Roosevelt now stood at the brink—of defeat. His "unit rule" states all tottered on defection's edge. Since November 1930 his greatest charm had been his inevitability. With that image dented, a Baker or a Young might finally emerge. They were, after all, far less longshots than the dark horses that had recently preceded them: Alton B. Parker and John W. Davis.

But no one waited for that to simply happen. William Gibbs McAdoo provided fulsome assurances of loyalty to Garner ("Sam, we'll vote for Jack Garner until Hell freezes if you say so"[134]), but seemed to be too involved in too many discussions with too many Roosevelt people for comfort. Huey Long redoubled his efforts to hold wavering Mississippi for Roosevelt. "If you break the [unit] rule, you so-and-so," the Kingfish threatened Pat Harrison, "I'll go into Mississippi and break you!"[135] Even prior to the third ballot, North Carolina threatened to defect. It simply could not decide where: to Garner or Young or even to Albert Ritchie?[136]

But, most significant, William Randolph Hearst had reconsidered his options.

The phone lines had been buzzing to San Simeon, with not only Joe Kennedy and Mayor Curley doing the calling. The phone also rang from staunchly Republican Louis B. Mayer. Hoover had directed his secretary Larry Richey to phone Mayer to similarly advise "W. R." (whose thirty-five-year old blonde mistress, Marion Davies, was under Metro-Goldwyn-Mayer contract) that if the sixty-nine-year-old Hearst really wanted to derail Baker, FDR was the quick, sure way to accomplish it.[137] Jim Farley—with Hearst's secretary Col. Joseph Willicombe and his star columnist Damon Runyon at his side—also phoned Hearst. All warned against Baker. Farley desperately pled that Roosevelt was nowhere near the interventionist that Hearst feared him to be.[138]

Hearst's Washington editor was one George Rothwell Brown, author not only of a laudatory serialized Garner biography[139] but also of its book form, published with the thoroughly inexplicable subtitle of *The Romantic Story of John N. Garner*.[140] Hearst now dialed Brown, ordering him to secure Garner's assent to releasing his delegates to Roosevelt. At 11:00 a.m., Friday, July 1, Brown and Garner met at the Capitol.[141] Depending on who told the story, Garner either agreed at that moment to drop out—or did not. In any case, he soon would.

Farley meanwhile pled his case to California's delegates: "Five states that have been in the Roosevelt column by the unit issue—Minnesota, Iowa, the two Dakotas, and Mississippi—will break and scatter on the fourth ballot,"[142] he confessed, adding, "Boys, Roosevelt is lost unless California comes over to us on the next ballot. I am 87 votes short, and I cannot hope to get them unless you switch to Roosevelt. . . ."[143]

McAdoo switched. Many in his delegation, however, wanted to fight for Garner to the end—and in the ensuing confusion never formally did vote to terminate their support.[144] If California proved reluctant, Texas proved, well . . . Texan. Few could stomach abandoning their crusade. Women cried at the news. "We had a horse all saddled up for a two-mile race," recalled *Fort-Worth Star-Telegram* publisher Amon G. Carter, "but one of our jockeys pulled up at the quarter mile post."[145] Texans finally switched to Roosevelt only by a slender 54–51 margin.[146]

Their vote had not transpired in a vacuum. The day swirled with plots and counter-plots, with one state threatening to defect one way and another another, but one thing is certain. At one point a deal was struck: John Nance Garner, and no one else, would be Franklin Roosevelt's running mate.

Yet, all was not quite settled. McAdoo angled with Hearst for a switch not to FDR—but to McAdoo himself. "W. R." wasn't interested. FDR was a sure bet. McAdoo's gambit threatened to send the party into a vortex of 1924-style, 103-ballot chaos. McAdoo regrouped, now hawking a Roosevelt-McAdoo ticket. Hearst remained unmoved. His deal—romantic or not—was with Garner, and he would honor it.[147]

Rumors circulated of California's move ("Bernie," Smith said to Baruch, "your long-legged friend has run out on us, just as I thought he would"[148]), but as the fourth ballot commenced, McAdoo—and his newly minted Roosevelt delegates—were nowhere to be seen. FDR's patchwork candidacy might still unravel. Smith's fragile mood recovered ("I have McAdoo's personal promise . . ."[149]), and he called out to New York alternate delegate Marion Dickerman (a close friend and business partner of Eleanor Roosevelt), "We've got this in the bag, Marion."[150]

McAdoo meanwhile sped to the stadium in a manner not akin to a western hero galloping to the rescue, but in the slapstick fashion of a silent movie comedic chase. Racing south from his delegation's Sherman House headquarters, his limousine sputtered to a sudden halt. Out of gas, pronounced his chauffeur (McAdoo always suspected sabotage). Thereupon, the gangly former treasury secretary hailed a passing motorcycle policeman and hitched a ride on the back of his vehicle. Unfortunately, he was too gangly, and his aforementioned long legs proved too elongated for comfort. Hopping off, he finally secured a taxicab to hustle him to the convention.[151]

The roll call had not reached California. McAdoo secured permission to speak. "Mr. Chairman, ladies and gentlemen," he commenced, "I thank you for the privilege accorded to me to say just a word in explaining the vote of the State of California."[152]

The galleries, packed by Chicago's uncouth, strong-arming Mayor Cermak with pro-Smith sympathizers, shared The Happy Warrior's delusion that California might flop down for him. They erupted in cheers, momentarily halting events. McAdoo, silently and patiently, a slight, cruel smile upon his lips, savored his moment. He appeared, thought California delegate Thomas Storke, like "a cat advancing craftily upon its prey."[153]

McAdoo finally continued: "California came here to nominate a President of the United States. She did not come here to deadlock this convention or to engage in another disastrous contest like that of 1924."[154] Even the densest Smith partisan knew what that meant. Cheers turned to boos and jeers—and personal insults.

The din subsided. With great glee, McAdoo announced the switch—his long-delayed payback against his great, still-hated, rival Smith: "As I was saying when this demonstration began, when a man comes into this convention with 700 votes in his favor, I take it as indicative of the public sentiment in this country for that candidate. I believe in democracy and in the rule of the majority. . . . California casts forty-four votes for Franklin D. Roosevelt."[155]

"If revenge is really sweet," noted H. L. Mencken, McAdoo "was sucking a colossal sugar teat."[156]

Texas and California switched. So did Maryland and Illinois and most other holdouts—but not Smith's acolytes. Only a handful—four Smith delegates—slunk toward Roosevelt. The remainder—190½—remained as stubbornly steadfast as their fallen hero.[157] New York's James W. Gerard requested Irene Gibson (years before the model of her husband Charles Dana Gibson's famed "Gibson Girl") to approach the embittered Smith to release his delegates to make it unanimous for FDR: "I won't do it. I won't do it. I won't do it,"[158] fumed Smith. And neither would they—neither would they—neither would they.

The furious Smith bolted out a side door. Clare Boothe Brokaw tracked him down at his Ambassador East Hotel suite. She expected to find him consoled by a crew of other loyalists. But precious few loyalists remain upon the decks of sunken political ships. Brokaw discovered Al and Catherine Smith quite alone, reciting their prayers before retiring for the night.[159] Soon the Smiths entrained for New York. Ely, Hague, and Tammany boss John F. Curry departed with them.[160] John W. Davis preceded their exit.[161] Back in Manhattan, Smith tersely told the press, "I have absolutely nothing to say to newspaper men . . . I am tired and I want to get a rest."[162]

Smith departed dramatically. FDR's arrival was electrifying.

It was also a great mask.

Smith had been at Chicago. So had Ritchie and Murray and Traylor and company. Only Garner, the ailing and coy Newton Baker—and Franklin Roosevelt—had absented themselves. Even low-key Warren Harding had been on the scene in 1920. But Franklin Roosevelt, like Woodrow Wilson in 1912, excused himself, a long-distance bystander while Farley and Flynn and Howe and Mullen and Kennedy and Curley sweated and schemed on his behalf, content to listen nervously on the radio[163] while Eleanor served eggs, frankfurters, sandwiches, and coffee to newsmen headquartered in the nearby Executive Mansion garage.[164]

But that image was about to change.

FDR would shatter tradition. He would not wait weeks to deliver his formal acceptance speech. Roosevelt, accompanied by Eleanor, secretaries Missy LeHand and Grace Tully, "his big, strong man" secretary Guernsey Cross, bodyguards New York City police officer Gus Gennerich (his part-time masseur[165]) and State Police sergeant Earl Miller, sons Elliott and John, and speechwriter Sam Rosenman,[166] piled into an American Airways mail plane bound for Chicago. Their fourteen-passenger, 1275-horsepower Ford tri-motor headed for an anxious convention. Even at a top speed of 130 mph, their trip required a grueling nine hours, including stops at Buffalo and Cleveland[167] (where Newton Baker pointedly refused to meet FDR[168]). Old salt FDR took matters in stride. Son John's stomach did not.[169] Ten thousand delirious Democrats (including the hitherto un-delirious Mayor Cermak) greeted FDR at the city's Municipal Airport for a twenty-mile triumphal procession toward the convention itself.[170]

As Roosevelt flew toward Chicago, delegates, however, concluded unfinished business: the nomination of a vice president. Cordell Hull hoped for the job. Some suggested a far-western progressive, such as Burton Wheeler, Clarence Dill, or even Utah governor George H. Dern.[171] Bernard Baruch (never for FDR) boldly inquired of Ed Flynn if it were too late to propose Governor Ritchie. Flynn tersely said, yes, it was.[172]

Sometimes, there is no deal so firm as a back-room deal. "Cactus Jack" Garner's nomination slid effortlessly along. Following four ballots of presidential rancor, delegates craved vice-presidential harmony. Iowa nominated former American Legion commander Gen. Matthew A. Tinley, but Tinley (formerly maneuvering for an unlikely Ritchie-Tinley ticket) quickly withdrew.[173] It was to be Garner—unlike Roosevelt—unanimously.

Boston's Mayor Curley, now riding high over his Massachusetts colleagues (he performed a little jig as he passed by them[174]), received the honor of seconding the Texan, though he seemed to have his eye on a bigger picture—the Depression. "Much has been said of the 'forgotten man,'" observed Curley. "Naturally, I have been a bit interested in him myself. Some have asked who he is and where he is, and I have made it my business to make my inquiry. To those who are unfamiliar with his existence, I want to say that within the last thirty days he could be found within the shadow of the national Capitol at Washington to the number of 15,000 sleeping in the open. To those who might visit the greatest industrial city in the whole world, the city of Detroit, he might be found with his dependents to the number of 600,000, out of a population of 2,000,000, or almost one in every three of the men, women, and children . . . To those who might journey to the richest city in the entire world, the city of New York, he would find the 'forgotten man' and his dependents to the number of 1,300,000 subsisting on public charity, victims in the richest land of the whole world to Hooverism."[175]

Aboard his tri-motor "Tin Goose," FDR and Rosenman continued fine-tuning Franklin's own address, snipping here-and-there, whittling it into fighting shape. In Chicago, meanwhile, Jesse Straus approached Ray Moley, who had co-authored its original draft with Rosenman. "Can we let Baruch see the acceptance speech?" Straus asked. "We want to be nice to him because he can contribute a good deal to the campaign."

"Please do!" Moley exploded, literally flinging his typescript at Straus. "It wouldn't be a regulation campaign, would it, if the nominee didn't tack and trim? This happens to be what Franklin Roosevelt believes and wants to say. But I'm sure he wouldn't be the first man to cave under pressure."[176]

Straus was easily cowed. The irascible Louis Howe was not. Greeting newly arrived FDR with his own draft of the document, he virtually demanded Roosevelt junk its Rosenman-Moley version. "Dammit, Louis," Roosevelt exploded, "I'm the nominee!"[177] But just as FDR had previously once ordered his Brains Trusters to reconcile grotesquely irreconcilable tariff positions, he calmly executed an instant merger of these competing efforts, by the strangely effective (though, yes, somewhat arbitrary) mechanism of simply tossing away Rosenman's first page and substituting Howe's.[178]

Thirty thousand Democrats cheered FDR's entrance to the convention, surging forward to greet him. Even the previously hostile galleries now warmed to him. His words rang out, in a great, if still vague, challenge to the existing order. "I have started out on the tasks that lie ahead," he informed them and the nation, "by breaking the absurd traditions that the candidate should remain in professed ignorance of what has happened for weeks until he is formally notified of that event many weeks later.

"My friends, may this be the symbol of my intentions to be honest and to avoid all hypocrisy or sham, to avoid all silly shutting of the eyes to the truth in this campaign. . . .

"I pledge you—I pledge myself to a new deal for the American people. Let us all here assembled constitute ourselves prophets of a new order of competence and of courage. This is more than a political campaign; it is a call to arms. Give me your help, not to win votes alone, but to win in this crusade to restore America to its own people."[179]

Smith, of course, wasn't there to hear him, but those who tarried came away impressed. Woodrow Wilson's widow extended her support. So, even, did the New Party's Clare Boothe Brokaw. Brokaw shared a ride from the convention with Baruch's henchman, Gen. Hugh S. "Iron Pants" Johnson and Wilson's former personal physician, Adm. Cary Grayson. Johnson grumbled that the party had nominated a son of a bitch. "Yes, Hugh," Grayson responded, "but he's our son of a bitch now."[180]

Beyond Chicago, even Republicans rallied to FDR's cause. Hiram Johnson praised his "fine and gallant and exhilarating" flight to the convention.[181] Nebraska's George Norris provided an outright endorsement—even before FDR's tri-motor had yet touched down. North Dakota's glass-eyed former attorney general William Lemke, now running for Congress as a Republican (in reality a member of the radical populist "Nonpartisan League"), openly plotted strategy with Roosevelt.[182] Senators Nye, Frazier,[183] Borah, and Norris's Nebraska colleague Robert B. Howell dared not go as far as Norris or Lemke. But neither would they voice any support for Hoover.[184]

Such matters worried Herbert Hoover nary a whit. He enjoyed a rare good mood when a White House usher brought news from press secretary Ted Joslin of his former friend's nomination. Message delivered, the emissary phoned Joslin to confirm delivery. Joslin itched to know The Chief's reaction. Hoover, he learned, had "smiled more broadly than he had in months. . . ."[185]

A presidential campaign was about to begin.

CHAPTER FIFTEEN

"Anti-Semitism may be a good starter . . ."

GERMANY'S TWO-STAGE PRESIDENTIAL CAMPAIGN HAD MERCIFULLY concluded, and though Adolf Hitler had not defeated Paul von Hindenburg, he had magically transformed his prognosis from the near side of improbable to the far side of inevitable. Hindenburg, on the other hand, would soon reveal himself as both a sore winner and a world-class ingrate.

Yes, he would never have to seek office again. Yes, he still might hire and fire chancellors at will or whim and dissolve legally elected legislatures. He continued to essentially rule by decree, wielding as much power as any breast-plated, ostrich-beplumed Kaiser. Heinrich Brüning bestowed that upon him. But Brüning's bequest failed to meet Hindenburg's prickly terms. The Old Gentleman had been forced to stand for election once more. Worse, his support had been reduced largely to socialists and Catholics. He won, but he won with the wrong army—he won with priests and proletarians, not Hohenzollerns and Junkers—and he hated that.

Such petulance might seem beneath such a great, George Washington–like national hero. It was par for the course. Paul von Hindenburg was, as his foremost biographer dubbed him, "The Wooden Titan"—in truth, more wooden than titan. Roused from retirement in 1914, he directed imperiled imperial eastern front forces to spectacular victories at Tannenberg and the Masurian Lakes. Genuine credit, however, properly resided with underlings, the already-famous Erich Ludendorff and the obscure Eighth Army staff officer Max Hoffmann. "See," a disgusted Hoffmann later sputtered to touring officers, "this is where Hindenburg slept before the battle [Tannenberg], this is where Hindenburg slept after the battle, and this is where Hindenburg slept during the battle."[1] By 1916, the somnolent, almost sixty-nine-year-old had, nonetheless, risen to army chief of staff. Again, reality diverged from rank. His supposed subordinate Ludendorff exercised actual control over both the army and of the nation as a whole. By September 1918, however,

Imperial Germany, already triumphant over Russia and so tantalizingly near to western front victory, was, in fact, cracking up—and so was Ludendorff, who recommended the nation seek an armistice, then changed what was left of his mind, and then resigned. He expected Hindenburg to follow his lead, but Hindenburg neither resigned nor possessed the courage to confront Wilhelm II with the news that war and empire were lost and that his imperial and royal majesty must abdicate.[2]

That unpleasant task thus fell to Ludendorff's successor, the master logician Gen. Wilhelm Gröner.

It was the Württemberg-born Gröner—not Hindenburg—who held the nation together in the difficult postwar period, cutting deals with the SPD to simultaneously preserve the integrity of the army and to squash whatever pesky Communist/Spartacist insurrections might arise. Hindenburg—through the SPD Reichskanzler Hermann Müller—appointed Gröner defense minister in January 1928. By October 1931, as the always shaky republic tottered still more, Gröner had become the unspectacular glue that held it together, now also serving as interior minister. But as Gröner acted as the Fatherland's great bulwark against anarchy, he, nonetheless, brought with him the seeds of profound intrigue, serial betrayal, and immense danger.

He brought with him Col. Kurt von Schleicher.

Key to understanding Colonel Schleicher was his very name, translated variously as "creeper,"[3] "intriguer," or "sneak."[4]

The Prussian-born Schleicher was, as his acquaintance, the historian Sir John Wheeler-Bennett, observed, "indeed, the evil genius of the later Weimar Period, symbolizing in himself all the worst traits of the General in politics. Vain he was, and unscrupulous, and unfaithful; with a passion, amounting almost to an obsession, for intrigue, and a marked preference for the devious and the disingenuous; but his ambitions were for power rather than responsibility, for influence rather than position."[5]

Posted pre-war to the Third Guards Regiment, he had befriended the lazy but brilliant future Reichswehr chief-of-staff Kurt von Hammerstein-Equord[6]—and, more important, Paul von Hindenburg's more than somewhat lazy[7] and considerably less brilliant son Oskar.[8] During the Great War, Schleicher served on the General Staff, increasing his circle of acquaintances even more: to include Hindenburg Sr. and Gröner, plus a tall, pleasant-enough Westphalian cavalry officer named Franz von Papen.[9] Gröner grew to regard Schleicher (fifteen years his junior) as his "adopted son."[10] As the 1920s progressed, Schleicher jockeyed himself into whatever intrigue Reichswehr officers might find themselves in, whether it be fostering Maj. Bruno Buchrucker's Black Reichswehr[11] or the equally violent Freikorps[12] or securing illegal armaments (including poison gas) through clandestine cooperation with the Soviets.[13] During Gröner's temporary departure from the government, Schleicher attached himself to Reichswehr chief Gen. Hans von Seeckt. By October 1926, however, he had betrayed the brilliant Seeckt (also a rival for a woman's favors) and helped force his retirement.[14]

When Gröner assumed the defense ministry in 1929, he created a special position for his protégé—the Reichswehr *Ministeramt* (Office of the Ministerial Affairs)—allowing Schleicher to devote full time to politicking throughout the government.[15] Gröner, fully trusting his young "cardinal in politics,"[16] permitted him full access to Hindenburg. Schleicher's influence grew even beyond his own considerable dreams, for he was, as Berlin high society columnist Bella Fromm conceded, "one of the few men who possess almost irresistible charm."[17] And so, when in 1930, Schleicher (now a general) suggested to Hindenburg that the colorless, relatively obscure Heinrich Brüning might constitute a worthy successor to the faltering Socialist Hermann Müller; Hindenburg took the bait. Master-schemer Kurt von Schleicher was now something a great more than a mere bureaucratic deal-maker.

He was indeed a king-maker, less a general than a Hindenburg, Seeckt, or Gröner, but ever more adept a politician than a Müller, a Brüning, or a Hugenberg.

"How soldierly at least [Schleicher's] title [of general] sounds," sneered the Nazis' innuendo-peddling *Völkischer Beobachter*, "but he is only a pale office general dabbling in politics. Surely he himself must think his uniform out of place. . . . A frock coat would suit him far better than a soldier's greatcoat. Nevertheless he will not give it up; perhaps he knows how colored cloth, particularly with broad red braid, works on women. His successes are like those of a hero in a novel! Some women have already attempted to give up their useless lives. But in the nick of time they thought better of it and saw that it was hardly worth the while. General von Schleicher is complete master of the Reichswehr Minister [Gröner] (family included)."[18]

At this late date, Schleicher's personal life is hard to judge. To the fair sex (and, it appears, he knew many of them), he played the dashing (if rather vague) blowhard. "The red cloak I wear as a general, Ladies," he oozed, "will some day become an executioner's cloak, when in the public squares, we have to deal with our enemies!"[19]

Historian Emil Ludwig termed him "depraved and weak, faithless and irresolute, his actions were in keeping with the soft sensuality of his aspect."[20] Rumors circulated of his being "abnormally inclined."[21] He did not marry until July 1932, when at age fifty, he wed the thirty-eight-year-old wife of his cousin, Bogislav Thilo Otto Hans-Karl von Schleicher, Elisabeth

Hennigs von Schleicher ("Slim and elegant, amiable and sincere"[22]). Kurt and Elisabeth might have wed earlier but she had taken her time in divorcing.[23] Franz von Papen sized up the once and future Frau Schleicher as "a lady of remarkable intelligence and personality, and of inordinate ambition" but theorized that it "may well have been her influence that decided [Schleicher] to abandon his position behind the scenes for the full responsibilities of power."[24]

And that would prove to be a dangerous game—for all.

Heinrich Brüning was no mere wooden mini-titan but a man of substance, serious and patriotic, intelligent and honest. "It is extraordinary," Hindenburg marveled, "how my little Brüning manages to get everything done!"[25] Even Hitler (rarely impressed with anyone) exclaimed after meeting him in October 1930, "That is a real man!"[26] American ambassador Frederic Sackett gushed to Secretary of State Stimson that Weimar's latest chancellor was "the discovery of Europe, a really great man."[27]

He might indeed have been that. But he was certainly not a great politician. In his own cold, ascetic way, he was as unlikely a successful politician as any former Vienna flophouse denizen. He was, in some sense, the German Hoover.

British journalist R. T. Clark observed of him:

> *Where Brüning may be criticized is in his conception of his mission, in his curious military attitude towards his chief [Hindenburg], in his aloofness from the nation. It was perfectly impossible for him to . . . identify himself with the nation and use the nation to impose his will on the politicians. He had [no] intense humanity. He was not the leader; he was the doctor working coldly to save the patient's life, always apart from it, forcing it to take remedies of extreme nauseatingness, never bringing it into active cooperation with him. There again it was the fault of the system, the fault that Hitler did not commit. There was no gulf between Hitler and his followers save . . . discipline and hierarchic distinction; they were a unity. Between the government and the nation there was still the impassable gulf . . . even in so dire an emergency and Brüning was the last man to create that unity. He was not a great man nor even a great statesman, but he was an honest man and a patriotic man whose defects were too big for him.[28]*

In the end, Brüning failed not only to create a bond with the people. He failed to create—or rather to sustain—one with Hindenburg.

And, so Kurt von Schleicher, having invented Heinrich Brüning, now endeavored to destroy him.

But first he had to smash Wilhelm Gröner.

Of all those inhabiting the top rungs of German government, Gröner exhibited the most profound apprehension of the Hitler menace, though his initial personal contact with the ascendant Führer was by no means totally negative. "Sympathetic impression; decent, modest chap with good intentions," Gröner observed in January 1932. "His air is that of a diligent self-made man . . . determined to wipe out revolutionary ideas . . . Hitler's purposes and goals are good; but [he is a] fanatic. So full of enthusiasm and volcanic force that he undoubtedly continues to use the wrong means now and then."[29]

German elections approached. SA violence increased. Gröner's sympathy evaporated. And here, he and Schleicher finally parted company.

Schleicher conceded the SA's faults. But, he, nonetheless, saw their militaristic squadrons as the perfect, nearly ready-made, auxiliary to the treaty-constrained Reichswehr. When the moment finally arrived to throw off Versailles's shackles and invigorate and augment the national army's restricted legions, each SA man might easily exchange his déclassé brown shirt for a far smarter field-gray tunic. Like Gröner, however, Schleicher saw Hitler as a distinctly mixed bag. "An interesting young man with exceptional speaking abilities," thought Schleicher. "In his plans he soars in the clouds. You have to hold him down by the coattails in order to keep him on the ground."[30]

Schleicher, though, fancied himself as just the man to seize those coattails. By now he thought he might manipulate *anyone*. And while Brüning and Hindenburg might be ardent monarchists, the cynical Schleicher was not. The game for him was not restoring thrones but elevating himself. "Republic or monarchy is not the question now," he said as far back as the mid-1920s, "but rather what should this republic look like."[31]

It should, he concluded very early on, look a lot like him.

Meanwhile, Gröner fretted about the SA—and not merely about its street-fighting aspects nor its overall numbers—though its exploding membership totals were quite amazing: from a hundred thousand in January 1930 to 290,000 in 1931 to 300,000 in March 1932, 400,000 in July, and 445,000 that August.[32] As March 1932's presidential election neared, Gröner sensed dangerous movements on the Sturmabteilung's part, aimed not at smashing Communist skulls, but at seizing power if—despite Joseph Goebbels's rosy predictions—their Führer's vaunted electoral bid failed. "[E]verything points to the conclusion that a *coup de main* may be expected," Gröner noted on March 8. "Frick, Goebbels and Strasser are said to have given Hitler a last chance to get into the saddle legally. If it should turn out after the end of the election that a victory for Hitler is precluded, then an attack may be expected."[33]

Schleicher supposed otherwise. "I am really quite happy," he wrote his superior barely a fortnight later, "that we have a counterbalance in the form of the Nazis, even though they are ill-behaved and to be used only with the greatest care. If there were no Nazis it would be necessary to invent them."[34]

Nonetheless, when Gröner finally decided to ban the fractious SA, as well as the whole raft of the Nazi strong-arm squads that augmented them—Heinrich Himmler's SS, the NSKK ("National Socialist Motor Corps" or *Nationalsozialistisches Kraftfahrkorps*), and the air auxiliary, the *Fliegersturme* ["Storm Flyers"])—Schleicher initially supported him.[35] Or, at least, he said he did, the latter proposition making more sense, for by the spring of 1932, Schleicher was already neck-deep in both open and clandestine negotiations with Nazi brass.

In March 1931, he had conferred with Ernst Röhm, securing promises that in the event of any crisis (i.e., another Red uprising and/or a Polish invasion) Röhm's SA would march to the aid of the Reichswehr.[36] That October he arranged not only for Hitler and Göring to meet Brüning, but later that same day for Hitler to confer with Hindenburg himself.[37] The ex-*feldmarschall* and the ex-meldeganger did not hit it off. Beforehand, Oskar von Hindenburg sniped regarding Hitler, "I suppose he wants a free drink."[38] Once introduced, Hitler could not shut up. Hindenburg's state secretary, Otto Meissner, recalled that the session had lasted for an hour-and-a-quarter—and that Hitler talked for a full hour.[39] Afterward the Reichspräsident fumed, "This corporal from Bohemia wants to be Reich Chancellor? Never! At the most he could be my Postmaster General. Then he can lick me on the stamps from behind. . . ."[40]

A lesser (or perhaps a greater) man might have been discouraged by such a result. Schleicher was not. Within the month, the French military attaché, Col. Édouard-Charles-François Chapouilly, disturbingly reported: "In Schleicher's view, Hitler knows very well how to distinguish between the demagogy suitable to a young party, and the needs of national and international life. He has already moderated the actions of his troops on more than one occasion, and one can secure more from him. Faced with the force he controls, there is only one policy to adopt—to use him and win him over, foreseeing with some reason the loss of the revolutionary wing of his party."[41]

In January 1932, Hitler, Brüning, Gröner, and Schleicher conferred regarding Hindenburg's short-term continuance in office.[42] This time, of course, it had been Hitler's turn to display intransigence, refusing to grant his assent.[43] "[T]he Presidency is not really in question," Goebbels observed of these sessions. "Brüning only wants to stabilize his own position indefinitely and that of his Cabinet. . . . The contest for power, the game of chess, has begun. It may last throughout the year. It will be a fast game, played with intelligence and skill."[44]

Schleicher not only deemed himself uniquely worthy for such a contest, but dismissed Hitler's band of parvenu malcontents as profoundly unequipped. National Socialists, he concluded, were "merely little children who had to be led by the hand."[45] But soon it was Schleicher nervously darting to meet Hitler. "The Leader has been to see Schleicher," Goebbels noted. "Everybody scuttling hither and thither like ants in an anthill. The Government has completely lost its head."[46]

Which returns us to Wilhelm Gröner's rapidly unraveling fate. By early February, Goebbels was confiding to his diary: "To put the thing in a nutshell: Gröner must go—followed by Brüning. . . ."[47]

It was Gröner's aforementioned hostility to the SA that finally capsized him. As Germans voted in March 1932, the Sturmabteilung grew increasingly restive, as a cordon of storm troopers surrounded Berlin. Röhm assured Schleicher that such ominous moves represented mere Nazi "precautionary measures,"[48] but Gröner, along with the nervous Prussian interior minister Carl Severing, knew better. A coup lay in the works. On March 17, Prussian authorities raided NSDAP offices. Seizing mounds of evidence (including the code word for action: "Grandma is dead"[49]), they quickly suspended twenty-five Prussian DNVP and Nazi newspapers.[50] In Bavaria, right-wing minister president Heinrich Held acted to prevent local military stores from falling into SA hands.[51]

In mid-April, Gröner banned the SA.[52] The move severely crippled the National Socialist movement and threatened to alienate Hitler from his more fractious and revolutionary SA. Nonetheless, Hitler, still wedded to a "legal" path to power, cautioned his momentarily defanged troops toward caution and restraint. "For years, true to my orders, you have followed the legal path to the conquest of political power," he declared. "Hundreds of your comrades have been assassinated during this period, and many thousands have been wounded. . . . April 24 [the date of local elections] will be a day of retribution. Give those who are now in power no chance whatever to postpone the election on any pretext. If you fulfill your duty, General Gröner's blow will fall back upon him and his confederates a thousand times over from the force of our propaganda will recoil on him and his allies with a thousandfold force."[53]

Banning the SA should have been a body blow to the rising movement. But God works in mysterious ways—and so does the devil. "There is reason to believe that the dissolution of the storm detachments was not entirely unwelcome to Hitler," Ambassador Sackett wired Secretary of State Stimson. "Various units of his army were dissatisfied with his principle of legality; they were tired of waiting for the promised Third Reich. Moreover, the two presidential campaigns had been a drain on Hitler's coffers and . . . financing these organizations threatened to become burdensome. The dissolution of the storm detachments removed also the main obstacle in the way of the Nazis' participation in a coalition government. . . ."[54]

Beyond the effect on Hitler was the greater effect on Gröner and the furtherance of Schleicher's schemes. Schleicher now skillfully employed the controversy to drive a huge wedge between the defense minister and his Reichspräsident. Already, Schleicher had circulated rumors that Gröner was a secret Social Democrat. To this he added whispers that Gröner's SA-banning edict should have also included the SPD paramilitary organization, the quite harmless *Reichsbanner*. "I find it incomprehensible," Kronprinz Wilhelm angrily wrote to Gröner, "that [you] wish to disperse the wonderful human resources which are united in the SA and SS which are receiving such valuable training there."[55]

Hitler's bloodthirsty minions had surrendered without a fight. Only in Edmund Heines's Breslau gau had any resistance been offered.[56] Left-leaning Count Harry Kessler (one-time librettist for Richard Strauss) pondered to his diary on how the Hitlerites had "allowed themselves with such lamb-like patience to be disarmed and broken up. . . ." He thought such "pretty chicken-hearted" and "pitiable" behavior "almost suspicious."[57]

The count might indeed have grasped something. For Hitler's Gandhi-like path of nonviolent least-resistance (now, *that's* an ironic phrase) would soon pay dividends, only re-enforcing Hindenburg's already existing sympathy toward Hitler's brownshirts. "Organizationally the S.A. and S.S. continued to exist," noted Hindenburg biographer Andreas Dorpalen, "in the guise of 'anti-Communist leagues,' sport clubs, or new party units. Yet their unwillingness to defy the decree openly served to convince the president, the army, and the bulk of their sympathizers that they were law-abiding groups that had been subjected to a grave injustice."[58]

Schleicher moved to remedy said "injustice," ordering his adjutant, Col. Eugen Ott, to draft a letter from Hindenburg demanding that Gröner justify his exemption of the Reichsbanner. "I have issued the Decree banning the S.A. and S.S. . . . ," Hindenburg now wrote Gröner. "I have been informed, evidence being provided at the same time, that other parties also have similar organizations to those banned here. In fulfilment of my duty to exercise my office in a supra-political manner and to apply the law equally, I must demand, that, if this is correct, these organizations shall also receive the same treatment. . . ."[59]

Schleicher's nonstop rumor machine hammered Gröner on matters of public policy—and personal foible. The "schemer" gleefully reminded Hindenburg that Gröner's son Walther had been born just five months following his parents' wedding ceremony. He had, Schleicher chuckled to The Old Gentleman, been nicknamed "Nurmi" in honor of the record-setting Finnish Olympic sprinter.[60]

And Hindenburg chuckled back.

The Nazis snickered too. Though, considering the striking similarities to Joseph and Magda Ritschel Quandt, Goebbels's own recent nuptials and accelerated parenthood, perhaps they might not have grinned at all.[61] In any case, they chuckled not at all at the SA ban, and Nazi Reichstag delegates arose to protest it.

And Wilhelm Gröner dared rise to defend it.

He blundered mightily. Göring forcefully reminded him of how not long ago, Gröner's Reichswehr had embraced these now supposedly despicable brownshirts: "But you were ready to have them under your own leadership!"[62] Gröner never had a chance. Dispirited from suspicions of Schleicher's betrayals, sick with diabetes,[63] and, for good measure, beset with a painful, bandaged boil upon his forehead,[64] the defense minister stood defenseless against an unceasing torrent of catcalls, insults, and invective. "Such an exhibition of inaptitude and helplessness has never before been witnessed," gloated Goebbels. "We overwhelm him with loud interruptions, so that the whole House is convulsed with laughter. At last one can only pity the man. He is done for, and has sung his swan song. One of us puts forward the motion to have this part of his speech broadcasted."[65] As Gröner staggered from the chamber, he met Schleicher, who callously informed his old mentor that he "no longer enjoyed the confidence of the Army and must resign."[66]

Wilhelm Gröner departed.

━◆━

Winston Spencer Churchill arrived.

Neither the stock market nor Winston's political fortunes had improved since 1929.

The British establishment desired no portion of him. Winston found himself reduced to flirting with the rising young fascist Oswald Mosley, going so far as to urge Mosley's return to Parliament.[67] Even Winston's usual amusements had turned on him. When Charles Chaplin visited Churchill's Chartwell estate in September 1931, The Little Tramp not only performed his famous *The Gold Rush* roll dance for his host—but mocked him for having fixed the disastrously wrong price for gold in 1925.[68] Back in New York, that December, and en route to Baruch's, Churchill found himself splayed across Fifth Avenue, hit by a taxi driven by a twenty-six-year-old Yonkers man named Mario Cantasano.[69] The battered Churchill feared complete paralysis. Even after recouping his mobility, the "never-give-up-never-never-never" Winston nearly did, confessing to his wife, Clementine, his fear that he might never "recover from the three blows"[70]—the Crash, his political exile, and this near fatality—recently visited upon him.

But he did *not* give up. He continued his American speaking tour (with Mr. and Mrs. Cantasano in attendance at the Brooklyn Institute of Arts[71]), returned home—and, in 1932, set out abroad once more—not to America, but to Bavaria. Researching a biography of his more-than-distinguished ancestor, the soldier and statesman, John Churchill, the 1st Duke of Marlborough, Churchill toured the site of the duke's decisive 1704 victory at Blenheim. There, he rendezvoused with twenty-one-year-old son Randolph, in Germany to cover electoral politics for Lord Camrose's *Sunday Graphic*, even occasionally traveling aboard Hitler's Junkers D1720. Randolph rang up Ernst "Putzi" Hanfstaengl with a request: "My mother and father are here and it would be awfully nice if you and your boss would come this evening at the Hotel Continental."

"Of course," Hanfstaengl responded, "it would be lovely. I will try what I can do, but of course Hitler is very busy."[72]

Hitler was indeed very busy, hurtling from city to city, limousine to plane, presidential to parliamentary campaign. Even before Hanfstaengl lay the proposition before him, Hitler was rushed, irritable.

"Herr Hitler," Hanfstaengl pled, "Mr. Churchill is in Munich and wants to meet you. This is a tremendous opportunity. They want me to bring you along to dinner at the Hotel Continental tonight."[73]

Adolf Hitler, however, no more coveted meeting Winston Churchill in 1932 than Franklin Roosevelt had three years earlier. "*Um Gotteswillen* ["For the Love of God"], Hanfstaengl," Hitler snapped, "don't they realize how busy I am? What on earth would I talk to him about?" It was an odd—indeed, an ignorant—rejoinder. For if Adolf Hitler were indeed the committed anti-Bolshevik he professed to be, he would have jumped at the opportunity to chat up the profoundly anti-Soviet Churchill ("Theirs is a war against civilized society that can never end"[74]).

"But, Herr Hitler," Putzi now argued, "this is the easiest man to talk to in the world—art, politics, architecture, anything you choose. This is one of the most influential men in England, you must meet him. . . ."[75]

Der Führer wouldn't budge. Hanfstaengl regrouped: "Herr Hitler, I will go to dinner and you arrive afterwards, as if you were calling for me, and stay to coffee."[76]

Hitler ("In any case, they say your Mr. Churchill is a rabid Francophile"[77]) remained adamant. Hanfstaengl knew why: insecurity. If Hitler could not dominate a situation he wanted no part of it. In no way might he dominate an evening with Winston Churchill.

Hanfstaengl kept his dinner date, apologizing for his Führer's absence. What might have transpired had Churchill and Hitler dined that evening? Their polite agreement? A glossing over of sticking points? A detonation of mutual rage—an irate storming out? Fireworks might very well have exploded, and not merely between Winston and Adolf. The Churchills brought to table with them not only Lord Camrose but also their German-born family friend, physicist Prof. Frederick Lindemann. Hitler might have savored Lindemann's racist and eugenicist views, but not all racists were pro-Nazi. Lindemann, as opinionated and egotistical in his own way as Hitler was in his, in fact, despised Nationalist Socialists.[78] Lindemann must, however, have remained relatively docile that night, for the evening went along relatively smoothly, considering (or perhaps due to) Hitler's absence. Hanfstaengl provided Churchill with a "mild" version of the Nazis' anti-Semitic views. For his part Churchill recalled that Hanfstaengl "gave a most interesting account of Hitler's activities and outlook. He spoke as one under a spell."[79] But Churchill also pointedly warned Putzi: "Tell your boss from me that anti-Semitism may be a good starter, but it is a bad sticker."[80]

By 2:00 a.m., enlivened by cigars and brandy, the conversation grew yet more serious. "Tell me," Churchill queried in a decidedly confidential tone, "how does your chief feel about an alliance between your country, France and England?" His words stunned Hanfstaengl. "Damn Hitler," he thought, before countering, "What about Italy?"

"No, no," answered Churchill, "we would have to leave them out for the time being. You cannot have everyone joining the club at once."[81]

Putzi excused himself to phone his wife, Helene. In reality, he desperately raced to reach Hitler to once more beg him to confer with Churchill. He phoned party headquarters. Hitler had departed. He rang Prinzregentenplatz. Frau Anni Winter informed him that Hitler had not been home all evening. Finally, Putzi did call his wife. But as he dejectedly returned to the Churchills, he clearly and miraculously spied . . .

Adolf Hitler.

A wealthy Dutchman, a friend of Göring's, accompanied him, and Hanfstaengl suspected that Hitler was occupied in soliciting yet another donation.

"Herr, Hitler," Hanfstaengl stammered, "what are you doing here? Don't you realize the Churchills are sitting in the restaurant? They may well have seen you come in and out? They will certainly learn from the hotel servants that you have been here. They are expecting you for coffee and will think this is a deliberate insult."[82]

Hitler alibied that he was a mess, and, indeed, he was. Attired in an ordinary green hat and a soiled white trenchcoat, badly in need of a shave, he hardly looked like an emerging European statesman. "I implore you," Hanfstaengl countered, "go home, shave, put a nice shirt on and come with me this evening. We'll have a great time. He's a real English gentleman. And his wife is charming. They're really looking forward to seeing you."[83]

"I have too much to do, Hanfstaengl," Hitler snapped. "I have to get up early in the morning."[84]

Hanfstaengl surrendered, returning to the Churchills, feigning that nothing had happened, playing the fool—and the piano—for them. All the while, he hoped Hitler might change his mind and join the gathering.

He never did.

A limousine arrived at Ernst Hanfstaengl's Gentzstrasse apartment not many hours afterward. It transported him to Hitler, ready to depart to Nürnberg and a meeting with its disreputable gauleiter, Julius Streicher. Tired and disappointed, Putzi, nonetheless, tendered to Hitler the details of the evening previous, emphasizing the possibilities of an Anglo-German alliance, gingerly omitting Churchill's anti-anti-Semitism.

Hitler remained unswayed. "In any case," he challenged his foreign press chief, "what part does Churchill play? He is in opposition and no one pays any attention to him."

"People," the frustrated Hanfstaengl answered, tossing caution to the wind, "say the same thing about you."[85]

CHAPTER SIXTEEN

"Soup is cheaper than tear bombs"

FRANKLIN ROOSEVELT ALSO REMAINED IN OPPOSITION, AND TO JOHN W. Davis and Newton Baker he may have seemed a dangerous radical to be avoided at all costs, less a Wilsonian than a dissembling Lord of the Manor Bryanite—or worse.

But there *were* worse.

Radicalism permeated the air. By no means, by any means, the extremism paralyzing German streets and legislatures, but by American standards, movements as radical as any its republic had yet witnessed. In desperate times, desperate men and women harbored desperate thoughts.

And sometimes they acted upon them.

—◆—

The year began with a priest and a protest—a jobless march formed in Pittsburgh led by stocky, bespectacled Fr. James R. Cox, pastor of that city's warehouse district's St. Patrick's Church. While Father Cox was no Father Coughlin, he was by no means at odds with him either, both sharing the same populist ideology. To Cox's own five-thousand-watt WJAS radio audience, he had already damned chain stores as "un-American" and "community wreckers," pleading to listeners—"with the help of God"—not to enter one "for one year, for six months, for ninety days or thirty days." He vowed to bring to Pittsburgh a noted US senator from the western states, "where real he-men live, real men who wear those ten-gallon hats and if necessary, will carry a gun to keep things right." He further confided that said mystery senator would "tell the effete East what they [sic] ought to do in the way of curbing monopolies."[1]

In January 1932, the forty-five-year-old Cox moved from garbled words to rash action, setting twenty thousand men and women on the march from Pittsburgh for Washington demanding direct federal aid for the destitute,[2] including five billion dollars in public works projects.[3] Twelve thousand completed his pil-grimage,[4] in the end, a very polite form of radicalism, with all involved pledging allegiance to the flag; Father Cox receiving a kiss on the cheek from his mother, Julia, as he spoke from the Capitol steps; and Herbert Hoover welcoming Cox, if not into the White House itself, onto its lawn.[5] "They really went further than we expected . . . ," burbled Cox, "everything was splendid."[6]

Radical priests can, however, only be mollified for so long. Back on the Monongahela, Cox quickly blasted the established order. "The United States is not the firm of Herbert Hoover Limited," he fumed. "I am the Mayor of Shantytown. That is a town in the heart of Pittsburgh, in the shadows of the skyscrapers owned by one of the richest men in America—Andrew W. Mel-lon. The men in my town want work but can't get it. So they live in huts and hovels. If the Pilgrim Fathers came here today, would they be satisfied? They came here to give us a country. Now it has been taken away. Who owns it now? The Andrew Mellons."[7]

And, yet, Andrew Mellons had their uses—and even their kindnesses. Cox stranded numerous protesters in Washington. Mellon quietly paid for 276 of them to return home by rail. Total cost: $1,242. Even before that Mel-lon had instructed his Gulf Oil stations along the route to provide marchers with free gas.[8]

Still, Cox was just getting started. Addressing fifty-five thousand at Pitt Stadium, he hinted at a third-party presidential run. "You have every right in the world to demand that the National Government shall come to your assistance." Gov. Gifford Pinchot wired Cox's audience, "It is your govern-ment, set up to protect and care for you—not to stand by and watch you go hungry and cold."[9]

Cox and Pinchot believed government possessed such obligations—as did a growing number of Americans, including, but hardly limited to, mem-bers of the Communist Party USA. Cox's protesters waved red-white-and-blue flags. American Communists waved red flags—and fists. Even before the Crash, a Communist-led Trade Union Unity League (TWUL) had formed to loudly advance their agenda. In February 1930, two- to three-thousand Communist-led unemployed stormed Cleveland's City Hall, injuring sev-eral police.[10] On Valentine's Day, 250 TWUL members attacked Philadel-phia's City Hall.[11] Twelve hundred rioters stormed Chicago's a week later.[12] By March 1930, Communists had proclaimed an "International Unemploy-ment Day"[13] and triggered massive riots at Boston[14] and at New York's Union Square.[15] January 1931 saw two thousand Communists battle three hundred nightstick-wielding police at Gotham's City Hall.[16] A similar battle rocked Newark City Hall.[17]

In December 1931, the Communist Party USA organized a National Hunger March to Washington.[18] On March 7, 1932, three thousand rock-throwing Communist-led protesters marched on the Ford Motor Co.'s River Rouge Plant in Dearborn, Michigan. One projectile felled Henry Ford's tough-as-nails chief security man, Harry Bennett, sending him to the hospital. Police opened fire. Four marchers died. Sixty thousand persons—and photographs of Lenin—accompanied their funeral.[19] May Day 1932 saw nine die in suburban Chicago rioting—including a Communist congressional candidate.[20] That same month the party nominated its general chairman William Z. Foster (arrested at the Union Square riot for attempting to march illegally downtown to City Hall) for president and the Moscow-trained (and a veteran of Communist activities in Frankfurt and Hamburg) black trade-unionist James W. Ford for vice president.[21]

But even in these fractious times, the Communist Party, though attracting an influential and energetic intellectual following, completely flopped at generating anything approaching a mass following. The American Masses, though battered, starved, and, above all, frightened, remained Americans first and Masses second—and, probably, Masses fourth or fifth—following their respective religions, races, or even regions. Beyond that, while Reds might attract a crowd by yelling about the "bosses" or "Wall Street," too often they bogged down in party-line jargon, employing gibberish, jargonesque phrases like "concretize the demands,"[22] and "semi-proletarian and petty-bourgeois elements"[23]—and inside baseball / inside the central committee arguments as:

It was a struggle on two fronts. First, against the centrist opportunism of Zivyon–Salutzky; secondly, against the "left" sectarian opportunism of the "United Toilers." At the same time it was a struggle against those Communist elements which manifested a tendency towards conciliation with centrism and "left" sectarianism.[24]

Such drivel made *Mein Kampf* and *The Myth of the Twentieth Century*—or the state papers of Herbert Hoover—scintillating by comparison. It was not the type of error a Father Coughlin or a Huey Long would commit.

But neither priests nor Communists nor Huey Long led the most spectacular march of 1932—or of the entire Depression for that matter. That honor fell to an obscure—and now-forgotten—former Army sergeant from Portland, Oregon.

Walter W. "Hot" Waters was by 1932 pretty much of a drifter, from state to state and job to job—farm hand, auto salesman, a worker in bakeries and canneries. He had at one time (for whatever reason, most likely not a good one) even changed his name to "Bill Kincaid."[25] The Depression hit Waters hard. He lost his savings and pawned what he had. When Portland veterans made vague moves to head for Washington to lobby for an accelerated payment of their World War bonuses, the well-spoken Walters slowly emerged as their "Assistant Field Marshal." Rail-thin, blue-eyed, smartly attired in riding boots and breeches, he looked very much like a jobless version of Charles Lindbergh. Quickly he replaced the asthmatic, sticky-fingered former sergeant Chester A. Hazen as the protesters' "Commander-in-Chief."[26]

In 1924, Congress overrode Calvin Coolidge's veto to enact a veterans bonus act allowing for the payment of up to $625 in 1945, with recipients empowered to borrow 22.5 percent of their benefit before that date. In February 1931, Congress (now over Herbert Hoover's veto) increased that amount to 50 percent;[27] and 2.5 million veterans filed for loans.[28] Pressure for immediate payment, however, grew louder, though the general public still preferred aiding the actually unemployed to shoveling cash at still employed veterans or those operating functioning businesses. Rep. Fiorello La Guardia (for the bonus in 1924), for one, shared such sentiments.[29] For his part Herbert Hoover declared the bill would impair the nation's credit[30] as the measure's projected $2.4 billion price tag amounted to roughly half the total current federal budget—this with one billion dollars already allocated for veterans relief.[31] In October 1930, and again in September 1931, even the American Legion declared itself opposed to immediate bonus payments.[32]

In January 1932, however, East Texas congressman Wright Patman, himself a veteran, introduced HR 7726, authorizing immediate disbursement.[33] In April, twelve hundred VFW members paraded to the Capitol in support.[34] Later that month, Father Coughlin boosted the bill before the House Ways & Means Committee, claiming he had received 2.5 million unsolicited letters on the subject.[35]

Meanwhile, bonus sentiment festered among the unemployed of Portland. By early May—to the tune of a borrowed drum—250 local veterans marched out of town headed for Washington, hoping to pressure Congress into action. To say they had no clear-cut plan would be an understatement. They possessed no transportation nor supplies nor publicity apparatus. They did not even yet have Waters in charge. But what they did have was this: the nuisance factor. Wherever they might go, people—even those in sympathy—desired them somewhere else. That's how they departed Portland. The Union Pacific, tired of their milling about its rail yard, finally determined that the easiest method to rid itself of these pesky loiterers was to simply grant them free outbound passage on its multitude of empty cattle cars.[36] At Council Bluffs, the Wabash line reached the same conclusion and transported them east to St. Louis.[37] By now, word of their odyssey had somehow spread nationwide. Before Portland's marchers even reached St. Louis, a handful of veterans from Chattanooga had already arrived at Washington. More tramped out of Philadelphia.[38]

A massive police presence greeted Bonus Marchers at St. Louis. But they too also followed the path of least resistance, quickly providing the veterans passage to the Baltimore & Ohio rail yards across the Mississippi at East St. Louis, Illinois. For three days, B & O officials refused them passage further eastward.[39] Finally, the B & O relented, but the standoff merely amplified national curiosity in their quixotic crusade. In Indiana, National Guard units trucked vets to the Ohio border. Similarly spirited through Ohio, Pennsylvania, and Maryland, before reaching Washington on May 29, they were greeted by District of Columbia Traffic Bureau patrolman James E. Bennett, who advised them of a local woman's tag sale to be held in their behalf before warning: "The minute you start mixing with Reds and Socialists, out you go."[40]

But where? They'd reached the end of their line, with no easy place for District officials to pack them off to. And soon this vagabond vanguard would be augmented by tens of thousands of other despairing men.

Responsibility for maintaining the District's public order fell not to Patrolman Bennett but to its newly installed police superintendent Pelham D. "Happy" Glassford. Glassford boasted minimal public safety experience. No career policeman, he was rather a retired army brigadier general, currently dabbling in oils and watercolors. In town from Arizona to facilitate logistics for a VFW convention, he had been hired not with any bonus march in mind, but rather to clean up traffic and bootlegging problems. Jauntily tooling around Washington on his blue motorcycle, he personally collared several traffic violators.[41]

Regarding the invading Bonus Marchers he initially exhibited a distinct toughness. "We must rid the city of the criminal element which has become so prevalent in Washington lately,"[42] he proclaimed on May 25, similarly serving notice that he would provide care for starving veterans for a mere forty-eight hours.[43] Yet, that same day, he directly interjected himself in the overall bonus issue, meeting at the White House to cajole support for Patman's bill and at the Capitol with Patman himself. While there he personally lobbied Senate Majority Leader James Watson and House Majority Leader Henry T. Rainey for passage.[44]

Glassford vowed "the elimination of radicals."[45] Radicals had indeed been at work. On May 19, the Communist-led Workers' Ex-Servicemen's League (WESL) had formed, and a provisional Veterans Bonus March Committee scheduled June 8 for their own march on Washington.[46] By

Wednesday, June 1, California Communist Party chairman Emmanuel Levin, a former Marine, hosted a Washington press conference to claim that Communists had organized the Portland Bonus March.[47] In Detroit that very day, Communist John T. Pace, another former Marine, led 450 demonstrators to City Hall, commandeering city streetcars along the way.[48] From New York the Secret Service's chief local agent Allen Straight reported to his agency's longtime chief, W. H. Moran, that Communists planned to "force an entrance into the White House, or on to the White House grounds and if possible draw fire from the guards. [If any Reds were] fortunate enough to be wounded or killed" the events would provide "excellent material for future activities." Agent Straight further described WESL (pronounced by the organization's foes as "weasel"[49]) as the "gorillas or shock troops of the party."[50] That night, at Washington's John Reed Club, party members threatened to forge "an organization of 100 men into a compact fighting unit to combat the police and render assistance to comrades by drilling them in the art of street fighting."[51]

Yet, these tough-talking Communists had their work cut out for them, not only versus Congress and Glassford's police but also against their fellow demonstrators. "My chief problem with the Communists," Waters recollected, "was to prevent the men of the B. E. F., literally, from almost killing any Communist they found among them. Had the men of the B. E. F. [the "Bonus Expeditionary Force"] had their way they would have refused the Communists any food and run the entire outfit out of Washington."[52]

The Communists fought alone. The B. E. F. had its friends. Glassford was certainly one of them—he had even coined the phrase the "Bonus Expeditionary Force."[53] Remarkably, the "army" elected him its "secretary-treasurer."[54] From Detroit, Fr. Charles Coughlin put his money where his mouth was—contributing five thousand dollars toward a fund for the marchers.[55] One night, Washington social butterfly Evalyn Walsh McLean (wife of *Washington Post* publisher Ned McLean) brought marchers coffee, cigarettes, and a thousand sandwiches.[56] Eleanor "Cissy" Patterson, editor (and eventually the owner) of Hearst's *Washington Times* and of his *Washington Herald,* dispatched five hundred dollars.[57] Washington Senators owner Clark Griffith allowed them use of his ballpark to stage a twenty-five-bout benefit boxing match.[58] From Albany, Franklin Roosevelt wired that he would furnish New York marchers transportation home.[59] And even Herbert Hoover exhibited sympathy, *sotto voce* providing bedraggled veterans with cots and foodstuffs.[60] When disease racked their camps, he allowed them access to a three-hundred-bed hospital at Fort Hunt, Virginia—again without fanfare.[61]

More Reds headed for Washington. John T. Pace's comrades departed Detroit. At Cleveland they joined with local party activists led by Clair B. Cowan ("I am a bolshevik of the American type"[62]), district organizer of the American Council of Unemployed. Even here, however, anti-Communist veterans expressed their hostility to their Red brethren. The thirty-four-year-old Pace's answer to such controversy was to simply lie. "I am not a communist," he proclaimed. "I don't believe in it, and we're all loyal to the government."[63] At Cleveland, one to two thousand protesters illegally occupied the local Pennsylvania Railroad roadhouse.[64] It was "a pretty bad situation in Cleveland . . . ," Pace ultimately acknowledged, "which made us very gleeful."[65]

Reds might have succeeded in seizing control of events in Washington but for one thing: The march had somehow managed to transform itself into a *very* big thing. Only three hundred Oregonians had accompanied Waters eastward, but once other desperate vets learned of his pilgrimage, they too trudged off toward the nation's capital. How many finally arrived, no one will ever know. Glassford and the War Department said eleven thousand.[66] The marchers themselves claimed twenty-two thousand.[67] By the standards of future protests neither count amounted to much, but by the standards of the time and by their destitution and disinclination to ever depart ("Stay til 1945"[68]), they constituted an immense throng.

In some sense, they were akin to Sturmabteilung or Stahlhelm men—disaffected veterans pounding their fists at the doors of national power. In very real senses they weren't. Despite all the hardships and heartaches they now endured, they—like Father Cox's earlier pilgrims—retained their old faith in America and in democracy and exhibited little curiosity for führers or traditional mass movements. And while brownshirts and blackshirts overflowed with youthful, rage-filled energy, their American counterparts seemed worn out, mustering barely enough strength to hop a boxcar or hitch a ride on the back of a pickup truck. The *Washington Star*'s Thomas R. Henry peered closely at them, concluding:

> *Nearly all have one thing in common—a curious melancholy, a sense of the futility of the individual struggle, a consciousness of being in the grip of cruel, incomprehensible forces. Their presence here is a supreme escape gesture. . . . They are fixing on a symbol—the symbol of the security and plenty of happier days. This symbol happens to be Uncle Sam and the war period with its military relief from responsibility. . . . This bonus march might well be described as a flight from reality—a flight from hunger, from the cries of starving children, the humiliation of accepting*

money from worn, querulous women, from the harsh rebuffs of prospective employers.[69]

They were, in an unkind, but hardly untrue word, failures. And, as they had failed (often only at the hand of forces greater than they) in their distant hometowns, they now failed at Washington. They aimed to convince (or frighten) the Congress into passing Wright Patman's bonus bill. Here they succeeded. Patman's bill cleared the House on Wednesday, June 15, 1932, by a comfortable, mostly Democratic, 209–176 margin.[70] Initially, their massive presence generated a positive effect on the Senate. Opposition dropped from sixty-four votes to sixty-one, then to fifty-six and fifty-one.[71] But as more marchers poured into Washington, and their speeches—and their panhandling—grew more aggressive, their efforts backfired. The *Washington Post* now decried "the descent of thousands of penniless men upon Washington for the purposes of browbeating Congress."[72] "I will not vote one penny for the veterans as long as they are in the Capital exerting pressure on Congress by their physical presence,"[73] declared Senator Borah. The Senate Finance Committee rejected the bonus bill 14–2.[74] On Friday, June 17, the Senate itself defeated it 62–28.[75]

It was a bitter blow. Bonus Marchers assembled at the Capitol. They did not riot. Instead, they listened quietly and respectfully as a buxom New York nurse seized the megaphone to lead them in singing "America."[76] But neither did they depart. Even prior to their Senate defeat they began construction of "Camp Camden" (later "Camp Marks") at Anacostia Flats.[77] Superintendent Glassford—mixing kindness with calculation—encouraged the move. The encampment lay safely distant, across the Anacostia River, from the White House, downtown, and the Capitol. Beyond that, access to and from Washington proper was controlled by the 11th Street Bridge—conveniently, a drawbridge. To isolate the marchers, all Glassford need do was order it raised.[78]

That strategy might have worked had the B. E. F. been willing to abide by it. It did not. In truth, Commander-in-Chief Waters never commanded matters as much as he would have desired. Seven times Waters resigned his post, only to be re-elected. Following the Senate vote, George Alman, the marchers' original leader, began occupying abandoned buildings downtown. "No men across the river," Alman proclaimed.[79] "I know where there are warehouses bursting with food in this town," he further threatened. "I'm going to march the boys down there and let them help themselves."[80]

John T. Pace's Communists ("The Central Rank and File Committee"[81]) departed from Alabama Avenue's "Camp Bartlett" (thirty acres owned on the district's outskirts by former New Hampshire Republican governor John Bartlett[82]) to occupy properties at 13th and B Streets, S. W., near to both the White House and the Washington Monument.[83] Two dozen-odd other "camps" dotted the district landscape.[84]

Some marchers, nonetheless, thought it time to sound retreat. When Superintendent Glassford urged their return home to "fight for their political interests at the polls,"[85] several hundred Massachusetts vets did just that.[86] The *Washington Post*, now conceding that "those who marched are true Americans," still wanted them sent homeward at government expense.[87] So did the Congress and Hoover—authorizing $100,000 for that purpose, the cost of transportation plus seventy-five cents a day for meals, as a loan against future bonuses.[88]

An estimated fifty-five hundred veterans took the loans.[89] Most didn't. What would they go home to? More starvation? More humiliation? "When Mr. Hoover insisted they leave Washington, he had no alternative to propose," wrote the *New Republic*. "In effect, he said to them: 'You are breaking my heart; go away and starve somewhere else, out of my sight.'"[90]

B. E. F. leadership, seeing their "troops" thus melt away, threatened the homeward bound. Some departing vets complained of beatings from Waters's thugs. Glassford provided squads of police to protect them and their families as they waited at the Veterans Administration offices or boarded trains at Union Station.[91]

From fear—or for whatever reasons—thousands did stay. New recruits arrived—two hundred from Syracuse alone.[92] A "Union of the Unemployed" vowed to dispatch twenty-five thousand marchers from New York's Columbus Circle to Washington.[93] "The Bonus revolutionary force in Washington," announced William Z. Foster's recent replacement as Communist Party general secretary, Earl Browder, "is the most significant beginning of the mass struggle against the deepening consequence of the crisis."[94]

Even among non-Communists the rhetoric escalated. On Sunday, June 19, the Washington Post headlined:

BONUS SEEKERS MAY NAME OWN 1932 CANDIDATE
Would Form Third Party if Democrats Choose Man Unfavorable.
150,000 IN CAPITAL, IS GOAL OF VETERANS
Army Ignores Plea to Quit U.S.-Owned Buildings in Southwest Area.
ARMY REFUSES TO LEAVE[95]

In early July, Waters traveled to New York to secure additional supplies. In his absence, B. E. F. chief lobbyist Harold B. Foulkrod, orating from the Capitol steps, excoriated Hoover and former Treasury Secretary Mellon, inciting lusty booing at the mention of their names.[96] Condemning the American Red Cross, he termed its president John Barton Payne "a political parasite, and a dirty contemptible cur."[97]

The increasingly ugly atmosphere alarmed Military Intelligence officer Maj. Paul Killiam, who concluded that the "marchers could easily be swayed to action one way or another, and that if some magnetic speaker had demanded an invasion of the Capitol and violence, he would probably get support with serious trouble resulting."[98]

A report on the boastings of upstate New York B. E. F. leader Charles M. Bundell from Killiam's fellow army intelligence operative, one Conrad H. Lanza, only exacerbated official Washington's jitters. The B.E.F., said Bundell, possessed machine guns—and support from District of Columbia Marine detachments. If push came to shove, like czarist troops in 1917 or imperial German units in 1918, these leathernecks could not be counted on to preserve order.[99]

The machine guns and Marines may have only existed in Bundell's (or perhaps Lanza's) imagination—although John T. Pace noted a significant sympathy of local Marines for his men.[100] But such talk did little to calm local nerves. Herbert Hoover feared appearing in public. There were, he grumbled, "too many assassins around."[101] To thwart any rush on the White House, authorities secretly billeted three hundred troops just to its southeast, at the massive Munitions Building.[102]

The largest contingent of B. E. F. reinforcements now arrived not from New York, but from far-off Southern California. Twelve hundred of them departed Los Angeles in late May, their 350 vehicle-caravan skittishly dodging "75 representatives of automobile finance companies."[103] Even by Bonus March standards, their leader caught the eye. Royal W. Robertson was indeed an injured Navy veteran, his head permanently supported with a sturdy metal brace—a bit like Erich von Stroheim in *Grand Illusion*. Robertson himself had even secured an occasional film bit part, most memorably in Rudolph Valentino's silent classic *The Four Horsemen of the Apocalypse*.[104] He had not, however, incurred his eye-catching injury in combat, but in basic training—by tumbling from his hammock.[105]

No boxcars transported Robertson. At one point he fancifully promised to enter Washington with a squadron of fifty aircraft. El Centro, California, locals supplied his men with fifteen tons of watermelons.[106] Tucson residents greeted them with enthusiasm, before concluding their visitors looked "like tramps" who exhibited "contempt for anyone not a marcher . . . the makings of an ill-controlled mob. . . ."[107]

Roy Robertson's July 9 arrival in Washington[108] created yet another disparate faction in already disunited B. E. F. ranks. But he had his uses—and his imagination. When authorities shooed protesters off the Capitol Grounds, Robertson inquired if his men might remain if they continued moving. No regulation, after all, prohibited walking across Capitol turf; no permit need be issued for such actions. And, so, for three days, 450 California Bonus Marchers (joined at some point by five thousand other B. E. F. members[109]) silently circled the Capitol. [110] Robertson's men had trudged cross-country to the tune of bass drum and bugle corps.[111] Now they marched—"The Death March"[112]—in ominous silence, akin to the zombie-like shuffling dead of Abel Gance's anti-war film *J'accuse*.

Congress still met. As long as it did, hope remained. But Congress finally did adjourn on Saturday, July 16,[113] and the atmosphere only grew tenser still. The normally accommodating Pelham Glassford nervously placed Waters under arrest—twice.[114] Herbert Hoover abandoned his normal plans to visit Capitol Hill for congressional adjournment.[115] That evening fifty B. E. F. members, mostly Communists, attempted to picket the White House.[116] White House physician Dr. Joel Boone, fearing an assault, remained on duty through the night.[117]

Congress departed. The B. E. F. remained. Authorities and local residents tolerated a mass of homeless veterans petitioning their legislature. It was something else to abide—and support—thousands of men essentially vowing to never leave. Worse, their presence—and their national public support—might attract thousands more to the resource-strained, increasingly nervous capital.

Roy Robertson departed. "Those men," he jeered, "know there is nothing to stay here for except to see Waters strut around with new boots on and a new black cane to swagger with."[118]

The thousands who remained lurched rightward. In the *B.E.F. News* Waters announced the formation of a new organization, the Khaki Shirts. "Inevitably," he took pains to explain, "such an organization brings up comparisons with the Facisti of Italy and the NAZI of Germany. . . . For five years Hitler was lampooned and derided, but today he controls Germany. Mussolini before the war was a tramp prin[t]er [sic], driven from Italy because of his political views. But today he is a world figure. . . . The Khaki Shirts, however, would be essentially American."[119] His second-in-command, the Cleveland veteran Doak Carter, further pledged that the Khaki Shirts will "leap into the breach between American institutions and threatened anarchy."[120] B. E. F. members not only reaffirmed Waters's leadership, they now voted him "complete dictatorial powers."[121]

"To hell with civil law and General Glassford!" Waters thundered, "I'm going to have my orders carried out."[122]

John T. Pace's Communists also remained. Supporting B. E. F. dissident leader George Alman against Waters, they openly assisted Alman's re-election as Oregon district commander. "We were using Alman to get control of the rank and file," Pace later revealed. "It was the plan of the party to use Alman as the front for gaining control of the entire bonus expeditionary forces."[123]

Even Pelham Glassford's patience wore thin, and he resigned as B. E. F. secretary-treasurer.[124] District authorities also had enough, both with the B. E. F.—and with him. On Thursday, July 21, district commissioners instructed Glassford to order the B. E. F. to evacuate all buildings seized without consent of the owners within twenty-four hours and for them to return all borrowed tents and rolling kitchens by August 1 and all other public property by August 4.[125] "While great latitude has heretofore been allowed with reference to the enforcement of regulations and ordinances," the commissioners commanded him, "after the times fixed above you will make no exceptions in their enforcement in the case of the bonus march."[126]

But Walter W. Waters, enjoying the virtual run of the city for nearly two months, was not to be cowed. "They can issue orders," he snapped, "but I don't know how they are going to enforce them."[127] Bonus Marchers refused to evacuate the Capitol Grounds.[128] Frustrated authorities merely reset their deadline.[129] John T. Pace led 210 Communists in another illegal attempt to picket the White House.[130]

Trouble centered on B. E. F.-occupied buildings ("Camp Glassford") on Pennsylvania Avenue N.W. scheduled for demolition to make way for new federal offices and to create jobs in the process. On Thursday, July 28, push came to shove. The day began with a *Washington Post* editorial. Clearing Camp Glassford, the *Post* fumed, wasn't enough. "Even if the bonus army evacuates the building sites along Pennsylvania Avenue," it declared, "serious problems as to their status here will remain unsolved. So long as the bonus seekers stay here they will be a menace to peace and order."[131]

At 10:00 a.m., *Superintendent* Glassford started clearing *Camp* Glassford, commencing with its largest structure, a partially demolished National Guard armory. His men moved methodically, dispersing occupants without incident. By then, Pace and Emmanuel Levin had hurried their respective followers to the scene. So had Waters ("I'm double crossed"[132]). Theoretically, major reinforcements should have been impossible but *Glassford had inexplicably neglected to raise the drawbridge from Anacostia.*[133] The B. E. F. camp named in his honor now turned ugly. Bonus Marchers rushed forward. One—most likely a Communist Navy veteran named Bernard McCoy—ripped the gold badge from Glassford's uniform jacket.[134] An officer grabbed an American flag belonging to the bonus army. A lead pipe bashed his head.[135] A brick landed square in Glassford's chest.[136] Another dislodged Patrolman George Scott's cap. Another smacked Scott in the temple—and down he went with a fractured skull.[137] "Be peaceful men," Glassford begged, "and let's not throw any more bricks! They are mighty hard and hurt. I want to say that you may have killed one of the best officers."

"Hell, that's nothing," retorted a B. E. F. man. "A lot of us were killed in France."[138]

Glassford ("This game is getting dangerous, and it's getting time for lunch"[139]) finally succeeded in calming the crowd. At two o'clock, his men returned to clear another building, 332 Pennsylvania Avenue N.W. The mob rushed the police, knocking thirty-eight-year-old Patrolman George W. Shinault to the ground where Oakland, California, veteran Eric Carlson began strangling him. Another vet slammed Shinault's partner Patrolman Miles Znamenacek on the head. Znamenacek shot Carlson dead. Shinault fired into the crowd, instantly killing an unemployed thirty-five-year-old Lithuanian-born Chicago butcher named William J. Huska.[140] A general bloodbath loomed. A man in the crowd drew a revolver from his coat. Glassford loudly ordered him to put it away. He did, and Glassford allowed him to simply disappear into the unruly multitude.[141] The crowd itself soon dispersed.

Glassford considered the situation under control. His superiors—Dr. Luther H. Reichelderfer and Herbert H. Crosby (who had hired Glassford in the first place[142])—thought otherwise. Reichelderfer, himself a World War veteran, dispatched a letter to Herbert Hoover requesting "the assistance of Federal troops."[143]

In the early afternoon of July 28, 1932, Secretary of War Patrick J. Hurley (also an A. E. F. veteran) gave the order: "Surround the affected area and clear it without delay."[144]

For weeks, tanks and cavalry at nearby Fort Myer, Virginia, had trained for such a moment.[145] A T-4 armored car parked conspicuously on the White House lawn.[146] In fact, troops had already once been called to the Capitol—by Vice President Curtis on Thursday, July 14. But that was a mere Keystone Cops episode. Two companies of Washington Navy Yard Marines arrived via trolley car. They departed ten minutes later—after Glassford provided assurances that order would be preserved.[147] Yet, even this farce possessed a dark side: Thirty-five Marines had reportedly refused to leave their barracks.[148]

Now, on July 28, Secretary Hurley dispatched orders to Army chief of staff Gen. Douglas MacArthur. The brilliant, obviously ambitious, MacArthur possessed precious little sympathy for the B. E. F. He believed most of them to be fakers—non-veterans. He gravely feared the influence of the movement's radical minority. Yet, his suspicions had their limits. Back when Waters and

Pace were wending their respective paths eastward, commandeering trains and trolley cars, MacArthur's deputy chief of staff, Brig. Gen. George Van Horn Moseley, advocated that the army disperse them before they ever reached Washington, lamely arguing that their advance was delaying US Mail trains. Neither MacArthur—nor Hoover—thought much of the idea.[149]

Neither acted then—but would now.

It need not have come to that. Bonus Marchers demanded what this current Congress—and a subsequent Democratic Congress—were not about to give. But Hoover might have employed a little—or a lot—more finesse in dealing with them. Privately, he furnished them with cots and supplies. Publicly, he gave them nothing save a loan for a ticket home. As they arrived, the man who had met repeatedly with Lenin's Bolsheviks to feed starving Russians instructed his staff, "If they ask for permission to see me and are veterans, tell them that I will receive a committee representing them. Make an appointment for the committee representing them. . . . but I won't receive any Communists. . . ."[150]

In January, Hoover met Father Cox. That summer, he saw no one, neither Communist nor anti-Communist.

He might have met again with Cox—by then busy organizing his own "Blue Shirt" movement[151]—in early June. Though Speaker John Nance Garner declined to confer with the priest (now garbed not in clerical collar—but in a brown-belted military uniform[152]), Vice President Curtis had. Cox then trundled over to the White House ("I was cordially received by police and secretaries. They remembered me from January 7"[153]) hoping to meet with Hoover.[154] Told the president was in conference but might make time for him, Cox nonchalantly declined the offer.[155] Another opportunity for Hoover had arrived and departed.

"[Warren] Harding," observed Evalyn Walsh McLean, "would have gone among those men and talked in such a manner as to make them cheer him and cheer their flag. If Hoover had done that, I think not even [the] troublemakers in the swarm could have caused any harm."[156]

It was now too late for speeches and for chats with priests. Violence had swept Camp Glassford. Dead men lay upon the street. Worse might lay across the horizon. "I do not believe that the Government had any alternative because of the rapid pace being made," John T. Pace would later testify before Congress. "It is my candid opinion that had this thing gone another week, the Communists would have gained the leadership of the bonus expeditionary forces, thereby resulting in forcing the Government to take the action that they did take, at a time when the results would have been much more disastrous."[157]

For such reasons MacArthur ("Another week might have meant that the government was in peril"[158]) determined to act quickly, with overwhelming force, to finally end this interminable game. Troops swarmed into the District—six hundred in all, including three hundred infantry. Six Renault FT-17 light tanks from the 1st Tank Regiment arrived, along with 217 cavalry and 213 horses[159] commanded by the recently assigned Maj. George S. Patton Jr.[160]

Badly wounded at the Argonne in fall 1918, Patton found himself dragged to safety by a Pvt. Joe Angelo. Now, Angelo, wearing the Distinguished Service Cross earned for saving Patton's life, testified before Congress for the Bonus.[161] No wonder, Patton described the day's work as "a most distasteful form of service."[162] Nonetheless, his horsemen set off from Fort Myer, reaching near the White House at approximately 5:00 p.m. Infantry units progressed by steamer and by truck northward from Maryland's more distant Fort Washington. MacArthur ordered them through Pennsylvania Avenue's rush hour traffic—steel-helmeted infantry, faces ominously obscured by gas masks, their rifles at the ready, Patton's cavalry with sabers drawn. MacArthur's half-dozen tanks had already sped as best they could down 3rd Street to finally block the 11th Street drawbridge to Anacostia.

Passersby and curiosity-seekers thronged city streets. Jeering Bonus Marchers hurled bricks and stones. Infantrymen lobbed tear gas grenades at them. Bonus Marchers hurled them back. Worse, the afternoon wind simply blew much of this noxious gas back at them. Numerous passersby (including Connecticut's Sen. Hiram Bingham[163]) choked on the fumes. Nonetheless, by 8:00 p.m., MacArthur had cleared downtown of any appreciable trace of Waters's B. E. F or Pace's Communists.

MacArthur might easily have remained at his War Department offices adjacent to the White House. Cognizant of his assignment's unusual nature and desiring maximum tactical flexibility, he assumed field command. Much has been written of his appearance that day, with much exaggeration—that he advanced upon civilians on horseback, in his fanciest dress uniform (for which he delayed the battle as aides scurried to Fort Myer to retrieve it), bedecked with every medal he might find. Reality was more mundane. There was no horse—at least none with MacArthur astride it. He advanced by auto. He retrieved his uniform because War Department staff ordinarily wore civilian clothes out of respect for the pacifistic Hoover's sensibilities[164]—and that is how MacArthur had started his day—every day. His uniform, while hardly combat fatigues, was by no means his fanciest. Its retrieval caused no unnecessary delay. He wore no medals, merely campaign ribbons—although, certainly enough of those to choke his nonexistent horse.

But he *was* damned conspicuous—and perhaps not from mere vanity. As he informed 16th Brigade commander Brig. Gen. Perry L. Miles: "I'm here to take the rap if there should be any unfavorable or critical repercussions."[165]

Slowly, his men and mounts advanced through clouds of tear gas, crowds of panic-stricken civilians, and knots of jeering and brick-tossing veterans. "Jeez, if we had guns! If we had guns!" the veterans chanted.[166] An angry spectator shouted, "The American flag means nothing to me after this!"

"Put that man under arrest if he opens his mouth again!" MacArthur barked.[167]

The Reds, for all their bluster (and all the projectiles hurled against Glassford's police) had no stomach for actual bayonets and sabers, fleeing their 13th Street encampment even before MacArthur's troops arrival. Unfortunately, however, W. W. Waters also fled, just when his presence was absolutely essential to negotiating a quick end to the night's sorry business.[168] But, nonetheless, he had vanished—just as he had disappeared several times previously in similarly difficult situations. Commander-in-Chief Waters really was, in fact, only sergeant material. At best.

Technically speaking, MacArthur's work was done. Or was it? Hurley had mandated pacifying "the scene of disorder." Was that merely downtown? Did it include Anacostia? While still downtown, MacArthur had informed Glassford: "We are going to break the back of the B. E. F. Within a short time we are going to move down Pennsylvania Avenue, sweep through the billets there, and then clean out the other two big camps. The operation will be continuous. It will be done tonight."[169]

The Anacostia River was MacArthur's Rubicon. At the White House, Hoover remained the Quaker. Originally, he had desired that MacArthur's troops advance without firearms.[170] Now, he decided against invading "Camp Marks" across the 11th Street Bridge. But getting those orders to MacArthur would prove to be no easy task.

Word went out from Hoover to Hurley to Brig. General Moseley—and perhaps but, only perhaps—to MacArthur. Long afterward Moseley claimed to have informed MacArthur to halt for the night.[171] But as historian Joseph Persico noted "on other occasions, Moseley boasted that he had made sure MacArthur never got the order."[172] Similar confusion surrounds another decades-later claim by then–MacArthur aide Maj. Dwight Eisenhower, who recalled that secretary of the general staff Col. Clement B. Wright had followed Moseley with the same orders. According to Ike, on hearing of Wright's approach, MacArthur had snapped that he was "too busy and did not want either himself or his staff bothered by people coming down and pretending to bring orders."[173] Yet perhaps that is not what happened at all.

Recent scholarship indicates that Colonel Wright arrived too early to actually convey Hoover's cease-and-desist message. He may have merely conveyed an army intelligence warning that Camp Marks residents were armed and would open fire if MacArthur dared breech their territory.[174]

So . . . either McArthur *did*. . . or *did not* . . . disobey Hoover's orders.

We do know this: He did not rush into Camp Marks. He delayed an hour—ostensibly for supper—to allow an evacuation.[175] Camp Marks commander Eddie Atwell requested another hour's delay—again to facilitate residents' evacuation. MacArthur granted it.[176] Inside Camp Marks, Atwell ordered his men that if any invader tried to "stampede our women and children" they should "kill the first man that steps over that line."[177]

Not until approximately 9:00 p.m. did MacArthur finally invade. Essentially, the scene remained as on Pennsylvania Avenue: shouting, insults, tear gas, some rock-throwing (a brick supposedly hit Patton in the head[178]), but with a trio of very large differences: the presence of women and children—and fire.

MacArthur's forces rumbled forward. "Give way boys, give way," Atwell yelled, "They've got the tanks and you haven't got a chance in hell!"[179] The B. E. F. fled. Their ramshackle shacks and shanties went up like kindling.

Who set those fires? Some (including Eisenhower[180]) claimed it was the marchers themselves, with soldiers eventually joining in to finish the job. Others contend it was MacArthur's men—either on their own initiative or following orders.[181] Whoever it was, the flames enveloping this great city of squatter's huts lit the summer sky. By morning, Camp Marks was a memory, as vanished as the more than ten thousand desperate men, women, and children who once huddled within its mud-caked confines.

It was a masterful military action. Two men had died in Glassford's botched operation of the morning. No one died in the afternoon and evening that followed. No one was wounded or seriously wounded (despite the lurid rumors of dead and bayonetted civilians that inevitably followed—and which still make their way into history books[182]). Not a single shot was fired—on either side.

T'was a glorious victory.

Or so it seemed at first. "Press opinion," editorialized the August 1 *New York Times*, "accurately reflecting public opinion, has been almost unanimous in holding up the hands of Mr. Hoover."[183] Even Hearst's *Washington Times* headlined, "The Bonus Riots—Use of Force was Necessary."[184] But soon, another Hearst paper, the *San Francisco Examiner*, railed: "For sheer stupidity, President Hoover's spectacular employment of the military in evicting a mere handful of the derelicts of the World War from their wretched billets in

Washington is without parallel in American annals."[185] Politicians also dissented. "Soup is cheaper than tear bombs," anti-bonus Fiorello La Guardia wired Hoover, "and bread better than bullets in maintaining law and order in these times of depression, unemployment and hunger."[186] Pennsylvania Rep. Louis McFadden, perhaps suspecting that "international bankers" were somehow involved, denounced Hoover's actions as "the greatest crime in modern history."[187]

"The use of federal troops against unarmed veterans," said New Mexico progressive Republican senator Bronson Cutting, "whether prompted by cowardice or stupidity, was an unpardonable outrage."[188]

In Albany, on Friday morning, July 29, Franklin Roosevelt lay abed, pondering the photos in the day's *New York Times*, pictures of tanks and bayonets and tear gas, of police and soldiers and protesters. With him was Rexford Tugwell, and FDR was simply disgusted at what he saw—and at Herbert Hoover. There was no more need to discuss Hoover, Roosevelt advanced: He was finished. Franklin felt compelled to apologize for having—a long time ago—thought Herbert Clark Hoover worthy of the presidency. Still, FDR mused, he had to admit that his rival had served well in the Cabinet and had at first *seemed* capable of dealing with the Depression. But he wasn't. "Now," said Roosevelt, "look where he was. He's surrounded himself with a guard *to keep away the revolutionaries*. There was nothing left inside the man but jelly; maybe there never had been anything."[189]

CHAPTER SEVENTEEN

"He doesn't need a head,
his job is to be a hat"

As Douglas MacArthur conferred with Secretary of War Patrick Hurley regarding how best to disperse the rival army occupying their nation's capital, events an ocean away triggered memories of two young officers who had met nearly twenty years before, at Veracruz, during America's pre-war Mexican intervention.

Their respective ambitions, he mused (speaking as he did in the third person[1]) had now been fulfilled "in *reverse* . . . one wanted to be the head of a great army, the other head of a great state. I speak . . . of von Papen and MacArthur."[2]

Meet Franz Joseph Hermann Michael Maria von Papen zu Köningen.

—◆—

The rather-too-bold Putzi Hanfstaengl had been technically correct: Adolf Hitler, like Winston Churchill, remained in mere opposition. But this was no normal political opposition. It was the opposition of a marauding medieval army, surrounding the starving defenders of an isolated castle, hurling hot pitch over its crumbling battlements, poised, with sharpened knives within firmly clenched teeth, to hoist their ladders high and mount a fierce and final bloody assault.

Which also meant that inside that castle, nerves were cracking very badly.

Kurt von Schleicher had engineered Wilhelm Gröner's posting to defense secretary. He guided Heinrich Brüning's ascent. Both had long served their purposes. Their popularity—and their utility—had plummeted. His ego and ambition merely increased. "What Germany needs today is a strong man,"[3] he bellowed a little too loudly one day to female admirers at a Berlin restaurant—before pointing even more crassly to his own jutting chest. Yes, Kurt von Schleicher was ambitious indeed.

To the casual observer, he had only behaved erratically concerning Gröner's SA ban. In reality, he maneuvered with expert cunning. True, he first supported the ban. Then, he zig-zagged to oppose it. But Gröner's crackdown served Schleicher immensely. It not only damaged Gröner, it also provided a marvelous carrot with which to lure Schleicher's new brown-shirted *kameraden* into a powerful nationalist alliance—that he itched to dominate.

On Thursday, April 22, 1932, he whispered his opposition to Gröner's policy to Ernst Röhm and Berlin SA leader Count Wolf von Helldorf.[4] By April 26 he upped the ante, informing them that he wanted "to alter the political course."[5] Two days later, he conferred with Hitler himself. "The Conference turned out well,"[6] Goebbels crowed privately.

In Nürnberg, on Monday evening, May 3, all three—Hitler, Schleicher, and Goebbels—met. "[W]e talk politics till late at night," Goebbels recorded, "Unanimous opinion: not to approach the Zentrum under any circumstances whatever. The matter must ripen by itself. It is always advisable to hold one-self a bit aloof. The others are already floundering into our nets."[7]

Goebbels did not exaggerate. These meetings, high level as they were, had been a mere prelude. On May 8, Hitler traveled to Schleicher's Berlin home. Also present were both Oskar von Hindenburg [8] (the French ambassador André François-Poncet sized him up as: "square-faced, brutal, and little educated, with nothing of [his father's] noble bearing"[9]) and his father's secretary of state Otto Meissner (François-Poncet: "ruddy, flushed . . . too tightly encased in his clothes, his glance lurking behind goggles, at home with all regimes . . ."[10]). Schleicher, Hindenburg, and Meissner promised Hitler nearly everything he hoped to hear. Gröner would fall—then Brüning. New Reichstag elections would follow. The SA ban would disappear.[11]

"We have news from General Schleicher," Goebbels recorded, "things are progressing according to plan."[12]

Indeed.

Berlin descended into steady chaos. Gröner fell, and so did other blows—physical blows—within the halls of power themselves. On May 12, Social Democrat leader Otto Wels and journalist Helmuth Klotz, who had published a pamphlet, "The Röhm Case," detailing the indiscreet Ernst Röhm's descriptions of his own sexual preferences, dined within the Reichstag restaurant.[13] Four Nazi deputies (including convicted murderer Edmund Heines) beat Klotz to a pulp then calmly returned to the chamber. Reichstag president Paul Löbe ordered them expelled for thirty days. They refused to leave. Löbe summoned the *Schupos* (the *Schutzpolizei* or state police), igniting a donnybrook among the 107 Nazi delegates. Brüning's Cabinet ministers, pleading that this was none of their business, fled. Police hauled Heines et al. to their headquarters, charging them with assault and battery.[14]

Such brutality, exploding within a national parliament's very gates, merely reflected the savagery raging outside—brutality not always inflicted by Hitler's minions. "[O]n the night of May 19, 1932," recalled the KPD operative Richard Krebs ("Jan Valtin"), "a group of young Nazis on their way home from a meeting were pounced on by Red Marines in a dark Street (Herrengraben), and dragged into the doorways of near-by houses. Here eight or nine of them were lacerated with knives. One Nazi had his eyes stabbed out with a screw driver. Another, the storm trooper [Karl] Heinzelmann, was stabbed eleven times. Members of the Red Marines then sat on their victim, slashed off his genitals, and severed his vertebrae. I and other comrades with me were stiff with horror on hearing the details of these exploits. But we had learned how to hold our tongues. In the Party, heresies were discovered with a facility and ingenuity that outrivaled the Spanish Inquisition."[15]

And, yet, somehow—notwithstanding torrents of Red and Brown violence, despite all Schleicher's machinations, and despite his lack of normal political skills—Heinrich Brüning survived. Not only through Reichspräsident Hindenburg's forbearance but also via parliamentary majority. In October 1931, *mirabile dictu,* the Reichstag tendered him a 294–270 vote of confidence.[16] In May 1932, he survived 287–257.[17]

Perhaps the system might somehow survive at all.

. . . or not.

For, at this moment Hindenburg chose to write *finis* to Germany's "best chancellor since Bismarck."

Brüning had not only failed to provide his master with a second term in the neat, gift-wrapped package the aged aristocrat had demanded of him, he had instituted policies, particularly those impacting East Prussia's heavily subsidized Junker estates, that immensely distressed him. The Reichspräsident's ire grew exponentially as the wily Schleicher—aided by Oskar Hindenburg (Brüning: "a fairly simple man, not really malicious"[18]) and Otto Meissner—filled the malleable Old Gentleman's ears with self-serving innuendo.

Hindenburg summoned Brüning. "I am told," he sputtered, "that the [latest] decree also includes a Bolshevik [East Prussian] resettlement plan. How about that?" Hindenburg's allusion to Bolshevism made little sense to Brüning. In Bolshevik Russia, Stalin was collectivizing farmland—and executing and starving millions in the process.[19] Brüning proposed the reverse—to distribute it. He ignored Hindenburg's insult. "You deal with finance questions, too?" Hindenburg snidely added, "I thought you were confining yourself to Bolshevism." Brüning again disregarded Hindenburg's accusation.

"But my dear Mr. Chancellor," Hindenburg came to his point, "this will never do. We cannot introduce Bolshevik wage laws and Bolshevik settlement schemes. The two trade unionists must leave the government."

"Yes," Hindenburg snapped, "I mean you and [Zentrum minister of labor Adam] Stegerwald. Of course you can remain as Foreign Minister."[20]

Hindenburg's anti-Stegerwald animus revealed much about his increasingly erratic affections. Not many months previously he decided that Brüning's Cabinet contained too many Catholics (five of eight members). Then, he specifically allowed Stegerwald to remain.[21] But was this current rant a result of Hindenburg's fickleness—or of Schleicher's machinations? Or even of Schleicher's fickleness. For, upon later reflection, Brüning discerned not only Schleicher's character significantly flawed but also his very psyche. "He's a very energetic man but very moody," Brüning noted. "He changes his mind repeatedly."[22] Gröner reached similar conclusions as well, considering his personal Judas, "resolute, but he frequently changes his aims."[23]

But whoever's capricious mind pulled the lever, the unfortunate Minister Stegenwald fell through the trap. So would Brüning, to be ingloriously demoted. The ingratitude, the sheer arrogance, of Hindenburg's autocratic proposition, stung him to tartly reply. "Thank you, Mr. General Field Marshal," he answered, "I cannot remain with a broken neck."[24]

He exited—most quickly. The Old Gentleman, priorities askew, had allotted the task of jettisoning a chancellor but a few minutes on his daily calendar—scurrying off to review a parade commemorating the World War's naval battle of Skagerrak (Jutland).[25]

But before Herr Brüning departs center stage, we might interpose in his defense a few words from the aforementioned historian R. T. Clark. Often accused of instituting a pre-Hitler "dictatorship," Brüning was, nevertheless, no more Hitler's "twin" in such matters than *Pravda* had accused the "Social Fascist" SPD of being Der Führer's twin. He was no twin—a distant cousin once-removed, perhaps—but no twin. Wrote Clark regarding Brüning's rule:

A dictatorship which depends for its continuance on a freely elected assembly is not a dictatorship in the unconstitutional sense. Although he had stretched the constitution to its limits Brüning was none the less a parliamentary chancellor. He may never have enjoyed the confidence of the Reichstag, but only once had he technically lost it, and had then resigned and referred the issue to the country. He had been unconstitutionally dismissed, although he had saved the President's constitutional face by resigning and [his successor] had been unconstitutionally appointed . . . because he had neither a party following nor any hope of a majority.[26]

But was Brüning's unconstitutional successor to be Kurt von Schleicher?

Not at all.

The German army—if not General von Schleicher—had long prided itself for its non-political status. Though Hindenburg had obviously dented that tradition, Schleicher still hesitated to formally assume any chancellorship. He dwelt—and prospered very well—as a dweller in shadows. Even now, he merely replaced Wilhelm Gröner at Defense, content to manipulate power behind any new chancellor's creaky throne.

But who might now ascend that throne?

Hitler was, well, a bit much—no matter how many Reichstag delegates or storm troopers he commanded. A more tractable member of his party might do—a Wilhelm Frick or a Gregor Strasser—but not Hitler. Not now.

Hugenberg and Seldte and Duesterberg remained heavily damaged goods. Not them, probably, not ever.

Hindenburg, more reactionary by the hour, would never stomach another Social Democrat. The KPD? A fine jest there.

Brüning's Zentrum Party rightly deemed itself betrayed and still stood by him. No, they would not easily provide his replacement.

Or would they?

One Zentrum member, a very minor cog, had always stood apart from its largely center-left leadership and policies. In 1925, he ditched party presidential nominee Wilhelm Marx in favor of the then-Nationalist Hindenburg.[27] Thus, he was a maverick, but a maverick not necessarily *verboten* at all to the prickly, grudge-holding Hindenburg.

Yes, meet Franz Joseph Hermann Michael Maria von Papen zu Köningen.

He was, all conceded, an unlikely choice for the chancellorship—even as a Schleicher pawn and front-man.

He was Catholic, if not as ascetic as Brüning, at least, more ostentatiously so. Trained as a cavalryman, he served with Schleicher on the general staff, and won diplomatic postings to Mexico and to America as a military attaché. When war came, he dabbled heavily in both espionage and sabotage, including plots to blow up Jersey City's Black Tom munitions depot (the resulting massive explosion damaged the Statue of Liberty and shook Philadelphia) and Canada's Welland Canal. Expelled from the New World, he helped foment Ireland's abortive 1916 Easter Rebellion and still later fought on both the Palestinian and Western fronts. From 1921 on, he served as a Zentrum Prussian Landtag delegate—though not even for a second as a Reichstag backbencher. The cautious Zentrum considered him unfit for even that limited honor.[28] After all, as 1932 commenced, American authorities still maintained a warrant for his arrest.[29]

Of Westphalian noble stock, Papen married into greater wealth (his bride being "as homely as she is rich"[30]). He was, observed Rudolf Olden, "a political dilettante, a Catholic romantic and imperialist, whom no one took seriously. His highest flights of ambition could not have extended beyond the prospect of becoming Minister in Luxembourg or in Munich . . . He was light-headed but courageous, a gambler whose luck was always out, slap-dash, fidgety. Almost everything he put his hand to failed; even when he succeeded, it would turn out for the worst."[31]

And so because his options were so very limited, Kurt von Schleicher placed this obscure, plucky, luckless baron on his short list for the chancellery.

His other possibilities had simply not worked out. In tandem with Meissner he had cajoled Hindenburg into suggesting former DNVP chairman (now with the splinter center-right Conservative People's Party) Count Kuno von Westarp to Brüning as his replacement. Westarp's support for Brüning's Cabinet had cost him the DNVP leadership, and by proposing the count as their new front-man, Schleicher and Meissner hoped to cajole Brüning into remaining in a new Cabinet. Brüning countered with suggestions of Hugenberg or the conservative Lutheran mayor of Leipzig, Carl Goerdeler (his former price commissioner). Hindenburg wouldn't bite.[32]

Scratch Westarp, Goerdeler, and Hugenberg, and that left . . . von Papen, as the national situation inexorably deteriorated. Absent anyone's working majority, Prussian chancellor Otto Braun's SPD-Zentrum-State Party coalition government staggered on in fitful caretaker-mode.[33] In late May, in Sachsen-Anhalt, the National Socialist vote skyrocketed from 2.1 to 40.9 percent, enabling them to form a coalition government.[34] In Oldenburg, in mid-June, Hitlerites won 48.4 percent, again triggering a ruling coalition.[35] Their Hessen vote soared to 44 percent.[36]

The Nazis' momentum had hardly escaped Papen's gaze. In October 1931, he lectured Brüning on the necessity "to forge these glowing [Nazi] masses before they overflow with hostility; above all, this youth, still undisciplined, to be sure, but valuable material, must be fitted into the state, and by education won for the state."[37] In mid-April 1932, he penned an article arguing that, as the Zentrum had domesticated the socialist SPD through shared power and responsibility, it might similarly house-break the fractious NSDAP.[38] The Nazi-accommodating Schleicher could only admire such marvelous pragmatism.

Papen would do.

Reckless though Papen might be, he was, nonetheless, not entirely delusional. To Schleicher, he pled his inadequacy ("I very much doubt if I am the right man"[39]) for national leadership. To the Zentrum party leader, the cultured intellectual papal domestic prelate, Monsignor Ludwig Kaas, he pledged fealty to Brüning.[40] But ego and Hindenburg ("Well, my dear Papen, I hope you are going to help me out of this difficult situation"[41]) could not long be denied. "You cannot possibly leave an old man like me in the lurch," The Old Gentleman pled. "In spite of my age I have had to accept the responsibilities of the nation for another period. I am asking you now to take over a task on which the future of our country depends, and I am relying on your sense of duty and patriotism to do what I ask you."

"I can remember to this day the deep, heavy tone of his voice," Papen would write, "so full of warmth, yet so demanding. 'It is immaterial to me if you earn the disapproval or even the enmity of your party. I intend to have people round me who are independent of political parties, men of good will and expert knowledge, who will surmount the crisis of our country.' The President's voice rose slightly. 'You have been a soldier and did your duty in the war. When the Fatherland calls, Prussia knows only one response—obedience.'"[42]

And, so Franz von Papen became reichskanzler of a republic neither he nor Hindenburg possessed much use for.

Berlin—and whatever portion of the world paying attention to it—greeted his ascent with undisguised astonishment. "No one but smiled or tittered or laughed because Papen [is] taken seriously by neither his friends nor his enemies," noted France's elegant ambassador André François-Poncet. "He bears the stamp of frivolity, he is not a personality of the first rank. He is one of those people who are considered capable of plunging into a dangerous adventure; they pick up every gauntlet, accept every wager. If he fails it doesn't bother him. . . . He was reputed to be superficial, blundering, untrue, ambitious, vain, crafty and an intriguer."[43] Count Harry Kessler found him to possess "the air of an irritable billy goat trying to adopt dignity and wears for the occasion a silk-lined black jacket, Sunday best. A character from *Alice in Wonderland*."[44] In Washington, a dumbfounded Secretary of State Stimson conveyed to British ambassador Sir Ronald Lindsay his chagrin that Hindenburg might dare select a reichskanzler who "if proposed as ambassador here would unhesitatingly be refused."[45]

Papen disconcerted observers, both foreign and domestic. "His" upper-class Cabinet appointments did little to provide any semblance of true national unity. Hindenburg—and Schleicher—had selected for him what Hindenburg enthusiastically dubbed a "cabinet of his friends,"[46] but which others quickly scorned as the "monocle cabinet"[47] or the "cabinet of barons."[48] Profoundly conservative, highly born, its nine other members included four barons: Konstantin von Neurath as foreign minister; the ultra-reactionary Wilhelm von Gayl at Interior; Magnus Alexander Maximilian von Braun at

Nutrition and Agriculture ("Dear Braun: Do you want to form a cabinet of gentlemen with me and take on the Ministry of Food?"[49]); and Peter Paul von Eltz-Rübenach at Mail and Transport. Bavarian Franz Gürtner (an old and reliable Hitler ally) directed Justice.[50] And, last, but absolutely not least, Kurt von Schleicher ruled Defense.

"The composition of the new government," groused even Bavaria's right-wing BVP premier Heinrich Held, "makes it seem as if the German nation were comprised of landed gentry, industrial magnates, and half-baked intellectuals."[51]

In its defense, this was, nonetheless, not an incapable Cabinet. It had its strengths. But it hardly represented a populace that delivered a plurality of its votes to socialists—or, for that matter, bestowed upon National Socialists second rank. It marked Weimar's first Cabinet bereft of labor representation.[52] "The overwhelming majority of the 19½ million Germans who only a few weeks ago set all party-political considerations aside and decided to support your re-election . . .," the SPD fruitlessly complained to Hindenburg, "have no representation in this new cabinet."[53]

This was the gratitude Hindenburg granted the SPD—*and* Heinrich Brüning *and* the Zentrum—for their recent support. Rarely had ingratitude been displayed so massively and so soon.

Such betrayal might logically have sent the SPD pouring into the streets in vengeful and righteous rage. Instead, Hindenburg's perfidy merely intensified the party's growing paralysis and, indeed, its increasing irrelevance. Heretofore, the Reich's various Catholic parties had pursued a consistent, indeed, a remarkably firm, anti-Nazi course. But when Brüning fell, something within his party snapped. Monsignor Kaas himself suffered what some characterized as "a total nervous collapse."[54] Zentrum loyalty to Brüning—and its nausea at Papen—triggered an attitudinal sea change. In January 1931, Kaas proclaimed, "If we were not restrained by a sense of decorum, we would, for pedagogical reasons, make room for the Nazis, [so] that the German people might become aware of their bloody ignorance. But the experiment seems risky, for I do not believe that afterwards there will be anything left to save."[55] Now, his party issued this momentous statement:

> *We condemn unanimously the events of the past few days, [leading] to the resignation of Chancellor Brüning. Irresponsible intrigues by persons having no authority under the Constitution have halted the work of . . . imminent international negotiations. The economic and social aspirations of every group in the country have had a grave obstacle placed in their path. . . . At a time of severe political unrest*

the Zentrum Party [demands] an overall policy leading to national freedom and equality, and a determined attempt to deal with the basic problem of unemployment. The Party therefore rejects the temporary solution provided by the present Cabinet, and demands that the situation should be clarified by placing the responsibility for forming a Government in the hands of the National Socialist Party.[56] *(emphasis added)*

With so many players scrambling about in this frantic, now dizzying, round of Weimar musical chairs, the Nazis were hardly about to be left out. As Papen negotiated with Schleicher and Hindenburg, in essence, another individual inhabited the room, quite invisible and, yet, very real: Adolf Hitler.

Schleicher coveted much from Hitler. In the short term, he required tacit Nazi support for Papen's new government. Eventually, Hitler's SA should augment his Reichswehr.

Hitler desired his own pound of flesh.

In December 1931, yet another transitory Schleicher scheme involved installing Wilhelm Gröner as chancellor, with Brüning demoted to the foreign ministry, and Wilhelm Frick arriving as an NSDAP minister.[57] That now seemed so very long ago. Gröner and Brüning were old news. Hitler could no longer be placated with a handful of lesser-rank Cabinet posts. He now insisted on two much bigger prizes, negotiating very hard with Schleicher for them, so seriously, in fact, that when the aforementioned Nazi journalist Albert Krebs published an article criticizing Schleicher, Krebs found himself summarily—and permanently—expelled from party ranks.[58]

Hitler, of course, had wanted Gröner's ban on Nazi paramilitary units lifted. He demanded new elections, because, with Nazi voting strength increasing at exponential levels, another round of voting might very well propel Hitlerites into an outright Reichstag majority—or, at least, with a voting bloc sufficiently large to fashion a ruling coalition with either the DNVP or the Zentrum. The chancellorship—and not merely a ragbag of worthless ministries—might then flutter gently into Hitler's lap.

Reichskanzler and Führer conferred. "We met at a flat belonging to Herr [Werner von] Alvensleben, a friend of Schleicher," Papen recalled. "I found him curiously unimpressive. Press pictures had conveyed no idea of a dominating personality and I could detect no inner quality which might explain his extraordinary hold on the masses. He was wearing a dark blue suit and seemed the complete petit-bourgeois. He had an unhealthy complexion and with his little moustache and curious hair style had an indefinable bohemian quality. His demeanor was modest and polite, and although I had heard much about the magnetic quality of his eyes, I do not remember being impressed by them."[59]

Impressed or not, Papen soon acceded to both new Reichstag elections[60] and the freeing of the SA.[61] Hitler in turn clandestinely pledged tacit support for Papen's newly minted regime. "Papen is . . . to be appointed Chancellor," Goebbels confided to his diary, "but that is neither here nor there. The Poll! [new elections] The Poll! It's the people we want. We are all entirely satisfied."[62]

But would they *ever* be satisfied? "The present Cabinet is a Cabinet of mutual deception . . . ," Britain's ambassador to Berlin Sir Horace Rumbold concluded. "Papen thinks he has scored off General von Schleicher and Hitler, General Schleicher thinks he has scored off Hitler, and Hitler, for his part, believes he has scored off both."[63]

Papen scheduled new balloting almost immediately; unleashing the Sturmabteilung took longer, only fueling Nazi frustration at both Papen and newly installed Interior Minister Gayl (Goebbels: "the weakling we held him for"[64]). "Modest and polite" Hitler now threatened Papen: "I regard your Cabinet only as a temporary solution, and will continue my efforts to make my Party the strongest in the country. The Chancellorship will then devolve on me."[65]

Goebbels was determined to force an SA emancipation. On Wednesday, June 15, he wrote in his diary:

> *In the evening I enter a large restaurant in the Potsdamer Platz, accompanied by forty to fifty S.A. leaders wearing full uniform, in spite of the prohibition. This is done expressly to irritate the authorities. Our purpose is to get ourselves arrested by the police. We wish Von Gayl joy of the business. Such a scandal would perhaps rouse him out of his complacency.*
>
> *Unfortunately the Alexanderplatz [the Headquarters of the Berlin Police], which has already rendered us many a good service, does not grant us this satisfaction. At midnight we proceed quite deliberately across the Potsdamer Platz and up Potsdamer Strasse. But nothing stirs. The policemen accord us a doubtful glance, and then turn shamefacedly away.[66]*

Goebbels didn't get his arrest. But he soon got his ban lifted.

All the while, Schleicher's ego raged. Around Berlin, Germany's puppetmaster-in-chief boasted that if he was "not the soul," he was, at least, "the will" of the new Cabinet.[67] And when a friend protested that Papen lacked any head for administration, Schleicher merely jeered, "He doesn't need a head, his job is to be a hat."[68]

Reichstag elections proceeded—often in unexpected ways. Interior Minister Gayl proudly announced that he was a monarchist—adding that so was the rest of the Cabinet.[69] Hugenberg seconded his sentiments.[70] In the run-up to Reichstag balloting, Nazis increased their representation in Mecklenburg-Schwerin local elections from two to thirty seats.[71] Hitler released an 8½-minute phonograph record, "Appeal to the Nation," fetching for five marks per disk.[72] From April through November, he—master of the art of speaking but increasingly fearful of vocal cord paralysis—subjected himself to secret speaking lessons from operatic tenor Paul Devrient.[73] Not always the most tractable of pupils, at one point he groused to Devrient, "You made me wait and now I have no desire to work. What gives you the right to deprive me of time? What do you make me do all these exercises for? And why do I need to dedicate all my free time to these lessons?"[74]

Lessons or not, it fell that June to Gregor Strasser ("The Nazis do not want reaction, but healing"[75]) to deliver the Nazis' first-ever radio address. Officials in Munich and Vienna refused to broadcast it. Local Hitlerites rioted in protest.[76] In the Prussian Landtag, National Socialist delegates snuck through a bill recommending the expropriation of property held by immigrant Jews ("a rapacious, nonproductive race"[77]).

That July, eighty-six persons—including thirty Communists and thirty-eight Nazis—died in political street violence.[78] Another 1,125 were wounded.[79] Even Hitler, surrounded by innumerable black- and brown-shirted legionnaires, could not count himself immune from danger. Thirty persons were wounded at a Hitler rally at Kiel.[80] On July 12, Goebbels wrote, almost joyously, in his diary:

> *We force our way through the howling mob in Düsseldorf and Elberfeld. A wild trip. We had no idea that things would get so serious. In all our innocence we drive into Hagen in an open car and wearing our uniforms. The streets are black with people. All of them mob and Communist rabble. They close off the road, so that we can go neither forward nor back. . . . We cut our way through the middle of the pack. Each of us has his pistol in his hand and is determined, if the worst comes to the worst, to sell his life as dearly as possible. . . . The meeting place is on a hill, framed by a forest of beeches in the background. The Communists have ingeniously set fire to this forest, so that it is almost impossible to carry on the meeting. Nevertheless, we make our speeches. . . . On our departure we are followed by a bombardment of stones. We manage to leave the city by detours. . . .[81]*

Intrigue piled atop intrigue in this topsy-turvy world. In normal times such machinations required discretion. But this epoch was hardly normal, and the nation's talent for betrayal outgrew any attendant sense of shame, progressing quite smoothly into a realm of brazen, utter cynicism. Within the Nazi press one might read notices such as this:

Halt! Before you leave your present party, convinced of the truth of the National Socialist idea, reflect if you cannot be more useful to the National Socialist Movement by remaining a member where you are and inform-ing us about all the occurrences and intentions of your present party com-rades . . . Your work will be valued as highly as the sacrifices of every party comrade and S.A. man who does his duty![82]

Such intrigues proved mere strange side show to von Papen's actions. Economically, he slashed unemployment benefits by 20 percent, while raising taxes and increasing business subsidies.[83] And, as he unshackled the SA, he banned the SPD paper *Vorwärts* for five days[84] and the Zentrum's *Kolnische Volkszeitung* (for labeling his appointment a "national embarrassment"[85]) for three.[86] On the foreign front, he built upon Brüning's earlier efforts, and at Lausanne, essentially secured an end to wartime reparations.[87] Still, this long-coveted foreign policy triumph yielded him little political capital.[88]

It was what he did in Prussia, however, that mattered far, far more.

CHAPTER EIGHTEEN

"The sinister faculty of making men like bad government"

ADOLF HITLER'S PARTY HAD HIS ERNST RÖHM.

Franklin Roosevelt's had Jimmy Walker.

Röhm ruled the SA.

Walker ruled City Hall in New York.

The Hon. James J. Walker—"Gentleman Jimmy," "Beau James," the mayor of the City of New York—bloomed as Tammany Hall's fairest flower. Years ago, FDR had initiated his career energetically crusading against the Hall's myriad peccadilloes. As a freshman state senator he had challenged their choice of "Blue Eyed Billy" Sheehan for US senator. He opposed it—quite unsuccessfully—in his own 1914 US Senate campaign.[1]

But that was then.

Youthful idealist Roosevelt had learned his lesson well. He might still tilt at windmills, but he no longer tilted at tanks. And in New York politics, Tammany (aka "The Hall" or the "Wigwam") fielded an entire armored division. So, he made his uneasy peace with them. They supported him in 1920. He supported their favorite son, Al Smith, in both 1924 and 1928, and they, in turn, boosted him for governor. The Tammany Tiger—and Smith, of course—had clearly underrated him, both physically and politically. Franklin, however, no longer underestimated the Hall. In fact, in 1929, by contributing to its building fund, he had technically enrolled as a member. "I am very glad to send you a check . . . ," he cheerfully jotted. "I regret that I cannot make it larger."[2]

Such coziness—among other reasons—contributed to a widespread liberal resistance to FDR's many charms. He was, reformers knew, not ready to cast aspersions against Tammany's boy Walker, unwilling to abandon the Wigwam's vote-rich turf.

Tammany had long been corrupt, whether under "Boss" Tweed, the Irish-born Richard Croker, or the savvier Charles Francis Murphy (FDR termed him a "genius"[3]). Murphy quietly transformed Tammany from not merely the patron of crooked pols and special interests but simultaneously to an incubator for such stellar progressives as Al Smith or US senator Robert F. Wagner. "Silent Charlie," expired, however, in 1924, leaving his party in less astute hands—leadership too eager to hoist the morally challenged state senator Walker into the mayor's office. Flamboyantly brilliant, but spectacularly lazy, "Beau James" was made for the Roaring Twenties. He had written a hit song—"Will You Love Me in December (as You Do in May)?"—shamelessly squired his showgirl mistress Betty Compton about town (he had, after all, also penned "There's Music in the Rustle of a Skirt"[4]), and refused to take much of anything very seriously. On appointing his mayoral predecessor, the famously obtuse Hearst-puppet John F. Hylan to the Children's Court, he could not help quipping, "The appointment of Judge Hylan means that the children now can be tried by their peer."[5]

He was bad—but he was fun. "He possesses," summarized *Vanity Fair*, "the sinister faculty of making men like bad government."[6]

Walker, however, was merely the dandified, wisecracking tip of an iceberg of bootleg gin and cash-filled envelopes. Times were flush, and the getting was good. Cops and judges and inspectors were all on the pad. Everything had a price. The fix was in from top down to bottom up.

Roosevelt's 1930 re-election landslide was presaged by Walker's own 1929 historic and humiliating rout of two men we have already met: GOP challenger Fiorello La Guardia and Socialist Party gadfly Norman Thomas.[7] But just as the stock market peaked that September merely to plunge over Niagara barely a month later, Tammany's travails were also soon in coming. Both La Guardia and Thomas had hammered Democrats over a recently discovered $19,600 "loan" tendered from the recently deceased organized crime figure Arnold Rothstein to Tammany magistrate Albert Vitale.[8] A month following Walker's landslide, Vitale presided over a dinner at the Bronx's Tepecano Democratic Club. Seven gunmen burst in, robbing guests, among them police detective Arthur C. Johnson. Vitale counseled patience ("don't start anything"), and sure and soon enough, Vitale suspiciously returned Johnson's service revolver to him—as well as all other guests' purloined cash and jewelry. The robbery had, in fact, been a setup, designed to retrieve documents incriminating to piquantly nicknamed mobster Ciro "The Artichoke King" Terranova (and his involvement in Brooklyn gangster Frankie Yale's 1928 rub-out). The public rightly pondered Vitale's gangland connections. Before long it clamored for a purging of the city's corrupt judiciary.[9]

Roosevelt's skirts were not nearly as clean as they might have been. True, he cavorted with no artichoke kings, but he was entirely too amenable to Tammany's judicial patronage recommendations. When Al Smith proposed the upright liberal Bernard L. Sheintag for a Supreme Court vacancy, FDR opted instead for Tammany choice, Joseph Force Crater.[10] When in October 1929, authorities indicted General Sessions judge Francis X. Mancuso in connection to Francesco Ferrari's City Trust Company failure,[11] FDR replaced him with Mayor Walker's patently unqualified boyhood chum, Amedeo A. Bertini.[12] Crater simply vanished into thin air one evening in August 1930. Bertini lasted hardly longer—though not departing before famously refusing to yield immunity concerning the purchase of his appointment.[13] During FDR's re-election campaign he faced charges of appointing a judge who had bought the position for thirty thousand dollars from Tammany.[14]

By 1930, the Wigwam stood upon dangerous ground. That September, Judge Samuel Seabury, the Democrats' 1916 gubernatorial candidate, was appointed to investigate the city's Magistrates Courts.[15] To say the Episcopalian Seabury was patrician was to understate the matter. "His dignity was Jove-like . . ." noted one observer, "there was a conviction, among his associates that anyone who called him Sam, chucked him in the ribs or offered him a cigar would be promptly dealt with by a heaven-sent bolt of lightning."[16] But Seabury was no mere stuffed shirt, no empty Brooks Brothers suit. He was smart, and he was thorough. And he meant to bring the machine low.

A month later an aggressive good government group, the City Affairs Committee, formed, with the ultra-progressive (a co-founder of *both* the NAACP and the ACLU) former Unitarian minister John Haynes Holmes as chairman, Reform rabbi Stephen S. Wise as vice-chairman, former *Nation* associate editor Paul Blanshard as executive director, and such heavyweights as Norman Thomas, Heywood Broun, and John Dewey among its fifteen hundred virtuous members.[17] Even they could not escape the immensity of their task. James J. Walker was not merely marvelously ornamental, he could be the most charming politician in the nation. Compared to "Beau James" even the charismatic FDR seemed as dull and dour as The Great Engineer. "Walker," Reverend Holmes never dared deny, "was easily and happily all things to all men. He could meet any situation with an adaptability, a *savoir faire*, a maximum of grace and a minimum of *gaucherie*, which stirred admiration [despite his affront] of every element of decency and honor."[18] A Walker appearance at the Metropolitan Opera House honoring Albert Einstein's birthday simply stunned Holmes. The mayor, late and unprepared as ever, "spoke with such ease of manner, such beauty of phrase, such flawless adaptation of his thought to the rigors of the occasion, as to make every person present, for this one evening at least, the Mayor's admirer and friend."[19]

This was not a crook to be taken lightly.

Yet, the stench of corruption was mighty, and even FDR's politically restrained nostrils flared. In March 1931, he wrote to William Randolph Hearst: "Our little Mayor can save much trouble in the future by getting on the job, cleaning his own house, and stopping wise cracks. If he does not do all this, he can only have himself to blame if he gets into trouble."[20]

Roosevelt's nostrils had their reasons. Seabury had uncovered a raft of judicial corruption, not merely the widely suspected purchase of judgeships but the spectacularly repulsive practice of framing innocent women on prostitution charges. Two magistrates were removed from office. Three more resigned under fire. Juries convicted six police officers.[21] The convictions did not come easy. In February 1931, a prospective witness, a thirty-two-year-old red-headed prostitute named Vivian Gordon, was found quite conveniently fatally beaten and garroted in the Bronx's sprawling Van Cortlandt Park.[22] The following month, New York's Republican-controlled legislature entrusted Seabury to investigate the entire municipal government.[23]

On Tuesday evening, March 17, 1931 (his twenty-sixth wedding anniversary), Franklin Roosevelt attended the Friendly Sons of St. Patrick dinner at Times Square's Hotel Astor. Returning home to East 65th Street, he discovered the invariably glowering, Hungarian-born Rabbi Wise and the tall, lean, Philadelphia-born Reverend Holmes encamped in his library. They tendered to him formal charges against Walker plus a four-thousand-signature petition demanding his removal.[24]

For two lions of reform, tonight their manner was strangely diffident, their terse presentation a nervous reflection of their host's distinct and unnerving coolness. As they prepared their leave, Franklin suddenly snapped, "I have listened to you. Now you sit down and listen to me."[25] For over a half hour he ripped into them, ostensibly over a letter Rabbi Wise had once dispatched to him over a judicial appointment.

His ill-tempered fusillade stunned his victims. Holmes never quite forgave him. But eventually he realized that Roosevelt had more on his plate than any mere judgeship. This was, Holmes would conclude only much later, "what would become a deliberate policy of [Roosevelt]—namely, to catch control of the situation at the start, and so monopolize the conversation that the meeting was over before the visitor had any chance to speak about the problem he had come to present. . . . Before the Rabbi, quite taken aback, could enter any plea in defense of his action, or I could intervene, our time was up and we were on the street."[26] A good offense was, indeed, Franklin Roosevelt's best defense—particularly, in defending the indefensible.

For, FDR knew trouble when he saw it. Tammany was now simultaneously both a Tiger and an albatross—and any move he made—or did not make—came with the gravest peril. The Hall might deny him the New York votes he would need at the 1932 convention. Worse, it might strike at him within New York. In 1913, Gov. William "Plain Bill" Sulzer, a populist Manhattan Democrat harboring presidential ambitions, had unwisely crossed Tammany's Charles Francis Murphy. "Silent Charlie" retaliated with a quick impeachment. Conversely, voters beyond the Hudson clearly loathed Tammany. Any Democrat perceived as hewing too closely to its soiled raiments risked national umbrage. Al Smith had surely paid that price in 1928. Wigwam support similarly helped capsize Champ Clark's nomination in 1912.

So, FDR had to proceed very, very carefully.

In August 1931, he, nonetheless, facilitated Seabury's ability to grant immunity to witnesses.[27] But he also initially resisted ousting New York county sheriff Thomas Farley, who, during the course of seven years (no doubt, one of those biblical seven-year periods of plenty), had mysteriously banked $360,000 while earning only $90,000.[28] The 250-pound Farley blandly rationalized that he had somehow accumulated this princely sum from "monies I saved" in "a little tin box." Seabury failed to follow Farley's logic. "Kind of a magic box?" he asked.

"It was a wonderful box,"[29] answered the sheriff.

When Manhattan's Grace Episcopal Church pastor, the Rev. W. Russell Bowie, demanded Farley's ouster, Franklin responded nearly sacrilegiously, citing: "the action of a certain magistrate by the name of Pontius Pilate, who acted upon public clamor after first washing his hands. When I re-read a certain poem, entitled 'IF' I am strengthened in any resolution not to let politics interfere with my decisions as Governor, nor to deny the right to be heard even to the meanest criminal in the State."[30]

Of course, FDR knew more about Sheriff Farley's miraculous finances than he avowed, having received $20,000 in campaign contributions from him in 1930.[31]

In the end, however, the once-silent FDR did remove Farley, and when he did his silence turned to politically opportune moralizing, suddenly cognizant that when a public official's "scale of living, or the total of his bank deposits, far exceeds the public salary which he is known to receive, he owes a positive public duty to the community to give a reasonable or credible explanation of the source of his deposits."[32]

Yet, other Tammany officials boasted similarly dubious income/savings ratios. Over a six-year period first deputy city clerk James J. McCormick (annual salary: $8,500) deposited over $250,000. Kings County (Brooklyn) sheriff James A. McQuade banked $510,597.35 while earning only $50,000.[33] City clerk Michael J. Cruise deposited $80,000 in six years while making just $17,246.91.[34] Over a four-year period, Judge Vitale earned $48,000 and saved $165,000.[35] The grossly fat Queens County Surrogates Court chief clerk (and Democratic county chairman) John Theofel's net worth exploded from $28,650 to $201,300. Perhaps not coincidentally, all Queens officials drove luxurious Pierce-Arrows—purchased from Theofel's son-in-law.[36] The law firm of Charlie Murphy's Tammany successor, Judge George Washington Olvany, banked $5,283,000 in legal fees.[37]

Still, FDR hesitated to strike *too* hard at the Hall. When he removed "Tin Box" Farley, he mollified the organization by appointing Olvany's friend, the loyal Tammanyite John E. Sheehy, as his replacement.[38] On March 17, 1932 (FDR's twenty-seventh wedding anniversary), Rabbi Wise and Reverend Holmes wrote to him, advocating McQuade and Theofel's removal on the same grounds FDR had employed against "Tin Box" Farley.[39] Rage FDR never dared exhibit versus Tammany, he again unleashed at Wise and Holmes: "Let me tell you two gentlemen straight from the shoulder, that I am becoming convinced from your letters that corruption in public office and unfit servants in public office are both far less abhorrent to you than they are to me," FDR now *publicly* lectured them. "A rushing into print early and often, with extravagant and ill-considered language, causes many of our decent citizens to doubt your own reliance on law, on order and on justice.

"The time which you two gentlemen now spend in bringing charges and asking your Governor to perform unconstitutional functions and to ignore the principles of representative government could be more profitably spent if you would exert yourself patiently and consistently in pointing out to the electorate of New York City that an active insistence on their part would result in better qualified and more honest and more efficient public servants, you would be performing a service to your community which at the present time you are not performing."[40]

But FDR was not through. From Hyde Park in early April he phoned reporters to further excoriate Wise and Holmes. "If they would serve their God with as much zeal as they seek to serve themselves," he charged, "the people of the city of New York would be the gainers."[41]

McQuade and Theofel and Tom Farley, however, were but small potatoes. Perched far away at Albany or grandly upon Hudson shores, FDR might still safely ignore such hacks' peccadilloes. He could not ignore Mayor

James J. Walker—and His Honor's rendezvous with Seabury's witness chair was soon approaching.

There existed in the Walker drama a worrisome sub-plot: the Catholic issue. Tammany was largely Catholic. Despite his once-fruitful alliance with Smith, FDR had long been suspected of harboring anti-Catholic prejudices. His break with—some would say his betrayal of—Smith merely complicated that issue. Wise and Holmes were not merely non-Catholics; they were the most liberal sort of clergy.[42] Their associate, Paul Blanshard, would later exhibit a visible and energetic anti-Catholicism. And, thus (as some Jews would later defend the Rosenbergs and some blacks Adam Clayton Powell Jr.) some Catholics would associate a spirited vindication of the corrupt Walker as a greater defense of their own faith and tribe.

Most prominent among Walker's champions was Detroit's obstreperous Father Charles Coughlin. Unlike Walker's Catholic Tammany associates, Coughlin was then a strident, even sycophantic, advocate ("I am with you to the end. Say the word and I will follow"[43]) for Roosevelt.

The year previously, FDR had received word of the rising radio priest from Detroit's city comptroller: his brother-in-law, Eleanor's younger brother, G. Hall Roosevelt:

> *Father Coughlin is probably known to you by this time and is famous for being the director of fifty-two secretaries, which he has found necessary to handle his mail which gets as high as 250,000 letters a day. He would like to tender his services. From what I can make out his brethren in the Church tolerate him. He would be difficult to handle and might be full of dynamite, but I think you had better prepare to say "yes" or "no." Of course, he has a following just about equal to that of Mr. Gandhi. We would probably enjoy the leadership of a lot of Indians however.*[44]

No one is quite sure what FDR made of an in-law's advice (Eleanor later said Franklin "disliked and distrusted [Coughlin]. . . . I never liked him"[45]), but, in any case, Coughlin's popularity only accelerated. By April 1932, Coughlin and his ally, Detroit mayor Frank Murphy, visited New York, meeting privately with FDR at a Manhattan hotel room. Coughlin departed confident that Roosevelt shared his visions on social justice, an inflated currency, and, for good measure, the repeal of Prohibition.[46]

Fine enough for an aspiring presidential candidate, but an April earlier Coughlin had also tarried in the big city. At a New York City Fire Department Holy Name Society Communion breakfast, he excoriated by name those attacking "Beau James" ("never . . . an angel, and if he were here . . . he would gladly . . . show you there are no wings sprouting from his shoulders").

By coincidence or not, soon afterward FDR found "insufficient evidence" to remove Walker.[47]

What a difference a year might make. In spring 1931, Coughlin and Walker might dismiss Wise and Holmes as dangerous Socialists, with Franklin Roosevelt not quite in agreement—but hardly disagreeing either. By spring 1932, Judge Seabury had concluded his bill's lesser acts and stood ready to stage his main attraction: "Gentleman Jimmy" himself. Seabury prepared himself well. Walker, his arrogance usually outshining even his wit and brilliance, rarely bothered to prepare anything. He would pay a heavy price for that latest dereliction of duty.

Times were flush in the 1920s but not so flush that Mayor Walker might enjoy all the pastimes he enjoyed on his $40,000 salary.[48] Aside from a mistress to support, he also had a wife. He enjoyed trips to Palm Springs,[49] "a much-needed rest in New England,"[50] and a grand August-September 1927 jaunt to Europe. An English-born admirer (and coincidentally a city functionary), Hector Fuller, even chronicled His Honor's continental adventures in a handsome little book, *Abroad with Mayor Walker*—fulsomely depicting the mayor refereeing a boxing match aboard the SS *Berengaria*, in Munich and Berlin (including a dinner at the elegant Kaiserhof),[51] losing at croquet at Cannes to Iraq's Mecca-born King Faisal I,[52] balancing a visit to Dublin with one to the Tower of London, traversing the Venetian canals via gondola, and meeting with Pius XI and then Benito Mussolini ("the greatest figure in modern times"[53]). Fuller dedicated his 264-page tome to "The Democratic Party of the City of New York."[54]

The mayor, of course, also enjoyed his domestic extravaganzas. In May 1932, with Seabury's noose closing around his exquisitely tailored neck, he led several hundred marchers up Fifth Avenue, across Central Park (where he had constructed a casino for the twenty-something Miss Compton's amusement[55]) and farther up Central Park West. His cause: Repeal. Walker's spectacular "Beer Parade" featured dozens of bands, captains of industry Walter Chrysler and E. F. Hutton, Broadway's William Gaxton and Victor Moore, plus a bevy of chorus girls, Gene Tunney, Mrs. William Randolph Hearst, the Anti-Profanity League, the House Wreckers Union, the Knights of Columbus, and the usual assortment of Tammany crooks. A million spectators cheered the six-hour-long procession.[56]

But for all the pageantry of "Gentleman Jimmy" swaggering up Fifth Avenue adorned in morning coat, striped trousers, and derby hat, a far more significant—and riveting—drama lay upon the horizon.

On Wednesday morning, May 25, 1932, Samuel Seabury finally summoned Walker to the witness stand. The picture remains ineradicable: the usually unflappable mayor squirming in his high-backed wooden chair as Judge Seabury, notes in hand, calmly looks askance as his prey self-destructs.

And Jimmy did self-destruct, though he had done it long before he had entered the New York County Courthouse, and Seabury had done his very best to document it, grilling two thousand witnesses (175 in public session) and securing seventy-five thousand pages of testimony. In most cases, such volume would constitute overkill. In Tammany's case, it merely scratched the surface.

His case against Walker hinged on a triptych of incredibly incriminating incidents. The first involved Walker's illustrious European jaunt. To fund it, "Beau James" had received a $10,000 line of credit from the Equitable Coach Company, an unusually unqualified bus company (it often helps in such cases to actually own a bus) that had just two days prior to Walker's sailing received the franchise to replace the city's existing trolley lines.[57] The second instance concerned twenty-six thousand dollars in stocks tendered quite gratuitously upon the mayor by Wall Street financier J. A. Sisto, a principal in the Checker Cab Company. Sisto desired a law limiting competition in the taxicab field. Not surprisingly, he got it.[58] Newspaper publisher (and close Hearst associate[59]) Paul Block, hoping to supply tiles for the city subway system,[60] bestowed even larger largesse upon the mayor. By August 1931, Walker had deposited $961,000 in various bank accounts—including $750,000 in cash—certainly suspicious amounts, and the misgivings only mounted when the mayor's bookkeeper, Russell T. Sherwood, hot-footed it to Mexico City.[61] Adding to the sordid mix were the activities of the mayor's pudgy, older brother, Dr. William H. Walker Jr., medical examiner of the city's Board of Education. To Dr. Walker's credit, his official position was not particularly lucrative (though, it must also be added, he was not particularly qualified), but his unofficial activities were quite remunerative: specifically a fee-splitting operation for city employees' compensation cases that netted him $216,000 in just three years. In four years, he banked $431,258.[62]

James J. Walker entered the New York County Courthouse like a conquering hero, surrounded by an adoring throng, shouting its encouragement, even, its love. He departed two days later wilted by Seabury's relentless marshaling of facts and testimony and bank records. Jimmy was smart and glib and cocky, but he was not enough of any of those qualities to withstand Seabury's very public unveiling of his own sordid record. "Walker," recalled Raymond Moley, "had no defense but evasion, amnesia, cheap theatrics and shallow, unbelievable rationalizations."[63]

He was essentially through.

Not, however, that Franklin D. Roosevelt particularly relished any of these developments. It may, of course, have been a matter of pure sentiment. It was "Beau James," after all, who had placed his name in nomination at Rochester in 1928.[64] It might indeed have been such memories, but more likely another convention motivated FDR: the upcoming national convention in Chicago and the sizable bloc of votes an increasingly enraged Tammany still controlled. As Bruce Bliven noted in the *New Republic*: FDR "has used his power of removal from office only once [the Sheriff Farley matter], and then not until the scandal had become so flagrant that he could no longer ignore it. . . . In the eyes of most people throughout the United States, his alliance with Tammany is his gravest liability."[65] Fiorello La Guardia aide Ernest Cuneo eventually put it more bluntly, "Roosevelt viewed the scene with absolutely unmixed emotions: . . . everyone knew he was out for himself."[66]

Any hopes, however, that FDR harbored of mollifying the Hall soon proved illusory. The Tammany Tiger remained for Smith—always had been, always would be. But what would Walker do? Smith, after all, had helped install him as mayor in 1925. Yet, gratitude had its limits in politics (indeed!), and it was Governor Roosevelt who now brandished a club over the embattled mayor's top-hatted head. Still, delegate-at-large Jimmy dared thunder: "I vote for Alfred E. Smith."[67]

"My God, that man's got nerve!" an observer exclaimed within earshot of Louis Howe's assistant Lila Stiles. "Voting against a man who has the toe of his boot right against the seat of the well-pressed Walker trousers."[68]

Yes, no one ever denied James J. Walker possessed nerve.

He certainly had it on Memorial Day 1932, present at the Bronx's Yankee Stadium to dedicate a bronze-and-granite outfield monument to the team's late manager Miller J. Huggins.[69] As the embattled mayor trekked from his box seat to deepest center field, a shower of booing commenced, swelling all the louder with each step advanced. This was a new thing for him. He heard no catcalls on entering Seabury's courtroom; none during his "Beer March," none honoring Einstein at the Met. No, these raucous sounds stung his ears and sickened his heart.

But he recovered to address his detractors thusly:

Politics is like baseball.

In baseball, the greatest star may be cheered for a home run today and then, on the very next day, be booed if he strikes out. That's the way it is, and that's the way it should be. Freedom of speech is guaranteed by that emblem up there [here he gestured to the Stars and Stripes fluttering overhead]. It also guarantees us the right to criticize, or even to boo. If a politician pops out, fouls out, or strikes out, he must expect adverse criticism. If he cannot withstand the boos—and I mean b-o-o-s, and not b-o-o-z-e—then he also should not pay attention to praise.

The great little fellow to whom this memorial tablet has been placed upon the scene of his many triumphs, Miller Huggins, sometimes heard his mighty team booed. Fame is a comet that chases its own tail in the sky. Huggins is now well beyond the reach of criticism or praise, but we still remember him as a wonderful man. It is so important to be a man first, and regard whatever else that comes to you or is denied you in the way of laurels as a secondary consideration. It is much more important, when all else is over, and one has been through the narrow door from which there is no returning, to have been loved than to have been exalted.[70]

And with that, he again crossed Yankee Stadium's great green expanse—this time to overwhelming cheers. "The return parade took on the aspect of a triumphal march,"[71] noted the *New York Times*, and the sound must have been sweet, but even "Gentleman Jimmy" was not so shallow as to not know the crowd—so often a mob—could turn on him once again. After all, it was he who had penned the question, "Will You Love Me in December (as You Do in May)?"

But Roosevelt still wavered, and beyond wavering, he lashed out—not at Walker but again at Walker's critics. "This fellow Seabury," FDR complained in a letter to Colonel House, "is merely trying to perpetrate another political play to embarrass me. His conduct has been a deep disappointment to people who honestly seek better government in New York City by stressing the fundamentals and eliminating political innuendoes."[72]

Many even suspected Seabury of harboring his own presidential ambitions.[73] But even if that were not so, he certainly favored Newton D. Baker over Franklin.[74] For that matter, so did Rabbi Wise.[75] Following the convention Wise had even written Baker: "It should have been you and only you. Personally I cannot give my support to the candidate for the party. I went into the party with Wilson. I go out thanks to Roosevelt. . . ."[76] And when William Gibbs McAdoo had plotted at the Waldorf-Astoria to support Baker, he had, in fact, conferred with Seabury—even dangling a Baker-Seabury ticket before him.[77]

So it was not surprising that in a statement issued by his secretary Guernsey Cross, Roosevelt now excoriated Seabury and the legislative committee he led: "The only information before the governor is in the form of very incomplete newspaper stories. . . . I act in each case definitely, positively and with due promptness. Get the facts straight. It is the duty of the legislative committee and its counsel, if they believe they have sufficient cause, to present evidence to the proper authorities without waiting to make formal report to next year's legislature . . . If the evidence in any case now before the legislative committee in their judgment or that of their counsel warrants, it is time for the legislative committee and their counsel to stop talking and do something. It is not the time for political sniping or buck-passing."[78]

It was all baloney. FDR had possessed transcripts of Seabury's hearings from the very beginning.[79]

At Hyde Park, that June, Eleanor's friend Marion Dickerman had witnessed FDR simply explode when confronted with the issue. Following a meeting with a trio of nationally prominent Democrats on the subject, she dared lecture him, "They're right, Franklin! You know they are! The convention will never nominate a Tammany-controlled candidate, and that's what your enemies will call you. You must remove the mayor."

He had remained calm during the conference. Now he flew into a rage. She had never seen him angrier. "Never, never will I let it be said that I climbed to a position of power on the back of someone else!" he fairly shouted. Calming down, he explained, "I have at times acted on the advice and counsel of others when it was contrary to my own judgment, and on occasion the results have been good. The advice proved to be good. But one act leads to another, and when the time comes to act again the same counselor may not be there. The first time, you acted out of character; the second time, you are confused. The path you are following is not the one that you would have chosen by yourself, and because it isn't you make mistakes. This is a vital matter. It's more important than any immediate political advantage. You must let me be myself."[80]

But all such prattling was in reality a gossamer rationale for inaction—and for his own conflicted political calculations. "This squalid [Walker] mess is due to nothing but Governor Roosevelt's own weakness and timidity . . . ," observed Walter Lippmann, "his mind is not very clear, his purposes are not simple, and his methods are not direct."[81]

But the time approached for artful evasion to conclude. The convention was over. The nomination was secured. The nation—not Tammany—needed mollifying. And Judge Seabury had dropped a damning series of charges against Walker right into Roosevelt's lap.

Again, Roosevelt delayed, but when he finally acted, he succeeded in summoning every ounce of the intelligence and strength of will that had so impressed Raymond Moley. Franklin Roosevelt—not any appointed counsel—would personally interrogate James J. Walker himself.

The scene: Albany's Executive Chamber. The date: Thursday, August 11, 1932—very late in the game with a presidential campaign still to run. Roosevelt seemed almost as nervous as Walker. He sweated. His voice wavered. He face was taut and grim.[82] But such angst proved merely transitory. Quickly, FDR recovered his *sang-froid*, forcing Walker on the defensive. "He was in full command of himself," noted his biographer Kenneth S. Davis. "He was in full command of the situation."[83]

More or less.

He was clearly proving—or, rather, reaffirming—that Walker was a crook and unfit for office. But he still had not quite decided what to *do* about it. From Michigan, Father Coughlin recalled certain unpleasant political facts. "Whether it is fortunate or unfortunate, religion does play a prominent part in major political campaigns," Coughlin wrote FDR. "I was thinking of the 20 odd million Catholics in this country, among whom are 5,000,000 voters. I was thinking of the tremendous influence which Mr. Walker has upon the majority of these voters. It was possible for clever Republicans and others who feel that they have been victims of circumstances to use this Walker case against your best interests." Recklessly scoring Seabury as a "member of the Klan," Coughlin continued, "You have gone to the extreme limit on the matter of this perilous case. I would not be loyal to you or to the Democratic party unless I spoke fearlessly and truthfully of those pertinent things."[84]

"I am, as you know, giving the defense every latitude," FDR responded, "and I am being scrupulously careful not to make up my mind in any way until their case is wholly in. I do hope I shall have the privilege of seeing you again soon."[85]

"What if I gave the little mayor hell and then let him off?" Roosevelt muttered to his staff, almost thinking out loud. Then, he thought again: "No, that would be weak."[86]

Lila Stiles inquired of Louis Howe, "Boss, what do you think the Governor ought to do?"

"I'm not thinking at the moment," Howe dodged.

"But boss, what have you told him he ought to do about it?"

"I have never mentioned the Walker matter to him but once," Howe replied, "and then I told him, Franklin, never mind what 'they' say about all this. You just search your heart and do what you think is right. You can't go very wrong if you do that and never mind the consequences."

He gave Stiles a wary glance to ascertain whether he had convinced her of that. He had.

But then he added, "As a matter of fact that's all I ever tell Franklin."

That she did not believe.[87]

And then death intervened.

The mayor's younger brother George, suffering from a "pulmonary malady," i.e., tuberculosis,[88] expired at New York's remote, far-northern Saranac Lake.[89] What fight Jimmy still possessed vanished. "Jim looks worse than George,"[90] whispered Jim Farley at George's interment at Queens' Calvary Cemetery.

Walker might still have toughed it out and forced Roosevelt to remove him. But he did not.

At the cemetery, Walker asked his younger sister Anna "Nan" Burke, "Sis, take a short walk with me. I've got something to tell you."

They visited the nearby grave of Tammany's Charles Murphy, and Jimmy confided, "Mr. Murphy once told me that most of the troubles of the world could be avoided if men opened their minds instead of their mouths. Sis, I'm going to resign."

"When, Jim?"

"Now, or as soon as I leave the meeting at the Plaza."[91]

Gathered at Manhattan's Plaza Hotel was what was left of the brains and heart of Tammany. Brooklyn's machine boss John H. McCooey remained in Walker's corner[92] but what of Tammany itself? During the recent Democratic Convention when Walker had defiantly stood by him against Franklin Roosevelt, Al Smith had exclaimed, "Good old Jimsie! Blood is thicker than water."[93] But today the straight-laced Smith, never sympathetic to Walker's shameless philandering, retained little room for sentiment. "Jim," Smith snapped, "you're through. You must resign for the good of the party."[94]

Almost simultaneously, FDR conferred with Farley, Sam Rosenman, Arthur Mullen, Basil O'Connor, and the newly installed Democratic National Committee treasurer, beefy theater-chain attorney Frank C. Walker (no relation to the mayor). Most argued against FDR removing "the little mayor." A stern slap on the wrist would suffice. But Roosevelt demurred. "So you'd rather be right than president," Basil O'Connor sputtered, so angry that he hurled a match he held in his hand at his old law partner.

"Well," FDR sadly pondered, "there might be something in what you say."[95]

The phone rang.

Jimmy Walker had resigned.

FDR had been literally saved by the bell. Fate would force no decision upon him either to remove James J. Walker or to merely chide him. Franklin Roosevelt would alienate no do-gooders nor machine pols, no Lippmanns nor Coughlins—though most likely he would have opted for removal.

Basil O'Connor, however, might have only imperfectly grasped the logic behind FDR's rationale. O'Connor was no politician, but Jimmy Walker was, and of Franklin Roosevelt, Walker ultimately deduced, "He was patient beyond reason, but finally I stood in his way . . . let me tell you something I have learned from experience: there are two things no one can do with impunity: stand in the way of a man and his woman, or a candidate and the presidency."[96]

Franklin Roosevelt now stood *this close* to the presidency. He was not about to stop now.

CHAPTER NINETEEN

"The swine within themselves"

FRANKLIN ROOSEVELT'S NEW YORK WAS AMERICA'S "EMPIRE STATE"—rich, powerful, populous, and boasting the nation's largest, most wide-open, teeming metropolis.

Prussia was Germany's New York—and more.

In reality, German unification had been Prussian annexation. The huge, militaristic Kingdom of Prussia had pushed lackadaisical rival Austria aside and in the wake of victory in 1870's Franco-Prussian War incorporated such smaller states as Bavaria, Hessen, Württemberg, Baden, Saxony, Mecklenburg-Schwerin, Oldenburg, and Braunschweig into the ascendant Hohenzollern monarchy.

The Reich's hodgepodge of lesser kingdoms, grand duchies, just regular duchies, principalities, and free cities chafed under Prussian domination. The new Weimar Republic might have remedied the situation and sundered the massive kingdom into more manageable components. It hadn't. And the German federal union remained fundamentally unbalanced, top-heavy with Prussian population, territory, and influence.

In the 1920s, Prussia's state government mirrored Weimar's, featuring a series of SPD-Zentrum coalitions. Hermann Müller's chancellorship departed the Wilhelmstrasse in March 1930. But despite forfeiting his working majority in April 1932's state balloting, another sickly Social Democrat, Prussian prime minister Otto Braun (Müller's great intraparty rival), clung tenuously to power.

Hardly anyone to the right of the SPD—Hitler, Hindenburg, Hugenberg, Schleicher, Papen—savored Braun's political survival, particularly since it enabled Social Democrats to retain control of Prussia's state police—at ninety thousand men, barely smaller than the hundred-thousand-man Reichswehr.

The Nazis might then have assumed power in Prussia. In May 1932, with Zentrum support, they elected one of their "old fighters," Dr. Hanns Kerrl, as

Prussian Landtag speaker.[1] It was, to say the least, not a red-letter day in the history of German democracy. "The Communists arraign one of our members as a murderer," noted Goebbels. "The Bolshevist faction-leader, [former Spartacist Wilhelm] Pieck, is speaking from the rostrum, and becomes insufferable. One of the Communists hits a Party member in the face. That is the signal for a general settlement. It is short, but to the point, and is fought out with inkpots and chair legs for weapons. Our faction is left alone in the hall, victorious, in three minutes. The Communists have been driven out; the parties of the 'Middle' have already taken to flight. We sing the Horst Wessel song. The casualties generally, amount to eight seriously wounded. That should be a warning: it is the only way to ensure respect. The Council Chamber is a scene of wreckage. We remain victorious amid the ruins."[2]

Barely a week later, Nazis and Communist Landtag deputies proved far more amenable to each other, combining to register no-confidence in the Braun government.[3] That was about as far as Hitlerites intended to go regarding replacing Braun. "We have a difficult decision to make," Goebbels concluded even before Kerrl's election. "Coalition with the Centre and Power, or opposition to the Centre minus the Power. From a parliamentary point of view, nothing can be achieved without the Centre—neither in Prussia nor in the Reich. This has to be thoroughly thought over."[4] In the end, Hitlerites judged it preferable to merely toss inkpots and chair legs than govern. "[W]e must not take any responsibility whatever upon ourselves in Prussia. Either we attain to power or we remain in opposition . . . ," Goebbels recorded in his diary. "It is all the better, then, to remain in opposition till we attain to undisputed power, so as to be able to take energetic measures when the right time comes. That is the Leader's idea."[5]

Ill and dispirited, the sixty-year-old Otto Braun clung shakily to power, his grasp upon office, even shakier, however, than even one merely dependent upon Herr Hitler's sufferance, for almost from the moment Franz von Papen had supplanted Heinrich Brüning, rumors circulated of Berlin (federal) soon supplanting Berlin (state).

For a while, nothing happened. Then, came the pretext.

Hitler had his strongholds. The Communists had theirs. Berlin was one. Hamburg was not far behind, nor was Hamburg's working-class, KPD-dominated suburb of Altona. On Sunday—"Bloody Sunday"—July 17, 1932, uniformed Nazis invaded Altona, itching for a fight. The American historian Otis C. Mitchell described the scene:

A week before . . . propaganda leaflets warning of upcoming Nazi demonstrations were scattered throughout the area by Hitler's followers. The

Reds . . . had, thus, been purposefully alerted and were ready for the brownshirted intruders. Before the march, the Communists distributed their own set of leaflets . . . These contained the sentence: "On Sunday, Fight in the Streets Against the Fascist Murderers!"

When Sunday finally came, the Nazis marched into the Communist stronghold. As SA columns strode down Altona's streets, drums intoning their solemn cadence, the storm troopers, unarmed in line with Hitler's "legal" policy, were paced on either side by armed policemen. Suddenly, rifle fire from the surrounding buildings began to rake the marching column. According to Nazi accounts, the first storm trooper to fall, a bullet through his heart, was a nineteen-year-old Heinz Koch of Altona Storm 2/31. The police returned the fire.[6]

Nineteen died; 285 were wounded.[7] More than two hundred more fell wounded nationwide in the day's tumult.[8]

Certainly, the Nazis themselves helped light the fuse that destroyed Prussian sovereignty. Perhaps Defense Minister Schleicher's fine hand also assisted—for on that very day Schleicher forwarded official Prussian Interior Ministry documents to Papen alleging Prussian police laxity toward KPD violence.[9] In truth, Prussian police tolerated street fighting only for fear that stricter law enforcement on their part would trigger federal repercussions.[10]

At day's end, "Bloody Altona" provided the excuse that both Papen and Interior Minister Wilhelm von Gayl coveted. If Otto Braun could not maintain Prussian order, they would—thanks to yet another of Hindenburg's Article 48 decrees.[11]

Not only should Braun have seen it coming (the rumors, after all, filled not only the Berlin papers but even the *New York Times*), he *did* see it coming. "Every Tom, Dick, and Harry knew,"[12] Prussia's New York City–born police president Albert Grzesinski later admitted. And Berlin in 1932, being a nest of spies spying on other spies (Brüning had thoroughly believed that Schleicher had both his phone tapped and his mail opened[13]) and loudmouths like Schleicher and Röhm openly boasting of their genius or their depravity, in early July (in other words, even before Altona) a Reich Defense Ministry source had informed Prussian finance minister Dr. Otto Klepper of a federal coup aimed at Prussia. Klepper, along with Prussia's social welfare minister Heinrich Hirtsiefer demanded that Prussian interior minister Carl Severing take action. A blasé Severing merely responded that he was not in the habit of planning action based on hypothetical circumstances. Klepper (a German State Party [DStP] member) and Hirtsiefer (of the Zentrum), trusting that their Social Democrat ally Severing knew what he was doing, meekly departed.[14]

Severing's attitude betrayed the SPD's growing paralysis—indeed, its outright irrelevance. At Weimar's outset, Social Democrats initiated a general strike to halt 1920's Kapp Putsch.[15] As late as 1930 Severing himself sponsored the federal "Law for the Defence of the Republic," proclaiming, "The right of assembly has become the wrongs of assembly, and press freedom has become press license. We cannot permit demagogues to inflame the masses any further."[16] SPD national chairman Otto Wels (unlike Hitler an actual former paper hanger) even blustered, "If there has to be a dictatorship, it will be ours!"[17]

But by 1932, the time for Social Democrat bluster—let alone action— had long since vanished. True, the SPD still boasted a million members (more adherents in 1932 than in 1928[18]), two hundred daily newspapers, the 3.5 million member Reichsbanner, five million trade union members,[19] and two hundred thousand men in Reichsbanner Defense Units (*Schufos*).[20] Yet, it no longer possessed any concept of what to do with any of these resources. With at least six million workers jobless, a general strike was out of the question. A KPD-led general strike that January had amply demonstrated that, with at best twenty thousand workers nationwide participating.[21] Yes, grown soft in power (and highly paid—some party municipal officials drew salaries of fifty thousand marks in gold[22]), the SPD seemed resigned to defeat, whether at the truncheon-wielding hands of Hitler's goons or the manicured hands of the Hindenburg-Schleicher-Papen camarilla. "We felt," sighed Goebbels's favorite target, Berlin police vice president Bernhard "Isidor" Weiss, "that what must be, must be."[23]

On July 16, the SPD's executive committee debated mobilizing Prussia's police. "You have no right," *Vorwärts*'s Jewish editor-in-chief Friedrich Stampfer lectured Carl Severing and anyone else who would listen, "to be brave at your policemen's expense."[24] Severing et al. possessed no answer for that, for as British journalist Sefton Delmer later noted, SPD leadership had by now been reduced to a coterie of "weak, pusillanimous little men."[25]

Which only emboldened the slightly stronger, slightly less pusillanimous little men who now composed the Reich government.

And adding to Papen's rationale was this: On June 4, the desperate Prussian Interior Minister state secretary Wilhelm Abegg (a partially Jewish State Party member) had launched into secret negotiations with KPD Reichstag leader Ernst Torgler and KPD Landtag leader Wilhelm Kasper to forswear violence and consequently prop up Braun's tottering government—a scenario exciting precious little KPD support. At Abegg's side, however, was his scar-faced crypto-Nazi aide, Rudolf Diels, who gleefully leaked details of the four-hour session to Papen and Schleicher. Before long Abegg's abortive initiative was being trumpeted in the Hugenberg press, only inflaming the Prussian SPD's multiplicity of dilemmas.[26]

Thus, on Wednesday morning, July 20, Papen summoned Severing, Klepper, and Hirtsiefer to the chancellery (*Reichskanzlei*). He informed them that Hindenburg had appointed him Reich Commissioner for Prussia, supplanting their government, an authority Hindenburg's predecessor, the Social Democrat Friedrich Ebert, had exercised in 1923 to restore order in Saxony.[27] "No, Herr Chancellor," Severing responded, "I am not going to [obey]. I'll yield only to force."

"What form of force do you desire?" Papen asked, and Severing supposedly answered, "You're mistaken, Herr Chancellor. This is not a question of appearance, but of right."[28]

There, the meeting essentially ended.

If only Severing exhibited such valor. Within a few hours, the Third Military District's Lt. Gen. Gerd von Rundstedt phoned Prussian police chief Grzesinski to confirm his government's ouster.[29] Soon Papen's henchman, Essen burgomaster Dr. Franz Bracht (a Zentrum Party member), arrived at Severing's offices by motorcycle.[30] Severing requested Bracht not to apply any force at 6:00 p.m.—he had a conference scheduled for that hour. "At what time, Minister," Bracht had famously inquired, "do you instruct force to be applied to yourself?"[31]

Two police officers[32] carried Severing—and the chair he sat in—out of the room.[33] Police Chief Grzesinski (he who had pledged to drive Hitler from Germany with a dog whip) and "Isidor" Weiss were not only dismissed from office—but very briefly arrested.[34]

What must be, after all, must be.

Carl Severing might have sounded the alarm for his police. They would have acted. It broke their heart not to. Some called out *Freiheit!* ("Freedom!"), the SPD's slogan, to encourage their leaders.[35] Tears filled their eyes as they helplessly stood by.[36] Severing might have sealed off Unter den Linden. He—and his party—did nothing but mutter increasingly hollow words against "the misgovernment of the barons and their National Socialist helpers."[37] *Vorwärts* editorialized: "The highest instance competent to judge on these monstrous processes is the people. It must pass judgment on July 31 and make it as overwhelming as possible."[38]

July 31 . . . the date of Reichstag elections. The SPD demanded that the people take action when they would not.

This latest electoral round featured many rings within its circuslike atmosphere. In mid-July, the *Munich Post*'s Dr. Fritz Gerlich published the article "Does Hitler Have Mongolian Blood?"[39]

On Friday, July 29, a barrage of rocks showered Hitler's Mercedes. One grazed his head. He jumped from the car, waved his whip, and scared his attackers off.[40] The next day, at a Hitler rally (one of four that day) at Nürnberg, a Communist fired a pistol at Der Führer, missing its target but wounding a bodyguard.[41] On Election Day itself, Vienna's *Weiner Sonn-und-Montags Zeitung*—instigated by Austria's newly installed chancellor Engelbert Dollfuss—provided embarrassing details (headlined "Heil Schicklgruber!"[42]) of the Hitler family history.

Everyone was attacking everyone. The SA's tone grew even more underworld in style. The organization boasted molls hiding their guns. It spoke in gangland slang. A truncheon was an "eraser" (*Radiergummi*); a pistol, a "lighter" (*Feurzeug*). Individual brownshirts boasted similar nicknames— "Pistol Packer" and "Potshot Müller," "Revolvernose" (*Revolversschauze*), and "King of the Beer Barrels" (*Mollenkönig*). In Berlin's working class, KPD-dominated Wedding district, embattled SA men dubbed themselves the *Raübersturm* or "Robber Band."[43] Central Berlin storm troopers fancied themselves as the *Tanzgilde* ("Dance Guild").

KPD goons did the SA one better, however, exercising a virtual monopoly in attacks on police. In August 1931, the national politburo (including future East German leader Walter Ulbricht) ordered out-of-town *Selbschutz* (the KPD version of the SS) gunsels Erich Ziemer and Erich Mielke (also a *Rote Fahn* newspaper reporter) to rub out Berlin Seventh Precinct Capt. Paul Anlau and Sr. Sgt. Max Willig (nicknamed "Pig Face" and "Hussar," respectively, by the KPD). Following a Bülowplatz rally featuring a rare joint Ulbricht-Goebbels appearance (and a KPD riot), Ziemer and Mielke opened fire on Anlau, Willig, and a third officer, Capt. Franz Lendt, as they strolled past Berlin's Babylon cinema. The KPD soon smuggled Mielke, ultimately chief of the East German *Stasi*, to the Soviet Union.[44]

On Reichstag Election Day alone—July 31, 1932—twelve died in political violence.[45]

⌐∿⌐

Hitler offered little more than negation. In 1932, that was more than enough. "Those who know the history of Bryanism [Populism] in America will find a striking resemblance in the German picture," *The Nation*'s Karl Frederick Geiser informed American readers, "though the colors there are heightened and more varied. Bryan voiced the financial distress of a single class; Hitler reflects the misery of all classes . . . There is not a grievance that he does not visualize, not a wish that he does not promise to fulfil. . . ."[46] German grievances lifted Hitler's vote totals higher . . . and higher . . . and higher. "In 1928 I paid a sales tax of 72 marks," a small Weimar shopkeeper complained to Geiser, "it is now 212 marks . . . and on this street we are for Hitler." Geisler questioned how Hitler might conceivably repair such a situation. "I don't know," came the response. "I only know that no party since the war has helped us, and I know that I never open my shop in the morning without a feeling of hopeless despair."[47]

Yes, the Nazis possessed no coherent program, but that mattered for little. Coherence had brought *Der Vaterland* only defeat and depression and misery upon misery. The American journalist H. R. Knickerbocker inquired of one of Hitler's followers, "What will you do when you get power?"

"He might have launched a long discussion of the party program," Knickerbocker recalled, "but his only reply was: 'Keep it.'"[48]

In this July Reichstag campaign, Hans Baur again piloted his rented triple-engined Junkers D1720 to fifty German cities.[49] Bad weather prevented his landing at Berlin. Detoured to Rechlin, he missed the tarmac entirely "and was digging up potatoes in an adjoining field."[50] At Stralsund, twenty-five thousand Germans waited six hours—until 2:30 a.m.—for their Führer.[51] At Hamburg and Kiel hostile Communist-influenced crowds confronted him. "Give me ten minutes, and they'll quiet," Hitler assured his staff. "By that time they want to hear what I've got to say—suspicious at first, but afterwards with enthusiasm."[52] He was right.

He was also—as circumstances warranted—either furiously histrionic or coolly detached. Ernst "Putzi" Hanfstaengl marveled at his ability to ratchet down his emotions once a tirade was delivered. At Munich, Putzi's eleven-year-old son, Egon, accompanied him to Hitler's election eve rally and then to the Brown House. "All right boy," Hanfstaengl instructed, "sit down somewhere, keep quiet and learn something!"[53] Egon's lesson: just how composed Der Führer might be—*when he so desired.*

A courier thrust a sheaf of papers into Joseph Goebbels's eager hands. "It was the [just-completed] transcript of Hitler's speech . . . ," Hanfstaengl recalled. "The Führer left the group and sat down behind his desk, with Goebbels standing behind him, looking over his shoulder. They [ran] through the speech to groom it for publication. Hitler [talked] to himself as he marked things with a pencil. 'That was good . . . this was effective . . . this must be cut . . .' Not more than an hour ago he had finished one of the most emotional speeches of his career. He had preached, entreated, thundered, and shrieked. Yet, here he was, as cool and rational as any man I've seen."[54]

Wednesday, July 27, 1932, stood as the current campaign's greatest day. As Hitler's Junker landed at Tempelhof, among the staff greeting him was a twenty-seven-year-old volunteer chauffeur, Albert Speer. Speer, a Mannheim architect and only a very recent party member, did not relish what he saw, as the testy Hitler furiously upbraided his higher-level staff. But what Speer soon witnessed negated that impression. "In Brandenburg," Speer would write decades later, "the sidewalks close to the stadium were occupied by Social Democrats and Communists. With my passenger wearing the party uniform, the temper of the crowd grew ugly. When Hitler with his entourage arrived a few minutes later, the demonstrators overflowed into the street. Hitler's car had to force its way through at a snail's pace. Hitler stood erect beside the driver. At that time I felt respect for his courage, and still do."[55]

At Brandenburg Hitler addressed a frenzied crowd of sixty thousand. At Berlin's Grunewald Stadium, 120,000 awaited him. A hundred thousand more jammed a nearby racetrack to hear him via loudspeaker.[56] Kurt Lüdecke recalled:

> *Inside the stadium, the stage-setting was flawless. Around the entire perimeter of the vast stone arena, banners were silhouetted against the darkening sky. Row under row, the seats stepped down to the center field, a murmurous, vast acreage of Germans, merged by the dimming light into one solid dun-colored cliff of humanity. The long oval was broken on one side by an opening which framed high poplar trees, through whose branches shone the level rays of the setting sun. Directly opposite reared a dramatic speaking-stand, its bold, cubical masses hung with giant Swastikas which gained significance through sheer magnification. Draperies likewise flaunting Swastikas made a simple and thrilling background. Picked men from the Schutzstaffel were drawn up in close ranks below the stand. Twelve huge SA bands played military marches with beautiful precision and terrifying power. Behind the bands, on the field itself, solid squares of uniformed men from the Nazi labor unions were ranged in strict military order, thousands strong. . . . Suddenly a wave surged over the crowd, it leaned forward, a word was tossed from man to man: Hitler is coming! Hitler is here! A blare of trumpets rent the air, and a hundred thousand people leaped to their feet in tense expectancy. All eyes were turned toward the stand, awaiting the approach of the Fuehrer.*[57]

Hyde Park, 1924. John W. Davis and Alfred E. Smith on Franklin Roosevelt's right. FDR LIBRARY

Herbert Hoover and his Belgian Shepherd "King Tut." Neither bore the strain of the White House very well.
THE LIBRARY OF CONGRESS

Adolf Hitler in 1923, the year of his Munich putsch. The future führer's style remains a work in progress.
COLLECTION OF THE AUTHOR

Pennsylvania Governor Gifford Pinchot, a progressive alternative to Hoover. WIKIMEDIA COMMONS

Weimar Defense Minister, Gen. Wilhelm Gröner. BUNDESARCHIV BILD

Financier Bernard Mannes Baruch, a Democrat studiously wary of FDR. THE LIBRARY OF CONGRESS

Paul von Hindenburg and Erich Ludendorff, partners during the Great War, rivals afterward. THE LIBRARY OF CONGRESS

The Catholic vote was not to be ignored in Germany—or America. Here John J. Raskob, Al Smith, and Jim Farley—all sons of the Church—hobnob with the hierarchy. THE LIBRARY OF CONGRESS

Adolf Hitler at the Bad Harzburg rally (October 10, 1931), designed to cement ties between the Weimar Republic's nationalist opponents. Rudolf Hess marches to his right. COLLECTION OF THE AUTHOR

Hitler confidant and former US resident Ernst "Putzi" Hanfstaengl. COLLECTION OF THE AUTHOR

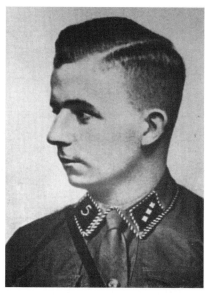

Berlin Stormtrooper and Nazi "martyr" Horst Wessel. COLLECTION OF THE AUTHOR

Reich President Paul von Hindenburg. COLLECTION OF THE AUTHOR

Berlin Gauleiter Joseph Goebbels, "the scheming dwarf." COLLECTION OF THE AUTHOR

FDR critics Walter Lippman and Heywood Broun dismissed FDR as "an amiable boy scout" and a "corkscrew" candidate. THE LIBRARY OF CONGRESS

Hitler with bodyguard Josef "Sepp" Dietrich and chauffeur Julius Schreck.
COLLECTION OF THE AUTHOR

The Brains Trust's "exhilarating" Rexford Guy Tugwell.
THE LIBRARY OF CONGRESS

Democratic National Committee Chairman and "wet" Al Smith ally John Jakob Raskob.
THE LIBRARY OF CONGRESS

Embattled Vice President Charles Curtis sweats out a Washington summer—and his re-nomination. THE LIBRARY OF CONGRESS

Franz von Papen's 1932 "Cabinet of Barons." Front row: Magnus von Braun (Nutrition and Agriculture), Wilhelm von Gayl (Interior), Papen, Konstantin von Neurath (Foreign Affairs). Rear: Dr. Franz Gürtner (Justice), Hermann Warmbold (Finance), Kurt von Schleicher (Defense). COLLECTION OF THE AUTHOR

Baronial life American style: Franklin and Eleanor Roosevelt and Franklin's mother, Sara Delano Roosevelt. FDR LIBRARY

FDR; daughter, Anna Roosevelt Dall; and Eleanor at Warm Springs, Georgia, 1932. FDR LIBRARY

Adolf Hitler speaking at Berlin's Lustgarten (his chief adjutant Wilhelm Brückner, Berlin SA leader Wolf-Heinrich Graf von Helldorf, and Berlin Gauleiter Joseph Goebbels to his rear). COLLECTION OF THE AUTHOR

Woodrow Wilson's Secretary of War Newton D. Baker: despised by William Randolph Hearst and feared by Herbert Hoover. THE LIBRARY OF CONGRESS

Reichstag President Hermann Göring, "half executioner, half clown." COLLECTION OF THE AUTHOR

One-armed Stahlhelm President, Franz Seldte. COLLECTION OF THE AUTHOR

Hitler exhorts his party leadership (Wilhelm Frick at his left, Gregor Strasser to his right, Joseph Geobbels to his rear). COLLECTION OF THE AUTHOR

The Roosevelts arrive at the Hoover
White House, April 28, 1932.
THE LIBRARY OF CONGRESS

Former Reichsbank President, Hjalmar
Horace Greeley Schacht.
COLLECTION OF THE AUTHOR

FDR's radical convention backer, Sen. Huey "The Kingfish" Long.
THE LIBRARY OF CONGRESS

Nomination won, FDR takes to the air; his flight stops in Cleveland.
THE LIBRARY OF CONGRESS

1932's Bonus March ends in tear gas, bayonets, and flaming shacks. FDR LIBRARY

Eleanor Roosevelt and the New York
State Police's Earl Miller. FDR LIBRARY

Financier and FDR booster Joseph
Patrick Kennedy, Sr.
THE LIBRARY OF CONGRESS

FDR on the stump with running mate John Nance "Cactus Jack" Garner in
Peekskill, New York, Sunday, August 14, 1932. FDR LIBRARY

New York City Mayor James J. Walker—his past threatens FDR's future. THE LIBRARY OF CONGRESS

Scandalously controversial SA leader Ernst Röhm. BUNDESARCHIV BILD

The Hoover-Curtis re-election campaign: a flag, a pair of white shoes, but not much more. THE LIBRARY OF CONGRESS

The Berlin transit strike of November 1932: Nazis join with their hated rivals, the Communists, to disrupt the nation's capital—and to thoroughly frighten their more moderate supporters. COLLECTION OF THE AUTHOR

Another alliance of convenience: von Papen, ousted by Schleicher, courts Hitler (Hitler's henchman Wilhelm Frick at left). COLLECTION OF THE AUTHOR

Former presidential rivals, Corporal Hitler and Field Marshal Hindenburg: their frosty relationship finally melts. COLLECTION OF THE AUTHOR

Nazis and their allies parade in triumph under the Brandenburg Gate, January 30, 1933.
COLLECTION OF THE AUTHOR

A victorious Hitler (at center window) surveys euphoric supporters, January 30, 1933. COLLECTION OF THE AUTHOR

A tense, silent ride to the Capitol, punctuated by the most of awkward small talk (Inauguration Day, Saturday, March 4, 1933). FDR LIBRARY

Eleanor, Franklin, and their son James on Inauguration Day, Saturday, March 4, 1933.
THE LIBRARY OF CONGRESS

Herbert Hoover departing Washington: the old order passeth.
THE LIBRARY OF CONGRESS

Hitler jammed the stadiums and indoor halls, the streets and the fields. The rest of the party toiled feverishly. "Work has to be done standing, walking, driving, flying," Goebbels boasted. "The most urgent conferences are held on the stairs, in the hall, at the door, or on the way to the station. It nearly drives one out of one's senses. One is carried by train, motor car and aeroplane criss-cross through Germany. One arrives at a town half an hour before the beginning of a meeting or sometimes even later, goes up to the platform and speaks."[58] Goebbels now followed up on his rival Gregor Strasser's initial Nazi radio broadcast, his performance disappointing him. "[S]omehow the speech is not effective," he alibied. "The censor . . . has maimed it. One cannot fly without wings, nor can one bite without teeth."[59]

Schleicher and Papen also took to the airwaves—Schleicher even praising Ernst Röhm's storm troopers—manpower that, after all, might eventually serve him as they now served Röhm or Hitler. "I should be a bad War Minister," he asserted, "if I were not pleased with every young German who by means of physical and particularly through voluntary discipline, is steeling his will, his courage and, in a word, his character. I am so often told that this hobby of getting drilled is in reality incomprehensible and almost unworthy. I can only answer that people who have no understanding for this do not know the elation of young lads who have got something extraordinary out of their bodies and have for the first time completely conquered the swine within themselves. It is the feeling that is expressed in the words: 'And if you do not risk your lives, you will never have won life.'"[60]

But Schleicher also declared his opposition to any "military dictatorship . . . The government must be supported by a strong popular sentiment. . . ."[61] Was "the schemer" simultaneously distancing himself from his creation Papen—a man bereft of discernable public support—and tossing an invitation to Hitler, a leader of vast "popular sentiment"?

Papen, meanwhile, addressed an unusual radio audience—the American people, whose property and liberty he had worked so hard to sabotage in the Great War. His English-language talk, delivered over a nationwide radio hookup, was couched in anti-Communist terms ("the Communist is directed against the cultural foundation of our national and social life"[62]) and attuned to American ears, but betrayed his growing myopia toward Hitler.[63] Ambassador Frederic Sackett relayed his analysis to Secretary of State Stimson:

> Papen referred to strong fighting units formed by the Communists. While the dangers of such units can not be ignored, one must not overlook the fact, as von Papen had done, that the Nazis maintain still stronger units

which, unlike those of the Communists, are not illegal, are permitted to wear uniforms and are for the most part housed in barracks.

According to von Papen, the Nazis are . . . striving only for national regeneration, while the aims of the Communists are purely destructive. As a matter of fact the Nazis have sponsored legislation . . . no less destructive than that of the Communists. The Chancellor overlooked the many socialistic, revolutionary and anarchistic motions which the Nazis, in cooperation with the Communists, have put through the Prussian Diet only a few weeks ago.

. . . the Nazis sponsored an amnesty bill in Prussia which practically constituted an inducement for irresponsible elements to attack political opponents. . . . [I]n cooperation with the Communists, they passed a motion to "tax away" all income in excess of 12,000 marks annually. These are only two instances of recent Nazi activity. That "national regeneration" can be achieved through cooperation with the Communists on such demagogic and anarchistic measures is at least open to doubt.[64]

July 31 drew near. But the German people had sickened of endless voting, sickened of parliamentary bickering, sickened of Depression and unemployment, sickened of Communist street gangs, sickened of spineless Social Democrats, sickened of "cabinets of barons," sickened of Weimar "sophistication," sickened of a Berlin that could boast a tourist handbook entitled "GUIDE TO VICIOUS BERLIN," describing "all of the 160 bars, cabarets and dance halls where the clients and performers prefer to wear the clothes and affect the manners of the opposite sex."[65] A writer for the Hugenberg press would later write the following regarding the leaders of Weimar's cultural decadence:

Women wearing décolletage down to their navels and diamonds on their shoes screeched their delight at the worst obscenities. . . . They claimed they were the German Geist [spirit], German culture, the German present and future. They represented Germany to the world, they spoke in its name . . . What they did not permit did not exist . . . Whoever served them was sure to succeed. He appeared on their stages, wrote in their journals, was advertised all over the world; his commodity was recommended whether it was cheese or relativity, powder or theatre, patent medicine or human rights, democracy or Bolshevism, propaganda for abortion or against the legal system, rotten Negro music or dancing in the nude. In brief, there was never a more shameless dictatorship than that of the democratic intelligentsia and the Zivilisationsliteraten.[66]

That was the top of the Weimar pyramid. At its bottom—fueled not only by Weimar morals, of course, but by worldwide Depression—was a growing lawless urban underclass. "In the big cities," British historian Michael Burleigh has noted, "some teenagers went around in anti-social packs—the 'Wild cliques,' numbering fourteen thousand in Berlin ("cesspool of the Republic, the spoiler of all noble and healthy life"[67]) alone, led by 'clique bulls' surrounded by simpering 'clique cows.' There was a rise in juvenile crime, prostitution, vagrancy and vandalism, and also in the population of remand homes and the juvenile wings of prisons."[68]

French anarcho-communist journalist Daniel Guérin observed the phenomenon firsthand: "They had the depraved and troubled faces of hoodlums and the most bizarre coverings on their heads: black or gray Chaplinesque bowlers, old women's hats with the brims turned up in 'Amazon' fashion adorned with ostrich plumes and medals, proletarian navigator caps decorated with enormous edelweiss above the visor, handkerchiefs or scarves in screaming colors tied any which way round the neck, bare chests bursting out of open skin vests with broad stripes, arms scored with fantastic or lewd tattoos, ears hung with pendants or enormous rings, leather shorts surmounted with all the colors of the rainbow, esoteric numbers, human profiles, and inscriptions such as *Wild-frei* (wild and free) or *Raüber* (bandits). Around their wrists they wore enormous leather bracelets. In short, they were a bizarre mixture of virility and effeminacy."[69]

And so, millions, forgetting that the enemy of their enemies was not necessarily their friend, chose the easy way out: They voted Nazi. The NSDAP again increased its vote, officially emerging as the nation's largest party, in the republic's crazy-quilt of parties. The results that night [70]:

Party	Votes	Seats	Percent	+/−
NSDAP	13,745,680	230	37.27	+123
SPD	7,959,712	133	21.58	−10
KPD	5,282,636	89	14.32	+12
Centre Party (Zentrum)	4,589,430	75	12.44	+7
DNVP	2,178,024	37	5.91	−4
Bavarian People's Party (BVP)	1,192,684	22	3.23	+3
German People's Party (DVP)	436,002	7	1.18	−23
German State Party (DStP) (formerly the German Democratic Party)	371,800	4	1.01	−16

Party	Votes	Seats	Percent	+/–
Christian Social People's Service (CSVD)	364,543	3	0.99	–11
Reich Party of the German Middle Class (WP)	146,876	2	0.40	–21
German Farmers' Party	137,133	2	0.37	–4
Agricultural League	96,851	2	0.26	–1
German Country People	90,554	1	0.25	–18
Socialist Workers Party of Germany (SAPD)	72,630	0	0.20	New
German-Hanoverian Party	46,927	0	0.13	–3
	36,711,482	607	99.54	

Excepting the Zentrum ("Brüning is the name of the leader, Center is the name of the party, freedom is the name of the goal!"[71]), the parties of the middle (the German People's Party, the German State Party, the Reich Party of the German Middle Class, and the Protestant-oriented Christian Social People's Service) largely evaporated. The SPD paid a price for its recent Prussian pusillanimity, losing ten seats. Totalitarianism (as fractured as it was) triumphed. Between them, the Nazis and the Communists enjoyed a majority of 319 of the Reichstag's 607 seats. And authoritarianism outpaced totalitarianism with 356 seats (58.6 percent of the total) parceled out between Nazis, Communists, and Nationalists. Even in Red Berlin, Hitlerites received 28.6 percent[72] (up from 1.4 percent in 1928)[73]—barely trailing the SPD and KPD.[74]

Hitler more than doubled his Reichstag representation, gaining 123 seats. More important, however, a Nazi alliance with the vitriolically anti-Papen Zentrum (it blasted him as among other things a front man for Hugenberg[75]) could deliver to Hitler a slim Reichstag majority. It was, however, a scenario the Nazis detested. "They would handcuff us and try to tame us down," wrote Goebbels. "We will have to be extremely wary and trust no one but ourselves. Things will not be made easy for us."[76]

No, they would not. Hitler had performed well but not as well as his circumstances demanded—"31st July," his press aide Otto Dietrich would later note, "brought the N.S.D.A.P. . . . a mighty triumph, but no decisive majority as yet."[77] Thirty-seven percent and change fell a long way from 50.1 percent. And, yes, the party had increased its April presidential runoff totals—but not by much; only from 36.8 to 37.72 percent and from 13,418,547 to 13,745,680 votes, a mere 327,133 vote increase. The rival KPD meanwhile augmented its April tallies by an enormous 1,575,877 votes.

That spelled trouble for Hitler. In April, he lost but triumphed. In July, he triumphed but did not triumph. His party was his nation's largest, but its enemies list larger still. "The National Socialists are now in a difficult position," Ambassador Sir Horace Rumbold wrote to Britain's foreign secretary Sir John Simon. "It would appear that they have shot their bolt and have exhausted their reservoir from which they drew many of their adherents, and yet have failed to obtain an absolute majority in the Reichstag. Their storm troopers will soon begin to ask themselves what their marching and their '*Alarmbereitchaft*' (being on alert) are leading to. In other words, the time is fast approaching when Hitler will be expected to deliver the goods."[78]

Yes, trouble loomed at the ballot box for Adolf Hitler, but luckily for him ballots rarely meant much to Gen. Kurt von Schleicher.

CHAPTER TWENTY

"Climb on the mule"

UNLIKE HERR MINISTER VON SCHLEICHER, AMERICAN POLITICIANS could not ignore elections, taking care to count the votes, nearly always fretful of all the little pieces of campaign folderol they generated. At Chicago, Franklin Roosevelt's campaign had jettisoned "Anchors Away." In New York, it did not. As millions still suffered from the deepening Depression, Bonus Marchers protested, and as Communists, Socialists, and populists railed against the existing economic order, Franklin Roosevelt—master of campaign optics, champion of the forgotten man—cast off anchors and boarded a yacht.

Alongside sons James, Franklin Jr., and John, on Monday, July 11, 1932, he had set sail from Long Island aboard the rented (but leaking) forty-foot yawl *Myth II*, bound eventually for Portsmouth, New Hampshire. Though Roosevelt conducted significant business at stops along the way (with Colonel House and Mayor Curley), it was a strange Depression-era message to send, though no one much seemed to notice.

Each evening his *Myth II* docked at a different port—from Stonington, Connecticut and Cuttyhunk to Sippican Harbor to Marblehead to Portsmouth. Trailing the *Myth II* was another chartered yacht, the luxurious ninety-five-foot[1] *Ambassadress*, hired by such party moneymen as Robert Jackson, Frank Walker, Jesse Straus—and Joseph P. Kennedy.

Despite his conspicuous efforts to secure Hearst's crucial support, his being the son of an East Boston Democratic alderman and son-in law of a Democratic Boston mayor, Kennedy surprisingly lacked genuine Democratic bona fides. In 1924, he jumped the party to support the LaFollette-Wheeler ticket (even lending the radical Burton K. Wheeler both his chauffeured Stevens-Duryea limousine and his own Rolls-Royce). Four years later JPK may have been the singular Irish Catholic supporting Hoover. Worse, when in that sorry year FDR wrote soliciting support for Smith within the motion picture industry, Kennedy simply ignored him.[2] Yet, among the most potent means of securing friendships in (or, or for that matter, out of) politics is money, and Joe Kennedy still possessed cash to spare. In 1932, he spared $25,000 for Roosevelt, plus another $50,000 in loans and raised $150,000 from other fat cats, including $25,000 from Hearst.[3] Joe Kennedy could be a very good friend to have.

At dusk, Kennedy would seaplane in to the *Ambassadress*, to confer with Jackson, Walker, Straus—and Roosevelt.[4] "I was really worried," Kennedy later explained, "I knew that big, drastic changes had to be made in our economic system and I felt that Roosevelt was the one who could make those changes. I wanted him in the White House for my own security and the security of our kids—and I was ready to do anything to help elect him."[5]

There may have been more to it. Kennedy had shrewdly accumulated fortunes in banking, taxicabs, finance, and (invariably bad) films. With the nonchalant skill of a tightrope walker, he vacated Wall Street just before the Crash—netting, some said, a cool $15 million.[6] Politics, however, remained a final challenge, an ultimate world to conquer. Always a social climber, adding a president of the United States (particularly a Harvard-bred one) to his list of souvenirs was merely another rung upon his social ladder. Still, his efforts to impress did not always succeed. When Joe phoned his estranged mistress, Gloria Swanson, to trumpet his clout with the next president ("I want you to say hello to him"), former silent film diva Swanson merely stormed, "Don't bother! I don't want to talk to him and I don't want to talk to you." She slammed the receiver down on both Kennedy—and FDR.[7]

He kept plugging FDR elsewhere. As Franklin sailed from Port Jefferson, Kennedy courted the Scripps-Howard chain's Roy Howard, his sales pitch revealing more about himself than his candidate. He was, noted Howard, "quite frank in his very low estimate of Roosevelt's ability"—and quite fearful of being undercut by both Louis Howe and Jim Farley.[8] He was indeed correct about Howe. At their first meeting, FDR's churlish henchman had greeted the parvenu Kennedy with a spectacular open contempt. The relationship had not improved much since.[9]

❧

FDR himself hit it off far better with . . . a matched set of Hohenzollerns. At Albany, on Monday morning, August 1, he received two of Kronprinz Wilhelm's four sons, twenty-four-year-old Louis Ferdinand ("Lulu"—more formally "Louis Ferdinand Viktor Eduard Albert Michael Hubertus Prinz von Preussen") and twenty-year-old Frederick ("Fritzi"), on their way from Malden-on-Hudson and the home of FDR's longtime friend and Hudson

Valley neighbor, the journalist Poultney Bigelow. Bigelow was a strange case. Described by historian Allan Nevins as "an eccentric American of Fascist tendencies,"[10] he had, in 1925, received the following message from his close friend (and virtual physical double) Wilhelm II, "Jews and mosquitoes [were] a nuisance that humankind must get rid of some way or other. I believe the best thing would be gas."[11] Bigelow himself would later allegedly propound, "I wish we had a hundred Hitlers in the United States."[12]

FDR, Frederick, and Louis Ferdinand presumably discussed significantly lighter matters—including Franklin's recent *Myth II* jaunt.[13] "They're nice kids," commented FDR. For his part, Louis Ferdinand, decidedly more anti-Hitler than Bigelow, considered FDR "like a father to me . . . a true aristocrat, in the finest sense of the word . . . a grand seigneur."[14]

It was not Louis Ferdinand's first meeting with FDR. That occurred in 1929, also arranged by Bigelow, this time at Hyde Park. FDR, with no time to meet Churchill that year, juggled and rejuggled his schedule to accommodate Bigelow and friend. Over contraband cocktails, Franklin had soft-soaped his young (and alcoholic[15]) visitor, "You know, there is a strange similarity between your family and mine. I was born the same year as your father. We were married the same year. We also have four sons, all about the same age as you and your brothers."[16]

A week later they met again, this time at Albany, with FDR providing Louis Ferdinand with an hour-long discourse on the American Constitution. "I hope I gave you a general idea of our constitution," he concluded. "I know it is not the most modern one. Your new Weimar Constitution, is much more up to date theoretically. But the main thing is that ours works, and we could not very well do without it. . . ."[17]

In 1932 "Fritzi" was bound for Los Angeles to take in the Summer Olympics. The finely featured "Lulu" was, however, definitely a different manner of German aristocrat—the first of his dynasty to earn a doctorate, a few years earlier smitten with sultry French-born American film star Lili Damita,[18] and now en route to Detroit. There, thanks to his imperial grandfather's influence, he toiled on one of Henry Ford's assembly lines, his Ford Motor Company tin badge (number 113) firmly pinned to his overalls, as neatly as his Prussian Order of the Black Eagle to his more formal attire.[19]

A different sort of Hohenzollern indeed.

◆～～

Finnish-American Emil Hurja toiled in quite another way. Polling in 1932 remained in its infancy. Self-selecting straw polls, such as those conducted by *Pathfinder* or Jesse Straus or the *Literary Digest* abounded. But scientific polling remained unknown. Hurja aimed to change that. He had volunteered to poll for the Democratic National Committee in 1928. But John J. Raskob wasn't interested. In 1932, however, Jim Farley accepted his proposal for "a division . . . to handle and collect this information and tabulate it on a uniform basis for . . . the national organization, and for various state and regional organizations . . . during the campaign." Beyond merely analyzing existing intelligence, however, Hurja also proposed to establish a group of "Minute Men of the Democratic Party" to harvest additional raw data.[20] A fellow like Emil Hurja might come in handy.

It required no scientific polling to determine Franklin Roosevelt's gravest problem: reconciling incensed Smith voters, a task easier in some cases than others. The very same day Franklin's *Myth II* sailed, Jersey City's Frank Hague addressed two thousand loyal Democrats (including six hundred members of the Hudson County Democratic Committee) at his city's Grotto Auditorium, fulsomely pledging his support.[21] John W. Davis jumped on board, if not enthusiastically for FDR, at least, in attacking the "panic-folly" of the Republicans.[22] Massachusetts's Governor Ely remained a far-harder sell. Nonetheless, by August 1, Ely announced that not only would he seek a second term, he now endorsed the once-hated Roosevelt.[23]

Which left Al Smith . . .

Smith restrained himself. Others didn't. Brooklyn's eleven-year-old Chester Burger wrote to Teddy Roosevelt's aged widow for an autograph, expressing admiration for "your cousin" FDR. "Franklin Delano Roosevelt is a distant cousin of my husband," Mrs. Rough Rider tersely responded. "I am a Republican and am voting for Herbert Hoover."[24] At Columbus, Secretary of War Patrick Hurley explained to Ohioans why they should vote for Hoover: "He stopped immigration by executive order."[25] The *Chicago Tribune's* John Boettiger, meanwhile, reported FDR's slogan to be "Hoover, the radical—Roosevelt, the conservative"—all part of a Democratic campaign opposing "Commissar Hoover."[26]

The embers of Anacostia's burnt-out shacks continued smoldering. Public opinion had turned against The Great Engineer on that issue—and stayed turned. San Antonio Democratic representative Maury Maverick spoke of "murder." Likening Anacostia to the "Boston Massacre," he decried Hoover's "military dictatorship."[27] The B. E. F. ("We're gonna get guns and go back to Washington"[28]) scattered—some to new camps in Maryland and Virginia,[29] most northward to Johnstown, Pennsylvania. Their former ally, Mayor Eddie McCloskey, now had no room in *his* inn for them—and quickly sent them packing. Governor Pinchot's interest in their cause ("the state has no funds to feed this army"[30]) similarly vanished. At Des Moines, sixteen hundred members (five hundred in uniform) of the bonus movement's bastard Khaki Shirts offspring, joined in a farmers' strike.[31] Within two days at Maury Maverick's San Antonio, forty veterans enlisted in the Khaki Shirts—quickly adopting the Hitler salute.[32]

A delegation of "intellectuals," including novelists Sherwood Anderson and Waldo Frank, poet James Rorty, and the *Baltimore Afro-American* managing editor William N. Jones, attempted to confront Herbert Hoover to protest his handling of the whole Bonus Army mess. Hoover hadn't been interested in meeting the Marchers—and he certainly wasn't interested in this quartet's lectures. "We are writers of reputation," sniffed Waldo Frank. "We are intellectuals, but the President prefers to listen to Boy Scouts and politicians."[33] In Albany, Franklin Roosevelt mused to Rexford Tugwell that Huey Long was "one of the two most dangerous men in the country." Tugwell surmised the other to be Father Coughlin. FDR corrected him: "Oh no, the other is Douglas MacArthur."[34]

Hoover didn't have time for Waldo Frank but did have time to finally (and nervously[35]) deliver his own acceptance speech, on his fifty-eighth birthday, at Washington's Constitution Hall.[36] Hoover had not flown to Chicago, but the nearly seventy-one-year-old Mrs. Theodore Roosevelt flew from Oyster Bay to Washington to attend.[37] Broadcasting over 1,160 radio stations to audiences as far away as Hawaii, Manila, and, as the *New York Times* put it, "the Antipodes,"[38] Hoover generated little news save for finally acknowledging that Prohibition had failed as "the final solution of the evils of the liquor traffic."[39] Accepting the vice-presidential re-nomination, at hometown Topeka, Charles Curtis made more news, sticking to his own substantial Prohibitionist guns. "I am opposed to the return of the saloon and I am opposed to the repeal of the Eighteenth Amendment. . . . ," spake Curtis. "The Republican Party pledges itself to the faithful, enforcement and the vigorous execution of the 18th Amendment to the Constitution and to oppose the return of the saloon."[40]

Startling enough, but less so than Curtis's explanation of—without explaining—his boss's efforts regarding that *other* national issue—the Depression. "I know the hearty cooperation of members of both political parties in the enactment of relief measures recommended by the President is deeply appreciated by the people," Curtis continued. "The President has so fully covered the economy and relief legislation that it is unnecessary for me to go into those subjects. We all know our country has a bright future, that when this business depression is over we will go forward as we have after every period of depression."[41]

Franklin Roosevelt possessed his own vice-presidential problems. John Nance Garner wasn't about to say anything untoward (or anything at all). He remained, nonetheless, a decided liability, with blacks distrusting him as a segregationist Texan. Rumors swirled that African Americans might not even reside within his hometown of Uvalde. Bitter Al Smith supporters also looked askance at Garner. Yes, "Cactus Jack" (*and* Hearst *and* McAdoo, to add salt to the gaping Smith wounds) had betrayed their hero for the thirty pieces of a vice-presidential nomination. But, beyond that, Smith partisans seethed at Garner's Lone Star State ("perhaps, bigotry's banner state"[42]) background. Texas had distinguished itself as the most spectacular defection from the 1928 Democratic column. It may not have been Garner's doing—but, then again perhaps it was. And, those charges stung. At a Manhattan campaign luncheon, tears filled his eyes as he denied deserting Smith in 1928. "I would like to apologize for the great State of Texas. . . . ," Garner begged, his voice choking with emotion, "I hear that I am considered a handicap to the ticket in the East."[43]

Huey Long also traveled to New York, though he retained a modicum more of his dignity—if The Kingfish ever maintained *any* dignity. William Jennings Bryan–style Populism had never quite bothered to expire, and Huey Pierce Long Jr. was merely its most fragrant surviving blossom. "Alfalfa Bill" Murray and Wright Patman and Maury Maverick marched to its tunes, and as FDR won nomination, North Carolina Democrat Robert Rice Reynolds captured his state's US Senate nomination. The "wet" Buncombe County attorney laid it on thick against "dry" incumbent Cameron Morrison. To accentuate his own "po' folks" image, tall, blond, thrice-married "Buncombe Bob" campaigned in threadbare suits and worn shoes, often faking car breakdowns before arriving in small towns.[44] To equally ragged audiences Reynolds would reveal that his wealthy rival Morrison lived in Washington's opulent Mayflower Hotel. Brandishing a Mayflower menu, he would read prices from it. "What do you think he eats?" Reynolds thundered, "He does not eat cabbage nor turnips nor ham and eggs, nor fatback like you or I do. My friends, think of it, Senator Morrison eats caviar."[45] Spicing his already-shocking narrative with some veiled (and most likely too subtle) anti-Romanism, Reynolds would slyly paint a picture of his opponent feasting upon "Eggs Benedictine."[46] As his coup de grace, Reynolds alleged that his fancy pants opponent had to change into evening clothes ("he can not eat in every day clothes like you or I do"[47]) to eat such fancy furrin' vittles!

Yes, Mr. Reynolds had his charms, but still had nothing on Senator Long. Fresh from his pro-FDR brow-beating of fellow southern convention delegates, The Kingfish endeavored to rescue one of his few Senate allies. "Silent

Hattie" Caraway had assumed her Arkansas senate seat upon the December 1931 death of her husband, Thaddeus Caraway. Serving as mere placeholder until the state's actual powers sorted things out and took the seat for themselves, in January 1932, she won a special election for the remaining year of her term. No one, however, expected her to run again or to win if she did—least of all, herself ("I'm in for a crucifixion . . . no wonder my hair won't stay in wave"[48]). It was here, however, that Long resolved to test his own unique powers and popularity. Muscling his way into Arkansas, he waged a whirlwind nine-day, 2,100-mile, thirty-seven speech campaign in Hattie's behalf, bringing with him his personal motorcar, a state police bodyguard, two sound trucks, five miscellaneous trucks[49]—and, most important, his own recondite gifts for vituperation and inspiration. "We're all here," he challenged curious Arkansans, "to pull a lot of potbellied politicians off a little woman's neck."[50]

"We have more food in this country . . . ," Long bellowed, "than we could eat up in two years if we never plowed another furrow or fattened another shote [piglet]—and yet people are hungry and starving. We have more cotton and wool and leather than we could wear out in two years if we never raised another boll of cotton, sheered another sheep, or tanned another hide—and yet people are ragged and naked. We have more houses than ever before in this country's history and more of them are unoccupied than ever before—and yet people are homeless."[51]

He traveled twenty-one hundred miles and delivered thirty-nine speeches before two hundred thousand persons. Hattie Caraway, previously left for dead, won re-nomination with 44.7 percent of the vote (against six opponents), sweeping sixty-one of the state's seventy-five counties.[52]

In California, William Gibbs McAdoo eyed a senate seat of his own, facing pioneering radio evangelist Rev. Robert P. Shuler. "Fighting Bob" didn't care much for many folks. Catholics, blacks, Jews, bootleggers, evolutionists, the ACLU, various Los Angeles crooked politicos, and fellow evangelists Aimee Semple McPherson and Billy Sunday all suffered Shuler's wrath. Suffice it to say, he had made his enemies, and in November 1931 the Federal Communications Commission revoked his broadcasting license. Now, he ran for the US Senate. Competing against both McAdoo and the "wet" San Franciscan Justus Wardell for the Democratic nomination, Shuler received only 16.1 percent of the vote[53]—but 22.93 percent in the state's four-way Republican contest.[54]

Not every loony ran for the US Senate. In Kansas, Dr. John R. Brinkley sought the governorship. Dr. Brinkley had grown rich peddling a "goat gland" treatment through his own powerful radio station KFKB ("Kansas Folks Know Best"). Dozens of his previously healthy patients died (and countless others sickened), and, in 1930, Brinkley forfeited both his medical and broadcasting licenses. Piloting his own plane statewide that year he secured 29.5 percent of the gubernatorial vote as a write-in. An early 1932 straw poll showed him crushing incumbent Democratic governor Harry Woodring and the GOP challenger, oil millionaire Alf Landon.[55]

In far-north Seattle, pencil-thin mustached, slick-haired, down-on-his-luck Seattle bandleader Victor Aloysius Meyers had first run for mayor as a joke, campaigning from a beer wagon, dressing as Mahatma Gandhi, and advocating graft for politicians and hostesses on local streetcars. Remarkably, the thirty-four-year-old Meyers didn't do badly at all and set his sights on the governorship. It cost fifty dollars to file for the Democratic nomination—fifty bucks he did not have. But he did possess the twelve dollars necessary to compete for lieutenant governor. He won his September primary.[56]

Hoover and Roosevelt faced their own competition. Norman Thomas (a "capitalist boot-licker"[57] according to the CPUSA) took leave from excoriating Tammany to launch his second White House run. His Socialists hoped the economic crisis might deliver a much-needed comeback for their waning party, with even one Republican journalist predicting that Thomas and his running mate, the Reading, Pennsylvania, trade unionist James H. Maurer, might garner as many as two million votes.[58] But intra-party strife and precious little interest from organized labor (the ticket's only national union endorsement came from the American Federation of Full-Fashioned Hosiery Workers)[59] made Thomas's difficult quest all the harder. So did a lack of funds. His campaign, energetic as it was with as many as seven speeches a day, raised a mere $26,000 nationwide.[60]

At Omaha, the Farmer-Labor Party designated ancient Jacob S. Coxey to replace Col. Frank E. Webb ("a tool of the Hoover administration"[61]) as their presidential candidate.[62] At St. Louis, three thousand delegates of the newly minted "Jobless Party" tapped our old acquaintance Fr. James R. Cox[63] running on a platform of federal control of banking and, through a great leap of illogic, a resultant elimination of taxation. "Interest is a modern conception," he lectured. "If you read history you know that interest used to be despised, called usury." Would the bankers be reimbursed? "What did they do with the saloon?" Cox answered, "They weren't compensated."[64] That summer, Cox had traveled to Europe, ostensibly to tour such shrines as Lourdes, but with his founding of the suspiciously fascist-sounding (and Hitler-style saluting) "Blue Shirts" in mind, more cynical observers speculated that his sojourn had far more to do with meeting continental fascists. Such may, indeed, have been the case, but by the time Father Cox reached Rome (a destination, of course, convenient for either religious or fascist pilgrimages), he had absolutely—and publicly—soured on Mussolinism.[65] His cross-country "Jobless Party" campaign tour fared little better, literally running out of gas in Tucumcari, New Mexico, and leaving him stranded.[66] Suspending his campaign that September, Cox tried tossing his support to Norman Thomas, before finally endorsing FDR.[67]

But by now few paid much attention to Cox. Many (or, at least, many intellectuals) tendered very serious notice to Communist Party standard-bearers William Z. Foster and James W. Ford ("THE CANDIDATES FOR THE WORKING YOUTHS"[68]). Even the so-called "Lovestoneites," expelled as a "Right Opposition" from the CPUSA in 1929, stubbornly supported the Foster-Ford ticket versus the "cursed" bourgeois status-quo[69]—a remarkable development in view of the CPUSA's policy of outright violence toward them. Particularly egregious was a July attack in Brooklyn's Brownsville neighborhood where "official 'Communist' hooligans . . . brandished knives, iron knuckles, and other weapons."[70]

Ignoring such incidents, in September, fifty-three intellectuals declared their fealty to Foster and Ford. The aforementioned Sherwood Anderson and Waldo Frank signed. So did Theodore Dreiser, John Dos Passos, Malcolm Cowley, Erskine Caldwell, Lincoln Steffens, Granville Hicks, Matthew Josephson, Sidney Hook, Clifton Fadiman, Edmund Wilson, Upton Sinclair, and Frederick L. Schuman.[71] *New Masses* editor James Rorty penned an open letter "Culture and Crisis" proclaiming, "It is capitalism which is destructive of all culture and Communism which desires to save civilization and its cultural heritage from the abyss to which the world crisis is driving it."[72] In the *Baltimore Afro-American* William N. Jones urged Negroes to vote Communist.[73]

Negroes weren't quite sure who they might vote for. They had always voted Republican—but so had a lot of folks no longer quite so firm in that loyalty. The Depression drove most African-American defections. But other issues predated their exit. In the 1920s, blacks hoped Republicans might finally enact federal anti-lynching legislation (the Dyer Anti-Lynching Bill). Southern Democratic senators blocked that initiative, but African Americans resented a perceived too-sanguine Republican acquiescence in that defeat. True, in 1928, Democrats had painted Hoover as some sort of wild-eyed integrationist. He had desegregated the Census Bureau, they fumed.[74] He had even, charged Mississippi's Governor Theodore "The Man" Bilbo (a Klansman), danced with Mrs. Mary Margaret Booze, his state's black female member of the Republican National Committee.[75] That might have won black support for Hoover. But it did not. Obsessed with wooing white southern Democratic support, his campaign denied their candidate had really desegregated much of anything—and, if he had, he hadn't meant to. His press secretary George E. Akerson excoriated Bilbo's allegation as "the most indecent and ignoble assertion ever made by a public man in the United States."[76] Beyond that, African Americans recalled Hoover's stiff-arming of black delegates at 1928's Republican National Convention and his botched Supreme Court nomination of North Carolina's Judge John H. Parker and his subsequent recriminations ("things are to be run by demagogues and Negro politicians"[77]). Controversy erupted over segregated, second-class accommodations ("cattle boats") provided to black Gold Star Mothers.[78]

In 1932 the number of black GOP delegates was reduced to just twenty-six—half its normal quotient.[79] Mary Booze's husband, the wealthy landowner Eugene P. Booze, chagrined over the seating of lily-white Mississippi delegates (not to mention local patronage), publicly blasted Hoover as "the only white man who ever made me a promise and didn't keep it"[80]—and called for dumping him from the ticket. When The Great Engineer appeared at all-black Howard University in June 1932, he rushed through his remarks.[81] Not until Saturday, October 1, 1932 did he even allow himself to be photographed with blacks.[82]

At Cleveland's St. James African Methodist Episcopal Church, *Pittsburgh Courier* editor Robert L. Vann proclaimed: "I see millions of Negroes turning the pictures of Abraham Lincoln to the wall. This year I see Negroes voting a Democratic ticket."[83]

Millions of Negro voters, however, still saw Franklin Roosevelt as the candidate of a traditionally racist party. When Will Rogers expressed his support for fellow-Indian Charles Curtis to his fellow Democrat H. L. Mencken, "The Sage of Baltimore" snorted, "The Republicans should not show so much race prejudice. They had an Indian last time. They ought to get a nigger this year."[84]

Beyond such gaucheries, FDR's Warm Springs, Georgia, clinic was itself segregated.[85] He himself owed his nomination to his party's most racist elements—Hull, Glass, Swanson, Daniels, Robinson, Harrison, and, most noticeably, John Nance Garner. That the so-called former "Klan candidate" William Gibbs McAdoo had so visibly pushed FDR over the top hardly allayed African-American fears, nor did the reports of Klan support that had preceded the convention. FDR thus wrote to NAACP executive director Walter F. White to disavow the KKK, disingenuously terming letters linking him to the organization "deliberate forgeries."[86] When the NAACP solicited writers to support FDR in its journal *The Crisis* (subtitled "A Record of the Darker Races"), volunteers proved to be in short supply.[87] "FDR has spent six months out of every twelve as Governor of New York and the rest swimming in a Georgia mudhole," worried the NAACP. "If he is elected president, we shall have to move the White House to Warm Springs and use Washington for his occasional vacations."[88]

While African Americans remained suspicious that they might only be pressed into service as Pullman porters aboard the Roosevelt campaign train, others besides Joe Kennedy hustled to stretch out in business class: most famously and furiously Bernard Baruch. As much a Wall Street specu- lator as Kennedy or any other "economic royalist," Baruch, however, enjoyed an enviable reputation as party elder statesman, dating back to his days chairing Woodrow Wilson's powerful War Industries Board. Beyond that, his sizable bank drafts might be deposited quite as conveniently as Ken- nedy or Hearst's. Suffice it to say, doors swung open widely and quickly for him at FDR-Garner headquarters. His instant rehabilitation with the Roosevelt camp, puzzled—and angered—its more progressive functionar- ies. "None of us quite understood the acceptance of Baruch . . . ,"[89] recalled Rexford Tugwell, who, for that matter, also could not fully understand why the invariably cool and composed Baruch now groveled before "the Boy Scout Governor."[90]

Perhaps Tugwell finally concluded, Baruch, "now wished to become Sec- retary of State; if he did, he was to be disappointed. Franklin would play him for the big fish he was, but what would be given to land him stopped short of a secretaryship."[91] FDR, nonetheless, allowed Baruch's factotum, Gen. Hugh S. "Iron Pants" Johnson entrance to his inner circle, granted a tantaliz- ing (though insincere) nod toward Baruch's generally conservative world- view, and extended to Baruch occasional highly personal perks (including being chauffeured about Hyde Park with Eleanor behind the wheel).[92] When Baruch fancifully proclaimed in a September 1932's *Nation's Business* article that "Taxes Can Be Cut a Billion," nary a protest emanated from either the candidate nor his Brains Trust.[93]

Not everyone, however, proved quite so tolerant of Baruch. For a variety of reasons, Father Coughlin was not—and continued pestering Franklin with offers of support—and outright adulation. "I have twenty-six of the most powerful [radio] stations in our network," he boasted to FDR. "The east is thoroughly covered as is the middle west and the west as far as Denver." Conversely, Coughlin begged the candidate to tout him in a speech as a cleric "who spoke for the rights of the common man."[94]

Huey Long similarly had little sympathy for such magnates as "Baruch, Morgan and Rockefeller,"[95] but, unlike Coughlin, probably not much more for Roosevelt. "By God, I feel sorry for him," he did admit. "He's got more sonofabitches in his family than I got in mine."[96]

The Kingfish, garishly clad in pink tie and an orchid shirt,[97] bounced into Hyde Park unannounced one Sunday in early October,[98] confronting a clearly amazed press at the Waldorf-Astoria the next day. "It's a cinch for Roosevelt," Huey prophesized, though he conceded that all was not perfect within the party. "The great trouble with the Democrats is that we have all the votes and no money," he diagnosed. "In the present situation I believe the best thing we could do is to sell President Hoover a million votes for half what he is going to pay to try to get them. We can spare the votes and we could use the money."

Reporters inquired if he was indeed the radical others painted him as. "I'm a conservative; I'm in," Huey expounded. "The radicals are the fellows who are out."

In fact, by Long standards, in October 1932, he seemed downright mellow and docile, pledging his loyalty—and efforts—wholeheartedly to Roosevelt. He meekly vowed to travel "wherever they tell me. You know that old song: 'I'll go where you want me to go; I'll say what you want me to say; I'll do what you want me to do.' That's me in this campaign."[99]

Queried if his lyrics emanated from the old Methodist hymnal, The Kingfish answered, "No, I'm a Baptist. That's a Baptist song. My great-grandfather was a Baptist minister of the Gospel in Greenfield, Ohio. He moved South in 1854 just after the Baptists adopted the first prohibition resolution. They held a conclave in Cincinnati and adopted a resolution that a minister shouldn't drink liquor on the Sabbath during the hours of service. My great-grandfather rebelled and moved South."

Huey lusted to hit the campaign trail. Herbert Hoover didn't. What passed for political thinking within the Hoover White House had ruled out such political activity. The Great Humanitarian should remain removed from such contact with actual humanity. He would stick to his last, working glumly 'round the clock to end the unending Depression. His, however, would not exactly be the McKinley- or Harding-style "Front Porch" campaign. For one thing his administration sorely lacked either "A Full Dinner Pail" or "Normalcy," but, with Hoover prepared to hunker down indefinitely, it would have to do. Other Republicans would take the field in his phlegmatic stead, establishing their eastern campaign headquarters in forty rooms of the newly relocated Waldorf-Astoria's sixth floor.[100] "It is safe to say," noted two contemporary observers, "that no fight of a political party was so magnificently housed."[101]

But when you are Herbert Hoover and the date is 1932, even 1600 Pennsylvania Avenue's gated and guarded confines possessed their hazards. Greeting conferees from the American Bar Association one evening at a White

House receiving line,[102] he possessed little energy. His aides soon discerned something even worse.

"We noticed splotches of red on the white gloves the women were wearing," recalled Press Secretary Ted Joslin. "The President's hand had been cut, presumably by a precious stone on the hand of someone who had passed through the line. He was tired out, too. He could barely go through the motions of shaking hands. There was only one thing to do. That was to stop the reception. The line was halted. The President and Mrs. Hoover were escorted to the living quarters on the second floor."[103]

In early September, Hoover prepared to receive a prestigious visitor, his old friend and fellow mining millionaire Col. Raymond Robins, once a key supporter of TR-style progressivism (and an associate of Pinchot and Ickes[104]) and more recently a vigorous booster of both Prohibition and Soviet recognition. Scheduled to arrive on Tuesday, September 6, to discuss Prohibition enforcement as well as Hoover's general campaign efforts, Colonel Robins departed midtown Manhattan's prestigious City Club at noon the previous Saturday afternoon . . . and simply vanished. His distraught wife feared his kidnapping by irate Florida bootleggers.[105]

Such events only added to the usually dour Hoover's now even grimmer demeanor, as witnessed by his behavior as he prepared to address the females of America over a nationwide broadcasting hookup. A woman inquired if he found it "a thrill to talk over the radio."

"The same thrill," he answered, "that I get when I rehearse an address to a door knob."[106]

Still worse, his audience now felt the same thrill in listening to him. Herbert Hoover ("the pathetic mud-turtle, Lord Hoover"[107]) had become, as H. L. Mencken observed, "the pebble in every American's shoe."[108]

Roosevelt, still shackled by obligations to grill Jimmy Walker, also remained slow to take the stump. On Saturday, August 20, 1932, he embarked on an overnight jaunt to Columbus, Ohio, to speak at the local ballpark but darted back just as quickly.[109] A similarly hurried pilgrimage to Woodrow Wilson's former haunt of Sea Girt, New Jersey, followed a week later.[110] His topic: Prohibition. "The experience of nearly one hundred and fifty years under the Constitution has shown us that the proper means of regulation is through the States," FDR pronounced, "with control by the Federal Government limited to that which is necessary to protect the States in the exercise of their legitimate powers."[111]

Huey Long had joked about campaigning where he might inflict the least harm and mused, "I think I'd like to speak in Vermont."[112] For some inexplicable reason, FDR did. On Wednesday, September 7 (perhaps more in search of foliage than votes), Franklin tore into the quintessentially Republican state, addressing crowds at Manchester, Bennington, and twice at Rutland (including ten thousand at the state fair), even babbling about winning the state as "another precedent." The state's Democratic chairman, Park Pollard (Calvin Coolidge's cousin; it was indeed a very small state), nonetheless, seemed dubious. Before addressing three thousand at Bennington, Roosevelt found his caravan blocked by a barricade on the back-road to the local college. Bodyguard Earl Miller drew his State Police service revolver, fired three shots at its lock, and the campaign sped merrily on.[113]

Franklin did not commence his first serious tour until very late Monday evening, September 12, departing Albany's Union Station on a three-week voyage taking his *Roosevelt Special* to Los Angeles and back.[114] Emil Hurja had, however, just reported trouble in the Midwest. FDR's sudden "wet" sympathies had caught the ear of midwestern women, and they were not at all pleased. "FARM BELT SHOWS HOOVER GAIN AMONG WOMEN," Hurja titled his warning.[115]

Polls were one thing, actual votes another. In September, Maine, as was its ancient custom, conducted local (but not presidential) elections. The rock-ribbed Republican state shocked just about everyone by electing not only a Democratic governor but two Democratic congressmen, one of the latter even defeating former Klan-supported GOP governor Owen Brewster.[116] Perhaps it seemed, Roosevelt had *not* wasted a day in Vermont. Perhaps something historic *was* in the wind. "A mighty phalanx of States will soon move into line," boomed Hearst's *New York American*. "Maine is only the first."[117]

"What's happened has happened," the devastated Hoover privately lamented. "It is a catastrophe for us. It means we have got to fight to the limit."[118] He furiously dispatched his original strategy into the trash can. Herbert Hoover would now leave the White House and face the American people.

Franklin Roosevelt was already meeting them. At Jefferson City, Missouri, a rail collapsed on a train car ramp, nearly taking FDR down with it. Supported by a straining Gus Gennerich, he lurched on to the podium, smiling as if nothing in the world had happened.[119] In Topeka, at Kansas's state capitol, he addressed twelve thousand farmers.[120] His research still needed work. "What half-baked student of agriculture and the tariff wrote his Topeka speech?" asked the patrician Upper East Side congresswoman Ruth Baker Pratt (not only New York State's first woman member of Congress, but Gotham's first female alderman). She fumed, "Typical of the ignorance . . . is his declaration that textiles, boots and shoes and coal had the 'highest subsidy in history' in 1926 and if elected President he would safeguard agricultural products as strongly. The truth is that leather boots and shoes received no protection in 1926. They were on the free list. Coal, too, was on the free list. And textiles were not as highly protected in 1926 as under the Payne-Aldrich tariff."[121]

But with FDR, the messenger transcended the message, the frame overshadowed the picture. The Associated Press's Lorena Hickok described not FDR's facts and figures but the Lochinvar that desperate men and women saw appear before them. "They stared intently at a tall man, with big, powerful shoulders," she would write. "As usual, his legs were concealed behind the speaker's stand, on which he kept a firm grip with one hand. He too was tanned, and he frequently wiped his forehead, for perspiration tricked down from his rumpled hair. His clothes were casual, loose-fitting, and somewhat wrinkled, as they always were because of his braces. He said he was a farmer, although he was not as ragged as they were."[122]

He could have told them anything. And they would have believed him. He was not a threadbare dirt farmer, but he was not Herbert Hoover either.

He rumbled westward. West of Butte, a train wreck delayed his advance by three hours.[123] At Portland, he spoke to five thousand regarding one of his favorite themes, public hydro-power.[124] Rex Tugwell pronounced that effort "enormously effective."[125] Next stop: California, one fraught with electoral peril. Charles Evans Hughes's visit there may have sealed his doom in 1916 as he stepped into a hornet's nest of competing Republican factions. Similar danger greeted FDR in 1932. Warring Democrats—divided still further by the May and August primaries—still hated each other, and Louis Howe argued against visiting California at all.[126] "Here was suspense, as when we crossed the [state] line . . . ," recalled Raymond Moley, "and . . . suspiciously waited for something disastrous to happen. We were jittery when two archenemies, William G. McAdoo and Justus Wardell, whom McAdoo had just defeated in a bitterly contested senatorial primary, boarded the train at almost the same moment. . . . There were moments of ecstatic relief as when McAdoo and Wardell came smilingly out of Roosevelt's car. . . ."[127]

That crisis surmounted, at Sacramento FDR received a nineteen-gun salute.[128] At San Francisco's Commonwealth Club, he delivered what must be ranked as his campaign's most significant address. Drafted largely by Adolf Berle, but with some assistance from Tugwell,[129] it endorsed massive controls on the nation's economic structure. "Sometimes, my friends, particularly in years such as these, the hand of discouragement falls upon us," FDR contended, diluting his message of hard times with generous dollops of jauntiness and optimism. "It seems that things are in a rut, fixed, settled, that the world has grown old and tired and very much out of joint. This is the mood of depression, of dire and weary depression. But then we look around us in America, and everything tells us that we are wrong. America is new. It is the process of change and development. It has the great potentialities of youth. . . . Whenever in the pursuit of this objective the lone wolf, the unethical competitor, the reckless promoter, the Ishmael or [Samuel] Insull whose hand is against every man's, declines to join in achieving an end recognized as being for the public welfare, and threatens to drag the industry back to a state of anarchy, the government may properly be asked to apply restraint. Likewise, should the group ever use its collective power contrary to public welfare, the government must be swift to enter and protect the public interest."[130]

Republicans and editorial writers fretted about such rhetoric. The man in the street did not. FDR's car was so "literally mobbed by friendly people," Ray Moley found the tumult "frightening."[131] Rexford Tugwell regarded the maelstrom concerning their chief's real sympathies equally disconcerting. Of the Commonwealth Club address, he sadly concluded, "we were on the verge of a vast expansion if we recognized our collective nature and socialized our product, but we all agreed well enough that collectivism was by now a commitment. . . The trouble was that Franklin did not write it and that he was actually, no matter what the speech said, in retreat from this position."[132]

And, so Roosevelt vacillated once more. Although, perhaps that was all for the best. Though Tugwell and his fellow academics failed to recognize it, 1932 was not the best of years for collectivization. For three years, the Soviet Union's Joseph Stalin had waged an unholy war on private farmland ("Liquidate the Kulaks as a class!"[133]), executing, deporting, or starving millions. At the Kremlin, in August 1942, he would personally admit (perhaps boast) to Winston Churchill that "ten million" obstinate peasants had been "dealt with."[134] No, not that anyone but the dead and the dying really noticed, but 1932 was not the optimal time to discuss collectivism.

Moving expeditiously away from such words in Northern California, FDR moved swiftly toward Southern California—territory once belonging not at all to Franklin Roosevelt, but to William Randolph Hearst—and his mistress Marion Davies. Hearst had advised Roosevelt to employ Hoover's original strategy: a sedate McKinley-style front-porch effort. But FDR *had* to move about the country, to sell himself, to dispel the rumors of mental or physical unfitness. Now, Franklin reached California, and, he, not Hearst, held the whip hand. They conferred privately at Santa Barbara. Then FDR spoke over Warner Brothers–owned radio station KFWB. Los Angeles mayor John C. Porter—a "dry" Republican, "Fighting Bob" Shuler protégé, and former Klansman[135]—refused to formally meet him,[136] but other

Republicans proved less coy. At a Biltmore Hotel luncheon, FDR addressed the newly rechristened "Roosevelt-Garner Republican League of Southern California," until recently—when a poll found 79 percent of its members for Roosevelt—simply the "Downtown Republican Club."[137] Roosevelt joyously announced: "If you are on a sinking elephant in the middle of the stream and a sturdy mule comes swimming past, isn't it the sensible thing to climb on the mule and let him take you out?"[138] Two hundred thousand Los Angelenos watched FDR process through city streets. By now, Mayor Porter was indecorously scrambling after his motorcade. A dozen ragged men held aloft a banner, "Welcome to Roosevelt from the Forgotten Men."[139] At the Hollywood Bowl, twenty-five thousand (some reports said fifty thousand) overflowed onto the hillsides, hearing Franklin intone, "I ask your support, not just to bring back better days but to bring us to a higher standard of morality, a greater faith in God."[140]

That night, Franklin D. Roosevelt, Galahad of "a higher standard of morality," highlighted a massive Los Angeles Coliseum rally doubling as a fundraiser for the "Marion Davies Foundation for Crippled Children."[141] Hearst pulled out every stop he could to entice a turnout, lassoing as many Hollywood stars as he could. Will Rogers hosted—and bought $1,800 worth of tickets to augment the crowd.[142] Comedian Joe E. Brown served as grand marshal. Two companies of soldiers, a military band, and thirty motorcycle police preceded the candidate's entrance. Red, white, and blue searchlights flashed across the night sky. Rogers—and Davies—introduced the candidate ("I wish to compliment those who by this method decrease suffering, especially to the kiddies"[143]) to the eighty thousand attending. Oddly enough, no footage of Davies—or Hearst—appeared in the Hearst Metrotone Newsreels distributed nationwide. Love, it appeared, was one thing; practical politics quite another.

Local Republicans deluded themselves into thinking that their competition had finally gone too far. As one GOP operative privately chortled to *Chicago Daily News* publisher (and former TR "Rough Rider") Col. Frank Knox:

> *I came to Los Angeles last night to witness the Roosevelt—Hearst—Marion Davies show. What a reaction it is to follow his unholy exhibition. Plenty of pictures were taken and the public thanking Governor Roosevelt for his part in making the party a big success was a "wow"—Nature will do the rest. . . . In a later letter I wrote . . . that Hearst, always inclined to overdoing things, would make a fatal mistake with Roosevelt before the campaign ended. I think the Hearst—Marion Davies—Roosevelt show*

here which Hearst promoted (of course) is the fatal mistake. The reaction is rolling up like mountains apparently everywhere. Will you imagine the fun I am having placing the dynamite around in strategic spots. When I see you I will give you many a laugh in my story of the crazy antics of the frothing, frantic Hearst crowd. In my own way I have hung the name William Rasputin Hearst on the old man. Up to now the "gang" have had no knowledge of just what I am doing. They will undoubtedly before long. Lots of good luck to you and many thanks for the opportunity of doing work of which am proud in a cause that will certainly win when the facts are known and they will be known.[144]

"Such things do one good,"[145] the for-once overly optimistic Herbert Hoover also wrote to Knox. Other things did him better. The economy finally upticked that summer. Prosperity might indeed be inching around the corner—or, better still, have turned a corner. The Republican National Committee issued a campaign textbook praising Hoover's "rugged leadership" in keeping the country "still American." He is, it asserted, "heaven-sent for the role."

"Prosperity is returning," it continued. "Courage and faith have been restored. The nation is moving ahead with its characteristic cheerful enterprise, the country is solvent. The industries that supply the jobs for the 40 million wage-earners and their families are sound and producing. The stores that employ 10 million wage-earners are doing business. The farms that support 25 million families are backed by the financial power of the government in their work of feeding the nation. Relief for the unemployed has been provided."

Nonetheless, for the first time in Republican National Committee history, such a publication was no longer free. The RNC, strapped for funds like the rest of the allegedly "solvent" nation, charged for its sale to cover costs.[146]

Yet, the polls indicated that something *was* in the air—a lingering uncertainty about the Democratic candidate. Baruch, Davis, Baker, Hague, and Ely may have submerged their doubts. Others—and they were no means all disgruntled Smith supporters—had not. In mid-September, Emil Hurja reported to Jim Farley that Democratic male support in Pennsylvania had increased from 47 percent on August 20 to 61 percent, but that female support had "shown a corresponding decline." Hurja predicted FDR would lose the state.[147] An independent Kansas straw poll revealed a sudden and substantial movement to Hoover.[148]

The hitherto-standoffish Calvin Coolidge now weighed in for his "wonder boy" successor. "He deserves reelection for what he has done and for what he has prevented," Silent Cal wrote in the *Saturday Evening Post*. "We know he is safe and sound."[149] In late September, the *Literary Digest* released the first results of its massive presidential straw poll. In years past, it had correctly called returns for Wilson, Harding, Coolidge, and, yes, Hoover. The sheer mass of its responses almost guaranteed accuracy. "[I]t might be a good idea hereafter quadrennially to quit holding elections and accept the *Digest's* polls as final. It would save millions in money and in time"[150]—so spake the *Raleigh News and Observer*, published by Franklin Roosevelt's old Navy Department boss Josephus Daniels.

And so on Saturday, September 24, 1932, the *Literary Digest* announced tallies from "five random States . . . the first to come from the hands of our tabulators"—Indiana, New York, Ohio, Pennsylvania, and West Virginia. Hoover led in New York and Indiana; FDR in Pennsylvania, West Virginia, and Ohio. Of 60,327 straw votes cast, Hoover garnered 28,193, Roosevelt only 27,654. Socialists, Prohibitionists, and Communists shared the remaining 4,480. [151]

"It is not the crushing blow I had feared,"[152] a relieved Hoover sighed, and he determined to fight on.

CHAPTER TWENTY-ONE

"Herr Hitler, I will shoot"

Hoover fought on.

So did Hitler.

But was Hitler still advancing—or, as so many said, had he reached his zenith?

Britain's Sir Horace Rumbold spoke of Hitler as having exhausted his reserves, and, perhaps he had. On July 31, though again increasing his vote, it was not by very much, and his party remained nowhere near achieving an unfettered parliamentary majority. Control of his movement—a horde of power-hungry, avaricious thugs—might well evaporate if he surged too near to power without grasping it. "[S]torm troopers will soon begin to ask themselves what their marching and their '*Alarmbereitchaft*' (being on alert) are leading to . . . ," Rumbold noted. "The time is fast approaching when Hitler will be expected to deliver the goods."[1] Even if Hitler played every card perfectly, he might still miscarry—and, having once failed, never recover.

For a very long time now—at least, since October 1930's Reichstag elections—his grasp of the political game he claimed to despise had been as masterful as his command of his audience at any chanting, saluting, swastika-bedecked, brown-shirted mass rally. Skillfully mixing contradictory dosages of rage and reason, of capitalism and socialism, of hatred and idealism, he was all things to all people—or, at least, to 37 percent of all people, and in a fractured multi-party society like Germany's—that was not so bad at all.

But, as he hovered ever closer to power, his innate "finger-tips" sense of strategy threatened to desert him. His bluster went too far, his back-room negotiating skills not far enough. And, worst of all, his armies of followers grew steadily impatient, with precious little he might do about it. Their Miracle Worker, it seemed, had run out of miracles.

August 1932 began well enough—on one level. Franz von Papen held out yet another public olive branch to the Hitlerites. Interviewed by the

Associated Press, he indicated that "the time has come for the Nationalist Socialist movement to take an active part in the reconstruction work of the country."[2]

On July 31, still only 14 percent of Catholics (as opposed to 40 percent of Protestants) had voted Nazi.[3] Nonetheless, the hitherto reluctant Zentrum also now inched toward Hitler. Convening at the Köln home of banker Baron Kurt von Schroeder (whose wife was now a Nazi), Zentrum party leaders bandied about the chances for a DNVP-National Socialist-Zentrum coalition. If such an awkward alliance developed, recorded Köln mayor Konrad Adenauer, the Zentrum "would be prepared to tolerate it and to judge it wholly without bias by its deeds alone."[4]

But such coalitions were not what Hitler wanted. He coveted not a "part" of governance. He wanted to *be* the government, to hold *all* power, not to share *some* power. He wanted to be chancellor.

Franz von Papen, of course, wanted Franz von Papen to remain chancellor, and besides that, Reichspräsident Hindenburg desired no part of any Hitler-led government. Hitler had proven too radical for such an honor. And, unless he seriously changed his act and displayed a willingness to work with non-Nazis, most sane Germans of whatever political stripe felt similarly.

Thus, Hitler needed to prove he was no longer a whip-wielding, putsch-planning monster. The road to power was paved with new-found restraint—not the caked, dried blood of opponents.

Moderation being absolutely necessary—he did the exact opposite.

Within twenty-four hours of Reichstag balloting, National Socialist terror rocked Silesia and East Prussia. At Königsberg, Hitlerites murdered local KPD leader Gustav Sauff and severely wounded not only Otto Wyrgatsch, publisher of that party's *Königsberger Volkszeitung*, but also local German People's Party leader Max von Bahrfeldt. Gunmen burst into KPD Reichstag deputy Walter Schütz's home, injuring both him and his daughter. Bombs racked the SPD headquarters, the Otto-Braun-Haus.[5] Predictably, Joseph Goebbels painted Königsberg not as Nazi carnage, but as simple Nazi self-defense. He saw *everything* as Nazi self-defense. "At Königsberg an S.A. man was attacked by the 'Reds,'" he wrote in his diary. "The day before the election a Communist cut his throat with a razor in broad daylight, in the middle of the street. The S.A. man died immediately.

"The next day bombs explode and pistols go off at Königsberg. Two Communist leaders are shot in the street. This is the only way to bring the 'Reds' to their senses: they are impressed by nothing less. We shall see more of this kind of thing in the near and remoter future. The timid *bourgeois,* of course, cannot understand that. They will only be brought to their senses when Bolshevism sets fire to their homes."[6]

It was all rubbish. "Prominent Socialists and Communists were surprised at night and murdered in their beds or shot down at the doors of their houses," Sir Horace Rumbold informed foreign secretary Sir John Simon. "The windows of shops owned by Jews were smashed and their contents looted."[7] American ambassador Frederic Sackett described "acts of atrocious violence at various places . . . from East Prussia to Bavaria."[8] The Nazis, theorized Count Harry Kessler, had "launched an operation which demonstrates in miniature what they proposed to do all over the country, on a bigger and far more thorough scale, if they had won the election."[9]

Murder and mayhem evidently counted for little with Kurt von Schleicher. On Friday, August 5, north of Berlin at the Reichswehr's Fürstenberg Barracks, he and Hitler secretly conferred. Der Führer demanded not only the chancellorship and the Prussian premiership for himself but also the ministries of Interior (for Strasser), Air Transport (for Göring), Popular Enlightenment and Propaganda (for Goebbels), with two additional Nazis-to-be-named-later at Justice and Agriculture—plus (and this was really the key) the ability to rule by decree. Schleicher would remain at Defense. Hjalmar Schacht would return to his old Reichsbank post. There might be a vice chancellor, though Papen's name remained unuttered—for anything.[10] Schleicher remained cagily circumspect. Hitler excitedly promised that he would strongarm a Reichstag majority "like Mussolini [had] in 1922." Schleicher blandly responded that if Hitler possessed a parliamentary majority, nary a soul might prevent him from governing. Hitler, intoxicated by recent events, failed to grasp the essential meaninglessness of Schleicher's comment, taking the ball and running with it across the wrong goal, toward a nonexistent endorsement of his fevered dreams—and Schleicher didn't bother correcting him. By meeting's end Hitler vowed to someday install a plaque, inscribed, "Here the memorable conference between General von Schleicher and Adolf Hitler took place."[11] The oily Schleicher again failed to disillusion him.

Not surprisingly, that plaque never got installed.

Nazi violence intensified. In Norgau, the mayor was gunned down in the streets.[12] In Lötzen, East Prussia, Nazis murdered local Reichsbanner chairman Kurt Kotzan.[13] At a Fröndenberg, Westphalia rifle club, three police and seven civilians were wounded. Top-level rhetoric more than matched street-level savagery. "Once we attain power," mused Goebbels, "we shall never relinquish it unless we are carried off dead."[14] Ernst Röhm vowed to deal with the party's enemies, "an eye for an eye and a tooth for a tooth,"[15] and Goebbels noted the growing thirst for action within Röhm's always-seething

Sturmabteilung: "The air is full of presage. . . . The whole Party is ready to take over power. The S.A. downs everyday tools to prepare for this. The political officials are preparing for the great hour. If things go well, everything is all right. It they do not, it will be an awful set-back."[16] Soon, he would note, "The S.A. are closely concentrated around Berlin. The manoeuvre is carried out with imposing precision and discipline."[17]

In truth, discipline was in short supply. "[A]n open outbreak of the National Socialist revolution was imminent . . . ," noted the then-Nazi president of the Danzig Teachers' Association, Dr. Hermann Rauschning. "It would have meant the end of the party. The rising would have been ruthlessly suppressed by the Reichswehr. Over and over again in conversation this sentence cropped up: 'Clear the streets for the brown battalions!' For himself and his friends, Hitler painted the chances of a surprise occupation of the key points of political economic power, and he lingered with special interest over the chances of a bloody destruction of Marxist resistance in the streets. Events of the summer revealed the extent to which plans for a *coup* were already elaborated. They were not the sporadic enterprises of local party leaders, but came from Hitler himself."[18]

On Tuesday, August 9, Gregor Strasser and Wilhelm Frick conveyed to Hitler worrisome news: The German people, disgusted with Nazi street violence, had grown increasingly wary of entrusting his party with national power. By coincidence, Hitler's economic aide, Walther Funk, arrived bearing word from Schacht: The Reich's business and industrial leaders held similar unpleasant conclusions; their fears regarding left-wing economic Nazism (a la Strasser and Gottfried Feder) only intensified.[19]

This very day, Franz von Papen, acting on the growing unease, restored martial law in Prussia and enacted a death penalty for political murders "in the passion of the political struggle undertakes, in rage and hatred. . . ."[20] As if to spit in the face of elemental decency, within an hour-and-a-half[21] Silesian Nazis murdered someone.

He was not a very great, or even very middling, someone. Not an editor nor a Reichstag deputy nor a Reichsbanner leader, just a Communist coal miner, and not even an ethnic German but a young Pole, Konrad Pietrzuch. At 1:30 that morning thirteen drunken, uniformed SA men broke into Pietrzuch's unlocked Potemba, Upper Silesia cottage—and proceeded to savagely kill him.[22] Wrote Hearst's International News Service of his death: "The Nazis invaded the house shouting: 'clear out, you dirty communists.' Pietrzuch, who was in bed at the time, hid in a closet when the troopers entered. The Nazis clubbed his brother [Alfons] into insensibility and then, finding Pietrzuch in the closet, shot him to death before the eyes of his [widowed] mother [Marie], who pleaded in vain for his life."[23] Before this coup de grace, they beat Pietrzuch with billiard cues and stomped him with their boots for half an hour.[24]

But if that were not horrifying enough, consider the police report:

The body bore the marks of 29 wounds, the deepest ones at the neck. The carotid artery was completely torn. The larynx was kicked in and had a gaping hole. Death occurred by suffocation as the arterial blood had entered the lungs by way of the larynx. Besides these wounds, Pietrzuch's body showed marks caused by severe beatings. He was beaten severely on the head with a blunt axe or club, and had other wounds probably caused by having the top of a billiard cue thrust in his face.[25]

Within such a blood-soaked context, Hitler demanded the chancellorship. At Berchtesgaden, he conferred with his staff. They remained deeply divided on what strategy to employ. Violence? A coup? A laughably pious legality? "The problems attendant upon seizing the reins of government are thoroughly talked out," recorded Goebbels, before adding a telling remark: "We must be as wary as serpents."[26]

Jittery as Hitler's subordinates were, more so was the camarilla surrounding the old feldmarschall. On the 10th, Hindenburg returned to Berlin from his East Prussian estate at Neudeck.[27] There he met with Schleicher, proving distinctly inhospitable ("I am told you want to hand me over to the Nazis"[28]) to any hint of capitulating to the "Bohemian Corporal." But soon events were in violent flux. "Phone call from Berlin from an intermediary of the Government," Goebbels now scribbled, "Wilhelmstrasse has again come to a different decision, and will now risk a bargain with us. The Leader coldly rebuffs them. . . . The Wilhelmstrasse is to decide to-day. We shall either be in Opposition or in Power."[29]

A day later, Papen signaled yet another march to the Right. Commemorating the Weimar Constitution's thirteenth anniversary, he studiously omitted any mention of the word "republic."[30] The following day found Papen and Schleicher clandestinely negotiating with Ernst Röhm and Count von Helldorf.[31] Anticipating his own rendezvous with the camarilla, Hitler discreetly motored from Obersalzberg to Munich to Berlin. To avoid detection, he halted at 10:00 p.m. at Goebbels's recently rented lakeside villa at wealthy suburban Caputh. Still, he enjoyed no real rest, pacing furiously about, before settling down to listen to some music. "Visibly a struggle is going on within him,"[32] observed Goebbels. Röhm arrived—with devastating news: Schleicher's Fürstenberg Barracks "promises" were no promises at all.[33] "For [Hitler] it is neck or nothing now,"[34] lamented Goebbels.

The next morning, the still-agitated Hitler established his headquarters at Berlin's Kaiserhof,[35] before embarking for the chancellery with Dr. Frick to meet Schleicher. The session did not go well, but it went quickly, as Hitler exploded in rage.[36] Next stop: Papen's. Again, neither side came away pleased. As head of Reich's largest party—and certainly after meeting with Schleicher at Fürstenberg—Hitler had convinced himself that he would finally be handed the chancellorship. Conversely, Schleicher and Papen assured themselves that Hitler had indeed peaked. Beyond that, the recent fortnight of Nazi thuggery had only steeled everyone's determination not to entrust this man with any meaningful power.

Particularly now.

"I soon realized," Papen would record in his memoirs, "that I was dealing with a very different man from the one I had met two months earlier. The modest air of deference had gone, and I was faced by a demanding politician who had just won a resounding electoral success."[37]

"*Herr Kanzler*," Hitler began, "I think you've drawn the necessary conclusion from the elections. The solution is in your hands. If you recommend me as your successor, the President cannot but follow your advice, especially in view of my parliamentary strength."

"I'm not so sure," Papen responded. "You overestimate my influence with the Field Marshal. You know how old men shrink from changes . . . It's not what I may say, but the way he feels that will decide. . . ."

Hitler had not raced from Berchtesgaden for that. Shifting gears, he resorted to a very un-Nazi-like theory of government: democratic majoritarianism. "Still," he archly informed Papen, "there are certain Parliamentary laws that must not depend upon the moods of the Chief of State. . . ."

Yet, Hitler possessed neither presidential favor nor a parliamentary majority. The Zentrum, despite despising Papen, had not joined with him. No one had. Not even his most logical ally, Hugenberg. "Herr Hitler," Papen counseled his would-be successor, "you forget one thing. Since you don't have an absolute majority, you could only be named head of a Presidential Cabinet. As such, you need to have the Old Gentleman's entire confidence. Why don't you wait a while longer? You're young. It's only a few months since you and Hindenburg opposed each other in a violent campaign."

Hitler burst out, "We can't go back to that . . ."

"The President," Papen interjected, refusing to be bullied, "also says that he must consider all possibilities. The Marxist reaction to your nomination would be extreme."

"I'll mow them down!" Hitler snapped.

"I had tried to be as serious and straightforward as possible," Papen later recollected, "and I had clearly given Hitler food for thought. But he still tried to convince me how impossible it would be for the leader of such a large movement to play second fiddle to another Chancellor. His movement expected to see him at the head of affairs, and although he did not doubt the honesty of my proposal, it was one that he could not accept. I then tried another tack, and suggested that he should remain outside the Cabinet, as leader of the National Socialist movement, and allow one of his colleagues to become Vice-chancellor. This would still give the President time to convince himself that the movement intended to co-operate in the general welfare."[38]

"Never!" Hitler shrieked. "If I am to take the responsibility, I must have the power! I have my own ideas about the way to conduct a government, and I can't submit myself to the concept of another person as to the use of the power! I ask you to make this clear to the President . . ."[39]

"You see," Papen continued, "in these grave circumstances my conscience doesn't allow me to put pressure on the President. He has taken an oath. He has the full responsibility. The decision must be his own." With that Papen ("The President is not prepared to offer you the post of Chancellor, as he feels that he does not yet know you well enough"[40]) suggested a meeting between Hindenburg and Hitler.

"So you decline to intervene, and the President isn't ready to appoint me," Hitler seethed. "Then why should I go and see him?"[41]

Hitler retreated to Hermann Göring's small Reichskanzlerplatz apartment, skittishly awaiting word from Hindenburg. At 3:00 p.m., Papen's state secretary, Erwin Planck, phoned: Hindenburg awaited Hitler at the Reichskanzlei. Planck promised no more than that. Hitler, unwilling to be rebuffed thrice in a single day, resisted. But Planck (quite competent, a Schleicher protégé, and the son of physicist Max Planck) bore on, and Hitler relented.[42] If it required one more meeting to procure the chancellorship, then so be it—for Hitler not only coveted the chancellorship, he *needed* it. For if he did not assume office—and soon—his fractious, impatient party might indeed disintegrate as speedily as it had so spectacularly grown.

He should have stayed at the Göring's. He should have stayed in Austria.

A thousand persons gathered on the Wilhelmstrasse as Hitler, Göring, Röhm, and Frick arrived at the Reichskanzlei.[43] Hindenburg, Papen, and Otto Meissner awaited them.[44] Röhm's presence, designed to instill fear of Nazi muscle, merely disgusted Hindenburg. He knew all too well about Röhm's proclivities.[45]

Paul von Hindenburg had few good days left to him, but August 13, 1932, was without contradiction certainly to be numbered among them.

Hitler demanded full power. Hindenburg did not even offer him a chair,[46] saying absolutely not, adding that Hitler had violated his pledge to support Papen and that his party was the least fit entity for such trust. He became downright agitated and read Hitler the riot act regarding Nazi provocations against the police—and even against the Jews. He cautioned him against inciting foreign tensions and urged him to cooperate with parties other than his own.[47] "Herr Hitler," he is said to have warned, "I will shoot."[48]

Befuddled and discouraged, Hitler merely reiterated his refusal to bargain with any other party leaders.

"You insist, therefore, on holding the premier position?" Hindenburg asked.

"I want the same position as Mussolini holds in Italy."

"I cannot square that with my conscience," retorted Hindenburg. "For the future I advise you to show chivalry in political struggles."[49]

The twain had not met. The old feldmarschall had inflicted upon the young corporal a massive dressing down. Hitler had arrived without power. He left without power. That was one thing. But he also left minus dignity. "That man for Chancellor?" Hindenburg barked to Meissner. "I'll make him a postmaster, and he can lick the stamps with my head on them."[50]

"So it has ended in failure," grieved Goebbels. "Everything has been denied him. Papen is to remain Prime Minister and the Leader has to content himself with the position of Vice-chancellor!

"A solution leading to no result! It is out of the question to accept such a proposal. No alternative offers but to decline it. The Leader did so immediately. He fully envisages the consequences, like the rest of us. It will mean a hard struggle, but we shall triumph in the end."[51]

That night, Hitler, accompanied by Hanfstaengl, bodyguard Sepp Dietrich, and adjutants Julius Schaub and Wilhelm Brückner, sped back to Berchtesgaden.[52]

"What sort of fellow is this Papen?" Hitler asked Hanfstaengl. "You must have known him during the war in New York?"

Hanfstaengl found Papen pleasant enough, "But politically he is a *Luftikus* [a light-weight]."

Hitler slapped his thigh, chortling, "*Ein Luftikus*, that just describes him."

Adolf Hitler struggled to place the most acceptable facade on the cruelest day of his political life since his failed putsch. "I can imagine that to work with Papen would, in a way, be quite good fun," he mused. "Somehow you feel he was a soldier in the war and quite the reckless fellow. Mind you, if it amuses his vanity to go on living in the Chancellor's palace and they confide the real power to me, I would not mind."

Awkward silence followed. *"Wir werden schon sehen,"* he concluded—"We shall see."[53]

What he saw instead was how public humiliation follows private humiliation. Normally, Dr. Goebbels's rabid, yet indefatigable, propagandists would have instantly proclaimed their stirring version of their Führer's heroic invasion of the Reichskanzlei. Instead, they did nothing, hunkering down within the Kaiserhof's plushy confines, rationalizing and fuming and, above all, hopelessly fretting. Meanwhile, Reaction's stodgy forces not only reacted, they acted, catching Goebbels and company completely flat-footed, as hardly sleek Otto Meissner struck the first, most powerful blow by issuing this damning public account of the late afternoon's events:

> *The President of the Reich opened the discussion by declaring to Hitler that he was ready to let the National Socialist Party and their leader Hitler participate in the Reich Government and would welcome their cooperation. He then put the question to Hitler whether he was prepared to participate in the present government of von Papen. Herr Hitler declared that, for reasons which he had explained in detail to the Reich Chancellor that morning, his taking any part in cooperation with the existing government was out of the question. Considering the importance of the National Socialist movement he must demand the full and complete leadership of government and state for himself and his party.*
>
> *The Reich President in reply said firmly that he must answer this demand with a clear, unyielding No. He could not justify before God, before his conscience or before the fatherland the transfer of the whole authority of government to a single party, especially to a party that was biased against people who had different views from their own. There were a number of other reasons against it upon which he did not wish to enlarge in detail, such as fear or increased unrest, the effect on foreign countries, etc.*
>
> *Herr Hitler repeated that any other solution was unacceptable to him.*
>
> *To this the Reich President replied: "So you will go into opposition?"*
> *Hitler: "I have now no alternative."*
> *The Reich President: "In that case the only advice I can give you is to engage in this opposition in a chivalrous way and to remain conscious of your responsibility and duty towards the fatherland. I have had no doubts about your love for the fatherland. I shall intervene sharply against any acts of terrorism or violence such as have been committed by members of the SA sections. We are both old comrades and we want to remain so, since*

the course of events may bring us together again later on. Therefore, I shall shake hands with you now in a comradely way."

This discussion was followed by a short conversation in the corridor between the Reich Chancellor and me, and Herr Hitler and his companions, in which Herr Hitler expressed the view that future developments would lead to the solution suggested by him and to the overthrow of the Reich President. The Government would get into a difficult position; the opposition would become very sharp and he could assume no responsibility for the consequences.

The conversation lasted for about twenty minutes.[54]

"Before the eyes of the German people," wrote Konrad Heiden, "[Hitler] had mounted the . . . steps to power; before the eyes of the people, he had slunk down them."[55]

Hitler, preacher of the gospels of strength and hardness, the beatitude of blessed are the merciless, had now exposed his own weakness, making the task of holding his forces together ever more demanding. That night he returned to the Kaiserhof "White as a sheet"[56] (in Hanfstaengl's words), and met with Röhm's SA commanders. Having summoned them to announce victory, he now could only make the best of a bad situation, reduced to cajoling his minions not to be the fool he had been in November 1923.[57] A few days later, he would explain to Kurt Lüdecke: "The Machiavellian method is the only one possible, the only one by which I can accomplish anything . . . What if the Reichswehr [sic—actually the Bavarian *Landespolizei*] should shoot again? No, *mein Lieber*, the Feldherrnhalle was enough—I've learned since then. No use being heroic in this world; if you want to get something done and get anywhere yourself, it's better to talk about it and let others do the work. If you can achieve something by cunning, don't try noble deeds— they might knock your teeth out."[58]

So, for that matter, might his SA leaders. Hitler and Röhm "outline[d] matters to them pretty fully," wrote Goebbels. "Their task is the most difficult. Who knows if their units will be able to hold together. Nothing is harder than to tell a troop already sure of victory that this victory has come to naught!"[59] No, one thing *was* harder, something Hitler well understood: jail. A contingent of heavily armed police waited secretly in trucks parked upon the Reichskanzerplatz. Had Hitler ordered the SA to advance, they would have struck first and arrested the entire Nazi leadership.[60]

Hitler felt ill. So did the duplicitous Schleicher. He reached out to Hitler to patch things up. Hitler, still irate, refused. Nervous and distraught, Schleicher barely commanded coherent sentences, finally conceding to associates, "The decision was right, one could not have given all the power to Adolf Hitler."[61]

A night's rest solved nothing for either he or for Hitler. "Deep despondency besets the Party,"[62] Goebbels recorded the following day.

Hitler fled Berlin. But he would not be silenced. For the *Rheinisch-Westfalische Zeitung*, he sat for an extensive interview with Dr. Otto Dietrich, affirming his official "opposition" to Papen's government and justifying his rejection of the vice-chancellorship. "I will never give away a birthright for a song. . . . ," he declared. "One cannot require heroism from a nation when its political leaders are ready to make any, even the cheapest compromise."[63]

At Berchtesgaden's Haus Wachenfeld, he posited his exculpations and rationales to an unlikely audience—the American press. Not all were impressed. Hearst's German-born correspondent Karl von Wiegand (an old intimate of the Hohenzollerns[64]) sputtered, "That man is hopeless. He gets worse every time I see him. I got nothing out of him. Ask him a question and he makes a speech. This whole trip has been a waste of time."[65] But others appreciated a rare extended close-up look at Europe's most newsworthy—and dangerous—man. To the Associated Press's Louis P. Lochner and the North American Newspaper Alliance's H. V. Kaltenborn (nee "Hans von Kaltenborn" and a Harvard classmate of Hanfstaengl's[66]), Hitler tackled such ticklish topics as anti-Semitism, dictatorship, and, of course, his recent flop at securing power.

"In your attitude of antagonism toward the Jews," asked Kaltenborn, "do you differentiate between German Jews and the Jews who have come into Germany from other countries?"

"You have a Monroe Doctrine for America," Hitler answered, quickly pureeing apples and oranges. "We believe in a Monroe Doctrine for Germany. You exclude any would-be immigrants you do not care to admit. You regulate their number. You demand that they come up to a certain physical standard. You insist that they bring in a certain amount of money. You examine them as to their political opinions. We demand the same right. We have no concern with the Jews of other lands. But we are concerned about any anti-German elements in our own country. And we demand the right to deal with them as we see fit. Jews have been the proponents of subversive anti-German movements and as such must be dealt with."[67]

Regarding democracy and dictatorship, he explained to Lochner: "Europe cannot maintain itself in the uncertain currents of democracy. Europe needs some kind of authoritarian government. Formerly it was the monarch who provided this authority. Or an institution like the Catholic Church. The Holy Roman Empire is an example. The authority can assume different forms. But parliamentarism is not native to us and does not belong to our tradition. The parliamentary system has never functioned in Europe.

"Yet we cannot substitute brute force. No government can maintain itself for any length of time by sitting on bayonets. It must have the support of the masses. You cannot establish a dictatorship in a vacuum.

"A government that does not derive its strength from the people will fail in a foreign crisis. The soldier and the policeman do not constitute a state. Yet dictatorship is justified if the people declare their confidence in one man and ask him to lead."[68]

Hitler now delved into a fuzzy math designed to transform his plurality party into a majority—or, at least, the majority of a majority. "Under the rules of democracy a majority of 51 per cent governs," he continued. "I have 37 per cent of the total vote, which means that I have 75 per cent of the power that is necessary to govern. That means that I am entitled to three-fourths of the power and my opponents to one-fourth.

"I have my safe position. I can wait. I now have 13.7 million voters. Next time I will have 14 to 15 million, and so it will go on. In the run-off elections for President, I stood alone, yet there were 13 million voters for me. That is my hard-earned capital which no one can take from me. I slaved for it and risked my life for it. Without my party no one can govern Germany today. We bring into the business of government 75 per cent of the capital investment. Whoever furnishes the rest, whether it be the President or the parties, contributes only 25 per cent.

"And this takes no account of the plain truth that every unit of my investment is worth twice that of the others. My 15 million voters are in reality worth 30 million. I have the bravest, the most energetic, and in every way the best German material in Germany—and the best disciplined, too. . . .

"My capital represents no mean investment. It can be put to work in the business of government forthwith, without any majority votes, commissions, or committees. It can be put to work on the say-so of one man."[69]

For, as he modestly phrased it, "*I have the right to complete control.*"[70]

Asked if he like Mussolini and his black shirts might march on Berlin, he snapped, "I don't have to march on Berlin as they say I propose to do. I am already there. The question is who will march out of Berlin."[71]

Meanwhile, Konrad Pietrzuch's murderers faced justice. Their trial commenced at Beuthen in the Upper Silesia highlands on August 19. It concluded three days later with three storm troopers acquitted, one receiving a two-year sentence—and five sentenced to death.[72] Hitlerites had packed the courtroom, and as the judges pronounced sentence, SA leader Edmund Heines leapt to his feet to proclaim, "The German people in the future will pass different sentences. This Beuthen verdict will become a beacon for German liberty."[73] Shouts of "Heil Hitler!" rang out as Nazis quickly exited. Police clubbed them with their carbines to roust them off courthouse grounds. Perched upon a nearby cafe balcony Heines harangued that Germany's "liberation" had started. Storm troopers smashed the windows of the local SPD and Zentrum newspapers as well as those of Jewish-owned stores.[74] "Several Jews were whipped,"[75] reported the International Press Service.

Yet, this was the mere beginning of a Nazi-generated firestorm. For if the Hitlerites were adept at anything it was propaganda. Konrad Pietrzuch's grizzly murder had certainly given them a huge black eye, but now, quickly and brazenly, shifting from bullying mode to snow-white victimhood, they shamelessly sniveled "Foul!" Hermann Göring dispatched a thousand reichsmarks[76] to the families of the convicted, expressing his "boundless bitterness and outrage" at this "terror-judgment."[77] The *Völkischer Beobachter*'s Alfred Rosenberg boldly proclaimed "All men are not equal,"[78] and Joseph Goebbels exhorted, "Never forget this, comrades! Repeat it to yourselves a hundred times a day until it haunts you in your deepest dreams: The Jews are guilty!"[79] Yes, black had once more materialized as white, wrong as right. Terror was not torture and murder before a mother's eyes; it was a legally-arrived-at, fully justified, moral verdict. Even the shorthand name of the incident was changed. No more was it *"Potemba"*; Nazis shouted *"Beuthen!"*

And, Hitler, still rankling from Hindenburg's dressing-down, only heaped petrol upon the pyre.

To the murderers, he instantly telegraphed: "My comrades:—In the face of this most monstrous and bloody sentence I feel myself bound to you in infinite loyalty. From this moment, your liberation is a question of our honor. To fight against a government which could allow this is our duty."[80]

In the next day's *Völkischer Beobachter*, he spelled out the connection between Beuthen on August 22 and his humiliation of August 13: "German racial comrades! Anyone amongst you who possesses any feeling for the struggle for the nation's honor and freedom will understand why I am refusing to enter this government. Herr von Papen's justice will in the end condemn perhaps thousands of National Socialists to death. Did anyone think they could put my name as well to this blindly aggressive action, this challenge to the entire people? The gentleman was mistaken! Herr von Papen, now I know what your bloodstained 'objectivity' is! I want victory for a nationalistic Germany, and annihilation for its Marxist destroyers and corrupters. I am not suited to be hangman of the nationalist freedom fighters of the German people!"[81]

It was as if Hitler had gone mad. But there existed a hard logic to his unabashed verbal barbarity. He again stood at the verge of power, but he stood frozen immobile. He could not go forward. The camarilla blocked him. He dared not march backward. His SA itched to fight. If he would not lead them, perhaps Röhm and Heines would. No, this was not madness on his part, it was a calculated gamble. He would risk losing votes in the middle rather than forfeit his strong-arm squads in the SA barracks. Yet, his mask *had* dropped a little too far. "At least now, if not before" postwar German historian Hannah Vogt would write, "anybody who retained even a rudimentary sense of justice must have recoiled in horror. For here was an open admission that murder was murder no longer if the murderer happened to belong to the 'Nazi movement,' and the victim belonged to the other side."[82]

Hitler already had other victims in mind. Millions of them. Still barred from power, humiliated at the goal line, he sought sanctuary in his old daydreams of world domination. In late July, a delegation of Nazis from the Free German City of Danzig arrived at Berchtesgaden. It was war he thought of—and declaimed on—war, not Danzig nor Papen nor Hindenburg.

War.

"I do not play at war," he told them. "I shall not allow myself to be ordered about by 'commanders-in-chief.' *I* shall make war. I shall determine the correct moment for attack . . . I shall not miss it. I shall bend all my energies towards bringing it about. That is my mission . . . I have no use for knights. I need revolutions. I have made the doctrines of revolution the basis of my policy. I shall shrink from nothing."[83]

And, indeed, he would not. Not in 1932—or ever.

CHAPTER TWENTY-TWO

"We always call her 'Granny'"

To some politics was a war not always worth fighting.

Just before midnight Monday, September 12, Joe Kennedy and his loyal henchman Eddie Moore had accompanied FDR and his usual crew as they departed Albany aboard the *Roosevelt Special*.[1]

Eleanor Roosevelt did not. She did not even see him off. That evening she—and lame-duck "dry" Florida congresswoman Ruth Bryan Owen (the late William Jennings Bryan's daughter)—instead delivered radio speeches from the NBC Red Network's 50,000-watt New York-affiliate WEAF.[2]

And, thereby, hung a tale of very long standing.

Mrs. Franklin Delano Roosevelt was very conflicted about Mr. Roosevelt's career. She was very conflicted about many things.

Franklin enjoyed a most enviable childhood. Handsome and loved, his family lavished upon him security and unwavering support.

Eleanor's childhood was the stuff of gothic nightmares.

Her parents' marriage had graced the daily press.[3] Dashing and handsome and rich, they were the beautiful people of their day. But underneath glamour lay disaster. Eleanor's father, Elliott Bulloch Roosevelt, was TR's younger brother, but such princely genetics did little to deliver him from a multiplicity of demons: a nervous breakdown,[4] opiate (morphine) addiction following a broken leg incurred while riding,[5] and finally self-commitment to the famed Keeley Center for Alcoholism.[6] Teddy traveled to the Dakotas to find himself—and succeeded. Elliott went off to Texas—and seemed all the more lost. "Elliott's writings during this period reveal a remarkable gender confusion," observed Eleanor's biographer Blanche Wiesen Cook regarding his travels, "He referred to himself as a woman on the range, and wrote stories about himself in which he was disguised as a woman."[7]

Marriage did little for him. He impregnated a servant girl, Katy Mann, leaving TR and the rest of the family to pay her off.[8] That, and the ample remainder of Elliott's vices, infuriated the Victorian Theodore. He cursed his sibling as "simply a selfish, brutal and vicious criminal" and "a maniac, morally no less than mentally."

"If he is not really irresponsible," concluded TR of his brother (Franklin's godfather[9]), "then his moral condition is one of hideous depravity."[10]

Elliott, often separated from wife and children, would occasionally re-enter into their life—and when not present physically faithfully corresponded with his beloved little Eleanor. Even so, his distressing faults endured. When she was six or eight, Elliott took her and his dogs out for a stroll. Passing his club, the hyper-exclusive Knickerbocker, he darted in for drinks, leaving her outside to hold the animals' leashes—for hours. They carried him out dead drunk.[11] On August 14, 1894, the increasingly dissolute Elliott tumbled to his death from the window at a mistress's West 102nd Street apartment.[12]

Such a parade of horrors might have drawn daughter and mother together. They did not. "Somehow it was always he and I," Eleanor recalled, "I did not understand whether my [two younger] brothers were to be our children or whether he felt they would be at school. . . . There started a feeling that day which never left me—that he and I were very close together, and some day we would have a life together."[13]

"He dominated my life as long as he lived," she revealed in her autobiography, "and was the love of my life for many years after he died."[14] She was not allowed to attend his funeral.[15]

In truth, she fairly detested her mother. Sheer physicality played its part. Eleanor ultimately possessed many admirers. Few, however, conceded that her appeal stemmed from beauty, a situation rendered more painful by Anna Hall Roosevelt's stunning splendor. "My mother," Eleanor recalled decades later, "was one of the most beautiful women I have ever seen."[16] The contrast only exacerbated Eleanor's unease regarding her own appearance, particularly when her own mother thoughtlessly drew attention to it. "She's such a funny child," Anna Roosevelt would say, "so old-fashioned, that we always call her Granny."[17] Anna preceded her husband in death, on December 7, 1892, from diphtheria following an operation.[18] Her "death meant nothing to me," Eleanor confessed with chilling candor, "and one fact wiped out everything else—my father was back and I would see him very soon."[19]

Eleanor was eventually sent to live at her maternal grandparents' estate at rural Tivoli, New York, not far north of Hyde Park. Her wealthy but reclusive grandfather was an odd figure of intense religiosity. Her uncles, Edward and Valentine ("Vallie"), were odder still. True, both were top-ranked tennis players, but, like her father, they suffered mightily from alcoholism.[20] Yes, "Vallie" taught Eleanor the game as well as to ride[21] and to shoot,[22] but he was also, according to Blanche Wiesen Cook, "arrested twice, once for rape of a ten-year-old girl. . . ."[23] Eleanor's grandmother—or possibly an aunt—placed three stout locks on her bedroom door for her protection, "To keep my uncles out,"[24] as she confided to a girlhood friend.

When Eleanor was nine, her grandmother discovered the effects of previous parental neglect. She was simply illiterate.[25] Worse was to come; her hired Alsatian companion's treatment caused her "many tears" (historian Geoffrey Ward hints at molestation).[26] At fifteen, however, poor, little rich girl Eleanor departed for England, headed for Mme. Marie Souvestre's Allenswood School. For once, fortune smiled upon her, the following three years being, as she recalled, "the happiest of my life."[27] For Easter 1901 the "short and rather stout"[28] Souvestre, an atheist[29] and a lesbian,[30] brought Eleanor with her to Pisa and Florence[31] and later to Rome, France, Belgium, and Germany.[32] "I often found," Mme. Souvestre reported to Grandmother Hall, "that she [Eleanor] influenced others in the right direction. She is full of sympathy for all those who live with her. As a pupil she is very satisfactory, but even that is of small account when you compare it with the perfect quality of her soul."[33] Considering her belated literacy her academic achievements were indeed laudatory.[34]

Before leaving for Allenswood, however, a seemingly inconsequential incident had occurred. At her paternal Aunt Corinne's Christmas party someone asked her to dance—and not many people did. Her sixteen-year-old cousin Franklin's kindness touched her so very much she never forgot it.[35] They met again years later, married, and had six children. Domestic life contained its disenchantments. Not only did Eleanor consider "sex an ordeal to be borne"[36] but would later confess that she found it unnatural "to understand little children or to enjoy them."[37]

Her husband's affair with her social secretary Lucy Mercer plunged her marriage upon still more difficult paths. His infidelity might have ended their union, but it did not. Despite what hurt Franklin inflicted upon her, she retained some very great bond toward him. Perhaps the model was her unlimited tolerance for her father's own ill-behavior. Perhaps not. We simply shall never know. Most likely, she never knew herself. But Franklin and Eleanor's relationship was now a very, very complicated one. On the one hand, she recoiled from being bound to his career and remarkable ascent. Yet, on the other, she never quite fully distanced herself from it—or from him.

When he campaigned for the vice-presidency in 1920, she rode the rails with him. When polio struck him down, she was there as well, bearing that anguish remarkably well. Only in 1922 was there an understandable incident, when she simply "sobbed and sobbed" for hours. Neither her sons nor Louis Howe could console her and soon abandoned trying. It was, she admitted, "the one and only time" in her life that she fell "to pieces."[38]

But when FDR continued his recovery, either in southern waters aboard his rented houseboat, the *Weona II,* or later upon his own seventy-one-foot houseboat, the *Larooco,* or at Warm Springs, she proved largely absent. Accompanying Franklin was his 5'7", blue-eyed, twentyish secretary, Marguerite "Missy" LeHand. From 1925 through 1928, FDR spent 116 of 208 weeks away from home, either at sea or in Georgia. Eleanor accompanied him for four weeks; his mother for two; Missy for 110.[39]

FDR curtailed—but hardly ended—such travels on assuming the governorship. Neither did he diminish his reliance upon Miss LeHand. According to Roosevelt's son Elliott, a physical bond now existed between Missy and his father. Of arrangements in Albany's executive mansion, Elliott wrote:

> *Mother allocated a back bedroom as her own. Around the corner and down the hall on the second floor, Father had the imposing master bedroom with big windows on two sides, next to Missy's. These two rooms were joined by a little door with clear glass panels, curtained on her side. Mother thought that this was a perfectly suitable arrangement in view of the role Missy played in Father's life.*
>
> *It was not unusual to enter his sunny corner room and find Missy with him in her nightgown. There was no attempt to conceal their relationship. . . .*
>
> *I would go in at the start of the day, and the three of us would talk with no embarrassment between us. It was no mystery. Mother had not shared life with Father for more than twenty years. . . .*
>
> *I am certain that she had no fear of sin in their relationship, in spite of her Catholic background.[40]*

As there had been trouble in Washington, trouble festered in Warm Springs's balmy paradise. In the summer of 1927, Missy, still only twenty-nine, became seriously unhinged, "a little crack-up . . . a nervous breakdown" in the words of another FDR secretary, Grace Tully.[41] It was, however, not so "little" a crack-up at all. Missy became argumentative (even with FDR), depressed, delirious, finally, even suicidal. She was essentially institutionalized, with all potential weapons (even her fountain pen) removed. By November, she had recovered but could not readily remember the first eleven days of her breakdown.[42] Some historians attribute her collapse to the sale of the *Larooco,* though that seems too slight a reason.[43] In fact, Missy, like Eleanor before her, may have discovered the truth about Franklin Roosevelt—and Lucy Mercer. The FDR-Lucy affair, or, at least, their involvement, had not at all ended. We do not know the details, but we do know this: In 2005, Lucy's two granddaughters discovered a cache of letters dating from May 1926 through September 1928 from Franklin to Lucy, now married to her next employer, the New York socialite Winthrop Rutherfurd, twenty-nine years Lucy's senior and a fox-hunting companion of Eleanor's late father Elliott.[44] Franklin's letters to Lucy are discreet, not so nearly lurid as those of, say, Warren Harding's to his own lover Mrs. Carrie Phillips. Not lurid at all, they are, nonetheless, remarkably specific regarding his upcoming whereabouts.[45] Lightning may have struck FDR's personal correspondence twice in the same place, and Missy may have reached the same painful conclusions torturing Eleanor a decade previously.

For her part, by the late 1920s, Eleanor gravitated to a new circle of friends, living in a world of suffragettes, female Democratic Party activists—and (though hardly exclusively) lesbians. Esther Lape and Elizabeth Read (Eleanor's personal attorney), cohabiting in Greenwich Village, were early acquaintances of this stripe.[46] Nancy Cook and Marion Dickerman soon followed. It was Cook and Dickerman who convinced Eleanor to teach at Manhattan's private Todhunter School, and it may have been for Cook (executive secretary of the State Democratic Committee's Women's Division) and Dickerman, rather than for Franklin, that Eleanor broke family ranks (as well as residual anti-Catholic feelings) to vociferously support Al Smith in 1924 against her own first cousin Theodore Roosevelt Jr., even installing a steam-belching, giant white canvas teapot (for Teapot Dome) atop her Buick touring car to stump for Smith. Teddy Jr.'s half-sister, Alice Roosevelt Longworth, conversely pondered affixing the flesh-and-blood Lucy Mercer to her own vehicle.[47]

In 1928, it was Eleanor whom Smith relied on to reach the reluctant Franklin regarding a possible gubernatorial run. "I am very proud and very happy, although I didn't want him to do it," she commented that October. "He felt that he had to. In the end you have to do what your friends want you to. There comes to every man, if he is wanted, the feeling that there is almost an obligation to return the confidence shown him."[48] That November, she displayed decidedly far less enthusiasm upon her husband's upset victory—and Smith's humiliating loss. "If the rest of the ticket didn't get in, what does it matter?" she tartly informed a *New York Post* reporter. "No, I am not excited about my husband's election. I don't care. What difference does it make to me?"[49]

Perhaps the *Post* misquoted her. Such things happen, but less than three weeks later she wrote to her friend and neighbor Elinor Morgenthau: "I felt

Gov. Smith's election meant something, but whether Franklin spends two years in Albany or not matters as you know comparatively little."[50]

And when two years later FDR achieved a triumphant re-election, she retired early, to ease the next morning's journey from Hyde Park to teach at Todhunter. "Much love and a world of congratulations," read the penciled note she left him. "It is a triumph in so many ways, dear and so well earned. Bless you and good luck these next two years."[51] Much love, but she was not there for him. As White House usher J. B. West later observed, he "never saw Eleanor and Franklin Roosevelt in the same room alone together. They had the most separate relationship I have ever seen between man and wife."[52]

Though Eleanor felt (or perhaps just displayed) little enthusiasm for her husband's success, she, nonetheless, doggedly pursued her own interests. In 1927, she, Nancy Cook, and Marion Dickerman purchased Todhunter. Soon they extended their partnership to founding Hyde Park's Val-Kill Industries, an endeavor employing local women. Louis Howe encouraged her to "Get out and talk,"[53] and she did. Pushing the day's social envelope, she publicly supported the American Birth Control League.[54]

There remained some question of her political influence over FDR. Louis Howe certainly continued to court and mold her. Rexford Tugwell concluded that Howe "regarded her as his agent in Albany."[55] Yet, her domain still had very real limits. Tugwell also found her to be of "a wonderful good will"[56] but "humorless."[57]

She was definitely not yet *Eleanor*.

For one, her liberalism had not yet uniformly crystalized. To an Alabama Democrat questioning Al Smith's racial stance, she had in 1928 calmly responded, "I want to assure you that Gov. Smith does not believe in intermarriage between white and colored people. He has a full understanding of conditions as they are in the South and would never try to do violence to the feelings of Southern people . . . the Democratic Party has always better understood and sympathized with Southern feelings and prejudices than has the Republican."[58]

Looking back upon it, Raymond Moley found that she "scarcely ever participated in the meetings, conferences and general activities of the campaign period or, in post-election days . . . Roosevelt never seemed to consult her beyond questions of housekeeping or family affairs. Except for her great dependence on Louis Howe and her minor contacts with Farley, she kept out of our way. Roosevelt seemed to place no reliance on her political judgment and, so far as I know, never permitted her to interfere in major decisions of government. She was generally regarded as a kindly woman who had torrential energy. Certainly, her curious economic and social concerns never crept into our concerns."[59]

Eleanor provided a clue to those "curious" concerns on January 12, 1932, when she addressed 150 members of the New York City League of Women Voters. Some might then have seen the Depression as a transient crisis to be ameliorated and conquered by temporary relief. She enunciated broader goals. "It is nice to hand out milk and bread," she declared as her husband stood upon the threshold of presidential nomination. "It gives you a comfortable feeling inside. But fundamentally you are not relieving the . . . reasons why we have to have this charity. . . . we may have to have great changes, . . . new solutions. . . ."[60]

She did not always concentrate on those solutions, having her distractions, among them one provided by Franklin. Originally assigned to guard newly elected Governor Roosevelt, New York State Police trooper Earl Miller quickly found himself reassigned to the already peripatetic Eleanor. To say the least, they hit it off. Miller, a former Navy middleweight boxing champion and ex-circus acrobat, was not only a magnificent specimen, he was as liberal as Eleanor. And beyond that, Sergeant Miller simply cared about "The Lady," as he called her. He made her feel special, different from her normal self-image.

They did not hide their friendship. "There was his arm around her waist and then around her shoulder, even when they were both in bathing suits," noted Blanche Wiesen Cook. "There was his hand in hers. Above all, there was his hand on her knee, in that time-honored expression of intimacy. And there was her hand on his knee, just casually there as they talked, knee to knee at poolside."[61]

"I believe there may have been one real romance in mother's life outside of marriage," theorized her eldest son, James. "Mother may have had an affair with Earl Miller. . . . If father noticed, he did not seem to mind."[62]

If FDR did not mind, Sara did. Disconcerted by the casual familiarity Miller enjoyed within official—and family—circles, she could only huff, "He used to be a Sergeant and now he's Earl."[63]

And yet Eleanor remained with Franklin.

"She was not in love with him," wrote her biographer and close friend Joseph P. Lash. "Yes, she was prepared to render him a labor of love by serving his work . . . if he would be thoughtful, considerate, and treat her as a partner and confidant."[64]

"Yet if there was not love—at least not love as commonly defined—between them," postulated Roosevelt family chroniclers Peter Collier and David Horowitz, "there was a deep chemistry that went past their shared history or even their pragmatic need for each other. They had both embarked on parallel journeys to rebuild selves damaged by cataclysms of illness and emotion. Each had even created an ideal community and alternative family. FDR built his at Warm Springs. Eleanor built hers at Val-Kill, . . . where she had decided to have not only a room but a house of her own she could share with her friends Dickerman and Cook."[65]

But, where, aside from the White House, was all this heading? Decades later, Earl Miller disclosed, "Mrs. R was going to stick with [the] Governor until he was elected and then she and the Sergeant were going to get married."[66] Yet nothing was ever as it seemed in the fun-house-mirror of the Roosevelts' soap opera household. Wheels spun within wheels. Sub-plots overwhelmed sub-plots. Suddenly—and for whatever reason—Earl Miller began pursuing Missy LeHand.[67] It was all very confusing. "My main purpose in playing up to Missy was because I knew The Lady was being hurt,"[68] Miller later contended.

When FDR flew to Chicago, Earl, Eleanor, and Missy accompanied him.[69] But before their departure, Eleanor, panicky at the thought of her husband's impending nomination, had dispatched a "hysterical" missive to her friend Nancy Cook, sputtering her refusal to be "a prisoner in the White House, forced onto a treadmill of formal receptions, openings, dedications, teas, official dinners."

"She won't do it." Cook would explain of the letter's contents, "She'll run away with Earl Miller. . . . She'll flee with Earl who loves and respects her as a woman as Franklin never did. Nor her sons. She'll file for divorce."

Cook shared these explosive contents with Marion Dickerman—and with Louis Howe. "You are not to breathe a word of this to anyone, understand? Not to anyone!"[70] Howe warned them. Neither did for decades.

But long before either spoke, Eleanor would. "I did not want my husband to be President," she wrote in 1949. "I realized, however, that it was impossible to keep a man out of public service if that was what he wanted and was undoubtedly well equipped for. It was pure selfishness on my part, and I never mentioned my feeling on the subject to him."[71]

Coincidentally—or not—Earl Miller's flight to Chicago proved to be his last with Franklin.[72] On Thursday, September 8, 1932, however, FDR motored down from Albany to Hyde Park to witness a bizarre ceremony at Eleanor's Val-Kill cottage: the marriage of his wife's supposed lover, the thirty-five-year-old Miller, to the seventeen-year-old Ruth Taylor Bellinger, a cousin of Miller's first wife. Elliott Roosevelt served as best man, his sister Anna Roosevelt Dall as matron of honor.

When Miller later revealed that Eleanor "and the Sergeant were going to get married" he added this: "That's why I got married in 1932 with plenty of publicity. I got married with someone I wasn't in love with. . . . But I was never successful in killing the gossip."[73]

Miller's loveless marriage ended in but a year—annulled by the under-aged bride's parents on the grounds of marrying sans their consent.[74]

Thus, with Franklin's campaign beginning in earnest, Eleanor's relationship with her Earl had been, if not sundered, at least, very greatly restricted. Her heart would not, however, be alone for very long.

Among the reporters covering FDR was the Associated Press's thirty-nine-year-old Lorena Hickok. Like Lape and Read, Cook and Dickerman, "Hick" was a lesbian, her former admirers including the great contralto Madame Ernestine Schumann-Heink, who had once appreciatively bestowed upon her an expensive sapphire-and-diamond ring.[75] The beefy (5'8", 200-pound), cigar-smoking, hard-drinking[76] Hickok wrote not so much about Franklin as about Eleanor, filling her dispatches with adulatory commentary regarding the candidate's spouse ("The new mistress of the Executive Mansion is a very great lady"[77]) and even allowing Louis Howe to vet them before filing them with her editors.[78] Eleanor and Lorena's lives, however, might have passed as mere footnotes to each other had not fate—and Mr. Roosevelt—intervened.

In October 1932, Missy LeHand's seventy-seven-year-old mother died at Potsdam, in New York State's northernmost reaches. FDR, concerned for Missy, suggested that Eleanor accompany her to the funeral. Accompanying Eleanor was Lorena Hickok.

"Hick," still in her role as a reporter, did not attend the funeral, but Eleanor tracked her down at a local restaurant and invited her to motor along the St. Lawrence River before their train departed southward. Onboard that night, Eleanor invited Lorena into her private drawing compartment. They talked. They shared life stories.[79] Eleanor revealed that she had been advised to open up to Hick by her personal secretary Malvina "Tommy" Thompson. "She's very fond of you," Eleanor explained, "and Tommy is a good judge of people. So I decided you must be all right. It was hard for me at first. I was brought up by a very strict grandmother, who thought no lady should ever have stories written about her, except in the society columns. To be frank with you, I don't like being interviewed. And that applied especially to you. For Franklin used to tease me about you. He'd say: You'd better watch out for that Hickok woman. She's smart. He wasn't criticizing you in any way he likes you. He was only teasing me."

At which point Eleanor, in the midst of her husband's still-unresolved presidential campaign, revealed to this reporter the details of her quite forlorn childhood, hiding little, narrating tales of her father's unseemly death, of an orphan farmed off to unloving relatives, and of a self-confessed "ugly duckling's" insecurities.

"May I write some of that?" Hickok asked nervously.

"If you like," Eleanor Roosevelt answered, "I trust you."[80]

And, indeed, she did.

CHAPTER TWENTY-THREE

"I saw Hitler cigarettes"

Eleanor and Lorena's bond would soon blossom.

The bloom had already vanished from the Hitler-Papen relationship's thorny, wilted rose.

It had never been much of a bloom anyway, a one-way relationship, with Hitler securing new elections and a liberation of the SA—and almost instantly welshing on his promises to support Papen's shaky regime.

Potemba and August 13 finally awakened Papen to those (and other) disturbing facts, and his once soothing words regarding National Socialism curdled into a warning tocsin. At Münster, on Sunday, August 28, he addressed the local Westphalian Association of Farmers and Peasants, blasting Hitler's Beuthen death sentence–fueled bellicosity. "No system of law can be regarded as the servant of one class or one party," he warned. "That is the Marxist conception, and it has been adopted by the National Socialists. It runs counter to all German and Christian ideals of law. . . . The contempt for all these principles, shown in the message that the Nazi leader has just sent, is a poor recommendation for his demands to lead the nation. I do not recognize his right to regard the minority that follows his standards as the nation, and the rest of us as vermin. I am determined to obtain respect for the law and put an end to these conditions of civil war and political violence."[1]

Which was almost well and good until he commuted the death sentences five days later.[2]

The Nazis remained on the march. Not long previously, Ira A. Hirschmann, advertising director for New York's Lord & Taylor department store, had visited Germany and found the Papen government to be "purely transitional, the NSDAP within nine months of taking power."

"No matter where I went," proclaimed the Jewish Hirschmann, "even in the fine little communities in inner Bavaria, I saw Hitler cigarettes, Hitler magazines and Hitler uniforms. He is the master of propaganda, and in my opinion nothing can stop his Nazi movement."[3]

In the five-day interregnum separating Papen's fine words at Münster and his commuting of the Beuthen sentences, the new, ever more National Socialist–dominated Reichstag convened. As parliamentary leader of the Reichstag's largest party, the Nazi's largest delegate, Hermann Göring emerged as Reichstagspräsident.[4] Nominated not by fellow National Socialists but by a Zentrum delegate, he had secured a solid 367 votes to the Social Democrat incumbent Paul Löbe's 135 and Communist Ernst Torgler's eighty. The SPD had retained the body's second biggest bloc but indicative of its fading fortunes, found itself excluded from even secondary Reichstag leadership, with that body's three vice-presidencies parceled out among the DNVP, the Zentrum, and the Bavarian Peoples Party (BVP)—all of which had supported Göring.[5]

The honors provided to the two Catholic parties were exceedingly normal given their usual participation in the republic's governance. Yet, they were also highly significant. Weimar's game of political musical chairs had struck up yet another confusing tune, this time with the embittered Heinrich Brüning (he who had banned the SA) now indicating his willingness to "establish contact" with Hitler.[6] In fact, such dialog had already commenced—as Kurt von Schleicher knew all too well. "Have a conference with General Schleicher . . ." Goebbels had already written. "Although he outwardly betrays nothing, he is, in reality, in deadly fear of a possible union of the Leader with the Zentrum. . . . I have the impression that they want to lure us into a trap again."[7] Monday morning, August 29, saw Hitler conferring with Brüning, whom Goebbels found "very humble and inclined to give in."[8] At midday, Hitler, Papen, and Schleicher lunched—and Hitler rejected yet another shopworn offer of a vice-chancellorship.[9] September 1 witnessed a joint NSDAP–Zentrum statement of cooperation against Papen's government.[10] That, however, was about all they could agree on.

Cooperation of all stripes filled the air—even the Nazi-KPD variety. As the new Reichstag convened, its rules mandated it be called to order not by the representative of its largest party nor by the longest-tenured delegate but simply by its oldest: in this case the KPD's feeble but distinctly elderly former Spartacist revolutionary, Klara Zetkin.[11]

Recently arrived from Moscow[12] and hoisted to the presiding officer's chair by two female associates, "Red Klara" struggled to toll the Reichstagspräsident's heavy brass bell before rasping, "It is a rule of this house that its oldest member shall preside over the opening of the new session. I was born July 5, 1857. Is there any one here older?" Shooting a particularly sharp glance at the sea of brown-shirted Nazis seated before her, she commenced to appoint three temporary aides—one apiece from the KPD, the SPD, and the Zentrum—before settling into a hoarse half-hour tirade against all non-Communist factions. For good measure she demanded Papen's ouster—as well as Hindenburg's impeachment for "violation of the Constitution."

"The world blaze has been started in the Far East [Manchuria]," the white-haired Frau Zetkin charged, "and its ocean of flames will bury Germany beneath horrors and atrocities worse than the work of murder and destruction of the last World War.

"Without consulting the Reichstag political power in Germany has for the moment been grasped by a Presidential Cabinet which is the servant of trust and monopoly capital and of the agrarians and whose only motive force is represented by Reichswehr Generals. In vain does it try to cover up its moral and political guilt through discussions with its allies as to how the power in the State is to be distributed. The blood that has been shed links it eternally with these Fascist murderers."[13]

Invariably, almost instinctively, Nazi delegates hissed and booed any KPD speaker—when they weren't tossing whatever they found nearby at whoever stood, sat, or cowered nearby. Today, however, Hitlerites behaved remarkably silently and respectfully—for, at least, two reasons, neither bearing much relation to propriety, courtesy, or respect for elders. First, on the day previously, Hitler had publicly warned them to display only their best manners ("You will give the German people who look on you an example of boundless discipline").[14] Following his August 13 dressing-down ("For the future I advise you to show chivalry in political struggles"), he remained at pains to demonstrate that Hitlerites were indeed fit to govern. Beyond that, his National Socialists would soon require cooperation from their Red adversaries.

Hermann Göring hinted at what was soon to come. "I assert to the German nation," the new reichstagspräsident announced, "that my election . . . has clearly demonstrated that the . . . Reichstag enjoys a large, workable majority and that therefore absolutely no legal state of emergency can be said to exist."[15]

Translation: Franz von Papen was heading for a fall.

How low a reichskanzler descended depended upon how high Kurt von Schleicher ascended—and Schleicher had grown all too weary of his latest protégé. Papen ("What do you say to that, *Fränzchen* has discovered himself!"[16]) was simply too independent. Worse, he enjoyed too great a popularity with The Old Gentleman, a clear stumbling-block to whatever devil's bargain Schleicher wished to strike with the National Socialists. "[B]oth Hindenburg and his son Oskar," noted Sir John Wheeler-Bennett, "were completely under the spell of von Papen's charm, and the President was determined to keep him at all costs. Von Schleicher's decoy duck had turned out to be a cuckoo and had supplanted him in the affections of the Hindenburgs, *père et fil*."[17]

And, most of all, Papen's popularity with the presidential clique was exceeded only—though it was exceeded mightily—by his unpopularity with the German people.

It was not that he hadn't tried. For a patently unqualified aristocratic front-man who spent weekends not at his desk but at the racetrack, *Fränz-chen* had proven remarkably energetic. Konrad Heiden surprisingly found him for "all his faults, a man of courage."[18] He had, after all, delivered on reparations. He had squashed Prussia. He had caused Nazi murderers to be condemned to death—and, then, caused Nazi murderers *not* to die at all. He had allowed Nazis to again don brown shirts. On the economic front, he proved similarly active, increasing unemployment insurance taxes and slashing benefits by 23 percent.[19] As the new Reichstag organized, he proposed tax credits for business, allowing employers engaging new employees to lower their staff's overall wages, even in contravention of existing contracts. The latter move endeared him, if it were possible, even less to the left.[20]

And so, Schleicher endeavored to jettison Papen, for as Wheeler-Bennett would later write of the general, "there was no vestige of loyalty or innate decency in him . . . friendship with von Schleicher was the Kiss of Death."[21]

Everyone seemed to be gunning for Papen. The Reichstag did not reconvene for actual business until Monday, September 12, 1932, when the KPD's Ernst Torgler introduced a no-confidence vote against Papen's Cabinet. Papen fretted not. It was all a stunt. Torgler had failed to place his motion on the official agenda. A single delegate's objection could block it. Beyond that, Papen possessed a presidential decree dissolving the nascent Reichstag. If by some longshot he needed to use it, he would—that is *if* he had it with him. Papen being Papen, however, he didn't. It sat, instead, peacefully upon his Reichskanzlei desk.

Which was unfortunate.

For, despite Nationalist promises to block Torgler's motion, they did *nothing*. They did nothing, and not a solitary delegate from *any* party bothered defending Papen.[22] Had Hermann Göring (woefully inexperienced in chairing much of anything), however, not been Hermann Göring, Torgler's motion would have sailed through with Papen meekly witnessing his own demise. Estimates of Göring's competence fluctuated from grossly inept to merely absurd. The *Manchester Guardian*'s R. T. Clark observed that "the stupidest trade union secretary on the Socialist benches could have bettered

Goering at conducting a meeting properly."[23] The French leftist Daniel Guérin, observing events from the gallery, thought him "a kind of large, beardless doll with a disturbing jaw—half executioner, half clown."[24]

And so, caught flat-footed by the Nationalists' failure to act, Reichstagspräsident Göring dithered, wasting time clearing everything with Hitler back at the Kaiserhof—who ordered the game to proceed. Provided with a half-hour's reprieve,[25] Papen had scrambled to retrieve the precious red leather portfolio containing Hindenburg's dissolution order, racing back to the Göring's Reichstag podium decree in hand. Göring, nonchalantly ignoring him, called the vote. Twice Papen ("pretentious, disagreeable, and very pale"[26] in Daniel Guérin's estimation) failed to garner the studiously inattentive Göring's notice. So too did Papen state secretary Erwin Planck. Torgler's motion sailed through 513–42, with only the suddenly-more-alert DNVP and the tiny center-right German People's Party (DVP) opposed. Only then did Göring recognize Papen but merely to rule him out of order since his government had already been voted out of office. Papen and his ministers, humiliated in unprecedented fashion, trooped furiously from the chamber. Hugenberg's Nationalists followed. Goebbels (Guérin: "a tiny, awkward monkey"[27]) sprang toward the dais, forcefully instructing the hapless Göring on what should now transpire, which, with precious little more damage left to inflict, was to simply adjourn the whole mess.[28]

It was a swollen, throbbing, black eye not merely for Papen, but for everyone—for the Reichstag itself, for the Nazis and the Communists, for authoritarianism and for parliamentary democracy. The German People's Party's organ, *Deutsche Allgemeine Zeitung*, observed, "The bridges have been destroyed. The dictatorship is reigning. In such a situation what are the use of new elections which are able to promote radicalization and check economic recovery?"[29] Franz Seldte's Stahlhelm conversely concluded that dictatorship was not a bad thing at all, particularly in view of this Marx Brothers–style Reichstag session. "The past 14 years," the Stahlhelm announced, "have proved that an independent, responsible government cannot be obtained with elections. Therefore, away with effete parliamentarianism! We demand that this government march forward and act, not talk. In this way it will gain the confidence of the whole nation."[30]

National Socialists bravely asserted that they looked forward to the coming campaign (The *Völkischer Beobachter*: "The conflict between the clique and the nation has come to a head"[31]). In reality many of them feared the path before them. Perhaps their ever-escalating vote totals had reached their zenith, perhaps the Reich had wearied of its electoral treadmill and would pin the blame for yet another pointless round of balloting on the Hitlerites—who finally did possess some responsibility for what transpired within the government (at least, its legislative component) and who had now fundamentally failed to improve anything. Beyond that, Papen had forged new friendships with his pro-business program; he had reached out to allies both new and old to discourage any continued funding for the NSDAP.[32] "[T]he Party exchequer is empty," Goebbels once more confessed. "The past elections have used up all the money at our disposal. . . . Now we are in for elections again! One sometimes feels this sort of thing is going on for ever. Through too much public speaking one becomes absolutely stupid; only now and then can one lash oneself up once more to make a respectable effort. Our adversaries count on our losing morale, and getting fagged out."[33]

Fagged out they were. Discord erupted—even infesting the party's elite Schutzstaffel (SS). Braunschweig's SS *Abschnitt* (Section) IV confessed to headquarters that the "dissolution of the Reichstag and the resultant delay in the seizure of power initially caused the SS to be somewhat depressed."[34] Schutzstaffel Gruppe South similarly reported that "our movement's failure to take power . . . has produced a certain amount of depression and insecurity."[35]

Endeavoring to provide Papen with badly needed breathing space, Hindenburg declared a state of emergency and refused to authorize new Reichstag elections within the sixty-day window mandated constitutionally. Soon, however, he retreated and grudgingly fixed their date for Sunday, November 6—two days before Americans trooped to their own polls.

With no further parliamentary fiascos to tend, Germany's leaders hectically traversed the political and geographic landscape. Having frightened the Nationalist Right with his Potemba/Beuthen ravings, Hitler now scrambled to reassure them. At Fritz Thyssen's home, he conferred with Thyssen's fellow industrialists, assuring all present that he was "peacemaker to the monarchy."[36] As if in lockstep, Göring sojourned to Doorn, Holland, to spend a week with the exiled Kaiser, disingenuously assuring him of a Hohenzollern restoration. Restoration or not, the Kaiser had his doubts about Hitler's corpulent paladin. A visit that May had seen Göring acting boorishly, spouting Nazi clap-trap, and even defiling the imperial presence by appearing in plus-fours. Wilhelm could barely contain himself. Had not his pro-Nazi wife intervened he might have exploded.[37]

Göring's buffoonery merely exacerbated Wilhelm II's growing unease over the Nazi movement. Impatient storm troopers weren't the only ones disturbed by Hitler's lack of action following August 13. The exiled Kaiser also thought that Hitler should have risen up in armed rebellion—not, however, to install a Nazi dictatorship but rather to install *him*. Now, the sight of Nazi cooperation with a KPD censure of Papen enraged him. Göring's Reichstag actions, Wilhelm II fulminated to the Crown Prince, were "first unworthy, second laughable, third absolutely *revolutionary*." [38]

The Kaiser did not utter the following conclusions regarding Göring's Führer until 1939, but most likely he had inched nearer and nearer to them by fall 1932:

> *There's a man alone, without family, without children, without God. Why should he be human? Oh, without a doubt, he's sincere: but this very sincerity keeps him apart, out of touch, with men and realities . . . He builds legions but he doesn't build a nation. A nation is created by families, a religion, traditions: it is made up out of the hearts of mothers, the wisdom of fathers, the joy and exuberance of children . . . Over there [in Germany] an all-swallowing State, disdainful of human dignities and the ancient structure of our race, sets itself up in place of everything else. And the man who, alone, incorporates in himself this whole State, has neither a god to honor nor a dynasty to conserve nor a past to consult . . .* [39]

Yes, by September 1932 the Kaiser, a slow learner, but faster than some, would finally (albeit understatedly) deduce that Hitler was, indeed, "no statesman." [40]

Neither was Göring—but he busied himself on many fronts. He contracted to compose an article for the Hearst press. [41] He sued Papen for libel for contending that his illegal actions of September 13 were . . . well . . . illegal [42]—and he conducted an interview with a very mysterious American by the name of John Franklin Carter Jr. To Carter Göring boldly asserted that he stood as a guardian, not a destroyer, of the Reichstag. "Those who are attempting to overthrow the Reichstag," he alleged, "are today only a clique of the antiquated." [43]

Interesting as Göring's comments are in their own perverse way, of far more interest was young Mr. Carter. Eventually, he would emerge as a New Deal official (and FDR's personal, if often erratic, spymaster), a confidant of Rexford Tugwell and Henry Wallace, a nationally syndicated (and quite liberal) newspaper columnist, an NBC radio commentator, a Thomas E. Dewey and Nelson Rockefeller speechwriter, and finally at life's end a staunch anti-Communist activist. [44]

He certainly got around.

But as varied as Mr. Carter's résumé proved to be in later years, it was, already in 1932, not only eclectic but incredibly convoluted. A veteran of the *New York Times*'s book review department, until recently he had served Coolidge and Hoover's State Department in both Rome and Istanbul. [45] More recently Clare Boothe Brokaw had importuned him to assist forming her ephemeral "New American Party." Carter had thus penned an article for *Vanity Fair*, properly entitled "Wanted: A New Party,"[46] promising "A new party for a new deal."[47]

Startlingly, however, in reporting his interview with Göring, the *New York Times* described Carter as the "chairman of an organizing committee for a New national party that is to introduce Hitlerism in the United States," and quoted Carter as saying that the point of the article was to dispel "the widely held idea that Hitler's objectives imply an immoderate German foreign policy should the Nazis assume control of the Reich government."[48]

What that meant one can only guess. Soon Carter denied to New York City's *Jewish Daily Bulletin* that his New Party was in any sense Hitlerite ("That intimation can well be thrown into the waste basket"), which might have settled the issue. Instead, he babbled on that "Ours is a progressive party, appealing mainly to the small community. It is meant to supplant the Socialist Party whose failure I attribute to both its name and personnel. By personnel I mean the predominance of Jewish, German and other foreign elements."[49] For good measure Carter confided the news that "the [Nazi] chieftain [Hitler] is moderating his anti-Semitic zeal."[50]

But if the circumstances of Carter's Berlin visit were not convoluted enough, consider this: Carter, having penned a profile of FDR for *Liberty Magazine*, had in January 1932 rated an invitation to Hyde Park.[51] FDR entrusted his new friend Carter ("You're going to be elected President"[52]) with a special mission—to deliver a very private message to Hitler's foreign press secretary Putzi Hanfstaengl.

FDR and Hanfstaengl shared a connection or two. So did Carter and Hanfstaengl. Carter's father had known Putzi's maternal relation, *Atlantic Monthly* editor Ellery Sedgwick (Colonel House's guest at Beverly). Further, Ellery's father had pastored an Episcopal parish at Williamstown, Massachusetts, immediately preceding Carter's father's tenure there.[53] Now, Hanfstaengl would assist Carter in securing his plum Göring interview. In return, Carter presently delivered FDR's message to old Harvard Club chum Putzi. By now, even Hanfstaengl (already the veteran of one lengthy mid-20s breach with Hitler) had grown increasingly anxious regarding Hitler's attitudes—both domestically and in regard to the United States, for Hitler had always underestimated American power. Now, fixated on Al Capone–style gangsterism and Jimmy Walker–style corruption, Hitler concluded, "Any country which cannot even master its own internal police problems cannot hope to play a part in foreign affairs."[54]

John Franklin Carter explained to Putzi FDR's cognizance of Hitler's growing importance, indeed, his inevitability. Roosevelt, Carter continued, hoped that Hanfstaengl might work to temper his Führer's wilder streaks. "Think of your piano playing and try and use the soft pedal if things get too loud," Carter quoted FDR. "If things start getting awkward, please get in touch with our ambassador at once."[55]

And as FDR's thoughts had turned backward to an old acquaintance, so did Adolf Hitler's, although in his case the acquaintance was of far nearer duration and much deeper sentiment. And that is why on Monday, September 19, 1932, with the Reichstag in disarray, his party flat broke, and his SS men depressed, he departed Germany, traveling to Vienna to secretly visit his niece Geli Raubal's grave.[56]

For even Adolf Hitler might, in his own way, be moved by very human sentiments of the heart.

CHAPTER TWENTY-FOUR

"Vote for Roosevelt and make it unanimous"

HERBERT HOOVER SEEMED ONLY MARGINALLY LESS DEAD THAN GELI Raubal.

Though if he was not deceased, everything else that might go wrong had gone wrong for him—which could hardly be said of his opponent. The Roosevelt luck held. Returning from his West Coast campaign swing he sojourned at Chicago, not merely to throw out the first ball of that year's Cubs-Yankees World Series, but to witness Babe Ruth's famed "called shot."[1] From Chicago, he invaded Detroit, Father Coughlin's home turf, where perhaps by sheerest coincidence, he delivered an address on "Social Justice" (a favorite Coughlin phrase), even quoting from the late Pope Leo XIII's encyclical on the subject[2]—"just as radical as I am"[3] he now proclaimed.

He returned home, and with the Walker matter finally resolved, and the winds of Maine's early election at his back, displayed his usual easy grace. Prior to his Chicago arrival, Franklin had visited the University of Wisconsin, planning to speak on the most mundane of matters—dairy farming and inland waterways. His advisers bluntly informed him that the topics were "dull."

"Very well, we'll do one on the university," FDR responded.

"If he can only hold tight to that modesty and honesty when he gets to be President," Raymond Moley thought, "if he can only keep free of false pride and listen to unselfish advice, he will be a very great man."[4]

Americans no longer believed The Great Engineer was a great man. The *Literary Digest* tallied more numbers, revealing significant Hoover slippage—a 28 percent drop in support from 1928.[5] That same day, Jim Farley trumpeted results from Emil Hurja's tabulation of 367 different straw polls: FDR, 626,331; Hoover, 385,464. Farley confidently predicted a ten-million-vote "sweep"[6] A week later, the *Literary Digest* reported that Hoover's 1928 support had declined by 32 percent.[7]

Hoover changed strategy. For the first time in his presidency he allowed himself to be photographed with blacks,[8] meeting with two hundred African-American leaders on the White House lawn.[9] He rolled out of Washington to campaign, though he remained terrified of assassination.[10] His Secret Service detail remained equally "jumpy."[11] "[W]e of the Detail were panic stricken,"[12] admitted the Secret Service's Col. Edmund Starling.

Hoover, nonetheless, rumbled along, gaining some confidence—until Detroit. "The city was in an ugly mood, and it was a four-mile run from the railroad station to the Olympic arena, where the President was to speak," recalled Starling. "I chose a route with as many wide streets and as few sharp turns as possible. I had every building along the line checked. I had plain-clothesmen at all points I considered dangerous."[13]

There was enough hostility in Detroit to start with. The presence of the Workers Ex-Servicemen's League only aggravated it. "Hoover Murdered the Bonus Marchers,"[14] read one of their banners. Longtime agent Starling had never previously seen a president jeered. Michiganders jeered Hoover—and loudly. Hoover press secretary Ted Joslin described "tumultuous booing and catcalling."[15] When police confronted the offenders, thousands literally thumbed their noses at the chief executive.[16]

In retrospect, such animus was hardly surprising. It was, in fact, inevitable and overdue. And as Detroiters booed Hoover, others now surprisingly (or, again perhaps not so surprisingly) hailed Franklin Roosevelt. "I shall vote cheerfully for Governor Roosevelt," Walter Lippmann blithely announced in early October. "That this means voting also for Mr. Garner does not add to my pleasure but I can endure it when I think of Mr. Curtis."[17]

A day later, from decidedly less elevated precincts, Khaki Shirts leader Art J. Smith proclaimed his nascent movement's preferences. Headlined the *Washington Post*: "America's Hitler Marshals Army to Demand New Deal Art J. Smith, National Commander of Khaki Shirts and Veteran of B.E.F., Says His Outfit Will Defeat Hoover."[18]

Lippmann and Art Smith were one thing (well, actually two). Al Smith remained quite another. The Unhappy Warrior's lingering bitterness threatened to dislodge significant numbers of eastern urban voters, particularly Massachusetts voters, from the Roosevelt column. Early *Literary Digest* polling had shown Hoover easily carrying Boston.[19] Rhode Island, also for Smith in 1928, exhibited similar wobbliness.[20] Pollster Emil Hurja privately warned Jim Farley of substantial Catholic Democratic defection from FDR: 6 to 8 percent in the Midwest, as much as 15 percent in the Northeast.[21] *The Nation* theorized "Massachusetts Drifts to Hoover."[22] The *New York Times* head-lined, "BAY STATE DOUBTFUL ON RESULT OF VOTING: Present Indications Point to Slight Advantage for President Hoover."[23]

The showdown occurred at Albany. Franklin Roosevelt desired his lieutenant governor Herbert Lehman to succeed him. Tammany possessed other ideas, wanting no part of anything Franklin Roosevelt wanted and plotting on jettisoning Lehman in favor of the Prussian-born liberal US senator Robert F. Wagner. Smith, a longtime Lehman admirer, threatened to run for mayor of New York if the Hall blocked his old friend Lehman.

"On what ticket?" Tammany's boss John F. Curry demanded.

"On a Chinese laundry ticket," Smith growled, "I can beat you and your crowd."[24]

At the state Democratic convention, Smith and Roosevelt, united, at least, for Lehman, finally came face-to-face. "Hello, Frank, I'm glad to see you," Smith greeted his old friend and protégé.

"Hello, Al," FDR responded, "I'm glad to see you too—and that's from the heart."

That was pretty much it, but it was enough. The United Press claimed that Smith had chortled, "Hello, you old potato."[25] He hadn't, but the make-believe "old potato" expression captured the public imagination and helped paper over a hitherto irreconcilable breech.

With so many horses now in his stable, FDR remained undecided about which ideological mount to whip across the finish line. Would his campaign's final lap feature the progressive themes of the "Forgotten Man" or the "collectivist" theme of his Oglethorpe or Commonwealth Club orations? Or would it highlight the budget-balancing, cost-cutting pronouncements of his actual platform? With capitalists like Joe Kennedy, Bernard Baruch, and Owen D. Young now pledging their support—and with millions of voters still wary of him—FDR tacked sharply starboard. At Pittsburgh's Forbes Field, he delivered an evening peroration on the budget and the deficit not merely to the right of his previous pronouncements but right of Hoover—and arguably even Coolidge. "[The tax] burden is a brake on any return to normal business activity," he proclaimed. "Taxes are paid in the sweat of every man who labors because they are a burden on production and can be paid only by production. If excessive, they are reflected in idle factories, tax-sold farms, and hence in hordes of the hungry tramping the streets and seeking jobs in vain. Our workers may never see a tax bill, but they pay in deductions from wages, in increased cost of what they buy, or (as now) in broad cessation of employment. There is not an unemployed man—there is not a struggling farmer—whose interest in this subject is not direct and vital."[26]

Four years later, having jettisoned just about everything that speech contained save an occasional "the" and "but," he queried Sam Rosenman how best to reconcile it with his subsequent, actual governance. Rosenman thought awhile (or perhaps not even that long) before cavalierly advising FDR that his only option was to dismiss it as "a giant misprint."[27]

That same trip also saw dissembling on the tariff. "I have never advocated," he informed ten thousand at the Wheeling, West Virginia, fairgrounds, "and I will never advocate a tariff policy which will withdraw protection from American workers against those countries which employ cheap labor, or who operate under a standard of living which is lower than that of our own great laboring people."[28] This, exclaimed a startled *Nation*, "is the doctrine of McKinley, of Lodge, of Smoot and Hawley, and all the rest. There is nothing Democratic about it."[29]

The issue of the Bonus would not go away, neither for Hoover nor for Roosevelt (the latter goaded on the subject by everyone from Calvin Coolidge[30] to Walter W. Waters[31]). Just prior to disconcerting pundits with his thoughts on the budget and the tariff, Franklin released a letter on the issue he had dispatched to Hartford veteran Dominick J. De Lucco (a future Democratic mayor). Again, he rang the tocsin of fiscal conservatism, prefacing his remarks with the dubious assertion that "we can cut down federal expenditures from 20 percent to 25 percent by the elimination of unnecessary offices and overlapping functions of government," and concluding with the dodgy judgment that he would not "consider" paying a bonus until a surplus existed in the Treasury.[32] He revisited the latter topic in Pittsburgh, and Felix Frankfurter (perhaps his most obsequious flatterer *ever*) wired him: "BONUS TREATMENT COULD NOT HAVE BEEN BETTER DONE."[33] *The Nation* ("If this is 'taking a stand,' heaven help us"[34]) remained dubious. Such equivocations inspired Hoover to a rare lively turn of phrase. Roosevelt's policy statements, he seethed, resemble "the dreadful position of the chameleon on the Scotch plaid."[35]

The Bonus was an irksome itch Roosevelt could not quite scratch; it was outright leprosy for Hoover. Dollars and cents for FDR, it was bayonets and burning shacks for The Great Engineer. His attorney general, William D. Mitchell, produced statistics demonstrating that the B. E. F. "brought into the City of Washington the largest aggregation of criminals that had ever been assembled in the city at one time"[36]—that of 4,723 Bonus Marchers fingerprinted in anticipation of their government-funded return home 1,069 (22.6 percent) had criminal records.[37] Few paid attention. Fewer believed. The once anti-Bonus American Legion now overwhelmingly endorsed immediate payment.[38] General Glassford continued sparring with the administration, charging that he had had the situation in control ("in this policy I had taken a leaf from the book of Mr. Herbert Hoover in the humanitarian relief work he accomplished in Belgium and Russia") until "the satellites of an intolerant and shortsighted administration saw fit to repudiate everything that had been done and to take matters into their own hands."[39]

As balloting drew near, Hoover addressed fifteen thousand supporters at St. Paul's Municipal Auditorium. Beset by protesters, frustrated and exhausted, Hoover literally wobbled on the platform, his vision blurred, his breath labored. "The President was 'out on his feet,' . . ." recalled Ted Joslin. "He spoke haltingly and without emphasis. . . . He lost his place in the manuscript again and again. . . . A man sat directly behind him gripping an empty chair throughout the time he was speaking, so that, if he should collapse, the chair could be pushed under him and he would not fall to the platform."[40] At one point, he quoted with some derision a Democratic partisan who had warned of rioting if he somehow won re-election. Here, The Great Engineer veered from his prepared text. "Thank God," he snapped, "we still have some officials in Washington that can hold out against a mob."[41] His remark triggered memories of tear gas and of tanks advancing upon ragged veterans. His Republican audience gasped. How voters listening on the NBC and CBS radio networks reacted can only be surmised. "Why don't they make him quit?" a Republican official angrily demanded of the Secret Service's Colonel Starling. "He's not doing himself or the party any good. It's turning into a farce."[42]

Yet, Hoover did occasionally deliver a few good licks. At Madison Square Garden, a crowd of twenty-two thousand (thirty thousand more heard him on the streets outside) provided him with a sixteen-minute standing ovation,[43] and he responded by warning that should Democrats assume office "grass will grow in a hundred cities . . . the weeds will overrun the fields of millions of farms . . . churches and school houses will decay."[44] At Indianapolis, he hammered FDR for his speculation in Weimar securities.[45] In Detroit, with Henry Ford at his side,[46] he informed twenty-two thousand supporters of FDR's ill-considered private promise "to provide employment for all surplus labor and at all times."[47] Charles Lindbergh, his 1927 "Lone Eagle" triumph having turned to the ashes of his son's fatal March 1932 kidnapping, wired Hoover: "Your single purpose of devotion to the American people deserves every support."[48] But such moments were exceedingly rare. Cynics pointed out that cities, farms, churches, and schoolhouses were already on the skids. Heckling delayed the beginning of his New York City talk.[49]

At Des Moines, locals attacked a caravan of four hundred Missourians in town for Hoover's visit, ripping apart their banners. Two thousand

Iowans (lame-duck "dry" Republican senator Smith Wildman Brookhart among them) caravanned with their own banners, including ones reading, "In Hoover we trusted; now we are busted," and "The Republican 4-H Club: Hoover, [Agriculture Secretary] Hyde, Hell, and Hard Times."[50]

At Des Moines's squat, tan-brick Coliseum, Hoover delivered a seventy-one-page speech ("Bad as our prices are . . .") to a packed house—of Republican postmasters. Few patronage appointees dared show on city streets as their candidate processed through town, at one point passing under a huge, eerily disturbing portrait of himself festooned across Locust Street. "As the glum and grim looking [Hoover] rode . . . in the parade," noted a Des Moines observer, "these same farmers [who supported him in 1928] favored him with boos and hisses from cars and trucks parked in alleys and frightened [secret] service men trotted beside his automobile, glancing wildly at windows and rooftops. Their passenger sat staring straight ahead, paying not the slightest heed to what he saw or heard."[51]

"Mr. Hoover's speech at Des Moines," sniped Sen. George Norris from next-door Nebraska, could be "boiled down and summed up in one sentence: 'It might be worse,' and taking into consideration the remote possibility of his re-election, I am inclined to agree with him."[52]

Kansans pelted Hoover's campaign train with rotting produce. He turned to his snow-white-tressed wife, Lou, to mourn, "I can't go on with it anymore."[53] To chief of staff Larry Richey, he soon confessed, "I'll tell you what our trouble is—we are opposed by six million unemployed, ten thousand bonus marchers, and ten-cent corn. Is it any wonder that the prospects are dark?"[54]

Back in Detroit Henry Ford posted this notice in his plants: "We are convinced that any break in Hoover's program would hurt industry and employment. To prevent times from getting worse and to help them to get better, President Hoover must be re-elected."[55] His employees weren't buying it, confessing to Franklin Roosevelt's young Hohenzollern friend, Prince Louis Ferdinand, that they "wore the Hoover button but voted for FDR."[56]

Hoover campaigned. So, unfortunately, did Charles Curtis. In 1928, in Iowa, the feisty vice-presidential candidate had shouted that the average voter was "too damn dumb" to appreciate his boss's efforts.[57] In October 1932, angry Iowans posted a banner retorting, "Mr. Curtis: We are not so damned dumb in 1932—Signed Mr. & Mrs. Iowa Farmer."[58]

At Layton, Utah, later that month, a gawking sixty-seven-year-old female motorist crashed into Curtis's limousine, injuring his right arm and shoulder.[59] Ten days earlier, he had similarly escaped serious injury.[60] Las Vegas residents should have appreciated the administration's public works efforts at nearby Boulder Dam. They clearly did not. "Why didn't you feed those ex-soldiers in Washington?" a local heckler demanded of Curtis. "I've fed more than you have, you dirty cowards! I'm not afraid of you!" the veep retorted. "Hurrah for Roosevelt!" chanted the crowd.[61]

The *Literary Digest* gathered still more straw ballots—Hoover by now had forfeited 36 percent of his 1928 totals. *Digest* internal numbers showed him winning Massachusetts but losing traditionally Republican Pennsylvania. It warned readers not to believe its numbers on Massachusetts.[62] Hearst polling showed Hoover swamped three-to-two (1,473,445–973,357), carrying only Maine, Vermont, New Hampshire, Rhode Island, Connecticut, and New Jersey.[63] FDR, like Farley, personally calculated a ten-million-vote triumph; Adolf Berle (perhaps a better speechwriter than either a prophet or a mathematician) projected a dizzying twenty-five million.[64] Hoover did, however, carry some straw polls—and handily. At FDR's alma mater, Groton, he triumphed four-to-one.[65] Princeton undergraduates, graduate students, and faculty leaned to Hoover. Among both graduate students and faculty, FDR ran behind Norman Thomas.[66] In a poll of students at forty-seven colleges in thirty-one states, Hoover crushed FDR 29,289–18,212. At the universities of Chicago and Minnesota, Roosevelt finished third behind Hoover and Norman Thomas, who not only drew a respectable 10,470 votes, but carried the University of Pennsylvania, Columbia and New York University.[67] At New York City's Riverside Church, New York Federation of Churches members supported Hoover 177 to three over Roosevelt.[68]

Protestant clergy aside, Hoover had not a prayer. For all intents and purposes his campaign ended not in any great, floodlit, flag-draped hall but in a lonely railroad car deep within the barren Nevada dessert. His plan was to reach Palo Alto, California, and to cast his vote—his first trip home in the four years of his presidency.[69] Advisers proposed he should fly—with none other than the willing Charles Lindbergh in the cockpit. Hoover vetoed that idea. Too much of a stunt, he muttered, too much like Roosevelt at Chicago.[70] So his forlorn train wended its way west, until he reached Elko, Nevada (population: 3,217), there to address a crowd of miners, sheepherders, and ranchers and, more important, deliver one last nationwide campaign address.

US senator Tasker L. Oddie flew in from Reno to greet him. Increasingly nervous regarding his own chances against the previously little-regarded challenger, the former state chief justice, Patrick A. McCarran, Oddie had spent much of the preceding year begging the administration for help. He entreated Hoover to jumpstart construction on Reno's new post office. Hoover refused.[71] He requested Navy aviators to stage a fly-over for the state's "Admission Day" festivities. The Navy said sure—if he paid for the fuel.[72] At Reno, Governor Fred Balzar warned him, "If you meet the President's train, you will be defeated."[73] Oddie flew out to greet the equally desperate Hoover anyway.

Hoover ("I see the handwriting on the wall. It is all over"[74]) greeted Oddie and then largely ignored him, devoting his time to drafting his radio speech. Nevadans confronted particularly hard times. The Silver State's mining revenues had evaporated, generating the nation's highest unemployment rate.[75] Its banking system had just collapsed, and Balzar's administration declared the nation's first "voluntary" bank holiday.[76] Elkoites, nonetheless, retained their sense of hospitality, mulling whether to present the Hoovers with mere flowers or a bouquet of sagebrush festooned with silver and blue ribbons. They also hoped to provide him with a twenty-one-gun salute but instead discovered that not only did Nevada not possess twenty-one cannons, it didn't possess any—nor any shells. What they had, however, was dynamite. Lots of it. Stringing together twenty-one sticks of the stuff, they exploded them one-by-one.[77]

Dynamite aside, Hoover still thought this was the most depressing trip he had endured since Warren Harding's transcontinental funeral.

The GOP booked two hours of national air time for the night, though Hoover would personally utilize only part of it. Calvin Coolidge and other more voluble dignities spoke for an hour-and-a-half. News photographers requested permission to snap Hoover as he spoke. He barred their entrance.[78] In New York City, the Republican left hand knew not its right, simultaneously booking both gubernatorial candidate Col. William J. "Wild Bill" Donovan on WOR and the substantially less wild Upper East Side congresswoman Ruth Baker Pratt on WMCA to compete with the beginning of their own national broadcast.[79]

Others besides Hoover's admirers possessed dynamite. Near Palisade, Nevada, two men ("one of whom, appeared to be a negro") fired on Paul E. Fish, safeguarding the Hoover train's route. A fight ensued. Fish's attackers fled, leaving behind two sticks of explosives evidently designed to derail or blow up the presidential locomotive. Authorities discovered twenty more nearby.[80]

Yet, Hoover was not out of the woods—or the sagebrush—yet. In Carlin, Nevada's cold mountain air, a man in the crowd shouted "Oh, Raspberries!"

"If that gentleman has an insult to deliver to the president of the United States," Hoover testily retorted, "if he will come up here I will take care of him."[81] At Sacramento, Hoover finally received his twenty-one-gun salute but faced old rumors that he refused to employ white labor ("No white men wanted") at his ranch. He denied anti-white discrimination. He denied even owning a ranch.[82] Oaklanders jeered him. Stink bombs exploded on San Francisco's Market Street.[83] Finally, he reached Palo Alto, and former interior secretary, Dr. Hubert Work, muttered into an open microphone, "Where the hell are we?"[84] Hoover opened a telegram bearing Ted Joslin's encouragements.[85] He opened another, and it read, "Vote for Roosevelt and make it unanimous."[86] Some thought he resembled a "walking corpse."[87]

Emil Hurja gleefully informed Jim Farley that the GOP "is going to sink to the lowest state that it has experienced since the Civil War. . . . we shall see a revolution at the ballot box."[88] But he also warned of Catholic defections from the Roosevelt juggernaut.

Al Smith was not quite as fond of "old potato" Roosevelt as he pretended to be, and, as a matter of fact, he scarcely bothered to pretend much at all. Finally taking the stump for the ticket, he said little about it. Smith speeches were about *Smith*—not FDR. Addressing two thousand at Tammany Hall, he hardly mentioned Roosevelt.[89] To thirty thousand at Newark's 113th Regiment Armory, he waited until his address's very end before even referencing Roosevelt or Garner by name.[90] The *Oregonian* observed that "the title of Al Smith's first address . . . might well be 'What the People Did to Me in 1928.'"[91] The *Christian Century* headlined, "Governor Smith Comes Out for Smith."[92] Said the *Denver Post*, "Al Smith's speech was one of the best that has been made for President Hoover in this campaign. Every bouquet he threw at the Democratic National ticket had a brick in it."[93]

Few tossed posies at Hoover, though the Oyster Bay Roosevelts remained at his side. TR's widow, Edith, introduced him at Madison Square Garden.[94] From Manila, Philippine governor general TR Jr. had earlier written his mother that "I have a distinctly hopeful feeling about November. Franklin is such poor stuff it seems improbable that he should be elected President."[95] Teddy Jr. resisted entreaties to return home and campaign,[96] instead delivering a long-distance Election Eve radio pitch on New York City stations WABC, WEAF, and WJZ for his embattled boss.[97]

Halfway, however, between Manila and the mainland lay Hawaii, where racial tensions had reached the boil—perhaps even more so than stateside. Domestic Communists promoted an autonomous African-American state in the Deep South "black belt."[98] The Scottsboro Boys case wended its way toward the Supreme Court, igniting international protests. The Communist Party–controlled International Labor Defense (ILD) Committee staged rally after rally in their behalf, including one attracting 150,000 workers to

Berlin's Lustgarten.[99] The organization transported Ada Wright, the widowed mother of two of the nine accused, on wide-ranging speaking tours. Careful observers, however, noted that at least eight different "Mother Wrights" simultaneously worked their protest circuit.[100] Injustice may indeed have resided in the verdicts and the (never carried out) death sentences, but, fortunately, there had been no lynch law, no vigilantism. That was not the case in Hawaii, where blonde, blue-eyed, twenty-year-old Mrs. Thalia Fortescue Massie accused five non-whites (two Hawaiians, two Chinese, one mixed Hawaiian-Chinese) of raping her as she walked along Waikiki Beach. Their trial ended in a mistrial (many doubted every aspect of her story, though she was certainly kidnapped and had her jaw broken), and Thalia's husband, Navy lieutenant Thomas H. Massie, assisted by his forty-eight-year-old mother-in-law and two ordinary seamen, Edward J. Lord and Albert O. "Deacon" Jones, abducted one of the defendants, the muscular, dark-skinned Joe Kahahawei. After the twenty-two-year-old Kahahawei allegedly admitted his guilt ("Yes, we done it") and "lunged" at Massie, Jones drew his .32-caliber revolver and shot him dead. The culprits hoped to get away with murder. They could not, however, get away with speeding, and, en route to disposing of Kahahawei, police gave chase and discovered the deceased under canvas in the back of Mrs. Fortescue's Buick.

Seventy-five-year-old Clarence Darrow had been defending the Scottsboro Boys until forced out by the Communist ILD.[101] Defending the upper-crust Massie clan was hardly the radical Darrow's preferred style, but when a $30,000 fee (plus expenses) was put on the table, he sailed for Honolulu anyway to defend the lot of them. His presence (and his four-hour summation—hardly his longest) failed to prevent a largely white jury from finding them guilty. Jurymen recommended leniency. The judge gave each ten years of hard labor. Race riots erupted. Authorities pondered imposing martial law. With local self-rule hanging in the balance, Gov. Lawrence M. Judd (under pressure from Washington) commuted their sentences to a single hour. For sixty minutes, they sat within the confines of his Iolani Palace office—and walked out free and clear.

It was not widely reported, barely reported at all, but Mrs. Massie was the bar-sinister granddaughter of Robert Barnwell Roosevelt, uncle of Theodore, great-uncle to Eleanor.

The Roosevelts, it appeared, were everywhere, in 1932.[102]

～～

Turmoil buffeted Hawaii. Tranquility bathed Hyde Park. True, there was the occasional glitch. Huey Long continued to be an unwanted presence—though his tour in behalf of the ticket proved remarkably effective. Father Coughlin noisily demanded that the price of gold be inflated to $41.34 an ounce.[103] Rumors spread of Democratic shakedowns of prospective federal contractors.[104] In Baltimore, FDR misspoke regarding the political nature of the Supreme Court.[105] But, otherwise, matters proceeded most smoothly. Felix Frankfurter wired FDR to praise his second campaign swing as an "unqualified success. You have probably heard John Davis' remark that it is a wonderful campaign speech that loses no votes. Your speeches held and gained votes."[106] On Monday, October 24, 1932, the United Press's Raymond Clapper reported that FDR was already contemplating his Cabinet appointments and would resign as governor as soon as he defeated Hoover.[107]

Even Al Smith seemed to be coming around, and the two men campaigned together at Boston (where Smith, accompanied by Baruch and Raskob,[108] requested "unqualified full and complete support"[109] for FDR) as well as at the Brooklyn Academy of Music.[110] He even took time to skewer the veteran Republican standpat senator, New Hampshire's George Moses, as "Hackshaw the Detective"[111]—a reference to a then-popular comic strip character. The *New York World-Telegram* reported that FDR was considering creation of a new super-Cabinet post "without portfolio" for his old— and now new—ally.[112] In Albany, Smith pronounced, "If we were a couple of Frenchmen, we'd kiss each other. As it is we have to rely on a handshake."[113]

For as one Gotham wit had pronounced:

In cities, towns and hamlets
The Democrats in joy
Cheered at the potent tidings
And shouted "Attaboy!"

"How are you, old potato?"
From Maine to Frisco,
They knew that Al and Frankie
Were friends—or nearly so![114]

Victory breeds unity. Defeat breeds discord. At Chicago, California's Hiram Johnson blasted Hoover, charging that the incumbent had conducted "our affairs as if there were divine right of big business to exploit all the rest of us."[115] His fellow Republicans Bob La Follette Jr., Bronson Cutting, and Henry Wallace similarly endorsed Roosevelt.[116] *The Nation* proclaimed: "Roosevelt Woos the Progressives: Insurgency Goes Democratic."[117]

At New York's Metropolitan Opera House, the dark horse who never made it into the starting gate, Owen D. Young, proclaimed, "I am not afraid of mobs if

Mr. Hoover is elected, and I am not afraid of markets and business if Mr. Roosevelt is elected. . . . It is time liberal parties came into power to save conservatives from their own destruction, and to save the rest of us who are victims too."[118]

Socialist Norman Thomas thought differently. Before three thousand persons at the packed Brooklyn Academy of Music (he had addressed eight thousand at the half-filled Bronx Coliseum earlier that day), Thomas tackled an issue neither Franklin Roosevelt nor Hoover seemed to notice: the specter rising in Germany. Thomas's analysis and comparisons, however, stood reality on its already dizzy head, pointing to recent developments in Germany as a harbinger of great things for the nation's Socialists and conversely warning of ascendant stateside fascism. "In America the menace of Hitler and Hitlerism is on the horizon," Thomas alerted listeners. "We can stand it off only by fighting it vigorously.[119]

"If you vote Republican you vote for a system of paternalistic capitalism under which the government gets deeper and deeper in business for the sake of saving business. And yet it has not succeeded in saving business and it has shamefully neglected to direct the human needs of the unemployed.

"If you vote Democratic you vote for the same capitalism under slightly different trimming. If anything, the Democratic party is more ramshackle and in sections more corrupt and more stupidly reactionary than the Republicans."[120]

Herbert Hoover headed home. FDR stayed close to home: campaigning furiously at Hudson Valley locales, from Poughkeepsie's Knights of Columbus Hall to Fishkill and North Tarrytown and Wappingers Falls, to Beacon's public square where two decades previously he had delivered his first public campaign speech, to Newburgh, Kingston, and Rhinecliff, speaking from his car at each stop.[121] Marveled a member of his traveling party: "You'd think that he was running for the State Senate and had to carry Dutchess County to win!"[122]

Like Hoover, he delivered one final radio address to voters, again drawing on those Hudson Valley roots. He began:

> *For twenty-two years it has been my custom to end every political campaign with my friends and neighbors of all political parties here in Dutchess County. I began my public service here many years ago. I have learned much of what I know of human life and of political affairs in country and in city from you, my friends. . . .*

He ended:

> *. . . A man comes to wisdom in many years of public life. He knows well that when the light of favor shines upon him, it comes not, of necessity,*

that he himself is important. Favor comes because for a brief moment in the great space of human change and progress some general human purpose finds in him a satisfactory embodiment. To be the means through which the ideal and hopes of the American people may find a greater realization calls for the best in any man; I seek to be only the humble emblem of this restoration. If that be your verdict, my friends of America and my next-door neighbors of Dutchess County, and that be the confident purpose behind your verdict, I shall in the humility that suits such a great confidence seek to meet this great expectation of yours. With your help and your patience and your generous good will we can mend the torn fabric of our common life.

On this very eve of the exercise of the greatest right of the American electorate, I bid you good night. And I add to that, God bless you all.[123]

In between he said not much at all. But he didn't have to.

Forty million Americans voted. Most were still Republicans. The GOP boasted a six-million-voter registration edge. Forty-eight percent of the electorate remained in their camp; just 42 percent Democratic.[124]

Which made no difference. In a great swelling, drowning tide Americans turned Democrats in and Republicans out. Democrats gained twelve Senate and ninety-seven House seats, providing them with an enormous 310–117 advantage in the latter house. Jim Watson, Tasker Oddie, and George Moses forfeited their Senate seats. Famous sponsors of famous bills disappeared as well—Reed Smoot (of Smoot-Hawley),[125] Gilbert Haugen (of the various McNary-Haugen initiatives; in the House since 1898)[126], and even St. Louis's Rep. Leonidas Dyer (of the Dyer anti-lynching bill). Not even the wettest, most progressive Republicans were safe. Fiorello La Guardia[127] and Hiram Bingham lost as well.[128] The Upper East Side's Ruth Baker Pratt, expecting a "larger majority"[129] than ever, flopped badly (one hesitates, but only momentarily, to say by a pratfall).[130]

Exceptions, of course, proved the rule. In Pennsylvania, the vociferously anti-Hoover (and anti-Semitic) Republican Louis McFadden captured 96 percent of the vote. South Side Chicago's Oscar De Priest defeated a white Democrat. In Kansas, the "goat gland doctor" John R. Brinkley merely split the vote and helped propel Alf Landon into the governor's mansion. A standing indictment failed to sink Pennsylvania's muscular, Welsh-born Republican US senator James J. "Puddler Jim" Davis. He defeated Lawrence H. Rupp 49.46 percent–43.18 percent.[131] In Pekin, Illinois, a thirty-six-year-old baker and city council member named Everett McKinley Dirksen first won election to the House. Hoover secured three-quarters of the West Branch vote.

He trounced Roosevelt and Thomas 176–45–17 at his home Stanford precinct.[132] Supposed Republicans (in reality Non-Partisan Leaguers) William Lemke (openly for FDR) and "Wild Bill" Langer won respectively for the House and for governor in North Dakota.[133]

A popular name helps win elections—even if you are not a Roosevelt. Oklahomans elected a Will Rogers (not that one) to the House. New Hampshirites re-elected a William Nathaniel Rogers.

North Carolina's hardline anti-caviar candidate Robert Rice Reynolds triumphed easily.[134] Californians sent William Gibbs McAdoo to the Senate—while still giving the volatile "Fighting Bob" Shuler 25.8 percent of their votes. Seattle bandleader Victor Aloysius Meyers, having won his primary for Washington State lieutenant governor, still occasionally campaigned in Gandhi-like garb, but settled down to occasionally discuss real issues. In 1932, his general election victory as a Democrat was not entirely inexplicable. That it marked the first of his *five* terms was.[135]

Leftism had its limits. In East Harlem, rising Communist Party functionary Earl Browder garnered a mere few hundred votes against Fiorello La Guardia and La Guardia's Democrat opponent alderman James J. Lanzetta. Socialist theologian Reinhold Niebuhr fared hardly better for Democrat Sol Bloom's Manhattan seat.

It was not good to be a Republican, worse to be a "dry," worse yet to be a "dry" Republican. Voters evicted ninety-eight "dry" House members and seven "dry" senators.[136] Eleven states conducted various referenda on repeal. "Wet" sentiment proved universal. Connecticut and Louisiana voters endorsed a national referendum on the subject. New Jersey, Louisiana, Washington, Michigan, North Dakota, Washington, Arizona, and Colorado rescinded their own prohibition acts. By huge margins Michigan, California, Oregon, and New Jersey junked enforcement statutes.[137]

People didn't much like the Bonus. But they liked people who voted against the Bonus even less; 42.6 percent of House members and 48.6 percent of senators casting anti-Bonus votes met defeat.[138]

And, it was not good at all to be Herbert Hoover.

He received the first reports, instantly knew the jig was up, wired congratulations to his opponent, bade farewell to all ("Good night, my friends, that's that!"[139]) and went to bed. He slept for twelve hours.[140]

It was, after all, a massacre. He carried but six states, providing FDR with a 472–59 Electoral College landslide. He fared not much better in the popular tally, losing 22,821,277 to 15,761,254 or 57.4 percent to 39.7, a startling mirror image of 1928 when he had walloped Smith 21,427,123 to 15,015,464. Third party candidates fared even worse. All of them combined—the Socialist

Thomas (at 881,781 votes[141]); the Communist Foster (103,307 votes); the crippled former Georgia congressman William D. Upshaw (81,905 votes) running on the Prohibitionist slate; the aged Farmer-Laborite Col. Jacob Coxey (7,431 votes) et al.—recorded just 1,169,367 votes, a piddling 2.9 percent.[142]

"Why was there so little radicalism in the ranks of so many and dissatisfied men?" mused the B. E. F.'s Walter W. Waters. ". . . They were Americans and as such they used one phrase, 'If I only got a break!' There was scarcely a man in the whole B.E.F. who did not believe that if only things 'broke' for him, he would be up at the top, along with the successful Americans who preach optimism in the *Saturday Evening Post* and the *American Magazine*."[143]

Optimism held. Democracy held. Capitalism held. So too had the two-party system. There would be no splintering of parties in America as had eternally plagued the Reichstag, no failure to stitch together a working coalition. Franklin Roosevelt had already done the stitching at Chicago. Herbert Hoover had done it four years before him, etc. etc. etc. The American political system was, indeed, not a bad one at all.

Despite its magnitude, Roosevelt's coalition was, nonetheless, not evenly spread across the map. Hoover retained a surprising popularity in the Northeast. Every state he carried lay in that region. The Midwest swung strongly for FDR; the trans-Mississippi West even more. But it was the white South that truly loved Franklin Roosevelt and now loathed Herbert Hoover. The Great Engineer's totals in usually intractable Dixie Democratic environs were of course abysmal: 14.1 percent in Alabama, 12.7 percent in Arkansas, 7.8 percent in Georgia, 7 percent in Louisiana, 3.5 percent in Mississippi— and a microscopic 1.9 percent in South Carolina. That was awful enough, but the most painful totals came from states he had *carried* just four short years previously: 30.1 percent in Virginia, 29.3 percent in North Carolina, 25 percent in Florida—and 11.2 in Texas.[144]

Southerners loved FDR. So did Jews. Herbert Hoover had appointed Benjamin Cardozo to the Supreme Court and Eugene Meyer first to the Federal Reserve and then to the newly formed Reconstruction Finance Corporation, but that counted for little for a president who bragged of shutting the door on immigration. Jews voted 70 to 80 percent for FDR, the highest percentage of any ethnic group.[145]

Not everyone backed FDR. Three groups held out. The wealthy still tendered their support to Hoover—though there were fewer of them every day. Northeastern rural areas (including Roosevelt's beloved Dutchess County) retained their GOP loyalties. So did African Americans. Hoover had not done much *for* them. Unemployment ran rife in their communities. But they feared what Roosevelt and Garner might do *to* them. True, FDR made inroads, carrying hitherto black Republican districts in Harlem, St. Louis, and Kansas City. But overall, from Chicago to Baltimore, Hoover shakily retained the national black vote.[146]

And, somehow, he managed to carry the city of Philadelphia[147]—as well as September's prodigal, the state of Maine.[148]

Herbert and Lou Hoover voted at the Women's Club House—he had helped with its construction—at Stanford's central social quadrangle.[149] At Springwood, Roosevelt and Missy LeHand ate lunch before voting at Hyde Park's town hall. He was number 716 ("two sevens, two lucky numbers"[150]). Eleanor had not eaten or arrived with them. At midnight, following a rally at Poughkeepsie, she had announced to her husband that she intended to drive to Manhattan for her 9:00 a.m. Todhunter School class. FDR was aghast. Not only was this now Election Day, the roads were windy and slick. At this hour, she might doze dangerously behind the wheel. Finally, he assented but only if Lorena Hickok went with her. Another female reporter asked to join them—Eleanor refused. They reached Manhattan at 2:00 a.m. Eleanor returned to Hyde Park barely in time to pose for the cameras casting her vote with Franklin.[151]

President and Mrs. Coolidge voted fairly early at Northampton, Massachusetts's Ward 4. "Come on," Calvin snapped at Grace, "or they'll keep you here all day."[152] At his Pocono Mountains home, Gifford Pinchot informed reporters that he "voted for the majority of the Republican ticket"—and then went fishing.[153]

But, at least, Coolidge and Pinchot voted. Ninety-three-year-old John D. Rockefeller, fearing that the weather made it too poor for him to trek from his Tarrytown estate to his New York City polling place, stayed home.[154] Ambassador and Mrs. Frederic Sackett traveled from Berlin to Louisville to campaign and vote for Herbert Hoover—only to discover that thanks to Kentucky's new election laws they were no longer registered. Democratic attorneys agreed to waive any objection, but a local circuit judge ruled that the law was the law: the Sacketts simply could not vote.[155]

Prince Louis Ferdinand, of course, could not vote in Detroit. But that hardly dented his pleasure at receiving the returns at the city's Grosse Pointe Yacht Club. A day short of his twenty-fifth birthday he raised his glass in thoroughly Germanic style to celebrate his upcoming natal day—and his friend's election as American president.[156]

Franklin Roosevelt had, of course, finally voted, and after retrieving Sara (she voted at 11:00 a.m.[157]), his entourage stopped first at Fishkill to pick up Mr. and Mrs. Henry Morgenthau and then at North Tarrytown for daughter Anna Dall. At North Tarrytown, Franklin halted at the local firehouse—his traditional Election Day good luck visit. He stopped again at East 65th Street—to eat again.[158] As Roosevelt dined, Sam Rosenman noticed two strangers enter. They did not eat. They merely stood near Franklin—Secret Service men, on duty even before the first polls had closed.[159] From there FDR traveled to Democratic election night headquarters at East 43rd Street's Biltmore Hotel.

Lorena Hickok also visited East 65th Street. As she entered, Eleanor, resplendent in a long white chiffon gown, kissed her, saying, "It's good to have you around tonight, Hick."[160]

At the Biltmore, Howe, Farley, Flynn, Moley, Missy LeHand, Grace Tully, and his skeletal press aide Marvin McIntyre (a veteran of the 1920 campaign) joined Roosevelt in a smoke-filled private room on the hotel's first floor. Two police guarded the entrance. Millicent Hearst—Mrs. William Randolph Hearst—was there too, her erstwhile husband having instructed her to keep an eye on things. He remained in California listening for results with Marion Davies.[161]

At 8:00 a.m., Eleanor, now in white fur (some said ermine; some said mere rabbit) and a light blue dress festooned with a huge spray of orchids and gardenias, arrived, accompanied, as the *New York Sun* observed, by "several members of her family and women friends."[162] She granted a few interviews for the press ("I was reminded of a fox, surrounded by a pack of baying hounds,"[163] reflected Hickok), ducked into FDR's "inner sanctum," ducked back out, and consented to a newsreel interview. Hickok was not allowed entrance, but as she recalled, "every now and then I would catch a glimpse of her. She was smiling and gracious as she greeted people who went in, but now and then, when she was not talking to anyone, her expression was sober, a little sad, I thought."[164]

Franklin remained inside. Sara arrived, hectored by the same photographers ("Mrs. Roosevelt, please look at the board!") who had waylaid Eleanor. Roosevelt *mère* forced a mechanical smile. At seventy-eight, she seemed as somber as her black dress and white pearls, noticeably more dazed than elated.[165]

Howe, chain-smoking and strangely pessimistic ("Losers always have a big spurt at the start"[166]), hid himself over at Democratic headquarters on Madison Avenue. Twenty secretaries tabulated results received via telephone. Franklin scribbled his own totals. The news remained good from just about everywhere, and FDR soon found his once-private lair invaded by jubilant well-wishers. Even Louis Howe, much cheerier now, returned. Reaching into his desk drawer, he pulled out, well . . . something he shouldn't. "I put this sherry away in Albany twenty years ago," he proclaimed, "right after Franklin had won his fight against Tammany Hall. I said then he'd be President someday and I made up my mind never to open this bottle until that time came."[167]

Round midnight, Roosevelt moved to the Biltmore's grand ballroom for his victory speech. "I want to say just a word," he advised the crowd and the nation. "There are two people in the United States more than anybody else who are responsible for this great victory. One is my old friend and associate, Colonel Louis McHenry Howe, and the other is that splendid American, Jim Farley."[168] Dignitaries poured in to extend congratulations: Jack Dempsey, Gene Tunney, John Jakob Raskob, John W. Davis, Owen D. Young, film star Mildred Harris (at sixteen, she had been the first of four Mrs. Charlie Chaplins), Edward G. Robinson—and, brown derby meekly in hand, Al Smith.[169] FDR draped his arm around his shoulder, booming to Raskob, "This is the man who killed Hackshaw the Detective!"[170] It was as good a way as any *not* to thank Al Smith for his final endorsement.

Franklin arrived back at East 65th Street at 1:40 that morning. His mother awaited his return. She embraced her president-elect only child, and reporters heard him say, "This is the greatest night of my life."[171] His biographer, Frank Freidel, would conclude that, "If Roosevelt had any such misgivings [about his triumph], he never voiced them."[172] But that was not so, not so at all. Soon, James would lay him to bed, and father would say to son, "You know, Jimmy, all my life I have been afraid of only one thing—fire. Tonight I think I'm afraid of something else."

"Afraid of what, Pa?"

"I'm just afraid that I may not have the strength to do this job."[173]

CHAPTER TWENTY-FIVE

"A primitive and stupid woman"

FRANKLIN ROOSEVELT POSSESSED REASONABLE DOUBTS ABOUT HIS abilities to assume national power, to reverse a Depression, to salve and save a nation.

After all, who wouldn't?

Adolf Hitler wouldn't.

Not at all.

And why should he? Neither homelessness and penury, nor blindness, nor imprisonment had permanently shattered him.

Neither had his great love's suicide—with his own pistol.

Yes, Geli Raubal's death had *temporarily* shattered Adolf Hitler. It had even by some strange turn of fate caused him to embrace vegetarianism[1] ("the world of the future will be vegetarian!"[2]). But her tragedy and his self-pitying reaction to it ("now this had to happen to *him*"[3]) had not permanently overcome him. And, by no means, did it close his eyes to the allure and the foibles of the fairer sex.

His adventures reminded many of the old joke about the dog not knowing what to do with the car after catching it. Hitler may—or may not—have known what to do with a woman once alone with her, but he certainly maintained his pursuit, craving female company, if not necessarily female passion. "I saw him often," recalled *Münchener Illustrierte* editor Stefan Lorant, "driving down Ludwigstrasse toward Schwabing to pick up girls. With his cronies around him he stood up straight in the open car, his whip in hand as always, like a hunter looking for prey. He was forever on the lookout for girls; his appetite was insatiable."[4] And, yet, Lorant could also not help but notice the man's trademark awkward mix of Viennese charm and provincial reticence. "His treatment of women was deferential, subordinately gallant," added Lorant. "He looked up to them as if they were goddesses."[5]

They often saw him as their god. At rallies, women were the first to collapse under his spell, reduced to hysterics and passing their frenzy on to the men accompanying them. Female admirers dispatched letters to Hitler by the basketful, often quite passionate in nature. Party functionaries ingloriously filed such correspondence under the heading "CRACKERS."[6] Wealthy female patrons showered him with surplus pieces of jewelry, even the occasional house, and, most important, with badly needed funds both for his party and his person.[7] Up close, even hitherto-skeptical women found him not at all as unpleasant as the brown-shirted ranter displayed in newsreels. "I was surprised at how nice-looking he was," recalled the anti-Nazi journalist Gitta Sereny of a 1940 meeting, "he wasn't ugly. . . . He liked to be surrounded by women, he enjoyed chit-chat, and was incredibly charming to those close to him."[8]

—◆—

In mid-June 1932, during his second "Hitler Over Germany" campaign, at Weimar's ornate Schloss Belvedere, Hitler chanced to remark to local gauleiter "Fritz" Sauckel, "See that we have some female companionship at table tonight, Sauckel. All day long I'm surrounded by men, and I'd like to hear women's voices for a change."[9]

Hitler's wish was, indeed, any gauleiter's command, but before a Sauckel-generated gaggle of young women appeared to dine with their Führer, still another attractive female motored past Hitler and his pilot, Hans Baur.

"Look, Baur: there's a lovely woman for you!" Hitler exclaimed, "As pretty as a picture!"

Hitler's odd tone, however, caused his companion to blurt out, "I feel quite sorry for you."

"Why, what do you mean, Baur?"

"I mean," the pilot answered, "that it sounds as though women were something only at a distance for you."

"As a matter of fact, you're right. And I have to keep it that way," Hitler responded. "I'm in the spotlight of publicity, and anything of that sort could be very damaging. Now if *you* were to have a passing affair, no one would bother his head about it, but if I did there'd be the devil to pay. And women can never keep their mouths shut."[10]

Shortly, thereafter, the balding, Hitler-mustachioed Sauckel arrived with a bevy of National Socialist mädchen. Their spellbound attention discomforted Hitler, but not enough to prevent him from inviting them to Weimar's Kunstler Café, where Putzi Hanfstaengl provided his usual keyboard stylings. Tinkling ivories or not, their awestruck manner only intensified—as did Hitler's own angst, driving him to almost cling to Putzi's piano for refuge.

One later confided to Baur that she could never marry as no man might live up to the standards set by her hero. Baur playfully (or cruelly) informed this twenty-two-year-old of Hitler's recent denigrations ("women can never keep their mouths shut") of female discretion. "He said that!" she protested, "Oh, how mistaken he is! Please, please tell him that I could [keep silent regarding an affair with Hitler]. I'd sooner have my tongue cut out than whisper a word."[11]

Hitler's magnetism—and reticence—at Weimar was, of course, par for the course. At Koblenz, that April, the British journalist Sefton Delmer observed not only his hypnotic effect on women—but their effect upon him. Having completed yet another campaign address, they sat privately together at the local train station, Hitler commenting on the possibility of a run on the mark when (*not* "if") he assumed power. His hulking adjutant, Wilhelm Brückner, burst in to announce, "Mein Führer, two girls have run all the way from the stadium. They want desperately to pay homage to you."[12]

Hitler broke off his interview to greet them. "I thought it discreet not to follow him," recalled Delmer. "But though I did not see, I could not help hearing. From the corridor came a series of convulsive sobs, hysterical cries and a slobbering kind of sound as the girls groveled, kissing the Führer's hands and boots. From Hitler I heard not so much as a word. Then he strode back into the compartment. He was extremely moved. On his face was a trance-like expression. Without a glance at me he flung aside the curtain, lowered the window and gazed out at the people on the platform. He gazed at them with his mesmeric stare turning in an arc light, a searchlight from left to right, exposing everyone within sight to the emotion the two girls had inspired in him and which he was now throwing back into the crowd. Then with the men and women on the platform still cheering and clapping, he slowly sat down to resume our conversation. And he resumed it at the exact point he had broken off."[13]

Shop girls and peasant maidens were one thing. Film stars were quite another—or were they?

Already, in the late 1920s and early 1930s, Hitler had embraced the company of glamorous performers, most notably (though still fleetingly), with operetta soprano Margarete "Gretl" Slezak, the bubblingly statuesque blond—but one-quarter Jewish—daughter of star operatic tenor, Leo Slezak.[14] "Please excuse me," Hitler wrote her in schoolboy fan-letter style, "if I, an unknown to you. . . ."[15] Film actress Renate Müller similarly received the Hitler charm treatment.[16]

Another popular entertainer, Leni Riefenstahl, not yet a director, but very much an established star of German cinema, sat among the Sportpalast crowd back in March, enthralled as Hitler unveiled his presidential candidacy. She watched—but did not meet him.

Her celluloid career continued. Late May found her scheduled to shoot a new project in Greenland—the German and English-language versions of yet another outdoor film, the rather forgettable *S.O.S. Eisberg* (*S.O.S. Iceberg*), starring, among others, Hermann Göring's former wartime flying comrade Ernst Udet, the American silent star Rod La Rocque, and "Nakinak—the Eskimo dog." She could not, however, shake Hitler from her mind and on May 18, 1932, took pen in hand to reach him. Ignorant of his actual address, she dispatched her missive simply to party headquarters, Munich. It read:

> *Dear Herr Hitler,*
>
> *Recently I attended a political rally for the first time in my life. You were giving a speech at the Sports Palace and I must confess that I was so impressed by you and by the enthusiasm of the spectators that I would like to meet with you personally. Unfortunately, I have to leave Germany in the next few days in order to make a film in Greenland so a meeting with you prior to my departure will scarcely be possible: nor indeed do I know whether this letter will ever reach you. I would be very glad to receive an answer from you.*
>
> *Cordially,*
>
> *Leni Riefenstahl*[17]

Two days before sailing aboard the British liner *Borodino*—her phone rang. "This is Brückner, adjutant to the Führer," said an unfamiliar voice. "The Führer has read your letter, and has asked me to ask you whether you could possibly come to Wilhelmshaven tomorrow for the day. We would pick you up at the railway station and drive you to Horumsiel, where the Führer is currently staying. . . . You could leave Berlin tomorrow morning and arrive in Wilhelmhaven at 4:00 p.m."

Was this a hoax? "Who is this?" she demanded. "Are you still there?"

"Wilhelm Brückner," he calmly answered. "What shall I tell the Führer?"

Eventually, she realized the call was genuine but also that she was also due to entrain from Berlin tomorrow for Hamburg and Greenland. Her studio expected her to conduct press interviews on that train. Her director, Dr. Arnold Fanck, *definitely* expected her on the *Borodino*. Disregard either engagement and she risked her career.

So, of course, she said, yes—yes to Wilhelm Brückner, yes to Adolf Hitler.

At Wilhemshaven, mufti-clad Brückner piled her into a big, black Mercedes driven by Hitler's chauffeur Julius Schreck. Der Führer's bodyguard Sepp Dietrich and his press aide Dr. Otto Dietrich traveled with them. Brückner explained that just before her letter had reached Hitler, an enormous motion picture devotee, he had coincidentally expounded to Brückner: "The most beautiful thing I have ever seen in a film was Riefenstahl's dance on the sea in [her 1926 silent] *The Holy Mountain*."

They reached Wilhelmshaven's beach. Heinrich Hoffmann jumped at the chance to record this meeting of film star and political messiah. "Don't Hoffmann," Hitler warned, "this could harm Fraulein Riefenstahl."

Der Führer had indeed seen all her films. He praised *The Holy Mountain* but gushed that her most recent title, the alpine-themed *The Blue Light*, counted as his favorite of her efforts. "Once we come to power, you must make my films," he entreated.

"I can't—," Leni protested. "Just two days ago I turned down a very prestigious offer from the Catholic Church on the grounds that I will never make prescribed films. I don't have the knack for it—I have a very personal relationship with my subject matter. Otherwise I can't be creative." It was true. She—a Berlin-born Protestant had received and rejected just such an offer from Köln's anti-Nazi monsignor (later archbishop and cardinal) Josef Frings.

Hitler barely reacted to Riefenstahl's nervous rebuff. "Please do not misunderstand my visit," she continued. "I have no interest whatsoever in politics; I could never be a member of your party."

That jarred Hitler. "I would never force anyone to join my party," he finally answered, "but maybe when you become older and more mature, perhaps you will be able to understand my ideas."

Riefenstahl drew back. "After all, you have racial prejudices," she chided her idol. "If I had been born an Indian or a Jew you wouldn't even speak to me, so how can I work for someone who makes such distinctions among people?"

Hitler brooked no opposition from fellow politicians or later from recalcitrant generals. Toward fellow artists or women, however, he might occasionally display uncharacteristic forbearance. "I wish," he advised Riefenstahl, "the people around me would be as uninhibited as you."

He must, he informed her, speed off to yet another campaign rally. She countered that she too must leave, for dockside at Hamburg. But he had other ideas and importuned her to spend the night with his traveling party at a nearby inn. He could be very persuasive. She stayed.

After dinner, they strolled alone on the beach. He made small talk then suddenly became startlingly serious. "More than anything else I am filled with my political mission," he protested. "I feel that I have been called to save Germany—I cannot and must not refuse this calling."

They walked on. They halted. He placed his arms about her.

She did not respond.

Several years previously, the young "Henny" Hoffmann had refused his advances. She later said it had been a mere kiss. Others alleged a far-less innocent incident.[18] When "Henny" refused, he instantly withdrew, acting as if what had happened had *never* happened. With Riefenstahl, it was the same. Backing away, he raised his arms skyward, wailing in face-saving excuse, "How can I love a woman until I have completed my task?"[19]

Flummoxed, but still dangerously intoxicated by this man, Riefenstahl remained mute. Hitler withdrew into the depths of his own silence.

"Good night," he finally announced.

And that was that.

But if Leni Riefenstahl—or Henriette Hoffmann—did not kiss on the first date, perhaps someone else did . . .

. . . Eva Braun.

Eva Anna Paula Braun was no soprano, no daredevil actress or dancing diva or budding director—not even half a niece.

She toiled as a salesgirl and general assistant at Heinrich Hoffman's studio, *Photohaus Hoffmann*. "She was no great beauty," recalled Hermann Göring, "but [hadn't] a bad figure. She had a sweet personality. . . ."[20] At Hoffmann's, in October 1929, three weeks into her new job, she first met Hitler. It was, to say the least, not a proper introduction.

"I'd stayed on after closing time," Eva confided to her older sister Ilse, "to file some papers and I'd climbed up a ladder to fetch the files kept on the top shelves of the cupboard. At that moment the boss came in accompanied by a man of uncertain age with a funny moustache, a light-colored, English-style overcoat and a big felt hat in his hand. They both sat down on the other side of the room, opposite me. I tried to squint in their direction without appearing to turn round and sensed that this character was looking at my legs . . . That very day I'd shortened my skirt, and I felt slightly embarrassed because I wasn't sure I'd got the hem even."[21]

Hoffmann dispatched Eva to fetch some beer and sausages for "this character."[22] He had not yet bothered disclosing his real identity.

"Do you know that man?" Hoffmann later asked.

"Only that he is a friend of yours."

"I mean, don't you recognize him? His name is not Herr Wolf. That is Adolf Hitler!"

"Who is Adolf Hitler?"[23] Eva Braun responded.

She was clearly *not* into politics.

Nor was she reminiscent of Hitler's current flame, Geli Raubal. "Geli," recalled Henriette Hoffmann, "was opera; Eva was operetta."[24]

Yet, she was blonde (albeit with a suspected "touch of peroxide"[25]) and, in her own way, attractive (Baldur von Schirach considered her "the most beautiful girl in Munich"[26]) and, once she deduced how significant this Hitler fellow was, quite amenable to his blandishments.

And Hitler ("She amuses me"[27]) knew how to blandish. "I would like to have you come to the house tonight, Eva," Hoffmann would soon say. "Hitler is going to stop by and he asked that you come too."[28]

"When I look at some of those old films of the female Hitler Youth," recalled Eva's younger cousin Gertraud Weisker, "pigtails were the thing, and usually your hair was piled up on your head. They were women who were supposed to be natural and unspoilt. Whether they were is another matter. We were told that German women don't smoke. German women don't drink. German women don't wear make-up. But she never fitted that stereotype.

"I think Hitler was attracted by her charm. And I think she was attracted by this man too. He was 23 years older. And Eva was what we call a teenager today; in those days she was a 'flapper' who wanted to break away from the family environment."[29]

Adolf brought Eva along on picnics. He showered her with gifts. He instructed Rudolf Hess's rising assistant Martin Bormann to investigate her ancestry. Fortunately, no Jews perched in the Braun family tree.[30] The budding couple shared a few basic traits: Though also raised Catholic, Eva also possessed a father none too supportive of that faith (Herr Braun being a Lutheran[31]). They both enjoyed the German writer Karl May's popular yet fanciful "Old Shatterhand" American Wild West stories.[32] She had even been educated at a convent school at Simbach, just across the border from Hitler's birthplace at Braunau am Inn.[33]

And yet, their relationship seemed, at least to others, bereft of any special meaning. The gifts? They constituted nothing special, reflected Heinrich Hoffmann, "flowers, chocolates, trinkets of modest value and the trivialities of the ordinary gallantry in which he delighted. . . . never, in voice, look or gesture, did he ever behave in a way that suggested any deeper interest in her."[34]

Yet, someone may have thought otherwise.

Geli Raubal.

Recall the note that Geli had discovered within her uncle's jacket pocket on the very night of her suicide, the one reading:

Dear Mr. Hitler,
Thank you again for the wonderful invitation to the theater. It was a
memorable evening. I am most grateful to you for your kindness. I am
counting the hours until I may have the joy of another meeting.[35]

That note came from Eva Braun.

Geli Raubal fired a 6.35 mm slug into her heart and left a void, no, a chasm, in Adolf Hitler's life. Eva Braun wasted no time in filling it. By that December, she had wangled an invitation to his Haus Wachenfeld mountain chalet.[36] She was, it seemed, exactly Adolf Hitler's type. "A highly intellectual man should have a primitive and stupid woman," he would later proclaim. "Imagine if I had a woman to interfere with my work."[37]

Yet, Eva's quest for Hitler's affections was not without its pitfalls. When she boasted to her fellow employees that she was conquering Hitler, Hoffmann threatened to fire her if she continued spinning such still fanciful tales.[38] Her family—had they known of the relationship—would have mightily disapproved. Her father, schoolteacher Friedrich "Fritz" Braun, simply detested Munich's rising demagogue, even having been blackballed for promotion for refusing NSDAP membership.[39]

"Hitler!" Herr Braun ranted, "He's a jack-of-all-trades, an imbecile who thinks himself omniscient and who wants to reform the world. He thinks he imbibed wisdom with his mother's milk. I cross to the other side when I meet him in the street."[40]

The heart has a way of overcoming parents. Overcoming the attitudes of a potential lover who proclaims his "bride is Germany,"[41] remained quite another, particularly in a year seeing him competing for Reich president in March and April and his Reichstag minions running that July and November.

Eva Braun was not only in love. She was alone, unacknowledged, and abandoned. It was not her. It was him. "In a sense," Joseph Goebbels's wife, Magda (herself rumored to have been in love with Hitler—and vice-versa[42]), confided to Kurt Lüdecke that August, "Hitler is simply not human—unreachable and untouchable."[43]

Oddly enough, we do not know when it happened. Some say mid-August.[44] Some say early November, just before the year's second round of Reichstag voting.[45] Whenever it happened, the circumstances eerily resembled Geli's.

Even the caliber of the bullet was the same.

Her sister Ilse found her. "My sister was lying on the right side of the bed," Ilse recalled, "but she had regained consciousness. There was blood everywhere, on the sheets with embroidered hems, on the pink cushion—I still remember the color—and on the floor in little pools. Eva, like Geli, had tried to shoot herself in the heart but had aimed very badly! The bullet had lodged just near the neck artery, and the doctor had no difficulty in extracting it. Eva had taken my father's 6.35 mm. caliber pistol, which he normally kept in the drawer of the bedside table beside him."[46]

Eva retained sufficient presence of mind to summon a properly discreet physician, Heinrich Hoffman's brother-in-law, a Dr. Wilhelm Plate. "This is a bad business," Plate informed Hoffmann. "During last night Eva rang me up. Speaking softly and with great difficulty, and obviously in great pain, she told me that she had shot herself through the heart . . . She had felt so lonely, she said, and so neglected by Hitler that she wanted to end it all."[47]

Hitler rushed to Photohaus Hoffmann, having already received a note from Eva containing her intentions.[48] Hoffmann informed him that she had not merely threatened—she had acted.[49] "Is the doctor a man who will hold his tongue?" Hitler asked, then demanded to see Plate.

They met at Hoffmann's home later that day. "Doctor—please tell me the truth." Hitler inquired, "Do you think that Fraulein Braun shot herself simply with the object of becoming an interesting patient and of drawing my attention to herself?"

Plate shook his head—"The shot was aimed directly at the heart." Plate departed. Hitler paced. Hitler always paced. "You hear, Hoffmann," he cried, "the girl did it for love of me. But I have given her no cause which could possibly justify such a deed." Then he added, "Obviously, I must now look after the girl."

Hoffmann disagreed. "I see no obligation," he interjected. "No one could blame you for what Eva has done."

"And who, do you think, would believe that?" Hitler retorted. "And another thing—what guarantee is there that something of the kind might not occur again?"

To that Hoffmann possessed no answer. Hitler continued, half to Hoffmann, half to himself, "If I take on the responsibility of looking after her, that doesn't mean that I intend to marry her. You well know my views. The great thing about Eva is that she is no political blue-stocking. I loathe politically-minded women. The *chère amie* of a politician must be quietly discreet."[50]

Armed with a bouquet of flowers, he rushed to the private clinic where Dr. Plate had sequestered her.[51]

But he could not stay long. He had yet another campaign to wage.

CHAPTER TWENTY-SIX

"You felt that they would do *anything*"

FOLLOWING HIS CAMPAIGN, FDR HAD PLEDGED BOLD ACTION. BUT HE took none. He could take none. None for four months. Not, that is, until he finally took office.

But, action or not, things had changed radically in America.

They got worse.

One might hardly discern it from any election return, but the summer and early fall of 1932 had witnessed tangible signs of economic recovery. The Depression was not over, but the nation was, indeed, turning several real corners. From July through September, blue chip stocks doubled in value; railroad stocks tripled. U.S. Steel and General Motors resumed paying dividends. Cotton cloth production surged. Business and bank failures declined.[1] By early fall, however, such factors reversed and kept heading south through the winter. Employment numbers as usual lagged behind financial indicators, but they too revealed a positive trend. Joblessness peaked at 27.9 percent in September 1932 but ratcheted sharply down to 22.3 percent by December. Again, however, the respite proved cruelly illusory. The next three months saw unemployment escalate respectively to 25.9 percent, 26.1 percent, and 28.3 percent.[2] Some blamed fear of the new administration; others that June's tax-hiking Revenue Act. Most likely it was a little—or a lot—of both.

In foreign affairs, Hoover's December 1931 debt moratorium had been just that, a "moratorium," a one-year breathing spell for the Europeans. Now, that year expired. Even before Hoover had returned from California, Britain's ambassador, Sir Ronald Lindsay, had written to him, strongly implying that Americans should forget resuming any payment schedule.[3] That game was up. Uncle Sam was again Uncle Sucker.

Hoover's moratorium simply infuriated Pennsylvania's Louis T. McFadden. In mid-December he rose in the House with a startling proposition: a 4,500-word resolution impeaching Herbert Clark Hoover. Congressmen didn't particularly like Hoover. They liked McFadden less. While Hoover lunched (the matter was over that quickly), hissing and booing House members tabled McFadden's motion 361–8.[4]

But Hoover needed not only congressional support, he needed FDR's and not merely regarding allied debt but in two other matters of foreign affairs: disarmament and an upcoming world economic conference. He requested a White House meeting with Franklin—and with his adviser Raymond Moley.

FDR evinced scant interest in pulling his vanquished rival's bacon out of the fire, sneering to Moley, "Ray, have you got any striped pants?" and then to Rexford Tugwell, "As a matter of fact, he will need a top hat too. I'll bet he doesn't have one of those. You know, Rex, they say Hoover is very formal. We could not afford to have our expert dressed wrong."[5] Complicating Franklin's now second-nature hostility to Hoover was this. The campaign had required FDR to jettison any semblance of internationalism. Appeasing Hearst was certainly a factor, but so too was FDR's naturally fine-tuned political instincts. Hoover had argued that much of the blame for America's Great Depression rested on European factors: abandoned gold standards, debts, reparations, failing Austrian and German banks, imports, and exports. Politically that would not do for the Democrats at all. Blame must be fastened on Hoover and on his party alone. During the campaign Roosevelt had derided Hoover's premise of European culpability as the "boldest alibi in history."[6]

Yes, in a single year FDR had transformed himself from starry-eyed Wilsonian internationalist to callous hard-shell isolationist. He wanted no part of blaming—or of rescuing—the Old World, and, certainly, nothing of rescuing Herbert Clark Hoover. Elements of his own party, like Colonel House and Owen D. Young, might lobby for a new debt restructuring, but his newest advisers, the Brains Trusters—Moley, Tugwell, and Berle—opposed wasting political capital on such moves.[7] "America First" was, in sentiment, if not in words, their primary foreign policy strategy. It was, in fact, their only strategy.

As ex-governor FDR wended his way south to Warm Springs that January, however, he did consent to meet with Hoover. Secretary of State Stimson (who fretted that Hoover's "distrust of his rival . . . will go far to prevent a profitable meeting"[8]) and Franklin's Hudson Valley neighbor, Treasury Secretary Ogden Livingston Mills, would accompany the lame-duck incumbent. Raymond Moley, no particular expert on the debt question, rode shotgun for Franklin, along with former Wilson Administration State and Treasury departments undersecretary, the Tennessee-born millionaire Norman H. Davis.

Puffing on a big black cigar, seated upon a plum-colored velvet sofa, Hoover monopolized the conversation. Moley found him to be the "best informed individual in the country on the question of debts. . . . [commanding] a mastery of detail and a clarity of arrangement that compelled admiration."[9] Hoover's presentation might command admiration. It did not command assent. Roosevelt—no cigars, only cigarettes for him—remained cagey during the session. Not possessing any great knowledge of European debt, he possessed the greater skill of convincing people that he had agreed with them. Hoover and Mills departed assured that Franklin had consented to a debt commission (with Hoover's appointees to be approved by Roosevelt). FDR and Moley exited the Red Room knowing damn well that he had not. Nonetheless, Roosevelt had not entirely gulled Hoover. "My impression at the moment," he confessed to Mills, "is that he will not carry through on the agreement."[10] He was right. Within the hour FDR announced to the world what he dared not inform Hoover face-to-face. There would be no debt commission. "I offered to share that great liability with him," Hoover privately confided to a United Press reporter, "to let him use me in any way he wished in these two months. I'm rid of a lot of grief now that he turned me down—but I'm filled with anxiety about what it means."[11]

The interregnum, it seems, was not to be employed for cooperation—but for yachting.

Herbert Hoover, bone weary physically, mentally, and emotionally, decided that if tens of millions of his employers no longer desired his services he would take some time off. Enjoying fishing far more than the presidency, he headed for Florida for some sail-fishing. At West Palm Beach, he boarded a special train. Trackside the leader of "a negro string band" doffed his hat and solemnly bowed toward Hoover. The little show merely embarrassed Hoover but not as much as their tune, FDR's theme song, "Happy Days Are Here Again."[12] Twice Hoover's yacht ran aground.[13]

Roosevelt, as ever, had the better of it, sojourning for eleven days upon southern waters aboard the 263-foot-long *Nourmahal*. That splendiferous craft belonged to yet another Hudson Valley neighbor, the Manhattan real estate magnate (and generous donor to the FDR presidential campaign) Vincent Astor. Five other wealthy men joined the Astor-FDR cruise, including Kermit Roosevelt (Alice and TR Jr.'s alcoholic brother[14]) and William Rhinelander Stewart, a habitué of Manhattan nightlife.[15] "The Hasty Pudding Club puts out to sea,"[16] mused an unimpressed Ed Flynn. Sailing from Jacksonville on February 4, 1933, the *Nourmahal* stopped at Nassau in the Bahamas, before reaching Miami on the late evening of Wednesday, February

15. "I didn't open [a] briefcase during the entire twelve days,"[17] FDR chortled. Rhymed the *New York Sun*:

On a splendid yacht in a climate hot
To tropical seas they ran
Among those they dismissed from mind
Was the Well-known Forgotten Man.[18]

Ray Moley had traveled south to brief FDR on Cabinet selections. They dined on board the *Nourmahal*, then headed toward a waterfront rally at the city's Bayfront Park: FDR via green Buick convertible; Moley, Astor, Kermit, and Stewart crammed into a small sedan. Astor nervously speculated on the danger of assassination in such immense crowds.[19] Moley had long known such unpleasant facts. As a teenager, he had been present at Buffalo in September 1901 when anarchist Leon Czolgosz twice fired his nickel-plated .32-caliber Iver Johnson revolver into William McKinley's ample gut—and watched in horror as the crowd nearly tore a president's murderer to pieces.[20]

Mayor R. B. Gautier and ten thousand of his fellow Miamians welcomed FDR. So did Chicago mayor "Ten Percent Tony" Cermak, in town to mend his fences. Cermak had backed a very wrong horse—Smith—at Chicago and desperately wanted to ensure Franklin of his new loyalties. FDR finished his brief speech, and Cermak stood alongside his convertible. They chatted. Six shots rang out. The first grazed Miss Margaret Kruis, a Dutch-born twenty-three-year-old Newark showgirl, standing not two feet from Roosevelt, in the head. A second grazed her hand.[21] Another plugged Cermak in the stomach, and he tumbled to the ground. Another wounded Gautier. Bodyguard Gus Gennerich leapt from the convertible's front seat to fling his body over Roosevelt's.[22] FDR ordered the badly wounded Cermak brought into his car. They sped to Miami's Jackson Memorial Hospital. A local police officer whispered to Roosevelt, "I don't think he is going to make it."

"I am afraid he isn't," Franklin conceded.

"Tony, keep quiet—don't move." FDR comforted Cermak. "It won't hurt you if you keep quiet."[23]

A trio of policemen tackled the prospective assassin, the mentally unstable, 5'1" Italian immigrant Giuseppe Zangara ("I hate all presidents"[24]), flinging him onto the trunk luggage rack of Astor's sedan. Moley grabbed hold of a police officer's belt to keep from falling from the car's running board to the pavement as they raced away. Later, aboard the *Nourmahal*, Moley marveled at Roosevelt's sang-froid:

*There was nothing—not so much as the twitching of a muscle, the mop-
ping of a brow, or even the hint of a false gaiety to indicate that it wasn't
any other evening in any other place. Roosevelt was simply himself—
easy, confident, poised, to all appearances. F. D. R. had talked to me once
or twice during the campaign about the possibility that someone would
try to assassinate him. To that extent, I knew, he was prepared for Zangara's attempt. But it is one thing to talk philosophically about assassination, and another to face it.*

    *And I confess that I have never in my life seen anything more mag-
nificent than Roosevelt's calm that night on the* Nourmahal.[25]

"A dastardly act!"[26] exclaimed Herbert Hoover on hearing the news. "There *is*
a star, you know," Missy LeHand reverently told Rexford Tugwell.[27]

Millions of other Americans shared Missy's belief. An assassin had fired
six rounds at close range at a crippled, stationary target. He killed one person and wounded four others. But he had not harmed—or even mildly disconcerted—Franklin Roosevelt. Providence must indeed possess some grand
plan for this man.

Eleanor ("I realize F.D.R. is a great man, & he is nice to me but as a
person I'm a stranger & don't want to be anything else"[28]) had long proven
tortured and uncertain regarding her husband's personality and ambitions.
She displayed no ambivalence regarding his physical safety. In late January, at
Washington's Mayflower Hotel, she had lunched with Lorena Hickok, Louis
Howe, and her second-oldest son, Elliott. Conversation turned to what she
might do if an assailant started shooting at Franklin. Eleanor hesitated not
at all: "I'd step in front of him, of course." Elliott pooh-poohed such bravado.
"That would be just dandy," he scoffed, "then you'd both get shot."

"Oh, but I have a weapon," Eleanor countered, removing a fountain pen–
like object from her purse. "You press this thing here," she illustrated, "and it
shoots out tear gas."[29] Eleanor's audience—particularly Elliott—deemed her
plan ludicrous. They burst out laughing. But later Hick would ponder Eleanor's constant nervousness at public events and how she invariably scanned
each venue for exits. "If a fire had broken out in one of those places," Eleanor
would explain to her, "and the crowd started to panic, it would have been
almost impossible to get Franklin out. Without his leg braces, two men can
pick him up and carry him easily and quickly. But when he is wearing his leg
braces, he is so awkward and unwieldy! He can't move himself or be moved
quickly."[30]

Something very large had been stolen from the Roosevelt marriage—
and yet an indestructible core remained.

—◦—

While FDR incongruously yachted, and America's economy sank, Eleanor pursued her own strange form of noblesse oblige for the starving. Not having accompanied Franklin south, she instead dined with Governor and Mrs. Gifford Pinchot at Harrisburg's executive mansion. The Pinchots served up a repast of foodstuffs secured from the local commissary for the unemployed: black bean soup, cabbage rolls, and bread sticks. Cost: 2.72 cents per plate. All well and good, but Eleanor Roosevelt and the Newport-bred Cornelia Bryce "Leila" Pinchot dined attired in elegant gowns, Pinchot Gifford in white tie and tails.[31] A critic blasted the affair as "an example of exhibitionism and bad taste . . . propaganda for radical causes."[32]

She, of course, was not with Franklin. He was already at Warm Springs, soon aboard the *Nourmahal*. But neither was she alone at this crucial period of her life. Her relationship with Lorena Hickok had blossomed quickly since Potsdam. On Christmas Day, Lorena bestowed upon her the expensive sapphire-and-diamond ring Madame Ernestine Schumann-Heink had lavished upon her back in 1916.[33]

A week before dining with the Pinchots, Eleanor traveled to Washington to meet with Lou Hoover and to inspect her future home. Lorena accompanied her. They lodged at the Mayflower Hotel's Presidential Suite ("we certainly were not crowded"[34]) and took a private breakfast.[35] Mrs. Hoover offered her successor an official limousine to traverse the five blocks separating the White House and the Mayflower. Eleanor and Lorena walked. Hickok, oddly unaware that reporters enjoyed access to the White House, halted at its northwest gate.[36] "I think [Eleanor] was there about an hour," Hickok remembered, "but it seemed much longer to me, as I stood waiting. . . ."[37]

—◦—

Radicalism festered. Communists staged a second hunger march on Washington. Vice President Curtis received their delegation, and an "unnamed negro" refused to shake his hand. "Well, you can go to the devil," snorted Curtis.[38] At Albany, that November, FDR ("I am just a private citizen. I cannot tell the President to do anything"[39]) surprised observers by receiving Communist hunger marchers for a full forty-five minutes. No undue incidents occurred.[40] In January, however, while Roosevelt met with eleven key Democratic congressional leaders, police battled a mob of five hundred Communists ("When do we eat. We want action!") outside his 65th Street townhouse. Fifty of them—egged on by female comrades—attacked the thirty-two police standing guard, knocking one to the ground.[41]

Another sort of marcher would visit New York. At some point, B. E. F. leader Walter W. Waters had made the acquaintance of Nazi agent Kurt Lüdecke. Together, that February, they journeyed from Washington to Manhattan. "Waters and one of his friends went to New York with me on business of their own," Lüdecke's memoirs recounted. "Waters was to drive my car back to Washington. The trip brought us closer together. Waters had made up his mind to go ahead with new organization plans, and was eager for me to get back. He inscribed for me his first copy of his book, *B. E. F.: The Whole Story of the Bonus Army.*"[42]

With Roosevelt's inauguration drawing near, Lüdecke kept busy before again returning to his homeland. "I made a point of getting in touch with persons who, directly or indirectly, had access to [FDR]," he said. "That done, I sought out other people of interest and influence. At his New York home I saw Colonel Edward M. House . . . I had a long and stimulating conversation with him. The little old man, with his gentle manner and the intently watching look of a mouse, listened to me with the greatest interest, and, though he did not commit himself, expressed sympathy with Hitler; he definitely saw . . . a great force behind our movement. He invited me warmly to see him again after my return, and to greet his old friends in Germany. 'Only,' he added, 'they will not be exactly in Nazi ranks.'"[43]

Loose talk floated regarding establishing an American dictatorship. Not merely from Lüdecke, but from quarters one might not easily suspect.

Well before Election Day, *Liberty*'s publisher, Bernarr Macfadden, had already trumpeted: "What we need now is martial law. The President should have dictatorial powers."[44] Pennsylvania's conservative Republican senator David Reed startled observers by exclaiming "if this country ever needed a Mussolini, it needs one now."[45] A young Greenwich Village type, a dealer in paint and floor wax named Howard Scott (a disgruntled veteran of Clare Brokaw's "New Party"[46]) peddled a brand of jibberish called "Technocracy" whereby scientists and "experts" would run things and the medium of exchange would be energy, in ergs and joules.[47] ("Individual income under technological control would consist of the quanta by which the flow of physical equipment is measured throughout the entire continental area. The unit income of the individual would be determined by the period necessary in the area to maintain a thermodynamically balanced load . . ."[48]). People took it seriously.

In January, Colonel House himself published an article in *Liberty* magazine, entitled, "Does America Need a Dictator? A Warning to Selfish Wealth and Narrow-Minded Politicians' Capitalistic Civilization." House predicted that if conditions did not improve the nation might indeed turn to dictatorship. His secret ghostwriter: the notorious German propagandist, George Sylvester Viereck.[49]

The deepening crisis only exacerbated such thinking. "For two years I've been called 'Dictator Ike' because I believe that virtual dictatorship must be exercised by our President,"[50] Maj. Dwight Eisenhower confided to his diaries. Late converts to FDR's cause proved particularly susceptible to similar sentiments. On January 12, Walter Lippmann, suddenly sounding like young Adolf Hitler following a visit to Vienna's Reichsrat, wrote: "[a]ny group of 500 men, whether they are called congressmen or anything else, is an unruly mob unless it comes under the strict control of a single will."[51] Nine days later he wrote directly to FDR: "The situation is critical, Franklin. You may have no alternative but to assume dictatorial power."[52] By early February, Al Smith, addressing the Catholic Conference on Industrial Problems, asked, "What does a democracy do in a war?" He promptly answered: "It becomes a tyrant, a despot, a real monarch. In the World War we took our Constitution, wrapped it up, and laid it on the shelf and left it there until the war was over."[53] Soon, Smith, Lippmann—and Rabbi Stephen Wise among others— would publicly express the "desire that [FDR] be granted immediately by the Congress such broad powers as may be necessary to enable the Executive to meet the present challenging emergency."[54]

Intimations of dictatorship filled the silver screen. Harry Cohn's Columbia Pictures released the documentary *Mussolini Speaks*, a Lowell Thomas–narrated paean ("a man of the people whose deeds will ever be an inspiration to mankind"[55]) to the Italian leader. Produced for a hundred thousand dollars, it grossed a phenomenal million dollars.[56]

Meanwhile, William Randolph Hearst bankrolled a highly fanciful tale (to say the least) of a concussed Hardingesque chief executive (Walter Huston as "Judson Hammond") transformed by the Archangel Gabriel into a progressive, dictatorial Roosevelt-like leader. In MGM's *Gabriel Over the White House*, Hammond turns his back on big business and expends billions on public works through his "Army of Construction." Ruling by martial law, he executes gangsters via Kafkaesque kangaroo courts and his newly deputized "federal police." He crudely bullies foreign leaders into sinking their nations' battleships. An aghast Louis B. Mayer ("Put that picture in its can and take it back to the studio and lock it up!"[57]) delayed the film's release until Roosevelt's inaugural. Conversely, Hearst forwarded the screenplay to FDR, who perhaps recalling his own stillborn screenwriting career, cheerfully provided his own suggestions.[58] FDR wired Hearst, "I want to send you this line to tell you how pleased I am with the changes you made in 'Gabriel Over the White House.' I think it is an intensely interesting picture and should do much to help."[59] Despite huge amounts of idiocy (including a scene in which gangsters motor up the White House driveway and tommy-gun the joint), the film earned a respectable profit.[60] FDR watched it three times and exhibited it to members of Congress.[61]

In newly elected Robert Rice Reynolds's Buncombe County, a goateed, occultish former novelist (*The Greater Glory, The Fog, Drag,* and *Golden Rubbish*), screenwriter (with a pair of Lon Chaney thrillers to his credit), and former toilet paper plant manager named William Dudley Pelley converted his existing polytheistic, spiritualist, pyramid-fixated organization, the "Liberators," into an openly anti-Semitic, fascist outfit called the "Silver Shirts." Despite its attire—which included an ample scarlet "L" over the heart—it looked like it had potential.[62]

And at Shreveport, a still small-time, but definitely rising, thirty-four-year-old Disciples of Christ radio preacher named Gerald L. K. Smith took time out from hooking his wagon to Huey Long's star to write to a German-American publisher in San Antonio, begging for an introduction to the even-more rising Adolf Hitler. "The Semitic propaganda in America," contended the economic progressive Smith, "is growing more serious every day . . . the Jews are trying to rob the American people just as they attempted to do in Germany and Germany and America will be closer together than any two nations in the world."[63]

Meanwhile, the economy remained abysmal. Rexford Tugwell walked the neighborhoods surrounding Columbia University where hundreds of ragged men, camped along the Hudson River, freezing in crude "Hooverville" shacks, patiently and pathetically queued for food handouts.[64] New Yorkers did not merely remain cold and hungry; twenty-nine starved to death that winter.[65] Such horrors only increased pressure upon Roosevelt. Hoover wanted him to proceed his way. His new budget director, the wealthy young Arizona congressman Lewis Douglas, lobbied for deep spending cuts.[66] New York's Senator Robert Wagner and midwestern progressives like Robert La Follette Jr. demanded *more* public works spending, more than even Hoover had spent. They wanted action—even before FDR's swearing-in.[67] They, of course, were moderates compared to Huey Long. "I'm going to talk turkey with Roosevelt," he fairly shouted at Washington reporters, before conferring with the president-elect. "I am going to ask you 'did you mean it or didn't you?' Goddamn it, there ain't but one thing I'm afraid of—and that's the people."[68]

〜〜

African Americans still feared Franklin Roosevelt. His southern roots were showing. That February, he and his daughter, Anna, visited Alabama's state capitol—site of Jefferson Davis's swearing-in as president of the Confederacy. He got a bit carried away.

"My friends and neighbors," he intoned, "it is a great privilege to stand on this sacred spot. . . . I can remember troubles caused in families caused by the [Civil] War. As some of you may remember one of the Roosevelts married a lady from Georgia. I recall that two distinguished gentlemen [TR's maternal uncles] who served in the Confederate Navy visited New York and there were Roosevelts who regarded these two distinguished gentlemen as pirates. I am sure that my daughter, who is here with me, and the other members of my families would laugh heartily at any manifestation of feeling. . . . I am glad as one who is to occupy another White House that I had the opportunity as I turned the corner to enter the capitol to see the 'White House' of the Confederacy."[69]

But before the nation turned a corner, things got even worse—much worse.

The problem involved the nation's very sick banking system. Even in the prosperous 1920s, thousands of small rural banks had collapsed. Before October 1929 prominent banks in New York City had also folded. FDR's banking superintendent found himself in Sing Sing. The Crash triggered yet more urban bank failures. Nervous depositors withdrew billions in their savings from even solvent institutions, weakening these otherwise reputable banks as well. Desperate businesses suffered still greater shortages of loan money. Hoover excoriated depositors' "hoarding." He utilized the new Reconstruction Finance Corporation to prop up troubled banks (John Nance Garner termed the RFC "Wall Street's three-billion dollar soup kitchen"[70]). By July 1932 the worst seemed over. Where bank failures had averaged 209 per month since September 1931, the average mercifully fell to just eighty-five from August through October 1932.[71]

Lull preceded typhoon.

Nevada's banks collapsed as Hoover's gloom-ridden campaign train chugged through the state. By February 1933, an unprecedented crisis gripped the country. In mid-month, two of Detroit's largest banks, the First National and the Union Guardian Trust Company, faltered. Newly minted Michigan Democratic governor (on his fourth try for the job) William A. Comstock declared a statewide eight-day bank holiday.[72] His holiday turned into a furlough. Michigan banks stayed uneasily shut. Other states rapidly followed suit. Barter replaced cash as a medium of exchange. "Detroit's Colonial

Department Store . . . ," historian William Manchester would record, "offered dresses for salted Saginaw herring, suits for livestock, assorted merchandise for eggs and honey."[73] Hoover pondered a national bank holiday to sort good banks from bad. Insolvent institutions would be immediately liquidated. Good banks would quickly re-open, with their deposits guaranteed by Washington. The national spiral of fear might finally, might mercifully, end.

A disquieting question nagged Hoover: Was his plan legal? He had serious doubts and wanted FDR's support on the matter. On Saturday, February 18, he dispatched a hand-delivered letter to Roosevelt, begging his public cooperation.

Roosevelt didn't answer. Some later charged him with playing high-stakes politics with the savings—the very lives—of millions. Such suspicions had good cause. Rex Tugwell had indiscreetly lunched with Remington-Rand's James H. Rand Jr. Tugwell, Rand contended, "said that they [the New Dealers] were fully aware of the bank situation and that it would collapse in a few days which would place the responsibility in the lap of President Hoover. We should not worry about anything except the rehabilitation of the country after March 4th."[74] To State Department economist Herbert Feis, Tugwell sneered even more directly, "Let 'em bust; then we'll get things on a sound basis."[75] FDR's gray-toupeed[76] Treasury secretary–designate William H. Woodin (also busy composing the "Franklin D. Roosevelt Inaugural March"[77]) confided similar sentiments to his departing predecessor Ogden Mills.[78]

Banks in over twenty states shuttered. Fear paralyzed the nation—and the White House. To his diary, Ted Joslin confided:

> *The Commercial [Bank] did open this morning and although I felt unpatriotic in doing so, I drew out most of the money in my checking account and had Rowena come in and withdraw her savings account. And I told the President what I had done. 'Don't hoard it, Ted,' was his only comment. 'Put it in another bank that is safe. I would suggest the Riggs. It is the most liquid.' But I am 'hoarding' temporarily. No bank is really liquid today and won't be until this panic is over. The daily hoarding figures from the Treasury are ghastly. That of yesterday was $165,000,000, bringing the total to in excess of $2,200,000,000. . . .*[79]

The next day—Tuesday, February 28—Hoover again wrote to FDR. The day following that, twelve days from Hoover's first missive, Roosevelt finally responded. Blandly alibiing that a secretary had lost Hoover's original correspondence, he protested that nothing could be done anyway ("frankly I doubt if anything short of a fairly general withdrawal of deposits can be prevented now").[80]

Wealthy, song-writing William Woodin was merely one of a trio of erst-while Republicans in FDR's new Cabinet. Progressive Republicans Harold Ickes (FDR: "I liked the cut of his jib"[81]) and Henry Wallace landed at Interior and Agriculture, respectively. Months before, FDR had confided to Woodrow Wilson's former tariffs and IRS chief Daniel C. Roper that he would name Newton Baker secretary of state. That was then. Rumors now held that said plum appointment would go either to the aforementioned Norman H. Davis (though many judged his business dealings too shady) or to Owen D. Young.[82] It went instead to the docile internationalist Cordell Hull. Despite all his angling for the job, Hull professed to be "thunderstruck"[83] on receiving it.

Jim Farley obtained the patronage-rich Post Office Department. New York's Frances Perkins emerged as the first female Cabinet member as sec-retary of labor. Virginia senator Claude Swanson received the Navy Depart-ment but only so that Harry Flood Byrd might slide into a Senate seat promised to him at the convention.[84] Moley emerged as an assistant secretary of state.[85] Tugwell, originally promised under secretary of Commerce, ulti-mately landed at Agriculture.[86] Rosenman, his eyes firmly fixed on a state supreme court judgeship, stayed behind in New York.[87]

FDR selected Montana senator Thomas J. Walsh, chair of the conven-tion, as his attorney general, but Walsh literally never made it to Washing-ton. At Havana, on February 25, the seventy-three-year-old Walsh married a wealthy, much-younger Cuban widow Mina Nieves Perez Chaumont de Truffin. The newlyweds flew to Miami, then entrained for Washington. Near Wilson, North Carolina, Walsh dropped dead of a heart attack.[88] Roosevelt had no idea of what to do: fill the vacancy quickly or delay until after his inaugural. Missy LeHand suggested a replacement: veteran Connecticut Democrat Homer Cummings, already tapped to succeed TR Jr. as governor general of the Philippines. FDR hesitated, then acceded to her wishes.[89]

Cummings got an unexpected promotion. Other hopefuls received . . . less. Macy's Jesse Straus coveted Commerce secretary, a post held by his uncle Oscar under TR. FDR conveyed the news of his rejection through a third party. As Ray Moley recorded it, Straus's "hurt and fury . . . knew no bounds."[90] Joseph P. Kennedy hankered after Woodin's Treasury post. He received nothing—but a condescending offer to become ambassador to Ire-land. He considered it an insult and turned it down.[91] Al Smith never got named "czar" of anything. Adding salt to his already enflamed wounds was the appointment of South Carolina's Dan Roper—like Cummings, a former McAdoo man—to Commerce.[92]

It was not a heavyweight Cabinet, no "team of rivals," no "best minds," not even a "cabinet of barons." "Scurrying through *Who's Who*, the *World*

Almanac, and the United States Fingerprint Department trying to find out who they were, I can say the forgotten man has been found," joshed Will Rogers. "There's nine of 'em and a woman."[93]

Joe Kennedy's buffoonish Massachusetts colleague, Boston's James Michael Curley, believed that FDR ("Well, Jim, if that's what you want, the job is yours"[94]) had promised him secretary of the navy. The "Rascal King" learned better on Sunday, January 7, when, at Calvin Coolidge's funeral, James Roosevelt sidled up to him and told him the deal was off. Franklin had filled his quota of Catholics in the Cabinet with Farley and Walsh. The best FDR might offer Curley was a posting to Paris or Rome. Soon that was reduced to ambassador to Poland. Curley indignantly refused.[95]

Curley feared Eleanor had poisoned FDR's mind against him.[96] She might have. But, if she did, that was the least of her mischief (if torpedoing a crook like Curley might be called mischief at all). As Franklin prepared to head south on the Baltimore & Ohio to assume his new office, he naturally assumed his wife might be, if not literally at his side, at least, somewhere on board. He—like Mayor Curley—assumed too much. Eleanor announced that her husband's plans were not her plans. Yes, FDR and his entourage might travel by rail, but she "would load up her roadster with belongings and drive down with a woman friend"[97]—Lorena. Aghast, FDR finally put his foot down. Eleanor *would* travel with the official party. Lorena, however, would also be along, chaperoning Eleanor's eight-year-old black Scottie "Meggie."[98]

Such contretemps aside, the overall atmosphere on board was upbeat, even giddy. "It's incredible," mused Henry Wallace. "The country is in ruins; and we seem to be on a kind of Sunday picnic."[99]

Eleanor again checked into the Mayflower—this time with Franklin (in adjoining suites[100]). Lorena stayed elsewhere. But she and Eleanor breakfasted the next morning, before the three of them—Eleanor, Lorena, and "Meggie"—scurried off by taxicab. They visited Mr. and Mrs. Henry M. Parrish (Eleanor had married at their home; she was Eleanor's cousin and godmother) at the New Shoreham.[101] They motored past Eleanor and Franklin's first Washington home, its current owners having placed a large sign out front—"Former Residence of Franklin D. Roosevelt." The sign disconcerted Eleanor, and she ordered the driver onward.[102] A far more significant visit followed—not to a person or persons—but to a statue.

They reached Rock Creek Cemetery, there to view Augustus Saint-Gaudens's bronze *Grief*, a memorial to Henry Adams's wife, Daisy—a suicide. "In the old days, when we lived here," Eleanor explained, almost to herself, "I was much younger and not so very wise. Sometimes I'd be very unhappy and sorry for myself. When I was feeling that way, if I could manage it, I'd come out here, alone, and sit and look at that woman. And I'd always come away somehow feeling better. And stronger. I've been here many, many times."[103]

Yes, this where Eleanor had gone to mourn her life . . . after Lucy.

And that she transported Lorena here on this of all days, a day of triumph, not tragedy, only reinforced the message of the hurt she still suffered.

Eleanor's personal drama was great, the nation's drama greater still. Banks continued failing. Farm foreclosures accelerated, as did ugly mob violence to prevent them. Trouble had been brewing for at least a year, with Iowa firebrand Milo Reno leading what he termed a "Farmers' Holiday Association," designed to force produce off the market. "Stay at Home— Buy Nothing—Sell Nothing,"[104] the wild-haired septuagenarian Reno demanded. "Let's call a Farmers' Holiday, a Holiday let's hold," his association rhymed, "We'll eat our wheat and ham and eggs, And let them eat their gold."[105]

"Farmers and workers!" read a typical handbill of the times, "Help protect your neighbors from being driven off their property. Now is the time to act. For the past three and a half years we have waited for our masters, who are responsible for the situation, to find a way out. . . . On Friday the property of ------------ is to be sold at a forced auction at the courthouse. . . . The Farmers Committee has called a mass meeting outside the sheriff's office to stop the above-mentioned sale."[106]

"They say blockading a highway is illegal," argued Reno, "I says, 'Seems to me there was a Tea Party in Boston that was illegal too.'"[107]

The veteran Communist agitator Ella Reeve "Mother" Bloor staged a midwestern tour. "I never saw anything like the militancy of those farmers,"[108] the seventy-year-old central committee member marveled. Neither had American Farm Bureau president Edward A. O'Neal III. "Unless something is done for the American farmer," O'Neal warned, "we'll have a revolution in the countryside in less than twelve months."[109]

Herbert Hoover, with barely twelve hours left in his term, invited Franklin to again confer at the White House, continuing to agitate for a national bank holiday. Their hour-and-ten-minute conversation went nowhere. FDR invited Hoover to call on him. Hoover stiffened. "Mr. Roosevelt," he answered, "when you are in Washington as long as I have been you will learn that the President of the United States calls on nobody."

"I shall be waiting at my hotel, Mr. President," an incensed FDR rejoined, "to learn what you decide."[110]

"Roosevelt returned from this visit visibly upset," recalled Ed Flynn. "It was, in fact, one of the few times I have ever seen him really angry."[111]

Back at the Mayflower, FDR conferred with William Woodin and Carter Glass. The phone rang. It was Hoover. Woodin and Carter overheard Franklin urge against any proclamation shuttering the banks.

The call complete, Glass inquired, "What are you planning to do?"

"Planning to close them, of course,"[112] FDR replied. His answer astounded Glass.

Banks would close. Saloons would open, though neither FDR nor Hoover had much to do with it. The lame-duck Congress had gotten the message on repeal. Everyone had. December witnessed a mighty shifting of House votes, not enough to pass repeal, but more than enough for everyone to notice.[113] In February, the Senate approved repeal 63–23; 79 percent of Democrats and 67 percent of Republicans voted in favor. The House now followed suit—289–121, with 85 percent of Democrats and 55 percent of the GOP voting aye.[114] Repeal went to the states.[115] Final enactment was only a matter of time.

The poison in the banking system spread almost minute by minute. At 4:20 Saturday morning, Herbert Lehman shuttered New York's banks.[116] Illinois did the same.[117] The Washington Hotel Association greeted inaugural attendees with this message: "Members find it necessary that, due to unsettled banking conditions throughout the country, checks on out-of-town banks cannot be accepted."[118] Eleanor fretted over how they would pay for their Mayflower suite.[119] Gifford Pinchot arrived in town with ninety-five cents in his pockets and could not lay his hands on anything more.[120] The New York Stock Exchange suspended trading. So did the Chicago Board of Trade.[121] With mere hours to go before departing the White House, Hoover—if it were possible—grew even more morose. "We are at the end of our string," he mourned to Ted Joslin. "There is nothing more we can do."[122]

But one can always pray. That morning, FDR summoned his Cabinet to St. John's, the small Protestant Episcopal church near the White House. "You know," he informed Jim Farley, "I think a thought to God is the right way to start off my administration. A proper attitude toward religion, and belief in God, will in the end be the salvation of all peoples. For ourselves it will be the means of bringing us out of the depths of despair into which so many have apparently fallen."[123]

Franklin's former Groton headmaster, Dr. Endicott Peabody, presided. Peabody had voted for Hoover as the "more capable man" but wasn't displeased to see his old student assume the nation's highest office.[124]

It was cold and dreary when the Roosevelts arrived in town. It remained so now, as their seven-car motorcade arrived at the White House's north portico to fetch the Hoovers. Franklin presented his invariably ebullient face to the world. The weight of his new obligations seemed nonexistent. Some urged him to cancel the lavish round of inaugural balls that highlighted each inauguration. Warren Harding had done so in less hard times back in 1921. Franklin vetoed that idea. A little gaiety remained in order, he said, perhaps now more than ever.

Hoover presented an even more dispirited image than was his wont. FDR attempted conversation. Hoover wanted no part of talk, small or grand, perched as rigidly mute as his predecessor, Silent Cal Coolidge, might on any ordinary day. The Depression might not rattle Franklin. His former friend's eerie immobility did. Desperate to jump-start a conversation, the suddenly jittery Franklin chattered about the "lovely steel"[125] underpinning the nearby under-construction Commerce Department Building. "It must have seemed insane," Eleanor recalled, "but it indicates how desperate [Franklin] was in search of small talk."[126]

Hoover, it must be admitted, was not the person Franklin wished to be conversing with that morning. He would have dearly preferred to chat with Lucy Mercer Rutherfurd, a circumstance not quite as far-fetched as one might suppose—for Lucy was not merely present in Washington that day, but firmly in possession of a ticket to her old lover's inauguration. Not only had Franklin ordered it supplied to her, he had behaved even more recklessly, dispatching a White House limousine to carry her from her temporary Q Street lodgings to the Capitol's East Portico.[127]

President-elect and president-defunct reached the Capitol. A hundred thousand persons, some of the more adventurous perched in icy tree limbs, awaited them in the morning chill.[128] So did troops with machine guns at the ready.[129] The venerable, black, silk skullcap–clad Charles Evans Hughes administered the oath. Franklin's family Bible lay before him, open to the words, "For now we see through a glass darkly; but then face to face: now I know in part; but then shall I know even as I am known. And now abideth faith, hope charity, these three, but the greatest of these is charity."[130]

"This is a day of consecration,"[131] FDR commenced his address, before pronouncing words that would electrify a nation that had recoiled in fear for almost four years:

> *Nor need we shrink from honestly facing conditions in our country today. This great nation will endure as it has endured, will revive and will prosper. So, first of all, let me assert my firm belief that the only thing we have to fear is fear itself—nameless, unreasoning, unjustified terror which paralyzes needed efforts to convert retreat into advance. In every dark hour of our national life a leadership of frankness and vigor has met*

that understanding and support of the people themselves which is essential to victory. I am convinced that you will again give that support to leadership in these critical days.[132]

That leadership, however, might very well not involve fretting about events abroad:

Our international trade relations, though vastly important, are in point of time and necessity secondary to the establishment of a sound national economy. I favor as a practical matter the putting off first things first. I shall spare no effort to restore world trade by international economic readjustment, but the emergency at home cannot wait on that accomplishment.[133]

"If I read the temper of our people correctly," Roosevelt continued, "we now realize as we never realized before our interdependence on each other; that we cannot merely take but must give as well; that if we are to go forward, we must move as a trained and loyal army willing to sacrifice for the good of a common discipline. . . . We are . . . ready and willing to submit our lives and our property to such discipline, because it makes possible a leadership which aims at a larger good. This I propose to offer. . . ."[134]

He paid homage to the Constitution, "so simple and practical that it is always possible to meet extraordinary needs by changes in emphasis and arrangement without loss of essential form." But then he issued a threat:

It is to be hoped that the normal balance of executive and legislative authority may be wholly adequate to meet the unprecedented task before us. But it may be that an unprecedented demand and need for undelayed action may call for temporary departure from that normal balance of public procedure.

I am prepared under my constitutional duty to recommend the measures that a stricken nation in the midst of a stricken world may require. These measures, or such other measures as the Congress may build out of its experience and wisdom, I shall seek, within my constitutional authority, to bring to speedy adoption.

But in the event that the Congress shall fail to take one of these two courses, and in the event that the national emergency is still critical, I shall not evade the clear course of duty that will then confront me. I shall ask the Congress for the one remaining instrument to meet the crisis— broad Executive power to wage a war against the emergency, as great as the power that would be given to me if we were in fact invaded by a foreign foe.[135]

"The thing that emerges most clearly," wrote *New Republic* associate editor Edmund Wilson, "is the warning of a dictatorship."[136] Eleanor found the moment "terrifying," confessing to Lorena—and thus, to Lorena's readers, "The crowds were so tremendous, and you felt that they would do *anything*— if only someone would tell them *what* to do."[137]

Perhaps someone had. As Hearst's million-circulation New York tabloid, the *Daily Mirror,* would approvingly headline the following day: "ROOSEVELT ASKS DICTATOR'S ROLE."[138]

Rhetoric ended. Parading began. Douglas MacArthur stood alongside Roosevelt as for three-and-a-half hours FDR reviewed column after column of marchers, fifty thousand alone from New York.[139] The ghosts of the Wilson Administration formed an honor guard about the platform—Wilson's widow and his personal physician, Adm. Cary Grayson, and the director of his War Industries Board—Bernard Baruch. There was no place for Al Smith upon that dais. But he traveled to Washington anyway, bedecked in full Tammany regalia, gamely heading its parade contingent.[140]

Parade concluded, Eleanor served hot dogs at the White House[141] before heading off to the inaugural ball. She went alone—the only First Lady to so attend an inaugural ball minus her spouse.[142] Franklin remained behind with Colonel House.[143]

Two mornings later FDR's black valet, Irvin "Mac" McDuffie, wheeled him into the Oval Office. McDuffie quickly departed. Quite alone, Roosevelt surveyed the scene. His obsessively organized predecessor had cleared all of his belongings from the office. Nary a piece of paper lay upon Franklin's desk. The emptiness profoundly unnerved him. He sat trancelike, immobile in body and in mind. Minutes passed. A thought invaded his suddenly befogged mind. He must break this ghastly spell, shatter the isolation, the nothingness, that trapped him. *He had to get help.* But how? He could not even locate the buttons that must be *somewhere* on this desk to summon staff. He shouted. *He shouted as loud as he could.* Missy LeHand ran in. His press secretary, Marvin McIntyre, hurried in from the other side of the room.

Life—and the nation's business—continued. But FDR never forgot that moment. Fear itself had gripped Franklin Roosevelt that morning, and seemed like it might never let go.[144]

But it would.

CHAPTER TWENTY-SEVEN

"Somebody hurled a spittoon"

HITLER HAD MISCALCULATED.

Humiliating Fränzchen von Papen was indeed marvelous fun. But triggering new elections was hardly enjoyable—or profitable—for anyone. Particularly for National Socialists. They should have seen their tribulations coming.

Everyone else did.

Money now proved a greater problem than ever. "Industrialists who hoped that Hitler's movement would help to break . . . the trade unions and reduce the onerous burdens of social legislation . . . have reason to be pleased with the present conservative regime . . . ," Ambassador Frederic Sackett informed Henry Stimson. "The energy with which [Papen's] Cabinet [carried] out its political and particularly its economic program, measures such as the reduction of the benefits of unemployment insurance, remission of taxes on a large scale and subsidies to business and industry as a means of stimulating economy, have served to win for the Government the active support of many who up to now helped to finance Hitler."[1]

Losing financial support was bad enough. Forfeiting public support was worse. In Washington, German ambassador Friedrich Wilhelm von Prittwitz und Gaffron predicted a forthcoming Hitlerite loss of "perhaps 20 seats."[2] In Berlin, Goebbels sullenly grasped a similar truth. "We must work like niggers," he mourned, "only thus we may hope to succeed."[3]

If Hitler himself saw trouble coming, he did not let on. "The Leader is optimistic as to the progress of affairs . . . ," Goebbels prattled. "He is a never-failing source of reinvigoration."[4]

Others viewed Hitler differently. "[T]here was a new harshness in his tone," lamented Putzi Hanfstaengl, "a conscious attitude of speaking from a higher level and keeping people in their place."[5]

Kurt Lüdecke had returned from America. Privately, old party acquaintances confided their own growing fears about the next election—and about their movement's dictatorial sun-god leadership style. "Hitler can wear you down—" Ernst Röhm confided, "he's incomparable in the art of making people believe in him. Now the situation is such that there's none among us who would dare throw the truth in his face, defy him openly, and fight it out. . . . And we, *we ourselves,* have made him what he is. . . . My position is so precarious I can't be too exigent; I'm becoming more and more an ostrich with my head in the sand. I stick to my job, following him blindly, loyal to the utmost—there's nothing else left me. It's wrong, I know, and believe me, I suffer under it. We do strange things sometimes to escape from ourselves."[6] Also betraying nervousness about Hitler was Gregor Strasser—an unease, however, never large enough to trigger any alliance with Röhm. "I'm not so crazy as to compromise myself with Röhm at this stage," Strasser argued. "What if he should talk?"[7] Strasser still preferred dealing with Schleicher.

Hitler, on the other hand, dealt desperately to retain his party's bloated quotient of Reichstag seats. It would not be an easy task. Voters recoiled from increased National Socialist violence. They shuddered at Hitler's famously intemperate defense of obvious Nazi murderers and at recent Nazi Reichstag antics. Göring and his stooges had proven no better than any other bunch of haggling Reichstag politicians. "Money is extraordinarily difficult to obtain," Goebbels again lamented. "All gentlemen of 'Property and Education' are standing by the Government."[8]

Exiled in Holland, Kaiser Wilhelm might indeed never stand with any portion of Weimar—but he was by now thoroughly disgusted with Hitler. His supposed friend Hermann Göring, somehow cognizant of Wilhelm's recent estimation of Hitler ("He is no statesman"), had threatened to bring the news to Der Führer and thus wreck any chance for a Hohenzollern restoration. Enraged, Wilhelm II threw all support to Hugenberg, for good measure even dumping his pro-Nazi aides Admiral Magnus von Levetzow and Leopold von Kleist, replacing Kleist with the steadfast anti-Nazi general Wilhelm von Dommes. In Germany itself, Kronprinz Wilhelm wrote to Hitler urging greater cooperation with the Stahlhelm. Hitler intemperately replied that he was sick of cooperation. He demanded total control—and the Hohenzollerns now grasped that Hitler's plans, indeed, included no imperial restoration.[9]

Giant rallies dominated the campaign. In Berlin, in early September, the Stahlhelm marshalled 150,000 supporters in a massive show of force.[10] A month later 110,000 Hitler Youth traveled to Potsdam to process for seven straight hours before their Führer. "You see?" Hitler exhorted Kurt Lüdecke, "No fear—the German race is on the march."[11]

Lüdecke and Hitler had traveled together from Munich to Potsdam. As they sped north, Hitler grilled him about America. "He was all ears . . . ," recalled Lüdecke. "Whenever I mentioned books . . . he would ask [his adjutant Julius] Schaub to write down the titles. He questioned me about the Roosevelt campaign, the American crisis, the probability of a great change in the United States. He was much interested in Prohibition. Though a teetotaler, he was no bigot on the question, and accepted my arguments against it. I tried to organize my talk somewhat to show Hitler the United States from a Nazi viewpoint, in order to give him a background for calculations of international policy. And so I told him of America's utterly different structure and tremendous resources, and suggested that even if Germany were to become a desert, America could get on without us despite the conviction of many worthy Germans that it couldn't, and that furthermore God wouldn't permit its destruction."[12] Lüdecke—unlike everyone else—thought Hitler was a good listener.

Shortly after his Hitler Youth rallied at Potsdam, Hitler launched a third installment of "Hitler Over Germany," campaigning in forty-nine cities,[13] delivering three, or even four, major speeches daily.[14] His rhetoric swung leftward. *Der Angriff* mercilessly pilloried Hugenberg's DNVP each day. "*Hugenzswerg* ['Hugendwarf"] *verrecke!*"[15] it threatened. Party speakers attacked Papen's "Dictatorship of the Moneybags,"[16] as lacking "any spark of social justice."[17] They trumpeted their latest new slogan: "Against reaction!"[18] But new slogans work only so well when the overall act wears thin, its novelty quickly eroding. Even Hitler struggled to fill meeting halls. His Nürnberg venue sat half-empty.[19] "[T]he outlook is still somewhat gloomy," Goebbels admitted, though he tried convincing himself that "it cannot be compared with the desolate outlook of a few weeks ago."[20]

Things were bad enough. Goebbels made them worse. In Berlin, the KPD instigated a city-wide transit strike. Neither the SPD nor local trade unions supported it.[21] But Goebbels did. Together, Nazis and Communists cooperated to "commit sabotage on a huge scale, to pour concrete into tramway points, to pull down high tension cables, to beat up workmen unwilling to strike, and to attack the police who protected them."[22] Goebbels, the one-time "German Communist,"[23] demonstrated side-by-side with Berlin KPD chairman Walter Ulbricht.[24]

His reckless move—unauthorized by Hitler—only further jeopardized waning moderate support. "The entire Press is furious with us and calls it Bolshevism . . . ," Goebbels confessed to his diary. "Middle-class people are being scared away from us. . . ."[25]

Yes, they were.

Germans voted on Sunday, November 6, 1932—"the most peaceful election in recent German annals," noted the *New York Times*, "there were no riots anywhere, and nobody was killed throughout the country. . . . The sole casualty of the day in Berlin was a Socialist who was beaten up in dispute with Nazis in the working class quarter, but even he was not seriously injured."[26]

Which was more than could be said for the Nazi vote total. It plummeted by two million votes, dropping from 37.4 to 33.1 percent of the vote. The party forfeited a whopping thirty-four Reichstag seats.[27] The election, however, had not been any victory for moderation. The KPD gained eleven seats, reaching the hundred-delegate threshold for the first time in its history. Counted together, the Brown-Red total had now reached an alarming 50 percent. The majority of Germans had, in one form or another, voted not simply for dictatorship but for totalitarianism.

The Zentrum lost five seats. The SPD continued its long slide, surrendering another dozen delegates. The DNVP reclaimed many of the rural Protestant[28] and urban middle class voters it had recently forfeited to the Hitlerites, including Hamburg schoolteacher Luise Solmitz. "For [Hitler], it's not a matter of Germany, but of power," she bristled. "Why has Hitler deserted us after showing us a future that we could welcome. Hitler awake!"[29] Hugenberg's DNVP gained fifteen seats.

Goebbels's transit strike antics had indeed gained him nothing. Not only had he forfeited votes to the DNVP, he lost 36,132 votes in the metropolis itself.[30] His former Communist allies increased their Berlin totals to 37.7 percent. They—and not the SPD—were now the capital's largest party.[31]

Worse yet for the Hitlerites, Nazi and Zentrum losses now meant that these two parties might no longer combine to fashion even a shakiest of Reichstag majorities. Papen and Hugenberg already barred Hitler's path to a presidial Cabinet. Now any hope of a parliamentary majority government evaporated.

Hitler had *clearly* miscalculated.

Observers galloped to write finis to the upstart Bohemian Corporal's unlikely career. From London, economist Harold Laski joked, "Accident apart, it is not unlikely that Hitler will end his career as an old man in some Bavarian village who, in the Tiergarten in the evening, tells his intimates how he nearly overturned the German Reich. . . . The old man they will think, is entitled to his pipe-dreams."[32]

Pipe-dreams, it seemed, was about all he had. Hitler had indeed missed the bus. His party was busted. "The financial situation of the Berlin organization is hopeless," Goebbels noted. "Nothing but debts and obligations."[33] It stood in arrears in taxes.[34] The *Völkischer Beobachter*'s unpaid printer threatened to cease publication.[35] Not very long before, brownshirts had flooded the streets smashing opponents' skulls. Now they took to the pavement literally begging for loose change.[36] Berlin's liberal *Vossiche Zeitung* jeered that the Nazis should junk their charity campaign slogan from "For the NSDAP Winter Aid program" for the more accurate "For the Winter Aid program for the NSDAP."[37]

Nazi internal dissent roared. The movement threatened to implode. Because the party "combined all extremes," observed former *Berliner Tageblatt* editor Rudolf Olden, "since it had no program, since it had promised all things to all men, since it had no tradition, since the most violent hatred prevailed among leaders big and small, since, finally, these staring incompatibles were held together by nothing except the Party's rapid rise, its unbounded financial resources and the heat of work, decline must mean complete collapse."[38]

And collapse it might have, save that Franz von Papen collapsed first.

Papen's two parliamentary backers, the DNVP and the German People's Party (DVP), had increased from forty-four to sixty-two seats, but representing a combined 19.03 percent of the voting public, his parliamentary mandate remained pitifully small—too slight to ever dream of crafting a ruling Cabinet.

But whether Papen claimed 19 or 91 percent support, he no longer boasted support from his defense minister, Kurt von Schleicher. Papen was in a great sense a conservative, at least, in the older European sense. Schleicher was merely militaristic. His politics ran well to the left of his unpopular protégé. Papen's pro-business program was not Schleicher's. Schleicher, a self-proclaimed "Social General,"[39] envisioned himself at the head of (or, at least, as at the ear of the head of) some vague coalition of army officers, conservatives, nationalists, trade unionists (perhaps, but not necessarily, including Social Democrats), and, with great good luck, all or part of the Nazi Party.

It was as much a pipe-dream as the one Harold Laski envisioned for Adolf Hitler, but it was now Schleicher's pipe-dream. He endeavored to implement it—and to jettison Papen.

His pretext was the Berlin transit strike. On the level of immediate election results, Goebbels's gambit had failed miserably. But it, nonetheless, generated a pair of contradictory but still very real unintended consequences invaluable in resuscitating National Socialist fortunes.

In bolstering the KPD's Berlin vote, and thus its national vote, the strike only served to remind voters of the nation's Bolshevik menace. The Nazi Party had ballyhooed itself as the muscular (and often bloody) bulwark against the Soviet-dominated KPD. So, for many, the NSDAP might again prove useful against a surging KPD. Yet, to Schleicher and the Reichswehr, the strike generated a vastly different conclusion. What havoc might transpire if storm troopers and Red Front Fighters united to topple Papen?

Or, at least, that's what they told Hindenburg.

Accordingly, Schleicher commissioned a Reichswehr study (a *kriegspiel*[40]) designed to demonstrate its inability to simultaneously combat Polish incursions into East Prussia and a combined Nazi-Communist uprising versus Papen—*and for good measure* how it might react to any disturbances in the key Ruhr-Rhine area and, *just to be on the safe side*, violence from the SPD's milquetoast Reichsbanner. Schleicher's *kriegspielers* thus created a perfect storm, worst-case scenario that they not very surprisingly concluded, the hundred-thousand-man Reichswehr could not control. It was essentially a Reichswehr vote of no confidence not so much in itself but in the nation's chancellor.[41]

Hindenburg thought little of Reichstag no-confidence votes. But Cassandra-like warnings from his beloved army caught and held his age-befogged eye.

Meanwhile, the mad minuet of the parties continued. Papen considered his position improved. Nobody else did. Aside from Hindenburg, all found his always improbable chancellorship highly expendable.

Papen calculated that importuning Hitler might finally prove beneficial. August had not been the right time at all. Hitler basked in his electoral triumph. Buy him then and buy him at peak price. Purchase him in November and secure him properly chastened—and at bargain rates. Feelers now went out for another Hindenburg-Hitler meeting.

Hitler had, however, not changed since August. As head of the nation's largest party (and as a practicing megalomaniac) he still wanted no part of any vice-chancellorship.

Yet, he had *learned*. Fearing another humiliating face-to-face session with Hindenburg—and, worse, an Otto Meissner–issued memo trumpeting that humiliation—his policy became: put it in writing.[42]

Correspondence filled the air. Offer countered offer. Nothing moved forward. Except . . . that Schleicher's machinations against Papen worked their magic. The Reichswehr's pessimistic kriegspiel unnerved Papen's Cabinet. It resigned en masse.[43] More important, it panicked Hindenburg. Papen struggled to survive. Schleicher mocked his efforts—sneering the same words at him that were hurled at Martin Luther centuries before as he embarked to face judgment at the Diet of Worms, "Little Monk, you have chosen a difficult path." (*Monchlein, Monchlein, du gehst einen schweren Gang.*)[44]

Papen's was not a difficult path. It was an impossible path.

Hindenburg summoned his Fränzchen. Tears filled The Old Gentleman's eyes, as he begged, "You'll consider me a cad, my dear Papen, if I change my mind now. But I am too old to take now, at the end of my life, the responsibility for a civil war. We'll have to let Herr von Schleicher try his luck in God's name."[45]

The tears were real. When it was all over, he inscribed a photo to his deposed chancellor, sentimentally reading "I had a comrade" ("*Ich hat einen Kameraden*").[46]

Perhaps the sobs and the inscription were mere factors of age, but, in truth, Hindenburg had grown incredibly fond of Franz von Papen. But fond or not, when the going got tough, you could count on not being able to count on Paul von Hindenburg.

Papen and Hitler desired the chancellorship. Schleicher didn't. It wasn't his style to assume such a high-profile—and now perilous—position. But who else remained? Certainly not Hugenberg or a Social Democrat. Not the Bohemian Corporal. Perhaps former Reichsbank president Hjalmar Schacht, but that scenario too went nowhere, with even Schacht publicly demurring: "There is only one man who can now become Chancellor, and that is Adolf Hitler."[47] Still, Schleicher protested. "I am the last horse in your stable," he argued to Hindenburg, "and ought to be kept in reserve."[48]

Some thought a revived Harzburg Front might sunder the deadlock. But talk of it rapidly deadlocked. "Strasser suggests negotiating with the Nationalists," Goebbels recorded. "The Leader unconditionally declines. This may come later, but for the time being it is impossible"[49]—impossible not only because of seething DNVP-NSDAP acrimony, but from Hitler's insistence that, like Brüning and Papen before him, he wield the powers of a presidial Cabinet.

Which was not about to happen under Hindenburg.

"You know that *I* represent the ideas of a presidial cabinet," Hindenburg wrote to Hitler on Monday, November 21, "meaning one that is led not by a party leader but by a supra-party personality who enjoys my confidence. *You* have stated that your movement would only be available for a cabinet headed by you, the Party leader. If I were to go along with this I would have to demand that such a cabinet commands a Parliamentary majority. Hence I request you, as leader of the largest party, to ascertain whether and on what conditions you could obtain a working majority for a Cabinet led by you with a firm programme. I would like your answer by Thursday evening."[50]

Hitler jumped to the conclusion that his appointment might finally be at hand. It wasn't. Hindenburg set him straight. On that Thursday, November 24, Otto Meissner wrote Hitler, "The Reich President thanks you for your readiness to accept the leadership of a presidial cabinet. But he . . . cannot give presidial power to the leader of a party which, over and over again, has stressed viewpoints not approved by the Herr Reich President. He cannot but fear that a presidial cabinet under your leadership would automatically lead to a Party dictatorship, causing increased and bitter strife within the nation. He cannot be responsible for such eventualities."[51]

On Friday, December 2, negotiations ended. Hindenburg named Schleicher chancellor. "That is the final choice left," Goebbels sneered. "When he is overthrown, our turn comes."[52]

But had their turn already come and gone? Each day brought more bad news for Hitler. On Saturday, December 3, Schleicher plotted with Gregor Strasser. Strasser would bring over as much support from the party as he could, perhaps as many as sixty Reichstag deputies. Schleicher would designate Strasser not only his vice chancellor but also minister president of Prussia.[53] The following day, the Nazi position grew yet more precarious. In Thuringian state elections, their vote tumbled from 42.5 percent on July 31 to just 37.1 percent.[54]

British journalist Sefton Delmer tipped off Putzi Hanfstaengl with details of a proposed Schleicher-Strasser deal. Putzi alerted Hitler.[55] So Hitler was loaded for bear when Strasser finally broached news of his negotiations with Schleicher, accusing him of the lowest form of disloyalty. His vitriol overwhelmed Strasser—just as at Bamberg in 1926. Again, Strasser folded. "I was so horrified, so speechless, so beside myself," Gregor later told his brother Otto, "that I could only ask 'Herr Hitler, do you really think me capable of such villainy?'"[56]

"Yes!" Hitler screamed, "I believe it! I am convinced of it! I have proof!"[57]

Strasser grabbed his briefcase, storming out of the Kaiserhof, barely grunting as he rushed past a clearly mystified Alfred Rosenberg, retreating to his headquarters at the Askanischer Platz's massive Hotel Excelsior. Defeated, disgusted, and exhausted (some saw him pacing the Wilhelmplatz talking to himself[58]), he precipitously resigned from all party offices.[59]

Gregor Strasser quickly vanished into history's woodwork (or, rather, to a vacation in Bolzano[60]). Hitler quickly moved to solidify his position, haranguing party leaders to stick with him. "If the Party ever falls apart," he raged, "I will take a gun and end it all in a minute."[61] As ever, Hitler's followers flung away all doubts, to pledge their complete, undying fealty to him—and to turn on anyone now accused of party disloyalty. Of top party leadership, only Gottfried Feder held out against denouncing Strasser. "Either you sign," Hitler screamed at his oldest remaining comrade, "or you'll be kicked out of the party."[62] Feder signed—and, for good measure, took a face-saving three-week leave of absence.[63]

"Rarely had the true nature of the Party been so revealed as on this occasion," observed Rudolf Olden, "with . . . its lack of discipline and dignity, its peculiar combination of mawkishness and sadism."[64] Or as Joseph Goebbels gleefully phrased it: "Strasser now is completely isolated, a dead man."[65]

Hitler's victory had been more closely run than he would have liked. He had carried this day. But the morrow might bring unpleasant headlines, massive rank-and-file defections, an end to his march on the Chancellery as inglorious as his retreat from the Feldherrnhalle in 1923. Life was not necessarily good.

A visitor came to call.

Leni Riefenstahl had called on Hitler and his acolytes several times since returning from filming in Greenland. At Berlin, she had found Magda Goebbels to be "a beauty . . . a lady" and Hermann Göring "not yet as fat as he became."[66] Almost immediately following the Nazis' dismal returns of November 6, she visited Hitler at Munich. He remained strangely buoyant, as confident as ever. Strasser's defection, however, left him morose, angry, and near despondency. Leni had not at all planned on seeing him on this fateful night—not at all. Strolling through Berlin streets, near to the Kaiserhof, a newsboy's bellowing caught her ear, with words of the Strasser imbroglio. Still the political neophyte, she barely knew who Schleicher was—let alone Strasser, but she bought a paper anyway, and ducked into the Kaiserhof lobby to learn of the day's Nazi soap opera. Wilhelm Brückner spotted her. They conversed. He ran upstairs to inform his master of her presence.

Hitler summoned her. She hesitated, possessing enough political (or just human) sense to know trouble when she saw it. She went anyway. Hitler "gave me his hand," she recalled, "then he walked up and down the room. His face was pale, his hair hanging down over his forehead, which was covered with beads of sweat. Then he burst out, 'Those traitors, those cowards—and shortly before the final victory at that—those idiots—we have fought, toiled, for thirteen years and given everything . . . and now, with the goal within reach, this betrayal!' Then he looked at me, held my hand and said, 'thank you for coming.' Without saying a single word, I left the room."[67]

Paul von Hindenburg also had company. Prince Louis Ferdinand was back from Detroit, bearing with him a personal written message for Hindenburg from his boss Henry Ford. He meant to just drop it off with Otto Meissner at the Chancellery and then to depart. Meissner had other ideas insisting "Lulu" visit with The Old Gentleman. The prince demurred, but Meissner persisted. Soon, "Lulu" was inside Otto von Bismarck's darkened old office, ushered before the ancient, frock-coated Reichspräsident. "To my great distress," Hindenburg pled, "I am accused by many people in Germany of being disloyal to your grandfather and your family. I am a monarchist and shall always be loyal to you and your house. At the same time I must do my duty towards the German people, who have twice shown me their confidence."[68]

Words that meant exactly nothing.

The Nazis struggled to maintain their own confidence. Goebbels bravely recorded such thoughts as, "We must summon all of our forces once more to hold the organization together"[69] and "We must cut down the salaries of our District Leaders, as otherwise we cannot manage to make shift with our finances."[70] On Friday evening, December 16, the visiting American Jewish trade union representative Abraham Plotkin decided on a big risk: attending that night's Sportpalast NSDAP rally. Goebbels was speaking, and friends advised Plotkin to arrive early. Yet, tonight the hall remained largely empty, the sparse crowd "disheartened and disappointed."[71]

"I had come to see a whale," concluded Plotkin, "and found a minnow."[72]

Like Riefenstahl, he too just silently . . . left.

Silence—quiet—was Schleicher's aim. He thought he had achieved it. "My policy is one of steadying the jarred nerves of the German people," he informed the Associated Press's Louis P. Lochner, "and especially our politicians. '*Ruhe, Ruhe, Ruhe*' ['Quiet, Quiet, Quiet'] is my motto. That policy is succeeding. Take today: everything is quiet. Why? Because I have suggested to all the parties that there should be a truce during the Christmas holidays. As you see, they have accepted my suggestion. These eight or ten days will do much to steady our political nerves.

"After the Christmas season is over I shall find other occasions for calling a political truce, and before we know it, the whole excitement that has characterized recent weeks and months will have subsided and we can go back to our constructive tasks again."[73]

Lochner thought Schleicher to be a fool. The nation's silence had nothing to do with Schleicher. It had everything to do with the Germans' reverence—indeed, almost obsession, for Christmas. And Lochner was right. January 1933 would contradict everything that Schleicher's December "silent nights" deceptively foretold.

The Nazis were divided, broke, and, yes, occasionally, suicidal. But they were not quite defeated. Nor were they incapable of rational strategizing. On Friday, December 8, the Reichstag, by a 404–127 vote, passed their motion to checkmate Schleicher in the case of Hindenburg's passing. Now, should any reichspräsident expire, his office would no longer pass onto the reichskanzler but rather to the chief justice of the supreme court.[74] The Nazis had other parliamentary tricks up their brown shirtsleeves, but those would wait for later days.

Still, their party remained somewhere between eight and twelve million marks in debt from its year of nonstop campaigning. Some estimated the total as high as twenty million.[75] "My most tragic moment was . . . when I had to sign all sorts of contracts," Hitler would recall in May 1942. "I signed . . . in the name of the Party, but all the time I had the feeling that, if we did not win, all would be for ever lost."[76]

Yes, lost. Strasser had bolted. Genuine NSDAP-Zentrum cooperation remained elusive. And, despite cooperation on transit strikes and the occasional resolution of no-confidence, any Nazi-KPD alliance proved the most fleeting of all. In the recent Reichstag session, Red and Brown acrimony went beyond the verbal. "Somebody hurled a spittoon," reported the *New York Times*. "After that everything movable was used. A Nazi was hit on the head with a telephone receiver. Two Communists were targets for inkwells. Tables were lifted high by Nazis and flung upon their Communist enemies. A glass chandelier was struck by the warring factions, and glass splinters showered the combatants."[77]

The public grew ever more disgusted with such nonsense. Speculation arose that if Hindenburg decreed still another round of elections, the Nazis' Reichstag membership might fall to just 150 seats—perhaps to as low as 120.[78] "The year 1932," grieved Goebbels as New Year's 1933 approached, "has brought us eternal ill-luck."[79]

Hitler, mercurial as ever, exhibited far better spirits. At Munich, on New Year's Day, he attended a coffee at Putzi Hanfstaengl's Gentzstrasse flat. Present was a recuperated Eva Braun.[80] "A pleasant-looking blonde, a slightly helpless type . . ." considered Hanfstaengl, "personable and eager to please."[81] As Hitler departed, he became oddly excited. Signing Putzi's guest book, he exclaimed, "This year belongs to us. I will guarantee you that in writing."[82]

Schleicher took to the radio to pronounce his middle way, the path of the progressive general that he was. "My heretical view," spake the new chancellor, "is I am a supporter neither of capitalism [n]or of socialism."[83] Such opinions—and loose talk of nationalizing the steel industry[84]—only alienated the industrialists who had previously supported Papen. "Schleicher," they grumbled to Hindenburg, "is no better than a Bolshevik. You should get rid of him."[85] For his part, The Old Gentleman had finally wearied of Schleicher's machinations, particularly his torpedoing of Hindenburg's favorite, "Fränzchen." The Schleicher game was getting old; his time growing short. In late November, Wilhelm Gröner summarized the growing anti-Schleicher movements, when he wrote to his former protégé:

You desire a meeting with me to learn the reasons for the "estrange-ment" that has taken place between us. My dear Schleicher, the expression "estrangement" is too mild. I will be open and honest. Wrath and fury boil within me, because I have been disappointed by you, my old friend, pupil, adopted son, my hope for the nation and fatherland. . . . Who has "confidence" in you now? Hardly anyone; you are considered exceptionally intelligent, clever, and cunning and one expects you to become chancellor because of your cleverness. You are welcome to it.[86]

Franz von Papen hankered for revenge against the puppet master who had created—and then mocked and destroyed—him. Schleicher had wanted to pack him off as ambassador to Paris,[87] but Papen demurred, wanting to remain on hand to now out-scheme the schemer. A trick of fate—and real estate—simplified his task. Assuming the chancellorship, Papen had found the presidential palace under repairs. He had allowed Hindenburg to reside in the chancellery, relocating to a nearby flat usually assigned to the per-manent secretary of the interior ministry at the back of 78 Wilhelmstrasse. When Papen forfeited his office, Hindenburg allowed him to remain there, convenient to his ear. Schleicher resided at the defense ministry—on the Bendlerstrasse, a half-mile distant.[88]

Papen swung into action. His opening salvo: a mid-December speech to Berlin's prestigious Herrenklub welcoming Hitler's participation in the govern-ment.[89] In early January, he and Hitler conferred at the Köln home of pro-Nazi banker Kurt von Schroeder.[90] The meeting was to have been top secret but pho-tographers from Berlin's *Tägliche Rundschau* (a Schleicher-subsidized paper) had bribed a Nazi official to learn Hitler's schedule. They snapped him and Papen shaking hands as they departed.[91] Hitler and Papen still could not agree on the chancellorship, but the ice had been broken. Beyond that, certain fiscal logjams again instantly and mysteriously evaporated. "[T]he financial situation has improved all of a sudden," Goebbels's diary entry of the 17th revealed.[92]

All the positive activity fell to Papen and Hitler. Schleicher receded into nothingness. The French ambassador François-Poncet found him "hesitant, at a loss, submerged, paler than ever, exhausted. . . ."[93] He continued to toy with the now pathetic idea of bringing Gregor Strasser into the government,[94] but that was about it. In mid-January, he even arranged a Strasser-Hindenburg meeting.[95] "I give you my word of honor as a Prussian general," The Old Gentleman informed the former Nazi majordomo, "that I shall never make the Bohemian corporal Chancellor of Germany."[96]

Perhaps it was such words—and assumptions that he was the only game in town—that propelled Schleicher into dangerous waters. Even Papen's maneuverings with Hitler failed to excite him. "I won't scold him," he con-descendingly declared regarding his predecessor. "I'll just say to him: 'my *Fränzchen*, you've committed another blunder!'"[97]

But Schleicher was already committing his own colossal blunders, most notably his resuscitation of Heinrich Brüning's abortive plan to resettle hard-luck urbanites onto eight hundred thousand acres of land belong-ing to Hindenburg's Junker *confrères*.[98] The Junkers' 5.6-million-member[99] organization, the influential Reichslandbund, hit the roof—as it had against Brüning. On the one hand, Junkers excoriated Schleicher as an "agrarian Bol-shevik" (*Agrabolschewik*).[100] On the other, they accused him of protecting "the almighty-money-bag interests of internationally oriented export industry and its satellites."[101]

Schleicher remained blissfully unperturbed. He had no real worries. Hit-ler, in fact, was useful to him, still strong enough to act as a bogeyman, but, with his party in disarray, progressing merely backwards.

And then came Lippe.

Lippe, among the very tiniest of the Reich's seventeen *lander*, conducted state elections on Sunday, January 15. National Socialists, desperate to jump-start their faltering movement shoved all their chips onto the table, flood-ing the state with money, manpower, and rallies, dispatching their grandest speakers to its meanest villages. They won big—39.6 percent of the vote, up from 17 percent in Lippe's last balloting. Social Democrats advanced from 31 to 35 percent, gaining largely from KPD defections. Nationalists forfeited a third of their votes.[102]

It was, however, not *that* much of a victory, amounting to too small a vote (only 99,812 ballots cast; just thirty-eight thousand for the Nazis—up by five thousand [103]) in too small a place (barely over 165,000 inhabitants). Beyond that, Hugenberg's local press had gone exceedingly easy on them.[104] But that counted for little as the Nazis' own press trumpeted the "miracle of Lippe."[105] "Hitler Victory!" crowed *Der Angriff*, "The People of Lippe Speak![106] . . . the great masses of the people are on the move—in our direction."[107] It was, as Hitler noted a decade later, "a success whose importance it is not possible to over-estimate."[108]

Fast upon Lippe's heels came the "Eastern Aid" (*Osthilfe*) Scandal.

The Osthilfe program dated from the late 1920s, earmarking approxi-mately two billion marks to aid hard-pressed eastern agriculture.[109] Much of it, however, simply lined the pockets of large Junker landholders. While millions of Germans starved, Osthilfe money funded the acquisition of race horses and travel to the Riviera.[110] SPD and Zentrum Reichstag delegates demanded an investigation. The Reichspräsident ordered Schleicher to quash their probe. Schleicher either couldn't or wouldn't. Some even said he tried to use the scandal as a club against Hindenburg.[111] *That* would have been a very dangerous game for even a Schleicher to play. Particularly, since this *Osthilfe-skandal* might eventually lead to the Hindenburgs themselves. In October 1927, as an eightieth birthday present, the Junker *Reichslandbunde* presented Hindenburg with the title to his ancient ancestral estate at Neudeck, East Prussia—except, they really hadn't. To evade future inheritance taxes, they had registered the transfer to Oskar.[112] By January 1933, with the Osthilfe-skandal cracking wide open, the Hindenburgs' Neudeck tax dodge suddenly threatened ominous consequences for all concerned.

Still more trouble confronted Hindenburg in the supposedly toothless Reichstag. National Socialists threatened to not only embarrass Hindenburg but to depose him. Articles of impeachment were now under consideration, charging the Reichspräsident with abusing the powers of his office, through the misuse of his various emergency decrees. Ordinarily, the fractured Reichstag could not agree on even the smallest matters. But on this huge matter, it just might. Hitlerites would vote "*ya*" (or threaten to) to pressure Hindenburg to finally name their leader reichskanzler. The KPD would also vote to impeach—merely out of their finely honed sense of crude anti-everything mischief. That totaled 296 votes—six more than necessary. Beyond that, any number of embittered Social Democrats, still incensed from Hindenburg's post–re-election ingratitude and his acquiesce in Papen's "Rape of Prussia," might join them.[113]

Paul and Oskar von Hindenburg, as well as Kurt von Schleicher, now felt the wall at their backs. Schleicher, moreover, no longer possessed the cards to toss anyone else overboard. The Hindenburgs did. And it would be Schleicher.

Which left the question of his replacement. Papen still fancied recapturing his lost chancellorship. Just about everyone opposed that. Hitler coveted it for himself. The Hindenburgs, as well as Alfred Hugenberg, remained, as ever, most opposed to that.

But ever was not always *for*ever.

Sunday, January 22, proved a busy day for Hitler. Morning saw him speeding across icy roads from Frankfurt-am-Oder to Berlin. At 2:00 p.m., he spoke at the city's St. Nicolai Cemetery, laying a wreath at Horst Wessel's grave ("Wessel has erected a monument to himself in ongoing history which shall prevail longer than stone and bronze"[114]). Virtually next door, thirty-five thousand storm troopers raucously taunted the KPD at its Karl Liebknecht House headquarters. That evening, Hitler delivered an atypically listless Sportpalast address.[115] He possessed, however, a very good reason for his disinterestedness.[116] At 10:00, that snowy evening, he, Göring, Röhm, Himmler, and Frick adjourned to suburban Dahlem and the luxurious home of the nouveau-riche (through marriage to his boss's daughter) and nouveau-Nazi (membership card number: 1,999,927[117]) Joachim von Ribbentrop.[118] Like Hanfstaengl Ribbentrop had once lived in New York City (temporarily at the Hotel Vanderbilt and earning his living as a freelance newspaper reporter[119]). Returning to protect the Fatherland in 1914, he had served on the Turkish Front alongside Papen.[120]

Not coincidentally at all, Papen would be there. So would Oskar von Hindenburg and Otto Meissner. Discretion ran at a premium. Meissner and Hindenburg had, under cover of darkened house lights, snuck out of Berlin's State Opera House to attend. At Ribbentrop's, Göring plied Meissner with insincere hints of a Nazi-assisted Hohenzollern restoration.[121] Hitler, meanwhile, conferred privately with Hindenburg, who held steadfastly committed to Papen's return to power and remained the camarilla's most adamantly anti-Hitler member. No one knows who said what in their hour-long conversation, though many assume Hitler employed a toxic combination of carrots and sticks (most likely, presidential impeachment and a Neudeck tax investigation[122]) on the hitherto recalcitrant Oskar. "In the taxi on the way back," Meissner recalled, "Oskar . . . was extremely silent, and the only remark which he made was that it could not be helped—the Nazis had to be taken into the government. My impression was that Hitler had succeeded in getting him under his spell."[123]

Meissner and Hindenburg's visit hardly passed unnoticed. Schleicher had not fully lost his knack for intrigue. The next day, he casually inquired of Meissner as to how he enjoyed the food at Ribbentrop's.[124] That same day, Papen proposed a Hitler chancellorship to Hindenburg Sr., who rejected it out of hand. Papen reported his failure back to Hitler, proposing a compromise Cabinet headed by Hjalmar Schacht. Hitler, tired of such variations on an unacceptable theme, exploded in rage.[125]

On Thursday, January 26, at Berlin's Friedrichstrasse Station, Kronprinz Wilhelm and his son, Prince Louis Ferdinand, entrained for Doorn. Riding past the Reichstag, "Lulu" asked, "Do you think Schleicher will hold out much longer?"

"I wonder,"[126] his father muttered forlornly.

Schleicher felt hardly better. By that same day, he had, at least momentarily, reached two unpleasant conclusions. First, he was finished as chancellor—though he might still retreat to his former bailiwick as defense minister.[127] Second, even a Hitler Cabinet was preferable to any headed by the execrable Papen (much as Papen now held that even a Hitler Cabinet was preferable to any headed by the execrable Schleicher). Schleicher, accompanied by his old friend and close ally Gen. Kurt ("The Red General") von Hammerstein-Equord, approached Hindenburg to solicit support for Hitler. They quickly discovered that Hindenburg shared only their first idea—that Schleicher's chancellorship was kaput—and demanded his resignation.[128]

Acceptable chancellors remained in short supply. Intrigue ran a surplus. Clandestine meetings, plots and counter-plots, shifting alliances and moments of sheer panic by all concerned, pervaded the air.

The free-for-all only accelerated on Saturday, January 28, when Reichspräsident Hindenburg accepted Schleicher's resignation.[129] "I have already one foot in the grave," Hindenburg excused himself to his now ex-chancellor, "and I am not sure that I will not regret this action in heaven later on."[130]

"After this breach of trust, sir," Schleicher—a man who knew such breaches all too well—acidly responded, "I am not sure that you will go to heaven."[131]

Only moderately less happy were the nation's Social Democrats. Frozen out of the federal government since Hermann Müller's ouster, betrayed and scorned by Hindenburg, swept from power in Prussia by Papen, a hundred thousand Social Democrats assembled in the Lustgarten to protest ("Berlin Stays Red"[132]) whatever government now awaited them. Six thousand Reichsbanner men staged military-style maneuvers at nearby Tegel. The *New York Times* reported that they "scouted 'the enemy,' leaped artificial ditches, crawled through wire obstacles and scaled like real soldiers."[133] In Berlin, SPD speakers vowed that "the working class" stood ready to "mount barricades to defend its constitutional rights."[134]

Would Hitler succeed Schleicher? That remained to be seen. The Zentrum proved unable to finalize a deal with Hitler. Or was that rather vice-versa?[135] Meanwhile a highly skittish Alfred Hugenberg, with Franz Seldte's Stahlhelm in tow, boarded the Hitler bandwagon. It remained an uneasy alliance. Hitler, desperate for power, ignored Theodor Duesterberg's Jewish roots, even offering the Stahlhelm vice president a Cabinet post. Duesterberg, still disgusted by the attacks launched against him as recently as November's race, said no.[136]

Papen and Hitler kept negotiating. Hitler now assumed a reasonable air, merely insisting on the chancellorship for himself, minor Cabinet posts for Frick (Interior) and Göring (Minister without Portfolio), and, through Göring, control of the Prussian police.[137] Papen could return as vice chancellor. Nationalists would hold all major Cabinet seats—Finance (Hugenberg), Labor (Seldte), Foreign Affairs (Baron Konstantin von Neurath), Finance (Count Lutz Schwerin von Krosigk), and Defense (Gen. Werner von

Blomberg[138]). Hitler agreed he would meet with Hindenburg only if accompanied by Papen.[139] Papen's friends still warned him of the threat Hitler posed. He countered that his new partner was boxed. Hitler would find himself surrounded by representatives of the camarilla, serving at Hindenburg's increasingly prickly will. Most important, the Bohemian Corporal would be compelled to actually govern, to finally take responsibility for events, to no longer stand so boldly, as Gregor Strasser had proclaimed, for "the opposite of what there is today."[140] And, so, Papen, insouciant as ever, comforted his critics, "You're wrong, we've hired him."[141] Even the vanquished Schleicher displayed equanimity. "If Hitler wants to establish a dictatorship," he remarked, "then the Army will be the dictatorship within the dictatorship."[142]

Yes, that is what *they* thought. After all, they were aristocrats and generals and magnates. He was but a failed dabbler in watercolors, the loudest of beer hall loudmouths, a mere corporal. Which is why, when time finally arrived to inform the Hitlerites that the doors to power had finally swung open, they conveyed that message not to Corporal Hitler directly but rather through Capt. Hermann Göring, proud wearer—like Blomberg and Ludendorff and, most important on this fateful day, Paul Ludwig Hans Anton von Beneckendorff und von Hindenburg—of Prussia's *Pour le Mérite*.[143]

The new year had not, however, treated Joseph Goebbels well. True, he had overseen the conquest of Lippe, but concentrating on that electoral triumph, he had been excluded from Hitler's January 4 Köln meeting with Papen. On December 23 his pregnant wife, Magda, miscarried. Taken to the hospital ("Everything is empty of joy"), her condition only worsened. And, as for Hitler's possible Cabinet, Goebbels was conspicuously absent—at least for now. Göring—not Hitler—had given him that news.[144] And, yes, everything might still fall apart. "We sit up till five o'clock in the morning," recorded Goebbels, "are ready for everything, and have considered the thing from all angles. The Leader paces up and down the room. A few hours' sleep and the decisive hour will strike."[145]

It was, however, to Goebbels's plush Reichskanzlerplatz apartment on Monday afternoon, January 30, that Göring rushed back with the gladdest of tidings: Hindenburg had finally given way. Hitler was chancellor. Der Führer conceded to Papen control of the overall Prussian government, and Hindenburg—egged on by Oskar—found the once loathsome Hitler suddenly sufficiently tolerable. If Hitler was the price one had to pay for a little peace and quiet, not to mention for the return of his beloved Fränzchen, well, so be it. So be it.

Events simply melted Göring. An observer found him "humble, sweetly reasonable, obviously overwhelmed by . . . his success."[146] Yet, success might still elude them. Rumors spread that Schleicher and Hammerstein-Equord plotted a military coup to arrest not only the Hitlerites but also Meissner and both Hindenburgs.[147] It was a thoroughly false alarm, spread by the aristocratic rightist busybody Werner von Alvensleben, but in this frantic, uncharted atmosphere no one could be sure of anything. Hitler ordered the SA into action. Göring, acting on no authority whatsoever, dispatched six police battalions[148] to protect Hindenburg, who by now had definitely concluded that enough was enough. The circus must end. Hitler would be his chancellor.

But the circus would not end. Hindenburg summoned defense minister–designate General Blomberg back from a disarmament conference at Geneva. Köln steel magnate (and former war profiteer[149]) Otto Wolff phoned Schleicher with the news, warning him to arrest not only Blomberg but also both Hindenburgs.[150] On January 30, Blomberg, never an admirer of Schleicher, detrained at Berlin's Anhalter Bahnhof, only to be met with conflicting orders. Hammerstein-Equord's adjutant, Maj. Adolf-Friedrich von Kuntzen, ordered him to the Bendlerstrasse to meet with Hammerstein-Equord and with Schleicher. Oskar von Hindenburg ("I intend to make the *traitor Schleicher* pay for this"[151]) demanded that Blomberg report to his father. Blomberg obeyed Oskar—to be hurriedly (and quite illegally) sworn in as defense minister.[152]

Speed was of the essence—before everything collapsed of its own weightlessness. Hitler and Hugenberg continued tussling. Hitler demanded new elections. Hugenberg, for once thinking clearly, feared them.[153] The two might yet simultaneously storm out the door and out of power. To the rescue trooped Otto Meissner. The Reichspräsident had been waiting for fifteen minutes, he snapped—he would not be kept "waiting any longer."[154] Hitler, Papen, Hugenberg et al. meekly trooped up to Hindenburg's second floor office. Suddenly finance minister–designate Krosigk tossed in one last roadblock, demanding to know chancellor-designate Hitler's proposed monetary and fiscal policies. The two had never previously met. Hitler, not particularly interested in either monetary or fiscal issues, might have loudly excoriated Krosigk. Instead, he merely mumbled a few words of assurance.[155]

Tens of thousands watched Franklin Roosevelt's inauguration. A select group witnessed Hitler's. Even men like Röhm and Goebbels found themselves excluded, nervously waiting from afar. "What is happening there?" the exhausted Goebbels agonized. "We are torn between doubt, hope, joy and despair. We have been deceived too often to be able whole-heartedly to believe in the great miracle. Chief-of-Staff Röhm stands at the window the whole time, watching the door of the Chancellery from which the Leader must emerge. We shall be able to judge by his face if the interview was happy."[156]

Hitler emerged, silent, tears swelling his once-blind eyes. Goebbels knew the answer—*Adolf Hitler was chancellor of Germany.*

Under a clear night sky, thousands and thousands of storm troopers, SS men, Hitler Youth, Stahlhelm—and just ordinary German men and women—combined to stage a six-hour display of torch-bearing, chanting, "Horst Wessel Lied"–singing, overwhelming power. Their sheer number, snaking their way past the *kanzlerie* and through the Brandenburg Gate, amazed the clearly out-of-touch Hindenburg. They would stage too many more. At one of the hundreds to come, reporter Dorothy Thompson stood watching in absolute horror, no longer quite so sanguine regarding Hitler's future.

"I saw them," she recorded of these vigorous, brownshirted men, "in my mind's eye, marching on and on, over frontiers, north, east, west and south. . . . I saw, in my mind's eye, the machine guns that would soon be in their hands, the planes that would fly over their heads, the tanks that would rumble and roll with their tread."

"Post-war Europe was finished," she sorrowed, "and pre-war Europe had begun. . . ."[157]

So had pre-war America.

An Epilogue of Blood

In my previous historical studies I have on occasion included an epilogue detailing the subsequent fate of each book's cast of characters. We shan't do that here but, nonetheless, we can—and should—list those mentioned in these pages who would subsequently fall afoul of Germany's Adolf Hitler. Granted, any number of FDR's high-level November 1932 supporters—Farley, Garner, Moley, Long, Coughlin, Smith, Davis, Raskob, Shouse, Ely, Lemke, Johnson, etc.—fell by their own various waysides. But America being America, and FDR being FDR, while all of them felt to some degree disappointed or betrayed, none of them were actually murdered—at least, not by Franklin Delano Roosevelt.

That was, of course, not the case in Adolf Hitler's Third Reich.

Those referenced in this book who suffered from Der Führer's thirst for revenge (or merely his paranoia) are many. Consider this list of fatalities from his June 1934 "Blood Purge" (aka "The Night of the Long Knives"): Dr. Otto Ballerstedt, Karl Ernst, Fritz Gerlich, Dr. Karl-Günther Heimsoth, Edmund Heines, Gustav Ritter von Kahr, Ernst Röhm, Elisabeth von Schleicher, Gen. Kurt von Schleicher, Hans Walter Schmidt, Fr. Bernhard Stempfle, and Gregor Strasser.

Among those arrested in (but surviving) that Blood Purge include: Konrad Adenauer, Werner von Alvensleben, Count Anton von Arco-Valley, Prince August Wilhelm, Theodor Duesterberg, Otto von Lossow, Franz von Papen, Paul Schulz, and Hans von Seisser.

Which, of course, was again only part of the picture. Along the way Hitler's government also imprisoned the following: Hjalmar Schacht, Fritz Thyssen, Rudolf Diels, Reichstag president Paul Löbe, Leipzig mayor Karl Goerdeler, SPD leader Rudolf Breitscheid, KPD leaders Ernst Torgler and Wilhelm Kasper, journalist Stefan Lorant, Prussia's social welfare minister Heinrich Hirtsiefer, and even the French ambassador André François-Poncet. They were, however, lucky. The following found themselves executed: Berlin SA leader Count Wolf von Helldorf, KPD chairman Ernst Thälmann, journalist Helmuth Klotz, the DNVP's Baron Hermann von Lüninck, and Undersecretary of the Reich Chancellery Erwin Planck. Ordered arrested by Hitler as his regime degraded in 1945 were Hermann Göring and Heinrich

Himmler. Ernst "Putzi" Hanfstaengl and Kurt Lüdecke both escaped arrest. Dr. Edmund Forster committed suicide. Capt. Karl Mayr died at Buchenwald; Werner Best at Dachau.

And, of course, escaping Hitler's "justice," hardly freed one from actual justice. Hung at Nürnberg were: Hans Frank, Wilhelm Frick, Joachim von Ribbentrop, Fritz Sauckel, and Julius Streicher.

Hung following Nürnberg was Rudolf Höss.

Hans Baur, Dr. Otto Dietrich, Sepp Dietrich, Walther Funk, Konstantin von Neurath, Franz von Papen, Baldur von Schirach, and Albert Speer found themselves receiving prison sentences, either at Nürnberg or later. Others might have been hung, but cheated the gallows (though not God) by choosing death at their own hand: Philipp Bouhler, Martin Bormann, Eva Braun, Walter Buch, Joseph Goebbels, Magda Goebbels, Hermann Göring, Robert Ritter von Greim, Rudolf Hess, Heinrich Himmler, Robert Ley, Reich Bishop Ludwig Müller, Bernard Rust, Ernst Udet . . .

. . . and, of course, and, least surprisingly of all, Adolf Hitler, himself.

ACKNOWLEDGMENTS

As always, I extend sincere thanks to the many wonderful institutions that have in some sense or other assisted in the compilation of my work, in this case, the University Library at the University at Albany, Albany, New York; the Albany Public Library of Albany, New York; the Begley Library at the Schenectady County Community College, Schenectady, New York; the MacArthur Memorial, Norfolk, Virginia; the New York Public Library; the New York Public Library for the Performing Arts; the Roosevelt House (Barnard College); the New York State Library; the Sage Libraries, Russell Sage College, Troy, New York; the Saratoga Springs Public Library, Saratoga Springs, New York; the Schenectady County Public Library, Schenectady, New York; the Lucy Scribner Library, Skidmore College, Saratoga Springs, New York; the Franklin D. Roosevelt Presidential Library and Museum, Hyde Park, New York; the District of Columbia Public Library, Washington, DC; the Smithsonian Institute; and the Library of Congress.

Sincere thanks are also extended to Robert N. Going, John Gizzi, Catherine Karp, and Amity Shlaes for their assistance in completing *1932*; to Lyons Press editorial director (and before that my editor at Carroll & Graf) Keith Wallman; to production editor Lynn Zelem, designer Sheryl Kober, layout artist Joanna Beyer, publicity manager Sharon Kunz, Lyons Press marketing manager Sara Given, copy editor Joshua Rosenberg, and proofreader Kristy Patenaude; and to my agent Robert Wilson at Wilson Media.

And, of course, to my beloved wife, Patty.

Notes and Sources

Chapter One: "A gentleman cast himself down fifteen stories"

1   Gold standard. Galbraith, p. 9; Thomas & Morgan-Witts, p. 32; Charmley, pp. 212-13.

2   Baruch accommodations. Gilbert (*Prophet*), p. 349; Sandys, p. 94; Thomas & Morgan-Witts, p. 322.

3   "bolshy in politics . . . in conversation". Soames, p. 347; Gilbert (*Prophet*), p. 348; Gilbert (*Wilderness*), p. 24; Thomas & Morgan-Witts, p. 322.

4   "*City Lights*". Gilbert (*Prophet*), p. 348; Gilbert (*America*), p. 118. They first met at Marion Davies's Santa Monica beach house. The Little Tramp found Churchill "Napoleon-like with his hand in his waistcoat," looking "lost and out of place." (Chaplin, p. 368)

5   McAdoo. Soames, p. 347.

6   "A grave simple child". Soames, p. 346; Gilbert (*Prophet*), p. 346; Gilbert (*Wilderness*), p. 24; Thomas & Morgan-Witts, p. 322.

7   San Simeon. Gilbert (*Prophet*), p. 348; Gilbert (*America*), p. 118.

8   Mrs. Hearst's. *NY Times*, 19 October 1929, p. 12.

9   Condé Nast. *NY Times*, 7 October 1929, p. 28.

10   "I can only . . . to her home." Pilpel, p. 96; Sandys, p. 95. It is generally believed that Maj. John Strange Churchill was only Churchill's half-brother, John's actual father not being Winston's, but rather Evelyn Boscawen, 7th Viscount Falmouth.

11   FDR declines. Gilbert (*America*), p. 122. Morgenthau indicated to Churchill that FDR's schedule "shows that unfortunately he will not be in New York on October 28th or 29th." (Gilbert [*America*], p. 122.). FDR was indeed not in New York City on the days in question. As noted, he addressed Springfield, Massachusetts Democrats on the evening of the 28th, and Margaret "Daisy" Suckley records his activities as "Lionberger Davis to dinner?" on the 29th. Davis was a St. Louis banker, philanthropist, and art collector. (Suckley; *NY Times*, 15 April 1973, p. 61).

12   "Do they take . . . mental defectives?" *NY Times*, 16 October 1929, p. 2.

13   Smith/Walker. *NY Times*, 16 October 1929, p. 1; *Brooklyn Standard-Union*, 18 October 1929, p. 18; Handlin, p. 151; O'Connor (*Hurrah*), p. 232.

14   Hoover visit. *NY Times*, 19 October 1929, p. 5; *NY Post*, 19 October 1929, p. 6; *Brooklyn Eagle*, 19 October 1929, p. 3; Pilpel, pp. 92-93; Jenkins, p. 417.

15   Hoover arrested. Jenkins, p. 427; Sandys, p. 97.

16   "I expected to . . . compelled to offer." Gilbert (*Prophet*), p. 350; Shachtman, p. 143; Thomas & Morgan-Witts, p. 259; Gilbert (*America*), pp. 122-23; Blumenthal, p. 38.

17   Baruch dinner. Gilbert (*Prophet*), p. 350; Gilbert (*Wilderness*), p. 25.

18   "Will they blame . . . on the Democrats?—Al". *Ogden Standard Examiner*, 29 October 1929, p. 1.

19   Springfield dinner. *Appleton Post-Crescent*, 30 October 1929, p. 17; *Troy Times*, 30 October 1929, p. 1; Davis (*New York*), p. 148.

20   Baruch fled. Baruch, p. 225; Miller (*New World*), p. 370; Horan, p. 88. He had also successfully advised Will Rogers to sell (Baruch, pp. 223-24).

21   "Under my very . . . the fire brigade." Gilbert (*Prophet*), p. 350; Kelly & Smyer, p. 168. Churchill recalled this as occurring on "Black Tuesday," October 29; it appears, however, to have transpired on "Black Thursday," October 24 (Kelly & Smyer, p. 168).
22   Churchill sails. *Brooklyn Eagle*, 30 October 1929, p. 28; *Troy Times*, 30 October 1929, p. 1; *NY Times*, 31 October 1929, p. 14; Gilbert (*Prophet*), p. 351; Gilbert (*America*), p. 123. Two porters stood guard at Churchill's door to bar reporters. One might surmise he was either hungover or still drunk.

CHAPTER TWO: "I WON'T BE READY UNTIL 1932"

1   Sixth cousins. Burns, p. 9; Pottker, p. 48.
2   First cousins. Davis (*New York*), p. 5; Black (*Champion*), p. 7; Persico (*Franklin*), p. 14; Pottker, p. 40; Simon, p. 54; Goodwin (*Ordinary*), p. 75; Ward (*Trumpet*), p. 33. Doris Kearns Goodwin and Michael Beschloss term Rebecca Brien Howland Roosevelt, the daughter of James's mother's *first cousin*, a second cousin. James's father, Isaac Roosevelt, had himself not married a blood relative but had rather, at age thirty-seven, wed a nineteen-year-old niece of his father's third wife (Miller [*F.D.R.*], p. 10; Beschloss, p. 23). At Hyde Park, in 1904, "Rosy" Roosevelt's daughter Helen married Theodore Douglas Robinson, son of TR's younger sister Corinne. Eleanor was a bridesmaid; Franklin served as usher; TR attended. (*NY Times*, 19 June 1904, p. 20; *NY Times*, 10 July 1962, p. 33; Cook [*Vol. 1*], p. 130)
3   Campobello. Brands (*Traitor*), pp. 23-24; Black (*Champion*), p. 15; Persico (*Franklin*), p. 19.
4   "In thinking back . . . regularity of things. . . ." Freidel (*New Deal*), p. 6; Schlesinger (*Crisis*), p. 317.
5   Democrat. Ward (*Trumpet*), pp. 44-45; Morgan, p. 32; Pottker, p. 45; Black (*Champion*), pp. 8-9; Beschloss, p. 25. James was formerly a Whig; his father, at first a Federalist. Sara's Republican father, Warren Delano II, was a successful opium trader (Ward [*Trumpet*], pp. 70-77; Miller [*F.D.R.*], p. 14), who noted: "James Roosevelt is the first person who made me realize that a Democrat can be a gentleman." (Black [*Champion*], p. 11; Pottker, p. 48)
6   Appointment. Morgan, p. 32; Miller (*F.D.R.*), p. 22; Black (*Champion*), pp. 17-18; Brands (*Traitor*), p. 18. "Rosey," formerly a Republican, had donated to Cleveland in 1884. By 1916, he had returned to the GOP, writing to Woodrow Wilson: "Your rotten administration will soon make us ashamed to live here!" Also, perhaps, aiding Rosey's appointment was Robert Barnwell Roosevelt, TR and Eleanor's uncle and great-uncle, respectively, Cleveland's minister to The Hague and later treasurer of the Democratic National Committee (see p. 301).
7   "My little . . . United States." *Iowa City Iowan*, 2 July 1932, p. 5; Schlesinger (*Crisis*), pp. 319-20; Kleeman, p. 146; Ward (*Trumpet*), p. 124; Miller (*F.D.R.*), p. 22; Black (*Champion*), p. 17; Farr, p. 40.
8   Supervisor. Pottker, p. 45.
9   School in Germany. Ward (*Trumpet*), p. 149; Black, p. 19.
10   Bad Nauheim. Ward (*Trumpet*), p. 146; Black (*Champion*), p. 19. In 1932, FDR revealed he was arrested four times in Germany when he was thirteen: "Once for running over a goose with my bicycle. A second time when we picked cherries hanging over a fence and a third time when we carried our bicycles into a station. We paid fines for all offenses. And when we cycled into the fortified city of Strassbourg [sic], a violation of a war regulation, we were taken before a colonel. He let us go with a warning." (*Charleston Gazette*, 2 August 1932, p. 8)
11   Groton. Miller (*F.D.R.*), p. 22. Both James and Sara had converted to Episcopalianism—James, first, previously being Dutch Reformed. Sara converted from Unitarianism upon their marriage, though they wed in a Unitarian ceremony. (Black [*Champion*], pp. 9, 13)
12   Harvard Law. Burns, p. 8.
13   "C." Burns, p. 18.
14   "the greatest . . . ever had." Miller (*F.D.R.*), p. 35; Smith (*FDR*), p. 33. That is how FDR described it to a distant relative.

15 *Crimson.* MacKenzie, pp. 54-55; Burns, p. 17; Davis (*Beckoning*), pp. 158-62; Miller (*F.D.R.*), p. 39. FDR also raised money for the Boer cause. Winston Churchill would not have been pleased. (MacKenzie, p. 52)

16 Republican Club. Schlesinger (*Crisis*), p. 324; Collier & Horowitz (*Roosevelts*), p. 108; Miller (*F.D.R.*), p. 34; Black (*Champion*), p. 27; Beschloss, p. 35.

17 March 17. MacKenzie, p. 45; Davis (*Beckoning*), pp. 191-93; Roosevelt (*Aunt*), p. 14; Brands (*Traitor*), p. 41.

18 "After the . . . forlorn." Roosevelt & Shalett, p. 214; Roosevelt (*Aunt*), p. 14; Collier & Horowitz (*Roosevelts*), p. 322.

19 "Dear Mummy . . . each other." Brands (*Traitor*), p. 39.

20 "Franklin D. . . . *etc., etc.*" Freidel (*Apprenticeship*), p. 82; Ward (*Temperament*), p. 70; Miller (*F.D.R.*), p. 56; Brands (*Traitor*), p. 44. The firm, however, handled far more than dogs and babies, for example, defending Standard Oil against cousin Theodore's high-profile 1906 anti-trust suit. (Brands [*Traitor*], p. 44)

21 "I went . . . full-fledged lawyer." Freidel (*Apprenticeship*), p. 83; Miller (*F.D.R.*), p. 56; Ward (*Temperament*), p. 71; Brands (*Traitor*), p. 44.

22 Small dogs. Mr. Ledyard himself had instructed his firm's office manager that "under no circumstances [was he] to put any serious piece of litigation" in FDR's hands. (Flynn [*Myth*], p. 260)

23 Senate nomination. MacKenzie, pp. 57-58, 166; Davis (*Beckoning*), pp. 220-23, 239.

24 Sheehan. MacKenzie, pp. 60-65; Davis (*Beckoning*), pp. 246-57; Morgan, pp. 117-22; Smith (*FDR*), pp. 70-78.

25 5'4". Schlesinger (*Ghosts*), p. 8; McElvaine, p. 105. Davis (*New York*, p. 45) and Lomazow & Fettmann (p. 18) saw him as just 5'0".

26 "spoiled silk-pants . . . of guy." Stiles, p. 25; Miller (*F.D.R.*), p. 76; Martin (*Bandwagons*), p. 251; Pietrusza (*1920*), p. 125.

27 "streak of . . . and insincerity". Ward (*Temperament*), p. 796; Collier & Horowitz (*Roosevelts*), p. 314; Downey, p. 90; Alter, p. 64.

28 "[A]lmost at . . . United States." Stiles, p. 22; Lomazow & Fettmann, p. 18; Pietrusza (*1920*), p. 126.

29 1904. Freidel (*New Deal*), p. 7. His father voted for TR for governor in 1898.

30 1914. Burns, pp. 57-59; Weintraub, pp. 68-71; Schlesinger (*Crisis*), p. 347; Cohen (*Fear*), p. 21; LaCerra, pp. 49-51.

31 Lucy Mercer. Schlesinger (*Crisis*), pp. 354-55; Lash (*Eleanor*), pp. 220-27; Davis (*Beckoning*), p. 493; Cook (*Vol. 1*), pp. 216-36; Persico (*Franklin*), pp. 86-122; Weintraub, pp. 141-43, 174-83.

32 "you know I . . . pretty good constitution." *NY Times*, 19 August 1920, p. 11; *Kingsport Times*, 20 August 1920, p. 9; *Chicago Tribune*, 26 August 1920, p. 3; *Providence Journal*, 19 October 1920, p. 14; Freidel (*The Ordeal*), p. 81; Morgan (*FDR*), p. 230.

33 "I was . . . reported". Morgan, p. 230. FDR was lying. Senator Borah was at Butte and heard him say it. Thirty local witnesses later supported Borah. (*Providence Journal*, 19 October 1920, p. 14; *Marion Star*, 20 October 1920, pp. 1, 7; *The Nation*, 6 October 1920, p. 364; Morgan, pp. 230-31)

34 "a pale and . . . resembles the Matterhorn". Teachout, p. 263.

35 "You might . . . until 1932." *New Outlook*, 1930, Vol. 156, p. 375; Martin (*Bandwagons*), p. 250. FDR's 1924 convention appearance so impressed Kansas City Democratic boss Tom Pendergast that he predicted Roosevelt would be the 1928 candidate. (Freidel [*Ordeal*], p. 180; Davis [*Beckoning*], p. 757)

36 Symptoms. MacKenzie, pp. 119-20; Freidel (*Ordeal*), pp. 98-99; Lash (*Eleanor*), pp. 267-68; Black (*Champion*), pp. 138-39; Davis (*Beckoning*), p. 650; Russell, p. 289; Lomazow & Fettmann, pp. 26-27; Willis, p. 63.

37 Sara/Eleanor/Howe. McKenzie, pp. 125-26; Roosevelt (*Aunt*), p. 4; Freidel (*Ordeal*), pp. 100-101, 104; Lash (*Eleanor*), pp. 273-75; Cook (*Vol. 1*), pp. 311-12; Collier & Horowitz (*Roosevelts*), p. 263; Black (*Champion*), p. 143; Cohen (*Fear*), p. 22.

38 "There are . . . by day." Martin (*Bandwagons*), p. 252; Neal, p. 168.

39 "Come here . . . along with him." Roosevelt & Shalett, p. 146; Ward (*Temperament*), p. 611; Collier & Horowitz (*Roosevelts*), p. 265; Black (*Champion*), p. 142.
40 "There had been . . . of philosophical concepts." Goodwin (*Ordinary*), p. 16.
41 "humiliation had not . . . a humble man". Tugwell (*Democratic*), p. 237.
42 "He was never . . . then more power." Tugwell (*Democratic*), p. 212.
43 Cockran. Freidel (*Ordeal*), pp. 175-76; Slayton, p. 209; Miller (*F.D.R.*), p. 204; Russell, p. 293. Smith, however, once recounted that FDR had begged him to deliver the speech.
44 Happy Warrior. Finan, pp. 178-80; Slayton, p. 209; Freidel (*Ordeal*), pp. 176-77; Miller (*F.D.R.*), p. 204; Martin (*Bandwagons*), p. 253; Black (*Champion*), pp. 164-65; Lomazow & Fettmann, p. 34; Russell, p. 294. Judge Nathan Proskauer wrote both the speech and the "Happy Warrior" phrase. FDR, having drafted his own horrendously dull version, never publicly acknowledged Proskauer's authorship.
45 "gripping so . . . it hurt". Miller (*F.D.R.*), p. 204.
46 "A figure tall . . . are lifted up." Tucker (*Mirrors*), p. 82; Peel & Donnelly, p. 30; Davis (*Beckoning*), pp. 822-23.
47 Senate. Schlesinger (*Crisis*), pp. 379, 530; Burns, pp. 98-99; Freidel (*Ordeal*), pp. 216-17, 299; Black (*Champion*), p. 175; Lomazow & Fettmann, pp. 35-36; Russell, p. 297. In December 1925, FDR, betraying his usually unfounded optimism regarding his paralysis, wrote to New York City Democrat Adolphus Ragan: "There are two good reasons why I can't run for the Senate next year. The first is that my legs are coming back in such fine shape that if I devote another two years to them I shall be on my feet again without my braces. The 2nd is that I am temperamentally unfitted to be a member of the uninteresting body known as the United States Senate. I like administrative or executive work, but do not want to have my hands and feet tied and my wings clipped for 6 long years."
48 Bond sales. Freidel (*Ordeal*), pp. 138-41; Farr, p. 138; Beschloss, p. 52.
49 Vending machines. Freidel (*Ordeal*), pp. 150-51; Farr, p. 139; Beschloss, pp. 54-55.
50 Cameras. Freidel (*Ordeal*), p. 151; Beschloss, p. 54.
51 Lobsters. Freidel (*Ordeal*), pp. 149-50; Farr, p. 139; Beschloss, pp. 52, 55.
52 Hyper-inflation. Freidel (*Ordeal*), pp. 145-46; Farr, p. 140; Beschloss, pp. 53-54. He made $5,000 over a three-year period.
53 Rosey's death. *NY Times*, 8 May 1927, p. 29; Davis (*Beckoning*), p. 811.
54 $100,000. *NY Times*, 24 May 1927, p. 38; Miller (*F.D.R.*), p. 212*fn*. FDR also inherited Rosey's Hyde Park estate following the deaths of his widow and daughter; Rosey's total estate was $1 million. Farr estimates FDR was left $600,000. The bequest may have arrived in the nick of time for FDR's finances—as well, of course, for his 1928 gubernatorial campaign. In January 1925, he had dispatched a collection of his precious ship models and naval prints to New York's Anderson Galleries for auction. He netted $4,537 (*NY Times*, 4 January 1925, pp. E3, E4; *NY Times*, 10 January 1925, p. 3; Farr, pp. 140-41; Miller [*F.D.R.*], p. 207). New Deal attorney Thomas "Tommy the Cork" Corcoran once explained the immensity of FDR's skills to fellow New Dealer James H. Rowe thusly: "Look, there you are. You have to work for a living. Here I am. I have to work for a living. This fellow has nothing to do all his life except politics. He's spent the bulk of his life in politics. He got to know every wrinkle of politics. He got to know how to handle anybody, and he worked at it 100 percent. You work at it 5 percent, and I work at it seven." (Louchheim, p. 287)
55 *Coronet*, February 1947, p. 37; www.wga.org/writtenby/writtenbysub.aspx?id=829. "Well, this much is certain—" FDR added, "if Paramount had taken that story, you and I wouldn't be chatting in the White House, would we?"
56 Warm Springs visit. Collier & Horowitz (*Roosevelts*), p. 309; Lomazow & Fettmann, p. 32. Even here, FDR's Georgia-connection was presaged by TR's. Theodore's mother, Martha "Mittie" Bulloch, hailed from Roswell, Georgia.
57 "I feel that . . . established here." Collier & Horowitz (*Roosevelts*), p. 310.
58 "I'll walk into . . . I'm a cripple!" Gould, p. 160; Collier & Horowitz (*Roosevelts*), p. 313; Persico (*Franklin*), p. 168.
59 "Warm Springs became . . . involvement with others." Collier & Horowitz (*Roosevelts*), p. 314.

60 "the longest wake any Irishman ever attended". Handlin, p. 126.

61 "My physicians . . . at Albany." Tucker (*Mirrors*), p. 95; Collier & Horowitz (*Roosevelts*), p. 230.

62 Eleanor. Schlesinger (*Crisis*), p. 382; Davis (*Invincible*), pp. 82-84; MacKenzie, p. 145; Cook (*Vol. 1*), pp. 376-77; Davis (*Beckoning*), p. 848; Rowley, p. 148. Via telephone. Eleanor was at Rochester, New York, Franklin at Warm Springs.

63 "Well, if . . . about it!" MacKenzie, p. 146; Burns, p. 101; Cook (*Vol. 1*), p. 377; Collier & Horowitz (*Roosevelts*), p. 321.

64 LeHand. Schlesinger (*Crisis*), p. 382; Davis (*Beckoning*), pp. 846, 850-51; Collier & Horowitz (*Roosevelts*), p. 230; Rowley, p. 148.

65 "Don't you dare! Don't you dare!" Schlesinger (*Crisis*), p. 382; Persico (*Lucy*), p. 183.

66 Howe. Schlesinger (*Crisis*), pp. 381-82; Rollins, p. 235; Davis (*Beckoning*), p. 846; Burns, p. 101; Cook (*Vol. 1*), p. 377; Rowley, p. 148.

67 "MESS IS NO NAME FOR IT". Stiles, p. 111; Schlesinger (*Crisis*), p. 382; Smith (*FDR*), p. 235.

68 "Now what . . . to you." Lash (*Eleanor*), p. 317; Cook (*Vol. 1*), p. 378.

69 "a governor doesn't have to be an acrobat". Stiles, p. 112; Lomazow & Fettmann, p. 36; Smith (*FDR*), p. 225.

70 Front men. New York's newly entrenched Albany County Democratic machine had already learned the trick, quickly placing Protestant aristocrats William Stormont Hackett (a Baptist and a 33rd degree Mason to boot) and John Boyd Thacher II in City Hall. Hackett, a lifelong bachelor, perished in a March 1926 auto accident at Havana. Had he not died, it is said, he—and not Franklin Roosevelt—might have succeeded Smith.

71 "And then . . . isn't it?" Rosenman & Rosenman, p. 290; Gosnell, p. 85; Rollins, p. 237; Burns, p. 103.

72 25,608. Smith (*FDR*), p. 228; Sinclair, p. 381. FDR, nonetheless, lost his home county of Dutchess quite handily. FDR lost Hyde Park 240–168, as he had lost the town in 1920. (*NY Times*, 7 November 1928, pp. 1-2; *NY Times*, 8 November 1928, p. 13) One is easily tempted to credit Roosevelt's narrow victory to his opponent Attorney General Albert Ottinger's Jewishness (as does historian Oscar Handlin), but this is not so. The Jewish Herbert Lehman ran far ahead of Roosevelt. (Handlin, p. 143)

CHAPTER THREE: "EVERYTHING SHOULD BE BLOWN UP"

1 "a beautiful woman . . . of her death". Kubizek, p. 44. Kubizek's description.

2 Alois Jr. Jetzinger, p. 42; Kubizek, pp. 45-46; Heiden (*Fuehrer*), p. 43; Langer, pp. 118-19; Shirer, p. 10; Payne, pp. 11, 21; Redlich, p. 257; Maser, p. 27. Alois Jr. twice served jail time and was also convicted of bigamy. Once writing to his stepmother, Klara, for assistance, he received a letter back in Adolf's handwriting, "To steal and be caught means that you are not even a good thief. In that case my advice is to go and hang yourself." (Payne, p. 94)

3 Gustav, Ida, Otto. Kubizek, p. 49; Jetzinger, pp. 16, 43; Olden, p. 13; Langer, pp. 117, 123; Hauner, p. 2; Waite, p. 140; Schwaab, p. 93; Stierlin, pp. 23-24; Murray, p. 104. A younger full brother, Edmund, also died young. (Maser, p. 29) It is possible that Ida was an "imbecile." (Langer, p. 117; Waite, p. 171) Paula has been described as "a little on the stupid side, perhaps a high-grade moron" (Langer, p. 117; Waite, p. 171) or as "mentally retarded." (Murray, p. 103) A little-noticed 1943 OSS report on Hitler mysteriously contends that Paula may have been at one time "the mistress of a Jew." (Murray, pp. 5, 103)

4 Klara's genealogy. Jetzinger, pp. 16, 40; Kubizek, pp. 46-49; Bullock, pp. 25, 29; Payne, pp. 9-12; Fest (*Hitler*), p. 17; Kershaw (*Hubris*), p. 9; Heiden (*Fuehrer*), p. 40; Shirer, p. 9. Hitler's attempts to expunge his family history may be seen within this streamlined, sanitized pro-Hitler account written in 1934: "So now [Alois] said good-bye to Vienna, returned home, married Klara Polzl, the daughter of a neighbour there with whom he had been playmates, and found himself appointed as Customs Officer to . . . Braunau on the Inn. A daughter was born to the couple, and then, a good many years later, came a boy [Adolf]." (Heinz, p. 14)

5   "uncle." Waite, p. 133; Kershaw (*Hubris*), p. 12; Stierlin, p. 23; Rosenbaum, p. 14.

6   Inbreeding. Waite, p. 125; Hayman, p. 7.

7   Veit. Lambert, p. 85. "[T]he Schicklgruber line has produced a string of idiots," noted David Irving. "Among the latter, was a tax official, Joseph Veit, deceased in 1904 in Klagenfurt, Austria. One of his sons had committed suicide; a daughter [Aloisia] had died in an asylum, a surviving daughter was half mad, and a third daughter was feebleminded." (Irving [*Hitler's War*], p. xxiii)

8   "People must not . . . my family is. . . ." Fest (*Hitler*), p. 14; Fest (*Face*), p. 312; Toland, p. 245; Hamann, p. 51; Rosenbaum, p. 4; Victor, pp. 13, 17. In *Mein Kampf*, he complained of press barons who "will poke into the most secret family affairs and not rest until his truffle-searching instinct digs up some embarrassing incident which is calculated to finish off the unfortunate victim." (Hitler [*Kampf*], p. 86)

9   "I'll kill myself . . . to my head." Unger, p. 67.

10   Czech blood. Jetzinger, pp. 32-33; Bullock, p. 24; Shirer, p. 8; Fest (*Hitler*), p. 15; Bracher, p. 58; Victor, pp. 35-36, 49. Alois Hitler's first wife "was of Czech origin . . ." (Langer, p. 118). His best friend was a Czech. (Jetzinger, p. 44; Redlich, p. 7)

11   Frankenberger. Jetzinger, pp. 20-24; Maser, pp. 12-13; Waite, pp. 126-27, 448; Kershaw (*Hubris*), p. 8; Roberts, p. 1; Rosenbaum, p. 5, Lukacs, p. 186; Bracher, p. 58; Toland, pp. 4, 247; Murray, pp. 5, 94; Victor, p. 17. Konrad Heiden, however, reports that Hitler's godparents—Vienna swimming pool attendant Johannes Prinz and his wife, Johanna—were "possibly of Jewish descent." (Heiden [*Fuehrer*], p. 44; Jones [*Vienna*], p. 3; Murray, pp. 5, 94; Tyson [*Eckart*], p. 258)

12   May have believed. Langer, p. 112; Redlich, pp. 6, 256; Rosenbaum, p. 31; Toland, p. 247; Maser, pp. 9-15; Kershaw (*Hitler*), p. 19.

13   "Jewishness to be . . . to be exorcised." Waite, p. 363. In his so-called "Secret Book," Hitler tellingly excoriated Weimar politician Matthias Erzberger as "the bastard son of a servant-girl and a Jewish employer." The description might very well, of course, fit Alois Hitler. (Hitler [*Secret*], p. 76; Toland, p. 231; Victor, p. 18) Germany's Nürnberg racial laws contained an interesting—and, perhaps, related—feature, banning all German women under forty-five from working for Jews. Maria Schicklgruber was forty-two when she delivered her illegitimate son Alois. (Victor, p. 13)

14   "My stepmother always . . . over any triviality." Toland, p. 9; Waite, p. 155.

15   "never witnessed a closer attachment". *Collier's*, 15 March 1941, p. 36; Payne, p. 57; Waite, p. 141; Hamann, p. 20; Kershaw (*Hubris*), p. 12; Victor, p. 24. Bloch, nevertheless, did not consider the relationship "pathological."

16   "challenged my father . . . were in vain." Toland, p. 12; Stierlin, p. 25; Flood, p. 7; Kershaw (*Hubris*), p. 13.

17   Parents' faith. Redlich, pp. 7-8; Kubizek, p. 49; Hamann, p. 18; Payne, pp. 28-29; Stierlin, p. 21. His obituary praised him as "a progressive man and a warm friend of the Free [non-religious] School."

18   "At thirteen, fourteen . . . be blown up." Hamann, p. 19; Hitler (*Table Talk*), p. 325. "I never remember his going to church," recalled August Kubizek. (Kubizek, p. 78)

19   Host. Heiden (*Fuehrer*), p. 45; Maser, p. 33. His contempt for the Sacred Host may be seen in his December 1941 observation: "A negro with his tabus [taboos] is crushingly superior to the human being who seriously believes in Transubstantiation." (Hitler [*Table Talk*], p. 144)

20   Wagner. Hitler (*Kampf*), pp. 16-17; Langer, pp. 103-4; Fest (*Hitler*), p. 22; Fest (*Face*), p. 7; Heinz, p. 30; Dietrich (*With*), pp. 72-73; Flood, pp. 8, 11-12; Hauner, p. 3, 56; Stierlin, p. 27. His affection for Wagner more than verged on Star Trek Convention devotion. Even by the time of his impoverished Vienna period, he recalled, "I had heard *Tristan* thirty or forty times, and always from the best companies." (Hitler [*Table Talk*] 252; Kershaw [*Hubris*], p. 47)

21   Pan-Germanism. Hitler (*Kampf*), p. 98; Toland, pp. 15; Fest (*Hitler*), p. 38. Hitler, like FDR, lived a portion of his childhood (1892–94) within Germany, Alois Sr. being stationed across the frontier at Passau in Bavaria. (Hauner, p. 1)

22   "Distinctly talented, though . . . and hot-tempered." Maser, p. 33; Hauner, p. 3.

23 "Few heads . . . unsatisfactory". Heiden (*Fuehrer*), p. 52; Langer, p. 203; Bullock, p. 30; Payne, p. 58; Maser, p. 40; Kershaw (*Hubris*), p. 24.

24 Architect. Hitler (*Kampf*), p. 20; Langer, p. 203; Heinz, pp. 31-32; Bullock, p. 31; Kershaw (*Hubris*), p. 24.

25 "Your father cannot . . . getting anywhere now." (Hitler [*Table Talk*], p. 361)

26 Pension. Bullock, p. 31; Maser, p. 43; Hamann, p. 21; Kershaw (*Hubris*), pp. 46-47; Hauner, p. 6; Bracher, p. 60.

27 "In all my . . . was that day." *Collier's*, 15 March 1941, p. 39; Maser, p. 41; Toland, p. 27; Payne, p. 59; Hamann, p. 35; Flood, p. 9; Lukacs, p. 196; Tyson [*Eckart*], p. 259; Murray, p. 101; Stierlin, p. 28; Kershaw (*Hubris*), p. 24.

28 Common laborer. Hitler (*Kampf*), pp. 21, 25, 34, 39-40; Heiden (*Fuehrer*), p. 56; Bracher, p. 61; Hauner, p. 7; Mitchell (*Obersalzberg*), p. 12.

29 Linz. Kubizek, p. 77; Kershaw (*Hubris*), p. 62; Flood, pp. 7-8; Lukacs, p. 184.

30 "Wherever I . . . to see Jews . . ." Hitler (*Kampf*), p. 56; Shirer, p. 26; Hamann, p. 348; Kershaw (*Hitler*), p. 20; Kershaw (*Hubris*), p. 61. Vienna's population in 1910 was 8.6 percent Jewish, up from 2 percent in 1857. (Schwaab, p. 112; Jones [*Vienna*], p. 110; Mitchell [*Obersalzberg*], p. 14)

31 "a pestilential whore". Hitler (*Kampf*), p. 38.

32 "the endless . . . mass demonstrations". Hitler (*Kampf*), p. 41.

33 "I gradually became . . . in my memory." Hitler (*Kampf*), p. 61; Victor, p. 142.

34 "absorbed with great . . . what suited him." Kubizek, p. 184; Jones (*Vienna*), p. 107.

35 "For let it . . . proclaim its will." Hitler (*Kampf*), pp. 106-7.

36 "a majority . . . and incompetents". Hitler (*Kampf*), p. 88.

37 Parliament. Hitler (*Kampf*), pp. 75-79, 92.

38 Führer principle. Hitler (*Kampf*), pp. 79-84.

39 "Sooner, will a . . . 'discovered' by an election." Hitler (*Kampf*), p. 88.

40 Lueger. Hitler (*Kampf*), pp. 98-101, 121; Heiden (*Fuehrer*), pp. 63-64; Olden, pp. 49-50; Bullock, pp. 37, 45-46, 186; Hamann, pp. 273-303; Jones (*Vienna*), pp. 153-57; Shirer, pp. 24-25; Schwaab, pp. 69, 111-12; Kershaw (*Hitler*), p. 20.

41 "sham". Hitler (*Kampf*), p. 121; Hamann, pp. 290-91. Proclaimed Lueger when he wished to protect a Jew from deportation: "I determine who is a Jew." Decades later, Hermann Göring applied the same principle (and virtually the same words) to his Luftwaffe appointments. (Snyder [*Encyclopedia*], p. 378)

42 Schönerer. Hitler (*Kampf*), pp. 98-99, 110-20; Olden, pp. 49-50; Shirer, pp. 23-24; Jones (*Vienna*), pp. 158-62; Burleigh, p. 87; Kershaw (*Hitler*), p. 20.

43 "Did you . . . Czech!" Kubizek, p. 229.

44 "incest incarnate". Kubizek, p. 229. Note that what Hitler describes has nothing to do with incest or inbreeding; it is indeed its very opposite. Yet, he naturally, obsessively returns to a sexual topic.

45 "Only loafers, drunkards. . . such a home". *New Republic*, 19 April 1939, p. 297; Heiden (*Fuehrer*), p. 56; Mitchell (*Obersalzberg*), p. 13.

46 Nuns/brothers. *New Republic*, 5 April 1939, p. 239; *New Republic*, 12 April 1939, p. 271; Toland, pp. 40-41; Payne, p. 82; Jones, p. 142; Victor, p. 49.

47 "On the very . . . terribly neglected condition." *Life*, 19 August 1940, p. 62; Bullock, p. 33.

48 Hunchbacked. Hayman, p. 7; Lambert, p. 63. A maternal cousin Edward was also hunchbacked.

49 Joanna. *New Republic*, 5 April 1939, p. 240; Toland, p. 42; Kershaw (*Hubris*), pp. 53, 57. Hanisch thought (or remembered) that Hitler had written to a sister, but that was clearly incorrect.

50 "It was . . . Hitler work". *New Republic*, 5 April 1939, p. 241; Hamann, p. 164.

51 "in the morning . . . read that too". Hamann, p. 164.

52 "When he got . . . with his hands". *New Republic*, 5 April 1939, p. 242; Toland, p. 44; Hamann, p. 168.

53 "I believe that . . . for an eccentric." Hitler (*Kampf*), p. 34; Shirer, p. 20; Fest (*Hitler*), p. 48; Kershaw (*Hubris*), p. 58.

54   Robinsohn. Kershaw (*Hubris*), pp. 63, 67; Jones, pp. 163, 241; Hamann, pp. 349-50; Kershaw (*Hubris*), pp. 63, 67.

55   Altenberg. *New Republic*, 19 April 1939, p. 300; Kershaw (*Hubris*), p. 56; Payne, p. 88; Jones, pp. 147, 201, 229-30; Hauner, p. 7.

56   Neumann. *New Republic*, 5 April 1939, p. 241; *New Republic*, 12 April 1939, p. 272; Heiden (*Fuehrer*), p. 61; Payne, pp. 85-86; Jones, pp. 149, 163; Maser, p. 48; Kershaw (*Hubris*), pp. 55, 67; Hauner, p. 7.

57   "it was only . . . to take chances." *New Republic*, 12 April 1939, p. 271; Jones, p. 148.

58   Löffner. *New Republic*, 19 April 1939, p. 270; Heiden (*Fuehrer*), p. 70; Payne, p. 87; Hamann, p. 349; Kershaw (*Hubris*), pp. 64, 67; Murray, p. 154.

59   Opportunities. Tyson (*Eckart*), p. 262.

60   Advertisements. *New Republic*, 5 April 1939, p. 241; *Life*, 19 August 1940, p. 62; Jones, pp. 176-78; Fest (*Hitler*), pp. 47-48; Tyson (*Eckart*), p. 261. In general, however, Greiner's accounts of life with Hitler are extremely suspect. (see Hamann, pp. 193-97, Kershaw [*Hubris*], pp. 30, 51)

61   Jesuits/"Reds". Kershaw (*Hubris*), p. 58.

62   "a different smell." *New Republic*, 12 April 1939, p. 271; Toland, p. 45; Kershaw (*Hubris*), p. 66.

63   "Without Jews. . . fatherland. Heil!" Jones, p. 158.

64   "The whole mass . . . have no ideals." Heiden (*Fuehrer*), p. 59. To Otto Strasser.

65   "enlightened me politically . . . and general education." Hamann, p. 397.

66   "He was full . . . radishes, etc." Hamann, p. 395.

67   Austrian draft. Hauner, pp. 10-11; Schwaab, p. 115; Bracher, p. 65; Kershaw (*Hubris*), pp. 85-86; Maser, p. 74; Victor, p. 50.

68   Birthday. Hamann, p. 395; Stierlin, pp. 28-29; Kershaw (*Hubris*), pp. 53, 68.

69   Eighty kronen. Zalampas, p. 27.

70   Anti-Semitism. As early as 1895, an observer wrote: "Like the Chinese to California came the Jews to Munich: diligent, frugal, numerous, and thoroughly hated." Local folksingers sang: "One sees these animals by the score / Hirsch and Low and many more / From Russia and Galicia they roam / settle here and call it home." (Large [*Munich*], pp. xxii-xxiii)

71   Pre-war Munich. Heinz, pp. 48-52, 55-56; Toland, pp. 50-56; Heiden (*Fuehrer*), pp. 72-75; Maser, pp. 52-53; Shirer, pp. 27-28; Bracher, pp. 64-65. Lenin had lived a block from Hitler's 34 Schleissheimerstrasse Munich lodgings a few years previously. Leon Trotsky also briefly resided in Schwabing. (Large [*Munich*], p. 5)

      Alois Jr.'s wife Bridget Dowling Hitler later circulated the story that Hitler had visited them in Liverpool and Dublin in 1912. The story appears to be quite false (Unger, *passim*; Payne, pp. 94-97; Waite, pp. 398, 432-33). In *Mein Kampf*, Hitler incorrectly provides 1912 as the date for his relocation to Munich. (Fest [*Hitler*], p. 61; Lukacs, p. 65)

72   Twenty mark. Zalampas, p. 28.

73   Popp. Fest (*Hitler*), p. 59; Maser, pp. 51-52, 70-72; Payne, pp. 98-99; Large (*Munich*), p. 39; Hauner, p. 9.

74   Deportation. Maser, pp. 74-76; Large (*Munich*), pp. 41-42; Zalampas, pp. 28-29; Payne, pp. 99-102; Hauner, pp. 10-11.

75   "Come on Adi . . . get an umbrella!" Hamann, p. 401. Following Hausler's departure Hitler's old Vienna acquaintance Josef Greiner shared the room for two months, sleeping on the sofa. He recalled Hitler performing odd jobs around the building in exchange for breakfast. (Payne, p. 99; Fest [*Hitler*], p. 63)

76   Odeonsplatz. *Life*, 19 August 1940, p. 63; Mowrer, p. 248; Langer, p. 99; Toland, p. 58; Fest (*Hitler*), p. 64; Fest (*Face*), p. 13; Bracher, p. 65; Payne, p. 106; Maser, p. 77. Hitler's official photographer Heinrich Hoffmann coincidentally snapped the famous image of Hitler in the Odeonsplatz crowd, not discovering it until 1932. In 2010, Düsseldorf historian Gerd Krumeich alleged the photo had been faked, primarily because of the absence of a negative. This contention, however, fails to explain where this excited, essentially unposed, early headshot of Hitler would have originated from to be pasted into Hoffmann's original crowd shot. (www.thelocal.de/20101014/30503)

77   "To me, those . . . live at this time." Hitler (*Kampf*), p. 161; Fest, (*Hitler*) p. 64; Maser, p. 77.

78   16th Bavarian. Williams (*Corporal*), *passim*; Hitler (*Kampf*), pp. 163-65; Payne, p. 107; Fest (*Hitler*), pp. 66-68; Flood, p. 12.

79   Meldeganger. Payne, p. 108; Kershaw (*Hubris*), p. 91.

80   Thirty-six battles. Flood, p. 25.

81   Iron Cross. Heinz, p. 60; Heiden (*Fuehrer*), p. 83; Hauner, p. 11; Fest (*Hitler*), p. 68; Lüdecke, p. 48; Payne, p. 113; Maser, pp. 83-88; Flood, pp. 15-16, 23-24; Delmer (*Trail*), pp. 151-55; Redlich, p. 40. To this writer the most reasonable explanation of how Hitler earned his Iron Cross was one he himself conveyed to the *New York Post*'s H. R. "Red" Knickerbocker in January 1932: that while travelling alone through "No Man's Land," he had stumbled upon a group of seven French soldiers and by calling out "Fix bayonets! Draw your hand grenades!" bluffed them into believing he commanded a far greater force—and surrendering. (Metcalfe, p. 54)

82   "As a runner . . . Iron Cross 1st class." Maser, p. 88; Williams (*Corporal*), p. 191.

83   "For Pfc. Hitler . . . was his homeland." Fest (*Hitler*), p. 70.

84   Bookish. Weber, pp. 139, 141; Flood, p. 20; Toland, pp. 63, 68; Kershaw (*Hubris*), p. 634.

85   Fuchsl. Hitler (*Table Talk*), pp. 232-33: Weber, p. 137; Toland, pp. 62, 67; Williams (*Corporal*), pp. 82, 178; Hauner, pp. 12-13; Kershaw (*Hubris*), p. 93.

86   Painted. Weber, pp. 11-12, 141; Toland, pp. 63, 66-68; Payne, pp. 108, 119-20; Zalampas, p. 29; Flood, p. 19; Hauner, p. 12; Lynch, p. 23; Victor, p. 56.

87   Furlough. Weber, pp. 123-25; Kershaw (*Hubris*), p. 92.

88   "We always called . . . 'woman-hater'". Waite, p. 202; Flood, p. 18; Olden, p. 62; Waite, p. 202. Kubizek uses that exact phrase to describe him. (Kubizek, p. 156)

89   Leave. Toland, p. 68; Fest (*Hitler*), p. 72; Machtan, p. 92; Flood, p. 18.

90   No leadership. Heiden (*Fuehrer*), p. 84; Fest (*Hitler*), p. 69; Victor, p. 56; Redlich, p. 40. One superior found him unsuited for further promotion because of mental instability.

91   "Some worshippers of . . . of machine-gun fire." Weber, pp. 100, 373. Writing in Braunschweig's Social Democratic paper *Volksfreund* in March 1932.

92   "Hitler had worked out . . . 'keep his position.'" Weber, pp. 99-100, 373; Lynch, pp. 22-23.

93   Anti-Semitism. Flood, pp. 19-20; Weber, p. 177; Toland, p. 66; Williams (*Corporal*), pp. 206-7.

94   Gutmann. Weber, pp. 107, 215-16; Maser, p. 88; Williams (*Corporal*), p. 191; Payne, p. 113; Redlich, p. 40.

95   "I think of Munich . . . any territorial gains." Hauner, p. 12; Weber, p. 70.

96   "We learn casually . . . of a convert." Kubizek, p. 11.

97   Propaganda. Hitler (*Kampf*), pp.176-90; Weber, p. 328; Maser, pp. 90-91; Flood, pp. 20-21; Payne, p. 114.

98   "Comrade Laced Shoe". Hauner, p. 11; Toland, p. 61. This relates to Austrian soldiers wearing laced boots rather than jackboots.

99   "There is almost . . . subject was art. . . ." Flood, p. 17. However, his comrade Hans Mend later described him as "an absurd braggart and a crazy chatterbox whom no one could take seriously." (Maser, p. 86)

100   Ambition. Fest (*Hitler*), p. 72.

101   "I was eating . . . it was killed." Toland, p. 64; Hauner, p. 12; Flood, p. 25. The List Regiment suffered 3,574 dead, 8,795 wounded, and 678 captured. (Weber, p. 222; Maser, p. 84)

102   "[H]e said that . . . time had arrived." Flood, p. 22.

103   "eyes had . . . glowing coals." Hitler (*Kampf*), p. 202; Fest (*Hitler*), p. 77; Payne, p. 120; Flood, p. 26.

104   Pasewalk. Weber, pp. 221, 296-97, 404; Redlich, pp. 41-43; Waite, pp. 350-51; Toland, p. 925; Lynch, p. 26.

105   "Hitler was diagnosed . . . symptoms of hysteria". Weber, p. 221. Early Hitler biographer Rudolf Olden also cast doubt on the physical nature of Hitler's blindness, terming it a "hysterical blindness." (Olden, pp. 67-68) An official World War II era US Government report found, "neither his symptoms nor the development of the illness corresponded to those found in genuine gas cases.

It has definitely been established that the blindness [was] of an hysterical nature. The physician [Dr. Edmund Forster] who treated him at that time found his case so typical of hysterical symptoms in general, he used it as an illustration . . . at a prominent German medical school." (Langer, p. 175) Dr. Henry Murray's October 1943 OSS report also references a "hysterical" cause for Hitler's blindness and accompanying "mutism." (Murray, pp. 4, 25, 87, 131-32; Victor, p. 57; Maser, p. 93) Neuropsychologist David Lewis's *The Man Who Invented Hitler (passim)* deals extensively with the subject.

106 "I could stand . . . had not wept." Hitler *(Kampf)*, p. 204; Fest *(Hitler)*, p. 78; Fest *(Face)*, p. 15; Kershaw *(Biography)*, p. 102; Flood, pp. 34-35. The American journalist Edgar Ansel Mowrer, however, tartly observed, "Later his tear glands became more active: in the course of a single interview with [Nazi] Otto Strasser he wept no less than three times." (Mowrer, p. 249)

107 "the Jews organized . . . Bavaria at once". Hitler *(Kampf)*, p. 194. As Konrad Heiden bluntly put it: "'It is the fault of the Jews,' was the best comfort bad losers could give themselves." (Heiden *[History]*, p. 67)

108 "There is no . . . go into politics." *Life*, 19 August 1940, p. 63; Hitler *(Kampf)*, p. 206; Maser, p. 93; Hauner, p. 15; Bracher, p. 65; Fest *(Face)*, p. 14; Kershaw *(Biography)*, p. 103.

CHAPTER FOUR: "MIRACLE MAN, WASHINGTON, D.C."

1 Resemblance. Photo insert facing Irwin, p. 16; Burner, p. 242.

2 "an enormous . . . meat pies". Hoover *(Adventure)*, p. 10; Smith *(Dream)*, p. 21.

3 High school. Jeansonne *(Hoover)*, p. 3.

4 Failed. Lane, pp. 95-96; Irwin, p. 34; Hoover *(Adventure)*, p. 14; Smith *(Dream)*, p. 23; Jeansonne *(Hoover)*, p. 3.

5 Nevada. Irwin, p. 69; Lane, pp. 180-82; Knox, pp. 30-31; Hoover *(Adventure)*, pp. 25-26; Burner, p. 23; Smith *(Dream)*, p. 25; Wilson *(Progressive)*, p. 12; Lyons, p. 102; Liggett, p. 48. There, working with Cornish-speaking miners, Hoover learned to speak Cornish. In China, he and his wife mastered Mandarin.

6 "I learned . . . paved with". Hoover *(Adventure)*, p. 26.

7 Bewick, Moreing & Co. Irwin, p. 74; Liggett, pp. 51-52; Hoover *(Adventure)*, p. 28; Hoff *(Progressive)*, p. 12; Smith *(Dream)*, p. 26; Schlesinger *(Crisis)*, p. 78.

8 Lou Henry. Lane, pp. 239-40; Irwin, pp. 83-84; Hoover *(Adventure)*, p. 36; Lyons, p. 110; Wilson *(Progressive)*, pp. 17-18; Burner, p. 32. In the absence of Protestant clergymen, the Quaker couple (she had converted from Episcopalism) was married by a Catholic priest.

9 Boxer Rebellion. Lane, pp. 264-82; Irwin, pp. 88-99; Liggett, pp. 77-83; Hoover *(Adventure)*, pp. 47-54; Lyons, pp. 114-18; Burner, pp. 36-38; Smith *(Dream)*, pp. 28-30; Schlesinger *(Crisis)*, p. 78.

10 .38 Mauser. Leuchtenburg *(Hoover)*, p. 13.

11 "The Chief." Jeansonne *(Hoover)*, p. 5; Wilson *(Progressive)*, p. 13.

12 "Great Engineer." Burner, p. 44.

13 $30 million. Wilson *(Progressive)*, p. 45.

14 Stranded Americans. Leuchtenburg *(Hoover)*, p. 25; Wilson *(Progressive)*, p. 44.

15 "He told . . . so many numbers." Schlesinger *(Crisis)*, p. 80.

16 "He's a . . . anybody's thanks." Nash *(Humanitarian)*, p. 96; Jeansonne *(Hoover)*, p. 7; Leuchtenburg *(Hoover)*, p. 30.

17 "Such men . . . with duty!" Nash *(Humanitarian)*, p. 150; Leuchtenburg *(Hoover)*, p. 32.

18 "Food will . . . the war". Hoover *(Adventure)*, p. 260; Lyons, p. 163; Nash *(Emergencies)*, p. 197; Burner, p. 96.

19 "I can . . . loving you." Smith *(Uncommon)*, p. 90; Wilson *(Progressive)*, p. 60; Leuchtenburg *(Hoover)*, p. 35.

20 1912. Wilson *(Progressive)*, p. 76.

21 FDR for Hoover. Schlesinger *(Crisis)*, p. 82.

22 "The smartest gink I know". Wilson *(Progressive)*, p. 122; Johnson *(Modern)*, p. 243.

23 "secretary of . . . other departments." *Outlook*, Vol. 150, p. 724; Schlesinger (*Crisis*), p. 84; Lisio (*Blacks*), p. 34; Leuchtenburg (*Hoover*), p. 63; Wilson (*Progressive*), p. 79.

24 "I have taken . . . in reading it." Schlesinger (*Crisis*), p. 372; Beschloss, p. 49.

25 Coolidge. Allen (*Why*), p. 88; Wilson (*Progressive*), p. 122; Shlaes (*Forgotten*), p. 38; Shlaes (*Coolidge*), p. 398.

26 "The Republican . . . in November." *NY Times*, 11 June 1932, p. 2; Allen (*Why*), p. 118.

27 "a pious old . . . fat Coolidge." Mencken (*Politics*), p. 191; O'Connor (*Hurrah*), p. 211; Behr, p. 238.

28 "In such an array . . . anything but success." Liggett, p. 322. "Each," noted Liggett, "had the temperament of a prima donna, and instead of presenting a united front they secretly knifed one another for the benefit of Hoover."

29 "We in . . . among us." Allen (*Why*), p. 106; Wilson (*Progressive*), pp. 127-28; Liggett, p. 337; Hicks, p. 210; Brands (*Traitor*), p. 221.

30 "Miracle Man, Washington, D. C." *Forum*, October 1917, p. 383; Ritchie, p. 21.

31 "is regarded . . . Tibetan home." *NY Post*, 6 June 1929, p. 3; *Rome Sentinel*, 6 June 1929, p. 9.

32 "fortunate enough. . . economic misery." Schwarz (*Kennedy*), p. 15; Kennedy (*Freedom*), p. 59. On November 15, 1929, Baruch had wired Churchill: "FINANCIAL STORM DEFINITELY PASSED." (Grant, p. 227)

33 6.3 percent. Vedder & Gallaway, p. 77.

34 "we have . . . rapidly recover". *NY Times*, 2 May 1930, p. 1; Hoover (*Great Depression*), p. 58; Wilson (*Progressive*), p. 146; Kennedy (*Freedom*), p. 58.

35 Immigration. *NY Times*, 2 January 1931, p. 18; Breitman & Lichtman, p. 43.

36 McNary-Haugen. Pietrusza (*Calvin Coolidge*), pp. 330-42; Leuchtenburg (*Perils*), pp. 102-03; Shlaes (*Coolidge*), pp. 353-54.

37 Economists. *Poughkeepsie Eagle News*, 6 May 1930, p. 6; Kull & Kull, p. 247; Shlaes (*Forgotten*), p. 96; Barone, p. 41.

38 "I almost . . . Hawley-Smoot tariff". Shlaes (*Forgotten*), p. 97.

39 "NOT ONLY A . . . OF RETURNING PROSPERITY". Procter, p. 158.

40 Smoot-Hawley signed. Shlaes (*Forgotten*), p. 99; Kull & Kull, p. 248; Barone, p. 41.

41 14.4 percent. Vedder & Gallaway, p. 77.

42 "Liquorsham Commission". *NY Sun*, 20 January 1930, p. 24; *NY Times*, 14 December 1930, p. N1.

43 Coolidge. Hard, p. 32. Aides alerted Coolidge to Hoover's attitude. "Can it be that Mr. Hoover is disturbed by these?" Coolidge coolly responded. "Weren't you disturbed by that magazine attack on you which the Democrats reprinted in the last campaign?" they then asked. "What attack?" Coolidge inquired. When informed of the specific incident, he answered, "I remember. The magazine [*The American Mercury*] had a green cover. So, I started to read the article, but it was against me; so I quit."

44 Wilson. Freidel (*Triumph*), p. 340*fn*.

45 "hair shirt." Allen (*Why*), p. 97.

46 "On the day . . . had opposed him." "Anonymous" (*Mirrors*), p. 7.

47 "I owe nothing . . . they know it." "Anonymous" (*Mirrors*), p. 7.

48 "No President must . . . has been wrong." Wilson (*Progressive*), p. 154.

49 "He would go . . . to hold on." Hoover (*42*), pp. 184, 187-88.

50 Johnson. *NY Times*, 6 December 1929, p. 1; Hoover (*42*), p. 216; Allen (*Why*), pp. 94-96. Johnson had defeated Hoover in the 1920 California GOP primary.

51 Hoovercrats/patronage. *Crisis*, November 1932, p. 362; Lisio (*Blacks*), pp. 76-78.

52 Anti-black. *Crisis*, June 1930, pp. 196-97; *Crisis*, November 1932, pp. 344, 362.

53 Urged to withdraw. Allen (*Why*), pp. 99-100; Watson, pp. 264-65.

54 41-39. *NY Times*, 8 May 1932, p. 2; Lisio (*Blacks*), p. 228.

55 "rejection is an . . . and Negro politicians." Lisio (*Blacks*), pp. 232-33.

56 "Hoover is . . . else keep out.'" Watson, p. 256.

57 "How in hell . . . St. Vitus Dance!" Allen (*Why*), pp. 81-82.

58   "knows less . . . about politics." "Anonymous" (*Mirrors*), p. 8.

59   "an effective poorhouse". *Wilmington Star*, 22 April 1934, p. 15; Allen (*Why*), p. 98.

60   Coolidge slights. Allen (*Why*), pp. 99-100.

61   "How much less . . . at Fort Myer?" Allen (*Why*), pp. 99-100.

62   Richey. Dorwart, pp. 3-4; Andrew, p. 74; Dickson & Allen, pp. 75, 312; Ritchie, p. 57; Calder, p. 11. O'Brien self-published the 1932 anti-Hoover work, *Hoover's Millions and How He Made Them*, after having assisted author John Hamill ("I am sorry I wrote it") in Hamill's even more egregiously anti-Hoover screed, *The Strange Career of Herbert Hoover Under Two Flags*. In 1933, New York Supreme Court justice Peter Schmuck ruled both works to be marked by "unfairness and untruthfulness" and to "sadden public decency." (*Collier's*, 20 February 1932, p. 8; *Brooklyn Eagle*, 3 January 1933, p. 5; *NY Times*, 13 January 1933, p. 13; *NY Sun*, 13 January 1933, p. 31; Jeansonne [*Hoover*], p. 397) Strauss, an acquaintance of Hoover since 1917, assumed leadership of the newly founded Atomic Energy Commission following World War II.

63   "I am being . . . some one is listening." *NY Times*, 21 December 1931, p. 12.

64   Coughlin. *Cumberland Times*, 5 January 1931, pp. 1-2; *NY Times*, 12 January 1931, p. 12; Ward (*Coughlin*), pp. 83-85; Fried, p. 41; Marcus, pp. 35-36; Brinkley, p. 304.

65   "the banker's friend. . . angel of Wall Street." Bennett (*Demagogues*), p. 34. In 1970, he praised Hoover as "the greatest president . . . in my lifetime." (Marcus, p. 44)

66   Brown. *NY Times*, 23 December 1931, p. 6.

67   Donovan. Andrew, p. 74. Hoover had double-crossed Donovan on being appointed attorney general, reneging on the deal in part for fear of opposition to appointing a Catholic to the post. (Waller, p. 41)

68   "Get out . . . not fail." *NY Times*, 15 May 1932, pp. 1, 11; Peel & Donnelly, pp. 58-59.

69   Lucas. *NY Times*, 17 January 1931, p. 4; *Plattsburgh Press*, 17 January 1931, p. 1.

70   "These men . . . the country." *NY Times*, 17 January 1931, p. 4. Lucas also improperly injected RNC funds into a 1930 primary against Nebraska's Sen. George W. Norris (who bolted Hoover for Smith in 1928) and compounded that crime by engaging a Klan-connected printer to produce anti-Norris cartoons. (*Collier's Weekly*, 7 February 1931, p. 21)

71   "trouble was . . . at all." Watson, p. 263.

72   "Hoover" terms. Wilson (*Progressive*), p. 142; Smith (*Dream*), p. 82; Alter, pp. 88-89; Ybarra, p. 102.

73   McCormick. *Chicago Tribune*, 5 January 1932, p. 9; Peel & Donnelly, p. 47.

74   Johnson. *NY Times*, 20 November 1931, p. 3; Peel & Donnelly, p. 47.

75   Pinchot, aide. Nash (*Humanitarian*), pp. 105-7; Burner, pp. 84, 101. Pinchot had been excoriating Hoover ("not a real Republican or a real American") since 1917. (Tucker [*Mirrors*], p. 222; Liggett, p. 245) In 1921 he (along with other progressives such as Senators Johnson, Borah, and Norris) opposed Hoover's appointment for the Harding Cabinet (Hawley, p. 19; Wilson [*Progressive*], p. 80). In October 1928, Pinchot, however, pledged allegiance to Hoover's presidential candidacy despite having been rejected as a pro-Hoover speaker by the Republican Speakers Bureau (*Berkeley Gazette*, 17 October 1928, p. 1; Tucker [*Mirrors*], p. 225; Liggett, p. 308).

76   "We in . . . to help." Richardson, Kindle Locations 302-7.

77   "vicious." *Iowa City Iowan*, 5 January 1932, p. 1.

78   Coolidge cabal. Joslin, pp. 226-27; Jeansonne (*Hoover*), pp. 407, 512.

79   Hearst, 1928. Carlisle, pp. 32-41; Hearst simply hated Al Smith. Religion and booze had nothing to do with it; he simply hated him.

80   "reactionary" "do-nothing administration." Carlisle, p. 46. Not helping matters was Hoover's fabled sensitivity to criticism. In 1924, the Hearst press had questioned his transfer of Alaskan fisheries. When the influential Hearst (for Hoover in 1928) visited the White House in early 1929 to congratulate him, Hoover barely had a pleasant word for him. (Swanberg [*Hearst*], p. 409)

81   "Back Coolidge and . . . Coolidge and Confidence". *San Antonio Light*, 3 June 1930, p. 13; Procter, p. 158.

82   Hearst/Coolidge. Swanberg (*Hearst*), p. 435; Procter, p. 166; Nasaw (*Chief*), p. 436; Carlisle, p. 52; Procter, p. 158.

83   "Only a strange mind. . . to those overseas". Carlisle, p. 50.

84   "It has no leaders and apparently no principles". Procter, p. 166.

85   "Not one . . . man's ambition." McGeary, p. 390; Mason, p. 25. *De jure* a Republican, Ickes rarely was. He supported Bryan over Taft in 1908, TR over Taft in 1912, Cox over Harding in 1920, La Follette over Coolidge in 1924, and Smith over Hoover in 1928.

86   "I once . . . policies were correct." Tugwell (*Revolution*), p. xiv.

87   Watson. Hoover (*Depression*), p. 101.

88   "the nicer offices in the Capitol." Hoover (*Depression*), p. 101.

89   "The ever . . . own work." Freidel (*Triumph*), pp. 163-65; Kennedy (*Freedom*), p. 94; Johnson (*Modern*), p. 249. Sections of Hoover's memoirs covering his early life surprisingly reveal a fairly deft, and, often quite charming, sense of humor. That touch largely disappears as he covers the Great Depression, a grim exercise devoted to grimly justifying his every grim move. Hoover's sympathetic biographer Glen Jeansonne, however, provides several examples of Hoover's wit. "Hoover," Jeansonne noted, "related a story about a circus in which the animals were starving. The owner had to kill the lion and feed him to the tigers. Soon afterward, the gorilla starved. A jobless banker applied for a job, and the circus owner agreed to dress him as a gorilla, and permit him to perform. Shortly, the lion charged out of his cage and the frightened banker-gorilla screamed for help. 'Shut up, you fool!' said the lion, "You're not the only banker out of a job!'" (Jeansonne [*Hoover*], p. 74)

90   "If you . . . would wilt." Miller (*New World*), p. 379. Borglum, though progressive, was also a former prominent Klan member. (Chalmers, pp. 106, 169, 282; Pietrusza [*1920*], p. 462)

91   "Here's a . . . 'em all." *Forum*, June 1932, p. 363; *Scribner's*, November 1932, p. 258; Peel & Donnelly, p. 56; Kennedy (*Freedom*), p. 91. (emphasis added)

CHAPTER FIVE: "THEY WILL REMAIN HANGING UNTIL THEY STINK"

1   "Russia is . . . their victims." Strawson, p. 140. Lloyd George thought Churchill suffered from "Bolshevism on the brain," and jested (or, perhaps, did not jest at all) that his "ducal blood revolted at the wholesale slaughter of the Grand Dukes." (Charmley, pp. 152-53)

2   Hungary. Watt, pp. 321-25; Flood, pp. 50-51; Burleigh, p. 37. Followed as in Munich by an equally vicious "White Terror."

3   Spartacists. Taylor, pp. 14-18; Knight-Patterson, pp. 481-83; Watt, pp. 254-72; Delmer (*Weimar*), pp. 40-41; Vogt, p. 38.

4   Comintern. Watt, pp. 297, 303; Lazici, p. xvii.

5   Back to Munich. Weber, pp. 227-28; Payne, p. 122; Toland, p. 73.

6   Half-Jewish. Flood, p. 49; Weber, p. 241; Watt, p. 293; Maser, p. 96; Delmer (*Weimar*), p. 42; Snyder (*Encyclopedia*), p. 347. Interestingly, German Jewish intermarriage with German Gentiles increased from 8 percent in 1910 to 23 percent in 1929. (Guérin, p. 32)

7   Eisner assassinated. Heinz, pp. 90-91; Payne, p. 124; Fest (*Hitler*), p. 110; Toland, p. 78; Maser, p. 96; Flood, p. 48; Craig (*Germany*), p. 410; Mitchell (*Hitler*), pp. 46-47; Watt, pp. 292-93; Delmer (*Weimar*), p. 42; Mosley, pp. 50-51.

8   Auer. Watt, pp. 293-94. In January 1922, Dietrich Eckart accused Auer of accepting bribes from Jewish cattle dealers. Auer sued for defamation and lost. (Tyson [*Eckart*], p. 402)

9   Toller regime. Flood, pp. 52-53; Davidson, pp. 120-21; Watt, pp. 325-26; Delmer (*Weimar*), pp. 42-43; Feuchtwanger, pp. 61-62. Within Toller's government was actor Ret Marut, who may (or may not) have re-emerged as "B. Traven," author of *The Treasure of the Sierra Madre*.

10   Thule Society. Taylor, pp. 33, 35; Heinz, p. 94; Payne, p. 127; Flood, p. 56; Davidson, pp. 122-23; Watt, p. 339; Maser, pp. 110-13. Leviné himself was belatedly (after his execution) cleared of shooting the hostages.

11   Recruited for Mayr. Hitler (*Kampf*), pp. 208-16; Fest (*Face*), p. 15; Toland, pp. 82-83; Payne, p. 129; Kershaw (*Biography*), pp. 73-75; Kershaw (*Hitler*), p. 41; Kershaw (*Hubris*), pp. 122, 128; Ryback, p. 31; Williams (*Corporal*), p. 207; Höhne, pp. 14-15.

12   Hitler's sympathies. Heinz, pp. 88-93; Flood, p. 55; Kershaw (*Hubris*), p. 116.

13   "totally unconcerned . . . their destinies." Murray, p. 133; Toland, p. 83; Kershaw (*Hubris*), p. 122; Williams (*Corporal*), pp. 206-7; Large (*Munich*), p. 127. Mayr, eventually a Social Democrat, died in Buchenwald in February 1945. (Redlich, p. 21)

14   First meeting. Bullock, pp. 64-65; Payne, pp. 135-36; Maser, pp. 113-14.

15   Twenty-two attended. Bullock, pp. 64-65; Payne, pp. 135-36.

16   "neither good nor bad". Hitler (*Kampf*), p. 218.

17   "The founder . . . of a club." Hitler (*Kampf*), p. 218.

18   Hitler tirade. Hitler. (*Kampf*), p. 219; Fest (*Hitler*), p. 118; Davidson, p. 126; Large (*Munich*), p. 130.

19   "astonished . . . one of my own." Hitler (*Kampf*), p. 220.

20   Joined party. Hitler (*Kampf*), p. 224; Payne, p. 138; Flood, p. 74.

21   Hofbräuhauskeller. Bracher, p. 84.

22   "After 30 minutes . . . three hundred marks." Hitler (*Kampf*), p. 355; Kershaw (*Hitler*), p. 22; Hauner, p. 17.

23   "unalterable". Hitler (*Kampf*), p. 373; Hauner, p. 19; Wistrich, p. 57; Bullock, p. 76; Nicholls, p. 122.

24   Point 22. Hauner, p. 19.

25   25 points. Heiden (*History*), pp. 14-18; Snyder (*Documentary*), pp. 23-25; Hauner, p. 19. The Darwinian aspect of Hitler's racism (and, indeed, his obsession with ruthlessness and hardness) cannot be ignored. "I dream of a state of affairs in which every man would know that he lives and dies for the preservation of the species," he said in December 1941. "It's our duty to encourage that idea: let the man who distinguishes himself in the service of the species be thought worthy of the highest honours." (Hitler [*Table Talk*], p. 145)

26   *Ordnerdienst*. Heiden (*History*), pp. 82-83; Hauner, p. 19; Orlow (*Nazi*), p. 41.

27   NSDAP/swastika. Hitler (*Kampf*), pp. 492-97; Shirer, p. 42; Fest (*Hitler*), p. 123; Evans (*Coming*), p. 174; Feuchtwanger, p. 113.

28   Thule members. Large (*Munich*), pp. 70-71, 88; Snyder (*Encyclopedia*), pp. 346-47. Other members included Rudolf Hess, Alfred Rosenberg, and Hans Frank. Anton Drexler was a "guest member."

29   "Come on Adolf. . . business here." Dietrich (*Knew*), p. 135; Dietrich (*With*), p. 35; Tyson (*Eckart*), p. 338; Ryback, p. 36; Flood, p. 122; Delmer (*Weimar*), p. 64. Internal passports were then necessary in Germany to travel between Bavaria and Prussia. (Louis Ferdinand, p. 46)

30   Airsick. Baur, p. 31; Large (*Munich*), p. 138.

31   Forged papers. Dietrich (*With*), p. 27; Payne, pp. 150-51; Ryback, pp. 36-37; Fest (*Hitler*), p. 133; Kershaw (*Biography*), pp. 93, 95; Hoffmann (*Security*), pp. 18-19; Read, pp. 52-53, 72; Baur, p. 31.

32   "DICTATORSHIP OF THE PROLETARIAT! . . . *without distinction as to sex or age*." Wheaton, p. 56.

33   Circus Krone. Heiden (*History*), pp. 44-45; Mowrer, p. 254; Wheaton, p. 47; Mitchell (*Hitler*), p. 60; Payne, pp. 153-55; Hauner, p. 25; Feuchtwanger, p. 113. Some, like Mowrer, calculated four thousand; Feuchtwanger at just six thousand; Heiden at four thousand.

34   "Entry one mark . . . free". Hauner, p. 25.

35   Ultimatum. Payne, p. 158.

36   "In recognition . . . dictatorial powers." Heiden (*History*), p. 53; Maser (*Hitler*), pp. 254-55; Bullock, p. 74; Payne, p. 158.

37   554–0. Orlow (*Nazi*), p. 30; Lewis (*Hitler*), p. 179. By 553–1 Hitler was then elected chairman.

38   "the Leader". Fest (*Hitler*), p. 133; Kershaw (*Myth*), p. 21.

39   *Völkischer Beobachter*. Heiden (*History*), p. 38; Fest (*Hitler*), p. 132; Shirer, p. 42.

40   "Here [in Germany. . . done about it." *Scribner's*, April 1932, p. 230.

41   "His critics charge . . . standard or not." *Scribner's*, April 1932, p. 230.

42 "A strange man . . . until he dies." Roberts (*Hitler*), p. 21.

43 "His was the . . . has already absorbed." Fest (*Face*), p. 313.

44 Photographs. Johnson (*Viereck*), opposite p. 117; Friedrich, p. 38. Heinrich Hoffmann recorded the first "official" photo in 1923 and was for a period the only person allowed to photograph him. (Bullock, p. 83; Snyder [*Encyclopedia*], p. 168; Wistrich, p. 155). "Everyone took me for something, but not for Hitler," Hitler later said, "And no picture of me existed. Those who didn't know me couldn't know what I looked like." (Machtan, p. 138)

45 Eckart. Mowrer, p. 249.

46 "National Drunkard in Chief". Kershaw (*Biography*), p. 536; Snyder (*Encyclopedia*), p. 289. Some thought the unusually befuddled Ley deserved that title. It may have been a toss-up. Hitler himself mused regarding his official photographer: "If Hoffmann were bitten by a serpent, I suppose the serpent would fall down stiff in a moment, dead-drunk." (Hitler [*Table Talk*], p. 231). Oddly enough, the invariably self-important Hitler also said fondly of the heavy-drinking, heavy-smoking Hoffman: "He's a man who always made fun of me." (Hitler [*Table Talk*], p. 334)

47 Funk. Wistrich, p. 87; Turner (*Business*), p. 152.

48 Rust. Barrows & Room, pp. 140, 142; Thacker, p. 120.

49 Ley. Shirer, p. 127; Kershaw (*Myth*), p. 101; Barrows & Room, pp. 140, 142; Goldensohn, p. 118.

50 "I am an immature and wicked man". Hancock, p. 98; Snyder (*Elite*), p. 61; Mitchell (*Hitler*), p. 73.

51 "I know Esser is a scoundrel". Heiden (*History*), p. 52.

52 Bormann. Snyder (*Encyclopedia*), p. 36; Snyder (*Elite*), p. 123; Wistrich, p. 23; Fest (*Face*), p. 129.

53 "If you really . . . quite different?" Fest (*Face*), p. 82. Göring's mother was the mistress of the Jewish Dr. Hermann Ritter von Epenstein. The young Göring titled an essay about Epenstein "The Man I Admire Most in the World." (Large [*Munich*], pp. 166-67; Manvell [*Göring*] pp. 9, 11, 13)

54 "Make room . . . old ones!" Bracher, p. 147; Maltitz, p. 216; Fest (*Face*), p. 220. Gregor Strasser in 1927.

55 "National Socialism . . . will of youth." Bracher, p. 146; Maltitz, p. 216; Mitchell (*Hitler*), p. 118. Historian Richard J. Evans points out that the NSDAP also did "particularly well" among female voters. (Evans [*Coming*], p. 262)

56 "Psychologists overdo . . . parental failures." Erikson, p. 337; Maltitz, p. 330. In *Mein Kampf*, Hitler reveals that he "had become a little ringleader in school [who] was rather hard to handle." (Hitler [*Kampf*], p. 6). Hitler's economic adviser Otto Wagener records a strange conversation with Hitler relating to Erikson's observation that Hitler "had reserved for himself the new position of the one who remains young in possession of supreme power." "For the healthy young body gives off its excess of force only to those who are worthy, only to people who are equally healthy and to those who know how to do something creative with the transferred force," theorized Hitler to Wagener. "That is why a baby cries and resists when his grandmother wants to keep hugging him; he doesn't want to pass on his powers to a dying person. And the only reason the grandmother picks up the baby is that she wants to draw to herself the child's excess force. . . . That is why an officer remains so youthful—because he is constantly among the young!" (Wagener, pp. 35-36; Tyson [*Surreal*], p. 41)

57 "Upon a broad . . . in the process." Krebs, p. 166. "He was to all intents and purposes an atheist by the time I got to know him," recalled Ernst Hanfstaengl, "although he still paid lip service to religious beliefs. . . ." (Hanfstaengl, p. 72) Otto Dietrich observed that Hitler "professed a highly general, monotheistic faith . . . sharply hostile to Christianity . . . the 'first Jewish-Communistic cell.'" (Dietrich [*Knew*], p. 127). Accordingly, the Jewish journalist Joseph Roth observed in 1933, "For the first time Jews are not being murdered for crucifying Christ but for having produced him from their midst." (Roth, p. 214) Hitler's faith, however, involved not so much believing in God but an unshakable conviction that God believed in him.

58 "The National Socialist . . . former countrymen." Bullock, p. 72; Shirer, p. 43; Flood, p. 175.

59 Ballerstedt. Fest (*Hitler*), p. 160; Bullock, pp. 72, 85; Redlich, p. 60; Flood, pp. 154, 253; Hauner, p. 23; Large (*Munich*), p. 145. Ballerstedt, murdered in 1934's "Night of the Long Knives," later also successfully sued Hitler for criminal defamation. (Flood, pp. 176-77)

60   Deportation. Bullock, p. 88; Hauner, pp. 33-34; Flood, p. 253; Bracher, p. 120; Eyck, p. 218; Large (*Munich*), p. 200.

61   "I made it . . . war experience." Hitler (*Kampf*), pp. 504-6; Hauner, p. 32.

62   "I was ready . . . I *alone*." Lüdecke, pp. 52-56; Toland, p. 118; Flood, p. 292. A similar cooperative effort had also totally flopped that May Day. (Strasser pp. 28-34; Large [*Munich*], pp. 168-70)

63   "Once I . . . cleansed of Jews." Redlich, p. 319; Fleming, p. 17.

64   Viereck. *American Monthly*, October 1923, pp. 235-38; Johnson (*Viereck*), p. 117.

65   List Regiment. Heiden (*Fuehrer*), pp. 77-78; Payne, p. 107.

66   Röhm. Bullock, p. 67; Machtan, p. 94; Fest (*Face*), p. 140.

67   Lippmann. Hanfstaengl, p. 26; Flood, p. 315; Conradi, p. 21; Persico (*Secret*), p. 192.

68   FDR. Hanfstaengl, p. 28; Conradi, p. 24; Flood, p. 316.

69   TR Jr. Hanfstaengl, p. 27; Persico (*Secret*), p. 192.

70   TR. Hanfstaengl, p. 27; Conradi, pp. 20-21; Flood, p. 322; Larson, p. 72; Persico (*Secret*), p. 192. Hanfstaengl's American attorney was TR's former secretary of state, Elihu Root. (Hanfstaengl, p. 29; Conradi, p. 32)

71   Hearst. Swanberg (*Hearst*), p. 443; Nasaw (*Chief*), p. 477.

72   Smith. Hanfstaengl, pp. 32-33, 37; Shirer, pp. 46-47*fn*; Conradi, pp. 5-8; Flood, p. 320; Wistrich, p. 120; Mitchell (*Hitler*), p. 65; Persico (*Secret*), p. 192; Nagorski (*Hitlerland*), p. 33. Smith, however, while not denying this, said he could not recall it.

73   "Sometimes he . . . indelicacy of utterance." Hanfstaengl, p. 36; Flood, p. 322.

74   *Völkischer Beobachter*. Hanfstaengl, pp. 55-56; Heiden (*History*), p 101; Shirer, p. 46; Bullock, p. 80; Wistrich, p. 120.

75   "Sieg Heil". Hanfstaengl, pp. 52-53; Conradi, p. 45; Toland, p. 135.

76   "You had . . . dislike him." Reynolds, p. 107; Larson, p. 72.

77   "an immense . . . incoherent clown." Kurth, p. 160; Nagorski (*Hitlerland*), p. 83.

78   Ludendorff. *NY Times*, 11 May 1924, p. E5; Heiden (*History*), p. 108; Wistrich, pp. 199-200; Shirer, pp. 63-64; Bullock, p. 99; Thyssen, p. 130; Hastings, pp. 140-41. Otto Strasser considered Hitler to be "profoundly imbued with paganism, more so, perhaps, than Ludendorff or Rosenberg himself." (Strasser, p. 59) In 1927, Hitler charged Ludendorff with himself being a Freemason. Ludendorff never answered the accusation. Hitler, however, possessed no noticeable aversion to welcoming actual freemason Hjalmar Schacht into his march to power and subsequent government. (Kershaw [*Hubris*], p. 356; Goldensohn, p. 229)

79   Erzberger. Heiden (*Fuehrer*), pp. 110, 112; Strasser, p. 22; Flood, pp. 214-17; Hauner, p. 27; Bracher, p. 102; Davidson, pp. 137-39; Burleigh, p. 53; Feuchtwanger, p. 115; Large (*Munich*), pp. 140-42; Watt, p. 521.

80   "Kill off . . . Jewish sow". Burleigh, p. 53.

81   Rathenau. Davidson, pp. 178-81; Heiden (*Fuehrer*), p. 117; Fest (*Hitler*), p. 122; Flood, p. 246; Hauner, p. 26; Bracher, p. 102; Burleigh, p. 53; Mitchell (*Hitler*), pp. 67-68; Vogt, p. 73; Delmer (*Weimar*), p. 70; Feuchtwanger, p. 116; Large (*Munich*), p. 145.

82   Scheidemann. Davidson, p. 178; Watt, p. 521.

83   Munich, 1921. Hitler (*Kampf*), pp. 502-7; Duffy & Ricci, p. 14; Hoffmann (*Security*), pp. 5-6; Hauner, p. 32.

84   Unemployment. Burleigh, p. 55.

85   Inflation. Knight-Patterson, p. 307; Craig (*Germany*), p. 450; Flood, pp. 234-35; Shirer, p. 61; Fest (*Hitler*), p. 122; Taylor, p. 57.

86   "Very cheap . . . a pint." Speer, p. 9.

87   "I had . . . half its value." Craig (*Germany*), p. 451.

88   Ruhr. Heiden (*Fuehrer*), pp. 161-64; Bracher, pp. 104-5; Hauner, p. 37; Lüdecke, p. 109; Shirer, p. 61; Fest (*Face*), p. 23; Jarman, p. 96; Feuchtwanger, pp. 119-22.

89   Blacks. Evans (*Coming*), pp. 186-87. Wrote the Nazis: "Haven't we seen the pest in Germany during the last ten years? Black Frenchmen and slimy Polacks in the service of international high finance. . . ." (Taylor, p. 78)

90   States of emergency. Shirer, p. 64; Hauner, p. 38.

91   Buchrucker. Wheeler-Bennett (*Nemesis*), p. 92; Shirer, p. 65; Fest (*Hitler*), p. 175; Kershaw (*Hubris*), p. 665*fn*; Wheaton, p. 70; Feuchtwanger, p. 130.

92   Communists. Taylor, p. 67; Heiden (*Fuehrer*), p. 177; Turner (*Stresemann*), pp. 124, 143, 151; Hauner, p. 41. The "Black Reichswehr" were clandestine units designed to circumvent troop strength limits imposed by the Treaty of Versailles.

93   Riots. Knickerbocker, p. 172.

94   Kahr/Protestant. Large (*Munich*), p. 139.

95   "for the purpose . . . I have behind me." Large (*Munich*), p. 144.

96   "on his word . . . make a putsch." Heiden (*Fuehrer*), pp. 155, 166; Heiden (*History*), p. 73; Payne, p. 187.

97   Rosenberg/Scheubner-Richter. Heiden (*Fuehrer*), pp. 182-83.

98   "a cross between Charlie Chaplin and a headwaiter". Large (*Munich*), p. 177. An eyewitness's characterization.

99   "The National Revolution . . . swastika banner." Bullock, p. 106; Shirer, p. 68; Fest (*Hitler*), p. 183; Singer, p. 68; Conradi, p. 60; Manvell & Fraenkel (*Göring*), p. 33; Dornberg, p. 70; Jarman, p. 99; Delmer (*Weimar*), p. 79; Large (*Munich*), p. 177; Strasser, p. 40.

100   "There is nothing . . . your beer!" Shirer, pp. 68-69; Manvell & Fraenkel (*Göring*), p. 33; Dornberg, pp. 72, 92; Read, p. 94; Large (*Munich*), p. 177; Snyder (*Elite*), p. 7. Less comically, Göring warned, "We do not have the right or authority to execute—yet." (Large [*Munich*], p. 179)

101   Pacelli. Dornberg, pp. 147-48.

102   Alienated Catholics. Hastings, pp. 140-41. A prominent example of this shift involves the young Heinrich Himmler. On joining the *völkisch* movement, he was still a devout and practicing Catholic. By summer 1924 he had both formally joined the NSDAP and ceased attending Mass. (Hastings, pp. 154-55; Höhne, pp. 35-36) Concluded historian Derek Hastings: "Whereas the pre-putsch Nazi movement had excoriated political Catholicism while defending and advocating religious Catholicism, the re-founded NSDAP tended increasingly—initially somewhat imperceptibly, then more overtly—toward outright anti-Catholicism, despite Hitler's public insistence on avoiding confessional disputes." (Hastings, p. 158)

103   No liberal. Heiden (*History*), p. 99. The cardinal even refused to have church bells rung in his archdiocese to mark the death of Reichspräsident Ebert. (Kershaw [*Hitler*], p. 93)

104   "our fellow Israelite citizens." Hastings, pp. 142, 159; Pridham, p. 152. Faulhaber, derided as "the Jewish cardinal," was soon blamed for Kahr and Seisser's repudiating the putsch. Hitler himself expressed that opinion to his economic adviser (and, fleetingly, his SA chief of staff) Otto Wagener (Wagener, pp. 102-3). Faulhaber could, however, also pull his punches, as in 1936, when he declared, "The Reich Chancellor undoubtedly lives in belief in God. He recognizes Christianity as the builder of western culture." (Kershaw [*Myth*], p. 105)

105   Graf. Dornberg, pp. 295, 346; Payne, p. 180; Hanfstaengl, p. 112; Large (*Munich*), p. 188.

106   Göring. Manvell & Fraenkel (*Göring*), pp. 34, 56; Mosley, p. 85; Payne, p. 179; Dornberg, pp. 296-97; Shirer, p. 74; Read, p. 97; Large (*Munich*), p. 188.

107   Ludendorff. Strasser, p. 45; Bullock, p. 112; Payne, p. 180; Toland, p. 170; Mosley, p. 85; Large (*Munich*), p. 189. Ludendorff had, however, initially and instinctively hit the ground, as did all the others.

108   "the first . . . turn back". Heiden (*History*), p. 106; Shirer, p. 74; Bullock, p. 112; Dornberg, p. 297; Langer, p. 223.

109   Fiat. Lewis (*Hitler*), p. 188. Some said it was an Opel.

110   "This is the . . . shoot myself first!" Hanfstaengl, p. 113; Dornberg, p. 326; Payne, p. 181; Conradi, p. 66; Large (*Munich*), p. 191. In prison, Hitler threatened suicide by hunger strike. Anton Drexler talked him out of it. (Langer, p. 88; Fest [*Hitler*], p. 190)

111   Pajamas, robe. Dornberg, pp. 327-28; Conradi, p. 66; Bracher, p. 117. Most estimates of Hitler's height run between 5'7" and 5'9", with most settling at 5'8".

112   Iron Cross. Fest (*Hitler*), p. 190; Bracher, p. 117.

113 "It was . . . a clothing firm." Mowrer, p. 252; Langer, p. 48.

114 "I am not a traitor but a German". Fest (*Hitler*), p. 191; Jarman, p. 102; Pridham, p. 17.

115 "I trusted him like a brother". Payne, p. 188.

116 "at the top of his lungs". *NY Times*, 28 March 1924, p. 10.

117 "The army we . . . she acquits us!" Bullock, p. 119; Wheeler-Bennett (*Nemesis*), p. 180; Payne, p. 191; Mitchell (*Hitler*), p. 88; de Sales, p. 83.

118 Ludendorff unaware. Bullock, p. 107.

119 Sentences. *NY Times*, 2 April 1924, p. 1; Strasser, p. 52; Bullock, p. 120; Toland, pp. 192-93; Payne, p. 192; Shirer, p. 78; Bracher, pp. 120-21; Jarman, p. 102; Pridham, p. 17; Large (*Munich*), pp. 193-94. The court considered but rejected deportation, in part because of Hitler's wartime service. Kershaw interestingly speaks of Landsberg as "a Nazi 'think tank.'" (Kershaw [*Hitler*], p. 32)

120 Released. Strasser, p. 58; Bullock, pp. 121, 127; Shirer, p. 78: Dornberg, pp. 337-38; Large (*Munich*), p. 197; Snyder (*Elite*), p. 80. According to Otto Strasser, Hitler's fellow prisoners had suggested the work to him—only so they might be spared listening to any more of his monologues. (Strasser, p. 53; Large [*Munich*], p. 197)

121 "spectacular . . . painter." *Emporia Gazette*, 5 August 1924, p. 5.

122 May 1924 elections. Heiden (*History*), pp. 108, 113; Wistrich, p. 199; Jarman, p. 143; Scheele, p. 149; Eyck, p. 218.

123 December 1924 elections. *NY Times*, 8 December 1924, p. 2; Wheeler-Bennett (*Nemesis*), p. 203; Jarman, p. 143; Scheele, p. 149; Eyck, p. 218. The *New York Times* attributed the setback to Ludendorff's anti-clerical and anti-Wittelsbach stance. During his 1924 trial he had devoted much of his defense to a great, booming anti-Catholic rant. (Pridham, p. 17)

124 Ludendorff vote total. Wheeler-Bennett (*Titan*), pp. 252-54; Wheeler-Bennett (*Nemesis*), p. 203; Halperin, p. 316; Wistrich, p. 199; Dorpalen, p. 67; Orlow (*Nazi*), pp. 61-62.

125 Röhm. Heiden (*History*), p. 112; Fest (*Face*), p. 141.

126 Göring. Mosley, pp. 98, 100-4, 326-27; Manvell (*Göring*), p. 43; Manvell & Fraenkel (*Goering*), pp. 36, 57-58, 61-62; Olden, p. 280; Singer, p. 128; Snyder (*Encyclopedia*), p. 122; Snyder (*Elite*), p. 7; Wistrich, p. 81; Reimann, p. 317.

127 Saxony. Broszat, p. 64.

128 Hamburg. Broszat, p. 65.

129 Braunschweig. Broszat, p. 65.

130 Unemployment. Johnson (*Modern*), p. 280.

131 May 1928 elections. Orlow (*Nazi*), pp. 128-31; Broszat, p. 65; Manvell (*Göring*), p. 38; Shirer, p. 146; Jarman, p. 143; Reuth, p. 98; Scheele, p. 149; Lüdecke, p. 333.

132 Berlin. Orlow (*Nazi*), p. 129; Large (*Berlin*), p. 226; Reuth, pp. 96-97; Evans (*Coming*), p. 209.

133 SPD, KPD. Reuth, pp. 96-97; Orlow (*Nazi*), p. 129.

134 Membership. Mowrer, p. 269; Lüdecke, p. 333; Heiden (*History*), p. 39; Taylor, p. 64; Orlow (*Nazi*), p. 25.

135 Young Plan. Heiden (*History*), p. 124; Davidson, pp. 276-77; Broszat, p. 74; Bracher, pp. 160-62; Kaufmann, pp. 191-92; Wheeler-Bennett (*Nemesis*), pp. 209-10; Leopold, pp. 56-67; Eyck, pp. 208-10. Young was, in fact, of German ancestry, his family name being originally "Jung."

136 Plebiscite. Davidson, p. 278; Hauner, p. 63; Broszat, p. 75; Bracher, p. 167; Kaufmann, p. 192; Noakes & Pridham, pp. 64-65; Pridham, pp. 90-91; Leopold, p. 70; Turner (*Stresemann*), p. 257; Eyck, pp. 208, 210-11, 222-24. The vote was stronger in Protestant than Catholic areas.

137 Two million. *NY Times*, 27 January 1931, p. 34.

138 Three million. *NY Times*, 24 September 1931, p. 15; Fest (*Hitler*), p. 269.

139 33.7/43.7 percent. Johnson (*Modern*), p. 280.

140 Communist rioting. *NY Times*, 2 January 1931, p. 19; Knickerbocker, p. 172.

141 Demonstration ban. Bullock, p. 167.

142 NSDAP/KPD ban. Broszat, p. 101.

143 "ruthlessly and without exception. . . ." Heiden (*Fuehrer*), p. 349; Heiden (*History*), pp. 125-28; Hauner, pp. 84-85.

144 Stennes. Lemmons, pp. 80-88; Heiden (*Fuehrer*), p. 350; Bullock, p. 168; Broszat, pp. 21-22; Fest (*Hitler*), p. 282; Payne, p. 118; Hauner, p. 85; Kershaw (*Hubris*), pp. 349-50; Weale, pp. 55-57; Reuth, pp. 100-101, 118-19, 127-33; Snyder (*Encyclopedia*), p. 333; Broszat, p. 97; Höhne, pp. 65-68; Mosley, p. 119.

145 Röhm. Heiden (*History*), p. 128; Bullock, pp. 168-69, 227; Fest (*Hitler*), p. 283; Fest (*Face*), p. 144; Hauner, pp. 65, 67; Lüdecke, p. 351; Bracher, pp. 181-82; Weale, p. 58; Höhne, p. 66.

146 Ill health. Wheeler-Bennett (*Nemesis*), p. 198.

147 Resigned. *NY Times*, 27 March 1930, pp. 1, 11; Knight-Patterson, p. 461; Davidson, p. 282; Hauner, p. 63; Burleigh, p. 125; Stachura, p. 82. Rudolf Olden, however, observed, "It fell without any reason; nothing had upset the majority coalition. The army [Gen. Kurt von Schleicher] simply put out a leg, and the Ministry simply tripped over it." (Olden, p. 239)

148 256–204. *NY Times*, 17 July March 1930, pp. 1, 9; *NY Times*, 2 January 1931, p. 19.

149 "petty Jesuit." Evans (*Coming*), p. 298.

150 "I decided . . . dangerous experiment. . . ." Grenville, p. 56.

151 1929-30 membership. Mowrer, p. 269; Lüdecke, p. 349; Payne, p. 257.

152 Twelve to 107. *NY Times*, 15 September 1930, pp. 1-2; *NY Times*, 2 January 1931, p. 19; Jarman, p. 143; Scheele, p. 149; Lüdecke, p. 344; Vogt, p. 94.

153 "Our solution depends . . . in advance." Knickerbocker, p. 112.

154 "If we give away . . . credit for it." Knickerbocker, p. 113.

155 "We know that . . . weapons of democracy." Heiden (*Fuehrer*), p. 348.

Chapter Six: "He has never consulted me about a damn thing"

1 1928 New York returns. *NY Times*, 7 November 1928, pp. 1-2.

2 1930. Bellush, pp. 172-73; Sinclair, p. 383. A good portion of FDR's historic margin resulted from a significant contrast in city (91.1 percent) versus upstate (70.6 percent) turnout. (Davis [*New York*], p. 190; Freidel [*Triumph*], p. 166; Smith [*FDR*], p. 245; Black [*Champion*], p. 207)

3 "I do not see . . . bring it about." *American Heritage*, August 1971, p. 40; Farley (*Story*), p. 6; Schlesinger (*Crisis*), p. 278; Russell, p. 306; Oulahan, p. 25; Smith (*FDR*), p. 249; Ritchie, p. 75. The aide was Jim Farley.

4 "The Democrats nominated . . . Roosevelt." Davis (*New York*), p. 190*fn*; Black (*Champion*), p. 208.

5 "his Christian Science smile". Teachout, p. 263.

6 6'2". *American Heritage*, August 1971, p. 38.

7 Jealousy. Howe displayed justifiable concern. As others joined FDR's inner circle, their star ascended, his dimmed. FDR biographer Ted Morgan described him, following 1933, as "a castoff, a threadbare coat given to charity." A New Dealer likened him to an "aging first wife in a harem." (Morgan, p. 442)

8 Howe/Rosenman. Moley (*Seven*), pp. 7-8. "Howe," recalled Raymond Moley, who refused to attend Howe's April 1936 funeral (Morgan, p. 443), "was forever trying to humiliate Rosenman," whom he also recollected as "capable [and] conscientious," but also "often brusque and tactless." Rexford Tugwell believed a key to Rosenman's success with Roosevelt was his ability to completely ignore FDR's infirmity. (Tugwell [*Brains*], p. 41) On the other hand, Farley, who got along fine with Moley and Berle, fared less well with Tugwell. (*American Heritage*, August 1971, p. 41)

9 "Why not go . . . the country?" Moley (*Seven*), p. 5; Tugwell (*Brains*), p. 9; Shlaes (*Forgotten*), p. 125. Not everyone was entranced with the idea of a "brains trust." In November 1941 Hitler publicly ridiculed it, pronouncing, "I have no experts at all. In my case, my own head alone is always enough. I need no brains trust to help me. Therefore, if there really is to be a change anywhere, then that change will be created in my brain and not in other people's brains. . . ." (Maltitz, p. 335)

10 "original and speculative . . . brain race along." Moley (*Seven*), p. 15; McElvaine, p. 126; Kennedy (*Freedom*), p. 122; Shlaes (*Forgotten*), p. 125; Alter, p. 96.

11   "I have gathered . . . make America over!" Schlesinger (*Crisis*), p. 194.

12   Since 1928. Moley (*Seven*), p. 2.

13   Moley and Rosenman. Schlesinger (*Ghosts*), p. 8.

14   "patient, amenable . . . indifferent to criticism." Moley (*27*), p. 45.

15   "The stories . . . good humor. . . ." Moley (*Seven*), pp. 10-12; Warren (*Presidency*), p. 230; Brands (*Traitor*), p. 250.

16   Berle/Baker. Tugwell (*Brains*), p. 85. Berle had supported Hoover in 1928. (Kennedy [*Freedom*], p. 121)

17   "not a handsome fellow. . . for his age." Tugwell (*Brains*), p. 139.

18   "He wasn't . . . it got across." *American Heritage*, August 1971, pp. 43, 90.

19   "never lied . . . with the truth". *American Heritage*, August 1971, p. 90.

20   "He had learned . . . a political habit". Tugwell (*Brains*), p. 78.

21   "Roosevelt would organize . . . known to us". Tugwell (*Brains*), p. 163.

22   "He seldom said . . . the least appreciation. . . ." Tugwell (*Brains*), p. 188. Tugwell displayed particular umbrage at FDR's lack of concern for his black valet Irvin "Mac" McDuffie. In 1939, McDuffie suffered a nervous breakdown. (Tugwell [*Brains*], p. 28)

23   "aldermanic". Oulahan, p. 17.

24   "amazingly detailed". Tugwell (*Brains*), p. 74.

25   "One of the . . . irrelevant and obsolete." Tugwell (*Democratic*), p. 212.

26   Farley trip. Farley (*Story*), pp. 11-12; Schlesinger (*Crisis*), p. 281; Martin (*Bandwagons*), pp. 269-72; Black (*Champion*), p. 210.

27   "Well, Jim Farley . . . nobody else did." Ritchie, p. 78.

28   "Wet". Farley (*Story*), p. 13; Freidel (*Triumph*), p. 236. In 1931, H. L. Mencken reported to his diary that Ritchie had informed him that "he could do little for himself, for the only feasible way was by making speeches, and he had run out of ideas for them." (Fecher, p. 36)

29   Bolivia. *Collier's*, 28 November 1931, p. 45.

30   Martial law. *Collier's*, 28 November 1931, p. 13.

31   Reed "wet." Okrent, p. 232.

32   Ford. *Time*, 28 March 1927, p. 78; *Jewish Tribune*, 15 July 1927, p. 27; Nevins (*Ford*), p. 318.

33   "a most . . . dark horse". Farley (*Story*), p. 13.

34   "Every time . . . get a hog". *World's Work*, January 1916, p. 275; Barone, p. 50.

35   Newsreels, radio. Carlisle, p. 9.

36   Hearst papers. Carlisle, pp. 9-11.

37   "a Wilsonite . . . at the end of Mr. Wilson's political blind alley". Carlisle, p. 55.

38   "a loyal American . . . Champ Clark." *NY Times*, 3 January 1932, p. 3; Carlisle, p. 55; Procter, p. 166; Davis (*New York*), p. 257; Martin (*Bandwagons*), p. 285; Procter, p. 166; Cramer, p. 249; Neal, p. 60. Wilson defeated then Speaker of the House Clark for 1912's Democratic nomination.

39   "presented at once . . . a new-born baby." Schlesinger (*Crisis*), p. 227; Procter, p. 171.

40   "a confused . . . of first." Tugwell (*Democratic*), p. 226. Hoover, however, regarded Garner as "a man of real statesmanship when he took off his political pistols. Philosophically he was a pragmatist, a bitter partisan and adroit. His program of public welfare in this session was simple—get the Republicans out and the Democrats in. His mental orbit during this period was dominated by political tactics and strategy and his capacities in this field were of a high order. He was engagingly frank and honored his undertakings. The few times when I secured his agreement for certain action, his word was always good." (Hoover [*Great Depression*], pp. 101-2; Kennedy [*Freedom*], p. 61)

41   Wilson. Moley (*27*), p. 71.

42   DeWitt Clinton Hotel. Flynn (*Boss*), p. 75; Schlesinger (*Crisis*), p. 386; Handlin, p. 143; O'Connor (*Hurrah*), p. 229; Caro, p. 294.

43   Taconic Parkway. Caro, pp. 288-91; Schlesinger (*Crisis*), p. 379; Handlin, p. 144; Freidel (*Ordeal*), pp. 219-20; Freidel (*Triumph*), p. 16.

44   Howe. Flynn (*Squire*), p. 39; O'Connor (*Hurrah*), p. 230; Caro, p. 287.

45 "You know . . . be better, Al." Perkins, pp. 52-53; Caro, p. 297; Gould, p. 206; Finan, p. 243. Even FDR knew—or soon would—that Cross's appointment was a joke. "I can't tell Guernsey Cross anything," he complained to Frances Perkins. "Guernsey Cross doesn't know anything." And, indeed, Cross hardly counted among his stellar hires. In April 1934, authorities revealed that Cross had received a $6,500 loan from mobster Waxey Gordon–connected Max Greenberg. Soon afterward authorities indicted him for bank fraud as a director with Sullivan County's First National Mortgage and Guarantee. (*NY Times*, 13 April 1934, p. 42; *Spokane Chronicle*, 13 April 1934, p. 5; *NY Times*, 5 June 1934, p. 3) Beyond that, FDR's excuse was even greater balderdash: his muscular bodyguard Gus Gennerich ("my humanizer") invariably placed him in and out of his wheelchair, etc. (*Spartanburg Herald*, 18 December 1936, p. 8; Cook [*Vol. 2*], pp. 401-2)

46 "By all signs . . . a firm stand." Lash (*Eleanor*), p. 323; Cook (*Vol. 1*), p. 388; Smith (*FDR*), p. 231; Breitman & Lichtman, p. 35.

47 "Gosh, the race . . . tentacles of steel." Lash (*Eleanor*), p. 323; Cook (*Vol. 1*), p. 388; Smith (*FDR*), p. 231; Breitman & Lichtman, p. 35.

48 "Do you know . . . ignored me." Schlesinger (*Crisis*), p. 387; Freidel (*Triumph*), p. 237; O'Connor (*Hurrah*), p. 249; Slayton, p. 370; Davis (*New York*), pp. 248-49; Handlin, pp. 154-55. Howell promptly revealed this conversation to FDR. (Burns, p. 129) Howell recommended that FDR reach out to Smith to mend fences. He never did.

49 "wishy-washy". Schlesinger (*Crisis*), p. 288; Martin (*Bandwagons*), p. 264; Morgan, p. 331.

50 "the Boy Scout Governor". Freidel (*Triumph*), p. 236; Davis (*New York*), p. 250; Miller (*FDR*), p. 258; Black (*Champion*), p. 219. The "boy scout" characterization seemed quite popular. In November 1931, Walter Lippmann wrote to Newton D. Baker, terming FDR a "kind of amiable boy scout." (Steel, pp. 291, 618)

51 Withdraws League support. *NY Times*, 1 January 1933, p. 20; *Scribner's*, April 1932, p. 201; Tugwell (*Brains*), p. 76; Hull, p. 150; Nasaw (*Chief*), p. 454; Ritchie, p. 84; Carlisle, pp. 57, 58*fn*; Davis (*New York*), p. 259; Warren (*Presidency*), p. 228; Black (*Champion*), pp. 220-21; Morgan, p. 340; Rosen, pp. 102-5; Martin (*Bandwagons*), p. 286; Carlisle, pp. 57-58. Wilson's former secretary Joseph Tumulty felt particularly betrayed. (*Jacksonville Journal*, 5 February 1932, p. 1)

52 Socialist candidate. O'Connor (*Broun*), pp. 159-65; Kramer, pp. 206-22. Broun was endorsed by (among others): Irving Berlin, the four Marx Brothers, Lunt & Fontanne, Ed Wynn (for Coolidge in 1924), George Jessel, Helen Hayes, Edna Ferber (for Harding in 1920), Fred Astaire, Stuart Chase, Theodore Dreiser, John Dewey, Clarence Darrow, David Belasco, and Walter Winchell. He still finished a very distant third.

53 Broun for Smith. Handlin, p. 163; Tugwell (*Democratic*), p. 227*fn*; Kramer, p. 241.

54 "[T]he banquet . . . hands and knees." *Pittsburgh Press*, 11 January 1932, p. 2; *Fitchburg Sentinel*, 25 January 1932, p. 6; Peel & Donnelly, p. 189; Kramer, pp. 239-40.

55 "Franklin D. Roosevelt . . . is too radical." Lippmann, p. 262; Tugwell (*Brains*), pp. 120-21; Steel, pp. 290-91; Morgan, p. 339; Oulahan, p. 42; Cashman, p. 134; Dobyns, p. 152; Ekirch, p. 86. Lippmann had not always so suspected FDR. Upon Franklin's 1920 vice-presidential nomination, Lippmann telegraphed him these congratulations: "When parties can pick a man like Franklin Roosevelt, there is a decent future in politics." Herbert Hoover conveyed similar felicitations. (Black [*Champion*], p. 124; Freidel [*Ordeal*], p. 69*fn*; Carlin, Cole, Miller & Walch, p. 8; Pietrusza [*1920*], pp. 331-32)

56 "not a man . . . moral stamina." *New Republic*, 1 April 1931, pp. 165-66; Schlesinger (*Crisis*), p. 291; Ekirch, p. 85; Kennedy (*Freedom*), p. 101.

57 "Roosevelt . . . had no . . . political suicide." Rosen, p. 105.

58 Syphilis. Morgan, p. 337; Neal, p. 126. While FDR's opponents might lie about the severity (and cause) of his infirmity, he invariably dissembled to minimize it, writing, for example on May 15, 1929, to Kansas editor George W. Marble, "I am not in any sense an invalid and have not been since an attack of infantile paralysis. Literally, the only thing the matter with my health is that I have to walk with braces on my legs and a couple of canes." Similarly, on December 29, 1931, to the editor of the *Butte Standard*, he denied use "of a wheelchair," though he would admit to employing "a little kitchen chair with wheels to get about my room while dressing . . . solely for the purpose of saving time. . . ." (Neal, pp. 166, 334)

59   Riordan. O'Connor (*Hurrah*), pp. 244-46; Handlin, pp. 147-50; Finan, pp. 246-48; Slayton, pp. 343-46; Thomas & Morgan-Witts, pp. 163-65, 403-4.

60   Flynn, Lehman. Flynn (*Boss*), p. 86; Golway, p. 273.

61   "Smith was a . . . the governorship myself." *Collier's Weekly*, 16 January 1932, p. 34; Handlin, p. 159; Freidel (*Triumph*), p. 237; Morgan, p. 329.

62   "I am . . . be rich." Freidel (*Triumph*), p. 85; Schlesinger (*Crisis*), p. 126.

63   Raskob's $100,000. *Chicago Tribune*, 17 June 1930, p. 3; Lomazow & Fettmann, p. 36.

64   1924. Hicks, p. 209; Schlesinger (*Crisis*), p. 126.

65   Republican enrollment. Hull, p. 141; Schlesinger (*Crisis*), p. 126.

66   "His heart still . . . big-business language." *Scribner's*, March 1932, p. 132.

67   Tariff. Schlesinger (*Crisis*), p. 126; Hull, pp. 140-41; Schlesinger (*Coming*), p. 190.

68   *Literary Digest* poll. *Literary Digest*, 30 April 1932, pp. 6-7, 39; Kyvig, p. 151; Kull & Kull, p. 247; Horan, p. 17.

69   1928. Sinclair, p. 380.

70   February 1931 meeting. Freidel (*Triumph*), p. 178; Hull, p. 141; Black (*Champion*), p. 209; Fried, pp. 33-34; Kyvig, p. 146.

71   Michelson. Michelson, *passim*; Schlesinger (*Crisis*), p. 274; Jeansonne (*Hoover*), pp. 145, 225, 398-400; Wilson (*Progressive*), p. 142; Hoover (*Depression*), p. 221. Oddly enough, most of the Michelson-generated criticism involved the tariff rather than the Depression.

72   "You cannot inscribe . . . of an outlawed trade". *NY Times*, 6 March 1931, p. 6; Dobyns, p. 149; Farber, p. 281.

73   Revolt. *NY Times*, 27 March 1931, p. 1; Hull, pp. 141-45; Handlin, pp. 152-53.

74   "just a naive amateur . . . him again." *Scribner's*, March 1932, p. 131. In July 1928, FDR warned Smith against appointing Raskob as he would "permanently drive away a host of people in the south and west and rural east. . . ." Smith supporter and Broadway producer Eddie Dowling found Raskob to be "a strange little man, a mixed-up man." (O'Connor [*Hurrah*], p. 202; Schlesinger [*Crisis*], p. 127)

75   Ally. *NY Times*, 18 April 1932, p. 14; Freidel (*Triumph*), p. 205; Davis (*New York*), p. 213.

76   April 1931 poll. Freidel (*Triumph*), p. 205; Davis (*New York*), p. 213.

77   March 1931 poll. *NY Times*, 30 March 1931, pp. 1, 15; Freidel (*Triumph*), pp. 204-05; Davis (*New York*), p. 213; Black (*Champion*), p. 216.

78   "If it's printed . . . *kaput*, finished." Houck (*Rhetoric*), p. 99; Houck & Kiewe, p. 16.

79   "No movies . . . [his car] boys!" Persico (*Lucy*), p. 188; Levin, p. 89; Lomazow & Fettmann, p. 37; Rowley, p. 149.

80   "while mentally qualified . . . utterly unfit physically." *Time*, April 27, 1931, p. 18; Neal, p. 165; Smith (*FDR*), p. 256; Houck & Kiewe, p. 65; Lomazow & Fettman, p. 43.

81   "We don't want . . . on the ticket." Mullen, p. 262; Schlesinger (*Crisis*), p. 286; Neal, p. 165. Roosevelt outlived both McAdoo and Mullen—as well as half of his original Cabinet: Walsh, Woodin, Dern, Swanson, and Roper—*plus* Al Smith, Louis Howe, Missy LeHand, and his very trusted bodyguard, "Gus" Gennerich. (*NY Times*, 6 December 1936, p. N3)

82   Medical examination. Smith (*FDR*), pp. 257-58; Neal, pp. 170-71.

83   *Liberty* article. *Liberty*, 25 July 1931, p. 78; Tugwell (*Brains*), p. 191; Freidel (*Triumph*), p. 211; Warren (*Presidency*), p. 225; Black (*Champion*), p. 211; Neal, pp. 170-71; Houck & Kiewe, pp. 65-70.

84   "I had noted . . . good to him." *Liberty*, 25 July 1931, page unknown; Freidel (*Triumph*), p. 211; Neal, pp. 170-71.

85   Looker. *NY Post*, 22 July 1932, p. 9; Roosevelt (*Government*), *passim*; Freidel (*Triumph*), p. 342*fn*; Tugwell (*Brains*), p. 191; Neal, pp. 170-71; Lomazow & Fettmann, pp. 45-48; Houck & Kiewe, p. 70. Its ironic title: *Government—Not Politics*. Once elected FDR dropped Looker ("I get it in the neck for being loyal to you") like a rock. Oddly enough, *Liberty* publisher Bernarr Macfadden was initially no great fan of FDR, dismissing him in 1931 as "nothing but a jellyfish." (Stiles, p. 149)

86   Copies mailed. Neal, p. 171; Lomazow & Fettmann, p. 46; Houck & Kiewe, p. 67.

87 "Roosevelt's supporters were . . . low tariff men." Burns, p. 130.
88 "I have seen . . . be a candidate." Freidel (*Triumph*), p. 167; Martin (*Bandwagons*), p. 264; Black (*Champion*), p. 208. To Mrs. Casper Whitney, an ardent "wet," on December 8, 1930. (Kyvig, p. 121) He was more honest eventually when he revealed to the *Times of London*: "For twenty years I had a perfectly natural and laudable ambition to become President and was obliged to behave like a man who wants to be President." (Martin [*Bandwagons*], p. 109; Oulahan, p. 25)
89 FDR announces. *NY Times*, 24 January 1932, p. 1; Rosenman (*Papers*), pp. 623-24; Oulahan, p. 37.
90 "availability". Martin (*Bandwagons*), p. 281.

CHAPTER SEVEN: "ARE YOU FRIGHTENED OF ME?"

1 Two rooms. Metcalfe, p. 74.
2 Wages. Menne, p. 57.
3 "Hunger Chancellor". Wheeler-Bennett (*Titan*), p. 345; Shirer, p. 152; Davidson, p. 287.
4 Thälmann. Evans (*Coming*), pp. 241-42; Snyder (*Encyclopedia*), pp. 344-45; Burleigh, p. 58.
5 "A block . . . a jelly". *Living Age*, January 1932, p. 421.
6 Despised Hugenberg. Dorpalen, pp. 228-29; Mommsen, p. 414; Leopold, p. 85.
7 "Bohemian Corporal". Dorpalen, p. 241; Turner (*Thirty*), p. 194; Shirer, p. 153; Hauner, p. 74; Wistrich, p. 116.
8 "the best . . . since Bismarck." Heiden (*History*), pp. 160, 167; Wheeler-Bennett (*Titan*), pp. 346, 348, 363; Wheeler-Bennett (*Nemesis*), p. 236; Knight-Patterson, p. 463.
9 Weimar constitution. pp. 253-75; Davidson, pp. 283-85; Manvell & Fraenkel (*Hundred*), pp. 188-89. The German Kaiser could similarly dissolve the Reichstag at will. (Cowles, p. 114) Weimar's constitution wildly inflated Hitler's Reichstag totals. In only one large district—Schleswig-Holstein—had the Nazis polled as much as 25 percent. In just twenty-three of the nation's 400 smaller districts did they secure over 30 percent. "In the vast majority of single-man constituencies," noted the German jurist and political scientist Arnold Brecht, "their share would have been far below 20 per cent. If the American or British plurality system of elections . . . had been in force in Germany, the National Socialists would have had no chance of gaining more than 10 or 20 seats, if that many. Nor would they have fared better under the French or imperial German systems, with their run-off elections, which tended to unite the moderate parties against the extremists." (Brecht, pp. 28-29; see also Vogt, p. 51) None of the Weimar constitution's flaws, however, might be blamed on the nation's authoritarian or totalitarian parties. This star-crossed mess was the work of the Center-Left. At Weimar, the Social Democrats (163), Zentrum (91), and the Democratic (75) parties controlled a hefty 329 of the convention's 421 delegates. (Vogt, p. 49)
10 "Any constructive element . . . complained of." Burke, p. 71. Dorothy Thompson more tersely summarized their appeal as a "peculiar mixture of Nordic myth, anti-Semitism, militaristic tradition, desperado nationalism and moronized socialism." (Kurth, p. 161)
11 "When finally I . . . of the Little Man. . . ." *Kansas City Star*, 10 February 1932, p. 24; *Syracuse Journal*, 16 February 1932, p. 13; Thompson, pp. 13-14; Kurth, p. 161; Metcalfe, pp. 56-67; Conradi, p. 87. She, however, continued, "But perhaps therein—exactly therein—lies the secret of his enormous success. When Charlie Chaplin created the eternal 'little man' and with him awakened the sympathy of millions he chose a mask which is uncannily like the face and bearing of Hitler." (Thompson, p. 23)
12 Drunk. Metcalfe, p. 57. The claim came from Putzi Hanfstaengl, under fire for having arranged the disastrous interview.
13 "We become Reichstag . . . longer among yourselves." Bracher, pp. 143-44.
14 "What made [Himmler] . . . a revivalist preacher." Krebs, p. 266; Padfield, p. 138; Höhne, p. 29.
15 Rust. Krebs, p. 291; Wistrich, p. 262; Snyder (*Encyclopedia*), p. 303; Heiden (*Fuehrer*), p. 287; Lewis (*Hitler*), p. 240.
16 "In 1920 a . . . its Reichstag delegation." Eyck, p. 358. Heines, released in a general amnesty, had also suffered expulsion from the party in May 1927 after insulting Hitler (Hauner, p. 56; Snyder

[*Encyclopedia*], p. 140; Heiden [*History*], pp. 390, 417-18) When the new Reichstag convened in October 1930, Heines allegedly added to the din by playing upon a fife. (Fischer, p. 173)

17   "The whole afternoon . . . about and demonstrating." Craig (*Germany*), pp. 542-43. "*Juda verrecke!*" translates roughly as "Perish Judah!" or "Death to the Jews!" with the extra meaning that this German form includes a slang term for the death of animals. (Vogt, p. 114*fn*; Kurth, p. 164)

18   Exit, re-entrance. Thacker, p. 114.

19   "a certain . . . embarrassment". Burke, pp. 91-92.

20   Shop windows. Heiden (*History*), p. 155; Thacker, p. 114. "The culprits were at once expelled from the Party," noted Konrad Heiden. "The *Beobachter* added that in the Third Reich the shop windows of Jewish businesses would be much better looked after than they were by the present Marxist police."

21   "Jewish provocation". Thacker, p. 115.

22   "bearers of state morality". Thacker, p. 115.

23   Goebbels. Richie, p. 398; Thacker, p. 115.

24   Snakes, stink bombs, mice. Heiden (*Fuehrer*), p. 403; Fischer, p. 174; Sigmund, p. 76.

25   Film banned. Fischer, p. 174; Sigmund, p. 76.

26   Reichstag boycott. *NY Times*, 5 April 1931, p. 51; *NY Times*, 1 January 1932, p. 25; Manvell (*Göring*), p. 42; Broszat, p. 96; Dorpalen, p. 228.

27   Gangs. Evans (*Coming*), p. 267; Siemens, p. 12.

28   "red districts". Evans (*Coming*), p. 237.

29   Unemployed. Evans (*Coming*), p. 236; Davidson, p. 296.

30   6,127,000. *Economist*, 2 July 1932, p. 18; Görtemaker, p. 46; Menne, p. 57; Snyder (*Encyclopedia*), p. 43; Kurth, p. 156; Davidson, p. 310; Burleigh, p. 124; Johnson (*Modern*), p. 280.

31   7.6 million. Burleigh, p. 124.

32   Fifteen percent. Taylor, p. 113.

33   Altona. Evans (*Coming*), p. 238.

34   67 percent. Weale, p. 56.

35   Suicide. Burleigh, p. 126.

36   "Every conversation I . . . must happen.'" Kurth, p. 157.

37   March 1931 bans. *NY Times*, 1 January 1932, p. 25; Hauner, p. 68.

38   Expel. Hauner, p. 69.

39   "I understand . . . bear arms." Wheeler-Bennett (*Nemesis*), p. 227; Snyder (*Encyclopedia*), p. 333; Toland, p. 249.

40   Customs union. *NY Times*, 1 January 1932, p. 25; Clark (*German Republic*), p. 317; Hoover (*Great Depression*), p. 62; Smith (*Dream*), p. 60.

41   Kreditanstalt. Broszat, p. 95; Dutch, pp. 119-20; Barone, p. 47; Leuchtenburg (*Perils*), p. 255; Peel & Donnelly, p. 11.

42   Polish border. Wheeler-Bennett (*Titan*), p. 350; Wheeler-Bennett (*Nemesis*), p. 227. Even in 1929 (with immense growth to soon follow), the SA at a hundred thousand members numerically equaled the Reichswehr. (Bracher, p. 167)

43   Stahlhelm. *NY Times*, 1 January 1932, p. 25; Knight-Patterson, p. 491.

44   Hoover to intervene. Hoover (*Great Depression*), pp. 68-69; Papen, p. 137; Clark (*German Republic*), p. 318; Peel & Donnelly, p. 12; Leuchtenburg (*Perils*), p. 256.

45   "The need of . . . are exhausted." Smith (*Dream*), p. 61.

46   Düsseldorf industrialists. *NY Times*, 1 January 1932, p. 25. In June 1931.

47   Reichstag resolution. Heiden (*History*), p. 132; Heiden (*Fuehrer*), pp. 403-4; Knight-Patterson, p. 483; Shirer, p. 144; Fest (*Hitler*), p. 301.

48   Feder disavowal. Broszat, p. 24; Manvell & Fraenkel (*Goering*), p. 72.

49   America. Goldensohn, p. 229.

50   "Schachtl". Muhlen, pp. 21, 29.

51   "the father of . . . of all time". Muhlen, p. 21.

52 Schacht. *NY Times*, 2 January 1931, p. 19; Broszat, p. 75; Knight-Patterson, pp. 457-58; Schacht, pp. 279-80; Hauner, p. 68; Kershaw (*Hubris*), p. 356; Davidson, p. 278; Eyck, p. 224; Turner (*Business*), p. 103; Manvell & Fraenkel (*Goering*), p. 72; Muhlen, p. 28. The German Democratic Party later became the German State Party.

53 Thyssen. Schacht, p. 279; Thyssen, p. 131; Bullock, p. 174; Snyder (*Encyclopedia*), p. 347; Kershaw (*Hubris*), pp. 356-57; Turner (*Business*), pp. 145, 148, 303. Thyssen, however, hung back from formally joining the NSDAP until December 1931. (Thyssen, p. 128)

54 Goebbels. Schacht, p. 279; Thacker, p. 114.

55 "I learned what . . . croaking voice." Schacht, pp. 279-80; Hauner, p. 68; Kershaw (*Hubris*), p. 357.

56 Cabinet. Kershaw (*Hubris*), p. 357.

57 "very little . . . entire manner". Röhl, p. 1202.

58 Harzburg Front. Heiden (*History*), pp. 161-62; Eyck, pp. 332-35; Scheele, p. 156; Evans (*Coming*), pp. 244-45; Bracher, pp.189-90; Kershaw (*Hubris*), p. 356; Davidson, pp. 304-6; Turner (*Business*), pp. 167-70; Leopold, pp. 98-104; Winkler, p. 446; Jonas, p. 171.

59 "suddenly decided . . . influential economic magnates." Dietrich (*With*), p. 12; Bullock, p. 174; Kershaw (*Hubris*), p. 358. This is the recollection of Nazi press aide Otto Dietrich. Hitler biographer Ian Kershaw considers Dietrich to be exaggerating, adding, "most [big business] support still went to . . . the conservative Right. The leaders of big business were no friends of democracy. But nor, for the most part, did they want to see the Nazis running the country."

60 Kirdorf. Heiden (*Fuehrer*), p. 356; Thyssen, pp. 129-31; Bullock, pp. 149, 173; Turner (*Business*), pp. 90-95, 131; Shirer, pp. 134, 144; Kershaw (*Hubris*), p. 357; Snyder (*Encyclopedia*), p. 195; Wistrich, pp. 171-72; Fest (*Hitler*), pp. 265, 301; Hauner, p. 57; Payne, p. 223. Kirdorf, a veteran of the Pan-German League, eventually also renounced Christianity to join Ludendorff's neo-pagan sect.

61 Strikes. Broszat, pp. 13, 24; Kershaw (*Hubris*), p. 358; Kershaw (*Hitler*), p. 200.

62 Cuno. Turner (*Business*), p. 75; Kershaw (*Hubris*), p. 357.

63 Krupp. Thyssen, pp. 134-35; Turner (*Business*), pp. 172, 214, 289, 320; Snyder (*Encyclopedia*), p. 201; Wistrich, p. 181.

64 Rosenberg. Pridham, pp. 161-63; Hanfstaengl, p. 85; Shirer, p. 149; Fest (*Face*), pp. 168-69; Kershaw (*Myth*), pp. 34, 115; Snyder (*Encyclopedia*), pp. 300-301. Even Hitler found the book to be "derivative, [a] pastiche, illogical rubbish!" Goebbels considered it a "philosophical belch." Göring damned it as "junk." (Reuth, p. 304)

65 Priests. Pridham, pp. 166-67.

66 Cardinals. *NY Times*, 8 March 1931, p. 10; Bracher, p. 188. "Bishops and priests belonging to the Centre party launched a fanatical attack against the Nazi movement," noted Kurt Lüdecke in 1937, "excommunicating its followers and even refusing them Christian burial. Indeed, much of the present hostility of the Nazi regime to the established churches of Germany can be traced to the memory of much un-Christian treatment at their hands in the years of struggle." (Lüdecke, p. 348)

67 Mainz. Pridham, pp. 165-66; Heiden (*History*), pp. 151-52. Paderborn Archbishop Kaspar Klein also declared party membership "not permissible for a Catholic Christian so long and in so far as it propagates political and educational theories that are irreconcilable with the Catholic doctrine."

68 "Yes, National Socialism . . . heathen to the core!" Lüdecke, p. 520. Hitler had traveled a long distance (at least overtly) from a widely publicized April 12, 1922 Bürgerbräukeller speech, in which he termed himself a "Christian" and claimed Jesus as his "Lord and Savior." (Langer, p. 39; Hastings, pp. 102-3)

69 Young Plan. *NY Times*, 2 January 1931, p. 19; Wheeler-Bennett (*Titan*), pp. 331-34; Bullock, pp. 148-49; Davidson, pp. 276-77; Eyck, p. 241.

70 "Herr Paul von Hindenburg . . . Field-Marshal." Knight-Patterson, p. 460; Wheeler-Bennett (*Titan*), p. 334; Davidson, p. 278*fn*; Eyck, p. 241.

71 Breakdown. Wheeler-Bennett (*Nemesis*), pp. 232-33, 259; Eyck, p. 351; Manvell & Fraenkel (*Hundred*), p. 23; Davidson, p. 306. Brüning termed it "a temporary blackout." State Secretary Otto Meissner denied the incident ever occurred.

72   "I am the . . . Emperor himself." Wheeler-Bennett (*Titan*), p. 354; Kaufmann, p. 206; Dorpalen, p. 260; Cowles, 423. Brüning had even secured some desperate SPD support for this scheme.
73   Bruckmann, Bechstein. Heiden (*History*), p. 101; Hanfstaengl, pp. 65, 112-14; Langer, pp. 96-97; Goebbels (*Early*), pp. 51, 119; Large (*Munich*), pp. 152, 197; Heiden (*Fuehrer*), p. 246; Shirer, p. 145; Fest (*Hitler*), p. 166; Infield (*Secret*), pp. 77-78; Davidson, p. 314; Halperin, p. 443; Sigmund, p. 8; Taylor, p. 65; Kershaw (*Hitler*), p. 42; Lewis [*Hitler*], pp. 182-83, 190.
74   *Mein Kampf.* Turner (*Business*), p. 154.
75   Nazi press articles. Heiden (*Fuehrer*), p. 279; Turner (*Business*), p. 154.
76   "Adolf Hitler's Own . . . Proposes to Remedy It". Jewett and Lawrence, p. 132.
77   Foreign articles. Nasaw (*Chief*), pp. 474-76; Jewett and Lawrence, p. 132.
78   Interviews. Bullock, p. 171; Turner (*Business*), pp. 154-55.
79    $20,000. McDonald, p. 15.
80   SA. Bullock, p. 172.
81   Dues, admission fees. Kershaw (*Hitler*), p. 57.
82   "looked like a . . . railway-station restaurant." Hanfstaengl, p. 34; Botting & Sayer, p. 66.
83   "boy scout . . . grudge." Botting & Sayer, p. 12.
84   "When dinner was . . . the dining hall." Cerruti, p. 123; Botting & Sayer, pp. 110-11.
85   1920s quarters. Hanfstaengl, pp. 48-49; Fest (*Hitler*), p. 214; Waite, p. 219.
86   Hundred marks. Read, p. 186.
87   Mensa Academica Judaica. Langer, pp. 120-21; Heiden (*Fuehrer*), pp. 43; Tyson (*Eckart*), p. 277; Sigmund, p. 126; Murray, pp. 103, 117. Reports indicated that "in the student riots Angela defended the Jewish students from attack and on several occasions beat the Aryan students off the steps of the dining hall with a club."
88   Housekeeper. Heiden (*Fuehrer*), pp. 278; Fest (*Hitler*), p. 236; Toland, p. 229; Görtemaker, p. 47. Heiden indicates that technically Angela had rented it.
89   16 Prinzregentenplatz. Heiden (*Fuehrer*), p. 356; Payne, p. 222; Waite, p. 219; Görtemaker, p. 43; Hauner, p. 63; Gun, p. 7. Even prior to the move to Prinzregentenplatz Geli resided next door to Hitler's Thierschstrasse lodgings. (Lambert, p. 104)
90   Stefanie Isak. Kubizek, pp. 60-71; Toland, pp. 24-25; Fest (*Hitler*), p. 22; Tyson (*Eckart*), p. 258; Victor, pp. 37-40; Stierlin, p. 27. There may have been an earlier abortive advance to a female in a barn in Spital. When she indicated her willingness (to whatever Hitler proposed) he merely fled.
91   Prostitution obsession. Hitler (*Mein Kampf*), p. 247. His ideas on prostitution most likely formed in Vienna, but streetwalkers also infested Munich—one "every six paces" according to a 1910 city guide. (Large [*Munich*], pp. xix-xx)
92   Syphilis. Hitler (*Mein Kampf*), pp. 59, 251-57.
93   "in the insane . . . in our—children". Hitler (*Mein Kampf*), p. 248.
94   "My bride is Germany". Hoffmann (*Friend*), p. 141; Wagener, p. 33; Infield (*Eva*), p. 34; Botting & Sayer, p. 54; Knopp, p. 14.
95   Liptauer. *Saturday Review*, 2 May 1970, p. 23; Hoffmann (*Friend*), p. 167; Waite, pp. 231, 239; Gun, p. 60; Botting & Sayer, p. 105; Tyson (*Surreal*), p. 22.
96   Reiter. *Saturday Review*, 2 May 1970, p. 22; Kershaw (*Hubris*), pp. 284-85, 352, 706; Machtan, pp. 155-56, 159; Redlich, pp. 78-79, 285; Waite, p. 239; Rosenbaum, pp. 109-17; Infield (*Secret*), p. 81; Botting & Sayer, pp. 35-44, 70-73; Mitchell (*Obersalzberg*), p. 19.
97   "She was a princess . . . done in Munich." Gun, p. 1.
98   "I was walking . . . anyone like that." Rosenbaum, p. 122.
99   "a brown-eyed brunette . . . extraordinarily self-possessed." Lambert, p. 119.
100   "an enchantress . . . especially her uncle. . . ." Hoffmann (*Friend*), p. 148; Infield (*Secret*), p. 82.
101   "Only Geli can . . . with her eyes". Gun, p. 1.
102   "[F]or a while . . . a youngster in love." Machtan, p. 162.
103   "If Geli wanted . . . to the lake." Toland, p. 229.
104   "he always . . . a faithful lamb." Hoffmann (*Friend*), p. 148; Toland, p. 236; Sigmund, p. 134. Emil Maurice later confirmed Hoffman's story of Hitler's shopping. (Gun, p. 8)

105 "He loved her . . . of an infatuation." Gun, p. 9; Toland, p. 252; Machtan, p. 158; Botting & Sayer, p. 46.

106 "coarse, provocative . . . little quarrelsome". Toland, p. 229.

107 "an empty-headed little slut". Hanfstaengl, p. 169; Toland, p. 229; Waite, p. 226; Large (*Munich*), p. 206; Rosenbaum, p. 125.

108 "Geli's charm couldn't . . . took of her." Lambert, p. 101*fn*.

109 "My uncle is . . . makes me do". Payne, p. 226; Kershaw (*Hubris*), p. 353.

110 "Geli told me . . . alone with him." Infield (*Eva*), p. 43.

111 "You know, Hoffmann. . . adventurer or swindler." Hoffmann (*Friend*), p. 150; Gun, p. 9; Machtan, p. 162; Hayman, p. 141.

112 "Uncle Adolf is . . . with my studies." Lambert, p. 116; Machtan, pp. 157-58; Sigmund, p. 123.

113 Shoot Maurice. Hoffmann (*Friend*), pp. 151-52; Large (*Munich*), p. 225. Otto Strasser contended that Hitler had caught Maurice and Geli in flagrante delicto. Maurice countered with a threat to blackmail Hitler. Hitler paid him 20,000 marks. (Strasser, p. 84; Machtan, pp. 158-61; Bullock, p. 392) Hanfstaengl provides a less dramatic version of events. (Hanfstaengl, p. 169) It later transpired that Maurice was partially Jewish. Hitler, by then reconciled with him, merely designated him an "Honorary Aryan." Maurice proved to be great utility during 1934's Blood Purge—assisting in the murder of both Fr. Stempfle and Edmund Heines. (Machtan, p. 164; Snyder [*Encyclopedia*], p. 223)

114 "Geli would associate . . . Hitler's favourite girlfriend." Infield (*Eva*), pp. 43-44; Lambert, p. 117; Hayman, p. 136.

115 "I used to . . . was no prude." Strasser, p. 83.

116 Hanfstaengl. Hanfstaengl, pp. 170-71, 175; Bullock, pp. 392-93; Payne, p. 226; Maltitz, p. 350.

117 Strasser. Strasser, pp. 84-85; Infield (*Secret*), p. 79; Maltitz, pp. 347-48; Rosenbaum, pp. 128, 132; Botting & Sayer, pp. 47-48.

118 Stocker. Hayman, p. 136. Said Stocker: "She admitted to me that at times Hitler made her do things in the privacy of her room that sickened her but when I asked her why she didn't refuse to do them she just shrugged and said that she didn't want to lose him to some woman that would do what he wanted."

119 Stempfle. Heiden (*Fuehrer*), p. 389; Strasser, p. 57; Snyder (*Encyclopedia*), p. 282; Kershaw (*Hubris*), pp. 242, 352, 515-16; Rosenbaum, pp. xlv, 129-30; Hastings, pp. 67-68, 116, 119-20, 141; Payne, p. 226; Hayman, pp. 142-43; Pridham, p. 250; Large (*Munich*), p. 197. Ian Kershaw believes Stempfle's murder might have been one of the evening's cases of mistaken identity. An even greater aid to Hitler in editing *Mein Kampf*'s unmanageable prose was the Czech *Völkischer Beobachter* editor Josef Czerny. (Hitler [*Kampf*], p. xviii; Heiden [*Fuehrer*], pp. 246, 291)

120 Oberzalzberg. Hoffmann (*Friend*), p. 154.

121 "I can shoot myself." Lambert, p. 121; Hayman, p. 161; Knopp, p. 15.

122 "For the last time, no!" Payne, p. 227. In February 1943, Hitler obliquely referenced her suicide, clearly indicating it had occurred after he "had made a few insulting remarks [to her] . . . nothing of importance. . . ." (Botting & Sayer, p. 62; Payne, pp. 454-55)

123 "I don't know . . . most uneasy feeling." Hoffmann (*Friend*), p. 152; Toland, p. 253; Botting & Sayer, p. 52.

124 "Really, I have . . . with my uncle." Toland, p. 253. Winter provided this version of their relationship: "His affection was that of a father. He was concerned only with her welfare. Geli was a flighty girl who tried to seduce everyone, including Hitler, and he merely wanted to protect her." (Bullock, p. 394)

125 Theater. Infield (*Eva*), pp. 47-48.

126 "Oh God! . . . Hess!" Hoffmann (*Friend*), p. 153; Hanfstaengl, p. 172; Hayman, pp. 173-74.

127 "the reverse . . . suicidal type." Hoffmann (*Friend*), p. 155.

128 Samthaber. Gun, p. 4; Payne, p. 227.

129 Pregnant by a Jew. Hanfstaengl, p. 175; Unger, pp. 61-62, 103; Toland, p. 255*fn*; Lambert, p. 121; Kershaw (*Hubris*), p. 353; Infield (*Eva*), p. 50; Hayman, pp. 161-62; Payne, p. 228; Botting & Sayer, p. 56; Sigmund, p. 142; Conradi, p. 82.

130 Pregnant by Hitler. Fest (*Hitler*), p. 323; Sigmund, p. 142.

131 Hitler killed her. Murray, p. 138; Rosenbaum, p. xliv; Infield (*Eva*), p. 50; Kershaw (*Hubris*), p. 354.

132 Speeding ticket. Kershaw (*Hubris*), p. 353; Rosenbaum, pp. 123-24; Sigmund, pp. 138, 142.

133 Himmler. Heiden (*Fuehrer*), pp. 388-89; Shirer, p. 132; Payne, p. 228; Fest (*Hitler*), p. 323; Hayman, p. 180; Sigmund, p. 142.

134 "Adolf Hitler's Chappaquiddick." Rosenbaum, p. 100.

135 "She [Geli] had previously . . . must happen to him." Rosenbaum, pp. 102-3.

136 "Hansi". Heiden (*Fuehrer*), p. 387; Snyder (*Encyclopedia*), p. 282; Rosenbaum, p. 122.

137 Pistol in towel. Payne, p. 227; Gun, p. 6*fn*; Hayman, p. 169. According to her sisters, Hitler had later confided this to Eva. Hitler, in fact, had instructed Geli on how to use his pistol. "You must learn to defend yourself," he informed her, "living as you do in a politician's house." (Gun, p. 5; Hayman, p. 158)

138 "When I come . . . Semmering an. . . ." Waite, p. 227; Lambert, p. 121; Payne, p. 228; Botting & Sayer, p. 55; Hayman, p. 160. Semmering was noted for its skiing.

139 "At the beginning . . . he once was." Hayman, p. 136. Stocker also noted, "She was a girl that needed attention and needed it often. And she definitely wanted to remain Hitler's favourite girl-friend. She was willing to do anything to retain that status."

140 Schaub. Riefenstahl, p. 300; Rosenbaum, p. 194. "There was no doubt that that letter was the trigger for Geli's suicide," Schaub informed Leni Riefenstahl.

141 "Dear Mr. Hitler . . . of another meeting." Gun, p. 13; Lambert, p. 121; Hayman, pp. 172-73; Botting & Sayer, p. 53; Large (*Munich*), p. 225.

142 "Some say that . . . facing the public." Sigmund, p. 140; Gun, p. 3; Infield (*Eva*), p. 49; Sigmund, p. 140; Hayman, pp. 163-64.

143 "The dead woman's . . . was never posted." Lambert, p. 122*fn*; Toland, pp. 255-56; Hayman, p. 165; Payne, p. 228; Kershaw (*Hubris*), p. 353; Hanfstaengl, p. 173; Sigmund, p. 140.

144 Argument. Lambert, p. 123*fn*; Toland, pp. 254-55; Hanfstaengl, p. 173. According to SA leader Otto Wagener, Hitler himself attended the autopsy, though his account of Raubal's suicide features myriad inaccuracies. (Wagener, p. 222) Historian Anna Maria Sigmund indicates no autopsy took place. (Sigmund, pp. 140, 142)

145 "It is untrue . . . my niece's engagement." Waite, p. 227; Lambert, p. 123*fn*; Kershaw (*Hubris*), p. 353; Sigmund, pp. 141-42; Hayman, p. 167.

146 "He really wanted . . . on the table." Lambert, p. 123.

147 "Geli's death had . . . find an answer." Hoffmann (*Friend*), p. 157; Botting & Sayer, p. 56.

148 Himmler, Röhm. Hanfstaengl, p. 174; Infield (*Eve*), p. 50; Lambert, p. 122; Redlich, p. 81; Maser, p. 202; Botting & Sayer, p. 57; Read, p. 219; Hayman, p. 184.

149 Catholic burial. Heiden (*Fuehrer*), p. 388; Strasser, p. 203; Infield (*Eva*), p. 50; Gun, p. 11; Payne, p. 229; Botting & Sayer, p. 60; Hayman, pp. 179, 189. Church officials ruled that she "was in a state of mental aberration and confusion and therefore not wholly responsible for her act."

150 Hitler's silence. Hoffmann (*Friend*), p. 158; Toland, p. 256.

151 "*So, now let . . . crowned with success.*" Hoffmann (*Friend*), p. 159; Toland, p. 256; Kershaw (*Hubris*), p. 354; Hayman, p. 199. Hitler remained, however, an emotional basket case for several weeks. Gregor Strasser, for one, claimed to have prevented his suicide during that period. Hess may have literally wrestled a gun from Hitler's hand. (Strasser, pp. 201-2; Shirer, p. 132; Heiden (*Fuehrer*), p. 388; Payne, pp. 229, 457; Sayer & Botting, p. 59; Read, p. 219; Hayman, pp. 188, 197-98; Maser, p. 209; Large [*Munich*], p. 224)

CHAPTER EIGHT: "I WILL TAKE OFF MY COAT AND VEST"

1 TERA. *NY Times*, 20 September 1931, pp. 1, 3. Straus, a Harvard-educated member of "Friends of Roosevelt," in turn recruited New York City social worker Harry Hopkins as TERA's executive director.

2   20 percent cut. *NY Times*, 26 February 1929, pp. 1-2; Freidel (*Triumph*), p. 51; Black (*Champion*), p. 190.

3   Dole. Rosenman (*Papers*), p. 43; Lyons, p. 289. This would be consistent with FDR's inclination for make-work schemes that Tugwell discerned. (Tugwell [*Brains*], pp. 75, 80)

4   FDR to Young Democrats. *NY Times*, 10 April 1932, p. 2.

5   "limited only by . . . without increasing taxation." *NY Times*, 25 November 1929, p. 5.

6   "final liquidation sale. . . marked several items." Cook (*Vol. 1*), p. 418; Smith (*FDR*), p. 243. The Anderson Galleries, however, was not a victim of the Crash, but rather of a pre-Crash merger. (*NY Times*, 30 September 1929, p. 30)

7   "without courage." *NY Times*, 18 January 1932, p. 7.

8   Long. Williams (*Long*), p. 553.

9   "Mr. Roosevelt, once . . . of American politics." Tucker (*Mirrors*), p. 81.

10   "If Thomas Jefferson . . . of economic power." *NY Times*, 27 April 1932, p. 1; *Brooklyn Eagle*, 27 April 1932, p. 1; Freidel (*Triumph*), p. 136; Davis (*New York*), pp. 161-62; Smith (*FDR*), pp. 242-43; Black (*Champion*), p. 203.

11   "Wisely or . . . to interfere." Late in 1932's campaign, Republican Upper East Side congresswoman Ruth Baker Pratt (Heywood Broun's 1930 congressional run opponent) would point out: "The sovereign State of New York can regulate and supervise, without stint or limit, the New York Stock Exchange and all other exchanges in the metropolis, if . . . so minded. Power, much greater than can be invoked by Congress and the President . . . in this regard is possessed by the legislature and the Governor of . . . New York. Of course all this was designedly forgotten by [Roosevelt] in his efforts to catch votes no matter how, and he still has the power, as Governor . . . , to convoke the Legislature in special session to give him additional power or to enact legislation if it be needed to achieve the unnamed reforms at which he vaguely hints. During the four annual sessions of the State legislature that Roosevelt has been Governor, he could have sent a message asking for this additional power; and with the aid of a special message he could have obtained action from the lawmakers almost overnight. But he took no such action." (*North American Review*, November 1932, p. 390)

12   "Roosevelt, too . . . stock market." Galbraith, p. 42.

13   Hundred thousand dollars. Rosen, p. 279.

14   1929, 1930, 1931 failures. Leuchtenburg (*Perils*), p. 256; Kennedy (*Freedom*), p. 65.

15   1932 failures. Kiewe, p. 14.

16   1.5 percent/25 percent. Lyons, p. 214.

17   Ferrari dies. *NY Times*, 3 February 1929, p. 1; Freidel (*Triumph*), p. 92; Morgan, p. 305; Black (*Champion*), p. 197.

18   Warder shutters bank. *NY Times*, 12 February 1929, p. 1; Freidel (*Triumph*), p. 93; Black (*Champion*), p. 197.

19   Warder resigned. Freidel (*Triumph*), p. 93.

20   Bribed. *NY Times*, 6 November 1929, pp. 1, 20; Lavine, pp. 49-50; Thomas & Blanshard, pp. 338-39. In November 1929, a jury convicted Warder of accepting a $10,000 bribe from Ferrari.

21   Moses appointed. Davis (*New York*), pp. 127-29; Flynn (*Squire*), p. 39. Lehman grew up two doors from the childhood home of Moses's wife. He greatly admired Moses. (Caro, pp. 33, 362)

22   Ignored Moses's commission. Morgan, p. 306. Among the hitherto completely unregulated private banks was Clark Bros. on Nassau Street, which failed in June 1929. Without actually being a bank, it, nonetheless, informed customers that it was "rendering a complete banking service" (Morgan, pp. 305-6). Eventually, Roosevelt took to bashing bankers, but his initial response to New York's banking crisis gravitated between disinterest and outright absenteeism. Notes historian Robert Lynn Fuller: "On the day of the closing of the Bank of United States, Governor Roosevelt returned from his vacation in Warm Springs . . . and held a brief meeting with . . . Lehman at Roosevelt's east-side town house. They issued no public statement." (Fuller, p. 22)

23   450,000. Freidel (*Triumph*), pp. 186-87. The name "Bank of United States" was purposely selected to confuse depositors into surmising that it was an official federal agency. Banking

Superintendent George C. Van Tuyl Jr., who later served on the bank's executive committee, was ultimately indicted for having issued it in 1913.

24   Bank of United States. Leuchtenburg (*Perils*), p. 256; Freidel (*Triumph*), p. 188; Morgan, p. 306; Kull & Kull, p. 248; Trager, p. 449; Rosen, p. 279; Kennedy (*Freedom*), p. 67.

25   Moses cites Bank of United States. Davis (*New York*), p. 224.

26   1929 audit. Davis (*New York*), p. 225.

27   FDR, Broderick inaction. Davis (*New York*), p. 225. By that point, New York's fellow banks refused to help.

28   "Why had . . . and later." Freidel (*Triumph*), pp. 186-87.

29   "with a . . . weeks later." Black (*Champion*), p. 212.

30   Hoarding. Leuchtenburg (*Perils*), p. 256.

31   Communists. *NY Times*, 26 December 1930, pp. 1, 3; Davis (*New York*), p. 225; Black (*Champion*), pp. 212-13. Authorities at Pontiac, Michigan, later uncovered a similar Communist plot. (*Chicago Tribune*, 28 July 1932, p. 6; *Chicago Tribune*, 6 August 1932, p. 6; *Literary Digest*, 13 August 1932, p. 8)

32   Broderick indicted. *NY Times*, 20 October 1931, pp. 1, 10; Lavine, pp. 44-46; Fuller, p. 22. Broderick, backed up by testimony from FDR (Davis [*New York*], p. 265; Morgan, p. 307), was eventually cleared. Among the co-indicted were Henry W. Pollock and the bank's president, Bernard Marcus, uncle of Sen. Joseph McCarthy's future investigator Roy Marcus Cohn and brother-in-law of Joshua Lionel Cowen, founder of Lionel Trains. Marcus went to Sing Sing. (*NY Times*, 11 February 1931, p. 16; Black [*Champion*], p. 212; Flynn [*Squire*], p. 39; Morgan, p. 306; Horan, pp. 28-29; http://quixoticjoust.blogspot.com/2011/08/roy-cohns-extended-family-marcus-and.html)

33   "the actual . . . the problem". Burns, p. 116.

34   "subsistence farms". Tugwell (*Brains*), p. 183. Impractical for several reasons, but, most basically because the nation already suffered from agricultural surpluses—including, of course, a surplus of farmers.

35   To counter Pinchot. *NY Times*, 28 May 1932, p. 1; Tugwell (*Brains*), pp. 176-80.

36   Cornelia Pinchot. McGeary, p. 394.

37   Pinchot, committee. Schlesinger (*Crisis*), pp. 335, 337.

38   Yacht Club. McGeary, p. 394.

39   Pinchot relief program. Beers, p. 97.

40   "Today the United States . . . international bankers". Richardson, Kindle edition, location 356.

41   Pinchot bitter. McGeary, p. 390.

42   "He wouldn't . . . first base." McGeary, p. 390.

43   "[George] Norris . . . Hoover 500 to 1." *NY Times*, 3 June 1931, p. 1; McGeary, p. 389.

44   Moley. Ekirch, p. 78.

45   Radio. *NY Times*, 6 April 1932, p. 2; Moley (*Seven*), p. 10; Shlaes (*Forgotten*), p. 127; Ritchie, p. 86. Lorena Hickok believed this "may have been the first speech he made over a national hook-up." (Hickok [*Road*], p. 187)

46   "Forgotten man." *NY Times*, 6 April 1932, pp. 1, 10; Rosenman (*Papers*), pp. 624-27; Moley (*Seven*), p. 5; Tugwell (*Democratic*), p. 214; Davis (*New York*), pp. 272-73; Miller (*F.D.R.*), pp. 262-63; Shlaes (*Forgotten*), pp. 12-13, 127; Barone, p. 52; Finan, p. 274; Ritchie, p. 86; Ekirch, p. 78. Roosevelt's pooh-poohing of public works projects would hardly have endeared him to the still skeptical Hearst, who broke with Hoover in part due to Hoover's reluctance to back Hearst's budget-busting, debt-creating $5 billion proposal. (Swanberg [*Hearst*], pp. 429-30; Procter, pp. 164-66; Nasaw [*Chief*], pp. 434-35; Carlisle, pp. 46)

47   Sumner. Tugwell (*Democratic*), pp. 214-15; Miller (*F.D.R.*), p. 262*fn*; Morgan, p. 346; Shlaes (*Forgotten*), pp. 12-13. Amity Shlaes, and many before her, makes the point that Sumner meant something very different by the phrase—the "forgotten man" being the individual who foots the bill for government programs. Cordell Hull used the phrase in a speech in February. (Hull, pp. 147-48)

48   "This is no . . . rich against poor." *NY Times*, 14 April 1932, pp. 1, 6, 8; *Plattsburgh Press*, 14 April 1932, p. 1; *Literary Digest*, 23 April 1932, p. 11; *Time*, 27 June 1932, p. 14; Dille, p. 49; Warner, p. 255; Martin (*Bandwagons*), p. 291; Eaton, p. 329; Ritchie, p. 86.

49   Bafflement. *NY Times*, 14 April 1932, p. 8.

Chapter Nine: "A poison-painted monkey on a stick"

1   "The year has . . . work begins again." Goebbels (*Part*), p. 13. Goebbels published his diary for this key period as *Vom Kaiserhof zur Reichskanzlei* ("From the Kaiserhof to the Reich Chancellery"; in the English edition: *My Part in Germany's Fight*). His biographer, Helmut Heiber, characterizes it as "a glorification of Hitler, a documenting of his monumental greatness, his unbending decisiveness, and his warm humanity [as well as] the aggrandizement of Goebbels himself." That puts it mildly.

2   "the most . . . the world". Winkler, p. 364.

3   Reichstag. Wheeler-Bennett (*Nemesis*), p. 230; Kaufmann, p. 205; Davidson, p. 309; Eyck, p. 350; Manvell & Fraenkel (*Hundred*), p. 189.

4   Anti-SPD. Dorpalen, pp. 257-58.

5   1925. *NY Times*, 5 April 1925, pp. 1, 18; *NY Times*, 27 April 1925, p. 1; Wheaton, pp. 82-83; Vogt, pp. 83-84. Marx had run only as a Zentrum candidate in the first round.

6   SPD-Zentrum. Dorpalen, pp. 257, 279; Evans (*Coming*), p. 279; Kershaw (*Hubris*), p. 362.

7   "Now I . . . my pocket". Heiden (*Fuehrer*), p. 433; Shirer, p. 154; Fest (*Hitler*), p. 302; Hauner, p. 76; Manvell & Fraenkel (*Hundred*), p. 25; Taylor, p. 101.

8   "dragged [Hindenburg] into . . . among his people." *NY Times*, 12 January 1932, p. 18; *NY Times*, 13 January 1932, p. 18; Wheeler-Bennett (*Titan*), p. 362; Dorpalen, p. 264; Bullock, p. 193.

9   Hitler evasive. *NY Times*, 12 January 1932, pp. 18, 22; *NY Times*, 13 January 1932, p. 18; Wheeler-Bennett (*Titan*), p. 362; Fest (*Hitler*), p. 317; Eyck, p. 352.

10   "I shall never . . . the present regime . . .". *NY Times*, 18 January 1932, p. 8.

11   Equal in invective. *NY Times*, 18 January 1932, p. 8; *NY Times*, 19 January 1932, p. 16; Wheeler-Bennett (*Titan*), pp. 362-63; Bullock, p. 194.

12   Testier. Wheeler-Bennett (*Titan*), p. 363.

13   Hindenburg announced. Goebbels (*Part*), p. 43; Shirer, p. 157.

14   "In full consciousness . . . hour of crisis." Clark (*German Republic*), p. 346; Wheeler-Bennett (*Titan*), p. 368; Eyck, p. 355.

15   Bremen, Mecklenburg. *NY Times*, 12 January 1932, p. 22; Feuchtwanger, p. 327.

16   Hamburg, Hesse, and Oldenburg. Thompson, p. 12; Feuchtwanger, pp. 271, 327; Bullock, p. 190; Burleigh, p. 125; Wheaton, p. 116.

17   Lippe. *NY Times*, 11 January 1932, p. 18; Goebbels (*Part*), p. 20; Childers, p. 196; Orlow (*Nazi*), p. 243; Feuchtwanger, p. 327.

18   "No other way . . . be carried through." *NY Times*, 11 January 1932, p. 18; Goebbels (*Part*), p. 20.

19   Frick, Epp. Orlow (*Nazi*), p. 245; Knickerbocker, p. 243.

20   Actors. Goebbels (*Part*), p. 41.

21   Garbo. Goebbels (*Part*), p. 34; Shirer, p. 156; Heiden (*Fuehrer*), p. 358.

22   *Mädchen in Uniform*. Goebbels (*Part*), p. 34.

23   *Die Fledermaus/Merry Widow*. Goebbels (*Part*), p. 36; Heiden (*Fuehrer*), p. 358.

24   Party headquarters. Goebbels (*Part*), pp. 34-35; Heiden (*Fuehrer*), p. 358.

25   "Everyone is nervous . . . waiting too long". Goebbels (*Part*), p. 35; Shirer, p. 156.

26   "We National Socialists . . . party of deserters—." Olden, p. 236; Davidson, p. 316; Thacker, p. 127. "Asphalt" was a favorite Goebbels term of opprobrium. (Thacker, p. 75)

27   "You bastard!" "Mongrel". Thacker, p. 128.

28   "in effecting the . . . of human stupidity". Eyck, p. 357.

29   Goebbels expelled. *NY Times*, 24 February 1932, p. 11; Clark (*German Republic*), p. 348; Manvell & Fraenkel (*Goebbels*), pp. 113, 299; Dorpalen, p. 278; Payne, p. 238; Eyck, p. 357; Winkler, p. 447. In

fact, the SPD (to Goebbels "the party of the deserters") boasted more veterans per capita of Reichstag members than did his Nazis.

30   Oskar/Nazi. Cowles, p. 424.

31   Hugenberg/Duesterberg. *NY Times*, 18 February 1932, p. 15; *NY Times*, 23 February 1932, p. 9; *NY Times*, 6 March 1932, p. 15; Dorpalen, pp. 272-73; Shirer, p. 157; Bullock, pp. 195-96; Kershaw (*Hubris*), p. 362; Wistrich, p. 58; Snyder (*Encyclopedia*), p. 75; Eyck, p. 356; Leopold, pp. 109-10.

32   Hildburghausen. Goebbels (*Part*), p. 36; Heiden (*Fuehrer*), p. 412; Domarus, p. 116; Eyck, p. 354; Friedrich, p. 257.

33   Professorship. Goebbels (*Part*), pp. 36-37.

34   Citizenship/*Regierungsrat*. *NY Times*, 18 February 1932, p. 15; *NY Times*, 24 February 1932, p. 11; *NY Times*, 26 February 1932, p. 9; *NY Times*, 27 February 1932, p. 8; *NY Times*, 16 March 1932, p. 8; Heiden (*History*), p. 167; Heiden (*Fuehrer*), p. 412; Reuth, p. 142; Dorpalen, p. 281; Hauner, pp. 51, 77; Payne, p. 238; Kershaw (*Hubris*), p. 362; Fest (*Hitler*), pp. 317-18; Snyder (*Encyclopedia*), p. 154; Wheaton, p. 118; Manvell & Fraenkel (*Hundred*), p. 190; Fromm, p. 45. Hitler renounced his Austrian citizenship effective April 30, 1925. (Jetzinger, pp. 164-65)

35   Goebbels announced. *NY Times*, 18 February 1932, p. 15; Reuth, p. 122; Shirer, p. 157; Broszat, p. 108; Heiber, p. 92.

36   "Four weeks ago . . . be our Reichspräsident." *Winnipeg Free Press*, 23 February 1932, p. 1; Heiden (*History*), p. 167; Davidson, p. 313; Winkler, p. 447; Friedrich, p. 258.

37   "Money is wanting . . . can't get it!" Goebbels (*Part*), p. 15; Bullock, p. 196; Mitchell (*Hitler*), p. 140.

38   "looked like an . . . engagingly." *NY Post*, 3 February 1932, p. 3; Knickerbocker, p. 229.

39   "the best diplomat in Hitler's service". *NY Post*, 3 February 1932, p. 3; Knickerbocker, p. 233.

40   "We shall not . . . similar German undertakings." *NY Post*, 3 February 1932, p. 3; Knickerbocker, p. 238.

41   Hardly swank. Turner (*Business*), pp. 204-05. Dues had been slashed from two hundred marks in 1930 to a hundred in 1932. Services in the Park Hotel, in whose grand ballroom Hitler spoke, were steadily declining.

42   Thyssen a member. Thyssen, p. 128.

43   Thyssen/Strasser. Thyssen, pp. 132-33; Turner (*Business*), p. 205.

44   Demonstrators. Turner (*Business*), p. 208.

45   Hitler effective. Thyssen, pp. 132-33; Toland, pp. 260-61; Bullock, p. 197; Davidson, p. 229; Broszat, p. 98.

46   Jews. Turner (*Business*), p. 208; Evans (*Coming*), p. 245.

47   "People say to me . . . thing that counts." Domarus, p. 113; de Sales, p. 122.

48   "Bolshevism will, if . . . perhaps like Buddha." Domarus, p. 99; de Sales, p. 107; Toland, pp. 260-61.

49   "Money affairs improve . . . is practically assured." Goebbels (*Part*), p. 39; Bullock, p. 196; Read, p. 40. One should, however, not overestimate the amount of big business funding that now flowed to Hitler. As Otto Dietrich later noted "a fund was collected at the door. But the contributions, though well meant, were insignificant in amount. Beyond that, there was no question of any significant subsidizing of Hitler's political efforts at that time by 'heavy industry,'. . . ." (Dietrich [*Knew*], p. 141; Turner [*Business*], p. 216)

50   Dutch/Javanese. Payne, p. 215; Manvell & Fraenkel (*Goebbels*), p. 2; Reuth, p. 6.

51   "a poison-painted . . . on a stick." Lüdecke, p. 416.

52   "There's no question . . . force behind it," *Journal of Historical Review*, January-February 1995, p. 5. From his cell at Nürnberg, Göring concurred. Goebbels, he contended, "forced Hitler to become anti-Semitic more than Hitler had been before. . . . Goebbels was the strongest representative of anti-Semitism. . . . Goebbels was just unscrupulous, clever, and dangerous. . . . I blame Goebbels for the atrocities." (Goldensohn, pp. 114-16)

53 Half-Jewish. Goebbels (*Early*), p. 21; Thacker, pp. 19, 23-24; Reimann, p. 65; Read, p. 153. Eventually Goebbels reached the conclusion regarding Else that she can "not disavow her Jewish blood. There is something destructive in her character, above all mentally. . . ."
54 "She is good and . . . makes me happy". Goebbels (*Early*), pp. 29, 52. For good measure, his wife Magda's stepfather, the leather manufacturer Richard Friedlander, was also Jewish. (Heiden [*Fuehrer*], p. 438; Manvell & Fraenkel [*Goebbels*], p. 89; Sigmund, pp. 70, 81; Knopp, p. 58; Lambert, p. 235)
55 "As you know . . . ignoble and unworthy." *Journal of Historical Review*, January-February 1995, pp. 5-6; www.ihr.org/jhr/v15/v15n1p-2_Irving.html.
56 "National and socialist! . . . between both opinions. . . ." Goebbels (*Early*), p. 34; Bramsted, p. 11; Kershaw (*Hubris*), p. 252.
57 "German Communist". Reuth, p. 66.
58 "stock exchange capital". Reuth, p. 68.
59 "gives in . . . war against Moscow." Goebbels (*Early*), p. 42.
60 "In the last . . . eternal capitalist servitude." Fest (*Face*), p. 89.
61 "A splendid . . . massive Bavarian". Goebbels (*Early*), p. 29; Heiber, p. 103. Goebbels's words.
62 "I feel devastated. . . of private property!" Goebbels (*Early*), p. 67; Payne, p. 216; Reuth, pp. 70-71; Reimann, pp. 53-54; Bramsted, p. 12; Kershaw (*Hubris*), p. 275; Davidson, pp. 261-62; Read, pp. 147-48.
63 "that the petty . . . the party." Bullock, p. 137; Shirer, p. 127; Fest (*Face*), p. 89; Hauner, p. 53; Reimann, p. 36; Wistrich, p. 77; Toland, p. 215; Read, p. 146; Snyder (*Encyclopedia*), p. 119.
64 "I want to cry . . . are socialist". Goebbels (*Early*), p. 67.
65 "Listen, Strasser . . . your worth should". Strasser, pp. 100-101; Bullock, p. 138.
66 "I stand shaken . . . how he is!" Goebbels (*Early*), p. 100; Payne, p. 218; Reuth, p. 75; Hauner, p. 54; Read, p. 151.
67 "How I love him . . . be my friend. . . ." Goebbels (*Early*), p. 50; Fest (*Face*), p. 85; Reuth, p. 67; Read, p. 5; Thacker, p. 59.
68 "Hitler and I . . . My heart aches. . . ." Hauner, p. 55; Payne, p. 218.
69 "those big blue eyes. Like stars". Thacker, p. 58. Goebbels thought at Braunschweig in November 1925.
70 "A man . . . like a flame". Heiden (*Fuehrer*), p. 289; Snyder (*Elite*), p. 103.
71 "responsible to me alone". Heiden (*Fuehrer*), p. 293.
72 Not to Strasser. Heiden (*History*), pp. 115-16; Manvell & Fraenkel (*Goebbels*), p. 65; Lüdecke, p. 335; Eyck, p. 219.
73 Gauleiter. Goebbels (*Early*), pp. 24, 115-16; Payne, pp. 218-19; Lemmons, pp. 10-11; Reuth, pp. 75-77; Reimann, p. 68; Evans (*Coming*), p. 206; Manvell & Fraenkel (*Goebbels*), p. 299; Read, pp. 152-53; Lüdecke, p. 335.
74 "New York of Europe." Large (*Munich*), p. 202.
75 "a self-important . . . from German soil." Thacker, p. 75.
76 KPD. Richie, p. 386.
77 4 percent. Ascher, p. 16. Germany's 503,000 Jews made up just 0.76 percent of its 66,029,000 population. (Guérin, p. 32)
78 "The only fly . . . in the place." Ascher, p. 16.
79 Berlin membership. Thacker, p. 75.
80 Berlin vote. Reuth, pp. 96-97; Evans (*Coming*), p. 209; Richie, p. 389.
81 "A Babylon of sins! . . . throw myself." Bramsted, p. 16; Richie, p. 384.
82 "Do you . . . elect me?" Bramsted, p. 33.
83 Reichstag deputies. Broszat, p. 65; Manvell (*Göring*), p. 38; Shirer, p. 146; Eyck, p. 219; Payne, p. 221; Reuth, p. 98; Evans (*Coming*), p. 209.
84 *Der Angriff.* Manvell & Fraenkel (*Goebbels*), pp. 76, 299; Lemmons, p. 31; Payne, p. 220; Reuth, p. 90; Bramsted, pp. 29-31; Wistrich, p. 97; Read, pp. 165-66, 192; Richie, p. 388; Childers, p. 194; Thacker, pp. 90-92.

85 *Reichspropagandaleiter.* Shirer, p. 148; Bullock, p. 141; Snyder (*Encyclopedia*), p. 120; Wistrich, p. 97; Heiden (*Fuehrer*), p. 301; Manvell & Fraenkel (*Goebbels*), p. 299; Read, p. 184; Richie, p. 394; Wheaton, p. 91; Mommsen, p. 335. Some give the date as November 1928.
86 "scheming dwarf." Heiden (*Fuehrer*), p. 290; Snyder (*Encyclopedia*), p. 335; Snyder (*Elite*), p. 103.
87 "The receptivity of . . . entirely cancelled out." Hitler (*Kampf*), pp. 180-81. For an alternate translation see Snell, p. 2.
88 "something of the . . . only too well. . . ." Hitler (*Kampf*), p. 232. For an alternate translation see Snell, p. 2.
89 "ANTI-SEMITISM is . . . DESPISE THE JEWS." Snyder (*Encyclopedia*), p. 274.
90 "we still have. . . . and narrow path . . .". Read, p. 184.
91 1930 strike. Broszat, pp. 13, 24; Kershaw (*Hubris*), p. 358.
92 "The struggle is . . . National Socialist Party. . . ." Knight-Patterson, p. 483.
93 "The stock-market hyenas . . . meager living standard." Broszat, p. 24.
94 "we have far . . . be our freedom . . ." Reimann, p. 46.
95 "literary clique." Reuth, p. 117.
96 "have Jewish blood . . . puffy, fleshy face." Reuth, pp. 88-89; Read, p. 164; Stachura, p. 56. Schweitzer had made such charges as early as 1927. Strasser countered with allegations of Goebbels's Jewishness. (Goebbels [*Early*], p. 142)
97 Hirelings. Bullock, p. 140.
98 "And he who . . . was always right". Bramsted, p. 33.
99 "Isidor". Lemmons, pp. 112-27; Reimann, pp. 93-97; Manvell & Fraenkel (*Goebbels*), pp. 76-77; Bramsted, pp. 36-37; Reuth, pp. 91-94; Burleigh, p. 131; Heiber, p. 98; Read, pp. 165-66, 174; Thacker, pp. 93, 348; Metcalfe, p. 203.
100 "a traveler in water closets." Fest (*Face*), p. 91.
101 "salon simpleton." Fest (*Face*), p. 91.
102 "Hugendwarf". Leopold, p. 124; Vogt, p. 137.
103 Sklarek scandal. *NY Times*, 2 November 1929, p. 7; *NY Times*, 29 June 1932, p. 6; *Syracuse Herald*, 3 July 1932, p. 3; Dunlap, pp. 153-59; Reuth, p. 109; Large (*Berlin*), pp. 232-33; Burleigh, p. 121; Richie, p. 390. The KPD also exploited the scandals, though not finding Jewishness as their root cause, but rather "bourgeois social fascist corruptionists."
104 "The rise of . . . these 'Sklarek elections.'" Dunlap, p. 156. The Nazi vote in Berlin's November 1929 municipal election jumped to 5.8 percent. (Reuth, p. 109; Read, p. 182; Richie, p. 392)
105 "THE JEW IS OUR GREATEST MISFORTUNE". Snyder (*Encyclopedia*), p. 274.
106 Anti-Semitism/Poles/Danes. Burleigh, p. 121.
107 Religion. Burleigh, pp. 252-67.
108 "says payment of . . . more consistent one?" Dunlap, p. 127.
109 Catholic. Manvell & Fraenkel (*Goebbels*), pp. 6, 9-10, 15; Reuth, pp. 11, 28, 31; Read, pp. 128, 131.
110 Schlageter. Halperin, p. 250,
111 Communists. Halperin, p. 272; Burleigh, p. 55.
112 *Blutfahne.* Heiden (*History*), p. 114; Snyder (*Encyclopedia*), pp. 33-34; Burleigh, pp. 265-66; Read, p. 157; Baird, p. 44; Large (*Munich*), p. 257.
113 "Day of Mourning". Burleigh, pp. 117, 264; Large (*Munich*), pp. 256-58; Snyder (*Encyclopedia*), p. 168. Nazis continued to observe the old German version of Memorial Day, but moved its commemoration from the fifth Sunday before Easter to March 16. (Snyder [*Encyclopedia*], p. 168)
114 Solstice. Snyder (*Encyclopedia*), p. 168.
115 Death totals. Burleigh, p. 117.
116 Kütemeyer. Reuth, p. 103; Read, pp. 186-87; Burleigh, pp. 117-18.
117 Fischer. Reuth, p. 110; Read, p. 187; Burleigh, p. 118; Lemmons, pp. 70-71.
118 Norkus. Baird, pp. 109-11; Reuth, p. 141; Lemmons, pp. 76-78; Roberts, p. 203; Friedrich, p. 263. Twenty-two Hitler Youth forfeited their lives in street-fighting before Hitler assumed power.
119 Trenchcoat. Thacker, p. 131.

120 "The delicate head . . . emptiness of death." Reuth, p. 141; Heiber, p. 97.

121 "A fine boy . . . incredible idealism". Siemens, p. 69.

122 "Note the face! . . . Murderer of Workers." Burleigh, p. 118; Baird, p. 80.

123 "You know . . . is for!" Baird, p. 80.

124 Close-range. Siemens, *passim*; Reuth, pp. 110-13; Burleigh, pp. 118-19; Read, pp. 187-89; Large (*Berlin*), p. 237. An estimated hundred thousand prostitutes toiled in Weimar Berlin. (Burleigh, p. 56; Magida, p. 103) Höhler's persona, points out historian Richard Evans, "illustrated the connections between Communism and criminality that were likely to be forged at a time when the party based itself in the poor districts and 'criminal quarters' of Germany's big cities." (Evans [*Coming*], p. 267) Höhler received just six years for his role in Wessel's murder.

125 "SA Leader . . . Out of Jealousy". Siemens, p. 13.

126 "A new martyr . . . Third Reich." Siemens, p. 15; Burleigh, p. 119.

127 "He went forth . . . end lies Germany!" Burleigh, p. 119; Reuth, p. 113; Read, p. 189.

128 Funeral. Reuth, p. 112; Siemens, p. 116; Read, pp. 189-90; Baird, pp. 83-86, 267; Heinz, p. 201. Hitler instead spent the weekend with Geli Raubal at Obersalzberg. (Irving [*Goebbels*], p. 177)

CHAPTER TEN: "THE HALF-WITTED YOKELS OF THE COW AND COTTON STATES"

1 Moley. Tugwell (*Democratic*), p. 218; Tugwell (*Brains*), pp. 48-49. Tennessee's Democratic senator, the free-trader Cordell Hull, a key to FDR's carrying southern convention delegates, for example, wrote FDR with effusive praise for the speech. Moley informed Tugwell that Hull was angling to be secretary of state—and probably would be. (Tugwell [*Brains*], p. 50)

2 "I am not . . . planned and regimented." Rosenman (*Papers*), p. 632.

3 "I favor economic . . . time to come." Rosenman (*Papers*), p. 632; Ekirch, p. 79. FDR had, in fact, long favored widespread centralized planning. To the Conference of Governors in June 1931 he advocated "concerted plans for the better use of our resources and the better planning of our social and economic life in general." (Ekirch, p. 78)

4 Molasses. *NY Times*, 11 May 1948, p. 25; Schlesinger (*Crisis*), p. 427; Moley (*Seven*), p. 45; Benjamin, p. 83. Berle was American Molasses Company counsel; Tugwell served as its vice president from 1936 through 1938. Taussig later chaired the national advisory committee of the New Deal's controversial National Youth Administration.

5 Taussig meeting. Tugwell (*Brains Trust*), p. 201; Benjamin, pp. 83-84. Other recruits, such as the researchers Robert K. Straus (son of Macy's Jesse Straus) and John Dalton (from Columbia's School of Business), proved immensely more utilitarian.

6 "The consequences . . . each other." *Otsego Farmer & Republican*, 6 May 1932, p. 1; Moley (*Seven*), p. 16; Shlaes (*Forgotten*), p. 127.

7 "The consequences . . . against each other." *Otsego Farmer & Republican*, 6 May 1932, p. 1; Moley (*Seven*), p. 16; Shlaes (*Forgotten*), p. 127.

8 *Post. NY Post*, 26 April 1932, pp. 1-2; Moley (*Seven*), p. 16; Shlaes (*Forgotten*), p. 127. Memory plays tricks upon even the closest of observers. Eleanor's confidante Lorena Hickok in a study of FDR's pre–White House years, noted that his speech was "almost word for word like one Al Smith . . . had made a few weeks earlier." Actually, it merely lifted that singular passage and was delivered five days, not a few weeks, after it. (Hickok [*Road*], p. 187)

9 "I don't . . . is mine." *Otsego Farmer & Republican*, 6 May 1932, p. 1.

10 *NY Post*, 27 April 1932, page unknown.

11 "So, I came . . . into a jam." Moley (*Seven*), p. 17.

12 White House incident. Suckley; Tugwell (*Democratic*), p. 258; Tugwell (*Brains*), p. 108; Freidel (*Triumph*), p. 324; Ritchie, pp. 92-93; Houck (*FDR*), pp. 48-49; Houck & Kiewe, pp. 63, 81-82; Smith (*Dream*), pp. 104-5; Smith (*Uncommon*), p. 153; Black (*Champion*), p. 342; Alter, p. 93.

13 Ritchie, p. 238.

14   Olson. "Unofficial Observer," p. 96. And just how long was Hoover's delay? FDR stood for a half hour at most—and more likely for just twenty minutes. But if he arrived early, that translates into Hoover's supposedly egregious delay amounting to no more than ten or fifteen minutes.

15   "Back in the . . . the White House." Houck & Kiewe, p. 82.

16   "They were horrible . . . down and cried." Houck & Kiewe, p. 82; Ritchie, p. 94.

17   Lindley. Tugwell (*Democratic*), pp. 218-19; Tugwell (*Brains*), pp. 103-4; Smith (*FDR*), p. 263*fn*; Ekirch, p. 80.

18   "the sincerest, most . . . attitudes and convictions." Tugwell (*Democratic*), p. 219.

19   "The country needs . . . within easy reach." Suckley; Rosenman (*Papers*), pp. 639-47; Ritchie, p. 87; Warren (*Presidency*), p. 231; Smith (*FDR*), p. 263; Ekirch, p. 80.

20   "the reward of . . . to be less." Tugwell (*Brains*), p. 104.

21   "[T]the Oglethorpe speech . . . of collectivism". Tugwell (*Democratic*), p. 219.

22   "presented the. . . in the campaign." Tugwell (*Democratic*), p. 219.

23   "only self-liquidating . . . be justified." *NY Times*, 23 May 1932, pp. 1-2; Tugwell (*Brains*), pp. 115-16.

24   "Mr. Hoover is . . . to be done." *NY Times*, 24 May 1932, p. 18; Tugwell (*Brains*), p. 116.

25   Blaine. *NY Times*, 16 October 1928, p. 15; Young (*LaFollette*), pp. 127, 183. Blaine's Senate colleague, Robert M. La Follette Jr., while refusing to support Hoover, did not formally, however, endorse Smith. His younger brother, Wisconsin Governor Philip La Follette, did.

26   Norris. *NY Times*, 25 October 1928, p. 1; *NY Times*, 30 October 1928, p. 30; Martin (*Bandwagons*), p. 366; Schlesinger (*Crisis*), p. 127.

27   Borah, McNary, Norbeck, Brookhart. *NY Times*, 4 November 1928, p. 2; Ritchie, pp. 33, 35; Wilson (*Progressive*), p. 133. At that year's convention, Norbeck had unleashed a scathing critique of Hoover. (*Sandusky Star-Journal*, 1 November 1928, p. 9)

28   La Guardia. *NY Times*, 6 August 1924, p. 6; "Unofficial Observer," p. 209.

29   Cornelia Pinchot. *NY Times*, 23 December 1931, p. 1; *Altoona Mirror*, 28 April 1932, p. 1; *NY Times*, 2 May 1932, p. 4; *NY Times*, 2 October 1936, p. 25; Beers, p. 104. Ironically, in her 1932 campaign against McFadden Mrs. Pinchot defended her husband's bête-noir Hoover.

30   "sold out". *NY Times*, 15 December 1931, p. 2.

31   "and paid . . . international bankers." *NY Times*, 16 December 1931, p. 20.

32   "If you don't . . . in power there." *NY Times*, 19 December 1931, p. 14. Democrats in opposition included Martin Dies, Sam Rayburn, Wright Patman, future Chief Justice Fred M. Vinson, Majority Leader Henry T. Rainey, and Alabama's Henry B. Steagall. "The House," noted the *New York Times*, "applauded [LaGuardia] wildly."

33   Brown. *NY Times*, 23 December 1931, p. 6.

34   McFadden "dry." *NY Times*, 23 December 1931, p. 1.

35   Enters North Dakota primary. *NY Times*, 14 February 1932, p. 28.

36   Anti-Semitic. McWilliams, p. 42; Carr, pp. 108-9; Arad, p. 174. When 20,000 attended a pro-Nazi "Friends of the New Germany" rally at Madison Square Garden in 1934, McFadden wired apologies for his absence. (*NY Times*, 18 May 1934, p. 3)

37   Macfadden drops out. *NY Times*, 14 February 1932, p. 28.

38   Wet. *NY Times*, 2 June 1932, p. 14; *Plattsburgh Press*, 10 June 1932, p. 1; Hart (*Convention*), pp. 174-75; Mertz, p. 310. France was one of only eight GOP senators to vote against the 18th Amendment—along with Penrose, Lodge, Wadsworth, Weeks, Brandegee, Calder, and Warren. With the exception of Wyoming's Frances E. Warren, the last Civil War veteran to serve in the Senate, all hailed from the Northeast.

39   Isolationist. Hart (*Convention*), p. 177. France was also one of fifteen "irreconcilable" senators voting against the League of Nations in any form. Others included Brandegee, Norris, La Follette Sr., Albert B. Fall, and Democrat James A. Reed.

40   Wealthy. Ritchie, pp. 96-97.

41   "stands for . . . is mentioned." *Scribner's*, May 1932, p. 260. The party's progressives, it seemed, were fractured not only by personality and ambition but by ideology. Some like La Guardia and Blaine were "wet." Borah, Norris, Brookhart, and McFadden were ardent "drys."

42   North Dakota. *Bismarck Tribune*, 16 March 1932, p. 1; *Billings Gazette*, 18 March 1932, p. 2. The state also voted in in a rare referendum to decide on the relocation of its capital. Bismarck trounced Jamestown to retain the title.

43   Nebraska. *NY Times*, 13 April 1932, p. 4; *NY Times*, 14 April 1932, p. 2.

44   West Virginia. *NY Times*, 10 May 1932, p. 9.

45   New Jersey. *NY Times*, 19 May 1932, p. 3.

46   Oregon. *NY Times*, 21 May 1932, p. 3; *Charleston Gazette*, 22 May 1932, p. 6. On the same day, primary voters defeated pro-administration Rep. Willis Hawley, he of Smoot-Hawley fame. (*Charleston Gazette*, 25 May 1932, p. 1)

47   Coxey. *American Mercury*, October 1932, p. 178.

48   Four delegates. Ritchie, p. 97.

49   Maryland. *NY Times*, 27 May 1932, p. 2; Ritchie, p. 97.

50   "the monotone which is his oratorical vehicle". *NY Times*, 1 June 1932, p. 12.

51   Hoover/Senate. *NY Times*, 1 June 1932, pp. 1, 12; Leuchtenburg (*Hoover*), p. 132; Shlaes (*Forgotten*), p. 130.

52   "diminishing returns". *NY Times*, 1 June 1932, p. 12.

53   Revenue Act of 1932. *NY Times*, 5 June 1932, p. 26; *NY Times*, 7 June 1932, p. 1; *Rochester Democrat & Chronicle*, 13 June 1932, p. 10; *NY Times*, 19 June 1932, pp. XX2; Joslin, p. 242; Hiltzik, p. 331; Kennedy (*Depression*), p. 81; Shlaes (*Forgotten*), p. 130. A stamp went from two to three cents.

54   Mineral water. *Schenectady Gazette*, 12 September 1932, p. 2.

55   Tariffs. *NY Times*, 5 June 1932, p. 26; Irwin, p. 191.

56   Dental work. *Troy Record*, 19 July 1932, p. 6; *Schenectady Gazette*, 20 July 1932, p. 5.

57   Sales tax. Zinn, p. 220; Hinshaw, p. 266; Liebovich, p. 185.

58   Unemployment. Vedder & Gallaway, p. 77.

59   *Pathfinder*. *NY Times*, 28 March 1932, p. 2; *Amsterdam Recorder*, 29 March 1932, p. 8; *Poughkeepsie Eagle-News*, 1 April 1932, p. 6; *Scribner's*, July 1932, p. 16. The *Pathfinder's* complete totals: Hoover, 115,042; Roosevelt, 49,626; Garner, 18,956; Smith, 12,299; Murray, 11,541; Borah, 4,387; Ritchie, 2,954; Baker, 2,780; Johnson, 2,130; Coolidge, 1,942; Pinchot, 1,213; Dawes, 1,509; Norris, 1,036; Norman Thomas, 948; James A. Reed, 656; McAdoo, 553; Joseph Robinson, 474; Young, 449; La Follette, 452; Hamilton Lewis (Illinois), 129; Gov. George White (Ohio), 102.

60   "If there is . . . the agricultural element". *Poughkeepsie Eagle-News*, 1 April 1932, p. 6.

61   "One could take . . . next November." *Amsterdam Recorder*, 29 March 1932, p. 8. In FDR's own backyard the *Poughkeepsie Eagle-News* postulated that "the remarkable lead enjoyed by Mr. Hoover would appear to indicate that he has a strong hold on the support of the farming population of America. The significance of that fact is not to be overlooked. . . . Hoover men and women aren't making much of a clamor, but their number is legion." (*Poughkeepsie Eagle-News*, 1 April 1932, p. 6)

62   "he would . . . be inevitable." *Scribner's*, March 1932, p. 130.

63   North Dakota. *Bismarck Tribune*, 16 March 1932, p. 1; Peel & Donnelly, p. 73; Schlesinger (*Crisis*), p. 293; Smith (*FDR*), p. 260; Neal, pp. 37-39.

64   Nebraska. *NY Times*, 13 April 1932, p. 4; *NY Times*, 14 April 1932, p. 2; Peel & Donnelly, p. 74; Schlesinger (*Crisis*), p. 293; Neal, p. 39.

65   West Virginia. *NY Times*, 11 May 1932, p. 3; Peel & Donnelly, p. 77; Schlesinger (*Crisis*), p. 294; Eaton, pp. 331-32; Freidel (*Triumph*), p. 279; Martin (*Bandwagons*), p. 301; Neal, p. 39.

66   Oregon. *NY Times*, 21 May 1932, p. 3; Peel & Donnelly, p. 78; Freidel (*Triumph*), p. 289; Martin (*Bandwagons*), p. 301; Schlesinger (*Crisis*), p. 294; Neal, p. 39.

67   Florida. Peel & Donnelly, p. 78; Schlesinger (*Crisis*), p. 294; Freidel (*Triumph*), p. 280; Martin (*Bandwagons*), p. 302; Neal, p. 39.

68   Georgia. *NY Times*, 1 January 1933, p. 20; Peel & Donnelly, p. 73; Schlesinger (*Crisis*), p. 293; Freidel (*Triumph*), p. 277; Smith (*FDR*), p. 260; Neal, p. 40.

69   O'Connell. *NY Times*, 17 April 1932, pp. 1, 26.

70   New Hampshire. *NY Times*, 1 January 1933, p. 20; Guilfoyle, pp. 94-102; Peel & Donnelly, p. 72; Freidel (*Triumph*), p. 281; Oulahan, p. 46; Warren (*Presidency*), p. 231; Smith (*FDR*), p. 261.

71   Wisconsin. Peel & Donnelly, p. 74; Neal, p. 41.

72   Maine. Guilfoyle, pp. 104-7; Peel & Donnelly, p. 73; Freidel (*Triumph*), p. 286; Schlesinger (*Crisis*), p. 293; Smith (*FDR*), p. 261; Neal, pp. 40-41.

73   "largely a fake movement." Freidel (*Triumph*), p. 281; Neal, p. 42.

74   Farley. Freidel (*Triumph*), p. 281.

75   Straus. Davis (*New York*), p. 216; Freidel (*Triumph*), p. 204; Neal, p. 42.

76   Ely. Neal, p. 42; Huthmacker, pp. 232, 239. It should not be assumed that because Ely so vociferously supported Smith that he was a Catholic. He was, like Marcus A. Coolidge, a Protestant Yankee Democrat.

77   Walsh. Trout, pp. 102-6; Huthmacker, p. 232; Neal, p. 42.

78   Fitzgerald. *NY Times*, 12 March 1932, p. 3; *NY Times*, 24 April 1932, p. E6; Koskoff, p. 43; Neal, p. 42. Fitzgerald, Ely, Walsh, Sen. Marcus Coolidge, and Rep. John McCormack all served as Smith delegates.

79   James Roosevelt. *NY Times*, 24 April 1932, p. E6; Guilfoyle, pp. 42, 87, 91; Curley, pp. 232-33; Freidel (*Triumph*), p. 282; Miller (*FDR*), p. 267*fn*; Martin (*Bandwagons*), p. 298; Huthmacker, p. 234; Oulahan, p. 46; Allison, p. 54. FDR had instructed James that he might "learn a great deal about practical politics from Brother Curley!" (Ritchie, p. 88) He ended up, perhaps, learning more from Governor Ely, who scolded him, "Your father has a lot of nerve to come to this state and try to knock down a Governor, two United States Senators, and four congressmen."

80   Feud with Smith. Huthmacker, pp. 176-77; Davis (*New York*), p. 217; Freidel (*Triumph*), p. 204; Oulahan, p. 46; Martin (*Bandwagons*), p. 297; Leinwand, p. 224; Rollins, p. 316; Neal, p. 42.

81   Roosevelt's family. *Scribner's*, January 1933, p. 2; House had known Sara Roosevelt prior to knowing Franklin.

82   "and the . . . have in November." Morgan, p. 218; Black (*Champion*), p. 118; Smith (*FDR*), p. 117; Pietrusza (*1920*), p. 138.

83   Advised FDR and Howe. Stiles, p. 140; Black (*Champion*), p. 210.

84   Baker. Neal, p. 78. In late April 1932, Walter Lippmann wrote to House: "I have information which I regard as entirely reliable that those who are very close to Governor Roosevelt, and probably the Governor himself are spreading the report that Newton Baker is disqualified because of his health." Lippmann testily continued, "It seems to be particularly distressing that the Governor, or people close to him, should inject into the discussion the question of physical fitness. That is a subject that they had better not discuss at all . . . For of course if this propaganda persists someone is sure to bring it out into the open and ask for a general showdown on the question of physical fitness." On May 4, Lippmann again chided House: "The very assurances you quote are not very reassuring. If I want to create the impression that a man is in bad health all I need to do is to keep inquiring solicitously about his health."

85   House's guests. Guilfoyle, p. 25; Freidel (*Triumph*), pp. 203-4; Davis (*New York*), pp. 212-13; Curley, p. 232. In February 1932, Sedgwick, a Baker man, viewed Hoover as looking "flabby and discouraged . . . a man of no resources of mind or spirit beyond his administrative duties. He never reads except along lines that may prove 'useful.'" (Nevins [*Adams*], p. 213)

86   "to discourage Smith . . . oppose our man." Davis (*New York*), p. 216; Beatty, p. 298. House had also planned to deliver his home state of Texas into FDR's hands; Garner's candidacy blew that goal into a cocked hat. (Guilfoyle, p. 27)

87   Williamstown. Davis (*New York*), p. 216; Guilfoyle, p. 28.

88   Curley. Guilfoyle, p. 28.

89   1930. Beatty, pp. 279-85. The scheming Curley coveted the re-election of Republican Gov. Frank G. Allen so that he himself might win the State House in 1932.

90   Blackmail. Beatty, pp. 136-39; Goodwin (*Fitzgeralds*), pp. 243-53; Schwarz (*Kennedy*), pp. 65-71. Curley threatened Fitzgerald (John F. Kennedy's maternal grandfather) with three public

lectures, "Graft, Ancient and Modern," "Great Lovers in History: From Cleopatra to Toodles," and "Libertines in History from Henry the Eighth to the Present Day." The latter two particularly riveted Mayor Fitzgerald's attention.

91 Walsh and Fitzgerald feuds. Huthmacker, pp. 176-77; Davis (*New York*), p. 217; Freidel (*Triumph*), p. 204; Oulahan, p. 46; Martin (*Bandwagons*), p. 297; Leinwand, p. 224; Rollins, p. 316; Neal, p. 42.

92 Hague/Walker/Cermak. *NY Times*, 1 May 1932, p. *xxi*; Case & Case, p. 571. FDR enjoyed his share of big-city crooks, not only in the form of support from Boston's Mayor Curley but also from mobbed-up West Harlem boss James J. Hines. (Handlin, p. 162)

93 Young. Guilfoyle, p. 20; Davis (*New York*), p. 217; Trout, p. 107; Guilfoyle, p. 20; Beatty, p. 297.

94 Jail. Curley, pp. 68-69; Beatty, pp. 80-83: Goodwin (*Fitzgeralds*), p. 243; Schwarz (*Kennedy*), p. 65. Curley served sixty days in the county's Charles Street jail for illegally taking a federal civil service examination for a colleague. He won re-election to the Board of Aldermen from his cell.

95 "We have been . . . nominate for the Presidency." Martin (*Bandwagons*), p. 298; Guilfoyle, pp. 28-29.

96 Smiled. Curley, p. 233; Martin (*Bandwagons*), p. 298.

97 Sphinx. *NY Times*, 10 December 1939, p. 62; *NY Times*, 14 April 1940, p. 4. An eight-foot-high papier mâché rendering of FDR as a smiling sphinx even graced Washington's 1939 and 1940 Gridiron Club Dinners. Since 1941 said sphinx has resided at the Franklin D. Roosevelt Presidential Library and Museum at Hyde Park. (*NY Times*, 9 November 1941, SM10, 30)

98 Brown. Huthmacker, p. 234; Neal, p. 43. Brown, a Harvard Law School classmate of Felix Frankfurter, had served as a special assistant to the attorney general under Wilson. (*Cambridge Tribune*, 27 April 1918, p. 1)

99 Jackson. Neal, pp. 42-43. New Hampshire's Jackson is not to be confused with the other "Robert H. Jackson," the future Supreme Court justice Robert H. Jackson, another 1932 FDR supporter.

100 "We strongly advise . . . to offset upstate vote." Martin (*Bandwagons*), p. 297.

101 "Please prepare . . . for the lady." Martin (*Bandwagons*), p. 297.

102 Ancient Order of Hibernians. Leinwand, p. 226; Allison, p. 54.

103 St. Patrick's Day. Beatty, p. 306; Neal, p. 43.

104 Massachusetts results. www.ourcampaigns.com/RaceDetail.html?RaceID=35485; *NY Times*, 28 April 1932, p. 2; Peel & Donnelly, p. 75; Huthmacker, p. 237; Warren (*Presidency*), p. 231; Neal, p. 44; Dille, p. 50.

105 Rhode Island. Peel & Donnelly, p. 75; Rosen, p. 228; Ritchie, p. 88.

106 172–23. Freidel (*Triumph*), p. 283.

107 Connecticut. *NY Times*, 22 April 1932, p. 11; Peel & Donnelly, p. 77; Freidel (*Triumph*), p. 283; Martin (*Bandwagons*), p. 301; Ritchie, p. 88.

108 Guffey. *NY Times*, 22 April 1932, p. 11; Freidel (*Triumph*), p. 283; Martin (*Bandwagons*), p. 299; Neal, p. 44. Guffey, educated at Princeton during Woodrow Wilson's tenure there, had been indicted for embezzling $400,000 from Wilson's wartime Alien Property Custodian's office. (*NY Times*, 19 April 1924, p. 2; *NY Times*, 13 June 1933, p. 6)

109 Pennsylvania. *Altoona Mirror*, 28 April 1932, p. 1; Peel & Donnelly, p. 75; Tugwell (*Democratic*), p. 224; Neal, p. 44.

110 "It was . . . impressive win." Tugwell (*Democratic*), p. 224.

111 "elimination". Houck & Kiewe, p. 82.

112 New Jersey. *NY Times*, 25 May 1932, p. 2; Freidel (*Triumph*), p. 283.

113 Texas. *NY Times*, 25 May 1932, p. 2; Peel & Donnelly, p. 78.

114 "If that man . . . the United States". Harbaugh, p. 339.

115 New York. *NY Times*, 16 April 1932, pp. 1, 10; *NY Times*, 17 April 1932, pp. 1, 26; Peel & Donnelly, p. 74; Neal, p. 45.

116 "Everything is . . . my views." *NY Times*, 16 April 1932, p. 10.

117 "Massachusetts and Pennsylvania . . . for an instant." Mencken (*Politics*), p. 260; O'Connor (*Hurrah*), p. 256. Mencken was remarkably awful in analyzing campaigns (in July 1931 he wrote:

"Mr. Hoover is almost as sure of re-election next year as he was in 1928"), but in this case he is more on the mark. As Cordell Hull admitted, supporting Roosevelt was indeed "the most effective way of killing off Smith." (Mencken [*Politics*], p. 225; Handlin, p. 153)

118   "I am convinced . . . of the state." Neal, p. 45.

119   Hearst papers. Carlisle, pp. 12, 59; Procter, p. 171. Hearst's five California dailies, in ascending order of circulation, were: the *Oakland Post-Enquirer*, the *San Francisco Call-Bulletin*, the *San Francisco Examiner*, the *Los Angeles Examiner*, and the recently merged *Los Angeles Herald-Express*.

120   "Tammany candidates . . . New York." Neal, p. 46.

121   Texans. *NY Times*, 6 May 1932, p. 4; Freidel (*Triumph*), p. 287; Neal, p. 46.

122   "If you are . . . for Roosevelt." *Sheboygan Press*, 22 May 1932, p. 14; Martin (*Bandwagons*), p. 299; Neal, p. 46. Garner came out for repeal that May 21.

123   Massachusetts/Howe. Neal, pp. 44-45.

124   "chaotic". Rosen, p. 233.

125   Divide delegates. Rosen, p. 233. Brown and Jackson had proposed a similar deal in Massachusetts. Ely and Walsh were amenable. Curley vetoed it. (Guilfoyle, pp. 85-88; Neal, p. 43)

126   McAdoo foe. *San Antonio Express*, 14 August 1926, p. 1. Dockweiler had vanquished a McAdoo slate in 1928 to deliver the state for Smith, a fellow Catholic.

127   "Roosevelt . . . will win". Rosen, p. 233.

128   California vote. Peel & Donnelly, p. 76; Freidel (*Triumph*), pp. 287-88; Ritchie, p. 88; Neal, pp. 46-47; Rosen, p. 233; Carlisle, p. 60. The raw totals: Garner, 211,913; Roosevelt, 167,117; Smith, 135,981.

129   "perhaps irreparable blow". Ritchie, p. 88.

CHAPTER ELEVEN: "DEAR OLD MAN . . . YOU MUST STEP ASIDE"

1   "pleasant chat . . . very close." *NY Times*, 26 February 1932, p. 3.

2   "on the rocks." Burke, pp. 8, 185-86.

3   Membership. Mowrer, p. 269; Bracher, p. 184; Lüdecke, p. 349; Payne, p. 257.

4   "Septemberlings." Speer, p. 20; Bracher, p. 184; Snyder (*Encyclopedia*), p. 320; Fest (*Hitler*), p. 289. Or, sometimes, "Septemberites."

5   Reichswehr account. Manvell & Fraenkel (*Hundred*), p. 190. Funneled to the campaign by Gen. Kurt von Schleicher.

6   "National Socialism . . . there is today." Stachura, p. 92; Wheaton, p. 49; Fest (*Face*), p. 296.

7   Entered race. Toland, p. 261; Reuth, pp. 142-43.

8   "I know your . . . in any case!" Magida, p. 125; Dietrich (*With*), pp. 17-18.

9   Greszinski. Greszinski, pp. 137-38; Goebbels (*Part*), p. 41; Orlow (*Prussia*), p. 189.

10   "Dear old man. . . to fight them." Domarus, pp. 119-20; Fest (*Hitler*), p. 318; Kershaw (*Hubris*), p. 362; Magida, p. 125; Richie, p. 400. Until 1934, Hitler habitually and conspicuously carried a whip with him. His rich patronesses, Elsa Bruckmann and Helene Bechstein, both gifted him with whips. (Rauschning, p. 162; Dietrich [*Knew*], p. 154; Bullock, pp. 135, 382; Waite, p. 240; Redlich, p. 266; Machtan, p. 18; Hanfstaengl, p. 172; Botting & Sayer, p. 12; Hayman, pp. 144, 156; Murray, p. 174; Large [*Munich*], p. 152). According to Paula Hitler, Alois Hitler carried a whip in their house. (Victor, p. 28)

11   "made a tremendous . . . first page." Bach, p. 86.

12   "fascinated . . . They are right.'" Bach, p. 80.

13   "Harry, you . . . coming man." Bach, p. 81.

14   "I'll work for them". Bach, p. 81.

15   "I had an . . . quite paralyzed." Riefenstahl, p. 101; Lynch, p. 89; Lambert, p. 218; Knopp, p. 113.

16   Cab. Riefenstahl, p. 101; Trimborn, p. 57.

17   "I was infected, no doubt about it". Trimborn, p. 57.

18   Moabit. Dorpalen, p. 284.

19   "a veritable mountain . . . no details." *NY Times*, 5 March 1932, p. 4; Dorpalen, p. 282.

20 "I cannot believe . . . new unity." Dorpalen, p. 284.
21 Brüning itinerary. *NY Times*, 4 March 1932, p. 11; Davidson, p. 313.
22 Mice. Davidson, p. 313.
23 "A vote for . . . and the people." *NY Times*, 10 March 1932, p. 7.
24 "vicious . . . Hindenburg." Dorpalen, p. 286.
25 "The present issue . . . ruin of Germany." Lüdecke, p. 362; Shirer, p. 157.
26 SPD. Dorpalen, p. 282; Toland, p. 262.
27 Converted. Dorpalen, p. 282; Toland, p. 262.
28 Daughters. Toland, p. 262.
29 Money. Davidson, p. 314.
30 "He betrayed . . . betray you too." Wheeler-Bennett (*Titan*), p. 367; Ludwig (*Hindenburg*), p. 309; Fromm, p. 43.
31 Thälmann/Winter. *NY Times*, 4 March 1932, p. 11; *Workers Age*, 19 March 1932, pp. 1-2; Olden, p. 245.
32 "Every vote . . . against Hitler." Reuth, p. 143.
33 Itinerary. Hauner, p. 78; Knight-Patterson, p. 526.
34 Eleven million. Fest (*Hitler*), p. 318; Kershaw (*Hubris*), p. 362.
35 "Hitler's activities were . . . carried out." Heinz, p. 204.
36 Meetings, pamphlets. Shirer, p. 158.
37 "Things have . . . one unemployed". Heiden (*Fuehrer*), p. 446.
38 "a man comes . . . the people". Heiden (*Fuehrer*), p. 446.
39 "What has this . . . a new dawn." Grenville, p. 56.
40 "hath kept . . . faithful unto him." Isherwood, p. 130.
41 "Honor Hindenburg . . . for Hitler." Toland, p. 262.
42 "foreign to . . . a weakling." *NY Times*, 5 March 1932, p. 4; *Oshkosh Daily Northwestern*, 5 March 1932, p. 3. Stephani later served as a Nazi Reichstag deputy.
43 *Echo der Woche*. Weber, pp. 100-101, 283-85; Heiden (*Fuehrer*), pp. 72-73.
44 Naturalization suit. *NY Times*, 16 March 1932, p. 8; Domarus, p. 125. Hitler returned to court in June, suing journalist Werner Abel for "libel and perjury." Abel, a former Nazi (and counterfeiter), had charged Hitler of accepting Italian government bribes to soft-pedal German claims on the South Tyrol. A screaming, fist-pounding Hitler ("That's a lie! Were such things true I'd shoot myself") refused to answer questions from "these Jew lawyers . . . though I will answer anything from the court." Judge Otto Bertram fined him $190 for contempt of court as well as $47 for unruly behavior. (*Syracuse Herald*, 9 June 1932, p. x; *Connellsville Courier*, 10 June 1932, p. 16; *Rome Sentinel*, 11 June 1932, p. 4; *Time*, 20 June 1932, p. 14; Morris [*Justice*], p. 268)
45 Train incident. *NY Times*, 16 March 1932, p. 8; Hoffmann (*Security*), p. 19; Duffy & Ricci, p. 15.
46 "On the way . . . harm ensues." Goebbels (*Part*), p. 60.
47 "Hate exploded . . . can't go on.'" Isherwood, p. 128; Toland, pp. 261-62; Rolfs, p. 143; Ritchie, p. 403; Johnson (*Modern*), p. 282.
48 "peculiarities". Heiden (*History*), p. 417; Machtan, p. 191; Lüdecke, p. 352.
49 "where they . . . sort of love." Lüdecke, p. 352.
50 1924. Machtan, p. 111.
51 *Münchener Post*. Large [*Munich*], p. 224; Höhne, p. 72; Machtan, p. 191.
52 "The Hitlerian party . . . horrible corruption." Tamagne, p. 288.
53 Buch. Hoffmann (*Security*), pp. 21-22; Höhne, pp. 73-75. Buch would later receive a six-month prison sentence for his part in the plot. He, nonetheless, retained his party position.
54 "That would be . . . he must go." Toland, pp. 263-64; Hauner, p. 78. Even before the war, Munich had seen "a proliferation of homosexuality and a growing trade in young boys." In the cabarets they sang: "Our city teems with creatures of this sway / Warm friendships bloom rank on rank / Aside the pretty Isar bank." (Large [*Munich*], p. xx)
55 "often had . . . in that direction." Machtan, p. 198.

56　Granninger. Höhne, p. 72; Hancock, pp. 114-15. There is the possibility that Granninger was really a "Peter Kronniger." (Tamagne, p. 288)
57　Heines. Heiden (*History*), pp. 417-18; Heiden (*Fuehrer*), pp. 294-95, 371; Machtan, p. 111; Weale, p. 91; Snyder (*Encyclopedia*), p. 141; Manvell & Fraenkel (*Göring*), p. 32; Höhne, p. 72.
58　Ernst. Heiden (*History*), p. 417; Hanfstaengl, p. 129; Magida, pp. 202, 205-11; Machtan, p. 208; Höhne, p. 72.
59　Helldorf. Heiden (*History*), p. 417; Heiden (*Fuehrer*), p. 371.
60　Schmidt. Heiden (*History*), p. 418.
61　"du." Lüdecke, p. 352; Machtan, p. 113; Read, p. 59; Kershaw (*Hubris*), p. 741; Weale, p. 25.
62　Wagener. Wagener, pp. 103, 105-6.
63　Strasser ally. Gisevius, p. 153; Patch, p. 224.
64　"the dangers . . . it in public." Machtan, pp. 187-89, 200. Goebbels also lobbied for a crackdown on homosexuality within the party. (Thacker, p. 120) Count Harry Kessler wrote to his diary in April 1932 of the "strongly feminine character of Hitler and his entourage." (Kessler, p. 414)
65　"Hitler had . . . [the Röhm-Heimsoth] correspondence." Lüdecke, p. 352.
66　"a lot of wavy-haired bugger-boys". Kurth, p. 161.
67　Lüdecke. Machtan, pp. 266-67; Conradi, p. 44; Max, pp. 15, 120. Lüdecke collaborated with his memoirs, *I Knew Hitler*, with homosexual Paul Mooney. (Max, pp. 3, 15, 119-28) Putzi Hanfstaengl was also convinced of Alfred Rosenberg's bisexuality (Caroli, p. 48)
68　Hess. Heiden (*History*), p. 418; Langer, p. 102; Waite, p. 264; Machtan, p. 143; Conradi, p. 73; Infield (*Secret*), p. 199; Tyson (*Surreal*), p. 272; Otto Strasser, however, considered the relationship "absolutely pure." (Strasser, p. 36)
69　Schirach. Langer, p. 99; Snyder (*Encyclopedia*), p. 309; Wistrich, p. 272; Machtan, p. 222; Tyson (*Surreal*), p. 381.
70　Bouhler. Tyson (*Surreal*), pp. 381, 410.
71　Brückner. Machtan, p. 222; Tyson (*Surreal*), p. 381.
72　Graf/Weber. Tyson (*Surreal*), p. 15.
73　Funk. Snyder (*Encyclopedia*), p. 106; Wistrich, p. 87; Tyson (*Surreal*), p. 381.
74　Frank. Heiden (*History*), p. 418.
75　Heimsoth raid. Machtan, p. 198.
76　Braun/Brüning. Machtan, p. 199. Brüning had similarly ignored the implications of papers famously seized at the Boxheim farm in Westphalia in December 1931 detailing a proposed Nazi coup. (Orlow [*Nazi*], p. 232; Evans [*Coming*], p. 274; Mitchell, p. 134; Longerich, p. 319) "He allowed the whole business to be minimized and smothered," thought the French ambassador François-Poncet. "From that day on I thought he was a doomed man." (François-Poncet, pp. 20-21)
77　"the most sinister. . . ever seen". The words of Martha Dodd, daughter of US ambassador William E. Dodd. (Larson, p. 116)
78　German State (Democratic) Party. Eyck, p. 412.
79　Diels. Machtan, pp. 194-99; Larson, p. 214. In 1943 Diels married Hermann Göring's cousin Ilse, also the widow of one of Göring's brothers. (Manvell & Fraenkel [*Himmler*], p. 32; Wistrich, p. 39; Metcalfe, p. 288)
80　"I have no . . . I must!" Krebs, p. 165; Hauner, p. 78; Toland, p. 264.
81　George Washington. *NY Times*, 7 March 1932, p. 1; *Buffalo Courier-Express*, 7 March 1932, p. 3; Fromm, p. 44.
82　March 13 voting. Hauner, p. 78.
83　"Our tactics are . . . vote [for Hindenburg]." *NY Times*, 8 March 1932, p. 8.
84　Himmler. Orlow (*Nazi*), p. 250.
85　"He was obviously . . . or against Hindenburg!" US Department of State, pp. 283-84; Burke, p. 190.
86　"In the desperate . . . freedom and bread!" Dorpalen, p. 287.
87　"Tomorrow, Hitler will . . . of the Reich." Domarus, p. 122; Fest (*Hitler*), p. 319.

88   "Newspapers have been . . . over the radio." *NY Post*, 10 March 1932, p. 7; *Rome Sentinel*, 10 March 1932, p. 1.
89   "Everyone confident of . . . is no consolation. . . ." Goebbels (*Part*), p. 58.
90   Results. Clark (*German Republic*), p. 352; Knight-Patterson, p. 526; Eyck, p. 360.
91   "The Party is . . . depressed and discouraged." Goebbels (*Part*), p. 58.
92   "the image of . . . his means." Fest (*Hitler*), p. 319.
93   "The Grand Army . . . in good health." Fest (*Hitler*), p. 319.
94   "Only a bold . . . the struggle begin. . . ." Hoffmann (*Friend*), p. 159; Toland, p. 256; Kershaw (*Hubris*), p. 354.
95   "'Phone to the . . . this experience." Goebbels (*Part*), p. 58.
96   "We must resume . . . shall lead it!" Dietrich (*With*), pp. 18-19; Fest (*Hitler*), p. 319; Domarus, p. 124.

CHAPTER TWELVE: "THE NOMINATION OF THIS MAN HOOVER IS INVALID"

1   "The Republican national . . . be reelected." *Chicago Tribune*, 12 June 1932, p. 5.
2   "Several gaudy cabarets . . . $7 a pint." *Literary Digest*, 11 June 1932, p. 30.
3   Indian blood. *Salt Lake Tribune*, 7 November 1928, p. 11. Mencken dismissed Curtis as a "Kansas comic character, who is half Indian and half windmill." (Mencken, p. 24) Will Rogers (9/32 Cherokee), not surprisingly, demurred: "Charlie Curtis is the last Indian in high office—and I'm not going to let anyone tomahawk him" (*Spokane Daily Chronicle*, 15 June 1932, p. 17). Curtis was not the first part-Indian vice president, that honor falling to Calvin Coolidge. He was, however, the first technically Roman Catholic veep, baptized by a Jesuit missionary to the Pottawatomies. Curtis, a Methodist, was very much surprised to learn of that in the 1920s—or, at least, said he was. (*NY Times*, 29 June 1928, p. 7)
4   Throttlebottom. Witcover, p. 68; Dickson & Allen, p. 292; Brock, p. 167; Oulahan, p. 59; Ritchie, p. 99.
5   "He'd rather . . . be President". Willis, p. 30; Persico (*Lucy*), p. 109.
6   Affairs. Caroli, pp. 412-15; Brands (*Traitor*), p. 91; Collier & Horowitz (*Roosevelts*), p. 301; Willis, p. 30. Longworth, it transpired, nonetheless, became quite the affectionate "father" to the Alice-Borah offspring.
7   "Well, we just . . . when Charlie deals . . .". Cordery, p. 346.
8   Meyer. *Milwaukee Journal*, 5 May 1929, p. 1; *NY Times*, 7 May 1929, p. 30; *NY Times*, 14 May 1929, p. 2; *Pittsburgh Press*, 14 May 1929, p. 3; Longworth, pp. 330-33; Cordery, p. 345; Oulahan, p. 59.
9   Hoover. Ritchie, p. 99.
10   TR Jr. *Spokane Daily Chronicle*, 15 June 1932, p. 17; *San Antonio Express*, 17 June 1932, p. 2.
11   Philippines. *Iowa City Iowan*, 10 January 1932, p. 1.
12   Smith. Collier & Horowitz (*Roosevelts*), pp. 295-300; Slayton, pp. 218-19; Handlin, p. 72.
13   "To nominate [Curtis] . . . from the Northeast. . . ." Collier & Horowitz (*Roosevelts*), pp. 332-33.
14   "She would add . . . color and pep." *Milwaukee Journal*, 8 February 1949, p. 20.
15   Whooping cough. *NY Times*, 15 June 1932, p. 13. Contracted via her daughter.
16   Dawes. *NY Times*, 16 June 1932, p. 12; Oulahan, p. 59.
17   Hoover. Oulahan, p. 59.
18   Pennsylvania. *Time*, 27 June 1932, pp. 12-13; Hart (*Convention*), pp. 215-17; Peel & Donnelly, p. 90; Oulahan, p. 59. Curtis received 634¼ votes. His nearest competition included the National Commander of the American Legion, Col. Hanford MacNider, 182¾; RCA President Gen. James G. Harbord, 161¾; former Massachusetts governor Alvan T. Fuller, 57; House Minority Leader Bertrand H. Snell, 56; Florida businessman J. Leonard Replogle, 23¾, Canadian-born Michigan US senator James J. Couzens, 11; and Charles G. Dawes, 9¾. Curtis thus became only the second GOP

vice president to be re-nominated. The first, James Schoolcraft Sherman, died before Election Day 1912.

19   "Don't change . . . over Niagara." *New Republic*, 22 June 1932, p. 141; *Reading Times*, 18 June 1932, p. 15; Kyvig, p. 155.

20   "We do not . . . and attendant abuses." *Time*, 27 June 1932, pp. 12-13; Hart (*Convention*), p. 120; Kyvig, pp. 154-55; Coffey, pp. 297-98.

21   "The Hoover plank. . . to simple folk." Mencken (*President*), p. 74; Kyvig, p. 155; Ritchie, p. 98. Said Will Rogers: "From now on you will just hear two kinds of arguments over prohibition—one fellow denouncing the Hoover plank and the other fellow trying to explain it." (*Joplin Globe*, 17 June 1932, p. 2) Embittered Prohibition Party keynoter Clinton Norman Howard, however, thought he understood the GOP plank quite well, denouncing it as "the most stupendous, titanic, colossal, calamitous, crimson, conscienceless, barbaric and cataclysmic fraud ever perpetrated upon the American people." (*Time*, 18 July 1932, p. 30; *Statesville Record & Landmark*, 19 July 1932, p. 4) The *Chicago Tribune*'s editorial headline read: "HOOVER PLANK IS SANE, FARCE, FAIR, HOAX, RIDICULOUS" (*Chicago Tribune*, 17 June 1932, p. 5)

22   Sabin. Kyvig, pp. 119-24; Dobyns, pp. 109-12; Kobler, pp. 342-45; Sinclair, pp. 343-44.

23   766,000. Tyrrell, p. 2.

24   372,355. *American Journal of Sociology* Vol. 61, No. 3 (1955), p. 222. A mid-1950s study of that group described the movement's diminished social standing—though that trend was already well in place by 1932. "When this union was organized, we had many of the most influential ladies of this city. . . . ," observed one discouraged member. "We have an undertaker's wife and a minister's wife, but the lawyer's and the doctor's wives shun us. They don't want to be thought queer. . . . I remember when I joined, women of prominence and social prestige were in it." (*American Journal of Sociology*, Vol. 61, No. 3 [1955], pp. 227-28)

25   Carnegie, Ford, Kresge, Wanamaker. Kobler, p. 184; Kyvig, p. 96; Behr, p. 59.

26   Rockefeller Jr. *Plattsburgh Press*, 7 June 1932, p. 1; *Time*, 20 June 1932, p. 10; Hart (*1932*), p. 35; Kyvig, p. 152; Kobler, pp. 350-51.

27   Butler. Hart (*Convention*), pp. 128-30; 134-36; Peel & Donnelly, pp. 86-87; Kyvig, p. 155; Eaton, p. 323.

28   Censured. *Congressional Record*, 4 June 1929, pp. 5131-32. Bingham was censured for placing a lobbyist on the Senate payroll so he might sit in on private legislative sessions.

29   "We adopted the . . . the depression". Hart (*Convention*), p. 129.

30   "almost the worst . . . with this subject". Hart (*Convention*), p. 135.

31   "What the word 'slavery' . . . 'repeal' is today." Hart (*Convention*), p. 136. "Drys" argued to blacks that repeal of the Eighteenth Amendment might foreshadow similar repeal of the Twelfth, Fourteenth, or Fifteenth Amendments. Historian Daniel Okrent posits this approach met "with some success." (*Middletown Times-Herald*, 14 July 1932, p. 1; *Amsterdam News*, 7 September 1932, p. 1; Root, p. 147; Okrent, p. 330)

32   "the only free State . . . my State pussyfoot." Hart (*Convention*), pp. 159-62.

33   Minority plank vote. *NY Times*, 16 June 1932, pp. 1, 12, 14; Hart (*Convention*), pp. 160-61; Eaton, p. 323. The by-no-means "dry" New York delegation, for example, voted 76–21 for the administration's "amphibian" plank.

34   Beer glasses. *NY Times*, 16 June 1932, p. 12; Ossian, p. 147.

35   Butler, Crocker. Wilson (*Challenge*), p. 223.

36   "gained for himself . . . dealt upon prosperity." Peel & Donnelly, p. 84.

37   Hoover edit. Jeansonne (*Hoover*), p. 411.

38   Washington/Hoover. Oulahan, p. 59.

39   "Press on with Hoover". *Time*, 27 June 1932, p. 11.

40   Scott. *NY Times*, 21 May 1932, p. N1. That Hoover would designate someone who had emigrated from Britain to America at age twenty-one—and only re-enforce his then prevalent image as an un-American Englishman—is puzzling. Consider that at 1928's convention Indiana agricultural advocate Edgar D. Bush had actually pulled out a Union Jack after being jeered by Hoover supporters. "Oorah for 'Oover," Bush mocked The Great Engineer. (*NY Times*, 14 June 1928, p. 6) Further, Louis Howe commissioned cartoons depicting Hoover as the British and pro-European "'Erbie" and distributed them by the millions. (Smith [*Dream*], p. 176)

41 Placed in nomination. Hart (*Convention*), pp. 167-72; Peel & Donnelly, pp. 87-88; Eaton, p. 323.

42 Priests. *Time*, 27 June 1932, p. 11; Dille, p. 51.

43 "to think of [Hoover] . . . aid mankind." Hart (*Convention*), pp. 168; Eaton, p. 323.

44 "a triple-tongued elocution hound". *Joplin Globe*, 17 June 1932, p. 2.

45 "as good . . . in the circumstances." Jeansonne (*Hoover*), p. 412.

46 Cabinet. *NY Times*, 15 June 1932, p. 13.

47 Hoover ally. Eyman, pp. 85, 137, 140-41, 144; Cary, pp. 64, 117-18, 140-41, 221; Marx, pp. 91, 98, 102. Conversely, the hitherto Republican Warner Brothers (irate over a Hoover Administration investigation of their finances) eventually donated $10,000 to FDR, staged rallies for him, arranged for pro-FDR broadcasts over their Los Angeles radio station, KFWB—and entrained a caravan of their biggest stars (William Powell, Douglas Fairbanks Jr., Jimmy Cagney, Ruby Keeler, Ginger Rogers, Loretta Young, Kay Francis, and Bette Davis) to his inaugural. (*Time*, 14 November 1932, p. 11; Muscio, pp. 60-61; Freedland, pp. 63-65)

48 White House guest. Marx, p. 113.

49 "I accused [Mayer. . . take it back." *NY Times*, 15 June 1932, p. 13.

50 Mayer. *Time*, 27 June 1932, p. 11; Dille, p. 51; Oulahan, p. 64; Ritchie, p. 99.

51 "The Presence failed to materialize." *New Republic*, 29 June 1932, p. 179.

52 Sandblast. *NY Times*, 17 June 1932, p. 14; *San Antonio Express*, 17 June 1932, p. 2; *Plattsburgh Press*, 17 June 1932, p. 1; *Time*, 27 June 1932, p. 11; Hart (*Convention*), pp. 173-79; Peel & Donnelly, p. 88; Eaton, p. 323; Oulihan, p. 64.

53 "You will have . . . intend nominating Coolidge." *San Antonio Express*, 17 June 1932, p. 2; *Joplin Globe*, 17 June 1932, p. 2. Just before the convention opened Senator Bingham urged drafting the former president on a "wet" plank. Calvin Coolidge got while the getting was good; he wasn't about to return when it was awful. (*Pittsburgh Post-Gazette*, 15 June 1932, p. 1)

54 Police. *NY Times*, 17 June 1932, p. 14; *San Antonio Express*, 17 June 1932, p. 2; *New Republic*, 29 June 1932, pp. 176, 179; Eaton, pp. 323-24; Ritchie, pp. 98-99; Oulahan, p. 64; Lorant, p. 588. Ironically, Sanders, soon to be appointed RNC chairman, had served as Coolidge's personal secretary. (*NY Times*, 13 May 1950, p. 17)

55 "The treatment was . . . was treated illegally." *NY Times*, 17 June 1932, p. 14.

56 "The nomination . . . is invalid". *Time*, 27 June 1932, p. 11.

57 Copies. *Joplin Globe*, 17 June 1932, p. 2.

58 "Say to Hoover. . . trod by him". *Time*, 27 June 1932, pp. 11-12; Dille, pp. 51-52; Hart (*Convention*), p. 191. The speaker was Col. Roscoe Conkling Simmons of Illinois, founder of the Lincoln League of America and often acclaimed as the greatest black orator of his day. (*Historical Journal*, Vol. 45, No. 1 [2002], p. 79; *Journal of American Studies*, Vol. 37 [2003], p. 79; Jeansonne [*Hoover*], p. 417)

59 Roll call. *Time*, 27 June 1932, p. 12; Hart (*Convention*), pp. 198-99; Peel & Donnelly, p. 89; Eaton, p. 324. France won four Oregon delegates but received only three votes from that state on the roll-call, so, perhaps, he really was in receipt of an Oregon delegate's credentials.

60 Hoover hoped for FDR. Houck & Kiewe, p. 85; Ritchie, p. 106.

CHAPTER THIRTEEN: "THERE WAS LITTLE OPPORTUNITY FOR AIR-SICKNESS"

1 KPD. *NY Times*, 13 March 1932, p. 24.

2 "influenced by . . . bourgeois nationalism." *NY Times*, 16 March 1932, p. 8.

3 "In . . . the Government . . . at a low ebb." www.shsu.edu/~his_ncp/Sackett.html.

4 "Yesterday, proved irrefutably . . . the National Socialist party." *NY Times*, 15 March 1932, p. 8.

5 "The fight goes . . . with the results." *NY Times*, 14 March 1932, p. 8.

6   "Never before had . . . person was immune." Krebs, p. 185.
7   "a real masterpiece". Krebs, p. 186.
8   "The individual elements . . . in the lurch!" Krebs, pp. 187-88.
9   No radio. Delmer (*Trail*), p. 151.
10   "[I]n any case. . . is largely psychological." Baur, p. 31. Hitler took the train back from Berlin. (Large [*Munich*], p. 139)
11   "The same lecture. . . or at night". Hitler (*Kampf*), p. 473.
12   "*Deutschlandflug*". Conradi, p. 90; Kershaw (*Myth*), p. 41; Kershaw (*Hitler*), p. 227.
13   "At the end . . . from now on!'" Baur, p. 32; Conradi, p. 91.
14   Hanfstaengl. Delmer (*Trail*), p. 148; Metcalfe, p. 60; Conradi, p. 92.
15   Goebbels. Heiber, p. 96.
16   "Berlin . . . is hardly . . . the Leader's address." Goebbels (*Part*), pp. 70-71.
17   "Röhmosexuality". Machtan, pp. 202, 368.
18   "For the moment. . . to be done." Goebbels (*Part*), p. 71.
19   Delmer. Delmer (*Trail*), p. 147; Conradi, pp. 91-92.
20   "For quite transparent . . . change this fact." Domarus, p. 129; Machtan, p. 201.
21   Genial. Goldensohn, p. 279.
22   "You couldn't get . . . Nor even Göring". Goldensohn, p. 282.
23   Sepp Dietrich. Conradi, p. 93. "At that period," Hitler alleged in January 1942, "the Lufthansa was infested by Jews. They let me fly when it was forbidden to fly all over the Reich territory. They obviously had one wish—that I should end my career in an aircraft accident!" (Hitler [*Table Talk*], p. 196)
24   April 7 and 8. Hauner, p. 78; Domarus, p. 129.
25   "It wasn't a . . . his next oration." Dietrich (*With*), p. 26; Infield (*Secret*), p. 59.
26   "On Furth airfield . . . the 'Walkure,' he said." Baur (KOBO edition).
27   "loyalty is everything . . . love of Adolf Hitler". *Bulletin of International News*, Vol. 11, July 1934-June 1935, p. 193; Wistrich, p. 272.
28   Schirach. *NY Times*, 9 August 1974, p. 36; Fest (*Face*), p. 228; Wistrich, p. 271; Snyder (*Encyclopedia*), p. 309.
29   Hosted reception. Sigmund, pp. 189-90. That Hitler would have witnessed the wedding of the Protestant "Henny" Hoffmann, as well as the 1926 nuptials of the nominally Lutheran (though actually violently anti-Christian) Martin Bormann and the December 1931 union of baptized-Catholic Joseph Goebbels and the divorced Magda Quandt (also a baptized Catholic), no doubt only reinforced Catholic skepticism regarding his loyalties.
30   "I eat everything . . . only eggs." Sigmund, p. 190.
31   "Vast implications for . . . leftist or Socialist." *American Mercury*, September 1932, p. 34.
32   "In order to . . . the chief enemy. . . ." Valtin, pp. 312-13.
33   "in reality twins." *NY Times*, 20 March 1932, p. E4.
34   DNVP. *NY Times*, 20 March 1932, p. 12.
35   Sportpalast. *NY Times*, 5 March 1932, p. 4; *Oshkosh Daily Northwestern*, 5 March 1932, p. 3.
36   Party Day. Röhl, p. 1246.
37   Crown Prince candidacy. Jonas, pp. 172-76; Cecil, pp. 337-38.
38   "Princess Hermine saw . . . of National Socialism before me. . . ." Jonas, pp. 175-76.
39   "Abstention at the . . . for Adolf Hitler. . . ." Jonas, p. 177; Domarus, p. 130; Knight-Patterson, p. 527; Wheeler-Bennett (*Titan*), p. 361; Wheaton, p. 119; Snyder (*Encyclopedia*), pp. 272, 381; Leopold, p. 111; Cecil, p. 338.
40   August Wilhelm. Gordon, p. 209; Röhl, p. 1248. Prussian police beat August Wilhelm and Joseph Goebbels with truncheons during a March 1931 Königsberg train station riot. "You may be proud that you have been permitted to be a martyr in this great national movement," his father wrote him. (*NY Times*, 18 June 1931, p. 5; *NY Times*, 26 March 1949, p. 17; Heiden [*History*], p. 157; Snyder [*Encyclopedia*], p. 272; Röhl, p. 1247) By April 1932, however, Wilhelm II was sternly warning

Prince Oskar that no other Hohenzollerns should stand for election. (Cecil, p. 337) Oskar eventually resigned from the Stahlhelm when they veered too sharply pro-Nazi. (Snyder [*Encyclopedia*], p. 272)

41 "Adolf Hitler is God's gift to Germany." *NY Times*, 18 June 1931, p. 5; *NY Times*, 26 March 1949, p. 17.

42 "the Communists from . . . storm is breaking!" Heiden (*Fuehrer*), p. 147.

43 "Germany has . . . the Communists." US Department of State, p. 283. Goebbels did concede: "On the extreme Left the irreconcilable Communists would remain immune to their propaganda campaign—a campaign which was intended to appeal to the racial instincts of the population—*das Nationalgefühl*. The power of State, when the Nazis came to power, would be used to bring the recalcitrants to heel." "A good many of these [Nazi brownshirts]," noted Konrad Heiden, "were workmen who had found other parties disappointing, and who hoped that Hitler would realize their aspirations. In the end, members of the SA troops were really socialist or Communist in spirit and organization. Humorists called them 'beefsteaks'—brown outside and red inside." (Heiden [*History*], p. 405)

44 "rainstorms and dismal weather". *NY Times*, 11 April 1932, p. 2; Snyder (*Documentary*), p. 74.

45 Turnout surged. *NY Times*, 11 April 1932, p. 2; Snyder (*Documentary*), p. 73.

46 Totals. Clark (*German Republic*), p. 352; Feuchtwanger, p. 327.

47 "His defeat is . . . 200,000 votes." Goebbels (*Part*), p. 73.

48 "National Socialists! . . . in the future." Domarus, p. 130; See *NY Times*, 11 April 1932, p. 2 and Snyder (*Documentary*), p. 74 for a far different translation.

49 "The game . . . once more." Strasser, p. 135.

50 "They are unclear on your economic program." Davidson, p. 229.

51 "Gramophone records . . . and placards designed." Goebbels (*Part*), p. 74.

52 Twenty-five speeches. Kershaw (*Biography*), p. 228.

53 "No one calls . . . into the people." Noakes & Pridham, p. 74; Kershaw (*Hubris*), pp. 363-64; Kershaw (*Myth*), p. 42; Grenville, p. 57; Lynch, p. 89.

54 "asking them for . . . can do this." Mowrer, p. 258. Comparisons to Aimee Semple McPherson were not unknown. (Thompson, p. 31)

55 Voting percentages. Kershaw (*Hubris*), p. 364.

56 "Back to Brüning". *Time*, 8 August 1932, p. 13.

57 Prussian returns. Goebbels (*Part*), p. 81; Grzesinski, p. 153; Heiden (*Fuehrer*), p. 360; Manvell & Fraenkel (*Hundred*), p. 33; Kershaw (*Biography*), pp. 227-28; Clark (*German Republic*), pp. 354-56; Wheeler-Bennett *(Nemesis)*, p. 252; Koeves, p. 156.

58 2.9 and 36.6 percent. Orlow (*Prussia*), pp. 27, 34, 159; Dutch, p. 133.

59 "It's a fantastic . . . is made of." Goebbels (*Part*), p. 82; Kershaw (*Hubris*), p. 364.

Chapter Fourteen: "Dammit, Louis, I'm the Nominee!"

1 Indiana. Peel & Donnelly, p. 79.

2 "an aristocrat, a demagogue . . . to excite sympathy." MacKenzie, p. 165. The exact quote is from FDR biographer Compton MacKenzie. The usually discreet Lomasney, by the way, must have been particularly incensed by FDR to orate so vehemently. It was he, after all, who first advised, "Never write if you can speak; never speak if you can nod; never nod if you can wink."

3 "The Democratic Party . . . the party success." *Niagara Falls Gazette*, 5 November 1932, p. 6; Peel & Donnelly, p. 92; Farley (*Ballots*), p. 115; Schlesinger (*Crisis*), p. 298; Dille, p. 52.

4 La Follette 1924. Tucker (*Tide*), p. 222.

5 Scripps-Howard. *Syracuse Herald*, 10 June 1932, p. 2; *El Paso Herald-Post*, 10 June 1932, p. 20; *Biloxi Herald*, 10 June 1932, p. 12; *Time*, 20 June 1932, p. 10; Dille, p. 51; Manchester (*Glory*), p. 47.

6 "a charming person . . . reform one bit." *The Nation*, 20 January 1932, p. 58; Ekirch, p. 85.

7 "notably progressive for . . . happens to be!" *New Republic*, 1 June 1932, p. 64; Ekirch, p. 87.

8 "the corkscrew candidate . . . betraying his friends." *Pittsburgh Press*, 29 June 1932, p. 2; *Sandusky Register*, 22 October 1932, p. 4; Moley (*Seven*), p. 32; Rosen, p. 250; Schlesinger (*Crisis*), p. 309.

9 Minnesota. Peel & Donnelly, p. 72.

10   Maine/Iowa. Guilfoyle, pp. 104-7; Peel & Donnelly, p. 73; Freidel (*Triumph*), p. 286; Smith (*FDR*), p. 261; Neal, pp. 40-41.

11   Michigan, Kentucky. April. Peel & Donnelly, pp. 74-75.

12   Alabama. Peel & Donnelly, p. 76; Freidel (*Triumph*), p. 278; Martin (*Bandwagons*), p. 300.

13   Kansas. Peel & Donnelly, p. 77; Dille, p. 50; Martin (*Bandwagons*), p. 301.

14   Montana. Peel & Donnelly, p. 77; Freidel (*Triumph*), p. 289; Dille, p. 50; Martin (*Bandwagons*), p. 301.

15   Vermont. Peel & Donnelly, p. 77; Dille, p. 50; Martin (*Bandwagons*), p. 301.

16   South Carolina. Peel & Donnelly, p. 77; Dille, p. 50; Schlesinger (*Crisis*), p. 294.

17   Nevada. Peel & Donnelly, p. 78; Freidel (*Triumph*), p. 289; Martin (*Bandwagons*), p. 302.

18   Delaware. Peel & Donnelly, p. 78; Schlesinger (*Crisis*), p. 294.

19   Utah. Peel & Donnelly, p. 78; Freidel (*Triumph*), p. 289; Martin (*Bandwagons*), p. 302.

20   Tennessee. Dille, p. 50; Schlesinger (*Crisis*), p. 294.

21   Oregon. Dille, p. 50; Schlesinger (*Crisis*), p. 294.

22   West Virginia. Schlesinger (*Crisis*), p. 294; Walsh, p. 296; Martin (*Bandwagons*), p. 301.

23   North Carolina. *Time*, 27 June 1932, p. 13; Peel & Donnelly, p. 79; Schlesinger (*Crisis*), p. 294.

24   "Colonel House was . . . of the Union." MacKenzie, p. 164.

25   Committees. Williams (*Long*), p. 561; Brinkley, p. 43.

26   "the two foghorns . . . on the right." Williams (*Long*), pp. 562-63.

27   "I didn't like . . . be for him". Wheeler, p. 285; Williams (*Long*), p. 573; Brinkley, p. 46.

28   Wheeler/Norris. Wheeler, p. 285; Williams (*Long*), p. 573.

29   "Well, if Norris . . . be for him". Wheeler, p. 285; Williams (*Long*), p. 573. Long favored Norris as the GOP nominee.

30   Long; ⅔ rule. Farley (*Ballots*), pp. 116-17; Martin (*Bandwagons*), pp. 313-14.

31   "If the Democrats . . . playing the game. . . ." *Pittsburgh Post-Gazette*, 25 June 1932, p. 2; *Plattsburgh Press*, 25 June 1932, p. 1.

32   Prickly. Tucker (*Tide*), p. 46.

33   "damaged goods . . . gambler's trick." *Reading Eagle*, 26 June 1932, p. 3; Schlesinger (*Crisis*), p. 299; Burns, p. 135.

34   "Why, we'll destroy . . . a third party." *Plattsburgh Press*, 25 June 1932, p. 1.

35   "foolhardy and asinine." Smith (*FDR*), p. 265.

36   "stormed into . . . then and there." Schlesinger (*Crisis*), p. 300; Martin (*Bandwagons*), pp. 313-14.

37   Supports, retreats. Peel & Donnelly, p. 92; Freidel (*Triumph*), pp. 299-300.

38   "the sensational . . . fine steel bracelets." *Sandusky Register*, 22 October 1932, p. 4; *Pittsburgh Press*, 29 June 1932, p. 2; Kramer, p. 241. Paavo Nurmi, the "Flying Finn," garnered a total of nine gold and three silver Olympic medals in running competition.

39   Klansmen. Lisio (*Blacks*), p. 267; Oulahan, p. 73; Chalmers, p. 307. The Klan's Atlanta-based Imperial Klonsel (chief attorney) Paul Etheridge chaired the group.

40   "[W]ith such damaging . . . convention in Chicago." *NY Times*, 21 June 1932, p. 8; Oulahan, p. 73.

41   Baruch-Brokaw. Morris (*Luce*), p. 192; Martin (*Henry*), p. 124; Persico (*Lucy*), p. 298; Beauchamp, p. 356; Shadegg, p. 68. Clare, who then wore a plain black band on her third finger, left hand, the "insignia of her divorced state," was at various times also said to be the mistress of Joseph P. Kennedy and Randolph Churchill. She was, nonetheless, also linked to George S. Kaufman, CBS's William Paley, sportsman multi-millionaire John Hay "Jock" Whitney (later wed to James Roosevelt's ex-wife Betsey)—and FDR pal Vincent Astor. (Shadegg, p. 67; Kessler, p. 210)

42   "Roosevelt has most . . . but no delegates." Lewis (*Swope*), p. 195.

43   Forrestal. Shadegg, p. 63. Forrestal had a $50,000 contribution from Mrs. Harrison Williams to work with.

44   "WANTED, A DICTATOR!" Morris (*Luce*), p. 195; Martin (*Henry*), p. 126; Shadegg, p. 68.

45   "If Roosevelt . . . as a member. . . ." Lewis (*Swope*), p. 196; Morris (*Luce*), p. 194.

NOTES AND SOURCES

46 February 20. *NY Times*, 21 February 1932, pp. 1, 3; Warren (*Presidency*), p. 227; Martin (*Bandwagons*), p. 282.

47 "We advocate . . . and needed revenue." Laporte, p. 155; *The State of Wisconsin Blue Book*, p. 451; *Review of Reviews*, Vols. 85-86, p. 16.

48 32–17. *NY Times*, 30 June 1932, pp. 1-2; Flynn (*Boss*), p. 94. Prohibition politics were often as messy as any other variety. Senator Glass, though "dry," absolutely detested "dry" leader Bishop James Cannon. And not every Catholic Democrat was "wet." Mahoney was "dry," as was Montana's Thomas Walsh.

49 "Has the prohibition . . . a barroom plank." *NY Times*, 30 June 1932, p. 2; Dobyns, p. 155; Oulahan, p. 102.

50 "This is the . . . anti-prohibition movement." *NY Times*, 30 June 1932, p. 2; Dobyns, p. 155.

51 "I'll smash . . . that." *Iowa City Iowan*, 26 June 1932, p. 1. Cannon was in full retreat mode, defensively averring at the recent GOP Convention that "drys" were "just as willing as the wettest of the wets to have the people speak on prohibition." (Hart [*1932*], p. 35)

52 1,489 words. Smith (*FDR*), p. 267.

53 "We advocate an . . . the common interest." Laporte, p. 147; *The State of Wisconsin Blue Book*, pp. 459-50.

54 "Roosevelt or Ruin". Bennett (*Demagogues*), p. 35; Brinkley, p. 107; Fried, p. 57; Kennedy (*Fear*), p. 231.

55 Coughlin. *San Antonio Light*, 27 June 1932, p. 5-A; Marcus, p. 46.

56 Hull. Rosen, p. 244.

57 McAdoo. Rosen, p. 244.

58 "unemployment and old age insurance." Laporte, p. 147; *The State of Wisconsin Blue Book*, p. 450.

59 "under state laws." Laporte, p. 147; *The State of Wisconsin Blue Book*, p. 450; Schlesinger (*Coming*), p. 301. The idea of a state-based social security system may seem foreign to contemporary ears, but that was, in fact, the (albeit tortoise-paced) trend prior to the Depression and the New Deal. The first historian of the Social Security Administration, Abe Bortz, noted: "By 1928, 11 states had enacted pension laws and between that year and 1933—more were added, making a total of 28 States, with 23 mandatory on the localities and 15 that provided State financial aid. The measures in effect up to 1929 were optional and locally financed. Like similar mother's pension legislation, they were either inoperative or defective. Many States had long residence requirements and other restrictive eligibility conditions. By 1932, only 102,000 persons were receiving pensions with $22,000,000 the annual cost of assistance." (www.socialwelfarehistory.com/programs/old-age-pensions-a-brief-history/)

It was Newton D. Baker who prevailed upon Palmer to call for the programs to be state-based. (Rosen, p. 245)

60 "These bankers . . . care of it later." Eaton, p. 341.

61 "Bernie, I don't . . . more intensely." *Chester Times*, 28 November 1932, p. 6.

62 "I am foolish . . . without egotism." Craig (*Progressives*), p. 312.

63 "the most . . . ever met." Johnson (*American*), p. 640; Pietrusza (*1920*), p. 189.

64 McAdoo's leaks. Anthony (*First Ladies*), p. 141.

65 "the greatest . . . I ever saw." Chase, p. 92; Craig (*Progressives*), p. 110; Pietrusza (*1920*), p. 189.

66 Farley. Neal, p. 124; Craig (*Progressives*), p. 318.

67 Waldorf. Mitgang (*Tiger*), p. 272.

68 "the citadel of . . . mercenary, and sordid." Kennedy (*Over*), p. 99.

69 "How're you . . . beat this fellow." Rosen, p. 247.

70 "If we go to . . . be there either." Davis (*New York*), p. 306; Rosen, p. 248.

71 Asthma. Davis (*Invincible*), pp. 103-4.

72 FDR in Albany. Farley (*Ballots*), p. 122; Flynn (*Boss*), p. 93; Stiles, p. 172; Davis (*Invincible*), p. 102; Eaton, p. 335; Warren (*Presidency*), p. 234.

73 Ritchie. Farley (*Roosevelt*), p. 19; Eaton, pp. 244, 349; Freidel (*Triumph*), p. 307*fn*.

74 Garner. Eaton, pp. 344-45, 349.

75 Byrd. Stiles, p. 186; Eaton, pp. 244, 349, 355; Manchester (*Glory*), p. 48. Byrd wanted a Senate seat. (Martin [*Bandwagons*], p. 348; Manchester [*Glory*], p. 48)

76 "We are not . . . Madison Square Garden." *American Heritage*, August 1971, p. 40; Farley (*Ballots*), p. 135; Farley (*Roosevelt*), p. 20; Eaton, p. 345; Martin (*Bandwagons*), p. 354; Davis (*New York*), pp. 320-21; Oulahan, p. 95; Hardeman & Bacon, p. 140.

77 "Roosevelt will . . . first ballot." Farley (*Ballots*), p. 120; Burns, p. 134; Eaton, p. 338; Freidel (*Triumph*), p. 300.

78 "Honest Mel . . . Abe Lincoln". Ritchie, pp. 89-90.

79 Treasury. Neal, p. 261. FDR aide Daniel Roper (an old McAdoo ally) offered McAdoo secretary of state. (Oulahan, p. 116; O'Connor [*Hurrah*], pp. 253-54)

80 First National. Wicker, pp. 112, 114.

81 "I've been posing . . . a fish on it." Slayton, p. 370.

82 "No, I know . . . didn't call me." Slayton, p. 370.

83 Smith/Rayburn. Hardeman & Bacon, p. 140.

84 "dry". *NY Times*, 27 June 1932, p. 13.

85 "In this tragic . . . show the way." Laporte, p. 5; *San Antonio Light*, 27 June 1932, p. 5-A; *NY Times*, 28 June 1932, p. 13; Peel & Donnelly, p. 94; Martin (*Bandwagons*), p. 319.

86 Statistics. Allen (*Yesterday*), pp. 45-47, 49, 59, 68.

87 "a crowd of . . . food like animals." Armstrong, p. 10; Allen (*Yesterday*), p. 50.

88 Barkley "dry." *NY Post*, 16 April 1932, p. 5.

89 "Two weeks ago . . . the Constitution. . . ." Laporte, p. 36; *NY Times*, 28 June 1932, p. 14; Martin (*Bandwagons*), p. 319; Neal, pp. 243-44. Barkley's speech lasted 2.5 hours. "As a history of the United States in modern times," noted one weary observer, "it left little untold." (Slayton, p. 370)

90 Four hours; ten minutes. *NY Times*, 30 June 1932, p. 1.

91 934¼-213¾. *NY Times*, 30 June 1932, p. 15; Eaton, p. 342; Davis (New York), p. 309; Sautter & Burke, p. 172; Lorant, p. 591; Neal, p. 248.

92 "demagogy and discourtesy". Hull, p. 152.

93 "a portable radio set". Martin (*Bandwagons*), p. 319.

94 Walsh/Shouse. Rosen, p. 250.

95 626–528. Laporte, p. 134; *NY Times*, 30 June 1932, p. 1; Eaton, p. 340; Neal, p. 235. Roosevelt's own New York delegation voted for Shouse.

96 638¾-514¼. Laporte, pp. 68, 71; *NY Times*, 30 June 1932, p. 1; Williams (*Long*), p. 580; Davis (*New York*), p. 307; Neal, p. 235; Schlesinger (*Crisis*), p. 301; White (*Kingfish*), p. 167. FDR's Minnesota slate won a similar battle by a slimmer margin.

97 "Absolutely, he'll get . . . afraid of Baker." Houck & Kiewe, p. 85; Houck, p. 51; Ritchie, p. 106.

98 "My impression is . . . easily be nominated." Lippmann, pp. 303-6; Rosen, p. 251; Davis (*New York*), p. 320; Cramer, p. 249.

99 "most probable nominee." *Time*, 27 June 1932, p. 14.

100 "There is no better . . . of the Depression." Farber, p. 283. John W. Davis similarly backed Smith but, in reality, preferred Baker. (Harbaugh, p. 339) Young meanwhile had issued a Sherman-like disclaimer of a candidacy in mid-May. (Case & Case, p. 572)

101 "As a speaker . . . heavyweight boxer". *Ames Tribune-Times*, 30 June 1932, p. 1.

102 "two boys who . . . entertainment than anyone . . .". Laporte, p. 621; *NY Times*, 30 June 1932, p. 17. In actuality, the white southerners Freeman Gosden ("Amos") and Charles Correll ("Andy").

103 "I'se regusted". Laporte, p. 621; *NY Times*, 30 June 1932, p. 17.

104 "the Carpenter from . . . Palo Alto." Laporte, p. 621; *NY Times*, 30 June 1932, p. 17; Warren (*Coughlin*), pp. 42-43.

105 Murray/Smith demonstrations. *Wisconsin State Journal*, 1 July 1932, p. 12; Kramer, pp. 240-41; O'Connor (*Broun*), pp. 178-79. The Communists, never a particularly forgiving bunch, despised Broun, at one point proclaiming, "Shooting may be deserved—and we do not exclude that from possibilities—but how about taking his gin away from him and putting him to work as a stoker in a steamer carrying workers to the Bermudas [sic] for their vacations?"

106 "Country-born . . . true American manhood." *NY Times*, 1 July 1932, p. 12; MacKenzie, pp. 166-67; Stiles, p. 182; Oulahan, p. 106. In 1927, Mack had gained the tabloid spotlight as attorney for fiftyish New York real-estate millionaire Edward W. Browning in his divorce against his teenaged bride Frances Belle Heenan "Peaches" Browning. (*NY Times*, 24 February 1958, p. 19)

107 Forty-three minutes. *Wisconsin State Journal*, 1 July 1932, p. 12. Mack, a third choice for the honor (after Sen. Robert Wagner and author and the "unapologetic racist" journalist and author Claude G. Bowers), witnessed his ovation bested, however, by that for Ely for Smith (fifty-two minutes) and that for Sen. Millard Tydings for fellow Marylander Albert Ritchie (forty-five minutes)

108 *"Happy Days Are Here Again"*. Flynn (*Boss*), p. 100; Stiles, pp. 181-82; Schlesinger (*Crisis*), p. 303; Davis (*Invincible*), pp. 103-4; Davis (*New York*), p. 322; Neal, p. 253; Black (*Champion*), p. 234; Smith (*FDR*), p. 268; Oulahan, p. 108; Ritchie, p. 103; Manchester (*Glory*), p. 48. Flynn recalled that the original idea for a change was his. For her part, Louis Howe's assistant Lela Stiles claimed virtually total credit. Organist Melgard had earlier played the same tune for the Republicans. For some reason it didn't catch on.

109 Ely not running. Huthmacker, p. 239.

110 "After his defeat . . . Alfred E. Smith." *NY Times*, 1 July 1932, p. 12; MacKenzie, p. 168. As grand as Ely's encomiums were for Smith, he also managed to plunge an occasional dagger into FDR, not only for his indecisiveness, but also for his infirmity. "To win this battle [for the White House]," contended Ely, "requires a man who can take the blows both physically and mentally. . . ."

111 Smith reaction. *The Nation*, 12 October 1932, p. 329; Curley, pp. 234-35. Ingersoll also delivered James G. Blaine's 1876 "Plumed Knight" nominating speech.

112 "in conformity. . . Spanish custom". Guilfoyle, p. 166; Allison, p. 58.

113 "Alcalde Jaime Miguel Curleo". Curley, p. 355; Guilfoyle, pp. 146-47, 166; Eaton, p. 340; Huthmacker, p. 239; Allison, p. 58.

114 "You have the . . . United States". Curley, p. 237; Martin (*Bandwagons*), p. 359.

115 "I learned something . . . his radio time." Farley (*Ballots*), p. 140; Eaton, pp. 346-47.

116 4:28. Farley (*Ballots*), p. 140; Eaton, p. 347.

117 First ballot tally. Eaton, p. 348; Freidel (*Triumph*), p. 306.

118 "Three ballots . . . maybe five". Eaton, p. 346; Ritchie, p. 103; Farley (*Roosevelt*), p. 20; Oulahan, p. 96; Hardeman & Bacon, p. 140.

119 "Well, we must . . . that we are." Eaton, p. 346.

120 Unit rule states. Eaton, p. 343; Martin (*Bandwagons*), p. 356. Working the southern delegations for Baker was his assistant floor manager Wendell Willkie. (Cramer, p. 250; Ritchie, p. 106; Shlaes [*Forgotten*], p. 133)

Other unit-rule FDR delegations included Iowa, Kansas, Minnesota, the Dakotas, and Michigan. (Peel & Donnelly, pp. 73-74; Eaton, p. 354; Smith [*FDR*], p. 261; Neal, pp. 40, 41, 278; Oulahan, p. 110).

121 Mississippi/Arkansas. Smith (*FDR*), p. 271.

122 Long. Oulahan, p. 104; Williams (*Long*), p. 581.

123 Gerard. Gerard, p. 322.

124 Second ballot tally. Eaton, pp. 349-50; Freidel (*Triumph*), p. 306.

125 "He was a tough . . . warcraft and materials. . . ." *Washington Post*, 9 November 1932, p. 9.

126 "Roosevelt was . . . down and cried." Maier, p. 99; Beschloss, p. 46.

127 "Joe called . . . you." Kessler, p. 94. According to Burton K. Wheeler a factor driving Kennedy toward FDR was his antipathy to Raskob ("if that so-and-so Raskob is against Roosevelt, I'll be for him"). (Wheeler, p. 297; Whalen, p. 120)

128 $5,000. Wheeler, p. 297.

129 Mid-April. Whalen, p. 122; Nasaw (*Chief*), p. 455; Nasaw (*Patriarch*), p. 173.

130 "Do you want . . . will you be?" Goodwin (*Fitzgeralds*), p. 429; Collier & Horowitz (*Kennedys*), p. 54; Kessler, pp. 95-96; Nasaw (*Patriarch*), p. 176. An organized Baker-for-President blitz of several thousand telegrams to the convention only fueled, what now seems to us, Hearst's seemingly irrational fear of Baker. (Cramer, p. 251)

131 "Can't . . . Ritchie?" Koskoff, p. 45; Ritchie, p. 106; Neal, p. 274; Kessler, p. 96. Earlier, Hearst had ordered his highly remunerated star columnist Arthur Brisbane to negotiate with Garner on releasing his delegates to Ritchie. Garner refused. (Oulahan, p. 104)

132 Adjournment. Martin (*Bandwagons*), pp. 344-45; Eaton, p. 350; Rosen, p. 255.

133 Third ballot tally. Laporte, p. 320; Eaton, p. 351; Freidel (*Triumph*), p. 306; Martin (*Bandwagons*), p. 346; Rosen, p. 255. The full tally: Roosevelt, 682.79, Smith, 190¾, Garner, 101¼, White, 52½, Traylor, 40¼, Reed, 27½, Byrd, 24.96, Ritchie, 23½, and Baker, 8½.

134 "Sam, we'll . . . you say so". Freidel (*Triumph*), p. 310; Martin (*Bandwagons*), p. 354; Oulahan, p. 119; Neal, p. 281; Brands (*Traitor*), p. 247.

135 "If you break . . . break you!" Flynn (*Boss*), p. 101; Williams (*Long*), p. 581; Brinkley, p. 46; White (*Kingfish*), p. 167. "There is no question in my mind," recalled Ed Flynn, "that without Long's work Roosevelt might not have been nominated."

136 North Carolina. Eaton, pp. 350-51; Martin (*Bandwagons*), p. 356.

137 Richey/Mayer. Ritchie, p. 106. Mayer later lobbied Hearst to forego Roosevelt and stick with Hoover. (Marx, p. 200)

138 Farley. Martin (*Bandwagons*), p. 351.

139 Biography. *NY Times*, 3 July 1932, p. 11; Carlisle, pp. 56, 60, 63; Procter, p. 166; Swanberg (*Hearst*), p. 426; Oulahan, p. 117; Martin (*Bandwagons*), p. 290; Procter, p. 168.

140 *The Romantic Story of John N. Garner*. Brown, *passim*; *Buffalo Courier-Express*, 22 May 1932, p. 4.

141 11:00 a.m. meeting. Schlesinger (*Crisis*), p. 308; Eaton, pp. 349, 353; Swanberg (*Hearst*), p. 437; Davis (*New York*), p. 326; Neal, p. 279; Procter, p. 170. The wily Hearst had such a meeting in mind long before the convention. Normally, Brown would have been assigned to cover the convention and was confused and initially disappointed when "The Chief" ordered him to remain in Washington.

142 "Five states that . . . fourth ballot". Oulahan, p. 120; Eaton, p. 354.

143 "Boys, Roosevelt . . . you switch to Roosevelt. . . ." Eaton, p. 353; Swanberg (*Hearst*), p. 437; O'Conner (*Hurrah*), p. 260; Neal, p. 277, Ritchie, p. 107; Martin (*Bandwagons*), p. 352; Alter, p. 109.

144 California delegation. Martin (*Bandwagons*), pp. 355-56; Neal, pp. 281-85. Hopelessly deadlocked, it abdicated responsibility to a three-person committee.

145 "We had a horse . . . quarter mile post." Hardeman & Bacon, p. 142; Neal, p. 282.

146 54–51. Hardeman & Bacon, p. 142; Oulahan, p. 119; Martin (*Bandwagons*), p. 357. Some provide the total as 54–52. Davis (*New York*), p. 327. Seventy-five delegates were absent.

147 McAdoo/Hearst. Oulahan, p. 123. Later, McAdoo would suggest to Hearst that he himself be the vice-presidential candidate.

148 "Bernie, your long-legged . . . he would". Oulahan, p. 122.

149 "I have McAdoo's personal promise . . .". *New Yorker*, 16 July 1932, p. 19.

150 "We've got . . . Marion." Martin (*Bandwagons*), p. 359; Davis (*Invincible*), p. 106.

151 McAdoo en route. Eaton, p. 357; Martin (*Bandwagons*), pp. 359-60; Neal, pp. 288-89.

152 "Mr. Chairman . . . State of California." *NY Times*, 2 July 1932, p. 5.

153 "a cat . . . upon its prey." Eaton, p. 358.

154 "California came here . . . that of 1924." *NY Times*, 2 July 1932, p. 5; Eaton, p. 358.

155 "As I was . . . Roosevelt." *NY Times*, 2 July 1932, p. 5; Schlesinger (*Crisis*), pp. 309-10; Rosen, p. 265; Martin (*Bandwagons*), p. 361.

156 "If revenge . . . sugar teat." Mencken (*President*), p. 163; Sinclair, p. 385; Slayton, p. 373; Alter, p. 110. Jouett Shouse soon wrote to Newton Baker: "If McAdoo had not broken the pledges he made, Roosevelt would not have been nominated. On the fourth ballot there would have been serious defections from his ranks with the result that some other nominee would have been certain. That nominee would have been you or Ritchie." (Rosen, p. 248)

157 190½. Eaton, p. 358. The final vote: FDR, 945, Smith, 190½, Baker, 5½, Ritchie, 3½, George White, 3, and James M. Cox, 1.

158 "I won't . . . do it". Slayton, p. 373; O'Connor (*Hurrah*), pp. 262-63.

159 Brokaw. Lewis (*Swope*), p. 197.

160 Ely. Hague, Curry. Tugwell (*Brains*), p. 254; Slayton, p. 373; Finan, p. 285.

161 Davis. *NY Times*, 3 July 1932, p. 9. FDR had not exactly broken *all* tradition in addressing the Chicago convention. Davis, in 1924, had delivered an eight-minute address at Madison Square Garden following his own nomination, but that, however, was not his formal acceptance, delivering that on August 11 in Clarksburg, West Virginia. (*NY Times*, 10 July 1924, p. 1; *NY Times*, 12 August 1924, pp. 1, 3; Tucker (*Tide*), pp. 98, 183-85)

162 "I have absolutely . . . get a rest." Roosevelt (*Letters*), p. 1000; Finan, p. 453; Slayton, p. 373.

163 Radio. Suckley.

164 Eleanor. *Time*, 11 July 1932, p. 10; Hickok (*Road*), p. 189.

165 Masseur. *NY Times*, 6 December 1936, p. N3; *Spartanburg Herald*, 18 December 1936, p. 8.

166 Passengers. *NY Times*, 2 July 1932, p. 1; *NY Times*, 3 July 1932, p. 9; Tully, p. 52; Cook (*Vol. 1*), pp. 446-47; Freidel (*Triumph*), p. 313; Smith (*FDR*), p. 276; Louchheim, p. 10. FDR's children James and Anna were already in Chicago.

167 Details of trip. *NY Times*, 3 July 1932, p. 9; *Time*, 11 June 1932, p. 11. A silent YouTube video posted by the FDR Library shows Roosevelt boarding this plane—and then inexplicably upon the rear platform of a train. This is what I believe is known in the film trade as a "continuity problem." (www.youtube.com/watch?v=SlaeMgrH7u8)

168 Baker. *NY Times*, 3 July 1932, p. 10; Neal, pp. 301-2.

169 John Roosevelt. Oulahan, p. 232; Neal, p. 306; Miller (*F.D.R.*), p. 277.

170 Procession. *NY Times*, 3 July 1932, p. 9; Suckley. All, however, was not entirely forgiven. Rexford Tugwell recalled that "hoodlums on the curb shouted epithets" at Roosevelt's motorcade. (Tugwell [*Brains*], p. 262)

171 Western progressives. Freidel (*Triumph*), p. 313; Oulahan, p. 132; Martin (*Bandwagons*), p. 363; Neal, pp. 302-33. Dern defeated incumbent Charles R. Mabey for governor in 1924 on the slogan, "We want a Dern good governor, and we don't mean Mabey."

172 Baruch. Eaton, p. 359.

173 Tinley. *NY Times*, 8 June 1932, p. 8; *NY Times*, 3 July 1932, p. 1; Freidel (*Triumph*), p. 313; Oulahan, p. 132; Martin (*Bandwagons*), p. 364.

174 Jig. *NY Times*, 3 July 1932, p. 9.

175 "Naturally, I have . . . world to Hooverism." Guilfoyle, p. 167; Allison, p. 58.

176 Straus/Baruch. Moley (*Seven*), pp. 31-32; Schlesinger (*Crisis*), p. 404; Morgan, p. 355.

177 "Dammit, Louis . . . the nominee!" Rollins, p. 347; Miller (*F.D.R.*), p. 278.

178 First page added. Moley (*Seven*), p. 33; Tugwell (*Brains*), pp. 258-60; Schlesinger (*Crisis*), p. 404; Schlesinger (*Ghosts*), p. 9.

179 "My friends. . . its own people." Rosenman (*Papers*), pp. 647-59; Eaton, p. 359. The phrase was hardly original. Walter Lippman's Harvard classmate Stuart Chase most famously employed it as the title of his August 1932 work (*A New Deal*) and a similarly titled four-part *New Republic* series, commencing that June 29. In it Chase asked "Why should the Russians have all the fun of remaking a work?" (Chase, *passim;* Schlesinger [*Crisis*], pp. 202, 532; Manchester [*Glory*], p. 57; Alter, p. 117) In April 1932, Norman Thomas published an article in *Scribner's* entitled: "Wanted—A New Political Deal" (*Scribner's*, April 1932, p. 216). *Vanity Fair* proclaimed that the ephemeral "New American Party" would be "A new party for a new deal." Youthful journalist John Franklin Carter got the byline; Clare Boothe Brokaw may have concocted the phrase. (Morris [*Luce*], p. 195; Shadegg, p. 64) Raymond Moley used the phrase in a memo to FDR in May. (Alter, p. 117) And, though *no one* seemed to have noticed, Alabama Rep. John McDuffie's nomination of Garner featured this sentence: "There is a demand for a new deal in the management of the affairs of the American people." Perhaps, FDR simply delivered the phrase a little better. (*NY Times*, 3 July 1932, p. 9; Freidel [*Triumph*], p. 315)

180 "Yes, Hugh . . . our son of a bitch now." Shadegg, p. 68.

181 "fine and . . . exhilarating". *NY Times*, 5 July 1932, pp. 1, 4.

182 Lemke. Bennett (*Demagogues*), pp. 92-93.

183 Frazier. *Ames Tribune-Times*, 5 October 1932, p. 2; *Salt Lake Tribune*, 6 October 1932, p. 2; "Unofficial Observer," p. 146.

184   Norris. *NY Times*, 3 July 1932, p. 11.
185   "smiled more . . . in months. . . ." Houck & Kiewe, p. 85.

Chapter Fifteen: "Anti-Semitism may be a good starter . . ."

1   "See, this is . . . during the battle." Tuchman, p. 365.
2   Abdication. Wheeler-Bennett (*Nemesis*), p. 3; Ludwig (*Hindenburg*), pp. 188-91; Eyck, pp. 146-47; Watt, p. 474; Wistrich, p. 108.
3   "creeper". Lüdecke, p. 364; Delmer (*Trail*), p. 120; Wheeler-Bennett (*Nemesis*), p. 184*fn*, 244; Payne, p. 255.
4   "intriguer" "sneak". Shirer, p. 150.
5   "indeed, the evil genius . . . rather than position." Wheeler-Bennett (*Nemesis*), p. 182.
6   Hammerstein-Equord. Shirer, p. 151.
7   Lazy. Koeves, p. 97.
8   Oskar Hindenburg. Heiden (*History*), p. 164; Heiden (*Fuehrer*), p. 408; Olden, p. 252; Lüdecke, p. 353; Knight-Patterson, p. 393; Papen, p. 124; Ludwig (*Hindenburg*), p. 279; Eyck, p. 273; Davidson, p. 319; Snyder (*Encyclopedia*), p. 310; Payne, p. 255; Wistrich, p. 273: Dorpalen, p. 302; Burleigh, p. 139; Mommsen, p. 441.
9   Papen. Papen, p. 124; Heiden (*Fuehrer*), p. 421; Rolfs, pp. 80, 138.
10   "adopted son". Wheeler-Bennett (*Nemesis*), p. 197; Heiden (*Fuehrer*), p. 408; Shirer, p. 162*fn*; Fest (*Hitler*), p. 335.
11   Black Reichswehr. Knight-Patterson, p. 322; Wheeler-Bennett (*Nemesis*), p. 184; Shirer, p. 150; Wistrich, p. 273.
12   Freikorps. Heiden (*Fuehrer*), p. 243; Shirer, p. 150; Snyder (*Encyclopedia*), p. 310; Wistrich, p. 273.
13   Soviets. Delmer (*Trail*), p. 120; Delmer (*Weimar*), p. 70; Shirer, p. 150; Craig (*Germany*), p. 535; Wistrich, p. 273; Davidson, p. 319.
14   Seeckt. Heiden (*Fuehrer*), p. 408; Papen, pp. 121-22; Knight-Patterson, pp. 390-91; Eyck, pp. 88-90; Ludwig (*Hindenburg*), pp. 278-79; Wheeler-Bennett (*Nemesis*), p. 183; Wistrich, p. 232; Rolfs, p. 98.
15   *Ministeramt*. Heiden (*Fuehrer*), p. 408; Wheeler-Bennett (*Nemesis*), p. 198; François-Poncet, p. 26; Wistrich, p. 224; Rolfs, p. 79.
16   "cardinal in politics". Wheeler-Bennett (*Nemesis*), pp. 199, 283; Davidson, p. 283; Shirer, p. 151; Craig (*Germany*), p. 535; Rolfs, p. 77.
17   "one of the few . . . irresistible charm." Fromm, p. 51. François-Poncet found him "a kindly, placid, blue-eyed giant of a man" but added he "was feared rather than liked. . . ." (François-Poncet, pp. 25, 28)
18   "How soldierly . . . (family included)." Olden, p. 248.
19   "The red cloak . . . with our enemies!" Ludwig (*Hindenburg*), p. 279.
20   "depraved and weak, faithless . . . soft sensuality of his aspect." Ludwig (*Hindenburg*), p. 279.
21   "abnormally inclined." Machtan, p. 209.
22   "Slim and elegant . . . sincere". Fromm, p. 52.
23   Cousin. Ludwig (*Hindenburg*), p. 279.
24   "a lady of . . . responsibilities of power." Papen, p. 249.
25   "It is extraordinary . . . everything done!" Ludwig (*Hindenburg*), p. 300.
26   "That is a real man!" Krebs, p. 25.
27   "the discovery . . . really great man." Craig (*Germany*), p. 537.
28   "Where Brüning may . . . too big for him." Clark (*German Republic*), p. 364.
29   "Sympathetic impression; decent. . . now and then." Eyck, p. 339; Fest (*Hitler*), p. 302; Reuth, p. 145.
30   "An interesting young man . . . on the ground." Toland, pp. 259-60.

31 "Republic or monarchy . . . republic look like." Turner (*Thirty*), p. 20.

32 SA membership. *Living Age*, March 1932, p. 24; *NY Times*, 10 July 1932, p. 13; Mommsen, p. 416; Kessler, p. 413; Olden, p. 254; Fest (*Hitler*), p. 335; Bullock, p. 218; Mitchell (*Hitler*), p. 146; Hauner, p. 81; Nicholls, p. 132; Mosley, p. 134; Taylor, p. 102; Ascher, p. 22*fn*.

33 "[E]verything points . . . may be expected." Knight-Patterson, p. 520.

34 "I am really . . . to invent them." Eyck, p. 368; Wheeler-Bennett (*Nemesis*), p. 235; Johnson (*Modern*), p. 282.

35 SA ban. Wheeler-Bennett (*Nemesis*), p. 240; Dorpalen, pp. 303-4; Koeves, p. 118; Wheaton, p. 122. "Schleicher," wrote Hindenburg biographer Andreas Dorpalen, "seemed to be driven by frenzied anxieties; Groener had the impression that he was close to a nervous collapse and that at times he was almost out of his mind."

36 Schleicher-Röhm. Wheeler-Bennett (*Nemesis*), p. 227.

37 October meetings. Fest (*Hitler*), p. 302; Manvell & Fraenkel (*Hundred*), pp. 23-24; Hauner, p. 74.

38 "I suppose . . . free drink." Fest (*Hitler*), p. 302.

39 Meissner. Olden, p. 252; Manvell & Fraenkel (*Hundred*), p. 24; Manvell & Fraenkel (*Goering*), p. 76; Bullock, p. 187. Hitler remained grief-stricken following Geli Raubal's suicide. Göring—on Hitler's command—very reluctantly abandoned his beloved wife Carin's deathbed to attend this meeting with Hindenburg.

40 "This corporal . . . from behind. . . ." Hauner, p. 74; Fest (*Hitler*), p. 302.

41 "In Schleicher's view . . . of his party." Bullock, pp. 190-91.

42 January 1932 conference. Shirer, p. 154; Bullock, p. 192; Wheeler-Bennett (*Titan*), p. 361.

43 Intransigence. Shirer, p. 154; Bullock, p. 192; Wheeler-Bennett (*Titan*), p. 361.

44 "[T]he Presidency is . . . intelligence and skill." Goebbels (*Part*), pp. 16-17; Shirer, p. 155; Hauner, p. 76; Fest (*Hitler*), p. 315; Manvell & Fraenkel (*Hundred*), p. 27; Toland, p. 260; Kershaw (*Hubris*), p. 361.

45 "merely little children . . . by the hand." Toland, p. 265; Dorpalen, p. 311.

46 "The Leader has . . . lost its head." Goebbels (*Part*), p. 18.

47 "To put the thing . . . followed by Brüning. . . ." Goebbels (*Part*), p. 37; Shirer, p. 161.

48 "precautionary measures". Wheeler-Bennett (*Nemesis*), p. 239.

49 "Grandma is dead". Koeves, p. 117; Olden, p. 253; Heiden (*History*), p. 172; Fest (*Hitler*), p. 334.

50 Prussia. *NY Times*, 6 April 1932, pp. 1, 11; Heiden (*History*), p. 172; Knight-Patterson, pp. 519-20; François-Poncet, p. 21; Eyck, p. 363; Lüdecke, p. 363; Hauner, p. 78; Koeves, pp. 116-17; Burke, p. 200.

51 Bavaria. Eyck, p. 364.

52 April SA ban. *NY Times*, 14 April 1932, pp. 1, 3; *Plattsburgh Press*, 14 April 1932, p. 1; Heiden (*History*), pp. 172-73; Kessler, p. 413; Wheeler-Bennett (*Nemesis*), pp. 240-41; Shirer, p. 160; Papen, p. 148; Eyck, pp. 362-63; Dorpalen, pp. 303-6; Singer, p. 129.

53 "For years . . . a thousandfold force." Domarus, p. 132; Knight-Patterson, p. 520; US Department of State, pp. 292-93.

54 "There is reason . . . a coalition government. . . ." US Department of State, p. 293.

55 "I find it . . . valuable training there." Eyck, p. 372; Fest (*Hitler*), p. 335; Mommsen, p. 420; Jonas, p. 178.

56 Breslau. Dorpalen, p. 306.

57 "allowed themselves with . . . almost suspicious." Kessler, pp. 412, 414.

58 "Organizationally the S.A. . . . a grave injustice." Dorpalen, p. 306.

59 "I have issued . . . the same treatment. . . ." *NY Times*, 17 April 1932, p. 5; Heiden (*History*), p. 179; Knight-Patterson, p. 528; Eyck, p. 369; Koeves, p. 121; Papen, p. 148. Similar indeed—at least, sartorially. Glance quickly at a photo of saluting Reichsbanner men and one might easily think one is looking at brown-belted, brown-shirted Hitlerites. Only the caps and the arc of salute are divergent. (Taylor, p. 116)

60 "Nurmi". Fischer, pp. 180-81; Lüdecke, p. 364; Shirer, p. 161; Fest (*Hitler*), p. 335; Koeves, p. 121; Mitchell, p. 148.

61   Goebbels. *Iowa City Iowan*, 12 January 1932, p. 8; Manvell & Fraenkel (*Goebbels*), pp. 109, 158; Reuth, p. 140.

62   "But you were . . . your own leadership!" Olden, p. 254.

63   Diabetes. Shirer, p. 162; Davidson, p. 309.

64   Boil. Davidson, p. 309.

65   "Such an exhibition . . . his speech broadcasted." Goebbels (*Part*), p. 90; Mitchell (*Hitler*), p. 148; Reuth, p. 147.

66   "no longer enjoyed . . . must resign." Shirer, p. 162; Dorpalen, p. 314; Watt, p. 527.

67   Mosley. Sidelsky, pp. 285-86; Charmley, pp. 265-66.

68   Chaplin. Soames, p. 354; Ahamed, p. 432.

69   Cab accident. *NY Post*, 14 December 1931, p. 1; *NY Post*, 21 December 1931, p. 3; *NY Sun*, 21 December 1931, p. 1; *Binghamton (NY) Sunday Press*, 13 December 1964, p. 9-A; Pilpel, pp. 100-102; Gilbert (*America*), pp. 131-32; Gilbert (*Wilderness*), p. 41; Soames, p. 357. The bulky fur coat he wore may have saved his life—or, at a minimum, prevented graver injuries.

70   "recover from . . . blows". Gilbert (*Wilderness*), p. 43. William Manchester contends that Bernard Baruch rescued Churchill from even worse losses. "Baruch," claimed Manchester, "had left instructions to buy every time Churchill sold and sell whenever Churchill bought. Winston had come out exactly even because, he later learned, Baruch even paid the commissions." (Manchester [*Lion*], p. 14; Cook [*Vol. 2*], p. 318)

71   Brooklyn Institute of Arts. *New York Sun*, 21 January 1932, p. 10; *Brooklyn Eagle*, 29 January 1932, p. 3; *Brooklyn Standard-Union*, 29 January 1932, p. 4.

72   "My mother . . . very busy." Conradi, p. 94. Winston, conversely, recalled the hotel as the Regina Palace; this would, of course, not be the final divergence of opinion separating Churchill and the Nazis.

73   "Herr Hitler . . . Hotel Continental tonight." Hanfstaengl, p. 193. Note how Hanfstaengl addresses Hitler as "Herr Hitler" and not "Mein Führer." Such *lèse majesté* (shared by Strasser and Röhm) played less and less well with Hitler as time progressed. All paid a price for it.

74   "Theirs is a . . . can never end". Somin, p. 49.

75   "But, Herr Hitler. . . meet him. . . ." Hanfstaengl, p. 194.

76   "Herr Hitler . . . stay to coffee." Hanfstaengl, p. 194; Conradi, p. 94.

77   "In any case . . . rabid Francophile". Hanfstaengl, p. 194; Gilbert (*Wilderness*), p. 50; Gilbert (*Winston Churchill, Vol. 5*), pp. 447-48.

78   Lindemann. Hanfstaengl, p. 194. Gilbert (*Winston Churchill, Vol. 5*), pp. 447-48. Lindemann had his revenge for the snub, overseeing the carpet bombing of Germany during the coming war. Camrose also published the *Manchester Evening Chronicle* and the *Daily Telegraph*.

79   "gave a most . . . under a spell." Gilbert (*Churchill*), p. 447.

80   "Tell your boss . . . a bad sticker." Hanfstaengl, p. 194; Gilbert (*Wilderness*), p. 50; Conradi, p. 95.

81   "Tell me . . . club at once." Hanfstaengl, p. 195; Conradi, p. 95.

82   "Herr, Hitler . . . a deliberate insult." Hanfstaengl, pp. 195-96; Conradi, p. 95.

83   "I implore you . . . to seeing you." Conradi, p. 94.

84   "I have too . . . in the morning." Hanfstaengl, p. 196.

85   "In any case . . . about you." Hanfstaengl, p. 196; Gilbert (*Winston Churchill, Vol. 5*), p. 448. Hitler's plans for an Anglo-German alliance differed greatly from Churchill's. At his first meeting with Brüning, he had outlined a German-British-Italian pact aligned against France. (Olden, p. 251) He said the same to British newsman Sefton Delmer. (Delmer [*Trail*], p. 115) In any case, he truly loathed Churchill, terming him in February 1942, "the very type of corrupt journalist. There's not a worse prostitute in politics. . . . an utterly amoral, repulsive creature." (Hitler [*Table Talk*], p. 318)

CHAPTER SIXTEEN: "SOUP IS CHEAPER THAN TEAR BOMBS"

1   Cox's broadcasts. *Western Pennsylvania Historical Magazine*, July 1972, p. 234. Such hostility toward chain stores was not unique to Fr. Cox. Article 16 of the Program of the Nazi Party demanded

"the immediate communalization of the large department stores, which are to be leased at low rates to small tradesmen. We demand the most careful consideration for the owners of small businesses in orders placed by national, state, or community authorities." (Lane & Rupp, p. 42; Heiden [*History*], p. 16)

2   Twenty thousand. *NY Times*, 6 January 1932, p. 3; *Western Pennsylvania Historical Magazine*, July 1972, p. 220; Shlaes (*Forgotten*), p. 124. The *New York Times* had no use for "freakish characters" such as Fr. Cox. "Hoover has set his face like flint against all such raids upon the Treasury at Washington. This does not indicate a hard heart, but a hard and cool head. Americans may as well make up their minds if they have no Great Father at Washington to relieve them of all their distresses. That work they must do themselves and in the places where they live." (*NY Times*, 19 January 1932, p. 20)

3 $5 billion. *Kansas City Star*, 7 January 1932, p. 2; *Oakland Tribune*, 7 January 1932, p. 14; Procter, pp. 164-65.

4   Twelve thousand. Smith (*Dream*), p. 69.

5   Hoover. *NY Times*, 8 January 1932, p. 3; *Western Pennsylvania Historical Magazine*, July 1972, pp. 222-23; Dickson & Allen, pp. 49-50; Smith (*Dream*), p. 69.

6   "They really went . . . everything was splendid." *NY Times*, 8 January 1932, p. 3; *Western Pennsylvania Historical Magazine*, July 1972, p. 223.

7   "The United States . . . The Andrew Mellons." Smith (*Dream*), p. 69.

8   Free gas. *NY Times*, 9 January 1932, p. 9; *Western Pennsylvania Historical Magazine*, July 1972, p. 224; Whisenhunt, p. 52.

9   "You have every . . . hungry and cold." *NY Times*, 19 January 1932, p. 20.

10   Cleveland. *NY Times*, 12 February 1930, p. 4; Laurie & Cole, p. 370.

11   Philadelphia. *NY Times*, 15 February 1930, p. 8; *Saturday Evening Post*, 10 September 1932, p. 16; Laurie & Cole, p. 370.

12   Chicago. *NY Times*, 22 February 1930, p. 8; *Saturday Evening Post*, 10 September 1932, p. 16; Laurie & Cole, p. 370.

13   "International Unemployment Day". Greenberg, p. 66.

14   Boston. *Amsterdam Recorder*, 8 March 1930, p. 11.

15   Union Square. *Brooklyn Eagle*, 14 March 1930, p. 2; *Brooklyn Weekly People*, 22 March 1930, p. 4; *Saturday Evening Post*, 10 September 1932, p. 16; Whalen, pp. 154-57; Thomas & Blanshard, p. 339; Walsh, p. 212.

16   NYC City Hall. *NY Times*, 21 January 1931, p. 20; *Buffalo Courier-Express*, 21 January 1931, p. 2; *Medina Journal*, 21 January 1931, p. 1.

17   Newark. *NY Times*, 8 January 1931, p. 20.

18   Hunger March. Douglas (*Veterans*), p. 23; Daniels, pp. 67-68; Dickson & Allen, p. 45; Barber (*Marching*), p. 81; Laurie & Cole, p. 370; Gott, pp. 4-5; Lohbeck, pp. 103-4.

19   River Rouge. *Workers Age*, 19 March 1932, pp. 1, 4; *Baltimore Afro-American*, 12 March 1932, p. 20; Gitlow, pp. 224-25; Dickson & Allen, pp. 52-53; Laurie & Cole, p. 370; Schlesinger (*Crisis*), p. 256.

20   Chicago rioting. *Oakland Tribune*, 7 May 1932, page unknown; *Saturday Evening Post*, 10 September 1932, p. 14; Gitlow, p. 226.

21   Foster-Ford ticket. Anonymous (*Foster-Ford*), pp. 3-24; Peel & Donnelly, pp. 203-4; Lazicì, pp. 121-22.

22   "concretize the demands". *Communist*, March 1932, p. 221.

23   "semi-proletarian . . . petty-bourgeois elements". *Communist*, March 1932, p. 213.

24   "It was a . . . centrism and 'left' sectarianism." *Communist*, March 1932, p. 433.

25   "Bill Kincaid." Waters, p. 5. Waters's career bore a superficial similarity to Hitler's: both being non-commissioned officers in the war in non-combat roles (Waters was a medic); at some point in their careers both were essentially drifters who then magically appeared before already-existing (but quite tiny) local movements and almost instantly took them over. Mercifully, the similarities end there.

26   Hazen. Daniels, p. 76.

27   50 percent. Dickson & Allen, pp. 37-38; Wilson (*Progressive*), p. 161; Kull & Kull, p. 248; Barone, p. 48; Gott, p. 2.

28   2.5 million. Barber (*Marching*), p. 78.

29   La Guardia. Daniels, p. 117; Dickson & Allen, p. 59; Barber (*Marching*), p. 78.

30   Hoover. *NY Times*, 1 January 1933, p. 20.

31 $2.4 billion/$1 billion. *Literary Digest*, 23 April 1932, pp. 5-6; Liebovich, p. 160; Rich, p. 168; Gott, p. 9.

32   American Legion. Joslin, pp. 121-24; Daniels, p. 42; Liebovich, p. 160; Archer, p. 13. In 1931, Hoover lobbied hard to secure Legion opposition.

33   Patman. *Literary Digest*, 23 April 1932, p. 5; Daniels, p. 54; Barber (*Marching*), p. 78; Miller (*Ike*), p. 262.

34   VFW. *Literary Digest*, 23 April 1932, p. 6; Daniels, p. 52; Dickson & Allen, p. 59. The VFW, however, later banned members from Bonus March participation. (*NY Times*, 9 June 1932, p. 19)

35   Coughlin. Dickson & Allen, p. 59; Daniels, p. 62l; Carpenter, p. 35; Tull, pp. 12-13.

36   Union Pacific. Waters, pp. 21-25; Smith (*Dream*), pp. 131-32; Barber (*Marching*), p. 77.

37   Wabash line. Waters, pp. 34-38; Douglas (*Veterans*), p. 29; Smith (*Dream*), pp. 133-34; Daniels, p. 79; Dickson & Allen, p. 65. At Council Bluffs they also received the key to the city.

38   Chattanooga/Philadelphia. *NY Post*, 29 July 1932, p. 3; *Niagara Falls Gazette*, 29 July 1932, p. 17; Bernstein (*Lean*), p. 441; Daniels, p. 80.

39   East St. Louis. *Political Science Quarterly*, September 1972, pp. 370-71; Waters, pp. 39-56; Douglas (*Veterans*), pp. 29-34; Bernstein (*Lean*), p. 441; Smith (*Dream*), p. 134; Daniels, pp. 80-81; Dickson & Allen, pp. 65-73; Gott, pp. 3-4.

40   "The minute you . . . out you go." *Washington Post*, 30 May 1932, p. 1; Dickson & Allen, p. 82; Barber (*Marching*), p. 80.

41   Glassford appointment. *NY Times*, 10 August 1959, p. 27; Dickson & Allen, pp. 43-44.

42   "We must rid . . . Washington lately". *Washington Post*, 26 May 1932, p. 18.

43   Forty-eight hours. *Washington Post*, 26 May 1932, p. 1.

44   Glassford/Patman/Watson/Rainey. Dickson & Allen, p. 76; Gott, p. 5.

45   "the elimination of radicals." Dickson & Allen, p. 85.

46   June 8 march. Douglas (*Veterans*), pp. 179-80; Gitlow, p. 226; HUAC, pp. 1928-30.

47   Levin. Dickson & Allen, pp. 93-94; Liebovich, p. 160; Lisio (*Protest*), pp. 92, 94. "The spontaneous outburst of the bonus march created a crisis in the central committee of the Communist Party," testified Communist Party central committee member Joseph Zack Kornfeder, "because the party, although working for the creation of such a movement, had . . . missed the boat in getting it started; so it started by itself and the problem then arose as to what could be done to get hold of this runaway movement and catch up with it." (HUAC, p. 1928; Lohbeck, pp. 104-5) Levin is sometimes known as "Levine."

48   Detroit. HUAC, p. 1932; Dickson & Allen, p. 91.

49   "weasel". Dickson & Allen, p. 82.

50   "gorillas . . . the party." Lisio (*Protest*), pp. 94-95.

51   an organization . . . street fighting." Lisio (*Protest*), p. 95. The figure of 100 is more significant than one might think. Pace later estimated there were only a hundred actual party members within the entire march. (HUAC, p. 1944) Glassford had placed the number at forty-five. (Gott, p. 5)

52   "My chief problem . . . out of Washington." Waters, p. 94; Liebovich, p. 160.

53   "Bonus Expeditionary Force." Barber (*Marching*), p. 83.

54   Secretary-treasurer. Bernstein (*Lean*), p. 443; Douglas (*Veterans*), p. 52; Smith (*Dream*), p. 137; Barber (*Marching*), p. 83. Said John T. Pace: "We were quite disturbed by the fact that the men began to think quite a bit of General Glassford, which didn't do our cause any too much good. And we found it rather difficult to carry on a smear campaign against a man who was giving them everything they asked for." (HUAC, p. 1937)

55   Coughlin. *Chicago Tribune*, 11 June 1932, p. 11; *Time*, 20 June 1932, p. 11; Douglas (*Veterans*), pp. 116-17; Bernstein (*Lean*), p. 445; Dille, p. 31; Daniels, p. 104; Marcus, p. 40; Carpenter, p. 35; Tull,

p. 13; Dickson & Allen, p. 106. Coughlin urged those benefitting from his largesse to "keep clear of all communistic leaders and all communistic suggestions."

56 McLean. *NY Times*, 15 July 1932, p. 2; Dille, p. 33; Daniels, p. 104; Dickson & Allen, pp. 98-99.

57 Patterson. Bernstein (*Lean*), p. 445.

58 Boxing card. *Washington Post*, 6 June 1932, p. 9; Daniels, p. 104; Dickson & Allen, pp. 102-4, 114. All was not altruism. "The Old Fox" Griffith kept the concession money.

59 Roosevelt. *Chicago Tribune*, 11 June 1932, p. 11; MacArthur, pp. 93-94.

60 Cots/food. Lisio (*Protest*), p. 59; Liebovich, p. 159; Dickson & Allen, p. 314; Gott, pp. 5, 13.

61 Fort Hunt. Lisio (*Protest*), pp. 80-81, 154; Liebovich, p. 159.

62 "I am a bolshevik of the American type". *Marion Star*, 23 February 1931, p. 6.

63 "I am not . . . the government." Dickson & Allen, p. 91. A famous photo of Bonus Marchers taken in Cleveland shows them astride a locomotive, all with raised-fist salutes. If they are not Communists, they are providing wonderful impersonations. (Dickson & Allen, p. 92)

64 Pennsylvania Railroad roadhouse. *Washington Post*, 4 June 1932, p. 1; *NY Post*, 29 July 1932, p. 3; *Niagara Falls Gazette*, 29 July 1932, p. 17; Dille, pp. 29-30; HUAC, pp. 1934-35; Lisio (*Protest*), pp. 96-97; Rich, p. 168.

65 "which made us very gleeful." HUAC, p. 1935; Dickson & Allen, p. 315.

66 Eleven thousand. *Political Science Quarterly*, September 1972, p. 372; Joslin, p. 263.

67 Twenty-two thousand. Dickson & Allen, p. 322. Specifically 22,574 persons, including women and children.

68 "Stay til 1945". Daniels, p. 111.

69 "Nearly all . . . prospective employers." *NY Times*, 9 June 1932, p. 19; Bernstein (*Lean*), pp. 339-40; Daniels, pp. 75-76; Rich, p. 168.

70 209–176. *NY Times*, 1 January 1933, p. 20; *Time*, 20 June 1932, p. 11; Hart (*1932*), p. 17; Daniels, p. 117; Liebovich, p. 162; Barber (*Marching*), p. 89. The vote was 153 Democrats, 55 Republicans, and 1 Farmer-Labor in favor; 126 Republicans, 50 Democrats against. Tennessee Rep. Edward Everett Eslick ("We hear nothing but dollars here. I want to go from the sordid side . . .") dropped dead on the House floor while advocating the bonus bill. His wife, seated in the gallery above, fainted. (*Washington Post*, 15 July 1932, pp. 1-2; *Pittsburgh Post-Gazette*, 15 June 1932, p. 1; *Iowa City Iowan*, 15 June 1932, p. 1; *NY Times*, 15 June 1932, p. 2; *Time*, 27 June 1932, p. 15; Douglas [*Veterans*], p. 148; Daniels, pp. 116-17)

71 Polling. Joslin, p. 265.

72 "the descent of . . . browbeating Congress." *Washington Post*, 5 June 1932, page unknown; Barber (*Marching*), p. 87.

73 "I will not . . . their physical presence". *Washington Post*, 5 June 1932, p. 1; Douglas (*Veterans*), p. 97; Barber (*Marching*), p. 86.

74 14–2. *NY Times*, 17 June 1932, p. 1.

75 62–28. *NY Times*, 18 June 1932, p. 1; *Iowa City Iowan*, 18 June 1932, p. 1; Joslin, p. 265; Daniels, p. 121; Liebovich, p. 162; Barber (*Marching*), p. 89. Eighteen Democrats, nine Republicans and one Farmer-Labor, Hendrik Shipstead, voted for. The more prominent GOP progressives (Borah, La Follette, Norris, and Johnson) all voted no; Huey Long, absent, was paired for.

76 "America." *NY Times*, 17 July 1932, p. 16; *Woodland Democrat*, 27 July 1932, p. 6; Waters, p. 152; Allen (*Yesterday*), p. 67; Dickson & Allen, p. 149; Barber (*Marching*), p. 90; Miller (*Ike*), p. 263.

77 "Camp Camden". Dickson & Allen, p. 96; Bartlett [*Bonus*], p. 123; Ritchie, p. 118.

78 Drawbridge. Barber (*Marching*), p. 89.

79 "No men across the river". Lisio (*Protest*), p. 118.

80 "I know where there are warehouses . . . let them help themselves." *Time*, 11 July 1932, p. 12.

81 "Central Rank and File Committee". Douglas (*Veterans*), p. 176.

82 Camp Bartlett. *NY Times*, 13 June 1932, p. 3; Bartlett [*Bonus*], p. 58; Daniels, p. 124; Dickson & Allen, pp. 161-62.

83 13th Street. HUAC, pp. 1936-37; Lisio (*Protest*), p. 119; Bartlett [*Bonus*], p. 85; Lohbeck, p. 107.

84   Other camps. *Political Science Quarterly*, September 1972, pp. 371-72; Smith (*Dream*), p. 136; Barber (*Marching*), p. 91; Rich, p. 169.

85   "fight for . . . at the polls". *Plattsburgh Press*, 24 June 1932, p. 4.

86   Massachusetts. *Iowa City Iowan*, 19 June 1932, p. 1.

87   "those who . . . true Americans". *Washington Post*, 9 June 1932, p. 6; Barber (*Marching*), p. 87.

88   Expenses authorized. *NY Times*, 9 July 1932, p. 2; *Plattsburgh Press*, 22 July 1932, p. 1; *NY Times*, 1 January 1933, p. 20; Laurie & Cole, p. 373; Rich, p. 168; Miller (*Ike*), p. 263.

89   5,500. Joslin, p. 265; Hoover (*Depression*), pp. 226, 228.

90   "When Mr. Hoover . . . of my sight.'" *New Republic*, 10 August 1932, p. 323. The *New Republic* opposed the bonus "as class legislation, extorted under threat of reprisals . . . We deplore the demagoguery which brought some of them to Washington and kept many of them there. . . ."

91   Violence. Lisio, p. 123.

92   Syracuse. *Plattsburgh Press*, 24 June 1932, p. 4.

93   Union of the Unemployed. *NY Times*, 6 July 1932, p. 2.

94   "The Bonus revolutionary . . . consequence of the crisis." Gitlow, p. 229.

95   "BONUS SEEKERS MAY . . . REFUSES TO LEAVE. *Washington Post*, 19 June 1932, p. 1.

96   Foulkrod. *NY Times*, 6 July 1932, p. 2; Dickson & Allen, pp. 140-41.

97   "a political parasite . . . contemptible cur." *NY Times*, 6 July 1932, p. 2; Dickson & Allen, p. 140. That April, Philadelphia authorities arrested Foulkrod for unlawful assembly and inciting to riot. (Dickson & Allen, p. 86)

98   "marchers could easily . . . serious trouble resulting." Dickson & Allen, pp. 141, 320.

99   Bundell. Dickson & Allen, p. 142; Smith (*Eisenhower*), p. 109*fn*.

100   Pace. HUAC, p. 1943. The *New Republic* reported: "Hadn't a detachment of Marines . . . thrown down its arms and refused to march against them?" (Congdon, p. 119)

101   "too many assassins around." Liebovich, p. 159; Ritchie, p. 118.

102   Munitions Building. Joslin, pp. 264-65.

103   Departed LA. Daniels, p. 85.

104   Films. Dickson & Allen, p. 145.

105   Hammock. Daniels, p. 85; Sonnichsen, p. 244.

106   Watermelon/aircraft. Smith (*Dream*), p. 144.

107   Tucson. Sonnichsen, p. 244.

108   Arrival. Dickson & Allen, p. 145; Liebovich, p. 166.

109   450/five thousand marchers. *NY Times*, 17 July 1932, p. 16.

110   Circled Capitol. *NY Times*, 13 July 1932, p. 2; *Washington Post*, 14 July 1932, p. 1; *NY Times*, 15 July 1932, p. 2.

111   Drum-and-bugle. *Denton Record-Chronicle*, 24 June 1932, p. 1.

112   "The Death March". *NY Times*, 17 July 1932, p. 16; Douglas (*Veterans*), pp. 195-97; Bernstein (*Lean*), p. 449; Gott, p. 9.

113   Adjournment. *NY Times*, 1 January 1933, p. 20; Dickson & Allen, p. 150; Barber (*Marching*), p. 95.

114   Waters arrested. *Christian Science Monitor*, 16 July 1932, p. 1; *NY Times*, 17 July 1932, p. 16; *Waterloo Courier*, 17 July 1932, p. 1; Waters, pp. 169-70; Dickson & Allen, p. 149; Gott, p. 10; Barber (*Marching*), p. 95.

115   Hoover visit. Waters, p. 171; Dickson & Allen, p. 150; Gott, p. 10.

116   Communist pickets. *Washington Post*, 17 July 1920, p. 1; Lisio (*Triumph*), p. 140; Dickson & Allen, p. 150; Barber (*Marching*), pp. 95, 97.

117   Boone. Dickson & Allen, p. 150.

118   "Those men know . . . to swagger with." *NY Sun*, 23 July 1932, p. 3.

119   "Inevitably, such an . . . essentially American." Lisio (*Protest*), p. 122; Dickson & Allen, p. 152.

120   "leap into the . . . threatened anarchy." Lisio (*Protest*), p. 148. Carter only served for twenty-one days in 1916. (Daniels, p. 183)

121   "complete dictatorial powers." *Time*, 22 July 1932, p. 12; Barber (*Marching*), p. 92.

122 "To hell with civil law and . . . orders carried out." *Time*, 11 July 1932, p. 12.

123 "We were using . . . expeditionary forces." HUAC, p. 1941; *Time*, 11 July 1932, p. 12.

124 Glassford resigned. Barber (*Marching*), p. 93.

125 Deadlines. Barber (*Marching*), p. 98; Gott, pp. 10-11.

126 "While great latitude . . . the bonus march." *Plattsburgh Press*, 22 July 1932, p. 1; Waters, pp. 263-65.

127 "They can issue . . . enforce them." *Plattsburgh Press*, 22 July 1932, p. 1.

128 Refused to evacuate. Gitlow, p. 229.

129 Reset deadline. Lisio (*Protest*), p. 122.

130 210 Communists. *Chicago Tribune*, 13 September 1932, p. 2; Dickson & Allen, p. 157.

131 "Even if the . . . peace and order." Liebovich, p. 166.

132 "I'm double crossed". Smith (*Dream*), p. 156; Dickson & Allen, p. 164.

133 Drawbridge. Daniels, p. 153; Gott, p. 11. Glassford did so on July 16, when Congress adjourned. (Gott, p. 10)

134 Badge. *Brooklyn Eagle*, 29 July 1932, p. 3; Dickson & Allen, p. 166; Waters, p. 215; MacArthur, p. 94; Barber (*Marching*), p. 100; Gott, p. 11; Miller (*Ike*), p. 264.

135 Flag. Dickson & Allen, p. 166; Waters, p. 214.

136 Chest. Dickson & Allen, p. 166; Miller (*Ike*), p. 264.

137 Scott. *Reno Gazette*, 28 July 1932, p. 1; *NY Times*, 29 July 1932, pp. 2, 3. *Brooklyn Eagle*, 29 July 1932, p. 3; *Emporia Gazette*, 30 July 1932, p. 1; *Plattsburgh Press*, 30 July 1932, p. 1; Horan, p. 79; Dickson & Allen, p. 166.

138 "Hell, that's nothing . . . killed in France." *NY Times*, 29 July 1932, p. 3; Horan, p. 79.

139 "This game is . . . time for lunch". Daniels, p. 150; Smith (*Dream*), p. 156.

140 Huska. *Reno Gazette*, 28 July 1932, p. 1; *NY Times*, 29 July 1932, p. 3; *Washington Post*, 3 August 1932, p. 1; *Brooklyn Eagle*, 29 July 1932, p. 3; *Time*, 8 August 1932, p. 5; Joslin, p. 266; Dille, p. 35; Dickson & Allen, pp. 169, 192-93; Liebovich, p. 167; Barber (*Marching*), p. 100; Horan, pp. 80, 82; Gott, p. 12. A grand jury later cleared both officers. Shinault soon died in the line of duty, on August 14, 1932. (*NY Times*, 14 August 1932), p. 1; Douglas (*Veterans*), p. 235; Waters, pp. 218-19; Dickson & Allen, pp. 197, 298)

141 Man pulled pistol. *Reno Gazette*, 28 July 1928, p. 1.

142 Hired Glassford. Dickson & Allen, pp. 43, 76.

143 "the assistance of Federal troops." Hoover (*Depression*), p. 227; Waters, pp. 268-69; Joslin, p. 266; Liebovich, p. 167; Rich, p. 171. The commissioners insisted that Glassford requested additional assistance; equally strenuously, he denied their contention.

144 "Surround the affected . . . it without delay." Joslin, p. 268; Hunt, pp. 142-43; MacArthur, p. 94; Smith (*Dream*), p. 157; Watkins, p. 138; Laurie & Cole, p. 376; Leary, pp. 35-36; Lohbeck, pp. 110-11; Rich, p. 171; Miller (*Ike*), pp. 265-66. The official time of Hurley's order was 2:55. It had obviously been dispatched well before then.

145 Fort Myer preparations. *Wisconsin Magazine of History*, Autumn 1971, p. 31; Smith (*Dream*), p.140; Lisio (*Protest*), p. 92; Dickson & Allen, p. 74; Smith (*Eisenhower*), p. 108; Leary, p. 39; Blumenson, p. 895.

146 T-4. Gott, p. 13.

147 Marines departed. *Washington Post*, 14 July 1932, p. 1; *NY Times*, 15 July 1932, p. 2; Douglas (*Veterans*), pp. 199-200; Bernstein (*Lean*), p. 449; Daniels, pp. 132, 228; Smith (*Dream*), pp. 149-50; Dickson & Allen, p. 147; Lisio (*Protest*), pp. 129-31; Gott, p. 9.

148 Thirty-five Marines. Gott, p. 9. The Navy Base stood directly across from Anacostia Flats. That these Marines did not see action on July 28 may be supportive of this report. Waters also noted: "Men in the regular army had already secretly revealed to us how we could get arms in Washington if we wanted them. One or two hotheads on my staff were eager to organize a marauding expedition and to break into a few Government storehouses. A telegram from a Marine officer stationed in Brooklyn was handed to me, 'Ready to march with my men to help you if you want me.'" (Waters, p. 237; Douglas [*Veterans*], pp. 230-31)

149 Moseley. *Wisconsin Magazine of History*, Autumn 1971, p. 31; Smith (*Dream*), pp. 134-35; Lisio (*Protest*), pp. 101, 104-5. Moseley also advocated "five years of martial law" and harbored (though not very silently) distinctly racial attitudes. "We pay great attention to the breeding of our hogs, our dogs, our horses, and our cattle," he wrote in 1932, "but we are just beginning to realize the. . . . effects of absorbing objectionable blood in our breed of human beings. The pages of history give us the tragic stories of one-time leading nations which . . . imported manpower of an inferior kind and then . . . intermarried with this inferior stock. . . . Those nations have either passed out of separate existence entirely, or have remained as decadent entities without influence in world affairs." (Bendersky, pp. 202-3; Dickson & Allen, p. 74; Laurie & Cole, p. 371)

150 "If they ask . . . committee representing them. . . . but I won't receive any Communists. . . ." Joslin, pp. 263-64.

151 Blue Shirts. *Western Pennsylvania Historical Magazine*, July 1972, p. 225; Whisenhunt, pp. 53-55.

152 Uniform. *Iowa City Iowan*, 15 June 1932, p. 4.

153 "I was cordially . . . from January 7". *Western Pennsylvania Historical Magazine*, July 1972, p. 227.

154 Meet Hoover. *Western Pennsylvania Historical Magazine*, July 1972, pp. 226-27. The largest Bonus March contingent hailed from Pennsylvania—16.5 percent by Waters' estimate. (Waters, p. 257)

155 Cox declines. *Western Pennsylvania Historical Magazine*, July 1972, pp. 226-27.

156 "[Warren] Harding would . . . caused any harm." Dickson & Allen, p. 142.

157 "I do not believe . . . much more disastrous." HUAC, p. 1942; Lohbeck, p. 113. Joseph Zack Kornfeder concurred: "There is no doubt in my mind that if they had obtained complete organization control of the bonus expeditionary forces they would have done everything possible to turn the life of Washington, D. C, upside down, including attempts at storming the White House, in order to dramatize the crisis in the United States before the world." (HUAC, p. 1945)

158 "Another week might . . . was in peril." MacArthur, p. 95.

159 Troop strength. Joslin, p. 269; Gott, p. 14; Blumenson, p. 895; Lohbeck, p. 111; Daniels, p. 167; Barber (*Marching*), p. 100; Dickson & Allen, p. 171.

160 Patton. Douglas (*Veterans*), p. 69; Blumenson, pp. 894-95; Gott, p. 14; D'Este (*Patton*), pp. 352-53; Miller (*Ike*), p. 266.

161 Angelo. *Brooklyn Eagle*, 29 July 1932, p. 1; *Wichita Times*, 29 July 1932, p. 4; *Logansport Pharos-Tribune*, 30 July 1932, p. 4; Dickson & Allen, pp. 16-17, 35-37, 42; Patton, pp. 183-84, 252-53. Patton had recommended Angelo for the Medal of Honor. Following the Armistice he periodically "lent" Angelo money, but Angelo's testimony embarrassed him. During the Anacostia eviction, Angelo attempted to meet with Patton. Patton ("Sergeant, I do not know this man. Take him away . . .") refused. They met much later.

162 "a most distasteful form of service." Patton, p. 212; D'Este (*Patton*), p. 354. "Distasteful" or not, Patton later composed a series of recommendations for "Federal Troops in Domestic Disturbances." While urging caution in many regards, they included: "Designate in advance certain sharpshooters to kill individual rioters . . . Gas is paramount . . . If they resist they must be killed . . . If you do fire do a good job—a few casualties become martyrs, a large number an object lesson." (Patton, p. 213)

163 Bingham. Smith (*Dream*), p. 161.

164 Civilian attire. Brendon, p. 62; Eisenhower, p. 216.

165 "I'm here to . . . or critical repercussions." Perret, p. 113. Gen. James M. Gavin, then a mere lieutenant, later wrote, "I have never read anywhere of the feeling of the junior officers towards MacArthur's participation. We all felt that it was a gesture of personal responsibility on his part, and it was deeply appreciated by us. It was an act that certainly could have destroyed him in the public mind. . . . He didn't delegate the responsibility; instead he, chief of staff, no less, strode into the midst of the affair and took full responsibility on his part. It was characteristic of him, and for this he was thoroughly respected." *Atlantic Monthly*, February 1965, p. 59; Manchester (*Caesar*), p. 150.

166 "Jeez, if . . . had guns!" Smith (*Dream*), p. 161.

167 "The American flag . . . his mouth again!" Douglas (*Veterans*), p. 240; Smith (*Dream*), p. 161; Manchester (*Caesar*), p. 150.

168 Waters missing. Douglas (*Veterans*), p. 243; Joslin, p. 270.

169 "We are going . . . be done tonight." *New York American*, 4 November 1932, page unknown; Daniels, p. 167; Lisio (*Protest*), pp. 204, 275; Dickson & Allen, p. 171. This might not have been MacArthur's first visit to the camp. A 1942 biography contended: "Intimate friends tell how MacArthur would go down into the Bonus Army camp at night and lend money to needy soldiers who had fought with him in the B.E.F. His heart was with them, his duty was to disperse them." Such a statement initially struck the author as obvious wartime propaganda—and transparent claptrap—until discovering the equally unlikely fact that in January 1935 MacArthur secured a War Department post for Walter W. Waters. (Miller [*MacArthur*], p. 127; Dickson & Allen, p. 299)

170 No firearms. Joslin, p. 268; Daniels, p. 170.

171 Moseley claim. *Wisconsin Magazine of History*, Autumn 1971, p. 34; Smith (*Dream*), p. 162; Korda, p. 199; Miller (*Ike*), pp. 266-67.

172 "on other occasions . . . got the order." Persico (*Centurions*), p. 131. Secret Service agent Edmund W. Starling, who had first advised Hurley to delay Anacostia's clearing, later wrote: "Hurley . . . was too late. Already the soldiers were in the camp. . . ." (Starling, p. 297)

173 "too busy and . . . to bring orders." Eisenhower, p. 217; Smith (*Dream*), p. 163; D'Este (*Eisenhower*), p. 222; Korda, p. 199; Miller (*Ike*), p. 266.

174 Wright too early? James (*vol.* 1), p. 402; D'Este (*Eisenhower*), p. 740. Many have noted that MacArthur once also characterized Eisenhower as the "Best *clerk* I ever had," but he also effusively praised him in formal evaluations as "Well suited for civilian contacts . . . In time of war [he] should be promoted to General rank immediately. His general value to the service is 'Superior.'" (Display, MacArthur Memorial)

175 Supper. Joslin, p. 271; Daniels, p. 169.

176 Commandant's truce. Joslin, p. 272; Daniels, p. 169; Dickson & Allen, p. 180.

177 "stampede our women . . . that steps over that line." *Brooklyn Eagle*, 29 July 1932, p. 3.

178 Patton/brick. Smith (*Dream*), p. 164; D'Este (*Patton*), p. 353.

179 "Give way boys . . . chance in hell!" *Brooklyn Eagle*, 29 July 1932, p. 3.

180 Ike. Miller (*Ike*), p. 267.

181 Who set fires? Evacuating their downtown camp, Communists set it ablaze; Soldiers lit counter-fires to control the original conflagrations. (*Washington Post*, 29 July 1932, p. 4; Joslin, p. 272; Dickson & Allen, p. 177)

The University of Pennsylvania's Bennett Milton Rich wrote: "To drive the Marchers out of their places of shelter during the night was a harsh measure. On the other hand, had they been given time to organize their forces, a much more serious situation might have developed." (Rich, p. 175)

182 Children. Smith (*Dream*), p. 164; Manchester (*Caesar*), p. 152; Korda, p. 200. See Dickson & Allen (p. 283) for a debunking of such fictions—myths only exacerbated by none other than Eleanor Roosevelt, who in July 1949 wrote quite incorrectly of "the Army actually being ordered to fire on the veterans." (Hoover [*Depression*], p. 232*fn*; Daniels [*Veterans*], p. 257; Dickson & Allen, p. 283)

183 "Press opinion . . . of Mr. Hoover." *NY Times*, 1 August 1932, p. 14; *Commonweal*, 10 August 1932, p. 16; Barber (*Marching*), p. 103.

184 "The Bonus Riots—Use of Force was Necessary." Joslin, p. 276.

185 "For sheer stupidity . . . in American annals." *San Francisco Examiner*, 30 July 1932, p. 1; Liebovich, p. 169.

186 "Soup is cheaper . . . unemployment and hunger." *Brooklyn Eagle*, 29 July 1932, p. 1; *Syracuse Herald*, 29 July 1932, p. 5; Franklin, p. 95; Mitgang (*Once*), p. 177.

187 "the greatest crime in modern history." Dickson & Allen, p. 203.

188 "whether prompted by . . . an unpardonable outrage." *Roswell Record*, 30 July 1932, p. 6.

189 "Now, look where . . . had been anything." Tugwell (*Brains*), p. 358; Morgan, pp. 356-57; Korda, p. 201; Miller (*Ike*), p. 267; Black (*Champion*), p. 342.

Chapter Seventeen: "He doesn't need a head, his job is to be a hat"

1   Third-person. Ambrose (*Eisenhower*), p. 94; Miller (*Ike*), p. 261.
2   "in *reverse* . . . Papen and MacArthur." Lisio (*Protest*), p. 287.
3   "What Germany . . . a strong man". Wheeler-Bennett (*Titan*), pp. 364-65; Wheeler-Bennett (*Nemesis*), pp. 237-38*fn*; Manvell & Fraenkel (*Hundred*), p. 26; Turner (*Thirty*), p. 20.
4   To Röhm and Helldorf. Wheeler-Bennett (*Nemesis*), p. 242; Heiden (*Fuehrer*), p. 360; Koeves, pp. 122-23.
5   "to alter the political course." Goebbels (*Part*), p. 83; Wheeler-Bennett (*Nemesis*), p. 242; Shirer, p. 161.
6   "The Conference turned out well". Goebbels (*Part*), p. 84; Wheeler-Bennett (*Nemesis*), p. 242; Heiden (*Fuehrer*), p. 361.
7   "[W]e talk politics . . . into our nets." Goebbels, pp. 86-87.
8   Oskar present. Manvell & Frankel (*Hundred*), p. 38.
9   "square-faced, brutal . . . noble bearing". François-Poncet, p. 24; Schwarz (*Ribbentrop*), p. 54.
10   "ruddy, flushed . . . with all regimes . . .". François-Poncet, p. 24; Schwarz (*Ribbentrop*), p. 54.
11   New elections, end SA ban. Wheeler-Bennett (*Nemesis*), p. 242; Heiden (*Fuehrer*), pp. 361-62; Manvell and Fraenkel (*Hundred*), p. 36; Bullock, pp. 208-9; Shirer, p. 161; Lüdecke, p. 364.
12   "We have news . . . according to plan." Goebbels (*Part*), p. 92; Wheeler-Bennett (*Nemesis*), p. 243; Broszat, p. 114.
13   Klotz publishes, dines. *Long Island Press*, 12 May 1932, p. 1; Reuth, p. 148; Machtan, p. 366.
14   Heines attacks. *Long Island Press*, 12 May 1932, p. 1; *NY Times*, 13 May 1932, p. 1; Goebbels (*Part*), p. 92; Manvell & Fraenkel (*Goebbels*), p. 107. Heines and two others ultimately received three-month sentences for the assault.
15   "[O]n the night . . . the Spanish Inquisition." Valtin, p. 315. Krebs seems to be discussing two separate incidents, as Heinzelmann was actually killed that October 20.
16   294-270. *Troy Times*, 16 October 1931, p. 1.
17   287-257. *NY Times*, 13 May 1932, p. 1; Knight-Patterson, p. 529; Dorpalen, p. 314.
18   "a fairly simple . . . really malicious". Manvell & Frankel (*Hundred*), p. 38.
19   Stalin. Johnson (*Modern*), pp. 268-76.
20   "I am told. . . as Foreign Minister." Heiden (*History*), p. 180; Fischer, pp. 179-80; François-Poncet, p. 19. This to a man to whom Hindenburg once pled, "Everyone has abandoned me in life; you must promise that your party must not leave me in the lurch at the end of my life." (Patch, p. 64)
21   Stegerwald. Heiden (*History*), pp. 179-80; Evans (*Center*), p. 373.
22   "He's a very . . . his mind repeatedly." Manvell & Frankel (*Hundred*), p. 37.
23   "resolute, but . . . changes his aims." Manvell & Frankel (*Hundred*), p. 37.
24   "Thank you . . . a broken neck." Fischer, pp. 179-80; Heiden (*History*), p. 180; According to Oswald Dutch he said, "I too have my name and my honour." (Dutch, p. 123)
25   Skagerrak commemoration. Fest (*Hitler*), p. 336; Mommsen, p. 446.
26   "A dictatorship which . . . of a majority." Clark (*German Republic*), p. 370.
27   For Hindenburg 1925. Papen, pp. 107-8; Dutch, p. 127; Eyck, p. 394; Evans (*Coming*), p. 283; Fest (*Face*), p. 152; Burleigh, p. 141.
28   Landtag but not Reichstag. Wheeler-Bennett (*Nemesis*), p. 247; Koeves, p. 90; Evans (*Center*), p. 376; Fest (*Face*), p. 153.
29   Warrant. *NY Times*, 5 June 1932, p. 5; Burke, p. 235.
30   "as homely as she is rich". Fromm, p. 53. The opinion of Berlin society columnist Bella Fromm.
31   "a political dilettante . . . for the worst." Olden, p. 265. Olden was not exaggerating about Papen's ambition to serve in Luxembourg. (Heiden [*Fuehrer*], p. 422; Dutch, p. 125)
32   Cabinet possibilities. Wheeler-Bennett (*Nemesis*), pp. 245-46; Mommsen, p. 433.
33   Prussia. Grzesinski, p. 153; Heiden (*Fuehrer*), p. 470; Rolfs, p. 137; Feuchtwanger, pp. 271-72.
34   Sachsen-Anhalt. Feuchtwanger, pp. 271, 327; Broszat, p. 79.

35 Oldenburg. *NY Times*, 30 October 1932, p. 1; Feuchtwanger, p. 327; Lüdecke, p. 364; Bullock, p. 210; Broszat, p. 79; Kershaw (*Hubris*), p. 368. Yet, they garnered only 37.2 percent of the seats. (Thompson, p. 12)

36 Hessen. Feuchtwanger, p. 327; Kershaw (*Hubris*), p. 368; Wheaton, p. 126; Hauner, p. 80; Clark (*Republic*), p. 375; Manvell & Fraenkel (*Hundred*), p. 191. They garnered only 40 percent of the seats. (Thompson, p. 12)

37 "to forge these . . . for the state." Heiden (*Fuehrer*), p. 423.

38 April 1932 article. Clark (*German Republic*), pp. 368-69; Koeves, pp. 121-22; Davidson, pp. 324-25.

39 "I very much . . . the right man". Papen, p. 152; Rolfs, p. 87.

40 Kaas promise. Papen, pp. 156-57; Dutch, pp. 128-29; Heiden (*Fuehrer*), p. 464; Koeves, pp. 142-43; Eyck, p. 396; Clark (*German Republic*), p. 372; Davidson, p. 328; Rolfs, pp. 90-91; Wheaton, p. 125.

41 "Well, my dear . . . difficult situation". Papen, p. 157; Toland, p. 265; Rolfs, p. 88.

42 "In spite of . . . one response—obedience.'" Papen, p. 158; Rolfs, p. 88; Toland, p. 266.

43 "No one but . . . and an intriguer." François-Poncet, p. 23; Shirer, p. 164; Rolfs, p. 90; Snyder (*Encyclopedia*), p. 266; Fest (*Face*), p. 153; Davidson, p. 324; Turner (*Thirty*), p. 40. François-Poncet's shock was amplified by this fact: significantly anti-clerical, he had abetted Schleicher in knifing the Catholic Brüning. Now, in a classic case of "be careful what you wish for," he found himself saddled with the equally Catholic, but far less impressive, Papen. (Metcalfe, p. 75)

44 "the air of an . . . *Alice in Wonderland*." Kessler, p. 419; Rolfs, p. 90.

45 "if proposed as . . . be refused." Eyck, p. 399; Burke, p. 233.

46 Friends. Wheeler-Bennett (*Nemesis*), p. 245.

47 "Monocle cabinet". *NY Times*, 3 June 1932, p. 5; *Time*, 6 February 1933, p. 20.

48 "Cabinet of barons". *NY Times*, 3 June 1932, p. 5; François-Poncet, p. 29; Wheeler-Bennett (*Nemesis*), p. 248; Shirer, p. 164; Kershaw (*Hubris*), p. 367; Knight-Patterson, p. 532; Davidson, p. 330; Mitchell (*Hitler*), p. 152; Lüdecke, p. 367; Vogt, p. 101.

49 "Dear Braun: . . . Ministry of Food?" Eyck, p. 397. Braun was the father of famed rocket scientist, Werner von Braun.

50 Gürtner. Heiden (*Fuehrer*), p. 465; Shirer, p. 164; Bullock, p. 211; Davidson, p. 330; Wistrich, pp. 115-16; Manvell & Fraenkel (*Hundred*), p. 189.

51 "The composition of . . . half-baked intellectuals." Eyck, p. 398.

52 No labor representation. Wheeler-Bennett (*Nemesis*), p. 248.

53 "The overwhelming majority . . . this new cabinet." *NY Times*, 3 June 1932, p. 5; Broszat, p. 116.

54 "a total nervous collapse." Evans (*Center*), p. 375.

55 "If we were not . . . left to save." Halperin, p. 456.

56 "We condemn unanimously . . . *National Socialist Party*." Papen, pp. 160-61; Shirer, pp. 165-66; Bullock, p. 213; Manvell & Fraenkel (*Hundred*), p. 40; Cary, p. 135.

57 December 1931 scheme. Knight-Patterson, p. 530. In early 1932, Schleicher negotiated with the DNVP to effect another potential Brüning demotion to foreign minister. Hugenberg would emerge as vice-chancellor; the DNVP's Baron Hermann von Lüninck as chancellor. (Mommsen, p. 414)

58 Krebs. Krebs, pp. 137, 188-89; Knight-Patterson, p. 530; Dutch, p. 139.

59 "I found him . . . impressed by them." Papen, p. 162; Manvell & Fraenkel (*Hundred*), p. 40; Rolfs, p. 93; Kershaw (*Hubris*), p. 367.

60 Reichstag. *NY Times*, 4 June 1932, p. 4; Papen, p. 161; Shirer, p. 164; Bullock, p. 213; Manvell & Fraenkel (*Hundred*), p. 39; Davidson, p. 327; Wheaton, p. 126.

61 SA. Papen, pp. 162-63; Davidson, p. 183; Bullock, p. 213.

62 "Papen is . . . all entirely satisfied." Goebbels (*Part*), p. 87; Wheeler-Bennett (*Nemesis*), pp. 247-48; Shirer, p. 164; Bullock, p. 210; Kershaw (*Hubris*), pp. 367-68; Manvell & Fraenkel (*Hundred*), p. 38. "An absolute majority in the Reichstag election did not seem out of the question," historian Ian Kershaw later concluded.

63   "The present Cabinet . . . scored off both." Manvell & Fraenkel (*Hundred*), p. 39; Eyck, p. 400.
64   "the weakling we held him for". Goebbels (*Part*), p. 97.
65   "I regard your . . . devolve on me." Papen, p. 162; Manvell & Fraenkel (*Hundred*), p. 38; Kershaw (*Biography*), pp. 165-66; Hauner, p. 80; Kershaw (*Hubris*), p. 368.
66   "In the evening . . . shamefacedly away." Goebbels (*Part*), p. 107; Fest (*Face*), p. 338.
67   "not the soul . . . the will". Olden, p. 255; Turner (*Thirty*), p. 18.
68   "He doesn't need . . . be a hat." Fest (*Face*), p. 154; Rolfs, p. 81; Davidson, p. 325; Mitchell, p. 151.
69   Gayl. Burke, p. 235.
70   Hugenberg. *NY Times*, 28 June 1932, p. 5.
71   Mecklenburg-Schwerin. *NY Times*, 6 June 1932, p. 7; Hauner, p. 80; Clark (*Republic*), p. 375; Manvell & Fraenkel (*Hundred*), p. 191.
72   Phonograph record. Hauner, p. 81; Kershaw (*Hubris*), p. 369.
73   Devrient. Redlich, p. 51, Lukacs, p. 49.
74   "You made me . . . to these lessons?" www.lermanet.com/cisar/germany/030818.htm.
75   "The Nazis do . . . reaction, but healing". *NY Times*, 14 June 1932, p. 9; Knight-Patterson, p. 438.
76   Munich, Vienna. *NY Times*, 16 June 1932, pp. 5, 6.
77   "a rapacious, nonproductive race". *NY Times*, 28 June 1932, p. 5; *San Antonio Light*, 27 June 1932, p. 5-A; Manvell & Fraenkel (*Hundred*), p. 193.
78   July deaths. Hauner, p. 81; Shirer, p. 164; Bullock, p. 213; Kershaw (*Hubris*), p. 368; Taylor, p. 102.
79   1,125. Eyck, p. 409; Vogt, p. 102; Manvell & Fraenkel (*Hundred*), p. 42.
80   Kiel. Hauner, p. 81.
81   "We force our . . . detours. . . ." Goebbels (*Part*), p. 106; Heiden (*Fuehrer*), p. 469.
82   "Halt! Before you . . . does his duty!" Heiden (*Fuehrer*), p. 472. For example, the Nazis had advised *Deutsche Bank*'s Emil Georg von Strauss to officially remain a member of the fast-fading liberal German People's Party (DVP).
83   Papen domestic policies. *NY Times*, 15 June 1932, p. 6; Turner (*Business*), p. 276; Koeves, pp. 151-52.
84   *Vorwärts*. *NY Times*, 2 July 1932, p. 8.
85   "national embarrassment". Rolfs, p. 89.
86   *Kolnische Volkszeitung*. *NY Times*, 6 July 1932, p. 10.
87   Lausanne. *NY Times*, 18 July 1932, pp. 1, 4; Papen, pp. 171-87; Heiden (*Fuehrer*), pp. 468-69; Eyck, pp. 392, 402-7; Knight-Patterson, pp. 533-35; Davidson, p. 330; Vogt, p. 97; Halperin, p. 490; Dutch, p. 131. François-Poncet had helped torpedo Brüning's efforts at Lausanne. (Metcalfe, p. 75)
88   Little political payoff. *NY Times*, 10 July 1932, p. 16; *NY Times*, 11 July 1932, p. 8; *NY Times*, 18 July 1932, p. 4; Eyck, p. 408.

Chapter Eighteen: "The sinister faculty of making men like bad government"

1   1914. Burns, pp. 57-59; Weintraub, pp. 68-71; Schlesinger (*Crisis*), p. 347; Cohen (*Fear*), p. 21; LaCerra, pp. 49-51.
2   "I am very . . . make it larger." Bellush, p. 154.
3   "genius". Connable & Silberfarb, p. 234.
4   "There's Music . . . of a Skirt". Fowler (*Walker*), p. 45; Davis (*New York*), p. 103; Morgan, p. 357; Black (*Champion*), p. 195.
5   "The appointment of . . . by their peer." Mitgang (*Tiger*), p. 169; Mitgang (*Once*), p. 76; Allen (*The Tiger*), p. 237; Mann, p. 60. Hylan's January 1930 appointment may have resulted less from Walker's magnanimity to a fallen foe than his threat to run independently for mayor in 1929. (*NY Times*, 17 March 1929, p. 2; *NY Times*, 12 January 1936, p. 21) In 1939, La Guardia "returned the favor" and appointed Walker to a badly needed $20,000-per-year city post. The appointment came at the behest of Ed Flynn—and of Franklin D. Roosevelt. (Moley [*27*], p. 212; Fowler [*Walker*], p. 357)

6   "He possesses the . . . like bad government." *Vanity Fair*, June 1931, p. 68.

7   1929. Thomas & Blanshard, p. 338; Walker won by 497,165 votes.

8   Rothstein loan. *NY Times*, 14 March 1930, pp. 1-2; Thomas & Blanshard, p. 339; Fowler (*Walker*), p. 270; Connable and Silberfarb, p. 278.

9   Tepecano robbery. *NY Times*, 16 February 1930, p. 29; Chambers, p. 217; Connable and Silberfarb, p. 278; Walsh, pp. 205-7; Cohen (*Graphic*), pp. 143-44; Pietrusza (*Rothstein*), pp. 332-33; Congdon, p. 190.

10   Crater. *NY Times*, 9 April 1930, p. 24; *NY Times*, 10 October 1930, pp. 1-2; Bellush, pp. 154-55; Lavine, p. 196; Fowler (*Walker*), p. 273.

11   Mancuso. *Albany News*, 10 May 1929, p. 6; *NY Times*, 20 September 1929, p. 1; Thomas & Blanshard, p. 116; Northrup & Northrup, p. 11; Fowler (*Walker*), pp. 269-70; Lavine, pp. 51, 200; Pietrusza (*Rothstein*), p. 370.

12   Bertini. *NY Times*, 18 October 1929, p. 1; *NY Times*, 10 October 1930, pp. 1-2; *NY Times*, 15 October 1930, p. 1; *NY Times*, 3 March 1931, p. 16; Chambers, pp. 222-23; MacKaye, p. 33; Thomas & Blanshard, p. 116; Northrup & Northrup, pp. 9, 11; Lavine, pp. 195-96; Bellush, p. 164. Rumor had it that Bertini purchased the post for $100,000.

13   Bertini, immunity. *NY Times*, 3 March 1931, p. 29; Freedman, p. 48.

14   1939 charges. Burns, p. 120.

15   Seabury appointed. Thomas & Blanshard, p. 341.

16   "His dignity . . . bolt of lightning." MacKaye, p. 298; Moley (*27*), p. 216.

17   City Affairs Committee. *NY Times*, 22 September 1930, p. 6; Voss, pp. 273-74; Urofsky, p. 244.

18   "Walker was easily . . . decency and honor." Holmes, p. 217.

19   "spoke with such . . . admirer and friend." Holmes, pp. 217-18.

20   "Our little Mayor . . . into trouble." Freidel (*Triumph*), p. 256; Bellush, p. 271; Freedman, p. 79; Urofsky, p. 247.

21   Prostitution. Lavine, pp. 155-68; Thomas & Blanshard, pp. 144-49; 342-43; Walsh, pp. 233-35; Congdon, p. 191; Horan, p. 40.

22   Gordon. *NY World*, 27 February 1931, p. 1; Lavine, pp. 168-70; Chambers, pp. 251-52; Fowler (*Walker*), pp. 74, 287; Cohen (*Graphic*), pp. 153-54, 160; Connable & Silberfarb, pp. 279-84; Allen (*Tiger*), pp. 242-44; Pietrusza (*Rothstein*), p. 336.

23   Legislature authorizes Seabury. *NY Times*, 9 March 1931; p. XX3; *NY Times*, 4 March 1931, p. 1; Bellush, p. 269; Freidel (*Triumph*), p. 256; Davis (*New York*), p. 235; Horan, pp. 39-40.

24   Wise, Holmes meeting. *NY Times*, 18 March 1931, p. 19; Thomas & Blanshard, p. 343; Fowler (*Walker*), p. 288; Davis (*New York*), p. 233; Black (*Champion*), p. 214; Bellush, p. 271; Mitgang (*Tiger*), p. 246.

25   "I have listened . . . listen to me." Voss, p. 275.

26   "what would . . . on the street." Holmes, pp. 216-17.

27   Immunity. Thomas & Blanshard, p. 346; Connable and Silberfarb, p. 282.

28   Farley finances. Bellush, p. 153.

29   "Kind of a . . . a wonderful box". Northrup & Northrup, p. 164; Walsh, p. 50; Mitgang (*Tiger*), p. 218; Chambers, pp. 330-31; Pietrusza (*Rothstein*), pp. 338-39; Allen (*Tammany*), p. 47; Congdon, p. 192. The reader is advised to google the song "A Little Tin Box" from the 1959 musical "Fiorello!" chronicling the aforementioned Kafkaesque testimony.

30   "The action of . . . criminal in the State." Freidel (*Triumph*), pp. 357-58.

31   $20,000. Mitgang (*Tiger*), pp. 217-18; Pietrusza (*Rothstein*), p. 440.

32   "scale of living. . . of his deposits." Freidel (*Triumph*), p. 258*fn*; LaCerra, p. 72; Allen (*Tiger*), p. 247. Farley's predecessor, Charles W. Culkin, a close friend to both Walker and Al Smith, also stood accused of financial improprieties. It may be significant—or not—that Smith had also served as New York County sheriff, leaving his position as Democratic leader in the Assembly to assume that lucrative post. (Handlin, pp. 68-70; Cohen [*Graphic*], pp. 165-67)

33 McQuade. *Lowville Journal-Republican*, 31 March 1932, p. 4; Thomas & Blanshard, p. 63; Northrup & Northrup, pp. 165-66; Connable and Silberfarb, p. 282; Cohen (*Graphic*), pp. 161-62; Bellush, p. 153; Chambers, pp. 334-38; Allen (*Tiger*), p. 248.

34 Cruise. *Olean Times-Herald*, 8 October 1931, p. 1; MacKaye, p. 206; Chambers, p. 334; Northrup & Northrup, pp. 164-65; Bellush, p. 153.

35 Vitale. Pietrusza (*Rothstein*), p. 334.

36 Theofel. *Long Island Daily Press*, 18 March 1932, pp. 1-2; Boydston, pp. 360-61; Mitgang (*Once*), p. 137.

37 Olvany. Thomas & Blanshard, p. 53; MacKaye, p. 61; Walsh, p. 284; Connable and Silberfarb, p. 76; Allen (*Tiger*), p. 239.

38 Sheehy. *NY Times*, 1 March 1932, pp. 1-2; *NY Post*, 15 March 1933, p. 9; Thomas & Blanshard, p. 347; LaCerra, p. 73. Upon Olvany's retirement, FDR praised him as "a very old friend of mine. He has rendered fine service to his party." (*NY Times*, 17 March 1929, p. 2)

39 Wise, Holmes write. *NY Times*, 18 March 1932, pp. 1, 12; *Long Island Daily Press*, 18 March 1932, pp. 1-2; City Affairs Committee (*McQuade*), *passim*; City Affairs Committee (*Theofel*), *passim*; Thomas & Blanshard, p. 347; Davis (*New York*), p. 263; Neal, p. 159; Black (*Champion*), p. 216; Voss, p. 280; Urofsky, p. 247.

40 "A rushing into . . . are not performing." *NY Times*, 31 March 1932, p. 13; Flynn (*Squire*), p. 45; Freidel (*Triumph*), p. 259; Neal, pp. 159-60; Davis (*New York*), p. 263; Voss, p. 280; Urofsky, p. 247. FDR biographer Kenneth S. Davis concluded that Roosevelt had not only attacked Wise and Holmes "on grounds palpably sophistic but also savagely impugned their motives."

41 "If they would . . . be the gainers." *NY Times*, 3 April 1932, p. 21; Voss, p. 281.

42 Liberal clergy. Walker took pains to warn: "The most dangerous individual is the parlor communist. He is the fellow who exercises the greatest influence and causes the most misery by his smooth approach. But the most dangerous of all is he who ascends the pulpit pretending to a background of Christ's holy word—or the Torah." (*Chicago Tribune*, 27 April 1931, page unknown)

43 "I am with . . . I will follow". Carpenter, p. 38; Tull, p. 15; Warren (*Coughlin*), p. 43; Fried, p. 43; Kennedy (*Freedom*), p. 231. Coughlin telegram to FDR July 2, 1932.

44 "Father Coughlin is . . . of Indians however." Marcus, p. 45; Carpenter, p. 38; Tull, p. 14; Warren (*Coughlin*), p. 41.

45 "disliked and distrusted . . . never liked him". Warren (*Coughlin*), p. 42.

46 NYC Coughlin meeting. Marcus, pp. 45-46; Warren (*Coughlin*), p. 41.

47 "Insufficient evidence". *NY Sun*, 27 April 1931, p. 2; Davis (*New York*), p. 234; Black (*Champion*), p. 214; Mitgang (*Tiger*), p. 246.

48 $40,000. *NY Times*, 20 December 1929, pp. 1, 32; *The Nation*, 5 October 1932, pp. 300-301; Thomas & Blanchard, pp. 35, 339; Voss, p. 271. Increased from $25,000 immediately following Walker's 1929 landslide; FDR's gubernatorial salary remained stalled at $25,000. (*San Antonio Light*, 26 September 1932, p. 1)

49 Palm Springs. Fowler (*Walker*), pp. 187-88; Allen (*Tiger*), p. 244; Voss, p. 273.

50 "a much-needed . . . New England". Fowler (*Walker*), p. 252.

51 Kaiserhof. Fuller, pp. 101-2; Fromm, pp. 37-38.

52 Faisal. Fowler (*Walker*), p. 299; Moley (*27*), p. 208. Portrayed by Alec Guinness in 1962's *Lawrence of Arabia*.

53 "the greatest . . . modern times". Fuller, p. 161. Praise for Mussolini was then strangely commonplace. In 1930, Hearst pronounced *Il Duce*: "A marvelous man. It is astonishing how he takes care of every detail of his job." (Procter, p. 165) Rexford Tugwell confessed similar admiration. FDR would later refer to Mussolini as "that admirable Italian gentleman" and confide to his Ambassador to Rome Breckinridge Long that he was "much interested and deeply impressed by what he has accomplished."(Schivelbusch, pp. 31-32)

54 Fuller dedication. Fuller, p. 9.

55 Casino. Walsh, pp. 189-91; Fowler (*Walker*), pp. 246-50.

56 Beer Parade. *NY Times*, 12 May 1932, p. 14; *Brooklyn Eagle*, 15 May 1932, pp. 1-2; *Long Island Press*, 15 May 1932, p. 2; Walsh, p. 298; Finan, p. 277; Fowler (*Walker*), p. 301; Horan, p. 66.

57 Equitable. *NY Post*, 9 June 1932, p. 14; *NY Times*, 11 August 1932, p. 3; Thomas & Blanshard, pp. 168-72; Walsh, pp. 98-99, 120-22, 300, 302-5; Mitgang (*Tiger*), pp. 248-51; Allen (*Tiger*), p. 249. Some alleged that the mayor's old friend, the almost equally flashy Brownsville (Brooklyn) state senator John A. Hastings, collected two million dollars from the deal.

58 Sisto. *NY Post*, 9 June 1932, p. 14; *NY Times*, 11 August 1932, p. 3; Thomas & Blanshard, pp. 175-76; Walsh, pp. 296-97, 306-14; Allen (*Tiger*), p. 249; Fowler (*Walker*), p. 301.

59 Hearst. *NY Times*, 23 June 1941, p. 17. Block, for Roosevelt as governor, for some reason supported Hoover in 1932.

60 Block. *NY Times*, 11 August 1932, p. 3; Thomas & Blanshard, p. 353; Mitgang (*Tiger*), p. 252; Allen (*Tiger*), pp. 249-50; Walsh, pp. 314, 324-25.

61 Sherwood. *NY Post*, 9 June 1932, p. 14; *NY Times*, 11 August 1932, p. 3; Thomas & Blanshard, p. 175; Fowler (*Walker*), pp. 295-96; Mitgang (*Tiger*), pp. 252-53; Chambers, pp. 315-19, 321; Allen (*Tammany*), p. 250; Walsh, pp. 323-33; Horan, p. 85. Among Seabury's findings: Sherwood had parceled out $75,000 to an "unnamed person"—Walker's mistress Betty Compton. (Fowler [*Walker*], pp. 322-23)

62 Dr. Walker. *NY Times*, 8 August 1932, p. 1; *NY Times*, 11 August 1932, p. 3; *NY Times*, 20 August 1932, p. 12; Thomas & Blanshard, p. 63; Walsh, p. 315.

63 "Walker, had no . . . unbelievable rationalizations." Moley (*27*), p. 208.

64 1928. Stiles, p. 111; Bellush, pp. 10, 162; Dobyns, p. 141; Davis (*New York*), p. 103. Eleanor returned the favor by serving on the committee importuning Walker to run again in 1929. Joining Eleanor among 681 others were Mrs. Alfred E. Smith, Mr. & Mrs. Bernard Baruch, David Belasco, Adolf Zukor, Lee Shubert, Jessy Lasky, Charles Dana Gibson, Bernard F. Gimble, Herbert Bayard Swope, George M. Cohan, George White, James Weldon Johnson, William Fox, and Generoso Pope. (*NY Times*, 15 July 1929, p. 10; Thomas & Blanshard, p. 179; Fowler (*Walker*), pp. 243-44)

65 "has used his . . . his gravest liability." *New Republic*, 1 June 1932, p. 63; Dobyns, pp. 144-45.

66 "Roosevelt viewed the scene with absolutely . . . everyone knew he was out for himself." Congdon, p. 192.

67 "I vote . . . Smith." Stiles, pp. 183-84; O'Connor (*Hurrah*), p. 262. However, it required Dudley Field Malone to first roust "Beau James" out of bed and hustle him to the hall.

68 "My God, that . . . well-pressed Walker trousers." Stiles, pp. 183-84.

69 Dedicating Huggins monument. *NY Times*, 31 May 1932; p. 24; Fowler (*Walker*), pp. 312-13.

70 "The great little . . . have been exalted." *NY Times*, 30 May 1932, p. 9; *NY Times*, 31 May 1932, pp. 3, 24; Fowler (*Walker*), pp. 312-13.

71 "The return parade . . . triumphal march". *NY Times*, 31 May 1932, p. 24.

72 "This fellow Seabury. . . eliminating political innuendoes." Schlesinger (*Crisis*), p. 395; Mitgang (*Tiger*), p. 273; Mitgang (*New York*), p. 160; Neal, p. 162.

73 Presidential ambitions. Moley (*27*), pp. 207-8; Mitgang (*Tiger*), pp. 275-81; Mitgang (*New York*), pp. 160-61; Neal, pp. 161-62.

74 Seabury for Baker. Mitgang (*Tiger*), p. 272; Cramer, p. 250.

75 Wise for Baker. Urofsky, p. 254. Wise had also favored a Baker run in 1920. (Cramer, p. 221)

76 "It should have . . . thanks to Roosevelt. . . ." Urofsky, p. 254.

77 McAdoo. Mitgang (*Tiger*), p. 272.

78 "The only information . . . or buck-passing." *Plattsburgh Press*, 4 June 1932, p. 1; Mitgang (*New York*), pp. 159-60.

79 Transcripts. Mitgang (*New York*), p. 160.

80 "Never, never will . . . me be myself." Davis (*Invincible*), pp. 257-58; Neal, pp. 162-63.

81 "This squalid [Walker] . . . are not direct." Lippmann, p. 250; Schlesinger (*Crisis*), p. 395; Neal, p. 161.

82 Nervous. Davis (*New York*), p. 354.

83 "He was in . . . of the situation." Davis (*New York*), p. 354.

84 "member of the . . . pertinent things." Tull, pp. 16-17; Marcus, pp. 46-47; Burns, p. 141; Warren (*Coughlin*), p. 42; Brinkley, p. 108. FDR was certainly cognizant of this factor. Not coincidentally he appointed the Catholic Martin Conboy as his counsel as he grilled Walker. (Moley [*27*], pp. 209-10; Flynn [*Boss*], p. 121)
85 "I am, as . . . you again soon." Tull, p. 17.
86 "What if I . . . would be weak." Moley (*27*), p. 209; Ellis, p. 548; Freidel (*Triumph*), p. 336*fn*; Neal, p. 163; Morgan, p. 358; Schlesinger (*Crisis*), p. 423.
87 Stiles-Howe. Stiles, p. 184.
88 "pulmonary malady". *NY Times*, 3 August 1932, p. 17.
89 Brother dead. *NY Post*, 29 August 1932, p. 15; *NY Times*, 30 August 1932, p. 2; Fowler (*Walker*), p. 324; Walsh, p. 326.
90 "Jim looks worse than George". Walsh, p. 326; Morgan, p. 360.
91 "Sis, take a . . . at the Plaza." Fowler (*Walker*), p. 325; Walsh, p. 327.
92 McCooey. Fowler (*Walker*), p. 325; O'Connor (*Hurrah*), p. 267.
93 "Good old Jimsie! . . . than water." Connable & Silberfarb, p. 285; O'Connor (*Hurrah*), p. 262.
94 "Jim, you're through . . . of the party." Fowler (*Walker*), p. 325, O'Connor (*Hurrah*), p. 267; Allen (*Tiger*), p. 253; Golway, pp. 280-81.
95 "So you'd rather . . . what you say." Moley (*17*), p. 211; Schlesinger (*Crisis*), p. 423; Morgan, p. 360. These were not his exact words. Moley describes them as "a comment somewhat to this effect."
96 "He was patient . . . and the presidency." Fowler (*Walker*), p. 263.

CHAPTER NINETEEN: "THE SWINE WITHIN THEMSELVES"
1 Kerrl. *NY Times*, 26 May 1932, p. 9; Goebbels (*Part*), p. 96; Heiden (*History*), p. 174; Orlow (*Prussia*), p. 210; Knight-Patterson, p. 535. Kerrl was only the Nazi faction's second-in-command. Its actual leader, Wilhelm Kube, a former DNVP Berlin city council member, was too leftist, anti-capitalist, anti-Catholic, and simply too eccentric to secure other parties' backing. (Orlow [*Prussia*], pp. 28, 104, 148; Wistrich, p. 148) Both Kube and Kerrl were Strasserites. (Orlow [*Prussia*], p. 214)
2 "The Communists arraign . . . amid the ruins." Goebbels, (*Part*), p. 96. In actuality, the Nazis started it. Kerrl ended up summoning the police. (Orlow [*Prussia*], p. 210)
3 No-confidence vote. Heiden (*Fuehrer*), p. 366; Dutch, p. 133.
4 "We have a . . . thoroughly thought over." Goebbels (*Part*), p. 83.
5 "[W]e must not . . . the Leader's idea." Goebbels (*Part*), p. 103.
6 "A week before . . . returned the fire." Mitchell (*Hitler*), p. 154.
7 19/285. *Chicago Tribune*, 18 July 1932, pp. 1-2; Wheeler-Bennett (*Nemesis*), p. 251; Broszat, p. 119; Toland, p. 266; Manvell & Fraenkel (*Hundred*), p. 42.
8 200 wounded. Mitchell (*Hitler*), p. 155.
9 Documents re: police. Wheeler-Bennett (*Nemesis*), p. 253.
10 Took no action. Eyck, p. 409; Mommsen, p. 441.
11 Article 48. Mitchell (*Hitler*), p. 155; Eyck, p. 413; Ludwig (*Hindenburg*), p. 336.
12 "Every Tom . . . Harry knew". Mommsen, p. 446.
13 Brüning. Patch, p. 89; Turner (*Thirty*), p. 89.
14 Klepper/Hirtsiefer /Severing. Kessler, p. 431.
15 General strike. Mowrer, pp. 6, 8; Knickerbocker, p. 136; Wheeler-Bennett (*Nemesis*), p. 255; Heiden (*Fuehrer*), p. 473; Knight-Patterson, p. 281; Shirer, p. 165; Bullock, p. 214; Davidson, p. 332; Breitman, p. 185; Evans (*Coming*), p. 287; Manvell & Fraenkel (*Hundred*), p. 193; Burleigh, p. 142; Delmer (*Weimar*), p. 108.
16 "The right of . . . masses any further." Papen, p. 132.
17 "If there has . . . it will be ours!" Mowrer, p. 1.
18 1928/1932. Nicholls, p. 135.

19   SPD strength. Knight-Patterson, pp. 424-25; Manvell & Fraenkel (*Hundred*), p. 193. Germany featured an immense number of newspapers—two thousand in all, more than the United Kingdom, France, and Italy combined. (Metcalfe, p. 69)

20   *Schufos.* Nicholls, p. 134.

21   KPD strike. Knickerbocker, pp. 168, 172.

22   Salaries. Knight-Patterson, p. 537.

23   "We felt that . . . must be." Ludwig (*Hindenburg*), p. 339.

24   "You have no . . . your policemen's expense." Eyck, p. 416; Mommsen, p. 447; Vogt, p. 102.

25   "weak, pusillanimous little men." Delmer (*Trail*), p. 158.

26   Abegg, KPD. Dutch, p. 134; Heiden (*Fuehrer*), p. 472; Rolfs, p. 145; Orlow (*Prussia*), p. 228; Mommsen, p. 448; Hett, pp. 31-32, 232.

27   1923. Papen, p. 189.

28   "No, Herr Chancellor . . . but of right." Koeves, p. 157; Mowrer, p. 2.

29   Rundstedt. Wheeler-Bennett (*Nemesis*), p. 254; Manvell & Fraenkel (*Hundred*), p. 41; Breitman, p. 185; Mowrer, p. 3.

30   Motorcycle. Koeves, p. 159.

31   Bracht. Kessler, p. 432; Dutch, p. 135; Davidson, p. 332; Ludwig (*Hindenburg*), p. 338; Knight-Patterson, pp. 535-36; Orlow (*Prussia*), p. 232; Mowrer, p. 2.

32   Two police. Ludwig (*Hindenburg*), p. 338; Davidson, p. 332.

33   Chair. Knight-Patterson, p. 536.

34   Grzesinski/Weiss. Heiden (*History*), p. 187; Knight-Patterson, p. 536; Mowrer, pp. 3-4; Mommsen, p. 449; Reuth, p. 151; Fromm, p. 55.

35   *Freiheit!* Fest (*Hitler*), p. 339.

36   Tears. Koeves, pp. 158-59.

37   "the misgovernment . . . National Socialist helpers." Childers, p. 252.

38   "The highest instance . . . overwhelming as possible." Knight-Patterson, p. 537. The courts also passed judgment on Papen's actions, vaguely but ineffectually condemning them. (Evans [*Coming*], pp. 452-53)

39   "Does Hitler Have Mongolian Blood?" Rosenbaum, pp. 155-58.

40   July 29 attack. Duffy & Ricci, p. 15; Hoffmann (*Security*), p. 19.

41   July 30 attack. *The Nation*, 16 October 1932, p. 474; Goebbels (*Part*), p. 129; Hoffmann (*Security*), p. 19.

42   *Weiner Sonn-und-Montags Zeitung.* Toland, p. 268.

43   Gangland style. Fest (*Hitler*), pp. 294-95; Richie, pp. 400-401.

44   Police attacks. Koehler, pp. 32-41; Burleigh, p. 131; Mommsen, p. 418. The KPD and the NSDAP, in the persons of Ulbricht and Goebbels, both supported a plebiscite aimed at dissolving the Prussian Landtag. (Dutch, p. 133)

45   Twelve dead. Burleigh, p. 142; Some put the number at only nine. (Richie, p. 401; Reuth, p. 151; Orlow [*Prussia*], pp. 152-53, 205)

46   "Those who know . . . promise to fulfil. . . ." *The Nation*, 16 November 1932, p. 474.

47   "In 1928 I paid . . . hopeless despair." *The Nation*, 16 November 1932, p. 474.

48   "What will you . . . 'Keep it.'" Knickerbocker, p. 47.

49   Air campaign. Hauner, p. 81; Bullock, p. 216.

50   "and was digging . . . an adjoining field." Baur (KOBO edition).

51   Stralsund. Hauner, p. 81; Dietrich (*Road*), p. 36; Bullock, p. 216; Toland, p. 267. Otto Dietrich claimed that forty thousand remained until 4:00 a.m.

52   "Give me ten . . . afterwards with enthusiasm." Baur (KOBO edition).

53   "All right boy . . . learn something!" Toland, p. 268.

54   "It was the . . . I've seen." Toland, p. 268. *Vössiche Zeitung* society columnist Bella Fromm recounted Wilhelm Brückner's explanation of why Hitler proscribed sound films of his talks: "You can't alter a sound film." (Fromm, p. 46)

55   "In Brandenburg . . . and still do." Speer, p. 23.

56 Brandenburg, Grunewald crowds. Goebbels (*Part*), p. 128; Shirer, p. 166; Jarman, p. 138; Hauner, p. 81; Mosley, p. 134; Heiber, p. 101.

57 "Inside the stadium . . . the Fuehrer." Lüdecke, pp. 376-77; Jarman, p. 138.

58 "Work has to . . . platform and speaks." Goebbels (*Part*), p. 115; Fest (*Hitler*), p. 321; Read, p. 238.

59 "[S]omehow the speech . . . bite without teeth." Goebbels (*Part*), p. 125; Bullock, p. 216; Heiber, p. 96; Reuth, p. 150.

60 "I should be . . . have won life.'" Knight-Patterson, p. 540.

61 "military dictatorship . . . strong popular sentiment. . . ." Heiden (*Fuehrer*), p. 476.

62 "the Communist is . . . and social life". *NY Times*, 30 July 1932, p. 2.

63 Papen radio talk. *NY Times*, 30 July 1932, p. 2.

64 "Papen referred to . . . least open to doubt." US Department of State, pp. 303-6.

65 "all of the 160 bars . . . the opposite sex." Knickerbocker, p. 32. The words of correspondent H. R. Knickerbocker.

66 "Women wearing décolletage . . . Zivilisationsliteraten." Roth, p. 191.

67 "cesspool of the . . . and healthy life". Weitz, p. 76. The opinion of the conservative, Protestant anti-Semitic journalist Wilhelm Stapel.

68 "In the big . . . wings of prisons." Burleigh, p. 126.

69 "They had the . . . virility and effeminacy." Guérin, p. 65.

70 Vote totals. Feuchtwanger, p. 326; Manvell & Fraenkel (*Hundred*), p. 42; Knight-Patterson, p. 542; Evans (*Coming*), pp. 293-94; Childers, p. 209; Eyck, pp. 425-46; Shirer, p. 166; Lüdecke, p. 380.

71 "Brüning is the . . . of the goal!" Evans (*Center*), p. 379.

72 Berlin vote. Reuth, pp. 96-97; Evans (*Coming*), p. 209; Richie, p. 389.

73 1928 vote. Orlow (*Nazi*), p. 129; Lemmons, p. 31; Large (*Berlin*), p. 245.

74 Election returns. Large (*Berlin*), p. 245.

75 Hugenberg front man. Cary, p. 135.

76 "They would handcuff . . . easy for us." Goebbels (*Part*), p. 130; Manvell & Fraenkel (*Hundred*), p. 42.

77 "31st July brought . . . majority as yet." Dietrich (*Road*), p. 38.

78 "The National Socialists . . . deliver the goods." Ascher, p. 18; McRandle, pp. 186-87.

CHAPTER TWENTY: "CLIMB ON THE MULE"

1 Ninety-five-foot. *Middletown Times-Herald*, 14 July 1932, p. 1.

2 1924, 1928. Whalen, pp. 68-69; Smith (*Hostage*), p. 65; Beschloss, pp. 60-61. Kennedy is conspicuous in his absence among top Smith donors. (Hoover [*Depression*], p. 220)

3 Fundraising. *Time*, 14 November 1932, p. 11; Nasaw (*Patriarch*), p. 183; Beschloss, p. 72; Koskoff, p. 47; Russell, p. 347; Pizzitola, p. 288.

4 *Ambassadress*. Cross, pp. 59-60; Whelan, p. 125.

5 "I was really . . . help elect him." Goodwin (*Fitzgeralds*), p. 428; Beschloss, p. 74. Joe Kennedy knew not only about economic radicalism, but possessed a little firsthand knowledge of domestic radicalism. When anarchists bombed Wall Street in September 1920, Kennedy coincidentally stood only a few hundred feet away. The blast knocked him to the ground. Had he been closer he might have been among the thirty-three dead or more than two hundred wounded. (Goodwin [*Fitzgeralds*], p. 317; Koskoff, p. 25)

6 $15 million. Russell, p. 346. Kennedy biographer Richard Whalen hints that JPK supported FDR in part to avoid congressional investigations of his Wall Street maneuverings. (Whalen, p. 121)

7 Swanson. Swanson, pp. 440-41; Kessler, p. 97; Schwarz (*Kennedy*), pp. 186-87. Eleanor Roosevelt was *not* impressed by this move. (Quirk, p. 106)

8 "quite frank in . . . of Roosevelt's ability". Smith (*Hostage*), p. 66; Beschloss, pp. 73-74. Howard's remarks to Newton D. Baker.

9 First meeting. Whelan, pp. 117-18; Beschloss, p. 70; Schwarz (*Kennedy*), pp. 180-81.

10   "an eccentric American of Fascist tendencies". Nevins (*Ford*), p. 168.

11   "Jews and mosquitoes . . . would be gas." Clark (*Wilhelm*), p. 247; McDonogh, p. 7; Röhl, p. 1238.

12   Bigelow. Nevins (*Ford*), p. 168; Herzstein, pp. 124-25; Clark (*Wilhelm*), p. 247.

13   *Myth II*. Suckley; *Charleston Gazette*, 2 August 1932, pp. 1, 8; *Salt Lake City Tribune*, 10 September 1932, p. 9; Metcalfe, pp. 191-92.

14   "like a father . . . a grand seigneur". Louis Ferdinand, p. 137; Fenyvesi, pp. 71, 75.

15   Alcoholic. Metcalfe, p. 192.

16   "You know, there . . . and your brothers." Louis Ferdinand, pp. 135-36.

17   "I hope I . . . do without it. . . ." Louis Ferdinand, p. 138.

18   Damita. *NY Times*, 2 May 1929, p. 20; *NY Times*, 3 May 1929, p. 30; *Yonkers Statesman*, 6 May 1929, p. 19; Louis Ferdinand, pp. 117-19, 166-77, 204; Fenyvesi, pp. 75-76. She later married Errol Flynn.

19   Ford Motor Co. *Troy Times*, 16 October 1931, p. 1; *NY Times*, 27 September 1974, p. B14; Louis Ferdinand, pp. 150-63, 172-73, 209-15; Fenyvesi, pp. 75-76; Metcalfe, p. 191.

20   Emil Hurja. Holli, p. 43.

21   Hague. *NY Times*, 11 July 1932, pp. 1, 3.

22   Davis. Harbaugh, pp. 339-40.

23   Ely. *Plattsburgh Press*, 1 August 1932, p. 1; *Time*, 8 August 1932, p. 8. Perhaps, not coincidentally, on the same day, FDR delivered a radio address tacking once more rightward, proclaiming, "High sounding, newly invented phrases cannot sugar-coat the pill. Let us have the courage to stop borrowing to meet continuing deficits. Stop the deficits." (Rosenman [*Papers*], p. 662; *NY Times*, 31 July 1932, p. 2; *NY Times*, 1 May 1938, p. 26; Hoover [*Depression*], p. 271; Lyons, p. 289)

24   "Franklin Delano Roosevelt . . . Herbert Hoover." *Chicago Tribune*, 16 July 1932, p. 4.

25   "He stopped immigration by executive order." *Iowa City Iowan*, 15 July 1932, p. 5.

26   Boettinger reports. *Chicago Tribune*, 1 August 1932, p. 5.

27   Maverick. *San Antonio Light*, 3 August 1932, p. 1.

28   "We're gonna get . . . back to Washington". Congdon, p. 121.

29   Maryland, Virginia. *Time*, 8 August 1932, p. 7.

30   "the state has . . . feed this army". *Gettysburg Times*, 2 August 1932, p. 1.

31   Des Moines. *Ames Tribune-Times*, 27 August 1932, p. 1; Schlesinger (*Crisis*), p. 267.

32   San Antonio. *San Antonio Light*, 3 August 1932, p. 1.

33   "We are writers . . . and politicians." *Chicago Tribune*, 11 August 1932, p. 2.

34   "one of the . . . Douglas MacArthur." Tugwell (*Democratic*), p. 349; Schlesinger (*Crisis*), pp. 417-18; Morgan, pp. 356-57; Manchester (*Caesar*), p. 152.

35   Nervously. Hoover (*42*), p. 218.

36   Constitution Hall. *Chicago Tribune*, 12 August 1932, p. 6; Ritchie, p. 121; Jeansonne (*Hoover*), p. 412.

37   Mrs. Theodore Roosevelt. *NY Times*, 11 August 1932, p. 1.

38   Radio. *NY Times*, 12 August 1932, p. 6.

39   "the final solution . . . the liquor traffic." Peel & Donnelly, p. 136; Jeansonne (*Hoover*), p. 413.

40   "I am opposed . . . of the saloon." *Plattsburgh Press*, 19 August 1932, p. 1; *Chester Times*, 19 August 1932, p. 17; *Time*, 29 August 1932, p. 10. North Carolina's Robert Rice Reynolds later informed audiences that New Yorkers had named a bridge on the Hudson the "Hoover Bridge" because "it's wet underneath, dry on top and faces both ways." (Pleasants, p. 56)

41   "I know the . . . period of depression." *Plattsburgh Press*, 19 August 1932, p. 1; *Chester Times*, 19 August 1932, p. 17.

42   "perhaps, bigotry's banner state". Handlin, p. 166. The words of the *Catholic Mirror*.

43   "I hear that . . . in the East." *NY Times*, 16 August 1932, pp. 1, 3.

44   Car. Pleasants, p. 31.

45   "What do you . . . Morrison eats caviar." Pleasants, p. 33.

46   "Eggs Benedictine." Pleasants, p. 33.

47 "he can not . . . or I do". Pleasants, p. 31.
48 "I'm in for . . . stay in wave". White (*Kingfish*), p. 169.
49 Long campaign. *Saturday Evening Post*, 15 October 1932, p. 88; Williams (*Long*), p. 587; Fried, p. 53.
50 "We're all here. . . little woman's neck." Williams (*Long*), p. 588; Kane, p. 95. Thaddeus Horatius Caraway was no slouch either, having once assaulted a veterans bureau attorney, the 5'4½" Harry Wallenstein, with a wet umbrella on a Washington streetcar. (*NY Telegram*, 5 March 1923, p. 18; Coan, p. 145)
51 "We have more . . . people are homeless." Williams (*Long*), p. 588.
52 Arkansas results. Williams (*Long*), pp. 592-93; White (*Kingfish*), p. 159. http://womenin congress.house.gov/member-profiles/profile.html?intID=37
53 California Democratic results. *San Mateo Times*, 31 August 1932, p. 1.
54 22.93 percent. *San Mateo Times*, 31 August 1932, p. 1.
55 Poll. *Literary Digest*, 24 September 1932, p. 8.
56 Meyers. *Charleston Gazette*, 14 February 1932, p. 5; *Walla Walla Union-Bulletin*, 13 December 1964, p. 35.
57 "capitalist boot-licker". Anonymous (*Ford-Foster*), p. 28.
58 Two million votes. Johnpoll, p. 94.
59 Union endorsement. Johnpoll, p. 95.
60 $26,000. Johnpoll, p. 95. Down from $110,000 in 1928.
61 "a tool . . . Hoover administration". Peel & Donnelly, pp. 205-06.
62 Farmer-Labor Party. *Washington Post*, 11 July 1932, p. 2; *American Mercury*, October 1932, pp. 177-79; Peel & Donnelly, p. 205.
63 "Jobless Party". *American Mercury*, October 1932, p. 180; *Western Pennsylvania Historical Magazine*, July 1972, pp. 227-28; Peel & Donnelly, p. 205; *Pittsburgh Bulletin-Index*, 1 September 1932, page unknown; www.clpgh.org/exhibit/neighborhoods/strip/strip_n10.html.
64 "Interest is a modern . . . They weren't compensated." *Pittsburgh Bulletin-Index*, 1 September 1932, page unknown; www.clpgh.org/exhibit/neighborhoods/strip/strip_n10.html.
65 Cox in Europe. Whisenhunt, p. 54.
66 Stranded. *NY Sun*, 21 September 1932, p. 1; Whisenhunt, p. 60.
67 Endorses FDR. *Western Pennsylvania Historical Magazine*, July 1972, p. 230; Peel & Donnelly, p. 207; Douglas (*Veterans*), p. 118; Whisenhunt, p. 66.
68 "THE CANDIDATES FOR THE WORKING YOUTHS". Anonymous (*Foster-Ford*), p. 3.
69 Lovestoneites endorse. *Workers Age*, 1 November 1932, p. 1.
70 "official 'Communist' hooligans . . . and other weapons." *Workers Age*, 16 July 1932, p. 1.
71 Intellectuals endorse Foster-Ford. Lewy, p. 42; Schlesinger (*Crisis*), pp. 436-37; Ekirch, p. 89; Johnson (*Modern*), p. 252. Not all left-leaning intellectuals supported Foster. Elmer Davis, George S. Kaufman, Stephen Vincent Benet, Reinhold Niebuhr, Morris Ernst, and Henry Hazlitt, for example, endorsed Norman Thomas. (Manchester [*Glory*], p. 51)
72 "It is capitalism . . . is driving it." Schlesinger (*Crisis*), p. 436; Ekirch, p. 89; Johnson (*Modern*), p. 252. Rorty, never an actual party member, nonetheless, broke with the CPUSA later that year. (*NY Times*, 26 February 1973, p. 34)
73 *Baltimore Afro-American*. *Baltimore Afro-American*, 22 October 1932, p. 1; Farrar, p. 151.
74 Census Bureau. Lisio (*Blacks*), p. 88; Wilson (*Progressive*), p. 129.
75 Booze. Lisio (*Blacks*), pp. 87-88; *Decatur Herald*, 20 October 1928, p. 1; Louchheim, p. 245; Wilson (*Progressive*), p. 129.
76 "the most indecent . . . the United States." *Decatur Herald*, 20 October 1928, p. 1; Lisio (*Blacks*), p. 88.
77 "things are to . . . and Negro politicians". Lisio (*Blacks*), pp. 232-33. It should be noted, however, that when Hoover first purchased a home in Washington, he refused to sign an anti-black, anti-Jewish covenant. (Neal, p. 145)

78   Gold Star Mothers. *Crisis*, November 1932, p. 362; Lisio (*Blacks*), pp. 235-36; Bartlett (*Race*), p. 112; Dickson & Allen, p. 120; Leuchtenburg (*Hoover*), p. 99; Black (*Champion*), p. 438.
79   1932 convention. Neal, p. 146.
80   "the only white man . . . didn't keep it". *Baltimore Afro-American*, 12 March 1932, p. 20.
81   Howard University. *Crisis*, November 1932, p. 343; www.presidency.ucsb.edu/ws/index .php?pid=23123&st=&st1=; Weiss, p. 25.
82   Photographed. *Crisis*, November 1932, pp. 343-44; Lisio (*Blacks*), pp. 271, 273; Weiss, p. 25; www.presidency.ucsb.edu/ws/index.php?pid=23264&st=&st1=. He met with 200 black leaders on the White House lawn. In June 1929, Lou Hoover, had, however, invoked a furor from Southern legislators by inviting Jessie De Priest, wife of newly elected black Republican Chicago congressman Oscar De Priest to a White House tea.
83   "I see millions . . . a Democratic ticket." Weiss, p. 15.
84   "The Republicans should not . . . nigger this year." *Time*, 27 June 1932, p. 44.
85   Warm Springs. Neal, p. 149.
86   "deliberate forgeries". Liseo (*Blacks*), pp. 268, 352. In January 1933, White requested a meeting with FDR. FDR refused "due to the pressure of work." (Weiss, p. 34)
87   *The Crisis. The Crisis*, November 1932, pp. 343-44.
88   "If he is . . . his occasional vacations." Leuchtenburg (*South*), p. 55. In 1971 Jim Farley responded with a forceful "No, no no" when asked if Democrats had courted blacks in 1932. (*American Heritage*, August 1971, p. 41)
89   "None of us . . . acceptance of Baruch . . .". Tugwell (*Democratic*), p. 239. Or, as the wit Dorothy Parker once mused, she could never figure out the theory of zippers or the exact function of Bernard Baruch. (Martin [*Henry*], p. 124) The exact function of Mr. Baruch, was, however, precisely $61,000—as the Democratic National Committee's largest reported donor. (*Time*, 14 November 1932, p. 11; Schlesinger [*Crisis*], p. 421)
90   "the Boy Scout Governor." Freidel (*Triumph*), p. 236; Davis (*New York*), p. 250; Miller (*FDR*), p. 258; Black (*Champion*), p. 219.
91   "now wished to . . . of a secretaryship." Tugwell (*Democratic*), p. 239.
92   Baruch chauffered. Tugwell (*Brains*), pp. 3-5.
93   *Nation's Business* article. *Nation's Business*, September 1932, pp. 16-17, 46, 48. Baruch had, in fact, also floated that idea at the Chicago convention. Clare Boothe Brokaw had helped him draft his statement. According to a biographer, her diary records that she slept in Baruch's compartment on their return to New York. (Morris [*Luce*], pp. 196, 198)
94   "I have twenty-six . . . the common man." Marcus, p. 47; Tull, p. 18; Brinkley, p. 108.
95   "Baruch, Morgan and Rockefeller". *NY Times*, 1 May 1932, p. E5.
96   "By God, I . . . got in mine." Brinkley (*Protest*), p. 58; Pottker, p. 264; Fried, pp. 54-55; White (*Kingfish*), p. 169. For her part, Sara Roosevelt famously inquired regarding Long, "Who is that awful man sitting next to Franklin?" (Caroli, p. 220; Schlesinger [*Crisis*], p. 418)
97   Tie, shirt. Fried, p. 54.
98   Long at Hyde Park. Suckley; Fried, pp. 54-55.
99   "wherever they tell . . . in this campaign." *NY Times*, 11 October 1932, p. 10; Schlesinger (*Crisis*), p. 430; Whalen, pp. 125-26.
100   Waldorf-Astoria. Peel & Donnelly, p. 109.
101   "It is safe . . . so magnificently housed." Peel & Donnelly, p. 109.
102   ABA reception. *NY Times*, 13 October 1932, p. 14; *Salt Lake Tribune*, 14 October 1932, p. 1; Joslin, p. 15.
103   "We noticed splotches . . . the second floor." Joslin, p. 315; *Fitchburg Sentinel*, 10 August 1963, p. 6.
104   Pinchot, Ickes. Kennedy (*Over*), p. 41.
105   Robins. *NY Times*, 9 September 1932, pp. 1, 13; *NY Post*, 1 September 1932, p. 1; *Iowa City Iowan*, 15 September 1932, p. 3; *Time*, 19 September 1932, p. 9; *The Spectator*, 22 September 1932, p. 6; *NY Times*, 8 October 1932, p. 36; *NY Times*, 27 September 1954, p. 21; Salzman, p. 334. Robins,

now sporting a beard and suffering from amnesia, was discovered panning for gold in North Carolina's Great Smoky Mountains following the election.

106 "a thrill to . . . a door knob." *Fitchburg Sentinel*, 10 August 1963, p. 6; Miller (*Ike*), p. 263. Oddly enough, Hoover did quite a bit of radio. He delivered only nine less radio talks (104 to 95) in his four years than did FDR in his first four, but most were perfunctory "glorified greetings," and, of course, he was just horrible at it. (Wilson [*Progressive*], p. 140)

107 "the pathetic mud-turtle, Lord Hoover". Teachout, p. 263.

108 "the pebble . . . American's shoe." Rodgers, p. 381.

109 Columbus. *NY Times*, 20 August 1932, pp. 1, 5; *NY Times*, 21 August 1932, p. 18; *NY Times*, 22 August 1932, p. 2; Suckley. A hopeful sign for his campaign at Columbus was a "long talk" with Newton D. Baker. (*NY Times*, 23 August 1932, p. 10; Suckley)

110 Sea Girt. *NY Times*, 28 August 1932, pp. 1, 20; Suckley.

111 "The experience of . . . their legitimate powers." Rosenman (*Papers*), pp. 684-92; Suckley; Kyvig, p. 166. By this time "wet" forces had significantly climbed aboard FDR's campaign effort. Brewers Col. Jacob Ruppert and Fred Pabst donated four thousand and three thousand dollars, respectively. Banker Charles Hamilton Sabin, husband of blueblood repeal activist (and former Republican National Committeewoman) Pauline Morton Sabin, donated a thousand dollars. (*Time*, 14 November 1932, p. 11)

112 "I think I'd . . . speak in Vermont." *NY Times*, 11 October 1932, p. 10.

113 Vermont. *NY Times*, 8 July 1932, p. 1. No Vermont Democrat had won statewide office since 1858.

114 Leaves Union Station. *NY Times*, 14 August 1932, p. 10; Suckley.

115 Hurja. Holli, p. 48.

116 Maine results. *Plattsburgh Press*, 14 September 1932, p. 1; Ritchie, pp. 129-30; Jeansonne (*Hoover*), pp. 418-19.

117 "A mighty phalanx . . . only the first." *Literary Digest*, 24 September 1932, p. 6.

118 "What's happened has . . . to the limit." Joslin, p. 301; Schlesinger (*Crisis*), p. 432; Smith (*Dream*), p. 179.

119 Jefferson City. Louchheim, p. 3.

120 Topeka. *NY Times*, 15 September 1932, pp. 1, 14, 20; Rosenman (*Papers*), pp. 693-711; Ritchie, pp. 129-30.

121 "Typical of the ignorance . . . Payne-Aldrich tariff." *North American Review*, November 1932, p. 391.

122 "They stared intently . . . as they were." Hickok (*Road*), p. 198.

123 Train wreck. *NY Times*, 20 August 1932, pp. 1, 4; Suckley.

124 Portland. *NY Times*, 22 September 1932, pp. 1, 16; Rosenman (*Papers*), pp. 741-56; Suckley.

125 "enormously effective". Tugwell (*Democratic*), p. 246.

126 Howe against visit. Flynn (*Boss*), p. 119.

127 "Here was suspense . . . out of Roosevelt's car. . . ." Moley (*Seven*), p. 57.

128 Nineteen-gun salute. Suckley.

129 Berle/Tugwell. Tugwell (*Democratic*), p. 246.

130 "Sometimes, my friends . . . the public interest." Rosenman (*Papers*), pp. 742-56.

131 "frightening". Moley (*Seven*), p. 57.

132 "we were on . . . from this position." Tugwell (*Democratic*), p. 246.

133 "Liquidate the Kulaks as a class!" Johnson (*Modern*), p. 271.

134 "ten million . . . dealt with." Johnson (*Modern*), p. 271.

135 Shuler/Klansman. Sitton, p. 219.

136 Porter. O'Brien (*Rogers*), p. 133; Louchheim, p. 7.

137 "Downtown Republican Club." *NY Times*, 25 September 1932, p. 32.

138 "If you are . . . take you out?" *Kansas City Star*, 25 September 1932, p. 1.

139 "Welcome to . . . the Forgotten Men." *NY Times*, 25 September 1932, p. 32.

140 "I ask your . . . faith in God." *NY Times*, 25 September 1932, pp. 1, 32.

141 "Marion Davies Foundation for Crippled Children." *San Bernardino Sun*, 25 September 1932, p. 1; *Syracuse Herald*, 25 September 1932, p. 1; Pizzitola, p. 290.
142 $1,800. O'Brien (*Rogers*), p. 133.
143 "I wish to . . . to the kiddies". *San Bernardino Sun*, 25 September 1932, p. 1.
144 "I came to . . . will be known." Pizzitola, pp. 291-92.
145 "Such things do one good,". Pizzitola, p. 292.
146 GOP campaign textbook. *Plattsburgh Press*, 16 September 1932, p. 1.
147 Hurja/Pennsylvania. Holli, p. 48.
148 Kansas poll. *Literary Digest*, 24 September 1932, p. 8.
149 "He deserves reelection . . . safe and sound." *Literary Digest*, 17 September 1932; p. 6.
150 "[I]t might . . . and in time." *Literary Digest*, 17 September 1932; p. 8.
151 *Literary Digest* poll. *Literary Digest*, 24 September 1932; pp. 7-8; Ritchie, p. 153.
152 "It is not . . . I had feared,". Joslin, p. 304; Smith (*Dream*), p. 191.

CHAPTER TWENTY-ONE: "HERR HITLER, I WILL SHOOT"

1 "[S]torm troopers will . . . deliver the goods." Ascher, p. 18; McRandle, pp. 186-87.
2 "the time has . . . of the country." Papen, pp. 193-94.
3 Protestant/Catholic vote. Evans (*Coming*), p. 294.
4 "would be prepared . . . its deeds alone." Williams (*Adenauer*), p. 199.
5 Königsberg violence. *NY Sun*, 1 August 1932, p. 17; *Reno Gazette*, 1 August 1932, p. 1; Longerich, p. 140; US Department of State, pp. 306-7; Kessler, p. 425; Broszat, p. 124.
6 "At Königsberg an . . . to their homes." Goebbels (*Part*), p. 130; Heiden (*Fuehrer*), p. 478.
7 "Prominent Socialists and . . . contents looted." Gilbert (*Winston Churchill, Vol. 5*), p. 447.
8 "acts of atrocious . . . Bavaria." US Department of State, pp. 306-7.
9 "launched an operation . . . won the election." Kessler, p. 425.
10 Proposed Cabinet. Wheeler-Bennett (*Nemesis*), pp. 258-59; Wheeler-Bennett (*Titan*), p. 406; Heiden (*Fuehrer*), pp. 478-79; Fest (*Hitler*), p. 340; Bullock, pp. 218-19; Hauner, p. 81; Manvell & Fraenkel (*Hundred*), p. 43; Kershaw (*Hubris*), p. 370; Kershaw (*Biography*), p. 232; Rolfs, p. 167; Wheaton, pp. 129-30.
11 "Here the . . . Hitler took place." Heiden (*History*), p. 194; Wheeler-Bennett (*Nemesis*), p. 259; Wheeler-Bennett (*Titan*), p. 406; Dutch, p. 131; Bullock, p. 219; Toland, p. 269; Fest (*Hitler*), p. 341; Olden, p. 279.
12 Norgau. Rolfs, p. 163.
13 Kotzan. *Lawrence Journal-World*, 8 August 1932, p. 3. In Berlin, Reds smashed the windows of a Nationalist newspaper.
14 "Once we attain . . . carried off dead." Goebbels (*Part*), p. 133; Kershaw (*Hubris*), p. 371; Fest (*Hitler*), p. 340; Shirer, p. 167; Johnson (*Modern*), p. 283.
15 "an eye for . . . for a tooth". Heiden (*Fuehrer*), p. 478.
16 "The air is . . . awful set-back." Goebbels (*Part*), pp. 133-34; Bullock, p. 218; Fest (*Hitler*), p. 341; Heiden (*Fuehrer*), p. 479; Pridham, pp. 285-86; Rolfs, p. 171.
17 "The S.A. are . . . precision and discipline." Goebbels (*Part*), p. 136; Bullock, p. 218; Toland, p. 269; Broszat, p. 124.
18 "[A]n open outbreak . . . from Hitler himself." Rauschning, p. 18.
19 August 9 meetings. Goebbels, pp. 134-35; Heiden (*Fuehrer*), pp. 480-81; Bullock, p. 219; Mitchell (*Hitler*), pp. 159-60; Shirer, pp. 167, 171.
20 "in the passion . . . rage and hatred. . . ." *Central European History*, September 1977, p. 243; Fest (*Hitler*), p. 341; Wheeler-Bennett (*Nemesis*), p. 259; Broszat, p. 124; Evans (*Coming*), p. 296; Halperin, p. 502; Rolfs, p. 164.
21 1.5 hours. *Central European History*, September 1977, p. 243.
22 Pietrzuch murder. *NY Times*, 23 August 1932, p. 1; *Central European History*, September 1977, pp. 246-47; Wheeler-Bennett (*Nemesis*), p. 259*fn*; Broszat, pp. 125-26; Heiden (*Fuehrer*), pp. 402-3;

Manvell & Fraenkel (*Hundred*), p. 193; Evans (*Coming*), p. 296; Halperin, p. 502; Davidson, p. 188; Burleigh, p. 151; Fest (*Hitler*), p. 341; Rolfs, pp. 164-65; Kershaw (*Hubris*), p. 381; Vogt, p. 114.

23   "The Nazis invaded . . . vain for his life." *New Castle News*, August 23, 1932, p. 6.

24   Billiard cues. Evans (*Coming*), p. 296.

25   "The body bore . . . thrust in his face." *Central European History*, September 1977, p. 247; Vogt, p. 114; Mitchell (*Hitler*), pp. 158-59; Halperin, p. 502.

26   "The problems attendant . . . wary as serpents." Goebbels (*Part*), pp. 133-34: Broszat, p. 124.

27   Returns from Neudeck. Toland, p. 269; Broszat, p. 124.

28   "I am told . . . the Nazis". Dorpalen, p. 351; Rolfs, p. 168.

29   "Phone call from . . . or in Power." Goebbels (*Part*), pp. 135-36.

30   Constitution day. Knight-Patterson, p. 542.

31   Röhm, Helldorf. Papen, pp. 195-97; Goebbels (*Part*), p. 137.

32   "Visibly a struggle . . . on within him". Goebbels (*Part*), p. 137; Heiden (*Fuehrer*), p. 481; Manvell & Fraenkel (*Hundred*), p. 44.

33   News from Röhm. Bullock, p. 219.

34   "For [Hitler] it . . . or nothing now". Goebbels (*Part*), p. 137.

35   Kaiserhof. Wheeler-Bennett (*Titan*), p. 408; Koeves, p. 162.

36   Schleicher meeting. Heiden (*Fuehrer*), p. 482.

37   "I soon realized . . . resounding electoral success." Papen, pp. 195-96; Manvell & Fraenkel (*Hundred*), p. 44; Kershaw (*Hubris*), p. 373.

38   "*Herr Kanzler* . . . the general welfare." Papen, p. 196.

39   "Never!" . . . clear to the President . . ." Koeves, pp. 164-65.

40   "The President is . . . you well enough". Papen, p. 196; Manvell & Fraenkel (*Hundred*), p. 44.

41   "You see . . . and see him?" Koeves, p. 165.

42   Planck-Hitler conversation. Wheeler-Bennett (*Titan*), p. 409; Domarus, p. 154; Dorpalen, pp. 353-54; Shirer, p. 168; Kershaw (*Hubris*), p. 373; Rolfs, p. 173; Mosley, pp. 135-36.

43   Crowd. *NY Times*, 14 August 1932, p. 1; Kershaw (*Hubris*), p. 373.

44   Those present. Noakes & Pridham, p. 104; Strasser, p. 137; Heiden (*Fuehrer*), p. 483; Davidson, p. 334; Dorpalen, p. 354; Halperin, p. 501; Reuth, p. 153.

45   Disgust for Röhm. Wheeler-Bennett (*Titan*), p. 409; Wheaton, p. 130.

46   No chair. Olden, p. 255; Heiden (*History*), p. 196. "Eye-witnesses," wrote Göring biographer Kurt Singer, "have told how Hitler wanted to shut the door after him, but it had already been shut by a servant. He stumbled as he walked towards Hindenburg." (Singer, p. 131)

47   Hindenburg to Hitler. Bullock, pp. 221-22; Shirer, p. 168; Kershaw (*Hubris*), p. 373.

48   "Herr Hitler . . . I will shoot." Davidson, p. 334; Smith (*Summer*), p. 58; Eyck, p. 427. *Time* reported it as "I'll rap your fingers." (*Time*, 6 February 1933, p. 20)

49   "You insist, therefore. . . in political struggles." *NY Times*, 14 August 1932, p. 1; Ludwig (*Hindenburg*), p. 349; Olden, p. 256; Singer, p. 132.

50   "That man for . . . head on them." Wheeler-Bennett (*Titan*), p. 410; Heiden (*History*), p. 194.

51   "A solution leading . . . in the end." Goebbels (*Part*), p. 138.

52   Back to Berchtesgaden. Goebbels (*Part*), p. 140; Manvell & Fraenkel (*Hundred Days*), p. 46.

53   "What sort . . . We shall see." Toland, pp. 270-71; Hanfstaengl, p. 197. Various accounts place these conversations at different intervals.

54   The President of the . . . about twenty minutes." *NY Times*, 14 August 1932, p. 9; Noakes & Pridham, pp. 104-5; Domarus, p. 152; Shirer, p. 168; Fest (*Hitler*), p. 342; Kershaw (*Hubris*), pp. 373-74; Heiden (*Fuehrer*), pp. 483-84; Davidson, p. 334; Dorpalen, pp. 354-55; Eyck, p. 427. Historian John Toland surmised that the memorandum "must have been prepared ahead of time." (Toland, p. 271)

55   "Before the . . . slunk down them." Heiden (Fuehrer), p. 483.

56   "White as a sheet". Toland, p. 270.

57   Rebellious SA leaders. Dorpalen, p. 355; Rolfs, p. 175.

58   "The Machiavellian method . . . your teeth out." Lüdecke, p. 470; Jarman, p. 140.

59 "outline[d] matters to . . . come to naught!" Goebbels, *(Part)*, p. 139; Bullock, p. 224; Shirer, p. 169.

60 Police. Delmer *(Weimar)*, p. 110.

61 "The decision was . . . to Adolf Hitler." Dorpalen, p. 356; Toland, p. 271.

62 "Deep despondency besets the Party". Goebbels, *(Part)*, p. 140; Heiden *(Fuehrer)*, p. 485.

63 "I will never . . . the cheapest compromise." Domarus, p. 156; Hauner, p. 81.

64 Wiegand/Hohenzollerns. Considine, pp. 96-97. Also the first American to interview Hitler— for Hearst's *New York American* in November 1922. (Nagorski *[Hitlerland]*, p. 22)

65 "That man is hopeless . . . a waste of time." Toland, p. 272; Payne, pp. 240-41; Nagorski *(Hitlerland)*, p. 87.

66 Classmate. Metcalfe, p. 156.

67 "In your attitude . . . be dealt with." Payne, pp. 240-41; Toland, p. 272.

68 "Europe cannot maintain . . . ask him to lead." Payne, pp. 244-45; Toland, p. 273.

69 "Under the rules . . . of one man." Payne, p. 241.

70 "*I have the . . . complete control.*" Payne, p. 241.

71 "I don't have . . . out of Berlin." Domarus, p. 158; Payne, p. 241; Kershaw *(Hubris)*, p. 381; Hauner, p. 82; Bach, p. 94.

72 Beuthen trial, sentences. *Brooklyn Eagle*, 28 August 1932, p. E7; *Central European History*, September 1977, p. 250; Clark *(German Republic)*, p. 393; Dietrich *(With)*, p. 45; Papen, p. 199; Broszat, p. 126; Bullock, p. 223; Fest *(Hitler)*, p. 342; Burleigh, p. 131.

73 "The German people . . . for German liberty." *NY Times*, 23 August 1932, p. 1; Domarus, p. 160.

74 Heines/newspapers/stores. *NY Times*, 23 August 1932, p. 1; *Washington Post*, 23 August 1932, p. 2; *Waterloo Courier*, 23 August 1932, p. 1; *Iowa City Iowan*, 23 August 1932, p. 1; *Central European History*, September 1977, p. 250; Kershaw *(Hubris)*, p. 382.

75 "Several Jews were whipped". *Waterloo Courier*, 23 August 1932, p. 1.

76 One thousand Reichsmarks. *Central European History*, September 1977, p. 252.

77 "boundless bitterness . . . terror-judgment." Evans *(Coming)*, p. 296.

78 "All men are not equal". *NY Post*, 25 August 1932, p. 4.

79 "Never forget this. . . Jews are guilty!" *NY Post*, 24 August 1932, p. 2; Vogt, p. 114; Goebbels *(Part)*, p. 141; Thacker, pp. 133-34.

80 "My comrades . . . is our duty." *Appleton Post-Crescent*, 23 August 1932, p. 1; *Clearfield Progress*, 23 August 1932; *NY Times*, 24 August 1932, p. 1; Domarus, pp. 158-59; Heiden *(History)*, p. 199; Papen, p. 299; Heiden *(Fuehrer)*, p. 484; Halperin, p. 503; Kershaw *(Hubris)*, p. 382; Manvell & Fraenkel *(Hundred)*, p. 193; Bullock, pp. 223-24; Vogt, p. 114; Davidson, p. 334; Olden, p. 262; Broszat, p. 126; Beck, p. 81.

81 "German racial comrades! . . . of the German people!" *Brooklyn Eagle*, 23 August 1932, p. 1; *NY Post*, 23 August 1932, p. 12; *NY Times*, 24 August 1932, p. 7; *Clearfield Progress*, 23 August 1932; *Central European History*, September 1977, pp. 252-53; Domarus, pp. 159-60; Heiden *(History)*, pp. 199-200; Evans *(Coming)*, p. 297; Ludwig *(Hindenburg)*, p. 350; Bullock, pp. 223-24; Kershaw *(Hubris)*, p. 382; Davidson, p. 334; Vogt, p. 114; Beck, p. 81. Hitler's reference to "objectivity" may refer to another verdict rendered on August 22. At Brieg, Silesia, four Reichsbanner men each received four-year sentences for assaulting Nazis. In Munich, Nazis groused that no Reichsbanner man had ever received the death sentence. (*Clearfield Progress*, 23 August 1932; *NY Times*, 24 August 1932, p. 1)

82 "At least now. . . the other side." Vogt, p. 114.

83 "I do not play . . . shrink from nothing." Rauschning, pp. 10-11; Hauner, pp. 82-83.

CHAPTER TWENTY-TWO: "WE ALWAYS CALL HER 'GRANNY'"

1 Kennedy. Smith *(Hostage)*, p. 98*fn*; Beauchamp, p. 325; Schwarz *(Kennedy)*, p. 188. Moore served as namesake for Sen. Edward Moore "Teddy" Kennedy.

2   WEAF broadcast. *Yonkers Statesman*, 11 September 1932, p. XX8; *Yonkers Statesman*, 12 September 1932, p. 12. She did not join FDR's party until he reached Flagstaff, Arizona. And that may have been only to rendezvous with her friend and bridesmaid, Arizona National Committeewoman Isabella Selmes Greenway. (*San Antonio Light*, 26 September 1932, p. 1; Louchheim, p. 6; Golay, p. 32) Rep. Owen, a "dry," lost re-nomination in 1932 over that issue.

3   Marriage, press. Ward (*Trumpet*), p. 263.

4   Nervous breakdown. Brands (*Traitor*), p. 34.

5   Addiction. Cook (*Vol. 1*), p. 53; Brands (*Traitor*), p. 34.

6   Keeley Center. Beasley, Shulman & Beasley, p. 448.

7   "Elliott's writings during . . . as a woman." Cook (*Vol. 1*), p. 35.

8   Katy Mann. Ward (*Trumpet*), pp. 272, 275-76; Cook (*Vol. 1*), pp. 59-62; Caroli, p. 241; Brands (*T.R.*), pp. 246-48; Brands (*Traitor*), pp. 34-35; Collier & Horowitz (*Roosevelts*), p. 82; Beasley, Shulman & Beasley, pp. 445, 448. Elliott Roosevelt Mann died in 1941. The family took little notice. (Cook [*Vol. 1*], p. 510; Caroli, p. 244)

9   Godfather. Lash (*Eleanor*), p. 28.

10   "If he is . . . of hideous depravity." Brands (*T.R.*), p. 248.

11   Knickerbocker Club. Cook (*Vol. 1*), p. 39; Collier & Horowitz (*Roosevelts*), p. 87. Franklin, a member, resigned in 1936.

12   Father's death. Ward (*Trumpet*), p. 286; Lash (*Eleanor*), pp. 56-67; Brands (*Traitor*), p. 36; Collier & Horowitz (*Roosevelts*), p. 87; Caroli, p. 243. Some contend he merely died trying to leap out the window.

13   "Somehow it was . . . a life together." Cook (*Vol. 1*), p. 80; Goodwin (*Time*), p. 94; Brands (*Traitor*), p. 35. Elliott admonished Eleanor to care for her little brother Hall (the future comptroller of Detroit). He lived with Eleanor and FDR until himself marrying. Unfortunately, he too was an alcoholic, dying of a "chronic liver ailment" on September 26, 1941. (Roosevelt [*Aunt*], p. 50; *NY Times*, 26 September 1941, p. 19)

14   "He dominated my . . . after he died." Roosevelt (*Autobiography*), p. 5; Brands (*Traitor*), p. 35.

15   Funeral. Brands (*Traitor*), p. 36.

16   "My mother was . . . ever seen." Roosevelt (*Autobiography*), p. 3; Cook (*Vol. 1*), p. 21; Brands (*Traitor*), p. 34.

17   "She's such a . . . call her Granny." Roosevelt (*Autobiography*), p. 9; Schlesinger (*Crisis*), p. 326; Davis (*Beckoning*), p. 177.

18   Mother's death. Ward (*Trumpet*), p. 281; Lash (*Eleanor*), p. 44; Goodwin (*Time*), p. 94; Collier & Horowitz (*Roosevelts*), p. 84; Caroli, p. 242; Davis (*Beckoning*), p. 181.

19   "Death meant . . . him very soon." Schlesinger (*Crisis*), p. 326; Lash (*Eleanor*), p. 44. The death of her younger brother Elliott Jr., also of diphtheria, soon followed.

20   Alcoholic uncles. Ward (*Trumpet*), p. 263; Davis (*Beckoning*), pp. 186-87.

21   Taught to ride. *Brooklyn Eagle*, 28 October 1934, p. 1.

22   Shoot. Cook (*Vol. 1*), p. 514.

23   "arrested twice. . . ten-year old girl. . . ." Cook (*Vol. 1*), p. 432. Joseph P. Lash, however, says this of him: "Vallie began associating with a young neighbor who had been arrested for raping a ten-year old girl and who managed to smuggle in liquor." This would be in the period when FDR was governor. (Lash [*Eleanor*], p. 454) Following a July 12, 1930, row at the Hall home at Tivoli, Eleanor's bodyguard Earl Miller convinced him to leave. (Cook [*Vol. 1*], p. 432; Lash [*Eleanor*], p. 341; Persico [*Lucy*], pp. 189-90) Eleanor found him dead in his sleep there in 1934. (*Brooklyn Eagle*, 28 October 1934, p. 1)

24   "To keep my uncles out". Ward (*Trumpet*), pp. 304, 365; Cook (*Vol. 1*), pp. 126, 517; Brands (*Traitor*), p. 37. Laura Chanler White, then a centenarian, revealed the story to author Geoffrey Ward.

25   Illiterate. Roosevelt (*Aunt*), p. 10.

26   "many tears". Ward (*Trumpet*), pp. 291-92, 364.

27   "the happiest . . . life." Ward (*Trumpet*), p. 294.

28 "short and rather stout". Roosevelt (*Autobiography*), p. 22; Cook (*Vol. 1*), p. 106.

29 Atheist. Davis (*New Deal*), p. 39; Ward (*Trumpet*), p. 298; Davis (*Beckoning*), p. 185; Brands (*Traitor*), p. 37.

30 Lesbian. Caroli, pp. 249-50.

31 Pisa & Florence. Ward (*Trumpet*), p. 298; Cook (*Vol. 1*), p. 114.

32 Trips. Ward (*Trumpet*), p. 301; Cook (*Vol. 1*), p. 116.

33 "that she [Eleanor] . . . of her soul." Ward (*Trumpet*), p. 301; Cook (*Vol. 1*), pp. 109-10.

34 Achievements. Cook (*Vol. 1*), pp. 110-12.

35 Christmas party. Ward (*Trumpet*), pp. 293-94; Persico (*Lucy*), p. 27.

36 "sex an ordeal to be borne". Cook (*Vol. 1*), p. 13. Their relationship appears to be sexless after her discovery of the Mercer affair. Nonetheless, she continued to share his bed at Hyde Park until 1921, moving to a separate room only because the immobile FDR required awakening and physical turning by a manservant several times each night to prevent bedsores. Eleanor simply required her own sleep. (National Park Service guide to author, 5 December 2012) On East 65th Street, however, Eleanor seemed to have taken separate quarters even before 1921. (Cook [*Vol. 1*], p. 112)

37 "to understand little children or to enjoy them." Lash (*Love*), p. 57; Lash (*Eleanor*), p. 275. "Playing with children was difficult for me because play had not been an important part of my own childhood," she would explain.

38 1922 incident. Roosevelt (*Autobiography*), pp. 119-20; Cook (*Vol. 1*), pp. 312-13; Willis, p. 67.

39 Weeks away. Black (*Champion*), p. 158; Persico (*Lucy*), p. 172; Alter, p. 55. According to Rexford Tugwell Eleanor "detested western Georgia and the western Georgians." (Tugwell [*Brains*], p. 91)

40 Mother allocated a back bedroom . . . spite of her Catholic background." Roosevelt and Brough (*Hyde Park*), pp. 258-59. Elliott Roosevelt's older brother James dismissed the idea of an FDR–LeHand affair as "utterly ridiculous," as he did regarding rumors involving Eleanor with Nancy Cook and Marion Dickerman. James, however, conceded that his mother "may have had an affair" with Earl Miller. (Roosevelt [*Parents*], pp. 105-6, 110-12; Willis, p. 86) Dissenting from the Miller-as-lover theory are Joseph P. Lash and Joseph E. Persico. (Persico [*Lucy*], pp. 194-96)

41 "a little crack-up . . . breakdown". Goodwin (*Ordinary*), p. 117; Willis, p. 100; Persico (*Lucy*), p. 170. Tully found Missy to be "a woman of great dignity and charm." (Tully, p. 338)

42 First eleven days. Persico (*Lucy*), p. 170; Rowley, pp. 143-44.

43 *Larooco* sale. Goodwin (*Ordinary*), p. 117; Willis, p. 100.

44 Winthrop Rutherfurd. *NY Times*, 12 February 1920; p, 11; Willis, pp. 45-56, 60-62; Persico (*Lucy*), p. 138; Pottker, p. 193; Weintraub, pp. 181-83. Rutherfurd's first marriage occurred at age forty, though he carried on numerous affairs beforehand, including one reputedly with Ada Astor, mother of FDR confidant Vincent Astor, nephew of James "Rosey" Roosevelt's wife Helen. (Cross, p. 71)

45 Whereabouts. Persico (*Lucy*), p. 171. Travel to Warm Springs for Lucy might have been less problematic than one would think. Her husband possessed an estate at Aiken, South Carolina, just across the Georgia state line. Missy may not have discovered any letters at Warm Springs. She may, however, have discovered Lucy.

46 Lape, Read. Cook (*Vol. 1*), pp. 13, 292-93; Black (*Champion*), p. 10; Streitmatter, pp. xviii-xix. Eleanor rented her Greenwich Village apartment at 20 East 11th Street from them. (Persico [*Lucy*], p. 190; Goodwin (*Ordinary*), p. 18) Alice Roosevelt termed the duo "female impersonators"—FDR as "squaws" and "she-men." (Cordery, p. 374; Beasley, p. 34; Black [*Champion*], p. 146)

47 1924 Smith campaign. Roosevelt (*Yesterday*), p. 164; Perkins, p. 68; Anthony (*First Ladies*), p. 403; Roosevelt & Brough (*Mother R.*), pp. 159-61; Perry, p. 181; Cordery, p. 313; Collier & Horowitz (*Roosevelts*), p. 299. In November 1893, Alice's mother had written to her own mother, "As you know I never wished Alice to associate with Eleanor so I shall not try to keep up any friendship between them" Cook (*Vol. 1*), pp. 92, 514.

48 "I am very . . . confidence shown him." Davis (*New York*), p. 29; Smith (*FDR*), p. 698.

49 "If the rest . . . it make to me?" *NY Post*, 8 November 1928, page unknown; Lash (*Eleanor*), p. 320; Black (*Champion*), p. 185; Davis (*New York*), p. 51; Smith (*FDR*), p. 235; Collier & Horowitz (*Roosevelts*), p. 321; Persico (*Lucy*), p. 184.

50 "I felt Gov. Smith's . . . comparatively little." Cook (*Vol. 1*), p. 554; Black (*Champion*), p. 185; Persico (*Lucy*), p. 184. Elinor was Mrs. Henry Morgenthau, Jr.

51 "Much love and . . . next two years." Black (*Champion*), pp. 207-8; Persico (*Lucy*), p. 197.

52 "It is a . . . man and wife." West & Kotz, p. 23; Persico (*Lucy*), p. 219. Harry Hopkins said much the same thing: "Watch them, because they do all their communication with each other in public."

53 "Get out and talk". Lash (*Eleanor*), p. 311.

54 Birth control. *NY Times*, 16 November 1929, p. 14; *NY Times*, 19 November 1929, p. 1; Cook (*Vol. 1*), p. 13; Beasley, p. 51; Persico (*Lucy*), p. 175. It was not until 1931 that any denomination condoned artificial contraception—and even then in rather limited circumstances.

55 "regarded her . . . in Albany." Tugwell (*Brains*), p. 88.

56 "a wonderful good will". Tugwell (*Brains*), p. 54.

57 "humorless." Tugwell (*Brains*), p. 54.

58 "I want to . . . has the Republican." Lash (*Eleanor*), p. 319; Beasley, p. 43. In the Hoover-Roosevelt interregnum, she wrote to White House chief usher "Ike" Hoover a note, which included the following: "I will also have my maid and my husband's valet, both colored. . . . Will you let me know which will be the best door for them to enter by?" (Roosevelt Houses display, second floor) The implication is obvious, and there was to be no social racial integration of her staff either at the White House or at Hyde Park. (Bartlett [*Race*], pp. 111-12)

59 "scarcely ever participated . . . into our concerns." Moley (*27*), pp. 38-39.

60 "It is nice . . . new solutions. . . ." *NY Times*, 13 January 1932, p. 8; Cook (*Vol. 1*), p. 423.

61 "There was his . . . knee at poolside." Cook (*Vol. 1*), p. 434.

62 "I believe there . . . seem to mind." Roosevelt (*Parents*), pp. 110-11; Cook (*Vol. 1*), p. 435; Persico (*Lucy*), p. 193.

63 "He used to . . . now he's Earl." Collier & Horowitz (*Roosevelts*), p. 327; Pottker, p. 252.

64 "She was not . . . partner and confidant." Lash (*Friends*), p. 311; Persico (*Lucy*), p. 230. Today many ponder why she remained with him. Others then pondered the opposite question. In 1925 or 1926, the rising British politician Oswald Mosley and his wife, Cynthia, visited the Roosevelts, and Cynthia puzzled: "What a contrast between this magnificent man with his fine head and massive torso, handsome as a classic Greek and radiating charm though completely immobile, and the exceptionally ugly woman, all movement and vivacity within an aura of gentle kindness but without even a reflection of his attraction." (Collier & Horowitz [*Roosevelts*], pp. 314-15; Black [*Champion*], p. 171)

65 "Yet if there . . . Dickerman and Cook." Collier & Horowitz (*Roosevelts*), p. 315.

66 "Mrs. R was . . . to get married." Cook (*Vol. 1*), p. 436; Smith (*FDR*), p. 248*fn.*

67 Miller/LeHand. Roosevelt (*Parents*), pp. 110-11; Cook (*Vol. 1*), p. 435. "If father noticed [the Miller-Eleanor affair]," recalled James Roosevelt, "he did not seem to mind. Curiously, he did promote a romance between Miller and Missy, but that did not last."

68 "My main purpose . . . was being hurt". Cook (*Vol. 1*), p. 437; Persico (*Lucy*), pp. 192-93; Willis, p. 86. Historian Joseph Persico dismisses Miller's story as "far-fetched."

69 Chicago flight. Cook (*Vol. 1*), pp. 446-47.

70 "You are not . . . Not to anyone!" Davis (*New York*), pp. 329-31; Persico (*Lucy*), p. 199; Beasley, p. 52. And, yet when McAdoo had placed Roosevelt over the top, Eleanor and Missy embraced at the news. Perhaps, it was the mere excitement of the moment; perhaps, Missy initiated the action, and Eleanor simply reacted to her. (Tully, p. 51)

71 "I did not want . . . subject to him." Roosevelt (*Remember*), p. 69; Persico (*Lucy*), p. 199; Beasley, p. 53.

72 Last Miller flight. Roosevelt (*This I Remember*), p. 70; Cook (*Vol. 1*), p. 447. When FDR became president he took his ultra-trusted (indeed, beloved) bodyguard Gus Gennerich with him to Washington but not Miller. Miller received the measly consolation prize of personnel director for the state department of corrections. (*NY Times*, 10 May 1973, p. 48; Beasley, p. 52; Black [*Casting*], p. 10)

73 "and the Sergeant . . . killing the gossip." Cook (*Vol. 1*), p. 436; Smith (*FDR*), p. 248*fn*.

74 Annulled. *NY Times*, 8 July 1932, p. 3; Cook (*Vol. 1*), p. 464; Persico (*Lucy*), p. 195. During this campaign season Anna—with the family's approval—took up with *Chicago Tribune* reporter John Boettiger. The family had never cared much for her husband, the financially failing investment banker Curtis Dall. (Collier & Horowitz [*Roosevelts*], pp. 363-64; Boettinger, p. 282; Streitmatter, p. 22*fn*)

75 Lesbian, sapphire ring. Cook (*Vol. 1*), p. 486; Streitmatter, pp. 10, 198; Persico (*Lucy*), p. 203; Beasley, p. 58.

76 Beefy, cigars, drinking. Streitmatter, p. xvi.

77 "The new mistress . . . very great lady". Persico (*Lucy*), p. 207.

78 Vetted articles. Hickok (*Reluctant*), p. 89; Streitmatter, p. 8.

79 Potsdam activities. Hickok (*Reluctant*), pp. 48-49; Streitmatter, p. 9; Cook (*Vol. 1*), pp. 466-68; Lash (*Eleanor*), p. 352.

80 "May I write . . . I trust you." Hickok (*Reluctant*), p. 59. Author Rodger Streitmatter indicates that on this night Hickok revealed to Eleanor that she had been raped as a child and that "When Eleanor . . . heard that shocking revelation, she instinctively reached out to [Hickok]. Eleanor's long, graceful arms embraced and comforted Lorena—assuring her she was safe, showing her that she was loved. Neither woman got much sleep that night, Lorena later wrote, but by the next morning their relationship had reached what the reporter called a new level of intimacy." He cites Hickok's account of the event, which in no way supports his version. (Streitmatter, p. 9)

CHAPTER TWENTY-THREE: "I SAW HITLER CIGARETTES"

1 "No system of . . . and political violence." Papen, pp. 199-200; Knight-Patterson, pp. 543-44; Heiden (*Fuehrer*), p. 486; Clark (*German Republic*), pp. 398-99; Halperin, p. 503. As late as August 28, Papen had delivered a radio address that Goebbels summarized as "from first to last out of our ideas." (Goebbels [*Part*], p. 145; Fest [*Face*], p. 156)

2 Commuted sentences. *NY Post*, 2 September 1932, p. 12; *NY Times*, 3 September 1932, p. 5; Fest (*Hitler*), p. 342, 345; Davidson, p. 188.

3 "No matter where . . . his Nazi movement." *NY Times*, 20 August 1932, p. 4. This was the *Nueu Front* ("New Front") brand. The anti-Hitler Iron Front already boasted *Drei Pfeile* ("Three Arrows") cigarettes. (Snyder [*Encyclopedia*], p. 246) In May 1932, printer Fritz Dittrich of Neustadt, Saxony, wrote to the non-smoking Führer suggesting putting "a *Hitler cigarette* and a *Hitler cigar* on the German market . . . *legally protected* under this name." Martin Bormann's younger brother Albert respectfully but firmly responded in the negative. (Eberle, pp. 60-61)

4 Göring Reichstagspräsident. Clark (*German Republic*), p. 405; Manvell & Fraenkel (*Hundred*), pp. 48-49.

5 DNVP, Zentrum, BVP. *NY Times*, 31 August 1932, pp. 1, 9; Goebbels (*Part*), p. 146; François-Poncet, p. 37; Dorpalen, p. 361; Clark (*German Republic*), p. 405; Heiden (*Fuehrer*), p. 491; Eyck, p. 428; Mommsen, p. 469; Orlow (*Nazi*), p. 279; Wheaton, p. 131.

6 "establish contact". Knight-Patterson, p. 544.

7 "Have a conference . . . a trap again." Goebbels (*Part*), p. 143; Shirer, p. 170.

8 "very humble . . . to give in." Goebbels (*Part*), p. 145; *NY Times*, 30 August 1932, p. 1.

9 Lunch meeting. *NY Times*, 30 August 1932, p. 1; Goebbels (*Part*), p. 145; Rolfs, pp. 177-78; Gilbert (*Winston Churchill, Vol. 5*), p. 447.

10 September 1. Kershaw (*Hubris*), p. 385.

11 Age rule. *NY Sun*, 2 August 1932, p. 16; *NY Times*, 31 August 1932, p. 9; Clark (*German Republic*), p. 404; Papen, p. 207; François-Poncet, p. 37; Eyck, p. 428; Wheeler-Bennett (*Titan*), pp. 413-14; Manvell & Fraenkel (*Hundred*), p. 48; Kershaw (*Hubris*), p. 384; Davidson, pp. 334-35. To block a Zetkin encore in the next Reichstag, Nazis nominated the even more ancient (and, perhaps, more ornery) Gen. Karl Litzmann (1850-1936).

12 Moscow. *NY Times*, 20 August 1932, p. 4; *NY Times*, 28 August 1932, p. 4; *NY Times*, 18 September 1932, p. XX2. Goebbels witnessed a Zetkin speech in November 1925 and summed her up as "Trenchant, acute, clear, full of hate, a pioneer of Bolshevism" (Goebbels [*Early*], p. 51)

13 "It is a rule of . . . these Fascist murderers." *NY Times*, 31 August 1932, p. 9; *NY Times*, 18 September 1932, p. XX2.

14 "You will give . . . of boundless discipline". *NY Times*, 30 August 1932, p. 1.

15 "I assert to . . . said to exist." Manvell & Fraenkel (*Hundred*), pp. 48-49; Manvell & Fraenkel (*Göring*), p. 45; Dorpalen, p. 361; Eyck, p. 428; Davidson, p. 335.

16 "What do you . . . discovered himself!" Fest (*Face*), p. 154; Mitchell, p. 165.

17 "[B]oth Hindenburg and his . . . *père et fil.*" Wheeler-Bennett (*Nemesis*), p. 259.

18 "all his faults, a man of courage." Heiden (*Fuehrer*), p. 486.

19 Unemployment insurance. Knight-Patterson, p. 545; Koeves, p. 151; Mommsen, p. 473.

20 Wage cuts. Heiden (*Fuehrer*), p. 487; Manvell & Fraenkel, p. 50; Koeves, pp. 151-52; Rolfs, pp. 180-83; Eyck, p. 429; Halperin, p. 504; Davidson, p. 335; Mommsen, pp. 472-73; Dorpalen, p. 359.

21 "there was no . . . Kiss of Death." Schofield, p. 62.

22 Nationalists. Manvell & Frankel (*Hundred*), p. 51; Papen, p. 208; Eyck, p. 430; Shirer, p. 170; Bullock, p. 226; Dorpalen, pp. 362-63; Rolfs, p. 192; Kershaw (*Hubris*), p. 385; Mommsen, p. 470; Koeves, p. 171.

23 "the stupidest trade . . . a meeting properly." *NY Times*, 13 September 1932, p. 11; Clark (*German Republic*), p. 410.

24 "a kind of . . . half clown." Guérin, p. 63; Large (*Berlin*), p. 249.

25 Delay. *Brooklyn Eagle*, 12 September 1932, p. 1; *NY Times*, 13 September 1932, p. 11; Papen, p. 208; Heiden (*History*), p. 203; Manvell & Frankel (*Hundred*), p. 51; Eyck, p. 430; Shirer, p. 170; Davidson, p. 336; Wheaton, p. 131; Koeves, pp. 171-72; Orlow (*Nazi*), p. 280; Rolfs, p. 192; Dorpalen, p. 363; Wheeler-Bennett (*Titan*), p. 413; Mommsen, p. 469; Mitchell (*Hitler*), p. 162.

26 "pretentious . . . very pale". Guérin, p. 64.

27 "a tiny . . . monkey". Guérin, p. 64.

28 Adjournment. *Brooklyn Eagle*, 12 September 1932, p. 1; *Brooklyn Daily Star*, 12 September 1932, p. 1; *NY Times*, 13 September 1932, pp. 1, 11; Papen, pp. 208-9; Clark (*German Republic*), p. 409; François-Poncet, pp. 38-39; Manvell & Fraenkel (*Hundred*), pp. 49-52; Eyck, pp. 430-31; Lüdecke, p. 484; Wheeler-Bennett (*Titan*), pp. 413-14; Davidson, p. 336; Kershaw (*Hubris*), pp. 385-86; Fest (*Hitler*), p. 345; Davidson, p. 189; Shirer, p. 170; Dorpalen, p. 363; Bullock, p. 227; Wheaton, p. 131; Koeves, p. 172; Mosley, p. 146. Five members abstained.

29 "The bridges have . . . check economic recovery?" *Literary Digest*, 24 September 1932, p. 15.

30 "The past 14 . . . the whole nation." *Brooklyn Eagle*, 12 September 1932, p. 1.

31 "The conflict between . . . to a head". *Literary Digest*, 24 September 1932, p. 15.

32 Funding. US Department of State, pp. 313-16; Wheeler-Bennett (*Titan*), p. 514.

33 "[T]he Party exchequer . . . getting fagged out." Goebbels (*Part*), p. 156; Bullock, p. 227.

34 "dissolution of the . . . somewhat depressed." Longerich, p. 142.

35 "our movement's failure. . . depression and insecurity." Longerich, p. 142.

36 "peacemaker to the monarchy." Thyssen, p. 142.

37 Kaiser incensed. Thyssen, p. 142; McDonogh, p. 448; Wheeler-Bennett (*Nemesis*), p. 231*fn*; Cowles, p. 424. Hitler had once similarly assured Kronprinz Wilhelm: "My goal is the restoration of the Empire under a Hohenzollern." (Jonas, p. 182; Cowles, p. 424)

38 "first unworthy, second laughable, third absolutely *revolutionary.*" Cecil, p. 318.

39 "There's a . . . to consult . . .". *Ken*, December 15, 1939, p. 17.

40 "no statesman." Cecil, p. 318.

41 Hearst. Nasaw (*Hearst*), pp. 476-77.

42 Libel. *NY Times*, 16 September 1932, p. 11.

43 "Those who are . . . of the antiquated." *NY Times*, 15 September 1932, p. 9; Mauch, p. 49.

44 Carter's later résumé. *Utica Press*, 3 May 1939, p. 4; *NY Times*, 24 December 1959, p. 11; *NY Times*, 29 November 1967, p. 47; *Brooklyn Weekly People*, 16 January 1960, p. 3; Persico (*Secret*), pp.

56-57. Some of the "information" Carter fed FDR was completely off the wall, e.g., that Gen. Charles de Gaulle and United Mine Workers leader John L. Lewis were plotting together to overthrow him. (Andrew, pp. 132-33; Persico [*Secret*], p. 190)

45   State Department. *NY Times*, 15 September 1932, p. 9; *Utica Press*, 3 May 1939, p. 4; *NY Times*, 29 November 1967, p. 47.

46   "Wanted: A New Party". *New Yorker*, 11 January 1941, p. 25.

47   "A new party for a new deal." Morris (*Luce*), p. 195. *Vanity Fair* had also headlined: "Appoint a dictator!" (Schlesinger [*Crisis*], p. 268)

48   "the widely held . . . the Reich government." *NY Times*, 15 September 1932, p. 9; *North Adams Transcript*, 20 September 1932, p. 17; *Oakland Tribune*, 26 September 1932, p. 24.

49   "That intimation can . . . other foreign elements." www.jta.org/1932/10/05/archive/denies-he-seeks-to-implant-hitlerism-here-scores-jews-in-socialist-party.

50   "the [Nazi] chieftain . . . anti-Semitic zeal." www.jta.org/1932/10/05/archive/denies-he-seeks-to-implant-hitlerism-here-scores-jews-in-socialist-party. Carter also claimed to have recently rejected an invitation to "a Swastika organization," presumably Kurt Lüdecke's "Swastika League of America."

51   Hyde Park. Mauch, p. 49. Joseph Persico said the meeting was in Albany. (Persico [*Secret*], p. 56) For some reason, years later FDR later informed Carter that he had known Hanfstaengl at Harvard. As Roosevelt had departed the university six years before Hanfstaengl's arrival, that is more than doubtful. Either FDR or (more likely) Carter remembered it wrong. (Persico [*Secret*], p. 193)

52   "You're going to be elected President". Persico (*Secret*), p. 56.

53   Sedgwicks/Carters. Persico (*Secret*), pp. 56, 193; Mauch, p. 49.

54   "Any country which . . . in foreign affairs." Hanfstaengl), p. 197.

55   "Think of your . . . ambassador at once." Conradi, p. 98. Hanfstaengl, pp. 197-98.

56   Raubal's grave. Lüdecke, p. 496; Goebbels (*Part*), p. 159; Sigmund, p. 145. Goebbels, Angela Raubal, and adjutant Julius Schaub went ahead to facilitate the pilgrimage.

Chapter Twenty-four: "Vote for Roosevelt and make it unanimous"

1   World Series. Mead & Dickson, pp. 79-80.

2   Detroit. Rosenman (*Papers*), pp. 771-80; Suckley; Fried, p. 43, Warren (*Coughlin*), p. 43.

3   "just as radical as I am". *Ames Tribune*, 4 October 1932, p. 7; Fried, p. 43; Golway, p. 199.

4   "Very well, we'll . . . very great man." Moley (*Seven*), p. 58.

5   28 percent. *Literary Digest*, 15 October 1932, pp. 8-9; Ritchie, p. 153. The *Literary Digest* ultimately came within 0.71 percent of 1932's actual results (Pietrusza [*1920*], p. 446 [paperback])

6   Farley. *NY Times*, 2 October 1932, p. 33.

7   32 percent. *Literary Digest*, 15 October 1932, pp. 1, 2, 8-9; Ritchie, p. 153.

8   Photographed. Weiss, p. 25; www.presidency.ucsb.edu/ws/index.php?pid=23264&st=&st1=.

9   White House lawn. *Crisis*, November 1932, pp. 343-44; Lisio (*Blacks*), pp. 271, 273.

10 Assassination. Fecher, p. 52.

11 "jumpy." Joslin, pp. 306-7.

12 "[W]e of the . . . panic stricken". Starling, p. 299.

13 "The city was . . . I considered dangerous." Starling, p. 299.

14 "Hoover Murdered . . . Marchers". *NY Times*, 23 October 1932, p. 1; Ritchie, p. 144.

15 "tumultuous booing and catcalling." Joslin, p. 321; Ritchie, pp. 144-45.

16 Nose-thumbing. Fecher, p. 52; Manchester (*Glory*), pp. 52-53.

17 "I shall vote . . . of Mr. Curtis." *Salt Lake Tribune*, 7 October 1932, p. 9; *Time*, 17 October 1932, p. 13; *NY Times*, 15 December 1974, p. 66; Steel, pp. 295-96.

18 "America's Hitler Marshals . . . Will Defeat Hoover." *Washington Post*, 9 October 1932, p. 3.

19 Boston. *Kansas City Star*, 25 September 1932, p. 1.

20 Rhode Island. *NY Post*, 15 October 1932, p. 2.

21 Hurja. Holli, pp. 51-52. Not all Catholics, of course, suddenly transformed themselves into Hoover partisans. "Undoubtedly anti-Catholic, as well as Catholic support was enlisted behind . . . Mr. Roosevelt," wrote *The Tablet*, the official publication of Brooklyn's archdiocese. "But to have the gentlemen who in 1928 used the dirtiest, vilest and most widespread anti-Catholic bigotry to win a tainted victory, trying to pull their chestnuts out of the fire, is more than we can stomach. Where was this partisan group, who are now so solicitous over Mr. Smith's religion in 1928? They were actually circulating and paying for the most diabolical lies about Mr. Smith's religion. The corpse of [Methodist] Bishop [James] Cannon is fastened to their backs, and it is embalmed in Fellowship Forum." (*Catholic Courier and Journal*, 19 August 1932, p. 6)

22 "Massachusetts Drifts to Hoover." *The Nation*, 12 October 1932, pp. 329-30.

23 "BAY STATE DOUBTFUL . . . President Hoover." *NY Times*, 23 October 1932, p. E5.

24 "On a Chinese . . . your crowd." Handlin, p. 168; O'Connor (*Hurrah*), p. 266.

25 "Hello, you old potato." *Yonkers Herald Statesman*, 5 October, 1932, p. 4; *NY Sun*, 6 October 1932, p. 28; *Time*, 17 October 1932, p. 12; O'Connor (*Hurrah*), p. 266; Ritchie, p. 143; Schlesinger (*Crisis*), p. 430; Smith (*FDR*), p. 279. Anti-FDR Albany County Democrats had not only endorsed Albany mayor George Boyd Thacher for governor, they turned out in large numbers to hail Jimmy Walker as he arrived to face Roosevelt's grilling. (*NY Times*, 10 August 1932, p. 1; *NY Sun*, 28 September 1932, p. 7)

26 "[The tax] burden . . . direct and vital." Rosenman (*Papers*), pp. 795-812.

27 "a giant misprint." Tugwell (*Democratic*), pp. 239-40; Freidel (*Triumph*), p. 362*fn*; Ritchie, p. 142. Tugwell thought the speech "most unfortunate" and "as contradictory as it was possible to be." (Tugwell [*Revolution*], p. 4)

28 "I have never advocated . . . great laboring people." Rosenman (*Papers*), pp. 795-812; *The Nation*, 2 November 1932, p. 414.

29 "is the doctrine . . . Democratic about it." *The Nation*, 2 November 1932, p. 414.

30 Coolidge. *NY Times*, 12 October 1932, pp. 1, 16; *NY Times*, 15 October 1932, p. 1; *NY Times*, 20 October 1932, p. 1; *The Nation*, 2 November 1932, p. 414; Peel & Donnelly, p. 141.

31 Waters. *Washington Post*, 8 September 1932, p. 2.

32 De Lucco correspondence. *The Nation*, 2 November 1932, p. 414. Actually, Roosevelt's position, though carefully hedged, had been consistent in its hedginess for months. (*San Antonio Light*, 26 September 1932, p. 1)

33 "BONUS TREATMENT COULD . . . BETTER DONE." Freedman, p. 90. Privately, Frankfurter wrote to Walter Lippmann: "If Roosevelt is elected, I think he will often do the right things, as it were, on inadequate and not wholly sturdy grounds. That's what I feel about the bonus statement."

34 "If this is . . . heaven help us". *The Nation*, 2 November 1932, p. 414.

35 "the dreadful position . . . the Scotch plaid." *Spartanburg Herald-Journal*, 29 October 1932, p. 1; Freidel (*New Deal*), p. 14; Mason, p. 35; Black (*Champion*), p. 246; Alter, p. 131*fn*.

36 "brought into the . . . one time". *LA Times*, 12 September 1932, p. 4; *Hartford Courant*, 12 September 1932, p. 1; *Plattsburgh Press*, 12 September 1932, p. 1.

37 1,069. Horan, p. 82. Of these, 829 (17.4 percent) were convicted.

38 American Legion. *Chicago Tribune*, 16 September 1932, p. 1; Hart (*Year 1932*), p. 36.

39 "the satellites of . . . their own hands." *Washington Post*, 4 November 1932, p. 2; *Plattsburgh Press*, 4 November 1932, p. 1.

40 "The President was . . . to the platform." Joslin, p. 324; Leuchtenburg (*Hoover*), p. 141; Smith (*Dream*), pp. 200-201.

41 "we still have . . . against a mob." *Time*, 14 November 1932, p. 10; Starling, p. 300; Dickson & Allen, p. 201; Ritchie, p. 155; Leuchtenburg (*Hoover*), p. 141; Smith (*Dream*), p. 201; Manchester (*Glory*), p. 52. Hoover also asked, "How does the gentleman explain the last 3 years of unparalleled social calm?"

42 "Why don't they . . . into a farce." Starling, p. 300; Schlesinger (*Crisis*), p. 437; Dickson & Allen, p. 201; Ritchie, p. 155; Leuchtenburg (*Hoover*), p. 141.

43 Ovation. Dille, p. 61.

44 "grass will grow . . . will decay." *NY Times*, 1 November 1932, pp. 1, 12; Schlesinger (*Crisis*), p. 435; Ritchie, p. 147; Smith (*Uncommon*), p. 147; Manchester (*Glory*), p. 52.

45 Indianapolis. *Geneva Times*, 29 October 1932, p. 3; Joslin, p. 322; Lyons, p. 300; Jeansonne (*Hoover*), p. 421. His press secretary Ted Joslin considered that "from a political point of view, [this] speech was the high point of his campaign."

46 Ford. *NY Times*, 23 October 1932, p. 1; Dille, pp. 59-60.

47 "to provide employment . . . at all times." *NY Times*, 23 October 1932, p. 29; *Time*, 31 October 1932, p. 10; Hoover (*Depression*), p. 316; Starling, p. 300; Dille, p. 60; Jeansonne (*Hoover*), p. 421.

48 Your single purpose . . . deserves every support." *Ames Tribune-Times*, 5 October 1932, p. 2; *Salt Lake Tribune*, 6 October 1932, p. 2.

49 Heckling. *NY Times*, 1 November 1932, p. 12.

50 Des Moines. *NY Times*, 5 October 1932, p. 19; Ossian, p. 171.

51 "As the glum . . . saw or heard." Ossian, p. 171.

52 "Mr. Hoover's speech . . . agree with him." *Ames Times-Tribune*, 5 October 1932, p. 2.

53 "I can't go . . . anymore." Leuchtenburg (*Hoover*), p. 141.

54 "I'll tell you . . . are dark?" Lorant, pp. 598-99; Ritchie, p. 135; Smith (*Uncommon*), p. 140; Jeansonne (*Hoover*), p. 414.

55 "We are convinced . . . Hoover must be re-elected." *Stevens Point Journal*, 24 October 1932, p. 4; Schlesinger (*Crisis*), p. 432; Manchester (*Glory*), p. 52.

56 "wore the Hoover . . . voted for FDR." Fenyvesi, p. 71.

57 "too damn dumb". *Buffalo News*, 20 September 1928, p. 7; Smith (*Dream*), p. 185.

58 "Mr. Curtis . . . Iowa Farmer." *NY Times*, 5 October 1932, p. 19.

59 Utah. *Chicago Tribune*, 16 October 1932, p. 1; *Ogden Standard Examiner*, 15 October 1932, pp. 1-2. *Brooklyn Eagle*, 15 October 1932, p. 1; *Greeley Tribune*, 15 October 1932, p. 1; *Santa Cruz Sentinel*, 15 October 1932, p. 1.

60 Earlier injury. *Santa Cruz Sentinel*, 15 October 1932, p. 1.

61 Las Vegas. *Time*, 8 August 1932, p. 5; Smith (*Dream*), p. 185.

62 *Literary Digest*. *Literary Digest*, 15 October 1932; pp. 10-11; Ritchie, p. 153.

63 Hearst poll. *San Antonio Light*, 21 October 1932, p. 3A; *Time*, 31 October 1932, p. 11. The United Press carried this report from New Jersey: "The wet issue, usually hot stuff with us, seems to be slumbering. Liquor is abundant and cheap so that none is suffering on that score. The idle hordes, the bonuseers and the middle class business boys, who have no business, are all going to vote against Mr. Hoover and they don't seem to care much what Mr. Roosevelt stands for—if anything." (*NY Post*, 15 October 1932, p. 2)

64 FDR/Berle. Freidel (*New Deal*), pp. 18-19.

65 Groton. Freidel (*New Deal*), p. 5.

66 Princeton. *Princeton Alumni Weekly*, 4 November 1932, p. 147.

67 Nationwide college poll. *NY Times*, 28 October 1932, p. 10; *Harrisburg News*, 28 October 1932, p. 7; *Princeton Alumni Weekly*, 4 November 1932, p. 147; *Time*, 7 November 1932, pp. 14-15; Johnpoll, p. 94.

68 Clergy poll. *NY Times*, 1 November 1932, p. 14; Ritchie, p. 154. Norman Thomas received 25 votes; Prohibitionist William D. Upshaw, 1. About 150 ministers abstained.

69 First trip. Ritchie, p. 155.

70 Lindbergh. Ritchie, p. 154. In 1928, a Hoover campaign song had boasted, "If he's good enough for Lindy, he's good enough for me." While Hoover wouldn't fly, Mrs. H. Foster Bain, 53, and Mrs. Samuel Dolber, 50, took to the skies in support of his candidacy. In mid-October, the two New York City "flying grandmothers" saluted the Hoovers' campaign train from the air, but Hoover luck being what it was that year, they crashed near Chicago before flying on to Iowa City via commercial airliner. Mary W. Bain, the duo's actual pilot, perhaps, not surprisingly, was the wife of a mining engineer. (*Greeley Tribune*, 15 October 1932, p. 1; *Brooklyn Eagle*, 31 October 1932, p. 2)

71 Post office. Ybarra, pp. 99, 112-13.

72 Navy. Ybarra, p. 119.

73 "If you meet . . . will be defeated." Wilson (*Challenge*), p. 231.

74 "I see the . . . It is all over". Wilson (*Challenge*), p. 231; Barber (*Character*), p. 40.

75 Unemployment. Ybarra, p. 100.

76 Bank holiday. Edwards, pp. 49-50; Kull & Kull, p. 251.

77 Dynamite. *Reno Gazette*, 7 November 1932, p. 1; Ybarra, p. 119.

78 Radio address. *Reno Gazette*, 8 November 1932, p. 2; *Plattsburgh Press*, 8 November 1932, p. 1; Ybarra, p. 123; Jeansonne (*Hoover*), p. 424.

79 NYC radio broadcasts. *Brooklyn Eagle*, 7 November 1932, p. 33.

80 Dynamite plot. *Nevada State Journal*, 8 November 1932, p. 1; *El Paso Herald Post*, 8 November 1932, p. 1; *Iowa City Iowan*, 9 November 1932, p. 9; *Charleston Mail*, 8 November 1932, p. 1; Ybarra, p. 123. Oddly enough, near Beloit, Wisconsin, two African Americans, Henry Vance and Hayes White, were arrested on suspicion of planning to remove spikes from the Chicago & Northwestern tracks on which Hoover's train would travel. Vance later admitted the two planned on loosening the rails and then collecting a reward for reporting their condition. (*Rome Sentinel*, 5 November 1932, p. 1; *Time*, 31 October 1932, p. 11; *Gloversville-Johnstown Herald*, 17 November 1932, p. 1; *New York Age*, 26 November 1932, p. 1; *Pittsburgh Courier*, 26 November 1932, p. 7; Jeansonne [*Hoover*], p. 424) A bomb containing six ounces of dynamite was mailed to FDR in April 1929 but made it only as far as New York City's general post office. (Ayton, p. 7)

81 "Oh, Raspberries!" . . . care of him." *El Paso Herald Post*, 8 November 1932, p. 1; *Charleston Mail*, 8 November 1932, p. 1.

82 Ranch. *El Paso Herald Post*, 8 November 1932, p. 1; Joslin, p. 37; Hoover (*Depression*), p. 225; Hinshaw, p. 227.

83 Stink bombs. Leuchtenburg (*Hoover*), p. 141; Wilson (*Progressive*), p. 167.

84 "Where the hell are we?" Starling, p. 301.

85 Joslin wire. Smith (*Dream*), p. 210.

86 "Vote for . . . it unanimous." Leuchtenburg (*Hoover*), p. 141; McElvaine, p. 131; Jeansonne (*Hoover*), p. 424.

87 "walking corpse." Leuchtenburg (*Hoover*), p. 141.

88 "is going to . . . the ballot box." Holli, p. 53.

89 Tammany Hall. *NY Times*, 20 October 1932, pp. 1, 16.

90 Newark. *Time*, 7 November 1932, pp. 14-15; Finan, pp. 288-99; Slayton, p. 374.

91 "the title of . . . Me in 1928.'" *NY Times*, 26 October 1932, p. 11.

92 "Governor Smith . . . for Smith." *Christian Century*, 2 November 1932, p. 1324; Slayton, p. 374.

93 "Al Smith's speech . . . a brick in it." *Literary Digest*, 5 November 1932, p. 7. On October 24, Dudley Field Malone, Wilson's 1916 Western campaign manager, endorsed Hoover (it would take FDR "four years to learn what Herbert Hoover now knows"). Observed Arthur Garfield Hays: "I am afraid he [Malone] is voting not so much for Hoover as against Roosevelt. It isn't hard to understand his personal resentment since we all know his friendship for Al Smith and Jimmy Walker."

94 Edith Roosevelt. Cook (*Vol. 1*), p. 470; Anthony, p. 451.

95 "I have a . . . be elected President." Collier & Horowitz (*Roosevelts*), p. 334.

96 Resisted entreaties. Roosevelt (*Yesterday*), pp. 298-301; Collier & Horowitz (*Roosevelts*), pp. 333-34; Smith (*Dream*), p. 186.

97 TR Jr. broadcast. *Brooklyn Eagle*, 7 November 1932, p. 44.

98 Communists. Anonymous (*Foster-Ford*), p. 30.

99 Lustgarten. Congdon, p. 171.

100 "Mother Wrights". Congdon, p. 171.

101 Darrow, ILD. Weinberg & Weinberg, pp. 367-68.

102 Massie case. *NY Times*, 10 January 1932, p. 31; *Weekly Kansas City Star*, 13 January 1932, p. 13; *Workers Age*, 19 March 1932, p. 3; Van Slingerland, pp. 316-22; Horan, pp. 67-68; Farrell, pp. 444-56; Weinberg & Weinberg, pp. 368-73; Stannard, *passim*. Massie's father was TR's military attaché and ostensibly Robert Barnwell Roosevelt's adopted son; in actuality he was his illegitimate son. There was never, by the way, any *Mr.* Fortescue, that merely being Robert Barnwell Roosevelt's pseudonym.

According to Deacon Jones only he and Massie were present when he fired the fatal slug into Kaha-wawei. By trial's end, Darrow was aware the narrative he presented in their defense was false.

103 Coughlin. Ward (*Coughlin*), p. 114; Marcus, pp. 47-48; Fried, p. 59; Brinkley, p. 111; Bennett (*Demagogues*), p. 46. From $20.67.

104 Shakedowns. *NY Times*, 30 October 1932, p. 16; *Chicago Tribune*, 31 October 1932, p. 2.

105 Supreme Court. Ritchie, p. 145.

106 "unqualified success. . . and gained votes." Freedman, p. 91.

107 Clapper. *Stevens Point Journal*, 24 October 1932, p. 1.

108 Baruch, Raskob. *NY Times*, 26 October 1932, p. 1.

109 "unqualified full and complete support". *NY Times*, 28 October 1932, p. 1; Finan, pp. 290-91.

110 Brooklyn. *Bluefield Telegraph*, 5 November 1932, p. 2; Suckley; Finan, pp. 292-93. Felix Frank-furter praised Smith's Boston speech to Walter Lippmann, but added, "If I had to bet, I should bet Massachusetts would go for Hoover." (Freedman, p. 92)

111 "Hackshaw the Detective". *Auburn Citizen-Advertiser*, 9 November 1932, p. 12.

112 New Cabinet post. *Sandusky Register*, 22 October 1932, p. 1. Not surprising Hearst opposed any Cabinet post for Smith. He also opposed appointments for Cordell Hull, William Woodin, and Owen D. Young. He had no problem with posts for Baruch, Carter Glass, or George Norris or "a woman" at Labor. (Carlisle, p. 71, 73) Meanwhile, British Socialist Harold Laski boosted Perkins—as well as Smith and (for attorney general) John W. Davis, while throwing cold water on McAdoo, Young, Traylor, Baruch, and James A. Reed. (*Living Age*, January 1933, p. 387)

113 "If we were . . . on a handshake." *NY Times*, 29 October 1932, p. 1; *Pittsburgh Press*, 29 October 1932, p. 1; *Time*, 7 November 1932, p. 15; Dille, p. 62.

114 In cities. . .or nearly so! *NY Sun*, 6 October 1932, p. 28.

115 "our affairs as . . . the rest of us." *Iowa City Iowan*, 5 November 1932, p. 3; *Bluefield Telegraph*, 5 November 1932, p. 2; *Time*, 17 October 1932, p. 14.

116 La Follette/Cutting/Wallace. Peel & Donnelly, p. 153. Borah didn't. But disgusted as he was with the GOP retreat on Prohibition, nor was he at all in favor of Hoover. The Prohibition Party mightily desired to nominate him. He rebuffed its fading siren call. (*Chicago Tribune*, 21 June 1932, p. 3; *Iowa City Iowan*, 21 June 1932, pp. 1, 5; *Time*, 18 July 1932, p. 20; *NY Times*, 3 August 1932, p. 1; Hart [*1932*], p. 37)

117 "Roosevelt Woos . . . Goes Democratic." *The Nation*, 12 October 1932, pp. 331-32.

118 "I am not . . . are victims too." *Brooklyn Eagle*, 4 November 1932, p. 19; *Plattsburgh Press*, 4 November 1932, p. 1; *Spartanburg Herald-Journal*, 4 November 1932, p. 1.

119 "In America . . . it vigourously. *NY Times*, 7 November 1932, pp. 1, 11.

120 "If you vote . . . the Republicans." *NY Times*, 7 November 1932, p. 1.

121 Itinerary. Suckley; *Charleston Mail*, 8 November 1932, p. 9.

122 "You'd think . . . County to win!" Hickok (*Road*), p. 201.

123 "For twenty-two years . . . to all." Moley (*Seven*), p. 402.

124 Registration. *Scribner's*, May 1932, p. 257; Jeansonne (*Hoover*), p. 414.

125 Smoot. *NY Sun*, 9 November 1932, p. 25.

126 Haugen. *Akron Register Tribune*, 24 November 1932, p. 2.

127 La Guardia. *NY Sun*, 9 November 1932, p. 25; *NY Sun*, 12 November 1932, p. 21; *Akron Register Tribune*, 24 November 1932, p. 2; Mann, pp. 313-20; Congdon, pp. 179-89.

128 Bingham. *NY Sun*, 9 November 1932, p. 25.

129 "larger majority". *NY Sun*, 4 November 1932, p. 9.

130 Pratt. *NY Sun*, 9 November 1932, p. 25; *NY Sun*, 12 November 1932, p. 21.

131 Davis. *Time*, 10 October 1932, p. 11; Beers, p. 105.

132 West Branch/Stanford. Jeansonne (*Hoover*), p. 424.

133 Lemke. Bennett (*Demagogues*), p. 93.

134 McAdoo, Reynolds. Pleasants, p. 57.

135 Meyers. *Charleston Gazette*, 14 February 1932, p. 5; *Walla Walla Union-Bulletin*, 13 December 1964, p. 35.

136 "dry" candidates. Hart (*Year 1932*), p. 37; Kyvig, p. 168.
137 Referenda. *NY Times*, 10 November 1932, pp. 1, 2, 9; Hart (*Year 1932*), p. 3; Kyvig, p. 168.
138 Bonus. Waters, p. 131.
139 "Good night, my friends, that's that!" Lyons, p. 308.
140 Twelve hours. Jeansonne (*Hoover*), p. 425.
141 881,781 votes. Johnpoll, p. 96.
142 Third party totals. Freidel (*Triumph*), p. 370.
143 "Why was there . . . *American Magazine.*" Waters, pp. 99-101.
144 South. Ritchie, pp. 223-24.
145 Jews. Breitman & Lichtman, p. 43.
146 Black vote. Lisio (*Blacks*), p. 272; Weiss, p. 32; Jeansonne (*Hoover*), p. 425.
147 Philadelphia. Beers, p. 30.
148 Maine. Ritchie, p. 223.
149 Hoovers voting. Wilson (*Challenge*), p. 233.
150 "two sevens, two lucky numbers". *Iowa City Iowan*, 9 November 1932, p. 5.
151 Eleanor. *NY Sun*, 8 November 1932, p. 2; *Charleston Mail*, 8 November 1932, p. 9; *NY Times*, 9 November 1932, p. 9; Hickok (*Reluctant*), pp. 53-54; Cook (*Eleanor*), pp. 470-71. Mother Sara's chauffeur transported her to the polls before eleven, making her the first woman to vote for her son for president. (*Iowa City Iowan*, 9 November 1932, p. 5; *Iowa City Iowan*, 12 November 1932, p. 1)
152 "Come on . . . all day." *Charleston Mail*, 8 November 1932, p. 9.
153 Pinchot. *Lebanon News*, 8 November 1932, p. 5; McGeary, p. 393.
154 Rockefeller. *Charleston Mail*, 8 November 1932, p. 9.
155 Sackett. *Iowa City Iowan*, 9 November 1932, p. 2; Burke, pp. 249-50. Hoover had also attempted to enlist Ambassador to Rome John W. Garrett, desiring Garrett to report that Mussolini supported his re-election. Garrett thought it a terrible idea.
156 Louis Ferdinand. Louis Ferdinand, p. 141.
157 Sara. *Charleston Mail*, 8 November 1932, p. 9; *Iowa City Iowan*, 9 November 1932, p. 5; *Iowa City Iowan*, 12 November 1932, p. 1.
158 East 65th Street. *NY Times*, 9 November 1932, p. 9; Suckley; Hickok (*Reluctant*), pp. 57-59.
159 Secret Service. Freidel (*Triumph*), p. 369; Freidel (*New Deal*), p. 4; Louchheim, p. 8.
160 "It's good . . . tonight, Hick." Hickok (*Reluctant*), p. 58.
161 Hearst. Pizzitola, p. 292.
162 Eleanor. *Brooklyn Eagle*, 9 November 1932, p. 5; *NY Sun*, 9 November 1932, p. 16.
163 "I was reminded . . . baying hounds". Hickok (*Reluctant*), p. 59.
164 "every now . . . I thought." Hickok (*Reluctant*), pp. 58-59.
165 Sara. *Brooklyn Eagle*, 9 November 1932, p. 5.
166 "Losers always have a big spurt at the start". Stiles, p. 216; Schlesinger (*Crisis*), p. 438.
167 "I put this . . . time came." Stiles, p. 216.
168 "I want to . . . American, Jim Farley." *Auburn Citizen-Advertiser*, 9 November 1932, p. 12; Stiles, p. 217; Freidel (*Triumph*), p. 370; Morgan (*FDR*), pp. 363-64.
169 Dignitaries. *NY Times*, 9 November 1932, p. 9; *Auburn Citizen-Advertiser*, 9 November 1932, p. 12. By Election Day the once hostile Davis had contributed $500 to FDR, though he was a piker. Tammany's John F. Curry swallowed his pride—hard—and kicked in a grand. (*Time*, 14 November 1932, p. 11)
170 "This is the . . . Hackshaw the Detective!" *Brooklyn Eagle*, 9 November 1932, p. 5; *Auburn Citizen-Advertiser*, 9 November 1932, p. 12. Smith's comments regarding Roosevelt's win were barely more enthusiastic, merely noting his joy regarding their party's overall sweep.
171 "This is the . . . my life." *Brooklyn Eagle*, 9 November 1932, p. 5; Freidel (*Triumph*), p. 371.
172 "If Roosevelt had . . . never voiced them." Freidel (*Triumph*), p. 371.
173 "You know . . . this job." Roosevelt & Libby, p. 142; Freidel (*New Deal*), p. 4; Manchester (*Glory*), p. 54; Brands (*Traitor*), p. 268.

CHAPTER TWENTY-FIVE: "A PRIMITIVE AND STUPID WOMAN"

1   Vegetarian. Murray, p. 138; Shirer, p. 132; Toland, p. 256; Victor, p. 63; Hayman, p. 224; Langer, pp. 56, 104, 191. Some, however, date his vegetarianism to his release from Landsberg and even to his early earliest days as a Wagner aficionado. (Kershaw [*Hubris*], pp. 261-62; Sigmund, p. 144)

2   "the world of the future will be vegetarian!" Hitler (*Table Talk*), p. 125. Uttered in November 1941.

3   "now this had to happen to *him*". Sigmund, p. 144. From police inspector Captain Sauer: "He said her death had deeply shaken him; she had been the only close relative he had and now this had to happen to *him*."

4   "I saw him . . . insatiable." *Saturday Review*, 2 May 1970, p. 21.

5   "His treatment . . . they were goddesses." *Saturday Review*, 2 May 1970, p. 21. Said Göring in 1946: "The Führer, like myself, had a great respect for women." Assessed Hans Frank: "I think that Hitler was abnormal in his sexual needs. That is, he needed too little from the opposite sex." (Goldensohn, pp. 39, 126)

6   "CRACKERS." Hoffmann (*Friend*), p. 167; Botting & Sayer, p. 83.

7   Wealthy women. Sigmund, pp. 7-9; 84-85.

8   "he wasn't ugly. . . . to those close to him." Lambert, pp. 9-10. Conversely, in early 1932, Thomas Mann's son Klaus (1906–1949) stumbled upon him at Munich's Hotel Carlton, and found him "surprisingly ugly, much more vulgar than I had anticipated." (Large [*Munich*], p. 224)

9   "See that we . . . for a change." Baur, p. 36.

10   "As a matter . . . their mouths shut." Baur, p. 36.

11   "women can never . . . whisper a word." Baur, p. 37; Maser, p. 206.

12   "Mein Führer . . . homage to you." Delmer (*Trail*), p. 155.

13   "I thought it . . . had broken off." Delmer (*Trail*), pp. 155-56; Toland, p. 264.

14   Slezak. *Saturday Review*, 2 May 1970, p. 22; Hanfstaengl, pp. 201-2; Botting & Sayer, pp. 106-7; Redlich, p. 284; Infield (*Secret*), p. 155; Maser, pp. 203-4; Lambert, p. 127; Riefenstahl, p. 124; Tyson (*Surreal*), p. 22. Gretl's younger brother was Hollywood character actor Walter Slezak (1902–1983).

15   "Please excuse me . . . unknown to you. . . ." *Saturday Review*, 2 May 1970, p. 22.

16   Müller. Lambert, pp. 132-33; Redlich, pp. 82-83; Langer, pp. 101-2, 192; Tyson (*Surreal*), p. 22; Mitchell (*Obersalzberg*), pp. 38-39. The lurid accounts of Müller's alleged sexual encounters (as well as those of actress Jenny Jugo [1904–2001]) with Hitler first published in *Liberty* magazine in 1940 and in later histories must, however, be taken with the proverbial grain of salt. (*Liberty*, 15 June 1940, pages unknown; Botting & Sayer, pp. 108-10, 126-28; Infield [*Eva*], pp. 95-97; Infield [*Secret*], pp. 79-81; Hayman, pp. 145-47). Two years earlier *Liberty* had also published a fanciful article ("Is Hitler in Love with a Jewess?") on Leni Riefenstahl, not only getting her ethnicity wrong but also the circumstances of their first meeting. (*Liberty*, 16 July 1938, pages unknown) "Gossips whispered that he had intimate relations with [Müller, Jugo and other female artists]," Otto Dietrich, by then no admirer of his Führer, would later write. "The stories are utterly false." (Dietrich [*With*], p. 182)

17   "Dear Herr Hitler . . . Cordially, Leni Riefenstahl". Riefenstahl, p. 103; Trimborn, p. 58; Bach, p. 90; Sigmund, p. 99; Knopp, pp. 113-14.

18   Hoffmann. Strasser, pp. 83-84; Tyson (*Surreal*), p. 16; Toland, p. 236; Langer, pp. 99, 191; Hayman, p. 156; Sigmund, p. 187.

19   "How can I . . . my task?" Riefenstahl, p. 99; Bach, p. 91; Knopp, p. 114.

20   "She was no great beauty . . . a sweet personality. . . ." Goldensohn, p. 126.

21   "I'd stayed on . . . the hem even." Gun, p. 42; Toland, p. 237; Wistrich, p. 28; Sigmund, p. 152; Knopp, p. 9; Large [*Munich*], p. 225.

22   "this character." Infield (*Eva*), p. 287; Toland, p. 237.

23   "Do you know . . . is Adolf Hitler!" Infield (*Eva*), p. 29; Infield (*Secret*), pp. 157-58; Toland, p. 237. Hitler often posed as a "Herr Wolf." (Goebbels [*Early*], p. 120; Victor, p. 35) He had also requested Mimi Reiter to address him as "Wolf" (Kershaw [*Hubris*], p. 284) and later convinced his younger, unmarried sister Paula to drop her now-famous surname for "Wolf." (Fest [*Hitler*], p. 157; Maser, p. 26; Lambert, pp. 83-84) "Adolf" derives from "Adelwolf"—"favored wolf"—and Hitler's early signature often appears to read like "Wolf." (Victor, p. 35)

Eerily, Joseph Stalin was also obsessed by wolves, often drawing them "numberlessly" as he conferred with foreign leaders. (Isaacson & Thomas, p. 213; Nagorski [*Stalingrad*], p. 163) FDR, luckily, fancied not wolves but sailing ships and postage stamps.

24 "Geli was opera . . . operetta." Lambert, p. 117.

25 "touch of peroxide". Maser, p. 205.

26 "the most beautiful girl in Munich". Hayman, p. 155. "She was not so pretty close up," dissented Berchtesgaden housemaid Rosa Krautenbacher Mitterer (www.dailymail.co.uk/news/article -1091768/Hitler-perfect-boss-Former-maid-breaks-silence-charming-dictator.html).

27 "She amuses me". Botting & Sayer, p. 54.

28 "I would like . . . you come too." Hoffmann (*Friend*), p. 161; Infield (*Eva*), p. 33; Infield (*Secret*), p. 158; Waite, p. 229.

29 "I think Hitler . . . the family environment." Knopp, p. 10.

30 Bormann. Sigmund, p. 155; Knopp, p. 11. Eva's sister Ilse, however, worked for a Jewish laryngologist, Dr. Martin Levi Marx until 1937 or 1938 and lived in his office. (Infield [*Eva*], p. 114; Görtemaker, pp. 36-37; Maser, p. 202; Gun, pp. 36, 49, 53-54)

31 Lutheran. Lambert, pp. 16, 130; Sigmund, p. 150; Knopp, p. 5.

32 Karl May. *Living Age*, November 1940, pp. 217-22; Knopp, p. 7; Sigmund, p. 151; Lambert, pp. 33, 209; Gun, p. 21; Hitler (*Table Talk*), p. 316; Ryback, pp. 179-80, 237; Maser, p. 120; Infield (*Secret*), pp. 230-32, 238-41; Lüdecke, p. 524; Jones, pp. 106, 122.

33 Simbach. Lüdecke, p. 528; Hoffmann (*Friend*), pp. 159-60; Payne, p. 347; Bullock, p. 229; Görtemaker, pp. 33-34; Sigmund, p. 152; Gun, p. 21; Knopp, p. 7. In 1925, Hitler startled Heinrich Hoffmann, a Protestant, by advising: "For young people the convent school is the best education we have. The Simbach convent, on the Inn opposite Braunau, had a great reputation when I was a young man." Even less in character, Hitler later drove Hoffmann's son to the school and personally enrolled him ("make a decent man out of him") with the Mother Superior—then advised Hoffmann to make the school a present of a "really good picture." Hoffmann donated an oil painting of the Holy Family. (Hoffmann [*Friend*], p. 132)

34 "flowers, chocolates, trinkets . . . interest in her." Hoffmann (*Friend*), p. 161; Botting & Sayer, p. 77; Kershaw (*Hubris*), p. 352. Hoffmann tended to downplay Braun, her relationship to Hitler, and even his own relationship to her. Berchtesgaden house-manager Herbert Döhring and his wife, Anni, however, alleged that Hoffmann "kept on encouraging them, serving Eva up on a silver platter . . . until Hitler took the hint." (Knopp, p. 10)

35 "Dear Mr. Hitler . . . another meeting." Gun, p. 13; Lambert, p. 121; Hayman, pp. 172-73; Botting & Sayer, p. 53; Large (*Munich*), p. 225. Geli knew Eva and did not care for her, referring to her (after spotting her in a monkey-fur trimmed overcoat) as "the monkey girl over there." (Hayman, p. 155; Infield [*Eva*], p. 46)

36 Haus Wachenfeld. Lambert, p. 125.

37 "A highly intellectual man . . . with my work." Speer, p. 92; Snyder (*Encyclopedia*), p. 40; Sigmund, p. 156; Waite, p. 52; Knopp, p. 11.

38 Nearly fired. Toland, p. 237; Hoffmann (*Friend*), p. 160; Bullock, p. 394; Sigmund, p. 156.

39 Blackballed. Infield (*Eva*), p. 31; Infield (*Secret*), p. 158.

40 "Hitler! He's a . . . in the street." Botting & Sayer, p. 12; Gun, p. 43; Hayman, p. 156.

41 "bride is Germany". Hoffmann (*Friend*), p. 141; Wagener, p. 33; Infield (*Eva*), p. 34; Botting & Sayer, pp. 54, 99; Knopp, p. 14.

42 Hitler/Magda. Thacker, pp. 121-22; Manvell & Fraenkel (*Goebbels*), p. 89.

43 "In a sense . . . unreachable and untouchable." Lüdecke, p. 420; Fest (*Face*), p. 523. Hitler's later interpreter Paul Schmidt said much the same thing at Nürnberg: "Hitler could not be classed as a human. He was too aloof from the very beginning and he never changed." (Goldensohn, pp. 441-42)

44   August. Hoffmann (*Friend*), p. 161; Görtemaker, p. 49. Based on Hoffmann and Baldur von Schirach's recollections.

45   November. Based on Ilse Braun's recollections. Sigmund, p. 157; Botting & Sayer, p. 98; Lambert, p. 134; Görtemaker, pp. 49-50; Toland, p. 273; Fest (*Hitler*), p. 524; Kershaw (*Hubris*), p. 388; Infield (*Eva*), p. 64; Maser, p. 203; Knopp, p. 13. If Eva's attempt occurred in November it pre-dated by only a few days the actual suicide (also by gunshot) of Joseph Stalin's thirty-one-year-old, partly-German wife, Nadezhda Sergeevna Alliluyeva. She had just excoriated her husband over his mass-murder of the USSR's peasantry. Some allege, however, that Stalin had her killed. (Johnson [*Modern*], pp. 272-73)

46   "My sister was . . . table beside him." Gun, p. 53; Botting & Sayer, p. 98; Görtemaker, p. 50.

47   "This is a bad . . . end it all." Hoffmann (*Friend*), p. 161.

48   Letter to Hitler. Hoffmann (*Friend*), p. 162; Infield (*Eva*), p. 65.

49   Had acted. Hoffmann (*Friend*), p. 162; Infield (*Eva*), p. 65.

50   "If I take on . . . be quietly discreet." Hoffmann (*Friend*), p. 162; Toland, p. 274; Görtemaker, p. 50; Infield (*Eva*), p. 65; Gun, pp. 53-54; Hayman, p. 206.

51   Clinic visit. Infield (*Eva*), p. 65; Infield (*Secret*), p. 160; Lambert, p. 134; Sigmund, p. 157; Kershaw (*Hubris*), p. 284; Knopp, p. 13; Hayman, p. 206. What their relationship actually became remains a mystery. The theories are endless, though she certainly loved him, and he was fond of her. Joachim Fest, however, theorizes that "far from being a natural sexual bond, [the relationship] was intended to provide a strained confirmation of his manhood in his own eyes and those of his closest followers." (Fest [*Face*], p. 264; Hayman, pp. 207-8)

CHAPTER TWENTY-SIX: "YOU FELT THAT THEY WOULD DO *ANYTHING*"

1   1932 recovery. Lyons, pp. 309-10; Jeansonne (*Hoover*), pp. 403-04; Wilson (*Challenge*), p. 225.

2   Unemployment. Vedder & Gallaway, p. 77; Wilson (*Challenge*), p. 225.

3   Lindsay. Freidel (*New Deal*), pp. 21-22; Miller (*FDR*), p. 292; Morgan, p. 368.

4   McFadden. *Congressional Record*, 13 December 1932, pp. 399-402; *Brainerd Daily Dispatch*, 13 December 1932, p. 1; *NY Times*, 2 October 1936, p. 25; Wilson (*Progressive*), p. 167; Dickson & Allen, p. 203. Wright Patman supported McFadden.

5   "Ray, have you . . . expert dressed wrong." Tugwell (*Search*), p. 210; Morgan, p. 368.

6   "boldest alibi in history." Davis (*New York*), p. 401; Black (*Champion*), p. 253. Nonetheless, during the campaign, FDR had confided to Moley: "Old Hoover's foreign policy has been pretty good." (Miller [*FDR*], p. 292; Leuchtenburg [*Hoover*], p. 125)

7   Brains Trust. Moley (*Seven*), p. 71; Freidel (*New Deal*), pp. 24-25.

8   "distrust of his rival . . . will go far to prevent a profitable meeting". Schlesinger (*Crisis*), p. 444.

9   "best informed individual . . . that compelled admiration." Moley (*Seven*), p. 73; Freidel (*New Deal*), p. 32; Kennedy (*Freedom*), pp. 108-9; Jeansonne (*Hoover*), p. 428. Tugwell asserted that this was not, however, Moley's contemporaneous opinion. (Tugwell [*Democratic*], p. 258*fn*)

10   "My impression at . . . on the agreement." Freidel (*New Deal*), p. 34; Kennedy (*Freedom*), p. 108.

11   "I offered to . . . what it means." Freidel (*New Deal*), pp. 43, 515.

12   West Palm Beach. Starling, p. 301.

13   Yacht. *NY Times*, 30 December 1932, p. 2.

14   Alcoholic. Collier & Horowitz (*Roosevelts*), pp. 323, 381; Denton, p. 77. Kermit's mother was present in Manila when reporters grilled TR Jr. regarding why his brother had accompanied FDR. Before Teddy Jr. could answer, she interrupted, "Because his mother was not there." (Roosevelt [*Yesterday*], pp. 301-2; Freidel [*New Deal*], p. 168*fn*; Caroli, p. 186)

15   *Nourmahal*. Suckley; Houck (*FDR*), p. 79; Denton, p. 76; Lomazow & Fettmann, p. 49. FDR's son, James, could only hazard a guess as to why his father chose their company at this desperate national juncture: they did not possess "deep intellectual or political affinity with him." He theorized,

that their "company may have been an escape for him, an escape back to the world of Groton, Harvard, Fly Club, Hyde Park. . . ." (Cross, p. 72)

16 "The Hasty Pudding Club puts out to sea". Davis (*New York*), p. 420; Freidel (*New Deal*), p. 168; Denton, pp. 78, 270; Cross, p. 71. Huey Long would soon enough deride FDR as "Prince Franklin, Knight of the *Nourmahal*." (Congdon, p. 315)

17 "I didn't open . . . entire twelve days". Miller (*FDR*), p. 297; Freidel (*New Deal*), p. 169; Picchi, p. 4; Denton, p. 83.

18 "On a splendid yacht . . . Forgotten Man." *NY Sun*, 9 February 1933, p. 22; *Rhinebeck Gazette*, 10 February 1933, p. 4; *Binghamton Press*, 10 February 1933, p. 13; Smith (*FDR*), p. 298; Denton, p. 78; Cross, pp. 71-72.

19 Astor speculation. Moley (*Seven*), p. 138; Miller (*FDR*), pp. 297-98; Denton, p. 84.

20 McKinley. Houck (*FDR*), p. 79.

21 Kruis. *Brooklyn Eagle*, 16 February 1933, p. 4; *Time*, 27 February 1933, p. 7.

22 Gennerich. *Spartanburg Herald*, 18 December 1936, p. 8; Picchi, p. 16.

23 "I don't think . . . you keep quiet." *Time*, 27 February 1933, p. 7; Miller (*FDR*), p. 299; Freidel (*New Deal*), p. 170; Davis (*New York*), p. 430; Houck (*FDR*), p. 81; Smith (*FDR*), p. 297; Lomazow & Fettmann, p. 49; Picchi, p. 24; Denton, p. 88.

24 "I hate all presidents". *Time*, 27 February 1933, p. 7; Davis (*New York*), p. 431, Smith (*FDR*), pp. 297-98.

25 "There was nothing . . . on the *Nourmahal*." Moley (*Seven*), p. 139; Miller (*FDR*), p. 300; Davis (*New York*), p. 432; Rowley, p. 175; Horan, p. 94. FDR later phoned the nervous Eleanor. His call concluded, she reflected to Louis Howe, "That drive to the hospital must have been awfully hard on Franklin. He hates the sight of blood."

26 "A dastardly act!" *Time*, 27 February 1933, p. 8.

27 "There *is* a star, you know". Tugwell (*Revolution*), p. 4.

28 "I realize F.D.R. . . . be anything else". Lash (*Love*), p. 311; Persico (*Lucy*), p. 230.

29 "You press this . . . out tear gas." Hickok (*Reluctant*), p. 76; Cook (*Vol. 1*), p. 491.

30 "If a fire had . . . be moved quickly." Hickok (*Reluctant*), p. 77. She had been dining with Hickok at an Armenian restaurant as Zangara fired his shots. (Golay, p. 26)

31 Pinchots. *Massillon Independent*, 3 February 1933, p. 1; *Titusville Herald*, 4 February 1933, p. 1; Beers, pp. 103-4; McGeary, p. 394.

32 "an example of . . . for radical causes." Beers, p. 104.

33 Ring. Cook (*Vol. 1*), p. 486; Streitmatter, p. 10; Persico (*Lucy*), p. 203.

34 "we certainly were not crowded". Hickok (*Reluctant*), p. 71.

35 Suite, breakfast. Hickok (*Reluctant*), pp. 71-72; Streitmatter, p. 11.

36 Walked. Hickok (*Reluctant*), pp. 73-74; Cook (*Vol. 1*), p. 490; Streitmatter, p. 11.

37 "I think [Eleanor] . . . I stood waiting. . . ." Hickok (*Reluctant*), p. 75. ER later inscribed a photo to Lorena: "We were only separated by a few yards dear Hick & I wonder which of us felt more oddly." (Cook [*Vol. 1*], pp. 490-91)

38 Curtis. *Plattsburgh Press*, 15 December 1932, p. 1.

39 "I am just . . . to do anything". Freidel (*New Deal*), pp. 29-30; Schlesinger (*Crisis*), p. 441.

40 No incidents. Suckley; Freidel (*New Deal*), pp. 29-30.

41 Communists, townhouse. *NY Times*, 6 January 12; *Time*, 16 January 1933, p. 11.

42 "Waters and one . . . *of the Bonus Army*." Lüdecke, p. 564.

43 "I made a . . . in Nazi ranks.'" Lüdecke, p. 565. Lüdecke's account may seem fanciful, but, perhaps, not so at all. Soon, House would advise FDR's new ambassador to Berlin, William Dodd, to certainly assist "to ameliorate Jewish sufferings" resulting from Hitler's new regime, but also not to allow "the Jews . . . to dominate economic or intellectual life in Berlin as they have done for a long time." (Larson, p. 38)

44 "What we need now . . . have dictatorial powers." Schlesinger (*Crisis*), p. 268.

45 "if this country . . . needs one now." *Congressional Record*, 72 Cong., I Sess. (5 May 1932), p. 9644; Manchester (*Glory*), p. 58.

46 "New Party". *New Yorker*, 11 January 1941, p. 25.

47 Technocracy. *Living Age*, December 1932, pp. 292-303; *Time*, 30 January 1933, p. 23; Schlesinger (*Crisis*), p. 461; Allen (*Yesterday*), pp. 71-72; Flynn (*Myth*), p. 157.

48 "Individual income under . . . balanced load . . .". *Living Age*, December 1932, p. 303.

49 House/dictatorship. *Liberty*, 7 January 1933, page unknown; *Brownsville Herald*, 5 January 1933, p. 4; *Syracuse Post-Standard*, 7 September 1954, p. 11; *Dixon Telegraph*, 8 September 1954, p. 4; Johnson (*Viereck*), pp. 158-59; Pietrusza (*1920*), p. 453 (paperback edition). Viereck and Hanfstaengl later plotted unsuccessfully to buy Kurt Lüdecke's silence when the latter became too talkative to congressional investigators. (Johnson [*Viereck*], pp. 163-64)

50 "For two years I've been . . . exercised by our President". Smith (*Eisenhower*), p. 116; D'Este (*Eisenhower*), p. 215; Ambrose, p. 89; Holland, p. 216; Bendersky, p. 311.

51 "[a]ny group of . . . a single will." *Pittsburgh Post-Gazette*, 18 January 1933, p. 3; *Salt Lake Tribune*, 19 January 1933, p. 9; Davis (*New Deal*), p. 36.

52 "The situation is . . . dictatorial power." Davis (*New Deal*), p. 36; Cohen (*Fear*), p. 37; Kennedy (*Freedom*), p. 111.

53 "What does a . . . war was over." *NY Times*, 8 February 1933, p. 1; *Hagerstown Mail*, 8 February 1933, p. 10; Davis (*New Deal*), p. 36; Kennedy (*Freedom*), p. 111. Smith publicly lobbied for the creation of a "Director General of Public Works" to sever such red tape—which just might have been him. (Handlin, p. 170)

54 "desire that [FDR] . . . challenging emergency." Davis (*New Deal*), p. 37.

55 "a man of the people . . . inspiration to mankind". Jewett and Lawrence, p. 133.

56 *Mussolini Speaks. Brooklyn Eagle*, 13 March 1933, p. 8; *NY Post*, 13 March 1933, p. 11; *NY Sun*, 14 March 1933, p. 13; Jewett and Lawrence, pp. 132-33. The film even played at Broadway's famed Palace Theater.

57 "Put that picture . . . lock it up!" Bernstein (*Wanger*), p. 86.

58 FDR edits. Pizzitola, p. 296; Denton, p. 177; Nasaw (*Chief*), p. 465; Jewett and Lawrence, p. 133.

59 "I want to send you this line to . . . should do much to help." Nasaw (*Chief*), p. 466; Alter, p. 185; Denton, p. 179; Jewett and Lawrence, p. 137. Film historian William K. Everson speaks of "a startlingly prolific cycle" of, what he termed, "Fascist-oriented gangster film[s], advocating police-state methods to rid the United States of crime . . . ." Among the most prominent of such efforts was 1932's *Beast of the City*, also bankrolled by Hearst and also starring Huston. (Everson, p. 233)

60 Made money. Nasaw (*Chief*), p. 466; Jewett and Lawrence, p. 137. The film, shot in two weeks, cost MGM only $180,000 and, at a time when most studios lost money, delivered $200,000 in profits. (Bernstein [*Wanger*], pp. 83, 86)

61 Three times. Pizzitola, p. 298. Walter Huston was by fortuitous coincidence FDR's favorite actor—"his favorite of favorites . . . ," noted the Secret Service's Michael F. Reilly, "whom he never missed on the screen and would occasionally see in legitimate shows in Washington although it meant climbing into the hated braces." (Reilly, p. 59)

62 Pelley. *American Jewish Congress Bulletin*, 24 August 1933, *passim*; *Syracuse Journal*, 17 October 1933, p. 26; *Ballston Spa Journal*, 21 October 1933, p. 2; *Niagara Falls Gazette*, 26 April 1934, p. 13; Beekman, *passim*; Bennett (*Party*), pp. 245-47.

63 "The Semitic propaganda . . . in the world." Jeansonne (*Smith*), pp. 30-31.

64 Tugwell. Tugwell (*Revolution*), p. 6.

65 Starved. Bennett (*Party*), p. 240.

66 Douglas. Tugwell (*Revolution*), pp. 6, 8-9; Freidel (*New Deal*), p. 70; Morgan, p. 372.

67 Wagner, LaFollette. Tugwell (*Revolution*), pp. 7-8.

68 "I'm going to talk . . . that's the people." *Time*, 20 February 1933, p. 12.

69 "My friends and neighbors. . . 'White House' of the Confederacy." *Time*, 20 February 1933, p. 12.

70 "Wall Street's three-billion dollar soup kitchen". Wilson (*Challenge*), p. 225.

71 Bank failures, 1931-32. Jeansonne (*Hoover*), pp. 403-4.

72   Comstock. *Michigan Political History News*, Summer 1997, p. 1; Brinkley, p. 116; Tugwell (*Revolution*), p. 18; Freidel (*New Deal*), p. 182; Jeansonne (*Hoover*), p. 443; Congdon, pp. 130-31; Kennedy (*Freedom*), p. 131; Manchester (*Glory*), p. 72.

73   "Detroit's Colonial Department Store . . . for eggs and honey." Congdon, pp. 131-32.

74   "said that they . . . after March 4th." Garrett, p. 251; Davis (*New Deal*), pp. 21-22; Freidel (*New Deal*), pp. 184-85; Shlaes (*Forgotten*), p. 142; Jeansonne (*Hoover*), p. 443; Hiltzik, p. 55; Namorato, p. 71; Lyons, p. 316.

75   "Let 'em bust. . . a sound basis." Jeansonne (*Hoover*), p. 443. Raymond Moley later revealed that FDR "preferred to have conditions deteriorate and gain for himself the entire credit for the operation." (Moley [*First*], p. 213; Hoover [*Depression*], p. 215; Garrett, p. 251; Jeansonne [*Hoover*], pp. 443-44)

76   Toupee. Manchester (*Glory*), p. 73.

77   "Inaugural March". Davis (*New Deal*), p. 21. Woodin's best campaign writing, however, remained his $35,000 check to the Democratic National Committee. (*Time*, 14 November 1932, p. 11) The song-writing Woodin found himself the object of much merriment, including this new ditty: "LITTLE WOODEN WILLIE/People thou't him silly/Cause he had a knothole/In the middle of his head,/But since he put a hat on./And since he's had that on/Those who thought him silly/Think him very nice indeed." (*Schenectady Gazette*, 2 March 1933, p. 8)

78   Woodin to Mills. Freidel (*New Deal*), p. 185*fn*; Jeansonne (*Hoover*), p. 444.

79   "The Commercial [Bank] . . . excess of $2,200,000,000. . . . *U.S. News & World Report*, 24 July 2006, p. 45.

80   "frankly . . . now". Walch and Miller, pp. 129-36; Moley (*New Deal*), p. 145; Moley (*Seven*), pp. 139-42; Black (*Champion*), pp. 264-65; Lyons, p. 316; Alter, pp. 179-82; Houck, p. 173.

81   "I liked . . . his jib." Moley (*Seven*), pp. 126-27; Schlesinger (*Crisis*), p. 472; Brand (*Traitor*), p. 293; Black(*Champion*), p. 262. FDR first selected Hiram Johnson. He declined. Carter Glass, sensing FDR's liberal tendencies, likewise rejected Treasury. (Smith & Beasley, pp. 336-37; Moley [*Seven*], p. 120; Tugwell [*Democratic*], p. 264; Freidel [*New Deal*], pp. 148-49; Allen [*Yesterday*], p. 79; Kennedy [*Freedom*], p. 127; Lyons, p. 315)

82   Baker, Davis, Young. Schlesinger (*Crisis*), p. 469.

83   "thunderstruck". Hull, p. 156.

84   Swanson. Freidel (*New Deal*), p. 150; Martin (*Bandwagons*), p. 348.

85   Moley. Freidel (*New Deal*), p. 67.

86   Tugwell. Namorato, p. 72.

87   Rosenman. Louchheim, p. 10.

88   Walsh. *Wisconsin State Journal*, 26 February 1933, p. 1; *NY Times*, 3 March 1933, p. 8; Tugwell (*Revolution*), pp. 21-22; Flynn (*Boss*), p. 125; Morgan, p. 372.

89   Cummings. Flynn (*Boss*), pp. 125-26. TR Jr., in Manila, pondered his fate thusly: "Fifth cousin about to be removed." (Roosevelt [*Yesterday*], p. 304; Caroli, p. 186; Collier & Horowitz [*Roosevelts*], p. 337)

90   "hurt and fury . . . knew no bounds." Moley (*Seven*), pp. 124-25; Freidel (*New Deal*), pp. 152-53; Schlesinger (*Crisis*), p. 470.

91   Kennedy. Quirk, pp. 105-6; Maier, p. 115. Kennedy feared that not only had Howe conspired against him but also Eleanor.

92   Smith/Roper. Moley (*Seven*), p. 124-25; Freidel (*New Deal*), p. 152; Finan, pp. 296-97; Neal, pp. 123, 321; Schlesinger (*Crisis*), p. 470.

93   "Scurrying through *Who's Who*, the *World Almanac* . . . and a woman." O'Brien (*Rogers*), p. 155.

94   "Well, Jim, if . . . the job is yours". Curley, pp. 247, 250.

95   Ambassadorships. Curley, pp. 248-52; Guilfoyle, pp. 201-8; "Unofficial Observer," p. 202.

96   Eleanor/Curley. Curley, pp. 249-50.

97   "would load up . . . a woman friend". Cook (*Vol. 2*), p. 13; Persico (*Lucy*), p. 202. Eleanor's original plans even made it into the *New York Times*. (see issue of 14 February 1933, p. 17)

98 "Meggie". Hickok (*Reluctant*), p. 90; Cook (*Vol. 2*), p. 13; Streitmatter, p. 12. "Major," FDR's police dog, however, traveled by truck with the saddle horses "Dot" and "Patches." Neither dog fared well in Washington. In separate incidents, "Major" bit Lorena Hickok, Sen. Hattie Caraway, Washington attorney Harry Johnson, and, most spectacularly, perhaps, even British prime minister Ramsay MacDonald. "Meggie" nipped Lorena's Associated Press successor Beth Furman on the face as she interviewed the First Lady. Eleanor exiled both canines from the White House. (*NY Times*, 25 February 1933, p. 6; *NY Times*, 31 August 1933, p. 4; *NY Times*, 29 December 1933, p. 2; Hickok [*Reluctant*], p. 155)

99 "It's incredible . . . of Sunday picnic." Tugwell (*Revolution*), p. 21; Hiltzik, p. 4.

100 adjoining suites. Rowley, p. 176.

101 New Shoreham. *NY Times*, 4 March 1933, p. 4.

102 Former residence. Hickok (*Reluctant*), pp. 90-91.

103 "In the old . . . many, many times." Hickok (*Reluctant*), p. 92; (*Vol. 2*), p. 13; Persico (*Lucy*), p. 203.

104 "Stay at Home—Buy Nothing—Sell Nothing". Cohen (*Fear*), p. 125; Rothbard, p. 235.

105 "Let's call a . . . eat their gold." Manchester (*Glory*), p. 59; Cohen (*Fear*), p. 125; Rothbard, p. 235.

106 "Farmers and workers. . . the above-mentioned sale." Allen (*Yesterday*), p. 69.

107 "They say blockading . . . was illegal too.'" Allen (*Yesterday*), p. 68; Manchester (*Glory*), p. 58. Similar radicalism visited German agricultural areas, particularly Schleswig-Holstein. There, noted historian Dietrich Orlow, "the anti-Weimar sentiments took the form of direct action and violence against governmental buildings and tax collectors, and the farmers' support of the NSDAP was based at least in part upon the party's image as a revolutionary political group." (Orlow [*Nazi*], p. 154)

108 "I never saw . . . militancy of those farmers". Schlesinger (*Crisis*), pp. 267, 460. Bloor toured the Midwest with her son, former Hoover Agriculture Department consultant (and future Soviet spymaster) Harold Ware, to organize agricultural elements. The Kremlin provided them with $25,000 for their various efforts. (Schlesinger, [*Coming*], p. 52)

109 "Unless something is . . . than twelve months." Manchester (*Glory*), p. 60. Raging resentment soon fueled the adulation of such rural Depression-Era outlaws as John Dillinger, Clyde Barrow and Bonnie Parker, "Baby Face" Nelson, "Pretty Boy" Floyd, and the "Ma" Barker gang.

110 "Mr. Roosevelt, when . . . what you decide." Davis (*New Deal*), p. 25; Freidel (*New Deal*), p. 193; Flynn (*Boss*), p. 125; Congdon, p. 125; Kennedy (*Freedom*), p. 133.

111 "Roosevelt returned from . . . him really angry." Flynn (*Boss*), p. 125; Congdon, p. 125.

112 "What are you . . . them, of course". Smith & Beasley, p. 341; Freidel (*New Deal*), p. 193.

113 December vote. Kyvig, p. 169.

114 House, Senate votes. Kyvig, p. 172.

115 To states. Kobler, p. 352.

116 Lehman. *NY Times*, 4 March 1933, p. 1; *NY Times*, 5 March 1933, p. E4; Allen (*Yesterday*), pp. 80-81; Congdon, p. 135; Schlesinger (*Crisis*), p. 481.

117 Illinois. Schlesinger (*Crisis*), p. 481.

118 "Members find it necessary . . . banks cannot be accepted." Congdon, p. 135; *NY Times*, 5 March 1933, p. E6; Pietrusza (*1920*), p. 436.

119 Eleanor. Pietrusza (*1920*), p. 436.

120 Pinchot. Congdon, p. 133.

121 NYSE, Chicago Board of Trade. Kennedy (*Freedom*), pp. 132-33.

122 "We are at . . . more we can do." Joslin, p. 366; Schlesinger (*Crisis*), p. 481; Smith (*Dream*), p. 228.

123 "You . . . fallen." Farley, p. 36; Perkins, pp. 139-41; Schlesinger (*Crisis*), p. 480. FDR possessed a strong religious streak. "As I watched him and thought about him from time to time," noted Frances Perkins, also devoutly Episcopal, "I realized his Christian faith was absolutely simple. As far as I can make out, he had no doubts. He just believed with a certainty and simplicity that gave him no pangs or doubts."

124 Peabody. *NY Times*, 5 March 1933, p. 3; *Washington Post*, 5 March 1933, p. 2; Farley (*Years*), p. 37; Lash, p. 360; Morgan, p. 373; Black (*Champion*), p. 269; Schlesinger (*Coming*), p. 570.

125 "lovely steel". Davis (*New Deal*), p. 28; Steinberg, p. 188; Alter, p. 213.

126 "It must have . . . of small talk." Roosevelt (*Memoirs*), p. 164; Pietrusza (*1920*), p. 437.

127 Lucy. Persico (*Lucy*), p. 201; Cook (*Vol. 1*), p. 492.

128 One hundred thousand. Schlesinger (*Crisis*), p. 1; Congdon, p. 125; Cohen (*Nothing*), p. 39.

129 Machine guns. Schlesinger (*Crisis*), p. 1; Congdon, p. 125.

130 "For now we . . . these is charity." Schlesinger (*Crisis*), p. 7; Congdon, p. 127; Cohen (*Nothing*), p. 37.

131 "This is . . . consecration". *NY Times*, 5 March 1933, p. 1; Davis (*New Deal*), p. 28; Schlesinger (*Crisis*), p. 7.

132 "Nor need we . . . these critical days." *NY Times*, 5 March 1933, p. 1; Moley (*New Deal*), p. 97; Davis (*New Deal*), p. 29; Schlesinger (*Crisis*), p. 8; Congdon, p. 127. It was Howe who inserted "the only thing we have to fear is fear itself." (Moley [*New Deal*], pp. 115, 127)

133 "Our international trade . . . on that accomplishment." Davis (*New Deal*), p. 31.

134 "If I read the . . . propose to offer. . . ." *NY Times*, 5 March 1933, p. 1; Davis (*New Deal*), p. 31.

135 "It is to . . . a foreign foe." *NY Times*, 5 March 1933, p. 1; Davis (*New Deal*), p. 32; Schlesinger (*Crisis*), pp. 7-8; Congdon, p. 127. From the United Kingdom, Cynthia Mosley, wife of Oswald Mosley, leader of the newly formed British Union of Fascists, wrote to her old friend FDR: "We were staying with Lloyd George last night at his place in the country. It was an extraordinary party consisting of us 2, Ll.G. & his son, the Soviet Ambassador and his wife, Oliver Baldwin (Stanley's son), a Labour and a Tory MP. We all listened to your speech which came over the wireless magnificently and completely bowled us all over—Ll.G. was terrifically excited about it and said it was the *most remarkable* utterance by a man in your position (*not* on the eve of an election but on taking up the job *after* the Election) that he ever heard. We were all tremendously thrilled. . . ." Following FDR's election, when Cynthia had extended her congratulations, he responded, "If answering your letter is a nuisance, I hope I may often be 'bothered' in this way! I was happy to have your good wishes and appreciate the confidence which you and that fine husband of yours have in me. You may be sure that I recognize both the great opportunities and the grave responsibilities of the days that lie ahead. However, there will still be occasional chances for fishing and I hope we may have a repetition of that jolly trip some time soon. Mrs. Roosevelt and my mother join me in warmest personal regards." (Sidelsky, p. 296)

136 "The thing that . . . warning of a dictatorship." Schlesinger (*Crisis*), p. 8; Congdon, p. 128.

137 "terrifying. . . them *what* to do." *NY Times*, 5 March 1933, p. 7; Hickok (*Reluctant*), p. 103; Davis (*New Deal*), pp. 37-38.

138 "ROOSEVELT ASKS . . . ROLE." Farr, p. 191. The Italian fascist newspaper *Giornale d'Italia* noted of FDR's inaugural address: "[T]he whole world feels the need for executive authority capable of acting with full powers of cutting short the purposeless chatter of legislative assemblies, . . . this method of government may well be defined as Fascist." (Davis [*New Deal*], p. 37) Startlingly, such unlikely figures as Rex Tugwell, Lorena Hickok ("If I were 20 years younger and weighed 75 pounds less, I think I'd start out to be the Joan of Arc of the Fascist Movement in the United States")—and FDR himself ("I am much interested and deeply impressed by what he has accomplished and by his evidenced honest purpose of restoring Italy") expressed sympathy for the Italian regime. (Schivelbusch, pp. 44-46)

139 MacArthur. Davis (*New Deal*), p. 33.

140 Smith. *LA Times*, 5 March 1933, pp. 3, 5; *Washington Post*, 5 March 1933, p. 13; *Oakland Tribune*, 5 March 1933, p. 1; *Syracuse Herald*, 5 March 1933, pp. 1, 3; *LA Times*, 15 April 1938, p. 1; Roosevelt (*My Parents*), p. 143; Anthony (*First Ladies*), p. 474; Alter, pp. 223-24; Davis (*New Deal*), p. 33.

141 Hot dogs. Davis (*New Deal*), p. 33. In his memoirs, Rex Tugwell complained about the food served by Eleanor and revealed that FDR himself "disliked most of it intensely." (Tugwell [*Brains*], p. 52)

142 Inaugural ball. Rowley, p. 181.

143 House. Suckley.

144 Oval Office. Tugwell (*Democratic*), pp. 270-71; Freidel (*New Deal*), pp. 213-14; Davis (*New Deal*), pp. 40-41; Miller (*FDR*), p. 300.

Chapter Twenty-seven: "Somebody hurled a spittoon"

1 "Industrialists who hoped . . . to finance Hitler." US Department of State, pp. 313-16.

2 "perhaps 20 seats." US Department of State, pp. 316-17. Prittwitz und Gaffron would become the only German ambassador to resign in protest of Hitler's appointment as chancellor.

3 "We must work . . . hope to succeed." Goebbels (*Part*), p. 163.

4 "The Leader is . . . source of reinvigoration." Goebbels (*Part*), pp. 165-66.

5 "[T]here was a new . . . in their place." Hanfstaengl, p. 190.

6 "Hitler can wear . . . escape from ourselves." Lüdecke, pp. 493-94.

7 "I'm not so . . . he should talk?" Lüdecke, p. 500.

8 "Money is extraordinarily . . . by the Government." Goebbels (*Part*), p. 172; Bullock, p. 228; Shirer, p. 172.

9 Wilhelm II. Cecil, pp. 339-40; McDonogh, p. 449.

10 Stahlhelm. Guérin, pp. 61-62; McDonald, pp. 17-18.

11 Potsdam. Lüdecke, pp. 515-16, 533-36; Goebbels (*Part*), pp. 165-66; Bullock, p. 229; Hauner, p. 85; Feuchtwanger, p. 296; Kershaw (*Hubris*), p. 387.

12 "He was all . . . permit its destruction." Lüdecke, p. 524.

13 Forty-nine cities. Thacker, p. 135.

14 Four speeches. Lambert, p. 134; Kershaw (*Hubris*), p. 388.

15 *Der Angriff.* Leopold, p. 124.

16 "Dictatorship of the Moneybags". Turner (*Business*), p. 279.

17 lacking "any spark of social justice." Turner (*Business*), p. 278.

18 "Against reaction!" Heiden (*Fuehrer*), p. 493; Fest (*Hitler*), p. 347.

19 Smaller crowds. Kershaw (*Hubris*), p. 389; Kershaw (*Myth*), p. 45; Evans (*Coming*), p. 298.

20 "[T]he outlook is still . . . a few weeks ago." Goebbels (*Part*), p. 172.

21 Transit strike. Lemmons, pp. 104-8; Heiden (*History*), p. 208; Heiden (*Fuehrer*), pp. 493-94; Olden, pp. 261-62; Richie, p. 404; Kessler, p. 434; Rolfs, p. 240; Reimann, p. 149; Orlow (*Nazi*), p. 285; Johnson (*Modern*), p. 282; Muhlen, p. 33.

22 "commit sabotage on . . . who protected them." Carsten, p. 377. The words of the German Jewish-born historian Francis Ludwig Carsten.

23 "German Communist". Reuth, p. 66.

24 Ulbricht. Reuth, pp. 155-56; Reimann, p. 149; Richie, p. 404; Hayman, p. 186.

25 "The entire Press . . . away from us. . . ." Goebbels (*Part*), pp. 181-82; Kershaw (*Hubris*), p. 391; Burleigh, p. 144; Heiber, p. 102; Shirer, p. 172.

26 "the most peaceful . . . not seriously injured." *NY Times*, 7 November 1932, p. 4.

27 Nazi vote. Clark (*German Republic*), pp. 422-23; Feuchtwanger, pp. 326-27; Wheeler-Bennett (*Nemesis*), p. 260; Nicholls, p. 137; Manvell & Fraenkel (*Hundred*), p. 53.

28 DNVP. Mommsen, p. 352.

29 "For [Hitler], it's . . . Hitler awake!" Kershaw (*Hubris*), p. 391; Evans (*Coming*), p. 299.

30 Nazi Berlin vote. Lemmons, p. 108; Reimann, p. 150. Dropping from 28.6 percent to 26.0 percent. (Heiber, p. 93)

31 KPD Berlin vote. Wheaton, p. 133; Large (*Berlin*), p. 251; Reuth, p. 156; Feuchtwanger, p. 298; Reimann, pp. 149-50. A raw total of 830,837 votes, the highest sum recorded by any party in Weimar Berlin.

32 "Accident apart, it . . . his pipe-dreams." Eyck, p. 441; Wheaton, p. 138; Davidson, p. 339; Burleigh, p. 145; Fest (*Hitler*), p. 356.

33 "Nothing but . . . obligations." Shirer, p. 176.

34 Taxes. Fest (*Hitler*), p. 358.

35 *Völkischer Beobachter*. Manvell & Fraenkel (*Hundred*), p. 198.

36 Begging. Olden, p. 264; Heiden (*History*), pp. 217-18; *NY Times*, 6 November 1932, p. E4; *Living Age*, February 1933, p. 498.

37 "For the NSDAP . . . the NSDAP." Reuth, p. 157; Davidson, p. 343.

38 "combined all extremes . . . mean complete collapse." Olden, p. 264.

39 "Social General". Turner (*Business*), p. 308; François-Poncet, p. 43.

40 *Kriegspiel*. Wheeler-Bennett (*Nemesis*), p. 264; Wheeler-Bennett (*Titan*), p. 421; Nicholls, p. 378.

41 Reichswehr report. Nicholls, pp. 382-84; Wheeler-Bennett (*Nemesis*), pp. 264-65; Wheeler-Bennett (*Titan*), p. 421-22; Dorpalen, p. 390; Davidson, pp. 340-41; Bullock, p. 236; Mitchell (*Hitler*), p. 166; Feuchtwanger, p. 302; Wheaton, p. 134; Davidson, pp. 340-41; Shirer, p. 174; Nicholls, p. 138.

42 Writing. Domarus, pp. 176-77, 181; Manvell & Fraenkel (*Hundred*), p. 58; Heiden (*Fuehrer*), p. 496; Eyck, p. 438; Rolfs, p. 241.

43 Cabinet. Wheeler-Bennett (*Titan*), p. 422; Dorpalen, p. 394; Feuchtwanger, p. 302; Eyck, p. 445.

44 "Little Monk. . . *schweren Gang*." Papen, p. 218; Shirer, p. 174; Rolfs, pp. 225, 245; Toland, p. 278.

45 "You'll consider . . . in God's name." Papen, p. 223; Dorpalen, p. 395; Bullock, p. 236; Davidson, p. 341; Mitchell (*Hitler*), p. 166; Manvell & Fraenkel (*Hundred*), p. 78; Toland, p. 279; Davidson, p. 341; Shirer, p. 175; Rolfs, p. 226.

46 "*Ich hat einen Kameraden*". Wheeler-Bennett (*Titan*), p. 422; Dorpalen, p. 395; Feuchtwanger, p. 302; Eyck, p. 447; Ludwig (*Hindenburg*), p. 355; Domarus, p. 202; Fest (*Hitler*), p. 352; Davidson, p. 341; Shirer, p. 175; Koeves, p. 186; Rolfs, p. 226.

47 "There is only . . . is Adolf Hitler." Muhlen, p. 33.

48 "I am the last . . . in reserve." Dorpalen, p. 395; Rolfs, p. 226.

49 "Strasser suggests negotiating . . . it is impossible". Goebbels (*Part*), p. 196.

50 "You know that . . . by Thursday evening." Heiden (*Fuehrer*), pp. 496-97; Heiden (*History*), p. 211; Wheeler-Bennett (*Titan*), p. 418; Manvell & Fraenkel (*Hundred*), p. 63; Domarus, p. 183; Rolfs, p. 219.

51 "The Reich President . . . for such eventualities." Manvell & Fraenkel (*Hundred*), p. 71; Domarus, p. 191; Eyck, p. 440; Davidson, p. 338; Hauner, p. 86; Kershaw (*Hubris*), p. 394; Fest (*Hitler*), p. 350.

52 "That is the . . . our turn comes." Goebbels (*Part*), p. 201; Reimann, p. 151.

53 Schleicher/Strasser. Kershaw (*Hubris*), p. 399; Orlow (*Prussia*), p. 222.

54 Thuringia. *NY Times*, 5 December 1932, p. 6; Goebbels (*Part*), pp. 202-3; Wheeler-Bennett (*Nemesis*), p. 269; Evans (*Coming*), p. 302; Shirer, p. 176; Wheaton, p. 135; Mitchell (*Hitler*), p. 168; Broszat, p. 129; Burleigh, p. 145; Hauner, p. 87; Halperin, p. 518; Koeves, pp. 191-92; Orlow (*Nazi*), p. 291.

55 Delmer. Hanfstaengl, p. 199; Kershaw (*Hubris*), p. 399.

56 "I was so . . . of such villainy?" Strasser, p. 140; Olden, p. 268; Payne, p. 244; Reimann, p. 152.

57 "Yes, I believe . . . I have proof!" Strasser, p. 140; Payne, p. 244.

58 Wilhelmplatz. Thacker, p. 137.

59 Resigned. *Living Age*, February 1933, p. 498; Reimann, pp. 152-54; Goebbels (*Part*), p. 206; Koeves, p. 192; Shirer, pp. 176-77; Kershaw (*Hubris*), p. 399; Fest (*Hitler*), p. 354; Orlow (*Nazi*), pp. 291-92; Thacker, p. 137. Yet, Strasser never did resign from the party and for a while remained under Hitler's special protection. (Kershaw [*Hubris*], p. 402; Orlow [*Nazi*], p. 292)

60 Bolzano. Koeves, p. 192; Heiden (*Fuehrer*), p. 505; Kershaw (*Hubris*), p. 402; Fest (*Hitler*), p. 355; Turner (*Thirty*), p. 84; Evans (*Coming*), p. 303; Jarman, p. 141; Delmer (*Weimar*), p. 110; Reuth, p. 159; Feuchtwanger, p. 302; Mitchell (*Hitler*), p. 168; Dutch, p. 166.

61 "If the Party . . . in a minute." Domarus, p. 198; Goebbels (*Part*), p. 207; Hauner, p. 87; Olden, p. 269; Kershaw (*Hubris*), p. 401; Fest (*Hitler*), p. 354; Heiden (*Fuehrer*), p. 507; Manvell & Fraenkel (*Hundred*), p. 87; Feuchtwanger, pp. 303-4; Ludwig (*Hindenburg*), p. 353; Toland, p. 282; Halperin, p. 519; Koeves, p. 189; Domarus, p. 198; Burleigh, p. 149.

62 "Either you sign. . . out of the party." Heiden (*Fuehrer*), p. 507; Bullock, p. 240. Strasser's few remaining followers were promptly denounced as "rats, finks and traitors" (*Schweinehunde, Lumpen, und Verräter*). (Orlow [*Nazi*], p. 294)

63 Feder. *NY Times*, 10 December 1932, p. 6; US Department of State, p. 321; Clark (*Republic*), p. 441; Turner (*Thirty*), p. 28; Manvell & Fraenkel (*Hundred*), p. 198; Domarus, p. 199. Strasser's main ally in his policy of entering the government had been Wilhelm Frick; Frick instantly caved. (Bullock, p. 238)

64 "Rarely had the . . . mawkishness and sadism." Olden, p. 269.

65 "Strasser now . . . a dead man." Goebbels (*Part*), p. 209; Payne, p. 244; Shirer, p. 177; Kershaw (*Hubris*), p. 402; Manvell & Fraenkel (*Hundred*), p. 90; Thacker, p. 137.

66 "not yet . . . he became." Riefenstahl, p. 124.

67 "gave me his . . . left the room." Riefenstahl, pp. 127-29; Sigmund, p. 100. Historian Anna Maria Sigmund, however, finds the entire incident apocryphal.

68 "To my great distress . . . me their confidence." Louis Ferdinand, pp. 221-22; Fenyvesi, p. 76.

69 "We must summon . . . the organization together". Goebbels (*Part*), p. 213; Heiden (*Fuehrer*), p. 510.

70 "We must cut . . . with our finances." Goebbels (*Part*), p. 214; Heiden (*Fuehrer*), p. 511; Shirer, p. 176; Fest (*Hitler*), p. 356; Bullock, p. 242; Halperin, p. 523.

71 "disenheartened and disappointed." Plotkin, p. 67; Nagorski (*Hitlerland*), p. 91.

72 "I had come . . . found a minnow." Plotkin, p. 70; Nagorski (*Hitlerland*), p. 79.

73 "My policy is . . . constructive tasks again." Lochner, pp. 39-40; Nagorski (*Hitlerland*), p. 90.

74 Presidential succession. *NY Times*, 8 December 1932, p. 4; Wheeler-Bennett (*Nemesis*), p. 270; Dorpalen, pp. 400-401; Wheaton, p. 136.

75 Party debt. *NY Times*, 12 January 1933, p. 5; Ludwig (*Hindenburg*), p. 359; Reimann, pp. 154-55; Bullock, p. 242; Manvell & Fraenkel (*Hundred*), p. 94; Delmer (*Weimar*), p. 110.

76 "My most tragic . . . for ever lost." Hitler (*Table Talk*), p. 465.

77 "Somebody hurled . . . the combatants." *NY Times*, 8 December 1932, p. 4.

78 150/120 seats. Olden, p. 275; Wheeler-Bennett (*Titan*), p. 416.

79 "The year 1932 . . . eternal ill-luck." Goebbels (*Part*), p. 215; Olden, p. 264; Manvell & Fraenkel (*Hundred*), p. 93; Shirer, p. 178; Bullock, p. 243; Fest (*Hitler*), p. 356.

80 Braun. Hanfstaengl, p. 203; Lambert, pp. 126-27; Turner (*Thirty*), p. 32.

81 "A pleasant-looking blonde . . . eager to please." Hanfstaengl, p. 204.

82 "This year belongs . . . that in writing." Hanfstaengl, p. 204; Turner (*Thirty*), p. 32.

83 "My heretical view. . . capitalism [n]or of socialism." Heiden (*Fuehrer*), p. 512; Bullock, p. 240; Turner (*Thirty*), p. 81.

84 Steel industry. Evans (*Coming*), p. 305.

85 "Schleicher is no better . . . rid of him." Delmer (*Weimar*), p. 115; Singer, p. 143.

86 "You desire a . . . welcome to it." Carsten, p. 385; Nicholls, p. 365.

87 Paris. Papen, pp. 323-24; Rolfs, p. 229.

88 78 Wilhelmstrasse. Papen, p. 164; Olden, p. 272; Wheeler-Bennett (*Nemesis*), p. 271; Heiden (*Fuehrer*), p. 519; Burleigh, p. 150; Turner (*Thirty*), pp. 96-97; Rolfs, p. 229; Burleigh, p. 150; Beck, p. 83. In November 1932, the Nazis established their Berlin headquarters also back-yard–to–back-yard to the chancellery. (*NY Times*, 6 November 1932, p. E4)

89 Herrenklub. Shirer, p. 178; Davidson, p. 193; Mitchell (*Hitler*), p. 169; Kershaw (*Hubris*), p. 413; Eyck, p. 464.

90 Schroeder. Papen, pp. 226-29; Olden, p. 270; Wheeler-Bennett (*Nemesis*), p. 272; Bullock, pp. 243-44; Clark (*Republic*), pp. 447-48; Manvell & Fraenkel (*Hundred*), pp. 96-101; Manvell (*Himmler*), p. 30; Williams (*Adenauer*), p. 204; Shirer, p. 180; Davidson, p. 194; Payne, p. 244. Papen had his work cut out in courting Hitler ("I did not trust Papen and wanted to work a coalition with General von Schleicher"). Schleicher's ill-fated plotting with Strasser derailed that scenario. (Bloch, pp. 27-28)

91 Photographed. Davidson, p. 194; Olden, p. 270; Turner (*Thirty*), p. 47; Wheaton, p. 139.

92 "[T]he financial situation . . . a sudden". Goebbels (*Part*), p. 228; Olden, p. 270; Singer, p. 140; Fest (*Hitler*), p. 358. In December, Göring met with Italian air minister Italo Balbo. Göring biographer Kurt Singer notes that on December 29 Goebbels recorded "Göring tells me all is in order" and speculates regarding Italian financial aid to Hitler. (Singer, p. 137)

93 "hesitant, at a loss . . . exhausted. . . ." François-Poncet, pp. 42-43.

94 Strasser in government. *NY Times*, 15 January 1933, p. 16; Manvell & Fraenkel (*Hundred*), p. 95; Turner (*Thirty*), p. 84; Dorpalen, p. 418; Kershaw (*Hubris*), p. 722.

95 Strasser/Hindenburg. Papen, p. 232; Wheeler-Bennett (*Nemesis*), p. 274; Shirer, p. 180; Domarus, p. 212; Manvell and Fraenkel (*Hundred*), p. 95; Davidson, p. 350; Turner (*Thirty*), p. 85.

96 "I give you my . . . Chancellor of Germany." Olden, p. 266; Koeves, p. 193.

97 "I won't scold . . . committed another blunder!'" Turner (*Thirty*), p. 50.

98 Eight hundred thousand acres. Knight-Patterson, p. 560; Heiden (*History*), p. 225; François-Poncet, p. 43; Clark (*Republic*), p. 441; Eyck, pp. 459-60; Manvell & Fraenkel (*Hundred*), p. 94; Rolfs, p. 234; Taylor, p. 107; Reimann, p. 158. Given in some sources as 750,000 acres.

99 5.6 million. Wheaton, p. 142.

100 "agrarian Bolsheviks". Olden, p. 272; Eyck, p. 461; Jarman, p. 141; Bullock, p. 241; Redlich, p. 87; Broszat, p. 136; Davidson, p. 343; Kershaw (*Hubris*), p. 416; Clark (*Republic*), pp. 447, 449; Rolfs, p. 246; Halperin, p. 522.

101 "the almighty-money-bag . . . and its satellites." *NY Times*, 12 January 1933, p. 5; Koeves, p. 197; Turner (*Business*), p. 310; Turner (*Thirty*), p. 99.

102 Lippe returns. *NY Times*, 16 January 1933, p. 4; *Literary Digest*, 28 January 1933, p. 13; Papen, p. 233; Turner (*Thirty*), pp. 53-66; Clark (*Republic*), pp. 448, 450; Dorpalen, pp. 418-19; Manvell and Fraenkel (*Hundred*), p. 94; Reimann, pp. 155-57; Wheaton, pp. 140-42; Shirer, p. 180; Davidson, p. 195; Redlich, p. 90; Mitchell, p. 170; Kershaw (*Hubris*), pp. 416, 721; Eyck, p. 470; Hitler (*Table Talk*), p. 496; Feuchtwanger, p. 307. The Nazis' Lippe campaign was complicated immeasurably by a prominent local Strasserite party leader's vocal defection.

103 99,812. Eyck, p. 470; Beck, p. 85*fn*; Heiber, p. 104; Manvell & Fraenkel (*Hundred*), p. 94.

104 Hugenberg. Leopold, p. 133.

105 "miracle of Lippe." Reimann, p. 157.

106 "Hitler Victory. . . Lippe Speak!" Reuth, p. 162.

107 "the great masses . . . in our direction." Manvell & Fraenkel (*Hundred*), p. 105.

108 "a success whose . . . possible to over-estimate." Hitler (*Table Talk*), p. 496.

109 *Osthilfe*. Knight-Patterson, pp. 486-87; Feuchtwanger, pp. 224, 243.

110 Corruption. Ludwig (*Hindenburg*), pp. 360-62; Papen, pp. 164-67; Olden, pp. 274-75; Turner (*Thirty*), pp. 100-101; François-Poncet, p. 46; Wheeler-Bennett (*Nemesis*), p. 275; Heiden (*Fuehrer*), pp. 443-44, 529-30; Singer, pp. 138-40; Shirer, pp. 180-81; Evans (*Center*), pp. 373-74, 383; Fischer, p. 179; Bullock, pp. 246-47; Kershaw (*Hubris*), pp. 416-17; Snell, pp. 23-24, 26; Clark (*Republic*), p. 359; Dutch, p. 115.

111 Threat to expose. Roberts, p. 61; Burleigh, p. 150; Singer, pp. 141-42.

112 Neudeck. Heiden (*History*), pp. 159-60, 227; Wheeler-Bennett (*Titan*), pp. 310-14; Dorpalen, pp. 135-36; François-Poncet, pp. 18-19; Bullock, p. 246; Feuchtwanger, p. 308; Snyder (*Encyclopedia*), pp. 148, 246.

113 Impeachment. Wheeler-Bennett (*Nemesis*), p. 270; Bullock, p. 247; Dorpalen, p. 426; Rolfs, p. 249.

114 "Wessel has erected . . . stone and bronze". Domarus, p. 220. Goebbels meanwhile fumed over a supposed interference in the day's events from Wessel's mother: "She is unbearable in her arrogance. Our dead belong to the nation." (Thacker, p. 138)

115 Sportpalast. Domarus, p. 221.

116 January 22 events. *NY Times*, 23 January 1933, p. 6; Goebbels (*Part*), pp. 229-31; Hitler (*Table Talk*), p. 497; Manvell & Fraenkel (*Hundred*), p. 106; Bullock, pp. 245-46; Toland, p. 285; Heiber, p. 105; Domarus, pp. 219-21; Turner (*Thirty*), pp. 110-11; Hauner, p. 88; Kershaw (*Hubris*), p. 418; Reuth, p. 162; Reimann, p. 158. Some said only twenty thousand. The former Kaiser and two of his sons also dispatched wreaths.

117 1,199,927. Bloch, p. 26; Read, p. 398.

118 Dahlem meeting. Papen, p. 235; Wheeler-Bennett (*Nemesis*), p. 278; Hitler (*Table Talk*), p. 497; Manvell & Fraenkel (*Hundred*), pp. 106-7; Toland, pp. 285-86; Bloch, p. 30; Shirer, p. 181; Davidson, pp. 350-52; Broszat, pp. 139-40; Eyck, p. 472; Wheaton, p. 143; Feuchtwanger, p. 307. "I was truly under Hitler's spell, that cannot be denied," Ribbentrop confessed in his cell at Nürnberg. "I was impressed with him from the moment I first met him in 1932. He had terrific power especially in his eyes. . . . until I met him . . . I was never a coward. . . ." (Goldensohn, p. 191)

119 New York. Goldensohn, p. 192; Read, p. 394. He soon moved to a less expensive boardinghouse.

120 Turkish Front. *American Mercury*, April 1941, p. 476; Papen, p. 235; Heiden (*Fuehrer*), p. 422; Shirer, p. 181; Manvell & Fraenkel (*Hundred*), p. 106; Wheaton, p. 143; Snyder (*Elite*), p. 158.

121 Göring to Meissner. Dorpalen, p. 424; Davidson, p. 352; Rolfs, p. 249.

122 Impeachment/investigation. Wheeler-Bennett (*Nemesis*), p. 279; Rolfs, p. 235; Bullock, p. 247; Dorpalen, p. 424; Turner (*Thirty*), p. 115; Broszat, p. 140; Bloch, p. 30; Davidson, p. 351; Snyder (*Encyclopedia*), p. 148.

123 "Oskar . . . was extremely . . . under his spell." Shirer, p. 181; Noakes & Pridham, p. 118; Dorpalen, p. 424; Wheeler-Bennett (*Nemesis*), p. 279; Rolfs, p. 235; Bullock, p. 247; Toland, p. 286; Broszat, p. 140; Wheaton, p. 143; Davidson, p. 351; Feuchtwanger, pp. 307-8.

124 Schleicher to Meissner. Rolfs, p. 249; Dorpalen, p. 425; Broszat, p. 140.

125 Hitler exploded. Bloch, p. 30. On January 6, Schacht had predicted to an American that Hitler would be in power in three weeks. (Muhlen, p. 34)

126 "Do you think . . . I wonder". Louis Ferdinand, p. 222.

127 Defense minister. Göring, pp. 97, 108.

128 Demanded resignation. Fest (*Hitler*), p. 362; Mommsen, pp. 522-23; Turner (*Business*), p. 313. Hammerstein-Equord was only recently, and temporarily, enamored of a Hitler chancellery. Following August 13, he expressed his relief that he could now count on Reichswehr troops to fire upon rebellious Nazis. (Carsten, p. 374; Wheaton, p. 130)

129 Resignation. *NY Times*, 29 January 1933, pp. 1-2; Snyder (*Documentary*), p. 80; Mommsen, p. 523; Domarus, p. 225.

130 "I have already . . . heaven later on." Papen, p. 238; Wheeler-Bennett (*Nemesis*), p. 280; Clark (*Republic*), pp. 454; Shirer, p. 182; Davidson, p. 355; Toland, p. 287.

131 "After this breach . . . go to heaven." Shirer, p. 182; Toland, p. 287; Fest (*Hitler*), p. 363.

132 "Berlin Stays Red". *NY Times*, 29 January 1933, p. 2.

133 "scouted 'the enemy,' . . . like real soldiers." *NY Times*, 30 January 1933, p. 5.

134 "mount barricades . . . constitutional rights." *NY Times*, 30 January 1933, p. 5.

135 Zentrum. Eyck, p. 481; Feuchtwanger, pp. 309, 311.

136 Duesterberg. Dorpalen, p. 437; Kershaw (*Hubris*), pp. 421, 723; Turner (*Thirty*), pp. 155-56; Wistrich, p. 58; Eyck, p. 475; Leopold, p. 124; Heiden (*Fuehrer*), p. 537.

137 Frick, Göring. Papen, p. 241. In August 1932, Papen had dangled a "Ministry of Propaganda, People's Education and Mass Persuasion" before Hitler, but as the months progressed Goebbels found himself shut out of any prospective Hitler Cabinet. (Goebbels [*Part*], p. 235; Heiden [*History*], p. 231; Heiber, pp. 91-92)

138 Blomberg. Wheaton, pp. 198-99; Mommsen, p. 526. Schleicher, not surprisingly, was quite sensitive as to who might serve as defense minister in a post-Schleicher chancellorship. First and foremost, of course, he hankered to retain the post. But he also feared (without much basis) that Hitler craved it for himself. Schleicher begged Hindenburg against bestowing it upon any Nazi. In selecting Blomberg, however, Hindenburg unknowingly designated an officer of distinct National Socialist (and sometimes Bolshevik) leanings: "I am not far short of becoming a Bolshevik myself". Konrad

Heiden indicates that Blomberg's thinking had been influenced by the East Prussian Military District's anti-Semitic Protestant chaplain, Ludwig Müller, later the leader ("Reich Bishop") of Hitler's officially Nazi "German Evangelical Church." (Göring, pp. 97, 108; Wheaton, pp. 198-99; Dorpalen, p. 435; Feuchtwanger, p. 310; Snyder [*Encyclopedia*], p. 30; Turner [*Business*], p. 319; Heiden [*History*], pp. 230, 405; Wistrich, p. 235)

139 Papen's presence. Hitler (*Table Talk*), p. 500; Mommsen, p. 528.

140 "the opposite . . . there is today." Stachura, p. 92; Wheaton, p. 49; Fest (*Face*), p. 296.

141 "You're wrong . . . hired him." Fest (*Face*), p. 39; Fest (*Hitler*), p. 366; Bracher, p. 195; Evans (*Coming*), p. 308; Kershaw [*Hitler*], p. 59; Kershaw (*Hubris*), p. 421; Hayman, p. 186. Davidson, p. 355. Following Hitler's appointment, the *New York Times* reported that "it is generally felt that the government is Colonel von Papen's show." (*NY Times*, 1 February 1933, p. 1; Dorpalen, p. 444*fn*)

142 "If Hitler wants . . . the dictatorship." Evans (*Coming*), p. 307.

143 *Pour le Mérite.* Manvell & Fraenkel (*Goering*), p. 75; Payne, p. 167; Reimann, p. 146; Wistrich, p. 102; Large (*Munich*), pp. 167-68; Snyder (*Encyclopedia*), p. 122; Orlow (*Nazi*), p. 132; Snyder (*Elite*), p. 5; Lewis (*Hitler*), p. 241.

144 Goebbels 1933. Thacker, pp. 137-38; Sigmund, pp. 82-83.

145 "We sit up . . . hour will strike." Goebbels (*Part*), p. 235.

146 "humble, sweetly reasonable. . . his success." Mosley, p. 147.

147 Coup rumor. Papen, p. 243; Heiden (*History*), p. 227; Wheeler-Bennett (*Nemesis*), pp. 283-84; Wheeler-Bennett (*Titan*), pp. 432-33; Singer, pp. 144-45; François-Poncet, p. 47; Shirer, pp. 182-83; Bullock, p. 248; Payne, p. 246; Goebbels (*Part*), p. 235; Carsten, p. 393; Delmer (*Weimar*), p. 115; Mitchell (*Hitler*), pp. 172-73; Toland, p. 288; Davidson, pp. 360-61; Koeves, pp. 206-7; Feuchtwanger, p. 310; Reuth, p. 163; Dorpalen, p. 440; Kershaw (*Hubris*), p. 422; Rolfs, p. 238; Manvell & Fraenkel (*Goering*), p. 89; Bloch, p. 32*fn*.

148 SA/police. Hitler (*Table Talk*), p. 499; Shirer, p. 183; Toland, p. 288; Wheaton, p. 147.

149 Profiteer. Turner (*Business*), pp. 258-59.

150 Wolff. Wheeler-Bennett (*Nemesis*), p. 282. Schleicher may have used Wolff to funnel funds to Gregor Strasser. (Turner [*Business*], p. 260)

151 "I intend to . . . pay for this". Eyck, p. 483.

152 Sworn in. Papen, p. 243; Wheeler-Bennett (*Nemesis*), p. 284; Papen, p. 243; Shirer, p. 183; Bullock, p. 249; Turner (*Thirty*), p. 153; Carsten, p. 393; Eyck, pp. 483-84; Davidson, p. 361; Broszat, p. 145; Feuchtwanger, p. 310; Wheaton, pp. 198-201; Dorpalen, p. 439; Kershaw (*Hubris*), pp. 420, 422; Rolfs, pp. 238-39. Hitler later claimed that it was he who ordered Blomberg to proceed to Hindenburg's. (Hitler [*Table Talk*], p. 500)

153 Elections. Papen, p. 243; Heiden (*History*), p. 229; Hitler (*Table Talk*), p. 498; Manvell & Fraenkel (*Hundred*), pp. 111-12; Koeves, pp. 207-8; Broszat, p. 146; Shirer, p. 184; Dorpalen, pp. 438, 441; Mommsen, pp. 522-23, 527; Domarus, p. 225; Kershaw (*Hubris*), p. 422; Leopold, p. 137; Rolfs, p. 239; Eyck, pp. 484-85; Davidson, pp. 362-63.

154 Meissner. Papen, pp. 243-44; Eyck, pp. 485-86; Fest (*Hitler*), p. 365; Turner (*Thirty*), p. 156; Shirer, p. 184; Toland, p. 289; Kershaw (*Hubris*), p. 423; Davidson, p. 363; Broszat, p. 146; Dorpalen, p. 441; Beck, p. 87.

155 Krosigk. Dorpalen, p. 443; Mommsen, p. 527; Turner (*Thirty*), p. 157.

156 "What is happening . . . interview was happy." Goebbels (*Part*), p. 236; Heiden (*Fuehrer*), p. 538; Manvell & Fraenkel (*100 Days*), p. 113.

157 "I saw them . . . had begun. . . ." Kurth, p. 164.

Bibliography

Addison, Paul. *Churchill: The Unexpected Hero.* New York: Oxford University Press, 2005.

Ahamed, Liaquat. *Lords of Finance: The Bankers Who Broke the World.* New York: Penguin Press, 2009.

Allen, Anne Beiser, and Jon L. Wakelyn. *An Independent Woman: The Life of Lou Henry Hoover.* Westport, CT: Greenwood Press, 2000.

Allen, Frederick Lewis. *Since Yesterday: The 1930s in America: September 3, 1929–September 3, 1939.* New York: Perennial Library, 1972.

———. *The Big Change.* New York: Harper, 1952.

Allen, George E. *Presidents Who Have Known Me.* New York: Simon & Schuster, 1960.

Allen, Oliver E. *The Tiger: The Rise and Fall of Tammany Hall.* Reading, MA: Addison-Wesley Publishing Company, 1993.

Allen, Robert S. *Why Hoover Faces Defeat.* New York: Brewer, Warren & Putnam, 1932.

Allen, William. *Al Smith's Tammany Hall: Champion Political Vampire.* New York: Institute for Public Service, 1928.

Allison, Robert. *James Michael Curley.* Beverly, MA: Commonwealth Editions, 2011.

Alonso, Harriet Hyman. *Robert E. Sherwood: The Playwright in Peace and War.* Amherst: University of Massachusetts Press, 2007.

Alter, Jonathan. *The Defining Moment: FDR's Hundred Days and the Triumph of Hope.* New York: Simon & Schuster, 2006.

Ambrose, Stephen E. *Eisenhower: Soldier, General of the Army, President-Elect: 1890–1952 Volume I.* New York: Simon & Schuster, 1983.

Andrew, Christopher. *For the President's Eyes Only: Secret Intelligence and the American Presidency from Washington to Bush.* New York: HarperCollins, 1995.

Anonymous. *Foster-Ford: The Candidates for the Working Youth.* New York: Youth Publishers, 1932.

———. *The Mirrors of Washington.* New York: G. P. Putnam's Sons, 1921.

Anonymous (Robert S. Allen and Drew Pearson). *Washington Merry-Go-Round.* New York: Horace Liveright & Co., 1931.

Anthony, Carl Sferrazza. *First Ladies: The Saga of the Presidents' Wives and Their Power, 1789–1961.* New York: HarperCollins, 1990.

———. *Florence Harding: The First Lady, the Jazz Age and the Death of America's Most Scandalous President.* New York: William Morrow and Company, 1998.

Arad, Gulie Ne'eman. *America, Its Jews, and the Rise of Nazism.* Bloomington: Indiana University Press, 2000.

Archer, Jules. *The Plot to Seize the White House.* New York: Hawthorn Books, 1973.

Armstrong, Louise Van Voorhis. *We Too Are The People.* Boston: Little, Brown and Company, 1938.

Ascher, Abraham. *Was Hitler a Riddle?: Western Democracies and National Socialism.* Stanford, CA: Stanford University Press, 2012.

Ayton, Mel. *Hunting the President: Threats, Plots and Assassination Attempts—From FDR to Obama*. Washington, DC: Regnery History, 2014.

Bach, Steven. *Leni: The Life and Work of Leni Riefenstahl*. New York: Vintage Books, 2008.

Baird, Jay W. *To Die for Germany: Heroes in the Nazi Pantheon*. Bloomington: Indiana University Press, 1990.

Barber, James David. *Presidential Character: Predicting Performance in the White House*. Upper Saddle River, NJ: Prentice-Hall, 1972.

Barber, Lucy G. *Marching on Washington—The Forging of an American Political Tradition*. Berkeley: University of California Press, 2004.

Barkley, Alben W. *That Reminds Me*. Garden City, NY: Doubleday & Co., 1954.

Bartlett, Bruce. *Wrong on Race: The Democratic Party's Buried Past*. New York: Palgrave Macmillan, 2008.

Bartlett, John Henry. *The Bonus March and the New Deal*. Chicago: M.A. Donohue & Company, 1937.

Barone, Michael. *Our Country: The Shaping of America from Roosevelt to Reagan*. New York: The Free Press, 1990.

Barrows, Susanna, and Robin Room, eds. *Drinking: Behavior and Belief in Modern History*. Berkeley: University of California Press, 1991.

Baruch, Bernard. *Baruch: The Public Years*. New York: Holt, Rinehart and Winston, 1960.

Baur, Lt. Gen. Hans. *I Was Hitler's Pilot*. London: Frontline Books, 2013 (KOBO edition).

Beasley, Maurine H. *Eleanor Roosevelt: Transformative First Lady*. Lawrence: University Press of Kansas, 2010.

Beasley, Maurine H., Holly C. Shulman, and Henry R. Beasley, eds. *The Eleanor Roosevelt Encyclopedia*. Westport, CT: Greenwood Press, 2001.

Beatty, Jack. *The Rascal King: The Life and Times of James Michael Curley 1874–1958*. Reading, MA: Addison-Wesley, 1992.

Beauchamp, Cari. *Joseph P. Kennedy Presents: His Hollywood Years*. New York: Vintage Books, 2009.

Beck, Hermann. *The Fateful Alliance: German Conservatives and Nazis in 1933: The Machtergreifung in a New Light*. New York: Berghahn Books, 2008.

Beekman, Scott. *William Dudley Pelley: A Life in Right-Wing Extremism and the Occult*. Syracuse, NY: Syracuse University Press, 2005.

Beers, Paul B. *Pennsylvania Politics Today and Yesterday: The Tolerable Accommodation*. University Park: Pennsylvania State University Press, 1979.

Behr, Edward. *Prohibition: Thirteen Years That Changed America*. New York: Arcade Publishing, 1996.

Bellush, Bernard. *Franklin D. Roosevelt as Governor of New York*. New York: Columbia University Press, 1955.

Bendersky, Joseph W. *The Jewish Threat: Anti-Semitic Policies of the U.S. Army*. New York: Basic Books, 2002.

Benjamin, Jules Robert. *The United States and Cuba: Hegemony and Dependent Development, 1880–1934*. Princeton, NJ: Princeton University Press, 1992.

Bennett, David Harry. *Demagogues in the Depression; American Radicals and the Union Party, 1932–1936*. New Brunswick, NJ: Rutgers University Press, 1969.

———. *The Party of Fear: From Nativist Movements to the New Right in American History*. Chapel Hill: University of North Carolina Press, 1988.

Bernstein, Irving. *The Lean Years: A History of the American Worker, 1920–1933*. Boston: Houghton Mifflin, 1969.

Bernstein, Michael. *Walter Wanger, Hollywood Independent*. Berkeley: University of California Press, 2000.

Beschloss, Michael. *Kennedy and Roosevelt: The Uneasy Alliance*. New York: W. W. Norton & Co., 1981.

Best, Gary Dean. *FDR and the Bonus Marchers, 1933–1935*. Westport, CT: Praeger Publishers, 1992.

———. *The Politics of American Individualism: Herbert Hoover in Transition, 1918–1929*. Westport, CT: Greenwood Press, 1975.

Black, Conrad. *Franklin Delano Roosevelt: Champion of Freedom*. New York: PublicAffairs, 2003.

Bloch, Michael. *Ribbentrop*. New York: Crown, 2002.

Blumenson, Martin. *The Patton Papers: 1885–1940*. Boston: Houghton Mifflin Co., 1972.

Blumenthal, Karen. *Six Days in October: The Stock Market Crash of 1929*. New York: Atheneum, 2002.

Botting, Douglas, and Ian Sayer. *Hitler and Women: The Love Life of Adolf Hitler*. London: Robinson Publishing, 2004.

Boydston, Jo Ann, ed. *John A. Dewey: Later Works, 1925–1953: 1933–1934*. Carbondale: Southern Illinois University Press, 1986.

Bracher, Karl Dietrich. *The German Dictatorship: The Origins, Structure and Effects of National Socialism*. New York: Praeger Publishers, 1970.

Brady, David W. *Critical Elections and Congressional Policy Making*. Stanford, CA: Stanford University Press, 1988.

Bramsted, Ernest K. *Goebbels and National Socialist Propaganda 1925–1945*. East Lansing: Michigan State University Press, 1965.

Brands, H. W. *T. R.: The Last Romantic*. New York: Basic Books, 2000.

———. *Traitor to His Class: The Privileged Life and Radical Presidency of Franklin Delano Roosevelt*. New York: Doubleday, 2008.

Brecht, Arnold. *Prelude to Silence: The End of the German Republic*. New York: Oxford University Press, 1944.

Breitman, Richard, and Allan J. Lichtman. *FDR and the Jews*. Cambridge, MA: Harvard University Press, 2013.

Brendon, Piers. *Ike: The Life and Times of Dwight D. Eisenhower*. London: Secker & Warburg, 1987.

Brinkley, Alan. *Voices of Protest: Huey Long, Father Coughlin, & the Great Depression*. New York: Knopf, 1982.

Brock, Pope. *Charlatan: America's Most Dangerous Huckster, the Man Who Pursued Him, and the Age of Flimflam*. New York: Random House, 2009.

Broszat, Martin. *Hitler and the Collapse of Weimar Germany*. Leamington Spa, UK: Berg Publishers Limited, 1987.

Brown, George Rothwell. *The Speaker of the House: The Romantic Story of John N. Garner*. New York: Brewer, Warren & Putnam, 1932.

Bullock, Alan. *Hitler: A Study in Tyranny*. New York: Harper & Row, 1962.

Burke, Bernard V. *Ambassador Frederic Sackett and the Collapse of the Weimar Republic from 1930 to 1933*. New York: Cambridge University Press, 1994.

Burleigh, Michael. *The Third Reich: A New History*. New York: Hill and Wang, 2000.

Burner, David. *Herbert Hoover: A Public Life*. New York: Alfred A. Knopf, 1979.

Burns, James MacGregor. *Roosevelt: The Lion and the Fox*. New York: Harcourt, Brace and Company, 1956.

Calder, James D. *The Origins and Development of Federal Crime Control Policy: Herbert Hoover's Initiatives.* Westport, CT: Praeger, 1993.

Cannadine, David. *Mellon: An American Life.* New York: Vintage, 2008.

Carlin, John W., Wayne S. Cole, Dwight M. Miller, and Timothy Walch, eds. *Herbert Hoover and Franklin D. Roosevelt: A Documentary History.* Westport, CT: Greenwood Press, 1998.

Carlisle, Rodney P. *Hearst and the New Deal: The Progressive as Reactionary.* New York: Garland Publishing, 1979.

Caro, Robert A. *The Power Broker: Robert Moses and the Fall of New York.* New York: Vintage Books, 1975.

Caroli, Betty Boyd. *The Roosevelt Women.* New York: Basic Books, 1998.

Carpenter, Ronald H. *Father Charles E. Coughlin: Surrogate Spokesman for the Disaffected.* Westport, CT: Greenwood Press, 1978.

Carr, Steven Alan. *Hollywood and Anti-Semitism: A Cultural History Up to World War II.* Cambridge, UK: Cambridge University Press, 2001.

Carsten, Francis Ludwig. *The Reichswehr and Politics: 1918 to 1933.* New York: Oxford, 1966.

Carter, John Franklin. *What We Are About to Receive.* Freeport, NY: Books for Libraries, 1968.

Cary, Noel D. *The Path to Christian Democracy: German Catholics and the Party System from Windthorst to Adenauer.* Cambridge, MA: Harvard University Press, 1996.

Case, Josephine Young, and Everett Needham Case. *Owen D. Young and American Enterprise: A Biography.* Boston: D. R. Godine, 1981.

Cashman, Sean Dennis. *America in the Twenties and Thirties: The Olympian Age of Franklin Delano Roosevelt.* New York: New York University Press, 1989.

Cecil, Lamar. *Wilhelm II: Emperor and Exile, 1900–1941.* Chapel Hill: University of North Carolina Press, 1996.

Cerruti, Elisabetta. *Ambassador's Wife.* New York: Macmillan, 1953.

Chalmers, David M. *Hooded Americanism: The History of the Ku Klux Klan.* Chicago: Quadrangle Paperbacks, 1965.

Chambers, Walter. *Samuel Seabury: A Challenge.* New York: Century Co., 1932.

Chaplin, Charles. *My Autobiography.* New York: Pocket Books, Inc., 1966.

Charmley, John. *Churchill: The End of Glory: A Political Biography.* New York: Harcourt Brace & Company, 1993.

Chase, Stuart. *A New Deal.* New York: The Macmillan Company, 1932.

Childers, Thomas. *The Nazi Voter: The Social Foundations of Fascism in Germany, 1919–1933.* Chapel Hill: University of North Carolina Press, 1983.

Churchill, Randolph S. *Twenty-One Years.* Boston: Houghton Mifflin, 1965.

City Affairs Committee. *Charges against James A. McQuade, Sheriff of Kings County, made by the City Affairs Committee of New York; Together with an Open Letter to Governor Roosevelt.* New York: City Affairs Committee, 1932.

———. *Charges Against John Theofel: Chief Clerk of the Surrogate's Court of the County of Queens, Made by the City Affairs Committee of New York Together with an Open Letter to Governor Roosevelt.* New York: City Affairs Committee, 1932.

Clark, Christopher M. *Iron Kingdom: The Rise and Downfall of Prussia, 1600–1947.* London: Penguin, 2007.

———. *Kaiser Wilhelm II.* Harlow, UK: Longman, 2000.

Clark, R. T. *The Fall of the German Republic: A Political Study*. London: G. Allen & Unwin, Ltd., 1935.

Clayton, James D. *The Years of MacArthur, vol. 1: 1880–1941*. Boston: Houghton Mifflin, 1970.

Clements, Kendrick A. *The Life of Herbert Hoover: Imperfect Visionary, 1918–1928*. New York: Palgrave Macmillan, 2010.

Coffey, Thomas M. *The Long Thirst: Prohibition in America: 1920–1933*. New York: W. W. Norton & Co., 1975.

Cohen, Adam. *Nothing to Fear: FDR's Inner Circle and the Hundred Days that Created Modern America*. New York: Penguin, 2009.

Cohen, Lester. *The New York Graphic: The World's Zaniest Newspaper*. New York: Chilton Books, 1965.

Collier, Peter, and David Horowitz. *The Kennedys: An American Drama*. New York: Summit Books, 1984.

———. *The Roosevelts: An American Saga*. New York: Simon & Schuster, 1994.

Congdon, Don, ed. *The '30s: A Time to Remember*. New York: Simon & Schuster, 1962.

Connable, Alfred, and Edward Silberfarb. *Tigers of Tammany: Nine Men Who Ran New York*. New York: Holt, Rinehart and Winston, 1967.

Conradi, Peter. *Hitler's Piano Player: The Rise and Fall of Ernst Hanfstaengl, Confidant of Hitler, Ally of FDR*. New York: Carroll & Graf, 2004.

Considine, Bob. *It's All News to Me: A Reporter's Deposition*. New York: Meredith Press, 1967.

Cook, Blanche Wiesen. *Eleanor Roosevelt, Volume I: 1884–1933*. New York: Penguin Books, 1992.

———. *Eleanor Roosevelt, Volume II: The Defining Years, 1933–1938*. New York: Viking, 1999.

Cordery, Stacy A. *Alice: Alice Roosevelt Longworth, from White House Princess to Washington Power Broker*. New York: Penguin, 2008.

Cowles, Virginia. *The Kaiser*. New York: Harper & Row, 1963.

Craig, Douglas B. *After Wilson: The Struggle for the Democratic Party, 1920–1934*. Chapel Hill: University of North Carolina Press, 1992.

———. *Progressives at War: William G. McAdoo and Newton D. Baker, 1863–1941*. Baltimore: Johns Hopkins University Press, 2013.

Craig, Gordon A. *Germany: 1866–1945*. New York: Oxford University Press, 1978.

Cramer, C. H. *Newton D. Baker: A Biography*. Cleveland: World Publishing Co., 1961.

Cross, Robert F. *Sailor in the White House: The Seafaring Life of FDR*. Annapolis: Naval Institute Press, 2003.

Culver, John C., and John Hyde. *American Dreamer: A Life of Henry A. Wallace*. New York: W. W. Norton, 2000.

Curley, James Michael. *I'd Do It Again: A Record of All My Uproarious Years*. Englewood Cliffs, NJ: Prentice-Hall, Inc., 1957.

Dallek, Robert. *FDR: Franklin D. Roosevelt and American Foreign Policy: 1932–1945*. New York: Oxford University Press, 1979.

———. *Lone Star Rising: Lyndon Johnson and His Times, 1908–1960*. New York: Oxford University Press, 1991.

Daniels, Roger. *The Bonus March: An Episode of the Great Depression*. Westport, CT: Greenwood, 1971.

Davidson, Eugene. *The Making of Adolf Hitler: The Birth and Rise of Nazism*. New York: Scribner's, 1977.

Davis, Kenneth S. *FDR: The Beckoning of Destiny 1882–1928*. New York: Putnam, 1972.

———. *FDR: The New Deal Years 1933–1937: A History*. New York: Random House, 1979.

———. *FDR: The New York Years 1928–1933*. New York: Random House, 1985.

———. *Invincible Summer: An Intimate Portrait of the Roosevelts Based on the Recollections of Marion Dickerman*. New York: Atheneum Press, 1974.

Day, Donald. *Franklin D. Roosevelt's Own Story: Told in His Own Words from His Private and Public Papers*. Boston: Little Brown & Co., 1951.

Delmer, Sefton. *Trail Sinister: An Autobiography*. London: Secker & Warburg, 1961.

———. *Weimar Germany: Democracy on Trial*. London: Macdonald, 1972.

Denton, Sally. *The Plots Against the President: FDR, A Nation in Crisis, and the Rise of the American Right*. New York: Bloomsbury Press, 2012.

De Sales, Raoul de Roussy, ed. *My New Order*. New York: Reynal and Hitchcock, 1941.

D'Este, Carlo. *Eisenhower: A Soldier's Life*. New York: Henry Holt and Co., 2002.

———. *Patton: A Genius for War*. New York: HarperCollins, 1995.

Dickson, Paul, and Thomas B. Allen. *The Bonus Army: An American Epic*. New York: Walker & Co., 2004.

Dietrich, Otto. *I Knew Hitler: The Memoirs of the Third Reich's Press Chief*. New York: Skyhorse Publishing, 2010.

———. *With Hitler on the Road to Power: Personal Experiences with My Leader*. London: 69, Fitzjohns Avenue, 1934. Publisher unknown.

Dille, John, ed. *Time Capsule/1932: A History of the Year Condensed from the Pages of Time*. New York: Time-Life Books, 1968.

Dobyns, Fletcher. *The Amazing Story of Repeal: An Expose of the Power of Propaganda*. Chicago: Willett, Clark, 1940.

Domarus, Max, ed. *Speeches and Proclamations, 1932–1945*. Wauconda, IL: Bolchazy-Carducci Publishers, 1990.

Dornberg, John. *Munich 1923: The Story of Hitler's First Grab for Power*. New York: Harper & Row, 1982.

Dorpalen, Andreas. *Hindenburg and the Weimar Republic*. Princeton, NJ: Princeton University Press, 1964.

Dorwart, Jeffrey M. *Conflict of Duty: The U.S. Navy's Intelligence Dilemma 1919–1945*. Annapolis: U.S. Naval Institute Press, 1984.

Douglas, Jack. *Veterans on the March*. New York: Workers Library Publishers, 1934.

Douglas, Paul H. *The Coming of a New Party*. New York: Whittlesey House, McGraw-Hill Book Co., 1932.

Downey, Kirstin. *The Woman Behind the New Deal: The Life of Frances Perkins, FDR's Secretary of Labor and His Moral Conscience*. New York: Nan A. Talese, 2009.

Duffy, James P., and Vincent L. Ricci. *Target Hitler: The Plots to Kill Hitler*. Westport, CT: Praeger, 1992.

Dunlap, Thomas. *Before the Holocaust: Three German-Jewish Lives, 1870–1939*. Bloomington, IN: Xlibris Corporation, 2010.

Dutch, Oswald. *The Errant Diplomat: The Life of Franz von Papen*. London: Edward Arnold & Co., 1940.

Eaton, Herbert. *Presidential Timber: A History of Nominating Conventions, 1868–1960*. New York: The Free Press of Glencoe, 1964.

Eberle, Henrik, ed. *Letters to Hitler*. Malden, MA: Polity, 2012.

Edwards, Jerome E. *Pat McCarran: Political Boss of Nevada*. Reno: University of Nevada Press, 1982.

Egan, Timothy. *The Worst Hard Time: The Untold Story of Those Who Survived the Great American Dust Bowl*. New York: Houghton Mifflin Harcourt, 2006.

Eisenhower, Dwight D. *At Ease: Stories I Tell to Friends*. Garden City, NY: Doubleday & Co., 1967.

Ekirch, Arthur A., Jr. *Ideologies and Utopias: The Impact of the New Deal on American Thought*. Chicago: Quadrangle Books, 1969.

Ellis, Edward Robb. *A Diary of the Century: Tales from America's Greatest Diarist*. New York: Union Square Press, 2008.

Erikson, Erik H. *Childhood and Society*. New York: W. W. Norton, 1963.

Evans, Ellen Lovell. *The German Center Party, 1870–1933: A Study in Political Catholicism*. Carbondale: Southern Illinois University Press, 1981.

Evans, Richard J. *The Coming of the Third Reich*. New York: Penguin Books, 2003.

Everson, William K. *American Silent Film*. New York: Da Capo Press, 1998.

Eyck, Erich. *A History of the Weimar Republic: From the Locarno Conference to Hitler's Seizure of Power*. Cambridge, MA: Harvard University Press, 1962.

Eyman, Scott. *Empire of Dreams: The Epic Life of Cecil B. DeMille*. New York: Simon & Schuster, 2010.

Faber, Doris. *The Life of Lorena Hickok: ER's Friend*. New York: William Morrow, 1980.

Farber, David. *Everybody Ought to Be Rich: The Life and Times of John J. Raskob, Capitalist*. New York: Oxford University Press, 2013.

Farley, James A. *Behind the Ballots: The Personal History of a Politician*. New York: Harcourt Brace and Company, 1938.

———. *Jim Farley's Story: The Roosevelt Years*. New York: Whittlesey House, 1948.

Farr, Finis. *FDR*. New Rochelle, NY: Arlington House, 1972.

Farrar, Hayward. *The Baltimore Afro-American, 1892–1950*. Westport, CT: Greenwood, 1989.

Farrell, John A. *Clarence Darrow: Attorney for the Damned*. New York: Vintage, 2012.

Fausold, Martin L. *The Presidency of Herbert C. Hoover*. Lawrence: University of Kansas Press, 1985.

Fecher, Charles A., ed. *The Diary of H. L. Mencken*. New York: Alfred A. Knopf, 1989.

Fenster, Julie M. *FDR's Shadow: Louis Howe, The Force That Shaped Franklin and Eleanor Roosevelt*. New York: Palgrave Macmillan, 2009.

Fenyvesi, Charles. *Splendor in Exile: The Ex-Majesties of Europe*. Washington: New Republic Books, 1979.

Fest, Joachim. *Hitler*. New York: Harcourt Brace Jovanovich, 1974.

———. *The Face of the Third Reich: Portraits of the Nazi Leadership*. New York: Pantheon Books, 1970.

Feuchtwanger, E. J. *From Weimar to Hitler: Germany, 1918–33*. New York: St. Martin's Press, 1993.

Finan, Christopher M. *Alfred E. Smith: The Happy Warrior*. New York: Hill and Wang, 2002.

Fischer, Louis. *Men and Politics: An Autobiography*. New York: Duell, Sloan and Pearce, 1941.

Fleming, Gerald. *Hitler and the Final Solution*. Berkeley: University of California Press, 1984.

Flood, Charles Bracelen. *Hitler: The Path to Power*. Boston: Houghton Mifflin Company, 1989.

Flynn, Edward J. *You're the Boss: My Story of a Life in Practical Politics*. New York: The Viking Press, 1947.

Flynn, John T. *Country Squire in the White House*. Garden City, NY: Doubleday, Doran & Co., 1940.

———. *The Roosevelt Myth*. Auburn, AL: The Ludwig von Mises Institute, 2008.

Fowler, Gene. *Beau James: The Life and Times of Jimmy Walker*. New York: Viking, 1949.

Fowler, Robert B. *Wisconsin Votes: An Electoral History*. Madison: University of Wisconsin Press, 2008.

François-Poncet, André. *The Fateful Years: Memoirs of a French Ambassador in Berlin, 1931–1938*. New York: Harcourt, Brace, 1949.

Franklin, Jay (pseud. of John Franklin Carter). *La Guardia: A Biography*. New York: Modern Age Books, 1937.

Freedland, Michael. *The Warner Brothers*. London: Harrap, 1983.

Freedman, Max, ed. *Roosevelt & Frankfurter: Their Correspondence, 1928–1945*. Boston: Atlantic Little, Brown, 1967.

Freidel, Frank. *Franklin D. Roosevelt: A Rendezvous with Destiny*. Boston: Little, Brown, 1989.

———. *Franklin D. Roosevelt: Launching the New Deal*. Boston: Little, Brown, 1973.

———. *Franklin D. Roosevelt: The Apprenticeship*. Boston: Little, Brown, 1952.

———. *Franklin D. Roosevelt: The Ordeal*. Boston: Little, Brown, 1954.

———. *Franklin D. Roosevelt: The Triumph*. Boston: Little, Brown, 1956.

Fried, Albert. *FDR and His Enemies*. New York: Palgrave, 1999.

Friedrich, Thomas. *Hitler's Berlin: Abused City*. New Haven: Yale University Press, 2012.

Fromm, Bella. *Blood and Banquets: A Berlin Social Diary*. New York: Birch Lane Press Book, 1990.

Fuller, Robert Lynn. *Phantom of Fear: The Banking Panic of 1933*. Jefferson, NC: McFarland & Co., 2011.

Galbraith, John Kenneth. *The Great Crash of 1929*. Boston: Houghton Mifflin, 1955.

Gallagher, Hugh Gregory. *FDR's Splendid Deception*. New York: Dodd, Mead, 1985.

Garrett, Garet. *The American Story*. Chicago: Henry Regnery Co., 1955.

Gerard, James W. *My First Eighty-Three Years in America: The Memoirs of James W. Gerard*. Garden City, NY: Doubleday & Company, Inc., 1951.

Gilbert, Martin. *Churchill and America*. New York: Free Press, 2005.

———. *Winston Churchill: The Wilderness Years: Speaking Out Against Hitler in the Prelude to War*. Boston: Houghton Mifflin Co., 1982.

———. *Winston S. Churchill, Volume Five: The Prophet of Truth 1922–1939*. Boston: Houghton Mifflin, 1966.

Gisevius, Hans Bernd. *To the Bitter End: An Insider's Account of the Plot to Kill Hitler, 1933–1944*. New York: Da Capo Press, 1998.

Gitlow, Benjamin. *The Whole of Their Lives: Communism in America, a Personal History and Intimate Portrayal of Its Leaders*. New York: Charles Scribner's Sons, 1948.

Goebbels, Joseph (Helmut Heiber, ed.). *The Early Goebbels Diaries, 1925–1926*. New York: Praeger, 1963.

Goebbels, Dr. Paul. *My Part in Germany's Fight*. London: Hurst & Blackett, Ltd., 1935.

Golay, Michael. *America 1933: The Great Depression, Lorena Hickok, Eleanor Roosevelt, and the Shaping of the New Deal*. New York: Free Press, 2013.

Goldberg, Richard Thayer. *The Making of FDR: Triumph Over Disability*. Cambridge, MA: Abt Books, 1984.

Goldensohn, Leon (Robert Gellately, ed.). *The Nuremberg Interviews: An American Psychiatrist's Conversations with the Defendants and Witnesses*. New York: Vintage Books, 2005.

von der Goltz, Anna. *Hindenburg: Power, Myth, and the Rise of the Nazis*. New York: Oxford University Press, 2009.

Golway, Terry. *Machine Made: Tammany Hall and the Creation of Modern American Politics*. New York: Liveright, 2014.

Goodwin, Doris Kearns. *No Ordinary Time: Franklin and Eleanor Roosevelt: The Home Front in World War II*. New York: Simon & Schuster, 1994.

———. *The Fitzgeralds and the Kennedys*. New York: Simon & Schuster, 1987.

Gordon, Mel. *Erik Jan Hanussen: Hitler's Jewish Clairvoyant*. Los Angeles: Feral House, 2001.

Görtemaker, Heike B. *Eva Braun: Life with Hitler*. New York: Alfred A. Knopf, 2011.

Gosnell, Harold F. *FDR: Champion Campaigner*. New York: Macmillan, 1952.

Gott, Kendall D. *Confrontation at Anacostia Flats: The Bonus Army of 1932*. Arlington, VA: The Institute of Land Warfare, 2007.

Gould, Jean. *A Good Fight: The Story of F. D. R.'s Conquest of Polio*. New York: Dodd, Mead, 1960.

Grant, James. *Bernard M. Baruch: The Adventures of a Wall Street Legend*. New York: J. Wiley, 1997.

Green, Paul M., and Melvin G. Holli, eds. *The Mayors: The Chicago Political Tradition* (3rd Edition). Carbondale: Southern Illinois University Press, 1987.

Greenberg, Ivan. *Surveillance in America: A Critical Analysis of the FBI, 1920 to the Present*. Lanham, MD: Lexington Books, 2012.

Grenville, J. A. S. *The Jews and Germans of Hamburg: The Destruction of a Civilization 1790–1945*. New York: Routledge, 2012.

Gribetz, Louis, and Joseph Kaye. *Jimmie Walker: The Story of a Personality*. New York: Dial Press, 1932.

Grzesinski, Albert C. *Inside Germany*. New York: E. P. Dutton & Company, 1939.

Guérin, Daniel. *The Brown Plague: Travels in Late Weimar and Early Nazi Germany*. Durham, NC: Duke University Press, 1994.

Guilfoyle, James H. *On the Trail of the Forgotten Man: A Journal of the Roosevelt Presidential Campaign*. Boston: Peabody Masters Printers, 1933.

Gun, Nerin E. *Hitler's Mistress: Eva Braun*. New York: Bantam, 1969.

Halperin, S. William. *Germany Tried Democracy: A Political History of the Reich from 1918 to 1933*. New York: T. Y. Crowell, 1946.

Hamann, Brigitte. *Hitler's Vienna: A Dictator's Apprenticeship*. New York: Oxford, 1999.

Hamill, John. *The Strange Career of Herbert Hoover Under Two Flags*. New York: W. Faro, Inc., 1931.

Hancock, Eleanor. *Ernst Röhm, Hitler's SA Chief of Staff*. New York: Palgrave Macmillan, 2008.

Handlin, Oscar. *Al Smith and His America*. Boston: Atlantic-Little Brown Books, 1958.

Hanfstaengl, Ernst. *Unheard Witness*. Philadelphia: J. B. Lippincott Co., 1957.

Harbaugh, William H. *Lawyer's Lawyer: The Life of John W. Davis*. New York: Oxford University Press, 1973.

Hard, William. *Who's Hoover?* New York: Dodd, Mead and Co., 1928.

Hardeman, D. B., and Donald C. Bacon. *Rayburn: A Biography*. Austin: Texas Monthly Press, 1987.

Harriman, W. Averell, and Elie Able. *Special Envoy to Churchill and Stalin, 1941–1946*. New York: Random House, 1975.

Hart, Albert Bushnell, ed. *The American Year Book: A Record of Events and Progress: Year 1931*. New York: The American Year Book Company, 1932.

———. *The American Year Book: A Record of Events and Progress: Year 1932*. New York: The American Year Book Company, 1933.

Hart, George L. *Official Report of the Proceedings of the Twentieth Republican National Convention Held in Chicago, Illinois, June 14, 15, and 16, 1932*. New York: Tenny Press, 1932.

Harwood, Michael. *In the Shadow of the Presidents: The American Vice-Presidency and Succession System*. Philadelphia: J. B. Lippincott Co., 1966.

Hastings, Derek. *Catholicism and the Roots of Nazism: Religious Identity and National Socialism*. New York: Oxford University Press, 2010.

Hauner, Milan. *Hitler: A Chronology of His Life and Time*. New York: St. Martin's Press, 1983.

Hawley, Ellis Wayne, ed. *Herbert Hoover As Secretary of Commerce: Studies in New Era Thought and Practice*. Iowa City: University of Iowa Press, 1981.

Hayman, Ronald. *Hitler and Geli*. New York: Bloomsbury, 1999.

Heaton, John L. *Tough Luck—Hoover Again!* New York: Vanguard Press, 1932.

Heiber, Helmut. *Goebbels*. New York: Hawthorne Books, Inc., 1972.

Heiden, Konrad. *A History of National Socialism*. New York: Alfred A. Knopf, 1935.

———. *Der Fuehrer*. Boston: Houghton Mifflin, 1944.

Heinz, Heinz A. *Germany's Hitler*. London Hurst & Blackett, Ltd., 1934.

Herzstein, Robert E. *Roosevelt and Hitler: Prelude to War*. New York, Paragon House, 1989.

Hett, Benjamin Carter. *Burning the Reichstag: An Investigation Into the Third Reich's Enduring Mystery*. New York: Oxford University Press, 2014.

Hickok, Lorena A. *Eleanor Roosevelt, Reluctant First Lady*. New York: Dodd, Mead, 1980.

———. *The Road to the White House: FDR: The Pre-Presidential Years*. New York: Scholastic Book Services, 1962.

Hicks, John D. *Republican Ascendency: 1921–1933*. New York: Harper & Brothers, 1960.

Hiltzik, Michael. *The New Deal: A Modern History*. New York: Free Press, 2011.

Hinshaw, David. *Herbert Hoover, American Quaker*. New York: Farrar, Straus and Company, 1950.

Hitler, Adolf. *Hitler's Secret Book*. New York: Bramhall House, 1986.

———. *Hitler's Table Talk 1941–1944: His Private Conversations*. New York: Enigma Books, 2000.

———. *Mein Kampf*. Boston: Houghton Mifflin Co., 1943.

Hodgson, Godfrey. *Woodrow Wilson's Right Hand: The Life of Colonel Edward M. House*. New Haven: Yale University Press, 2006.

Hoffmann, Heinrich. *Hitler Was My Friend*. Barnsley, UK: Frontline, 2011.

Hoffmann, Peter. *Hitler's Personal Security*. New York: Da Capo Press, 2000.

Höhne, Heinz. *The Order of the Death's Head: The Story of Hitler's S.S.* New York: Coward-McCann, Inc., 1970.

Holland, Matthew F. *Eisenhower Between the Wars: The Making of a Soldier and a Statesman*. Westport, CT: Praeger, 2001.

Holli, Melvin G. *The Wizard of Washington: Emil Hurja, Franklin Roosevelt, and the Birth of Public Opinion Polling*. New York: Palgrave Macmillan, 2002.

Holmes, John Haynes. *I Speak for Myself: The Autobiography of John Haynes Holmes*. New York: Harper & Brothers, 1959.

Hoover, Herbert (George H. Nash, ed.). *Freedom Betrayed: Herbert Hoover's Secret History of the Second World War and Its Aftermath*. Stanford, CA: Hoover Institution Press, Stanford University, 2011.

Hoover, Herbert. *The Memoirs of Herbert Hoover: The Cabinet & The Presidency 1920–1933*. New York: MacMillan, 1952.

———. *The Memoirs of Herbert Hoover: The Great Depression 1929–1941*. New York: MacMillan, 1952.

———. *The Memoirs of Herbert Hoover: Years of Adventure 1874–1920*. New York: MacMillan, 1951.

———. *The Ordeal of Woodrow Wilson*. New York: McGraw-Hill, 1958.

Hoover, Irwin Hood "Ike." *42 Years in the White House*. Boston: Houghton Mifflin, 1934.

Horan, James D. *The Desperate Years: A Pictorial History of the Thirties*. New York: Bonanza Books, 1962.

Houck, Davis W. *FDR and Fear Itself: The First Inaugural Address*. College Station: Texas A&M University Press, 2002.

———. *Rhetoric as Currency: Hoover, Roosevelt and the Great Depression*. College Station: Texas A&M University Press, 2001.

Houck, Davis W., and Amos Kiewe. *FDR's Body Politics: The Rhetoric of Disability*. College Station: Texas A&M University Press, 2003.

House Committee on Un-American Activities [aka HUAC]. *Communist Tactics Among Veterans' Groups (Testimony of John T. Pace) Hearing Before the Committee on Un-American Activities, House of Representatives, Eighty-second Congress, first session. July 13, 1951 (1951)*. Washington: US Government Printing Office, 1951.

Hull, Cordell. *The Memoirs of Cordell Hull*. New York: The Macmillan Company, 1951.

Hunt, Frazier. *The Untold Story of Douglas MacArthur*. New York: Devin-Adair, 1954.

Huthmacker, J. Joseph. *Massachusetts People and Politics 1919–1933*. New York: Atheneum, 1969.

Ickes, Harold L. *The Secret Diary of Harold L. Ickes. 3 vols*. New York: Simon & Schuster, 1954.

Infield, Glenn B. *Hitler and Eva*. New York: Grosset & Dunlap, 1974.

———. *Hitler's Secret Life: The Mysteries of the Eagle's Nest*. New York: Stein & Day, 1979.

Irving, David. *Goebbels: Mastermind of the Third Reich*. London: Focal Point Publications, 1996.

———. *Hitler's War and the War Path*. London: Focal Point Publications, 2001.

Irwin, Douglas. *Peddling Protectionism: Smoot-Hawley and the Great Depression*. Princeton, NJ: Princeton University Press, 2011.

Isaacson, Walter, and Evan Thomas. *The Wise Men: Six Friends and the World They Made*. New York: Simon & Schuster, 1988.

Isherwood, Christopher. *Mr. Norris Changes Trains*. New York: William Morrow, 1935.

James, Dorris Clayton. *The Years of MacArthur, Volume 1: 1880–1941*. Boston: Houghton Mifflin, 1970.

Jarman, T. L. *The Rise and Fall of Nazi Germany*. New York: New York University Press, 1956.

Jeansonne, Glen. *Gerald L. K. Smith: Minister of Hate*. New Haven: Yale University Press, 1988.

———. *The Life of Herbert Hoover: Fighting Quaker 1928–1933*. New York: Palgrave Macmillan, 2012.

Jeffers, H. Paul. *The Napoleon of New York: Mayor Fiorello La Guardia*. New York: Wiley, 2002.

Jenkins, Roy. *Churchill: A Biography*. New York: Farrar, Straus and Giroux, 2001.

Jetzinger, Franz. *Hitler's Youth*. London: Hutchinson, 1958.

Jewett, Robert, and John Shelton Lawrence. *The Myth of the American Superhero*. Grand Rapids, MI: Wm. B. Eerdmans Publishing Company, 2002.

Johnpoll, Bernard K. *Pacifist's Progress: Norman Thomas and the Decline of American Socialism*. Chicago: Quadrangle Books, 1970.

Johnson, Neil M. *George Sylvester Viereck: German-American Propagandist*. Urbana, IL: University of Illinois Press, 1982.

Johnson, Paul. *A History of the American People*. New York: HarperCollins, 1997.

———. *Modern Times: The World from the Twenties to the Eighties*. New York: Harper & Row, 1983.

Jonas, Klaus W. *The Life of Crown Prince Wilhelm*. London: Routledge & K. Paul, 1961.

Jones, J. Sydney. *Hitler in Vienna 1907–13*. London: Blond & Briggs, 1983.

Joslin, Theodore G. *Hoover Off the Record*. Garden City, NY: Doubleday, Doran and Co., 1934.

Kane, Harnett T. *Louisiana Hayride: The American Rehearsal for Dictatorship, 1928–1940*. New York: William Morrow, 1949.

Kaufmann, Walter H. *Monarchism in the Weimar Republic*. New York: Bookman Associates, 1953.

Kelly, C. Brian, and Ingrid Smyer. *Best Little Stories from the Life and Times of Winston Churchill*. Nashville, TN: Cumberland House, 2008.

Kennedy, David M. *Freedom from Fear: The American People in Depression and War 1929–1945*. New York: Oxford University Press, 1999.

———. *Over Here: The First World War and American Society*. New York: Oxford University Press, 1980.

Kershaw, Ian. *Hitler*. London: Longman, 1991.

———. *Hitler 1889–1936, Hubris*. New York: W. W. Norton & Company, 1999.

———. *Hitler: A Biography*. New York: W. W. Norton & Company, 2008.

———. *The 'Hitler Myth': Image and Reality in the Third Reich*. Oxford: Oxford University Press, 1987.

Kessler, Graf. *Harry in the Twenties: The Diaries of Harry Kessler*. New York: Holt, Rinehart, and Winston, 1971.

Kiewe, Amos. *FDR's First Fireside Chat: Public Confidence and the Banking Crisis*. College Station: Texas A & M University Press, 2007.

Kleeman, Rita Halle. *Gracious Lady: The Life of Sara Delano Roosevelt*. New York: Appleton-Century, 1935.

Knickerbocker, H. R. *The German Crisis*. New York, Farrar & Rinehart, Inc., 1932.

Knight-Patterson, W. M. (pseud. of Władysław Wszeboìr Kulski). *Germany from Defeat to Conquest, 1913–1933*. London: G. Allen and Unwin, Ltd, 1945.

Knopp, Guido. *Hitler's Women*. New York: Routledge, 2003.

Knox, John. *The Great Mistake: Can Herbert Hoover Explain His Past?* Baltimore: The Grace Press, 1932.

Kobler, John. *Ardent Spirits: The Rise and Fall of Prohibition.* New York: Putnam, 1973.

Koehler, John O. *Stasi: The Untold Story of the East German Secret Police.* Boulder, CO: Westview Press, 1999.

Koeves, Tibor. *Satan in Top Hat: The Biography of Franz von Papen.* New York: Alliance Book Corporation, 1941.

Korda, Michael. *Ike: An American Hero.* New York: HarperCollins, 2009.

Koskoff, David E. *Joseph P. Kennedy: A Life and Times.* Englewood Cliffs, NJ: Prentice-Hall, 1974.

Kramer, Dale. *Heywood Broun: A Biographical Portrait.* New York: Current Books, Inc., A. A. Wyn, Publisher, 1949.

Krebs, Albert (Henry Ashby Turner, Jr., ed.). *The Infancy of Nazism: The Memoirs of ex-Gauleiter Albert Krebs, 1923–1933.* New York: New Viewpoints, 1976.

Krock, Arthur. *Memoirs: Sixty Years on the Firing Line.* New York: Funk & Wagnalls, 1968.

Kubizek, August. *The Young Hitler I Knew.* New York: Tower Publications, 1971.

Kull, Irving, and Neal Kull. *An Encyclopedia of American History in Chronological Order.* New York: Popular Library, 1965.

Kurth, Peter. *American Cassandra: The Life of Dorothy Thompson.* Boston: Little, Brown & Co., 1990.

Kyvig, David E. *Repealing National Prohibition.* Chicago: University of Chicago Press, 1979.

LaCerra, Charles. *Franklin Delano Roosevelt and Tammany Hall of New York.* Lanham, MD: University Press of America, 1997.

Lambert, Angela. *The Lost Life of Eva Braun: A Biography.* New York: St. Martin's Press, 2006.

Lane, Rose Wilder. *The Making of Herbert Hoover.* New York: The Century Company, 1920.

Lane, Barbara Miller, and Nancy J. Rupp. *Nazi Ideology Before 1933.* Austin: University of Texas Press, 1978.

Langer, Walter C. *The Mind of Adolf Hitler: The Secret Wartime Report.* New York: Basic Books, 1972.

Laporte, Ewing. *Official Report of the Proceedings of the Democratic National Convention held at Chicago, Illinois, June 27th to July 2nd, inclusive, 1932, Resulting in the Nomination of Franklin D. Roosevelt (of New York) for President and John N. Garner (of Texas) for Vice-President.* Washington, 1932.

Large, David Clay. *Berlin.* New York: Basic Books, 2000.

———. *Where Ghosts Walked: Munich's Road to the Third Reich.* New York: W. W. Norton, 1997.

Larson, Erik. *In the Garden of the Beasts: Love, Terror, and an American Family in Hitler's Berlin.* New York: Crown, 2011.

Lash, Joseph P. *Eleanor and Franklin: The Story of Their Relationship Based on Eleanor Roosevelt's Private Papers.* New York: W. W. Norton & Co., 1971.

———. *Love Eleanor: Eleanor Roosevelt and Her Friends.* Garden City, NY: Doubleday, 1982.

Laurie, Clayton D., and Ronald H. Cole. *The Role of Federal Military Forces in Domestic Disorders, 1877–1945.* Washington: Government Printing Office, 1997.

Lavine, Emanuel H. *"Gimme" or How Politicians Get Rich.* New York: The Vanguard Press, 1931.

Lazicì, Branko M. *Biographical Dictionary of the Comintern.* Stanford, CA: Hoover Institute Press, 1986.

Leary, William M., ed. *MacArthur and the American Century: A Reader.* Lincoln: University of Nebraska Press, 2001.

Leinwand, Gerald. *Mackerels in the Moonlight: Four Corrupt American Mayors.* Jefferson, NC: McFarland & Co., 2004.

Lemmons, Russel. *Goebbels and* Der Angriff. Lexington: University Press of Kentucky, 1994.

Leopold, John A. *Alfred Hugenberg: The Radical Nationalist Campaign Against the Weimar Republic.* New Haven: Yale University Press, 1978.

Leuchtenburg, William E. *Franklin D. Roosevelt and the New Deal.* New York: Harper & Row, 1963.

———. *Herbert Hoover.* New York: Times Books (Henry Holt and Co.), 2009.

———. *The Perils of Prosperity 1914–32.* Chicago: University of Chicago Press, 1959.

———. *The White House Looks South: Franklin D. Roosevelt, Harry S. Truman, Lyndon B. Johnson.* Baton Rouge: Louisiana State University Press, 2007.

Levin, Linda Lotridge. *The Making of FDR: The Story of Stephen T. Early, America's First Modern Press Secretary.* Amherst, NY: Prometheus Books, 2008.

Lewy, Guenter. *The Cause That Failed: Communism in American Political Life.* New York: Oxford University Press, 1990.

Lewis, Alfred Allan. *Man of the World: Herbert Bayard Swope: A Charmed Life of Pulitzer Prizes, Poker and Politics.* Indianapolis: The Bobbs-Merrill Co., Inc., 1978.

Lewis, David. *The Man Who Invented Hitler: The Making of the Führer.* London: Bounty Books, 2005.

Lichtman, Allan J. *Prejudice and the Old Politics: The Presidential Election of 1928.* Chapel Hill: University of North Carolina Press, 1979.

Liebovich, Louis W. *Bylines in Despair: Herbert Hoover, the Great Depression, and the U.S. News Media.* Westport, CT: Praeger, 1994.

Liggett, Walter W. *The Rise of Herbert Hoover.* New York: The H. K. Fly Company, 1932.

Lindley, Ernest K. *Franklin D. Roosevelt: A Career in Progressive Democracy.* Indianapolis: Bobbs-Merrill, 1931.

Lippmann, Walter (Allan Nevins, ed.). *Interpretations, 1931–32.* New York: Macmillan, 1932.

Lisio, Donald J. *Hoover, Blacks, & Lily-Whites: A Study of Southern Strategies.* Chapel Hill: University of North Carolina Press, 1985.

———. *The President and Protest: Hoover, Conspiracy and the Bonus Riot.* Columbia: University of Missouri Press, 1974.

Lochner, Louis P. *What About Germany?* New York: Dodd, Mead & Co., 1943.

Lohbeck, Don. *Patrick J. Hurley.* Chicago: Henry Regnery Co., 1956.

Lomazow, Steven, MD, and Eric Fettmann. *FDR's Deadly Secret.* New York: PublicAffairs, 2009.

Longerich, Peter. *Heinrich Himmler: A Life.* New York; Oxford University Press, 2012.

Longworth, Alice Roosevelt. *Crowded Hours: Reminiscences of Alice Roosevelt Longworth.* New York, Charles Scribner's Sons, 1933.

Lorant, Stefan. *The Glorious Burden: The History of the Presidency and Presidential Elections from George Washington to James Earl Carter, Jr.* Lenox, MA: Author's Edition, Inc., 1977.

Louchheim, Katie, ed. *The Making of the New Deal: The Insiders Speak*. Cambridge, MA: Harvard University Press, 1983.

Louis Ferdinand, Prince of Prussia. *The Rebel Prince*. Chicago, Regnery, 1952.

Lowitt, Richard. *Bronson M. Cutting: Progressive Politician*. Albuquerque: University of New Mexico Press, 1992.

Lüdecke, Kurt. *I Knew Hitler: The Story of a National Socialist Who Escaped the Blood Purge*. New York: Scribner's, 1937.

Ludwig, Emil. *Hindenburg and the Saga of the German Revolution*. London: W. Heinemann, Ltd., 1935.

———. *Roosevelt: A Study in Fortune and Power*. New York: Viking Press, 1938.

Lukacs, John. *The Hitler of History*. New York: Alfred A. Knopf, 1997.

Lynch, Michael J. *Hitler*. Oxford, UK: Taylor & Francis, 2012.

Lyons, Eugene. *Our Unknown Ex-President: A Portrait of Herbert Hoover*. Garden City, NY: Doubleday & Company, 1948.

Machtan, Lothar. *The Hidden Hitler*. New York: Basic Books, 2002.

MacArthur, Douglas. *Reminiscences*. New York: McGraw-Hill Book Company, 1964.

MacKaye, Milton. *The Tin Box Parade: A Handbook for Larceny*. New York: R. M. McBride, 1934.

MacKenzie, Compton. *Mr. Roosevelt*. New York: E. P. Dutton & Co., 1944.

Magida, Arthur J. *The Nazi Séance: The Strange Story of the Jewish Psychic in Hitler's Circle*. New York: Palgrave Macmillan, 2011.

Maier, Thomas. *The Kennedys: America's Emerald Kings: A Five-Generation History of the Ultimate Irish-Catholic Family*. New York: Basic Books, 2004.

Maine, Basil. *Franklin Roosevelt: His Life and Achievement*. London: John Murray Ltd., 1938.

von Maltitz, Horst. *The Evolution of Hitler's Germany: The Ideology, the Personality, the Moment*. New York: McGraw-Hill, 1973.

Manchester, William. *American Caesar*. Boston: Little, Brown & Co., 1978.

———. *The Glory and the Dream: A Narrative History of America: 1932–1972*. New York: Bantam Books, 1975.

———. *The Last Lion: Winston Spencer Churchill, Alone 1932–1940*. Boston: Little, Brown & Co., 1988.

Mann, Arthur. *La Guardia: A Fighter Against His Times, 1882–1933*. Philadelphia: J. B. Lippincott, 1939.

Manvell, Roger (advised by Heinrich Fraenkel). *Göring*. New York: Ballantine Books, 1972.

Manvell, Roger, and Heinrich Fraenkel. *The Hundred Days to Hitler*. London: J. M. Dent & Sons Ltd., 1974.

———. *Dr. Goebbels: His Life and Death*. New York: Simon & Schuster, 1960.

———. *Goering: The Rise and Fall of the Notorious Nazi Leader*. New York: Skyhorse Publishing, 2011.

———. *Heinrich Himmler: The Sinister Life of the Head of the SS and Gestapo*. New York: Putnam, 1965.

Marcus, Sheldon. *Father Coughlin: The Tumultuous Life of the Priest of the Little Flower*. Boston: Little, Brown & Co., 1973.

Markey, Morris. *This Country of Yours*. Boston: Little, Brown & Co., 1932.

Martin, Ralph G. *Ballots and Bandwagons*. Chicago: Rand McNally, 1964.

———. *Henry and Clare: An Intimate Portrait of the Luces*. New York: Putnam, 1991.

Marx, Samuel. *Mayer and Thalberg: The Make-Believe Saints.* New York: Random House, 1975.

Maser, Werner. *Hitler: Legend, Myth & Reality.* New York: Harper & Row, 1973.

Mason, Robert. *The Republican Party and American Politics from Hoover to Reagan.* New York: Cambridge University Press, 2011.

Mauch, Christof. *The Shadow War Against Hitler: The Covert Operations of America's Wartime Secret Intelligence Service.* New York: Columbia University Press, 2003.

Max, Gerry. *Horizon Chasers: The Lives and Adventures of Richard Halliburton and Paul Mooney.* Jefferson, NC: McFarland & Co., 2007.

McDonald, James G. *Advocate for the Doomed: The Diaries and Papers of James G. McDonald 1932–35.* Bloomington: Indiana University Press, 2007.

McDonogh, Giles. *The Last Kaiser: The Life of Wilhelm II.* New York: St. Martin's Press, 2000.

McElvaine, Robert S. *The Great Depression: America 1929–1941.* New York: Times Books, 1993.

McGeary, Nelson. *Gifford Pinchot: Forester Politician.* Princeton, NJ: Princeton University Press, 1960.

McKenna, Marian C. *Borah.* Ann Arbor: University of Michigan Press, 1961.

McRandle, James H. *The Track of the Wolf.* Evanston, IL: Northwestern University Press, 1965.

McWilliams, Carey. *A Mask for Privilege: Anti-Semitism in America.* New Brunswick, NJ: Transaction Publishers, 1975.

Mead, William B., and Paul Dickson. *Baseball: The Presidents' Game.* Washington: Farragut Publishing Co., 1993.

Mencken, H. L. *Making a President—A Footnote to the Saga of Democracy.* New York: Knopf, 1932.

———. *On Politics: A Carnival of Buncombe.* Baltimore: Johns Hopkins University Press, 1996.

Mend, Hans. *Adolf Hitler im Felde.* Munich: Diessen, 1931.

Menne, Bernhard. *The Case of Dr. Brüning.* London: Hutchinson & Co., 1942.

Mertz, Charles. *The Dry Decade.* Garden City, NY: Dounleday, Doran & Company, Inc. 1931.

Metcalfe, Philip. *1933.* Sag Harbor, NY: The Permanent Press, 1988.

Michelson, Charles. *The Ghost Talks.* New York: G. P. Putnam's Sons, 1944.

Miller, Francis Trevelyan. *General Douglas MacArthur: Fighter for Freedom.* Chicago: John C. Winston Co., 1942.

Miller, Merle. *Ike the Soldier: As They Knew Him.* New York: Perigee Books, 1987.

Miller, Nathan. *F.D.R.: An Intimate History.* Garden City, NY: Doubleday, 1983.

———. *New World Coming: The 1920s and the Making of Modern America.* Cambridge, MA: Da Capo Press, 2004.

Mitcham, Samuel W., Jr. *Why Hitler?: The Genesis of the Nazi Reich.* Westport, CT: Praeger, 1996.

Mitchell, Arthur. *Hitler's Mountain: The Führer, Obersalzberg and the American Occupation of Berchtesgaden.* Jefferson, NC: McFarland & Co., 2007.

Mitchell, Otis C. *Hitler Over Germany: The Establishment of the Nazi Dictatorship (1918–1934).* Philadelphia: Institute for the Study of Human Issues, 1983.

Mitgang, Herbert. *Once Upon a Time in New York: Jimmy Walker, Franklin Roosevelt, and the Last Great Battle of the Jazz Age.* New York: Free Press, 2000.

————. *The Man Who Rode the Tiger: The Life and Times of Judge Samuel Seabury.* Philadelphia: J. B. Lippincott Co., 1963.

Moley, Raymond. *After Seven Years.* New York: Harper & Bros., 1939.

————. *27 Masters of Politics: In a Personal Perspective.* New York: Funk & Wagnalls Co., 1949.

Moley, Raymond (with Elliot A. Rosen). *The First New Deal.* New York: Harcourt, Brace & World, Inc., 1966.

Mommsen, Hans. *The Rise and Fall of Weimar Democracy.* Chapel Hill: University of North Carolina Press, 1998.

Moore, Edmund A. *A Catholic Runs for President: The Campaign of 1928.* New York: Ronald Press Co., 1956.

Morgan, Ted. *FDR: A Biography.* New York: Simon & Schuster, 1985.

Morris, Douglas G. *Justice Imperiled: The Anti-Nazi Lawyer Max Hirschberg in Weimar Germany.* Ann Arbor: University of Michigan Press, 2005.

Morris, Sylvia Jukes. *Rage for Fame: The Ascent of Clare Booth Luce.* New York: Random House, 1997.

Mosley, Leonard. *The Reich Marshal: A Biography of Hermann Goering.* New York: Doubleday & Company, Inc., 1975.

Mowrer, Edgar Ansel. *Germany Turns the Clock Back.* New York: William Morrow, 1933.

Muhlen, Norbert. *Schacht: Hitler's Magician: The Life and Loans of Dr. Hjalmar Schacht.* New York: Alliance Book Corporation, 1939.

Mullen, Arthur Francis. *Western Democrat.* New York: W. Funk, Incorporated, 1940.

Murray, Henry A., MD. *Analysis of the Personality of Adolph Hitler: With Predictions of His Future Behavior and Suggestions for Dealing With Him Now and After Germany's Surrender.* Washington, DC: Office of Strategic Services (Confidential Report), 1943.

Muscio, Giuliana. *Hollywood's New Deal.* Philadelphia: Temple University Press, 1996.

Myers, William Starr, ed. *The State Papers and Other Public Writings of Herbert Hoover: Volume One: March 4, 1929 to October 1, 1931.* Garden City, NY: Doubleday, Doran & Company, 1934.

————. *The State Papers and Other Public Writings of Herbert Hoover: Volume Two: October 1, 1931 to March 4, 1933.* Garden City, NY: Doubleday, Doran & Company, 1934.

Myers, William Starr, and Walter H. Newton. *The Hoover Administration: A Documented Narrative.* New York: Charles Scribner's Sons, 1936.

Nagorski, Andrew. *Hitlerland: American Eyewitnesses to the Nazi Rise to Power.* New York: Simon & Schuster, 2012.

————. *The Greatest Battle: Stalin, Hitler, and the Desperate Struggle for Moscow That Changed the Course of World War II.* New York: Simon & Schuster, 2007.

Namorato, Michael. *Rexford G. Tugwell: A Biography.* New York: Praeger, 1988.

Nasaw, David. *The Chief: The Life of William Randolph Hearst.* New York: Houghton Mifflin, 2000.

————. *The Patriarch: The Remarkable Life and Turbulent Times of Joseph P. Kennedy.* New York: Penguin Press, 2012.

Nash, George H. *The Life of Herbert Hoover: Master of Emergencies, 1917–1918.* New York: W. W. Norton & Co., 1996.

————. *The Life of Herbert Hoover: The Humanitarian, 1914–1917.* New York: W. W. Norton & Co., 1988.

Neal, Steve. *Happy Days Are Here Again: The 1932 Democratic Convention, the Emergence of FDR—and How America Was Changed Forever.* New York: HarperPerennial, 2005.

Nevins, Allan. *Ford: Decline and Rebirth 1933–1962*. New York: Scribner's, 1963.

———. *James Truslow Adams: Historian of the American Dream*. Urbana: University of Illinois Press, 1968.

Nicholls, A. J. *Weimar and the Rise of Hitler*. New York: St. Martins, 1991.

Noakes, Jeremy, and Geoffrey Pridham, eds. *Nazism 1919–1945, Vol. 1, The Rise to Power 1919–1934*. Exeter, UK: University of Exeter Press, 1983.

Northrup, William B., and John B. Northrup. *The Insolence of Office: The Story of the Seabury Investigations*. New York: G. P. Putnam's Sons, 1932.

O'Brien, John J. *Hoover's Millions and How He Made Them*. New York: J. J. O'Brien Publishing Company, 1932.

O'Brien, P. J. *Will Rogers: Ambassador of Good Will, Prince of Wit and Wisdom*. Chicago: John C. Winston Company, 1935.

O'Connor, Harvey. *Mellon's Millions: The Biography of a Fortune; the Life and Times of Andrew W. Mellon*. New York: The John Day Company, 1933.

O'Connor, Richard. *Heywood Broun: A Biography*. New York: G. P. Putnam's Sons, 1975.

———. *The First Hurrah: A Biography of Alfred E. Smith*. New York: G. P. Putnam's Sons, 1970.

Okrent, Daniel *Last Call: The Rise and Fall of Prohibition*. New York: Scribner's, 2010.

Olden, Rudolf. *Hitler*. New York: Covici, Friede, 1936.

Orlow, Dietrich. *The History of the Nazi Party: 1919–1933*. Pittsburgh: University of Pittsburgh Press, 1969.

———. *Weimar Prussia: 1925–1933: The Illusion of Strength*. Pittsburgh: University of Pittsburgh Press, 1991.

Ossian, Lisa L. *The Depression Dilemmas of Rural Iowa, 1929–1933*. Columbia: University of Missouri Press, 2011.

Oulahan, Richard. *The Man Who . . . The Story of the 1932 Democratic National Convention*. New York: The Dial Press, 1971.

Padfield, Peter. *Himmler*. New York: Mjf Books, 1990.

von Papen, Franz. *Memoirs*. New York: E. P. Dutton, 1953.

Patch, William L., Jr. *Heinrich Brüning and the Dissolution of the Weimar Republic*. New York: Cambridge University Press, 2006.

Patton, Robert H. *The Pattons: A Personal History of an American Family*. New York: Crown Publishers, 1994.

Payne, Robert. *The Life and Death of Adolf Hitler*. New York: Praeger, 1973.

Peel, Roy V., and Thomas C. Donnelly. *The 1932 Campaign: An Analysis*. New York: Farrar & Rinehart, 1935.

Perkins, Frances. *The Roosevelt I Knew*. New York: Viking, 1946.

Perret, Geoffrey. *Eisenhower*. New York: Random House, 1999.

Perry, Elisabeth I. *Belle Moskowitz: Feminine Politics and the Exercise of Power in the Age of Alfred Smith*. New York: Oxford University Press, 1987.

Persico, Joseph E. *Franklin & Lucy: President Roosevelt, Mrs. Rutherfurd, and the Other Remarkable Women in His Life*. New York: Random House, 2008.

———. *Roosevelt's Centurions: FDR and the Commanders He Led to Victory in World War II*. New York: Random House, 2013.

———. *Roosevelt's Secret War: FDR and World War II Espionage*. New York: Random House, 2001.

Picchi, Blaise. *The Five Weeks of Giuseppe Zangara: The Man Who Would Assassinate FDR*. Chicago: Chicago Academy Publishers, 1998.

Pietrusza, David. *Calvin Coolidge: A Documentary Biography*. Scotia, NY: Church & Reid Books, 2013.

———. *1920: The Year of the Six Presidents*. New York: Carroll & Graf, 2007.

———. *Rothstein: The Life, Times, and Murder of the Criminal Genius Who Fixed the 1919 World Series*. New York: Carroll & Graf, 2003.

Pilpel, Robert H. *Churchill in America: An Affectionate Portrait 1895–1961*. New York: Harcourt, Brace, Jovanovich, 1976.

Pizzitola, Louis. *Hearst over Hollywood: Power, Passion, and Propaganda in the Movies*. New York: Columbia University Press, 2002.

Pleasants, Julian M. *Buncombe Bob: The Life and Times of Robert Rice Reynolds*. Chapel Hill: University of North Carolina Press, 2000.

Plotkin, Abraham. *An American in Hitler's Berlin: Abraham Plotkin's Diary, 1932–33*. Urbana, IL: University of Illinois Press, 2009.

Pool, James, and Suzanne Pool. *Who Financed Hitler: The Secret Funding of Hitler's Rise to Power, 1919–1933*. New York: Dial Press, 1978.

Pottker, Jan. *Sara and Eleanor: The Story of Sara Delano Roosevelt and Her Daughter-in-Law, Eleanor Roosevelt*. New York: St. Martin's Press, 2004.

Pridham, Geoffrey. *Hitler's Rise to Power: The Nazi Movement in Bavaria 1923–1933*. New York: Harper & Row, 1973.

Pringle, Henry F. *Alfred E. Smith: A Critical Study Book*. New York: Macy-Masius, 1927.

Procter, Ben. *William Randolph Hearst: Final Edition, 1911–1951*. New York: Oxford University Press, 2007.

Quirk, Lawrence J. *The Kennedys of Hollywood*. New York: Cooper Square Press, 2004.

Rauschning, Hermann. *The Voice of Destruction*. New York: Putnam, 1940.

Read, Anthony. *The Devil's Disciples: Hitler's Inner Circle*. New York: W. W. Norton, 2004.

Redlich, Fritz. *Hitler: Diagnosis of a Destructive Prophet*. New York: Oxford University Press, 1998.

Reilly, Michael F. *Reilly of the White House*. New York: Simon & Schuster, 1947.

Reimann, Viktor. *Goebbels: The Man Who Created Hitler*. Garden City, NY: Doubleday & Co., 1976.

Reuth, Ralf Georg. *Goebbels*. New York: Harcourt Brace & Co., 1993.

Reynolds, Quentin. *By Quentin Reynolds*. New York: McGraw-Hill Book Co., 1963.

Rich, Bennett Milton. *The Presidents and Civil Disorder*. Washington: The Brookings Institution, 1941.

Richardson, Darcy G. *A Toast to Glory: The Prohibition Party Flirts with Greatness*. Jacksonville, FL: Uncovered Politics, 2012.

Richie, Alexandra. *Faust's Metropolis: A History of Berlin*. New York: Carroll & Graf, 1998.

Riefenstahl, Leni. *Leni Riefenstahl*. New York: Picador USA, 1995.

Ritchie, Donald A. *Electing FDR: The New Deal Campaign of 1932*. Lawrence: University Press of Kansas, 2009.

Roberts, Stephen H. *The House That Hitler Built*. New York: Harper & Bros., 1938.

Rodgers, Marion Elizabeth. *Mencken: The American Iconoclast*. New York: Oxford University Press, 2005.

Röhl, John C. G. *Wilhelm II: Into the Abyss of War and Exile, 1900–1941*. Cambridge, UK: Cambridge University Press, 2014.

Rolfs, Richard W., S. J. *The Sorcerer's Apprentice: The Life of Franz von Papen*. Lanham, MD: University Press of America, 1996.

Rollins, Alfred B., Jr. *Roosevelt and Howe*. New York: Alfred A. Knopf, 1962.

Roosevelt, Eleanor. *The Autobiography of Eleanor Roosevelt*. New York: Da Capo Press, 1992.

———. *This I Remember*. New York: Harper & Brothers, 1949.

Roosevelt, Eleanor II. *With Love, Aunt Eleanor: Stories from My Life with the First Lady of the World*. Petaluma, CA: Scrapbook Press, 2004.

Roosevelt, Elliott. *Eleanor Roosevelt, with Love: A Centenary Remembrance*. New York: E. P. Dutton, 1984.

Roosevelt, Elliott, ed. *F.D.R.: His Personal Letters, The Early Years*. New York: Duell, Sloan and Pearce, 1947.

———. *F.D.R.: His Personal Letters, 1928–1945*. New York: Duell, Sloan and Pearce, 1947.

Roosevelt, Elliott, and James Brough. *A Rendezvous with Destiny: The Roosevelts of the White House*. New York: G. P. Putnam's Sons, 1977.

———. *An Untold Story: The Roosevelts of Hyde Park*. New York: G. P. Putnam's Sons, 1973.

———. *Mother R.: Eleanor Roosevelt's Untold Story*. New York: G. P. Putnam's Sons, 1975.

Roosevelt, Franklin D. *Government—Not Politics*. New York: Covici-Friede, 1932.

———. *The Happy Warrior: A Study of a Public Servant*. Boston: Houghton Mifflin Co., 1928.

Roosevelt, James, with Bill Libby. *My Parents: A Differing View*. Chicago: A Playboy Press Book, 1976.

Roosevelt, James, with Sidney Shalett. *Affectionately, F.D.R.: A Son's Story of a Lonely Man*. New York: Harcourt, Brace, 1959. N. B. the book was later published under the title *Affectionately, F.D.R.: A Son's Story of a Courageous Man*.

Roosevelt, Mrs. Theodore, Jr. *Day Before Yesterday: The Reminiscences of Mrs. Theodore Roosevelt Jr*. Garden City, NY: Doubleday & Company, Inc., 1959.

Root, Grace C. *Women and Repeal: The Story of the Women's Organization for National Prohibition Reform*. New York: Harper, 1934.

Rosen, Elliot A. *Hoover, Roosevelt, and the Brains Trust: From Depression to New Deal*. New York: Columbia University Press, 1977.

Rosenbaum, Ron. *Explaining Hitler: The Search for the Origins of His Evil*. New York: HarperCollins, 1998.

Rosenman, Samuel I., ed. *The Public Papers and Addresses of Franklin D. Roosevelt: 1928–1932, The Genesis of the New Deal*. New York: Random House, 1938.

———. *Working with Roosevelt*. New York: Harper & Row, 1952.

Rosenman, Samuel I., and Dorothy Rosenman. *Presidential Style: Some Giants and a Pygmy in the White House*. New York: Harper & Row, 1976.

Roth, Joseph. *What I Saw: Reports from Berlin, 1920–1933*. New York: Norton, 2003.

Rothbard, Murray. *America's Great Depression*. Princeton, NJ: Van Nostrand, 1963.

Rowley, Hazel. *Franklin and Eleanor: An Extraordinary Marriage*. New York: Farrar, Straus & Giroux, 2010.

Russell, Francis. *The President Makers: From Mark Hanna to Joseph P. Kennedy*. Boston: Little, Brown, 1976.

Ryback, Timothy W. *Hitler's Private Library: The Books That Shaped His Life*. New York: Alfred A. Knopf, 2008.

Salzman, Neil V. *Reform and Revolution: The Life and Times of Raymond Robins*. Kent, OH: Kent State University Press, 1991.

Sandys, Celia. *Chasing Churchill: The Travels of Winston Churchill*. London: Unicorn Press, 2014.

Saposs, David Joseph. *Communism in American Politics*. Washington: Public Affairs Press, 1960.

Sautter, R. Craig, and Edward M. Burke. *Inside the Wigwam: Chicago Presidential Conventions, 1860–1996*. Chicago: Wild Onion Press, 1996.

Schacht, Hjalmar Horace Greeley. *Confessions of "The Old Wizard": The Autobiography of Hjalmar Horace Greeley Schacht*. Boston: Houghton Mifflin, 1956.

Schapsmeier, Frederick H., and Edward L. Schapsmeier. *Henry A. Wallace of Iowa: The Agrarian Years, 1910–1940*. Ames: Iowa State University Press, 1968.

Scheele, Godfrey. *The Weimar Republic: Overture to the Third Reich*. London: Faber and Faber Limited, 1946.

Schivelbusch, Wolfgang. *Three New Deals, Reflections on Roosevelt's America, Mussolini's Italy, and Hitler's Germany*. New York: Metropolitan Books, 2006.

Schlesinger, Arthur M., Jr. *The Age of Roosevelt: The Coming of the New Deal, 1933–1935*. New York: Houghton-Mifflin, 1958.

Schlesinger, Arthur M., Jr. *The Age of Roosevelt: The Crisis of the Old Order, 1919–1933*. New York: Houghton-Mifflin, 1957.

Schlesinger, Robert. *White House Ghosts: Presidents and Their Speech Writers*. New York: Simon & Schuster, 2008.

Schmidt, Hans. *Maverick Marine: General Smedley D. Butler and the Contradictions of American Military History*. Lexington: The University Press of Kentucky, 1998.

Schofield, Victoria. *Witness to History: The Life of John Wheeler-Bennett*. New Haven: Yale University Press, 2012.

Schwaab, Edleff H. *Hitler's Mind: A Plunge Into Madness*. New York: Praeger, 1992.

Schwarz, Jordan A. *The Interregnum of Despair: Hoover, Congress and the Depression*. Urbana: University of Illinois Press, 1970.

Schwarz, Paul. *This Man Ribbentrop: His Life and Times*. New York: J. Messner, Inc., 1943.

Schwarz, Ted. *Joseph P. Kennedy: The Mogul, the Mob, the Statesman, and the Making of an American Myth*. Hoboken. NJ: John Wiley & Sons, 2003.

Scroop, Daniel. *Mr. Democrat: Jim Farley, The New Deal & The Making of Modern American Politics*. Ann Arbor: University of Michigan Press, 2006.

Shachtman, Tom. *The Day America Crashed: A Narrative Account of the Great Stock Market Crash of October 24, 1929*. New York: Putnam, 1979.

Shadegg, Stephen. *Clare Boothe Luce: A Biography*. New York: Simon & Schuster, 1970.

Sherwood, Robert E. *Roosevelt and Hopkins, an Intimate History*. New York: Harper, 1948.

Shirer, William L. *The Rise and Fall of the Third Reich: A History of Nazi Germany*. New York: Simon & Schuster, 1960.

Shlaes, Amity. *Coolidge*. New York: HarperCollins, 2013.

———. *The Forgotten Man: A New History of the Great Depression*. New York: Harper Perennial, 2007.

Shuler, Robert, III *"Fighting Bob" Shuler of Los Angeles*. Indianapolis: Dog Ear Publishing, 2012.

Sidelsky, Robert. *Oswald Mosley*. New York: Macmillan, 1975.

Siemens, Daniel. *The Making of a Nazi Hero: The Murder and Myth of Horst Wessel*. London & New York: I. B. Tauris, 2013.

Sigmund, Anna Maria. *Women of the Third Reich*. Richmond Hill, ON: NDE Publishers, 2000.

Simon, James F. *FDR and Chief Justice Hughes: The President, the Supreme Court, and the Epic Battle Over the New Deal*. New York: Simon & Schuster, 2012.

Sinclair, Andrew. *Prohibition: The Era of Excess*. Boston: Little, Brown & Co., 1962.

Singer, Kurt. *Göring: Germany's Most Dangerous Man*. London: Hutchinson & Co., Ltd., 1940.

Sitton, Tom. *John Randolph Haynes: California Progressive*. Stanford, CA: Stanford University Press, 1992.

Slayton, Robert A. *Empire Statesman: The Rise and Redemption of Al Smith*. New York: Free Press, 2001.

Smith, Amanda, ed. *Hostages to Fortune: The Letters of Joseph P. Kennedy*. New York: Viking, 2001.

Smith, Gary Scott. *Faith and the Presidency: From George Washington to George W. Bush*. New York: Oxford University Press, 2006.

Smith, Gene. *The Dark Summer: An Intimate History of the Events That Led to World War II*. New York: Collier Books, 1987.

———. *The Shattered Dream: Herbert Hoover and the Great Depression*. New York: William Morrow, 1970.

Smith, Jean Edward. *Eisenhower: In War and Peace*. New York: Random House, 2012.

———. *FDR*. New York: Random House, 2007.

Smith, Richard Norton. *An Uncommon Man: The Triumph of Herbert Hoover*. New York: Simon & Schuster, 1984.

———. *The Colonel: The Life and Legend of Robert R. McCormick, 1880–1955*. Chicago: Northwestern University Press, 2003.

Smith, Rixey, and Norman Beasley. *Carter Glass: A Biography*. New York: Longmans, Green & Co., 1939.

Snell, John L. *The Nazi Revolution: Germany's Guilt or Germany's Fate?* Boston: D. C. Heath, 1959.

Snyder, Dr. Louis L. *Encyclopedia of the Third Reich*. New York: Paragon House, 1989.

Snyder, Louis L. *Hitler's Elite: Biographical Sketches of Nazis Who Shaped the Third Reich*. New York: Hippocrene Books, 1989.

Snyder, Louis L., ed. *Hitler's Third Reich: A Documentary History*. Chicago: Nelson-Hall, 1981.

Soames, Mary, ed. *Winston and Clementine: The Personal Letters of the Churchills*. New York: Houghton Mifflin Harcourt, 1999.

Sobel, Robert. *Coolidge: An American Enigma*. Washington, DC: Regnery Publishers, 1998.

———. *Herbert Hoover at the Onset of the Great Depression 1929–1930*. Philadelphia: J. B. Lippincott Company, 1975.

Somin, Ilya. *Stillborn Crusade: The Tragic Failure of the Allied Intervention in the Russian Civil War, 1918–1920*. New Brunswick, NJ: Transaction Publishers, 1996.

Sonnichsen, C. L. *Tucson: The Life and Times of an American City*. Norman: University of Oklahoma Press, 1987.

Speer, Albert. *Inside the Third Reich*. New York: Simon & Schuster, 1970.

Stachura, Peter D. *Gregor Strasser and the Rise of Nazism*. London: George Allen & Unwin, 1983.

Stannard, David E. *Honor Killing: Race, Rape, and Clarence Darrow's Spectacular Last Case*. New York: Penguin Books, 2006.

Starling, Edmund W. (as told to Thomas Sugrue). *Starling of the White House*. Chicago: Peoples Book Club, 1946.

Steel, Ronald. *Walter Lippmann and the American Century*. Boston: Little, Brown & Co., 1980.

Stierlin, Helm. *Adolf Hitler: A Family Perspective*. New York: Psychotherapy Press, 1976.

Stiles, Lela. *The Man Behind Roosevelt: The Story of Louis McHenry Howe*. Cleveland: World Publishing Co., 1954.

Strasser, Otto. *Hitler and I*. Boston: Houghton Mifflin Co., 1940.

Strawson, John. *Churchill and Hitler: In Victory and Defeat*. New York: Fromm International, 2000.

Streitmatter, Rodger. *Empty Without You: The Intimate Letters Of Eleanor Roosevelt and Lorena Hickok*. New York: Free Press, 1998.

Suckley, Daisy. *FDR Chronology (1925–1945)*. Unpublished.

Swanberg, W. A. *Citizen Hearst: A Biography of William Randolph Hearst*. New York: Scribner's, 1961.

———. *Luce and His Empire*. New York: Charles Scribner's Sons, 1972.

———. *Norman Thomas: The Last Idealist*. New York: Scribner's, 1976.

Tamagne, Florence. *A History of Homosexuality: Europe between the Wars*. New York: Algora, 2003.

Taylor, Simon. *The Rise of Hitler: Revolution and Counter-Revolution in Germany, 1918–1933*. New York: Universe Books, 1983.

Teachout, Terry. *The Skeptic: A Life of H. L. Mencken*. New York: HarperCollins, 2003.

Thacker, Toby. *Joseph Goebbels: Life and Death*. London: Palgrave Macmillan, 2009.

Thomas, Gordon, and Max Morgan-Witts. *The Day the Bubble Burst: A Social History of the Wall Street Crash of 1929*. Garden City, NY: Doubleday & Co., 1979.

Thomas, Norman, and Paul Blanshard. *What's the Matter with New York: A National Problem*. New York: The Macmillan Company, 1932.

Thompson, Dorothy. *I Saw Hitler!* New York: Farrar and Rinehart, 1932.

Thyssen, Fritz. *I Paid Hitler*. New York: Farrar & Rinehart, Inc. 1941.

Timmons, Bascom N. *Garner of Texas*. New York: Harper, 1948.

———. *Jesse H. Jones: The Man and the Statesman*. New York: Holt, 1956.

Toland, John. *Adolf Hitler*. Garden City, NY: Doubleday & Co., 1976.

Trager, James. *The New York Chronology: The Ultimate Compendium of Events, People and Anecdotes from the Dutch to the Present*. New York: HarperResource, 2003.

Trimborn, Jürgen. *Leni Riefenstahl: A Life*. New York: Faber and Faber, 2007.

Trout, Charles H. *Boston, the Great Depression, and the New Deal*. New York: Oxford University Press, 1977.

Tuchman, Barbara. *The Guns of August*. New York: Random House, 1962.

Tucker, Garland S., III *The High Tide of American Conservatism: Davis, Coolidge and the 1924 Election*. Austin, TX: Emerald Book Company, 2010.

Tucker, Ray Thomas. *The Mirrors of 1932*. New York: Brewer, Warren & Putnam, 1931.

Tugwell, Rexford Guy. *A Chronicle of Jeopardy*. Chicago: University of Chicago Press, 1955.

———. *In Search of Roosevelt*. Cambridge, MA: Harvard University Press, 1972.

———. *Roosevelt's Revolution*. New York: Macmillan, 1977.

———. *The Brains Trust*. New York: Viking, 1968.

———. *The Democratic Roosevelt*. Garden City, NY: Doubleday & Co., Inc., 1957.

Tull, Charles J. *Father Coughlin and the New Deal*. Syracuse: Syracuse University Press, 1965.

Tully, Grace. *F.D.R., My Boss*. New York: Charles Scribner's Sons, 1949.

Turner, Henry Ashby, Jr. *German Big Business and the Rise of Hitler.* New York: Oxford University Press, 1987.

———. *Hitler's Thirty Days to Power.* New York: Addison-Wesley, 1996.

———. *Stresemann and the Politics of the Weimar Republic.* Princeton, NJ: Princeton University Press, 1963.

Tyrrell, Ian. *Woman's World/Woman's Christian Temperance Union: The Women's Christian Temperance Union in International Perspective, 1800–1930.* Chapel Hill and London: University of North Carolina Press, 1991.

Tyson, Joseph Howard. *The Surreal Reich.* Bloomington, IN: iUniverse, 2010.

———. *Hitler's Mentor: Dietrich Eckart, His Life, Times, & Milieu.* New York: iUniverse, 2008.

Underhill, Robert. *FDR and Harry: Unparalleled Lives.* Westport, CT: Praeger, 1996.

Unger, Michael, ed. *The Memoirs of Bridget Hitler.* London: Duckworth & Co., 1979.

United States Department of State. *Foreign Relations of the United States: Diplomatic Papers, 1932. Volume II. The British Commonwealth, Europe, Near East and Africa.* Washington, DC: United States Government Printing Office, 1947.

"Unofficial Observer" (pseud. of John Franklin Carter). *American Messiahs.* New York: Simon & Schuster, 1935.

Urofsky, Melvin I. *A Voice That Spoke for Justice: The Life and Times of Stephen S. Wise.* Albany: State University of New York Press, 1982.

Valtin, Jan. *Out of the Night: Memoir of Richard Julius Hermann Krebs alias Jan Valtin.* Oakland, CA: AK Press/Nabat, 2004.

Van Slingerland, Peter. *Something Terrible Has Happened.* New York: Harper & Row, 1966.

Vedder, Richard K., and Lowell E. Gallaway. *Out of Work: Unemployment and Government in Twentieth-Century America.* New York: New York University Press, 1997.

Victor, George. *Hitler: The Pathology of Evil.* Washington, DC: Brassey's, 1998.

Vogt, Hannah. *The Burden of Guilt: A Short History of Germany, 1914–1945.* New York: Oxford University Press, 1964.

Voss, Carl Hermann. *Rabbi and Minister: The Friendship of Stephen S. Wise and John Haynes Holmes.* Cleveland, OH: The World Publishing Company, 1964.

Wagener, Otto (Henry Ashby Turner, Jr., ed.). *Hitler: Memoirs of a Confidant.* New Haven, CT: Yale University Press, 1985.

Waite, Robert G. L. *The Psychopathic God: Adolf Hitler.* New York: Da Capo Press, 1993.

Walch, Timothy, and Dwight M. Miller. *Herbert Hoover and Franklin D. Roosevelt: A Documentary History.* Westport, CT: Greenwood Press, 1998.

Waller, Douglas. *Wild Bill Donovan: The Spymaster Who Created the OSS and Modern American Espionage.* New York: The Free Press, 2011.

Walsh, George. *Gentleman Jimmy Walker: Mayor of the Jazz Age.* New York: Praeger Publishers, 1974.

Ward, Geoffrey C. *A First-Class Temperament: The Emergence of Franklin Roosevelt.* New York: HarperCollins, 1989.

———. *Before the Trumpet: Young Franklin Roosevelt, 1882–1905.* Old Saybrook, CT: Konecky & Konecky, 1985.

Ward, Louis B. *Father Charles E. Coughlin: An Authorized Biography.* Detroit: Tower Publications, 1933.

Warner, Emily Smith. *The Happy Warrior: A Biography of My Father Alfred E. Smith.* Garden City, NY: Doubleday, 1956.

Warren, Donald E. *Radio Priest: Charles Coughlin, The Father of Hate Radio*. New York: Free Press, 1996.

Warren, Harris Gaylord. *Herbert Hoover and the Great Depression*. New York: Oxford University Press, 1959.

Warren, Sidney. *The Battle for the Presidency*. Philadelphia: J. B. Lippincott Co., 1968.

Waters, Walter W. (as told to William C. White). *B.E.F.: The Whole Story of the Bonus Army*. Cary, NC: Cincinnatus Press, 2007.

Watkins, T. H. *Righteous Pilgrim: The Life and Times of Harold L. Ickes, 1874–1952*. New York: Henry Holt & Co., 1990.

Watson, James E. *As I Knew Them*. Indianapolis: Bobbs-Merrill, 1936.

Watt, Richard M. *The Kings Depart: The Tragedy of Versailles and the German Revolution*. London: Weidenfeld & Nicolson, 1968.

Weale, Adrian. *Army of Evil: A History of the SS*. New York: Penguin, 2010.

Weber, Thomas. *Hitler's First War: Adolf Hitler, the Men of the List Regiment, and the First World War*. New York: Oxford University Press, 2010.

Weinberg, Arthur, and Lila Weinberg. *Clarence Darrow: A Sentimental Rebel*. New York: G. P. Putnam's Sons, 1980.

Weintraub, Stanley. *Young Mr. Roosevelt: FDR's Introduction to War, Politics, and Life*. New York: Da Capo, 2013.

Weiss, Nancy Joan. *Farewell to the Party of Lincoln: Black Politics in the Age of FDR*. Princeton, NJ: Princeton University Press, 1983.

Weitz, Eric D. *Weimar Germany: Promise and Tragedy*. Princeton, NJ: Princeton University Press, 2007.

Werner, M. R. (Morris Robert). *Little Napoleons and Dummy Directors: Being the Narrative of the Bank of United States*. New York and London: Harper & Brothers, 1933.

West, J. B. (with Mary Lynn Kotz). *Upstairs at the White House: My Life with the First Ladies*. New York: Coward, McCann & Geoghegan, 1973.

Whalen, Grover A. *Mr. New York: The Autobiography of Grover A. Whalen*. New York: G. P. Putnam's Sons, 1955.

Wheaton, Eliot Barculo. *The Nazi Revolution 1933–35: With a Background Survey of the Weimar Era*. Garden City, NY: Anchor Books, 1969.

Wheeler, Burton K. (with Paul F. Healy). *Yankee from the West: The Candid, Turbulent Life Story of the Yankee-Born U.S. Senator from Montana*. New York: Octagon Books, 1962.

Wheeler-Bennett, John. *The Nemesis of Power: The German Army in Politics 1918–1945*. London: Macmillan, 1967.

———. *Wooden Titan: Hindenburg in Twenty Years of German History 1914–1934*. New York: William Morrow & Co., 1936.

Whisenhunt, Donald W. *Utopian Movements and Ideas of the Great Depression: Dreamers, Believers, and Madmen*. Lanham, MD: Lexington Books, 2013.

White, Richard. *Kingfish: The Reign of Huey P. Long*. New York: Random House, 2006.

White, William Allen. *Masks in a Pageant*. New York: The MacMillan Co., 1928.

White, William S. *Majesty & Mischief: A Mixed Tribute to F.D.R.* New York: McGraw-Hill, 1961.

Wicker, Elmus. *The Banking Panics of the Great Depression*. Cambridge, UK: Cambridge University Press, 2000.

Williams, Charles. *Adenauer: The Father of the New Germany*. New York: Wiley, 2000.

Williams, John F. *Corporal Hitler and the Great War 1914–1918: The List Regiment*. New York: Frank Cass, 2005.

Williams, T. Harry. *Huey Long*. New York: Alfred A. Knopf, 1960.

Willis, Resa. *FDR and Lucy: Lovers and Friends*. New York: Routledge, 2004.

Wilson, Carol Green. *Herbert Hoover: A Challenge for Today*. New York: The Evans Publishing Company, 1968.

Wilson, Joan Hoff. *Herbert Hoover: Forgotten Progressive*. Boston: Little, Brown and Company, 1975.

Winfield, Betty Houchin. *FDR and the News Media*. Urbana: University of Illinois Press, 1990.

Winkler, Heinrich August. *Germany: The Long Road West, 1789–1933*. New York: Oxford, 2006.

Wisconsin Legislative Reference Library. *The Wisconsin Blue Book: 1933*. Madison, WI: Democratic Printing Company, 1933.

Wistrich, Robert. *Who's Who in Nazi Germany*. New York: Bonanza, 1982.

Witcover, Jules. *Crapshoot: Rolling the Dice on the Vice Presidency*. New York: Crown, 1991.

Ybarra, Michael J. *Washington Gone Crazy: Senator Pat McCarran and the Great American Communist Hunt*. Hanover, NH: Steedforth Press, 2004.

Young, Donald, ed. *Adventures in Politics: The Memoirs of Philip LaFollette*. New York: Holt, Rinehart, Winston, 1970.

Young, Nancy Beck. *Lou Henry Hoover: Activist First Lady*. Lawrence: University of Kansas Press, 2004.

Zalampas, Sherree Owens. *Adolf Hitler: A Psychological Interpretation of His Views on Architecture, Art and Music*. Bowling Green, OH: Bowling Green University Popular Press, 1990.

Zinn, Howard. *La Guardia in Congress*. Ithaca, NY: Cornell University Press, 1959.

Periodicals

American Heritage

The American Journal of Sociology

American Mercury

American Monthly

Atlantic Monthly

Bulletin of International News

Central European History

Christian Century

Collier's Weekly

Commonweal

Communist

Congressional Digest

Congressional Record

Coronet

The Crisis

The Economist

The Forum

The Historical Journal

The Jewish Tribune: The American Jewish Weekly

Journal of American Studies

Journal of Historical Review

Ken

Liberty

Life

Literary Digest

The Living Age

Michigan Political History News

The Nation

Nation's Business

The New Outlook

The New Republic

The New Yorker

The North American Review

The Outlook

Political Science Quarterly

Princeton Alumni Weekly

Review of Reviews

The Saturday Evening Post

Saturday Review

Scribner's Magazine

The Spectator

Time

U.S. News & World Report

Vanity Fair

*The Western Pennsylvania Historical
    Magazine*
The Wisconsin Magazine of History
The World's Work: A History of Our Time

Newspapers
Akron (IA) Register Tribune
Albany (NY) Evening News
Albert Lea (MN) Tribune
Altoona Mirror
Ames (IA) Daily Tribune-Times
*Amsterdam (NY) Evening Recorder and
    Daily Democrat*
Amsterdam News (New York, NY)
Appleton (WI) Post-Crescent
Auburn (NY) Citizen-Advertiser
Ballston Spa (NY) Daily Journal
Baltimore Afro-American
Berkeley (CA) Gazette
Billings Gazette
Biloxi (MS) Daily Herald
Binghamton (NY) Press
Bismarck (ND) Tribune
Bluefield Daily (WV) Telegraph
Brainerd (MN) Daily Dispatch
Brooklyn Daily Eagle
Brooklyn Daily Star
Brooklyn Standard-Union
Brooklyn Weekly People
Brownsville (TX) Herald
Buffalo (NY) Courier-Express
Buffalo (NY) Daily News
Burlington (IA) Hawk Eye
Cambridge (MA) Tribune
Catholic Courier and Journal (Rochester,
    NY)
Charleston (WV) Gazette
Charleston (WV) Mail
Chester (PA) Times
Chicago Tribune
Christian Science Monitor
Clearfield (PA) Progress
Connellsville (PA) Daily Courier
Cooperstown (NY) Farmer & Republican
Cumberland (MD) Evening Times
Dansville (NY) Daily Breeze
Decatur (IL) Evening Herald
Denton Record-Chronicle

Dixon (IL) Evening Telegraph
El Paso Herald-Post
Emporia (KS) Gazette
Fitchburg (RI) Sentinel
Geneva (NY) Times
Gettysburg (PA) Times
*Gloversville-Johnstown (NY) Morning
    Herald*
Greeley (CO) Tribune
Harrisburg (PA) Evening News
Hartford Courant
Iowa City Daily Iowan
Jacksonville (FL) Daily Journal
Joplin (MO) Globe
Kansas City Star
Kingsport (TN) Times
Lawrence (KS) Journal-World
Lebanon (PA) Daily News
Logansport (IN) Pharos-Tribune
Long Island (Jamaica, NY) Daily Press
Los Angeles Times
Lowville (NY) Journal-Republican
Marion (OH) Star
Massillon (OH) Independent
Medina (NY) Daily Journal
Middletown (NY) Times-Herald
Milwaukee Journal
Monessen (PA) Daily Independent
Nevada State Journal (Reno, NV)
New Castle (PA) News
New York Age
New York American
New York Evening Post
New York Sun
New York Telegram
New York Times
New York World
Niagara Falls (NY) Gazette
North Adams (MA) Evening Transcript
Oakland Tribune
Ogden (UT) Standard Examiner
Olean (NY) Times-Herald
Oshkosh (WI) Daily Northwestern
Otsego (NY) Farmer & Republican
    (Cooperstown, NY)
Pittsburgh Bulletin-Index
Pittsburgh Courier
Pittsburgh Post-Gazette

Pittsburgh Press
Plattsburgh (NY) Daily Press
Portland Oregonian
Poughkeepsie Eagle-News
Providence (RI) Journal
Reading (PA) Times
Reno Evening Gazette
Rhinebeck (NY) Gazette
Rochester (NY) Democrat and Chronicle
Rome (NY) Daily Sentinel
Roswell (NM) Daily Record
Salt Lake Tribune (Salt Lake City, UT)
San Antonio (TX) Express
San Antonio (TX) Light
San Bernardino (CA) Sun
San Francisco Examiner
San Mateo (CA) Times
Santa Cruz (CA) Sentinel
Sandusky (OH) Register
Sandusky (OH) Register Star News
Sandusky (OH) Star-Journal
Schenectady (NY) Gazette
Sheboygan (WI) Press
Spartanburg (SC) Herald-Journal
Spokane Daily Chronicle

Statesville (NC) Record & Landmark
Stevens Point (WI) Daily Gazette
Stevens Point (WI) Journal
Syracuse Herald
Syracuse Journal
Syracuse Post-Standard
Titusville (FL) Herald
Troy (NY) Record
Troy (NY) Times
Utica (NY) Daily Press
Walla-Walla (WA) Union-Bulletin
Washington Post
Washington Star
Waterloo (IA) Sunday Courier
Wichita (TX) Daily Times
Wilmington (DE) Sunday Morning Star
Winnipeg Free Press
Wisconsin State Journal (Madison, WI)
Woodland (CA) Democrat
Workers Age (New York, NY)
Yonkers Herald Statesman
Yonkers Statesman

Miscellaneous
American Jewish Congress Bulletin

Index

ABOUT THE AUTHOR

David Pietrusza has appeared on *Good Morning America*, *Morning Joe*, *The Voice of America*, The History Channel, AMC, ESPN, NPR, and C-SPAN. He has spoken at the John F. Kennedy Presidential Library and Museum, the National Baseball Hall of Fame, the Franklin D. Roosevelt Presidential Library and Museum, and various universities and festivals. His books include *1920: The Year of the Six Presidents*; *Rothstein: The Life, Times, and Murder of the Criminal Genius Who Fixed the 1919 World Series*; *1948: Harry Truman's Improbable Victory and the Year That Transformed America*; and *1960: LBJ vs. JFK vs. Nixon: The Epic Campaign That Forged Three Presidencies*. He lives in upstate New York. Visit davidpietrusza.com.